PRINCIPLES OF SEMANTIC NETWORKS

EXPLORATIONS IN THE REPRESENTATION OF KNOWLEDGE

THE MORGAN KAUFMANN SERIES IN REPRESENTATION AND REASONING

Series editor, Ronald J. Brachman (AT&T Bell Laboratories)

BOOKS

James Allen, James Hendler, and Austin Tate, editors
Readings in Planning (1990)

James F. Allen, Henry Kautz, Richard Pelavin, and Josh Tenenberg
Reasoning About Plans (1991)

Ronald J. Brachman and Hector Levesque, editors
Readings in Knowledge Representation (1985)

Ernest Davis
Representations of Commonsense Knowledge (1990)

Matthew L. Ginsberg, editor
Readings in Nonmonotonic Reasoning (1987)

Judea Pearl
Probabilistic Reasoning in Intelligent Systems: Networks of Plausible Inference (1988)

Glenn Shafer and Judea Pearl, editors
Readings in Uncertain Reasoning (1990)

John Sowa, editor
Principles of Semantic Networks: Explorations in the Representation of Knowledge (1991)

Daniel S. Weld and John de Kleer, editors
Readings in Qualitative Reasoning about Physical Systems (1990)

David E. Wilkins
Practical Planning: Extending the Classical AI Planning Paradigm (1988)

PROCEEDINGS

Principles of Knowledge Representation and Reasoning: Proceedings of the Second International Conference (KR 91)
edited by Ronald J. Brachman, Hector J. Levesque, and Raymond Reiter (1989)

The Frame Problem in Artificial Intelligence: Proceedings of the 1987 Conference
edited by Frank M. Brown (1987)

Reasoning about Actions and Plans: Proceedings of the 1986 Workshop
edited by Michael P. Georgeff and Amy L. Lansky (1987)

Proceedings of the Second Conference (TARK 1988)
edited by Moshe Y. Vardi (1988)

Proceedings of the Third Conference (TARK 1990)
edited by Rohit Parikh (1990)

PRINCIPLES OF SEMANTIC NETWORKS

EXPLORATIONS IN THE REPRESENTATION OF KNOWLEDGE

Contributors:

Alexander Borgida
Ronald J. Brachman
Michael J. Coombs
J. M. Crawford
Roger T. Hartley
Barbara Hayes-Roth
Rattikorn Hewett
Paul S. Jacobs
Alfred Kobsa
Benjamin Kuipers
Hector J. Levesque
Robert Mac Gregor
Deborah L. McGuinness
Bernhard Nebel
Lori Alperin Resnick
Peter F. Patel-Schneider
Lenhart K. Schubert
Bart Selman
Stuart C. Shapiro
Lokendra Shastri
Douglas Skuce
Lynn Andrea Stein
Richmond H. Thomason
David S. Touretzky
Robert Wilensky
W. A. Woods
Wlodek Zadrozny

EDITED BY **JOHN F. SOWA**, IBM Systems Research

MORGAN KAUFMANN PUBLISHERS, INC.
SAN MATEO, CALIFORNIA

Sponsoring Editor *Michael B. Morgan*
Production Editor *Sharon E. Montooth*
Cover Designer *Gary Head*
Electronic Copyediting and Composition *Ocean View Technical Publications*
Text Programming *Bruce Boston*
Proofreader *Kathleen McClung*
Index *Linda Fetters*

Library of Congress data is available.
ISBN 1-55860-088-4
MORGAN KAUFMANN PUBLISHERS, INC.
Editorial Office:
2929 Campus Drive
San Mateo, California 94403
(415) 578-9911

Printed in the United States

CONTENTS

PREFACE

Graphic notations for knowledge have been used for centuries in logic, philosophy, psychology, and linguistics. In the 1960s, the early days of artificial intelligence, network notations were among the first knowledge representation schemes to be developed. They were especially popular for natural language processing because they clarified linguistic relationships that other notations tended to obscure. By the late 1970s, the family of semantic networks had reached a high degree of sophistication and logical rigor.

During the 1980s, the proliferation of commercial applications of AI caused attention to shift to linear notations: most applications used languages like Lisp and Prolog or rule-based expert systems, which have notations that can easily be typed on a keyboard. By the end of that decade, however, two developments rekindled interest in networks: the ubiquity of graphical user interfaces made it possible to show networks on the screen; and the increasing size and complexity of applications made it desirable to have graphic ways of organizing and displaying the contents of a knowledge base. Today, many expert system shells supplement their rule-based and frame-based notations with a semantic network that shows the hierarchy of object types and subtypes.

Developments in related fields of computer science have also enhanced the interest in semantic networks. Procedural object-oriented languages, such as Simula, Smalltalk, and C++, have type or class hierarchies that parallel the hierarchies in semantic networks. Database designers have been using graphic systems for drawing entity-relationship diagrams, which are simplified versions of the kinds of networks used in AI. Many of the issues that those developers are encountering are ones that have long been addressed in the AI research on semantic networks. In particular, recent attempts to apply the object-oriented style of programming to database systems have run into difficulties in reconciling the procedural languages with the purely declarative databases. Semantic networks can help to bridge that gap: like the object-oriented languages, they have type hierarchies with inheritance; and like the database systems, they are purely declarative. In fact, some of the authors who contributed to this book prefer to characterize semantic networks as *object-centered knowledge representations*.

Despite the importance of the subject, there was no book that adequately covered the current theory and applications of semantic networks. To remedy that lack, this book was written as a collaboration with some of the leading researchers in the field. Most of the authors are professors of computer science with long experience in teaching the subject to advanced undergraduate and beginning graduate students. In writing their chapters, they organized the material as they would like to present it to their students. Although each chapter leads the reader to the forefront of research in its area, it starts with systematic definitions and presents the material in an accessible format. The general prerequisites for reading the book are a knowledge of logic and an introductory course on artificial intelligence. The book could be used in a course on knowledge representation or a seminar on semantic networks. Most of the chapters are suitable as supplementary reading for related areas of cognitive science, including linguistics, philosophy, and cognitive psychology.

The idea for the book grew out of a conversation between Norm Sondheimer and John Sowa. We realized that an impressive body of research and development had accumulated on various aspects of semantic networks, but that it was scattered throughout the AI literature. To bring together the most active researchers in semantic networks, we organized a three-day workshop on Catalina Island in 1989. For a sampling of the lively and stimulating discussion at the workshop, the reader should turn to the opening chapter of this book, which is an edited transcript of the concluding panel discussion. After the workshop, the program committee decided on the organization of this book and the selection of chapters to be written. Each chapter was written during the following year, and each was reviewed by two other authors. Not every participant contributed a chapter, and some chapters have coauthors who were not able to participate in the workshop.

The process of developing this book has helped to make it a cohesive and comprehensive review of the state of the art: the authors held extensive discussions with one another at the workshop; they reviewed each other's chapters; and in many cases, they worked closely with one another and the editor to decide what topics to present and how to present them. The chapters fall into three major groups: seven chapters on issues in knowledge representation, which discuss theoretical topics independent of particular implementations; six chapters on formal analyses, which treat the methods of reasoning with semantic networks and their computational complexity; and seven chapters on systems, which show how the theory has been implemented in working systems for knowledge representation.

As the editor, I gratefully acknowledge the collaboration of the workshop organizers and participants, whose help was essential in producing this book and maintaining its quality. Funds for the workshop were provided by a grant from the AAAI and an advance from Morgan Kaufmann Publishers. The general chairman of the workshop was Norm Sondheimer of General Electric Research; the program chairman was John Sowa of the IBM Systems Research Institute; and the local arrangements chairman was Robert MacGregor of the USC Information Sciences

Institute. The program committee members contributed generous amounts of time in helping to plan the workshop, review the preliminary abstracts, and select the talks to be presented and the chapters to be written; they include

- Ron Brachman, AT & T Bell Laboratories,
- Jaime Carbonell, Carnegie Mellon University,
- David Etherington, AT & T Bell Laboratories,
- Norman Foo, Sydney University,
- Christopher Habel, Hamburg University,
- Len Schubert, University of Rochester,
- Stuart Shapiro, State University of New York at Buffalo,
- Robert Simmons, University of Texas,
- Doug Skuce, University of Ottawa,
- James Slagle, University of Minnesota,
- Rich Thomason, University of Pittsburgh,
- Robert Wilensky, University of California at Berkeley.

Finally, this book could not have been produced without the support of Mike Morgan and his able assistants, especially Sharon Montooth, who saw it through to completion.

John F. Sowa
February 1991

PART I

ISSUES IN KNOWLEDGE REPRESENTATION

A semantic network is a structure for representing knowledge as a pattern of interconnected nodes and arcs. The first semantic networks were implemented in machine translation systems in the early 1960s. Since then, dozens of different versions have been designed and implemented. Although the terminology and notations vary widely, the following themes are common to most of them:

- Nodes in the net represent concepts of entities, attributes, events, and states.
- Arcs in the net, usually called conceptual relations, represent relationships that hold between the concept nodes. Labels on the arcs specify the relation types.
- Some conceptual relations represent linguistic cases, such as *agent*, *patient*, *recipient*, or *instrument*. Others represent spatial, temporal, causal, and logical connectives. Still others specify the role that one entity plays with respect to another, such as *mother*, *owner*, or *residence*; but the representation of roles as relations or concepts is one area of divergence between different systems.
- Concept types are organized in a hierarchy according to levels of generality, such as ENTITY, LIVING-THING, ANIMAL, CARNIVORE, FELINE, CAT. This hierarchy is often called a *type hierarchy* or a *taxonomic hierarchy*. It is also called a *subsumption hierarchy*, since the instances of a general type such as ANIMAL *subsume* the instances of a more specialized type such as CAT.
- Relationships that hold for all concepts of a given type are *inherited* through the hierarchy by all subtypes. Since every animal requires oxygen, the property of requiring oxygen is inherited by every carnivore, feline, and cat.

Despite these common themes, the networks diverge on a number of issues such as philosophical questions of meaning, methods for representing all the quantifiers and operators of logic, techniques for manipulating the networks and performing inferences, and stylistic conventions for drawing the nodes and arcs and labeling them with words or other symbols. Some systems emphasize the ability to assert propositions and reason with them, and others place more emphasis on ways of defining new concepts in the type hierarchy. Some are designed for representing natural language, and others are designed for expert systems applications. Some have a formal basis in logic, while others are much more informal. Despite the differences, their resemblances are sufficient to characterize them as a distinctive family of knowledge representation systems.

SURVEY OF CHAPTERS IN PART I

The chapters in Part I discuss issues in knowledge representation that are independent of any particular implementation. The opening chapter is a transcript of the panel discussion that concluded the Catalina workshop. Although the panel discussion came at the end of the workshop, this chapter belongs at the beginning of the book, since all the other chapters were written after the panel. Its informal style makes it a very readable introduction that displays the motivation for the more formal presentations in later chapters. Among the themes it covers are expressive power vs. computational complexity, formal semantics vs. informal heuristics, methods of integrating knowledge from diverse sources, relationships between theory and applications, relationships of connectionism to semantic networks, and the need for standard test cases or problems that can guide the theoretical studies and measure their success.

The next four chapters address ways in which the knowledge representation supports the reasoning methods. William Woods, the author of Chapter 1, published a classic paper entitled "What's in a Link" in 1975. In it, he criticized the poorly defined semantics of many early networks and he established principles that have helped to guide much of the research in the 1970s and early 1980s. In this book, he analyzes subsumption and taxonomy, two themes from his earlier paper. He discusses their role in knowledge representation and generalizes them to accommodate probabilistic and default rules as well as abstract and partial definitions. Len Schubert also worked with semantic networks in 1975 and was the first to introduce modal operators and definitional mechanisms based on the lambda calculus. In Chapter 2, he argues that the syntax of logic and the inference mechanisms based on it are fundamentally network-like. For that reason, he believes that semantic networks are not competitors to logic, but allied representations that exhibit the underlying logical structure in a perspicuous way. Although Schubert is a strong advocate of network representations, he has reservations about the term "semantic network" since it diverts attention from the fundamental unity between logic and networks. Lokendra Shastri, by contrast, believes that semantic networks are much more than notational variants of other languages or logics. In Chapter 3, he argues that their structure can determine the effectiveness of certain kinds of inferences and the optimal methods for performing computations. In particular, when semantic networks are realized as massively parallel networks, they may provide an appropriate framework for modeling reflexive reasoning—reasoning that can be performed rapidly, effortlessly, and without conscious effort. Stuart Shapiro, who implemented the first semantic networks that could support all of first-order logic, also believes that a properly structured network can support important kinds of "subconscious" reasoning that are not directly representable in the linear form of logic. In Chapter 4, he discusses *cables* and *paths*: a cable represents a set of nodes all linked to a given node by the same relation type; a path is a sequence of arcs through a network. Both of these constructions allow many propositions to be represented implicitly or "subconsciously" and only realized explicitly when there is a specific need for them.

The last two chapters of Part I address aspects of language that are not easily represented in predicate calculus. In Chapter 5, John Sowa argues that a graph logic, such as C. S. Peirce's existential graphs, can represent linguistic structures more faithfully than the predicate calculus. He combines Peirce's graphs with representations from AI and linguistics to form his version of *conceptual graphs*. For a variety of linguistic constructions, he shows that the graphs are simpler than predicate calculus. The differences are most significant in the representation of contexts, indexicals, plurals, and generalized quantifiers. In Chapter 6, Robert Wilensky explores issues related to situation semantics. With a series of examples that illustrate the distinctions between situations and propositions, he shows the inadequacies of various knowledge representations. Some semantic networks, for example, can represent either propositions or situations, but not both. To provide a more general representation for sentences in natural language, Wilensky proposes an extended ontology of situations that clarifies the relationships between different kinds of situations and the propositions that describe them.

GENERAL BACKGROUND

Readers who have had an introductory course in artificial intelligence should be able to read most of the chapters in this book, but they may encounter some unfamiliar terms from philosophy. A word that has become increasingly popular in discussions of knowledge representation is *ontology*, which comes from the Greek *ontos* [being] and *logos* [word]. Ontology is therefore the study of being, or, the basic categories of existence. With the indefinite article, the term *an ontology* is often used as a synonym for a taxonomy that classifies the categories or concept types in a knowledge base. The word *taxonomy* itself comes from the Greek *taxis* [arrangement] and *nomos* [law]. Literally, a taxonomy could be an arrangement based on any kind of law or principle. The most common principle is generalization; in that case, the taxonomy would be a *generalization hierarchy*, more often called a type hierarchy or subsumption hierarchy. A taxonomy could also be based on the part-whole relation. Such an arrangement is called a *meronomy* from the Greek *meros* [part]. Some people use the word *partonomy* for *meronomy*, but the word *part* (from the Latin *pars, partis*) is out of place among all those Greek terms. Another term derived from *meros* is *mereology*, which is the study of parts and wholes and the axioms for relating them. Philosophers and linguists are beginning to consider mereology as an alternative to set theory, since the plurals and mass terms in natural language can be represented more easily in mereology. Chapter 5 includes a brief discussion of mereology. One other term that is often used in AI is *epistemology*, from the Greek *episteme* [knowledge]. In philosophy, epistemology is the study of the limits and validity of knowledge and the criteria that distinguish it from belief. In AI, the term *epistemology* is sometimes applied to the categories of knowledge; but since those categories are the same as the categories of existence, the term *ontology* would be more appropriate.

Logic is also used throughout this book. Len Schubert's observation about the network-like nature of logic has some support from the history of predicate calculus. In 1879, the German philosopher Gottlob Frege used a tree notation for his *Begriffsschrift* [concept writing], which was the first complete system of predicate logic; no one else, however, adopted his notation. In 1883, the American philosopher Charles Sanders Peirce independently developed the linear notation that is used today. Peirce's notation was adopted by the German logician Ernst Schröder. The Italian mathematician Giuseppe Peano adopted the system from Schröder, but changed the symbols. He started the practice of turning letters upside down and backwards to represent logical operators: the letter E for existence became the existential quantifier $\exists$; the letter C for consequence became the implication symbol $\supset$; the letter V for the Latin *vel* [or] became the symbol for disjunction $\vee$; and the V turned upside down became the symbol for conjunction $\wedge$. Meanwhile, Peirce was not satisfied with the linear notation and experimented with networks, which he felt would show the structure of logic more clearly. In 1896, he developed his *existential graphs*, a graphical system for logic with complete rules of inference. In his later work on logic, Peirce mainly used the graphs, which he considered "the logic of the future." The modern interest in semantic networks suggests that Peirce may have been right.

Since most chapters in this book freely use the notation and terminology of propositional and predicate logic, an introduction to logic is a prerequisite. However, many of the terms would not be mentioned in an introductory course. Following are some of them:

- *Monotonic logic* is standard logic. It is called monotonic because the number of provable theorems increases monotonically as the number of assumptions increases. Adding a new axiom can never cause a previous theorem to become unprovable. If the new axiom causes a contradiction, then everything becomes provable.

- *Nonmonotonic logic* is the name for a family of new logics used to represent defaults and exceptions. Tweety the penguin is a commonly used example. If Tweety is a bird, then one might assume that Tweety can fly. But the additional information that Tweety is a penguin should block the proof that Tweety can fly. That kind of blocking, which is characteristic of nonmonotonic logics, is not possible in standard logics. Examples of nonmonotonic logics include *default logic*, logics with *negation as failure*, and logics based on the principle of *circumscription*. Some of the chapters in Part II discuss *path-based* methods for nonmonotonic reasoning in semantic networks.
- *Sorted logic* restricts each variable to a specific sort. In standard logic, a quantifier like $(\forall x)$ is completely unrestricted, and x could range over any entity in the universe. In sorted logic, however, a quantifier like $(\forall x\text{:DONKEY})$ limits x to entities of the sort DONKEY. The sorts of sorted logic correspond to the types of a semantic network, and the same kinds of inheritance mechanisms may be used to improve the efficiency of proof procedures.
- *Higher-order logics* allow variables to range over functions and predicates, unlike *first-order logic*, where quantified variables can only range over simple individuals. Allowing quantifiers to range over functions and predicates makes a major increase in expressive power, but at the expense of serious computational overhead. For many purposes, first-order logic is adequate, but sometimes a single statement in higher-order logic can express a generalization that would require infinitely many statements in first-order logic.
- *Fuzzy logic* is a family of logics that have a continuous range of truth values. Instead of the two values *true* and *false*, they allow an arbitrary number of values, such as 1.0 for certainly true, 0 for certainly false, 0.9 for very strong likelihood, 0.7 for mild likelihood, and 0.5 for unknown or indifferent. Fuzzy logic has some affinity with probability theory, and it has important applications in control systems. However, many people have serious reservations about its philosophical foundations.
- *Modal logics* represent modalities, as expressed by the English modal auxiliary verbs, *may, can,* and *must.* The two basic modal operators are *possibility*, often represented by a diamond symbol $\Diamond$, and *necessity*, represented by a small box $\Box$. Other versions of modal logic include *deontic logic*, which represents the two modes *permissible* and *obligatory*.
- *Intensional logics* are closely related to modal logic. They are used to represent *propositional attitudes*, or they are used to represent verbs that express some mental attitude toward a proposition. Such verbs include *know, believe,*

think, hope, wish, fear, and *imagine*. If the only intensional verbs are *know* and *believe*, the logic is called *epistemic logic*.

- *Temporal logics* deal with time, which raises complications that are not handled by the static models of standard logic. Some versions of temporal logic have a close affinity with modal logic, with the □ symbol representing *always* and the ◊ symbol representing *sometimes*. *Tense logics* represent the multiple reference times implied by the tenses in natural languages. A sentence such as *Tom will have been traveling* implies a time t_1 when the sentence is spoken, a later time t_2 when Tom is traveling, and a time t_3 when Tom's travel started.

Every system of logic, whether represented by networks or by linear strings, has a notation that is purely syntactic. Calling something a semantic network does not confer any deeper semantics upon it. To give it semantic content, there must be an independent basis for determining the meaning of its nodes and arcs. In talking about meaning, philosophers have drawn a distinction between the *intension* of a term (its basic meaning in itself) and its *extension* (the set of things it refers to). Frege used the example of the *evening star* vs. the *morning star*. These two terms have different intensions: one means a star that is seen in the morning, and the other means a star that is seen in the evening. Yet both of them have the same extension, namely the planet Venus. A semantic basis could be extensional or intensional. An extensional definition of COW, for example, would be a catalog of all the cows in the world; an intensional definition would specify the properties or criteria for recognizing cows without regard to their possible existence.

The usual semantic basis for logic is an extensional approach called *model theory*, which was originally developed by Alfred Tarski. For propositional logic, model theory reduces to the theory of truth tables, which are covered in most introductory courses. For predicate logic, however, the models must include the entities over which the quantifiers range. To represent those entities, a model is constructed as an abstract data structure with two components: a set of elements called *individuals*, which represent every entity in the domain of discourse, and a set of relations defined over those individuals. Besides the data structure, a model has an *interpretation function* that maps formulas and terms into their *denotations*. The denotation of a formula is a truth value **T** or **F**. The denotation of a constant is an individual: the constant *Mary*, for example, would denote an individual named Mary.

Model theory can be adapted to graphs in a concise and elegant way, since the data structure of a model is naturally graph-like. Any set of individuals and relations can be represented by a graph with the individuals as the nodes and the relations as the arcs; each arc is labeled with the name of the relation. A relation with more than two arguments can be represented by a node for each n-tuple of the relation linked by an arc to each individual in that n-tuple. When the formulas and the models are both represented by graphs, the interpretation function can be defined by a graph-matching algorithm that maps the formula graphs to the model graphs. Sowa defined models like these for conceptual graphs, but a similar technique could be applied to almost any version of semantic networks.

Tarski's version of model theory, either for graphs or for linear logic, is purely extensional. For a given model, the meaning of a predicate is completely determined by a list of the individuals for which it is true. Modal logic, however, is intensional: it deals with possibilities that do not exist and may never exist. Saul Kripke defined a model theory for modal logic in terms of families of possible worlds together with an accessibility relation that shows how the worlds are related. For such a logic, extensional definitions are impossible because the sets of individuals may be infinite. Instead, meaning must be defined by some rule that can compute the referent of a term only when needed.

The logician Richard Montague developed a model theory for intensional logic in his approach to natural language semantics. He set the standard for rigor in model-theoretic semantics, but his system implied infinite families of infinite possible worlds, whose computational complexity was staggering. Much of the later work in semantics could be characterized as a revolt against that complexity. Rich Thomason, one of the coauthors of Chapter 7, had been working with those logics and edited a collection of Montague's original papers; but he turned to semantic networks in order to develop theories that were computationally more realistic. Situation semantics represents another revolt led by the philosophers Barwise and Perry. Instead of the infinite possible worlds, they defined their semantic systems in terms of finite, representable situations. In Chapter 6, Robert Wilensky discusses situations and their implications for knowledge representation.

In a type hierarchy, the position of a concept type is determined by intension rather than extension. The type UNICORN, for example, has no instances, since there are no existing unicorns. Therefore, its extension is empty. Since the empty set is a subset of all other sets, the extension of UNICORN is a subset of every other set, including the extensions of COW, TREE, and ASTEROID. The description of a unicorn, however, defines it as an animal, or more specifically, a mammal. According to its intensional definition, the type UNICORN should therefore be placed under MAMMAL rather than TREE. In Chapter 1, Woods discusses the intensional nature of concept definitions; other authors refer to the distinctions between intensions and extensions at various points throughout the book.

The distinction between intension and extension also applies to mathematical objects like functions. A rule or procedure for computing the value of a function is an intensional definition; and a set of ordered pairs (argument,value) is an extensional definition. But a problem arises when two different rules generate the same set of ordered pairs. Are two functions considered the same if they have the same ordered pairs, but different generating rules? What happens if two procedures generate the same values for every argument tested, but the equivalence of the two procedures is undecidable? To distinguish the intension and extension of functions and to formalize the rules for defining them, Alonzo Church developed a system called the *lambda calculus*. In the traditional notation for defining functions, the name of a function f and its formal parameter x are specified together:

$$f(x) = 2x^2 + 7x - 2.$$

Church separated the name from the definition by using the Greek letter λ to mark the parameter:

$$f = (\lambda x)(2x^2 + 7x - 2).$$

Whenever a term like $f(5)$ is used, it may be *expanded* by replacing it with the expression that follows λ and substituting the argument 5 for every occurrence of the parameter x. The process of parametrizing an expression with the λ symbol is called *lambda abstraction*.

As a notation, the lambda calculus has little advantage over the traditional method of defining functions. Its advantages come from the operations on lambda expressions: the ability to define a function independent of the act of naming it; the ability to use a lambda expression anywhere that a function name could be used; and the *conversion rules* for expanding and contracting lambda expressions. With those rules, Church was able to answer the question of when two functions are equal. They are equal by extension if they have the same set of ordered pairs; they are equal by intension if their definitions are reducible to the same canonical form by the rules of lambda conversion. Church observed that there is only one notion of equality by extension, but that different notions of equality by intension are possible if different conversion rules are used. If the sets are infinite or very large (such as the set of all cows), the extensions are noncomputable, and intensional criteria are necessary.

The methods of lambda conversion and the issues concerning intensions and extensions have exact counterparts for semantic networks. Ron Brachman emphasized the distinction between the *T-box* or taxonomic system for definitions and the *A-box* or assertional system for stating propositions. There are two ways of building a T-box. One approach is used in *hybrid systems*, which have a special language for defining terms; those terms are also used in a separate language for stating propositions. The other approach uses the same language for both purposes: it starts with an assertional language and defines new concepts and relations by lambda abstractions that parametrize the propositions. In Chapter 11, Bernhard Nebel discusses some of the logical and computational problems created by definitions. Both hybrid systems and systems based on lambda abstraction lead to the same logical and computational issues.

Besides the question of the semantic basis, other logical questions concern the *soundness* and *completeness* of the rules of inference. A rule is *sound* if it preserves truth, i.e., if the starting premises are true of some model, the conclusions are guaranteed to be true of that same model. A set of rules is *complete* if every true statement is provable; more specifically, every statement that is true of all models for which a set of axioms are true must be provable from those axioms by that set of rules. Kurt Gödel proved two important theorems about logic: in 1930, he showed that first-order logic is complete. And in 1931, he showed that higher order logic is not complete—in other words, it has true statements that are not provable.

Although soundness and completeness are desirable properties of logic, many AI researchers deliberately abandon them. The default rules of nonmonotonic logic, for example, are not sound. A person who doesn't know that Tweety is a penguin might erroneously conclude that Tweety can fly. In the panel discussion in the opening chapter, Graeme Hirst argued for heuristic rules, such as a preference for options with a short semantic distance in the type hierarchy, even though those options are not guaranteed to be correct. Norm Sondheimer disagreed; he preferred to use heuristics only for speeding up a proof, not for deriving possibly erroneous conclusions. Completeness is highly desirable when it can be done efficiently, but a complete theorem prover for first-order logic can take an exponential amount of time. For higher order logics, modal logics, and intensional logics, there is no hope of achieving completeness in any reasonable amount of time. Many systems therefore support a limited set of inference rules that are incomplete, but efficient. In Chapter 10, Crawford and Kuipers provide an alternative, which they call *Socratic completeness*. The implementations described in Part III make different compromises to achieve reasonable efficiency with a level of completeness that is adequate for their applications.

The rules of inference for logic also have counterparts for semantic networks, but the various networks have diverged in the kinds of rules that are permitted. In some systems, the networks are treated as static data structures that can be manipulated by rules for copying, joining, and transforming graphs. Those rules are similar in nature to the rules that transform linear formulas during the steps of a proof. The *unification algorithm*, which is used in most theorem proving programs, in languages like Prolog, and in many new formalisms for grammar, also has a counterpart for networks. Conceptual graph systems have four basic formation rules, which together support a graph unification algorithm called *maximal join*. Systems for performing inheritance through the type hierarchy use a kind of unification for merging the attributes inherited from a supertype with the attributes of the subtype.

Another branch of the semantic network family uses rules that generate *spreading activations*. This branch was started by Ross Quillian's work in 1966. His system was not the first semantic network, because networks were used in machine translation at least six years earlier. Quillian's innovation was to mark the nodes to indicate which ones were active for a particular computation. He then let the activations spread in parallel to determine paths through the network. Quillian's nets and related ideas in Petri nets and neural nets have stimulated a great deal of research. In NETL, Scott Fahlman extended the ideas to a very rich, but informally defined system. Much of the work on inheritance theory reported in this book refers to these systems and builds upon them.

Besides logical and philosophical terms, many of the chapters in this book use terms from linguistics. Following are some of them:

- *Anaphora*, from the Greek *ana* [back] and *pherein* [carry], is the process of referring back to something that was mentioned earlier in the text. The most common *anaphoric expressions* are pronouns, but other words and phrases can also be used.
- *Case grammar* was developed by Charles Fillmore as a system for showing the relationships between a verb and the noun phrases it governs. Linguists who follow Chomsky's approach have similar relations, which they call *thematic relations* or θ-*roles*. Whatever their origin, these relations are often used as labels on the arcs of a semantic network. The most common include *agent, patient, recipient, instrument, result, experiencer,* and *beneficiary*.
- *Disambiguation* is the process of resolving the ambiguities in language. Syntactic ambiguities, also called *structural ambiguities*, arise when more than one parse tree could be generated for the same sentence. Semantic ambiguities, also called *lexical ambiguities*, arise when a word has multiple meanings that fit a given syntactic category. Resolving the ambiguities may require a considerable amount of background knowledge.
- An *elliptical expression* is one in which something has been omitted because it can be understood from context. In a dialog, many responses are elliptical sentences, as in *Where did you get that book? From Tom. Why? Because he wanted to thank me for helping him.*
- An *indexical* is a term whose reference depends on context. Two common indexicals are the pronouns *I* and *you*, whose reference changes with each turn of a conversation. Other kinds of indexicals include words like *this* and *that*, which are *deictics* or pointing words that indicate something in the context. Anaphoric references, including definite noun phrases like *the boy*, also have an indexical effect. Even tenses are indexicals, since they indicate reference times before or after the implicit speech time. Predicate calculus makes no provision for any of these context-dependent features of language.
- *Metonymy*, from the Greek *meta* [beyond] and *onyma* [name], is the process of referring to something by the name of something else that is associated with it. In the sentence *The White House announced the budget*, the building didn't do the announcing; instead, some people associated with it did. Metonymy is a frequent cause of shifts in the meaning of words, and a knowledge engineer who is unaware of it can easily be misled.

As this survey indicates, every major issue in knowledge representation has had an impact on the development of semantic networks. Ideas that originated in linear notations for logic were later adapted to networks, but others were first discovered in the network forms. Although various systems and schools of thought have developed their own notations and terminology, the underlying mechanisms are so similar that almost any idea that arises in one system can be adapted to any of the others. The motivation for using networks is that many operations that are complex or difficult to describe in a linear form become simpler and more direct on networks. Sometimes the converse is true, and a student of artificial intelligence should acquire a basic familiarity with all approaches.

CURRENT ISSUES IN SEMANTIC NETWORKS

Panel Discussion with All Participants

At the end of the Catalina workshop, there was a panel discussion with all participants. It began with short position statements by John Sowa, Bill Woods, Graeme Hirst, Norm Sondheimer, and Rich Thomason, and continued with a discussion of issues, problems, and directions for future research. This chapter is an edited transcript of the tape-recorded discussion. Because of its conversational style and lively interchanges, it makes a good introduction to the more formal chapters that follow.

STATEMENT BY JOHN SOWA

Since I'm the first speaker, I'd like to start with a review of the ancient history of semantic networks. In doing so, I'd also like to respond to a question that Graeme Hirst raised this morning: "Why don't we just use natural language as our knowledge representation language?" I have a great deal of sympathy for using natural language. But a good notation can often clarify relationships that are obscure in natural language. Aristotle's syllogisms, which were the first system of formal logic, used stylized natural language as the representation. But in the third century A.D., the Greek philosopher Porphyry clarified the relationships among Aristotle's categories by drawing them in a tree.

The tree of Porphyry

Figure 1 is the *Tree of Porphyry* as it was usually drawn by the Scholastic logicians in the middle ages. At the top of the tree is SUBSTANCE, the supreme genus or most general concept type. The differentiae *material* and *immaterial* are attributes of SUBSTANCE that distinguish the two major subtypes, BODY and SPIRIT. Below BODY are the more specialized subtypes LIVING, ANIMAL, and HUMAN. Below HUMAN are instances of individual humans, such as Socrates, Plato, and Aristotle. All the features of Porphyry's tree are still important aspects of the semantic networks in AI.

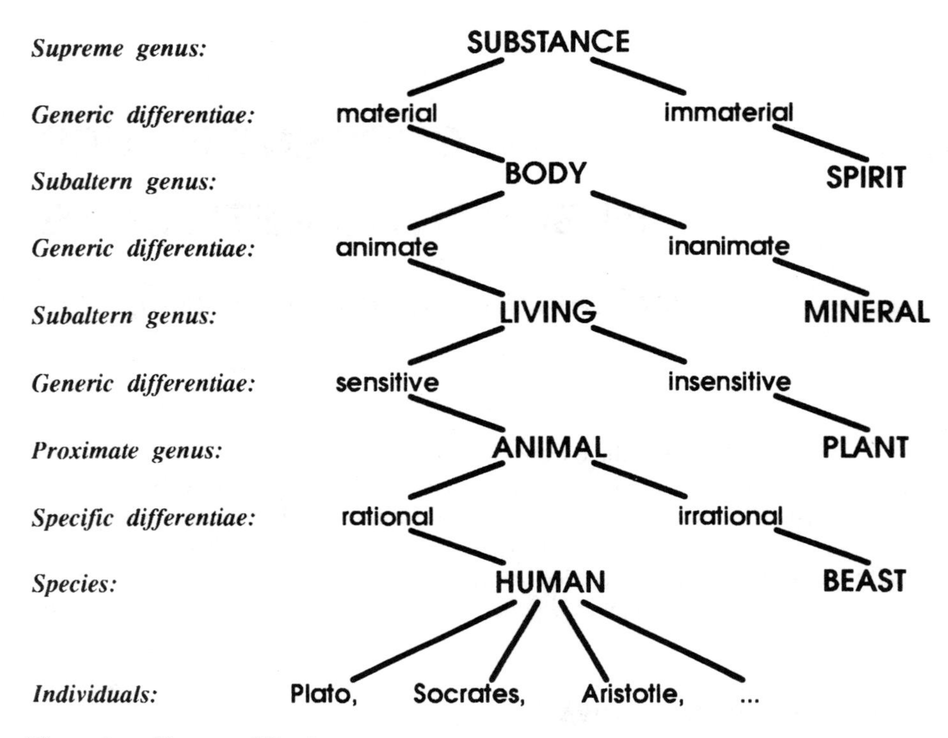

Figure 1: The tree of Porphyry

My next example is from Charles S. Peirce, who emphasized the role of logic in "making our ideas clear" [Peirce, 1878]. Around 1896, he developed his *existential graphs* as a graphical system of logic [Roberts, 1973]. Figure 2 shows his graph for the sentence *You can lead a horse to water, but you can't make him drink.* The linked bars represent existential quantifiers. There are three sets of them: one for a person, one for a horse, and one for some water. The ovals represent negations; a nest of two ovals represents if-then, since $(p \supset q)$ is equivalent to $\sim(p \wedge \sim q)$. A shaded area represents possibility; a shaded area inside an oval represents impossibility. Literally, Figure 2 could be read *If there exists a person, a horse, and water, then it is possible for the person to lead the horse to the water and not possible for the person to make the horse drink the water.* This graph corresponds to the following formula in predicate calculus:

```
~(∃x)(∃y)(∃z)(person(x) ∧ horse(y) ∧ water(z)
∧ ~(◊leadsto(x,y,z) ∧ ~◊makesdrink(x,y,z))).
```

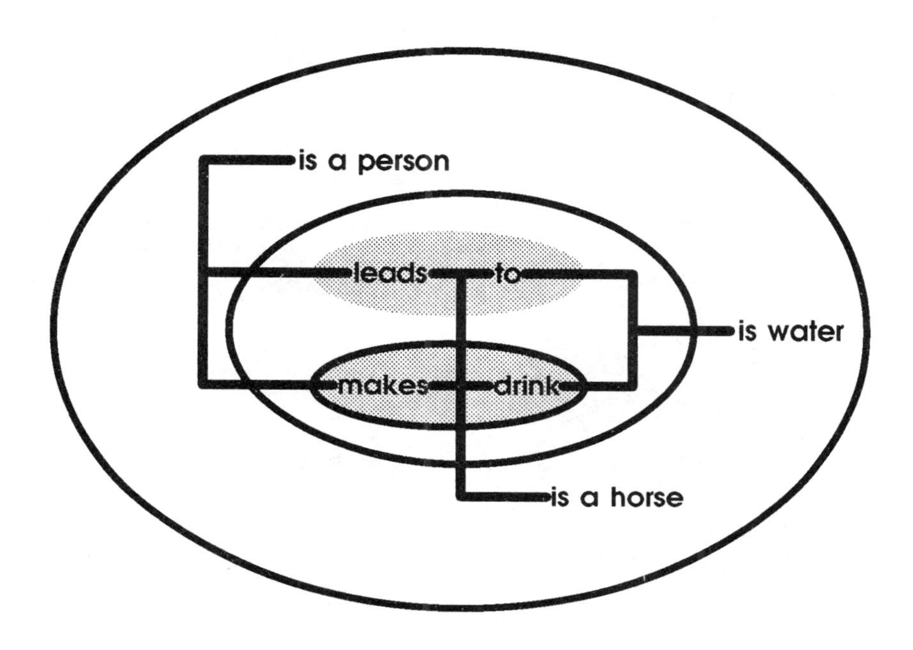

Figure 2: An existential graph by Charles S. Peirce

Peirce's graphs formed a complete system of first-order logic with extensions to modal and higher-order logic. The semantic networks in AI didn't have complete notations for logic until the 1970s.

The examples by Porphyry and Peirce show that long before AI, there was a dichotomy between the taxonomic and the assertional systems. Porphyry's trees formed a taxonomic system or T-box for organizing concepts in types and subtypes. They also showed the definition of each type in terms of its supertype plus its differentiae or distinguishing characteristics. The definition of HUMAN, according to Figure 1, would be rational, sensitive, animate, material SUBSTANCE. Peirce's graphs formed an assertional system or A-box. Peirce considered them to be simpler and preferable to the linear notation for logic (which he also happened to invent in 1883].

Another theme that originated before AI was the use of graphs in psychology. Figure 3 shows a concept hierarchy by the psychologist Otto Selz [1913, 1922]. He used it to study human reaction times and the thinking processes in problem solv-

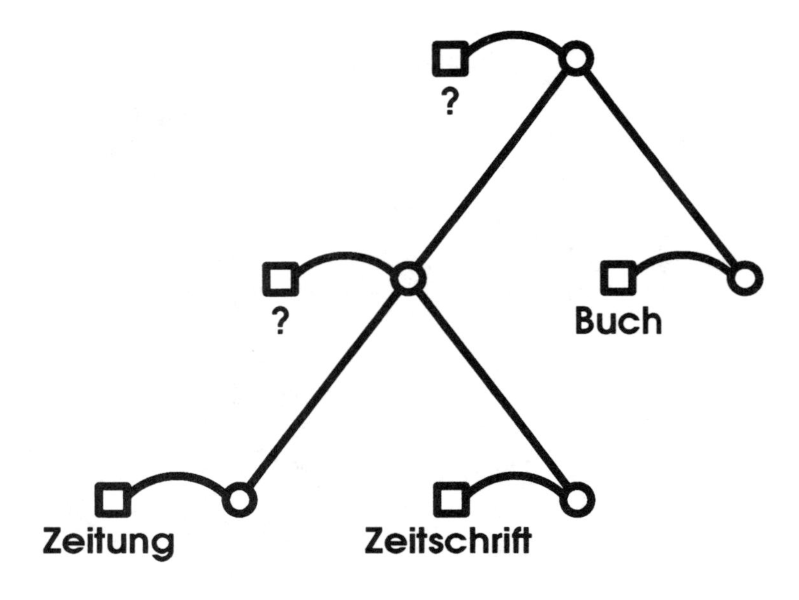

Figure 3: A concept hierarchy by Otto Selz

ing. The circles represent concepts, and the boxes represent the corresponding words. The subject is supposed to think of a word or phrase for each box with a question mark. The concept in the middle is the supertype of the concepts for *Zeitung* [newspaper] and *Zeitschrift* [magazine]. The one at the top is the supertype of that concept and the concept of *Buch* [book]. This problem is actually easier for English speakers than for German speakers, because English has a single word *periodical*. In German, the middle box requires two words, *periodische Druckschrift* [periodic publication]. The word for the top one is just *Druckschrift*. Besides using networks to represent concepts and relations, Selz also studied the operations on them. He developed the notion of *schematic anticipation*, which was a kind of pattern directed inference. For him, thinking was initiated by a consciousness of the goal [Zielbewußtsein], which serves as a guide to the thinking process. Selz described these operations in great detail and even anticipated the AI mechanisms of forward chaining and backward chaining.

Although Selz's work in psychology was not widely known, he did have an indirect influence on AI. His theories were applied by Adriaan de Groot [1965] in his studies of thinking in chess. De Groot visited Carnegie Tech where he introduced Selz's work to Newell and Simon, who cited Selz in their book on human problem solving [1972]. Their student Ross Quillian also cited Selz in his disserta-

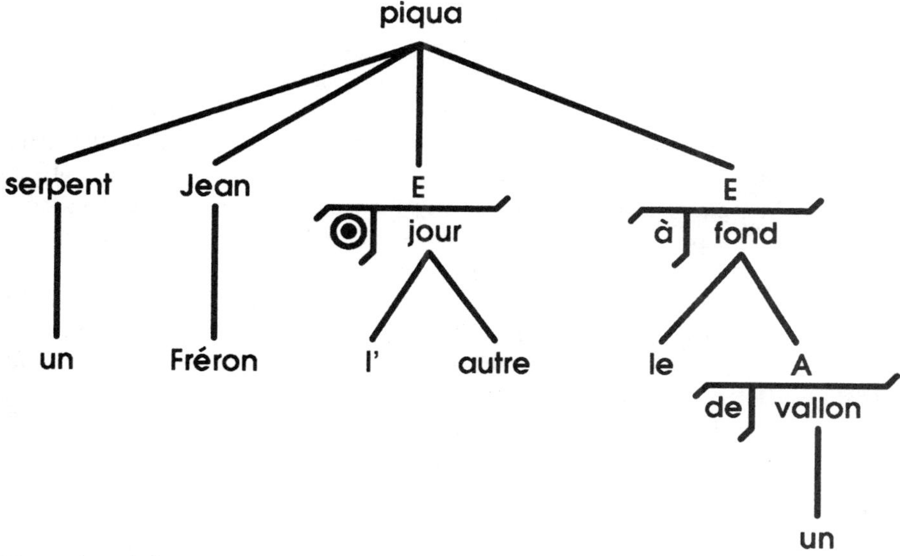

Figure 4: A dependency graph by Lucien Tesnière

tion on semantic memory [1966], which Minsky reprinted in his highly influential collection of papers [1968].

Another influence from the early days was the theory of dependency grammar by the French linguist Lucien Tesnière [1959]. Figure 4 shows Tesnière's representation for the following sentence:

L'autre jour, au fond d'un vallon,
Un serpent piqua Jean Fréron.

[The other day, at the bottom of a valley,
a snake stung Jean Fréron.]

The verb *piqua* is at the top of the tree. The two arcs hanging down on the left link to the subject and object, which Tesnière considered two of the *actants* or principal participants in the action. The two arcs on the right link to adverbial modifiers, which Tesnière called *circonstants*. For prepositional phrases, the letter E marks an adverbial phrase, and A marks an adjectival phrase. The bull's eye symbol represents a dummy preposition, since a noun phrase representing time (*l'autre jour*) may be considered a kind of prepositional phrase with a missing preposition.

In his work on machine translation, David Hays [1964] adopted Tesnière's dependency grammar and introduced it into the U.S. One person who cited Hays in his early work was Roger Schank, who shifted the emphasis from grammatical dependency to conceptual dependency [Schank and Tesler, 1969]. So Tesnière could be considered the greatgrandfather of much of the work by Schank and his students.

These notations from logic, philosophy, psychology, and linguistics make the implicit structures in natural language explicit. That has been one of the main motivations for many of the semantic networks in AI as well. As I said at the beginning, I have a great deal of sympathy for Graeme's comment, and I also have a great deal of respect for the underlying logic that is implicit in natural language. In my own work with conceptual graphs [Sowa, 1984], I have tried to stay as close as possible to the spirit of the original language. Conceptual graphs are more explicit than natural language in showing the logical structure, the attachment of phrases, the anaphoric references, and the contextual scoping of quantifiers and modalities. But in the content of what is represented, I believe that it is important to maintain a nearly one-to-one mapping to and from natural language.

STATEMENT BY BILL WOODS

After listening to the talks here, I feel like I've been walking through a metaphorical forest, looking at the trees but not necessarily seeing the forest. I've seen a lot of very interesting trees, and I'm asking myself, "Well, what does the forest look like, and how much of it have I seen?" Did I just take a random path through a bit of it? Are we just working around the edge? Or have we in some sense sampled the forest in a comprehensive way? Are all the pieces represented?

I think, in fact, that we've seen only a small part of the forest and that the pieces we have seen only become coherent when viewed as part of a much larger picture, many of whose pieces are not here. The coherence comes from interpreting semantic networks broadly as networks of nodes and links used for representing knowledge for use by mechanical reasoning systems of various sorts. The reasoning in question here includes all of common-sense reasoning, natural language understanding, learning models of the environment from experience, perceiving situations, and planning to act. If we take this broad a view of the goal, however, then we also have to recognize that there are many parts of the forest that we haven't seen on our tour, some of which are serious gaps in the current state of research in knowledge representation. A major gap, I believe, is the lack of sufficient emphasis on algorithmic uses of network representations to support various kinds of inference.

There has been a recurring theme in many of the talks here that building a model theory underneath a network structure is a good way (almost implicitly **the** only way) to give it a formal foundation. While I think that is a good and a useful thing to do—I argued strongly for clarity about semantics in my paper "What's in a Link" [Woods, 1975]—I want to raise the suggestion here that it isn't necessarily the only way to put a formal foundation under a semantic network and that there are some issues for which that isn't the right foundation to use.

First of all, I want to suggest that for most of what we want a knowledge network to do, the presumption that the formal foundation is primarily truth-theoretic is probably grossly myopic. I think that the foundation one really needs is something more like a theory of rational action, a theory that involves state change, models of belief, models of intention, and so forth, a theory in which a truth clearly plays an important part, but only a part. A Tarskian model theory doesn't have all the attributes needed to fill out the rest of the paradigm (see my "Don't Blame the Tool" paper, [Woods, 1987]. A few of the things that it takes to flesh out the paradigm more fully showed up in some of the talks here. I was glad to see at least one paper that addressed some probabilistic reasoning issues. I think there are places where you just obviously can't do what people do in common-sense reasoning, in understanding language, and in planning to act, without at some point being able to judge relative likelihoods of states and outcomes. Thus probabilities are an important part of the picture. (For those of you who have a spontaneous adverse reaction to numbers, I encourage you to at least recognize the value of someone pursuing probabilistic reasoning issues, even if it doesn't fit into the paradigm that you're using. It's an important part of the overall picture.)

Second, there's an issue that hasn't really surfaced here, and hasn't really surfaced in the field very well, although I guess it's related to the concept of hybrid representation. The issue is that we're really in desperate need of some kind of overall architecture that would enable us to integrate something like a probabilistic model and something like the classification and inheritance models into a coherent framework where the right pieces play the right roles with respect to each other. Currently, each discipline pursues separate issues in separate compartments without a view of how they would interrelate with each other. We need some high-powered intellectual talent devoted to the question of how one could sensibly combine some of these things.

Another important part of the picture is the ability to use a theory to make predictions. One of the things that one should be able to do with a knowledge representation is to answer questions like, "What's true that I haven't looked at, that I haven't measured myself, given the other things I know at this moment in time?," and "What's going to be true over time as a projection of those things that I know or believe at this moment?" These are modeling capabilities that are certainly not just truth functional, but have to do with behavior of things over time. The frame problem is a central part of this.

A general way to put it is that there's a list of very hard problems in common sense reasoning: things like modeling intentional behavior, modeling change over time, modeling hypothetical reasoning, and modeling people's propositional attitudes with respect to things. For every one of these hard reasoning problems, there's a corresponding set of challenges imposed on the knowledge representation system.

Another major need is in the area of natural language understanding. Years ago, we talked about language understanding primarily in terms of separate components of syntax, semantics, and some kind of reasoning system—each with its own special representation. The perspective that's more useful now is very much like the one that Paul Jacobs suggested, where you'd have the same knowledge representation framework cut across these components so that one can integrate knowledge from different sources in a common framework.

When you look at what goes on in language understanding today, you find that an actual surface utterance merely imposes a set of constraints on what you might have been intending to say. A lot is left unsaid. Somehow, the context in which the words occur imposes some additional constraints, and other things you know about social conventions and the way the world works impose still further constraints. The problem is to find a solution to this very complex set of constraints.

Let me illustrate that with two examples. One is a notice that a colleague of mine found posted next to an elevator during the height of an energy crisis. It said, "Walk up one floor, down two floors." So he thought, "Oh, well, the elevator is broken somehow," and he walked up a floor to catch the elevator. There he found another sign next to the elevator on that floor that said exactly the same thing—"Walk up one floor, down two floors." After a bit of puzzlement, he finally realized that the intent of this communication was to tell him that he should save energy by not using the elevator. If he only had one floor to go up, he should walk. If he had only two floors to go down, he should walk. It takes a lot of inference as well as topical knowledge about the issues of the times to come up with that interpretation on the basis of such a little bit of evidence.

The other example, a favorite of mine, is the information one used to find printed on toothpaste tubes (before the invention of pump toothpaste dispensers) that said, "For best results, squeeze tube from bottom and flatten as you go up." The interesting question is: what kind of "best results"? Will you get whiter teeth? And what does "as you go up" mean? It takes a lot of general world knowledge and sophisticated deduction to make sense of this message—including why it's printed on the toothpaste tube (which gives a lot of information) and what people do with toothpaste tubes (which it takes to understand the phrase "as you go up").

The point I want to make is that a knowledge representation network needs to support reasoning processes like these. That requires more than a mere truth-theoretic account of the semantics of the network representation. It requires attention to the structure of the network links as associational connections between concepts that support reasoning algorithms in operating on the knowledge. Notice that the importance of the associational connections lies not so much in the visual appeal of network pictures to the human eye, but in the use of the link connections by algorithms to trace out connections and draw conclusions. When you look at diagrams like the ones John just put up, they always seem to make sense for small pedagogical examples. But when you take any kind of a nontrivial problem and start to draw it pictorially with all the links, you very quickly get spaghetti. The links in such full scale networks are clearly not a felicitous notation to help a person understand what's going on.

The links in a knowledge network, whether or not they have a truth-functional semantics, are of little use if they do not support efficient algorithms for performing various kinds of inference, including classification of descriptions, inheriting information from more general concepts to more specific ones, following connections between objects, their parts, their names, their typical properties, their uses, their roles in larger contexts, etc. These links must express facts and support processes—processes for recognizing instances of concepts, for predicting consequences of actions, for planning to achieve goals, for recognizing the plans behind linguistic communications, and for proposing generalizations and specializations of rules for learning algorithms.

So when we talk about semantic networks of links and relations, we need to devote more attention, I think, to issues of what algorithms they support and what they contribute to reasoning processes—not just whether they have a formal semantic model. The formal foundation, in such cases, may be grounded in the theory of computation and algorithms, not logic.

I'd like to close by suggesting some forcing functions for driving research to address problems in need of solution. I was very pleased to see a number of people present their work in the context of having a real application that's driving the process, because I think real applications tend to reveal problems that can be missed by pure theory. But usually the application was suppressed in the background: we didn't see much detail about the application; we didn't see what problems the application raised or the representational challenges it posed.

One useful forcing application is story understanding. This problem has been around for some time, but I would advocate a much stronger performance criterion than has been used in the past. The goal is not merely to analyze a story in the context of a knowledge base designed for that specific story and to answer questions about it. Rather, one criterion is to understand a variety of stories on the basis of a standard body of general knowledge plus what has been learned from previous stories—with no new twiddling of the knowledge base for the new story. Another criterion is to understand the point of the story. (Doing this for children's stories is possibly frivolous, but detective stories and science fiction stories would be great. I was glad to hear one talk on science fiction stories.)

Finally, I think it would be an excellent challenge to build two systems that approximate children at different stages of development. One is the "sponge," an approximation of a child at the age of about four when he starts asking, "Why, why, why," and absorbs everything. The other is the "know-it-all," an approximation of an older (say nine-year-old) child who loves to explain things and will explain anything you want.

Even to attempt to build something that was as good at knowledge acquisition as a four-year-old "sponge," or as good at explaining things as a nine-year-old "know-it-all," would reveal important issues for representing and using knowledge in semantic networks.

STATEMENT BY GRAEME HIRST

With regard to Bill's toothpaste-tube example, one problem is that there are some kinds of containers that just have nice little mottos and advertisements on them, like Celestial Seasonings Tea—wisdom to live your life by. If you try to understand them in context, you get nowhere. And I've lived a lot of my life by a motto that I once found on a dry-cleaning bag, which said, "To avoid suffocation, keep away from children."

With regard to the conference in general, I was very heartened by a sign that I saw in many of the talks. Coming as I do from Toronto, I see one side of knowledge representation research from my colleagues like Hector Levesque, Ray Reiter, and their students Bart Selman, Gerhard Lakemeyer, and Peter Patel-Schneider. In their paradigm, knowledge representation has much the same status in the world as, say, number theory in mathematics. It's fun to do, you can play around all day with symbols and invent wonderful new theorems. If it's some use to the world, well, that makes you feel warm inside, and if it's absolutely no use, then who cares? Well, the answer is, I care, because my work is in natural language understanding and I want to use knowledge representation as a tool. And so I'm glad to see, typified mostly but not exclusively in the papers by Bob MacGregor and Debbie McGuinness, people who are building knowledge representations and are thinking first and foremost, "What are the people who are going to use these things going to do with them. What do the users want?" And, as a user, that's what I want all you guys to be thinking when you go out there and design knowledge representations. So the good sign is a greater emphasis on the user and a greater emphasis on the expressive power of languages—again especially in Classic. That's what the users want, more expressive power. I went into that in my remarks this morning, and I don't have to elaborate on it again.

Now, I said my work is really in natural language understanding, and I'm at this workshop as a user. But the fact is that people in natural language understanding do do an awful lot of research in knowledge representation. It's just that when we do it, we don't call it knowledge representation, we call it semantics. But it's really the same thing in disguise, or very much the same thing. People in linguistics or in philosophy, when they're looking at semantics, are doing knowledge representation too.

And my students and I in Toronto have been doing various projects in natural language understanding that ultimately come down in some way to knowledge representation. I mentioned one this morning, the work of Judy Dick [1987] on legal texts. Dan Lyons, another one of my students, is looking at representations and semantics of focusing subjuncts, words like *again, even, only,* and so on, which turn out to be very problematic for compositional representations [Lyons, 1989]. Brenda Fawcett [1985; Fawcett and Hirst, 1986] looked at how to represent descriptions. In natural language we can refer to entities by descriptions that the speaker implicitly attributes to another agent without making any commitment to it. Certain kinds of such descriptions simply can't be represented in any kind of first-order or modal logic. And Mara Miezitis [1988] looked at the problem of how to make a conceptually-organized hierarchic lexicon meet the needs of lexical choice in language generation. These are all examples of natural language research that is largely knowledge representation, and I offer them as examples of the things that the users of knowledge representation systems actually want.

Complexity, as I said this morning, has to be a secondary issue compared with expressive power. It has been discussed a lot at this conference, and I don't think that's a bad thing. But ultimately we have to remember that we first have to answer the questions, "What are knowledge representations for? What is their job out there in the world? What do we want them do?" For all the work we have in knowledge representation, we don't have definitive answers yet. Until we do have some good answers, it's perhaps a little premature to worry too much about tractability issues.

Something else that came up in the first panel and then again this morning, especially in Wlodek's talk, is proximity-based reasoning. Bob Wilensky was rather critical of it. Now, of course, there are limits to proximity-based reasoning. And the example he gave about the president in Nicaragua is a good one. But I think it's incontrovertible that people do do something like spreading activation. We have an extremely strong intuition of the concept of semantic distance between two concepts, and we use that in our reasoning and thinking. In the second session this morning, Roger Hartley in particular kept using the word "abduction." He didn't really talk about semantic distance as a measure for relevance and abduction, but people like Eugene Charniak [1986], Jim Hendler [1988], and others have done work that implicitly or explicitly addresses that issue. And it always comes back in some way to semantic distance as measured by some kind of physical distance in a network.

In my own work on lexical ambiguity [Hirst, 1987, 1988], I looked at semantic distance as one factor in the resolution of word senses, and I emphasized that factor. One of the good parts of my work, I think, was that I integrated a number of different factors, all of which help resolve word senses. But semantic distance was the first and most important because of the psycholinguistic work of people like Lynne Reder [1983] at Carnegie Mellon, who showed that people misunderstand certain negatively primed sentences, and they seem to do so exactly because they use semantic distance to reason with. Negatively primed sentences are sentences such as, "The watchmaker removed the tick," "The sailor ate the submarine," and so on, all of which have perfectly reasonable literal interpretations, but which often give people lots of trouble. Yes, I see people smiling. Some you of see both meanings, perhaps some only see the anomalous meaning and not the literal meaning at all. Most people have trouble with these sentences most of the time.

So I want to put in a very strong plug for proximity-based reasoning. I think everything Len Schubert said in his talk was true, except at the end when he said, "Oh yeah, there's this proximity stuff on the side." It's not on the side, it's in the center, and that's what makes it important.

STATEMENT BY NORM SONDHEIMER

The problem with being the fourth panelist is that you find yourself either repeating or disagreeing with the earlier panelists. But I thought I'd use my time to comment on the entire undertaking we are engaged in, this field of formal knowledge representation. You'll see in my comments that I come to this as a user with a computational viewpoint.

I want to start with what we should point to as the true contributions of our work compared to other knowledge representation work. That's the commitment to an explicit semantics. More than anything else, the ability to understand what the notation expresses sets us apart. As Bill Woods discussed, it would be useless to have an explicit semantics unless there were some inference engine that goes with it. We've been able to create some of those. As Graeme Hirst discussed, these inference engines must support the expressiveness users desire and be efficient enough for use inside other systems. We have been contributing here too.

In addition, what's important on a socio-economic level is that we've been able to form schools of thought, that we've been able to build on each other's work. This has not been a single juggernaut, certainly. But we have ongoing studies that have been able to develop some understanding of a technology which others have developed.

But there are things that are wrong with the field that match almost one-to-one what's right with it. First, there is a willingness to compromise. Graeme's comments, as a matter of fact, encouraged you to look away from dependable, explicit semantics captured in an inference engine towards one where truth depends on heuristics, like semantic distance. That's a useful move in some cases. But for the sake of the users, I really would like to distinguish such techniques from those employed in dependable inference engines. Just to clarify, I'm not discussing heuristics that help guide the search and get the best answer quicker. I'm opposed to those that lead you to pick answers out of the air on informal criteria.

We should also be concerned about subjective measures of our work. I only heard it once here when someone talked about the perspicuity of graphic notations. That's not something we should get involved with.

We should also curb the rampant data structurism, where there may be an explicit publication semantics for the notation, but in an actual program, it's up to you and your maker as to what gets done with the notation. What you gain in the explicit semantics, you lose when you treat the knowledge as merely a data structure.

I agree with Graeme's point that we're emphasizing some of the wrong things—for example, the worst case behavior for computational complexity when the typical case is more appropriate. We're emphasizing theoretical completeness, both trying to attack all problems and trying to answer all questions completely, when something short of that would be useful.

And finally, just as there's a socio-economic tendency to form schools of thought, there's a socio-economic tendency based on the reward system of academia to fragment and develop a "not-invented-here" attitude.

I think there are also some elements missing. I've mentioned before, and I think Bill and Graeme mentioned too that we need a systems perspective. We need to understand that the issue here involves tools, manuals, and a global view of our enterprise.

Another missing piece, as Bill mentioned, is to measure our work against real tasks, as opposed to measuring it against the mathematical criteria that we've adopted along with the tools of mathematics that we're currently using. We must measure ourselves against the needs of natural language understanding, expert systems, database access, etc. We must measure so that we can identify progress. And then we have to do the same thing that goes on in philosophy, where we see the philosophy of language parallel to the philosophy of logic. We have to develop a theory of use. For each of our notations, we have to understand as we attempt an application what options we have in approaching it.

So what's next? I'd argue, of course, that we move to cover what's missing, build the systems, worry about the applications, and build a theory of use. And I'd suggest, as before, that the most important possible applications are tools like database management systems and rule-based systems. We should see our work as an important addition to those systems. Exclusive of notation, this should represent efficient access mechanisms and inference engines that could make those tools more powerful and easier to use.

In conclusion, I would borrow here from Paul Jacobs's vaporware, AI-ware, and software distinction. Where we are today is at the vaporware stage, heading to AI-ware. With all due respect to the folks who prove theorems, that's vaporware.

The AI-ware is produced by the people who claim that they are building systems. I know some of those systems, and I know that they're not "software." That is what we have to produce next.

So tomorrow, I think we should be building those software systems, the systems that the people beyond this small field, beyond AI, out in the world, can use. I say keep going.

STATEMENT BY RICH THOMASON

One theme that I want to touch on, since it seems to have something to do with this conference, is the question of achieving a healthy relationship between theory and applications. There is always a gap between theory and practice in subjects that really address applications, but in our field it's particularly hard to close this gap. We shouldn't pretend that it's easy to have nice theories that really relate to problems, that are inspired by, that guide and help to improve applications.

The process of relating theory to practice can't be just top down or bottom up. We ought to strive for a kind of tight feedback loop where the theoretical work pays close attention to the problems of practitioners, and practitioners look to theories for models that help them to deal with their concerns. This sort of relation is crucial for all kinds of engineering applications, of course. But in well developed areas with a long history, we tend to lose sight of the relationship, because there will be many intermediate niches between theoretical and practical extremes. So you have a long chain, with people at one extreme not paying much direct attention to the people at the other. Nevertheless, the connections are there.

AI is not well enough developed to have niches at these intermediate points, but over the last few years we have seen some differentiation into theoretical and applied communities. Paul Cohen has documented this well in a recent study [1990]. It's vital to keep this from becoming a process of polarization. We can't have separate communities each doing their thing and ignoring the other; we've got to have a lot of communication. At least until the subject develops enough to have intermediate niches, we need to have some people who are able to work on both sides at once, and many people who are well able to understand both sorts of problems. We need to encourage and reward amphibious people, and, of course, one of the most important things about meetings of this kind is that they can help to achieve this purpose.

The theory that's most important for us is computer science. It has matured to the point now where it has absorbed the kinds of theoretical disciplines that bear on all sorts of computational problems, including the problems of AI. For instance, if you're going to be using logic, you can find most of the logic you need in theoretical computer science. So I mean theoretical computer science when I talk about theory.

There are many, many areas, I think, where people are addressing in their own way issues that are similar to the ones we're addressing here. Some of them have come up in the meeting, but there are a lot of others. What's so difficult, since this is a rapidly evolving field, is to keep track of all of these things and to try to figure out what they have in common, and how to bring them to bear on these sorts of problems.

For instance, work on types in the theory of programming languages is quite relevant to studying types and inferences in networks and inheritance-based systems. See, for instance, Ait-Kaci [1986] and Cardelli and Wegner [1985]. Ait-Kaci's work, in particular, has some similarities to the work on roles presented in the chapter by Touretzky and me.

I don't think that work on grammar formalisms has been mentioned at this meeting, but this work is very relevant, too. Grammatical knowledge is knowledge, so it isn't surprising that the kinds of formalisms people have come up with in unification grammar for describing linguistic structures are very like some of the things we've been talking about. The work that has grown up out of unification grammar formalisms and feature structures is very relevant. This has been a very active area. See, for instance, Kasper and Rounds [1986], Shieber [1986], Johnson [1988] and Pollard and Sag (forthcoming).

Database theory and technology is another area that's extremely important and that eventually has to be integrated with what we're doing, especially if we are going to think about building large systems. As databases get more complicated and people begin to worry about how to make them hierarchically structured and capable of more intelligent inferencing, the gap between databases and knowledge representation systems begins to close, and the difference is really one of size. See, for instance, Zdonik and Maier [1989] for a survey of such work. But the issue of size is one that we all have to address in one way or another. It seems to me that we really have to begin to work with the database community in order to identify and address the common problems together.

With such difficult problems, and so much going on, it's difficult to find out how to focus on strategic problems. I myself am inclined to begin with real technology that's working, performing some useful reasoning task that can be evaluated. This means, for instance, that if a system is used as a representation of natural language input, there must be some reasoning on the representations too.

One surprising lesson we've learned from AI, is that you can simulate intelligence in microworlds. You can find domain-specific, relatively small-scale systems that really do interesting things, but then it turns out to be very hard to transport what you've done in one domain or to scale up the work by an order of magnitude. I don't expect that we're going to be able to find brilliant insights that launch us out of this situation into a new age of AI. We're going to have to settle for the slower-paced kind of progress you find in well established sciences. In an incremental spirit, I think we need to look at the systems that work—that is, to look at expert systems, or domain-specific natural language translation systems, or natural language interfaces to expert systems. We have to try to understand what makes them work, to try to isolate the knowledge representation component, and to see whether what makes the job get done can be preserved if the knowledge is represented in a more general, principled way. The problems that are encountered in this process should then become high-priority issues for theory. And the theories that emerge should be tested by building new systems.

I don't think, by the way, that we're going to get too much help from the theory of natural language. This just comes from my own experience. I've done work in natural language semantics and syntax, to some extent, and I still work in these areas, but I find myself not using that experience much when I'm thinking about knowledge representation. It doesn't seem to be of much direct help. And it seems to me that the reason for that is that the natural language people have made their science work by exploiting the modularity of language. That is, they want to look at language as a separate, distinctive cognitive module, concentrating only on language and linguistic structure. But AI can't ignore the problem of how language processing, along with our other cognitive abilities, is smoothly integrated with massive amounts of real-world knowledge. The linguists have avoided all kinds of problems by systematically ignoring such issues, and these are just the problems we're interested in.

OPEN DISCUSSION

Norm Sondheimer:

That's the end of the prepared statements by our five panelists. We can now open up the discussion to comments from anyone who wants to join in.

Stuart Shapiro:

Just a quick answer to Norm's challenge. I'd like to announce a SNePS-2 User's Manual that I finished recently. I'm willing to send it to anyone who wants it, or, indeed, I'm willing to send copies of the system. We've been distributing it. So if anyone is interested, either in just looking at the manual, getting a copy of the system, or both, let me know, and I'll send it through the mail.

Lokendra Shastri:

I think the issues of complexity are important for helping us to determine the best representation or to make choices between representations. Worrying about complexity is a very important constraint that forces us to look in particular directions. It can tell us that certain choices are obviously incorrect, because they can never lead to appropriate complexity behavior. So for example, any operation that has to be executed repeatedly or quite often during natural language understanding cannot have complexity on the order of the size of the knowledge base. You should immediately know that you're doing something wrong if you're coming up with representations for which there is no obvious way of operating on them or doing inferencing on them in real time. And this constraint does not depend on technology.

Norm Sondheimer:

Again, the issue is worst case complexity. And if average case complexity and consideration of the space of problems being addressed is part of the analysis, then that's perfectly correct.

Lokendra Shastri:

Yes, worst case analysis is probably not important, but I'm using this only as an example; I realize that it's only a small component of the big puzzle. For example, if you don't have a representation scheme in which you can do inheritance, say, in time sublinear in your knowledge base size, then clearly there is something missing. You cannot assume that one can take a million steps, let's say.

Participant:[1]

I'd like to say a bit about worst case complexity. Rich mentioned some systems like databases and expert systems. I think one reason why these large systems actually work is that their worst case complexity is very good. I don't think there's any clear evidence that we can go with very expressive and very intractable computations, just scale them up to make them very large, and then hope that they're going to work on average. I would argue that the evidence we've seen so far in AI is that that is not the case. The systems that do scale up are the ones that are very restrictive. So I don't think there is evidence for the average case behavior being significantly better than the worst case.

John Sowa:

I would like to comment on the point about expressive power, because I'm one of the people who have been advocating very great expressive power. I certainly agree that we must have systems that can scale up. We also need things that are simple and efficient, like database systems, which don't do very much reason-

[1] Some participants who did not give their names when they spoke are identified only as "Participant."

ing, but do it very fast, very efficiently, and on very large volumes of data. But at the same time, we also need some way of dealing with ordinary text in ordinary language. We have to take things as they come in language and relate them to some of the simpler things that are computable. I think there's a lot that we can do. We can take complex sentences with nested contexts and break them down into their components. For example, somebody may say "John believes that he can swim." There you have a belief with a nested modal proposition. Instead of doing deep reasoning with some sort of epistemic modal logic, you can just add that new information to your mental database about John's beliefs. That would be more of a database update than a kind of deep reasoning. So it may be possible to keep the operations simple, even when the representation is complex.

Participant:

I basically support that view, that natural language on the surface is a very expressive system. You can express incomplete information, and it may make reasoning very hard. However, there's no reason why you can't translate it into a form with which you can reason fast, like close to a database form. And I think that's why looking at complexity is important, because you have to find reasoning methods that are fast.

John Sowa:

Yes, but expressiveness and complexity are equally important. You have to capture everything that was said, and then you need a systematic way of taking a big statement and breaking it down piece by piece. You need knowledge representation schemes that are very expressive, but can be subsetted to handle the simpler parts.

Participant:

Yes.

David Gardiner:

I have a question that concerns Bill Woods's comments. I'd like to stand back and look at the global issue of connectionist models versus semantic networks. One of the first questions that comes up when you're dealing with semantic networks is whether we're on the right track or whether we're completely in the wrong ballpark. Obviously everybody here thinks we're in the right ballpark, at least to a certain extent.

But a question that comes up is that semantic networks are symbolic in nature, yet there's some indication that some things are very difficult or virtually impossible to represent symbolically. That is basically a connectionist point of view. I'm looking for opinions from the panelists on whether nonsymbolic representations are necessary—not just neural networks, but any nonsymbolic representation. If so, what should such a representation look like?

Lokendra Shastri:

I'd like to say something about connectionism. What I want to clarify is that there are three separate camps: The first are the strict connectionists or the neural network types. They have intuitions that describe the physics or the mechanics of how neurons interact. The second group are the parallel distributed processing group, who talk about network computations independent of the underlying physics. And then there's a third group, which you can describe as the local connectionist group or the structure connectionist group. I believe that the structure connectionist group can be viewed as a natural extension of the semantic network approach. They have the same motivations that drive the work in semantic networks. The issues are making things vivid, making things explicit, making explicit all the forms of dependencies, and laying out the structure of the underlying knowledge. Besides that, they emphasize that the processing takes place in the active networks, so that there are efficiencies in terms of computational time taken and all that. But I don't understand what it means to say "a nonsymbolic representation." To me, that sounds like an oxymoron.

David Gardiner:

Let me clarify that. The general idea with a symbolic representation is that you can open up the system, look at it, and see what you've got. You can tell that this node is a representation of a dog; it's something of a mapping from the world to the system. Yet the point that connectionists make is that that's very artificial in some cases. For example, in a reasoning system, the meta knowledge that determines how the system works isn't coded symbolically in the same knowledge representation language; it is embedded in lower-level procedures that just make it work. In the brain, there's no direct mapping to the world, as far as anybody has found. Nobody can tell you how their neurons work. Is there going to be a need for representations where you just can't look inside and tell what you've got?

Alfred Kobsa:

I've been working for some time on finding the relationships between those representation systems that have been developed in the field of AI knowledge representation and those that have recently been developed in the field of connectionism. I wanted to compare the expressiveness of these connectionist systems to traditional systems and to see to what degree one could combine these two kinds of representations. My result [Kobsa, 1989] was that connectionist systems still show great deficiencies in expressiveness as compared to the classical systems. However, there are certain kinds of things which you can do much more easily in a connectionist architecture. For instance, certain inference processes—particularly certain extensions of classification—can be performed more easily in connectionist systems. This includes concretion, classification in inheritance hierarchies with exceptions, and classification in inheritance hierarchies which possess primitive concepts. These kinds of things can be much more easily performed with connectionist schemes. So it already makes sense to combine classical knowledge representation systems with a connectionist architecture.

Bill Woods:

There are two points to make about the question of nonsymbolic representations. One of them is, that there are some representations that people have called nonsymbolic in the sense that they have quantitative values proportional to aspects of the thing being represented—e.g., mental maps in visual imagery. There's some debate about whether these are nonpropositional representations since they can be represented in computers as vectors and arrays of numbers, which can in turn be expressed as predicate assertions in a formal logical system. There's a big argument there, and I don't want to get into it. But the argument that you raise is somewhat different. It is the claim that a representation is not symbolic because you can't understand it. This seems to me to be a fallacious argument. For example, Quillian's semantic networks, which were originally motivated by the desire to do a connectionist-style spreading activation, were relatively understandable. Does that make them symbolic? On the other hand, the intended semantics for Quillian's nodes came only from the names on the nodes, and Quillian at one point deleted the names, leaving a structure that one could not understand, but which still worked the same way. Did the same representation suddenly become nonsymbolic at that point? Or if I were to take away all of the debugging tools that support a LISP program and just give you a memory dump, you would have the same kind of apparent chaos that seems to reside in a connectionist network, but would that make the program any less symbolic?

In both of the above cases, we have pairs of systems that work identically, one of which is understandable and one not. Clearly in these cases there is no advantage in moving from a system that you can understand to one that you cannot. Moreover, algorithms for learning hidden Markov models of language strings have characteristics like a connectionist model in that they come up with a matrix of connection strengths. But the interesting thing about those models is that when you look at them, there is structure, and one can frequently interpret the structure and it makes sense. My suspicion is that in connectionist networks, also, if one looks for it, one can discover structure, and it will make sense, too. Moreover, for the group that Lokendra referred to as the structure connectionist group (the group that is producing some of the most successful connectionist results), the structure is actually designed into the network and the structures do make sense. There is a growing tendency in connectionist research to take this approach, in which a specific high-level connectivity pattern or connection architecture, is designed into the network to achieve a certain behavior. This approach is one of the innovations in modern connectionist research that I think is responsible for much of its success. I think the preponderance of evidence, both within and outside the connectionist community, supports a conclusion that understandable representations perform better than totally unguided networks with arbitrary connectivity. The people who argue that there's an advantage to a representation simply because it doesn't make sense, I think, are just confused.

Rich Thomason:

The issue with the connectionist architectures is not the presence or absence of symbols; it's the ability to manipulate them in certain systematic ways that most people in AI would like to have available. And that's not available in most connectionist architectures. Dave Touretzky does try to mix them both (he's one of the few people who do that) and in practice, he builds lists on top of the connectionist architecture. But there are horrible engineering problems. It's painfully, painfully slow. The interesting difficulties seem to be in getting the ability to do both and to do it without taking a century of machine time.

Len Schubert:

I'd like to react to Bill Woods' and Rich Thomason's remarks about optimal research strategy. I think the truth falls somewhere between them and perhaps a little closer to Bill. Their positions really are quite different, in that Rich is urging us to concentrate on domain-specific applications and Bill is asking us to work on story understanding, with emphasis on understanding the point of a story.

Now, I think the problem with emphasizing practical applications is that we may end up working on various arbitrary microworlds that happen to be economically or socio-economically important, but don't necessarily address the problems that are crucial to understanding our cognitive apparatus. And I think there's been a lot of experience in AI in developing systems that address particular microworlds, and then finding them nonextensible. Also, when you try to move incrementally out of the microworlds, you go in a very different direction than when you tackle a bigger problem head-on and let the difficulties you run into determine your research emphasis.

On the other hand, I felt that Bill Woods was really giving us too tough a job in calling for understanding the point of a story, even though there've been some attempts in that direction. We're still a long way from knowing what's involved in understanding fairy tales to extent of being able to answer straightforward content questions. Of course, there's been a lot of interesting work on that, but I think the work has been aimed at specific sets of stories and at a fairly coarse-grained analysis of stories and questions. So I think we need to work hard to get greater breadth in understanding and greater depth in simple question answering, quite apart from figuring out the point of a story.

Norm Sondheimer:

I think Len just presented two very seriously wrong-headed views to use in motivating an entire field. The first is the cognitive view. It's wrong for an entire field to take that view, given the slow progress that people have had in impacting the computational world. In and of itself, just as mathematics is self-justifying, psychology is self-justifying. But knowledge representation is a computational endeavor. Not everyone should be pursuing cognitively valid knowledge representations.

The second mistake is to take the view that in dealing with the knowledge of the world, we must address massive issues. I find it really appalling that you think that things that have only socio-economic or economic consequences are to be ignored. If you look in a field as important to the world as database management systems, we find that the developers are well aware of the fact that some tiny percentage of the semantics of their application is taken care of by the automatic processing of the database management system. Numbers are thrown around, like five or ten percent. The other ninety or ninety-five percent of the semantics resides in the programs. It's only politic of us to realize that our work will only be able to increase that five or ten percent to ten or twenty percent. The right view to take is that we should be working on making those contributions.

Len Schubert:

What I was trying to say is that there is a rather arbitrary connection between the specific problems that arise in our economic environment, and the problems that are most central to cognition and intelligence. For instance, there may be no essential connection between the central problems of cognition, and, say, the requirements of a financial advisor system, or of a particular database application. But we know that all children enjoy and understand stories, so there's something fundamentally appropriate about looking at that kind of domain.

Bill Woods:

If you were to succeed in making the point that there was no such connection, you would have rationalized away most of the funding for anything of the kind you want. Fortunately, I think it's false to believe that there is no connection. In particular, there are interesting cognitive issues involved in mundane practical applications, and there are often significant practical benefits that result from research with no apparent practical goal. With respect to your other point, while I recognize the point that you were making, and the spectrum that you were able to identify with me at one end and Rich at the other, I don't see any real dissidence between what Rich said and what I said. In fact, I agreed with everything he said. I think as a field, you've got to be doing both kinds of activities. If you don't have some grand challenges to shoot for, things get stale. In fact, I think one of the things that's making database research interesting now is that it's being somewhat challenged and some vision is trickling in from the kinds of things that AI has been doing. Artificial intelligence has had that effect on a lot of other disciplines. So I think that some of the grand challenges, although they may be out in the distance and difficult to reach, are often worth thinking about to remind us how far we are from those goals and what future possibilities might be.

With respect to what people are trying to do with story understanding, yes, people have tried it, and as you said, a lot of them were sort of ad-hocish in the flavor and approach. I don't think anybody has given understanding the point of a story the kind of theoretical horsepower that one might put on it if somebody were to try to really understand what goes on there. I think that could be a useful challenge, because we probably only begin to understand about 5% of what it takes to solve the problem. When children's stories start to deal with people's models of other people's models of the way the world works, there's real rich, subtle stuff there. People's models of other people's propositional attitudes are a real challenge.

Rich Thomason:

Well, I don't think Bill and I disagreed that much, either. So the truth is somewhere in between us; we've really cornered it. I was trying to say that I'm a little uneasy about using whole hog natural language understanding as the target for knowledge representation, because I think we lose sight of the target. Unless there is real output for the system and reasoning going on, it's really just translating the input into some notation with no constraints on whether you got it right or not. So I feel much better about cases where there is some reasoning going on and some output. And I think these are likely to be cases that are domain-specific and less ambitious in their goals. So I don't feel bad about story understanding as long as it's some fairly local task of getting the point of a story, where people can agree on what the point is and what a summary would include. I also think it probably would have to be domain-specific to work. I don't think Bill would disagree with that.

Stuart Shapiro:

I want to reflect on, or highlight a distinction among different people's motivations. It's been mentioned once or twice in the last couple of days, and it relates to this last discussion. Someone put a diagram on the screen that showed the knowledge representation being a rather small knowledge server to a large system. That's one approach. That is, there are people who are working on knowledge representations with the idea that they are going to be a kind of intelligent database for use by a programmer who's building a knowledge-based system for other users. These people view a knowledge representation system as merely one of the tools for constructing this larger system.

The other approach, which I follow, is that the knowledge representation system is the entire system. The ultimate goal is to build an Artificial Intelligence—to build an intelligence system that one can communicate with via the natural sorts of communications that people use to communicate with each other. So the knowledge representation is, as I said in my talk, the mind of the entire agent. When we draw these diagrams or write these linear notations, that's for communication among us as researchers. The way someone will communicate with the system is in English or German or pointing, the way everyday people communicate with each other. So using natural language understanding as the driving force for knowledge representation work is, I think, very much to the point. Rich contrasted "using whole hog natural language understanding as the target for knowledge representation" with there being "real output for the system and reasoning going on." I don't see a contrast between these two. Natural language understanding doesn't mean anything unless the understander can reason about what it understood and is able to contribute back to the interlocutor something that it inferred as a result of that reasoning. And so it's valuable not to lose track of that general AI goal as a goal for knowledge representation systems.

Wlodek Zadrozny:

I would like to change the topic and ask a question. Perhaps it would be useful to list a number of problems—I don't know whether it should be ten or one hundred problems—which we believe should be discussed at the next workshop. We could then say to what extent our theories or our systems address these problems. This should make the next workshop more cohesive than this one. We have talked on various systems of notations applied to different problems; all this was quite stimulating, and I enjoyed most of the talks. But there was no clearly formulated focus of these talks; I find "semantic network" too general a term. Perhaps the titles of sessions should be formulated as questions, not as noun phrases. So I would like to see a list of specific problems whose solution would mean something. I have in mind something like the 23 problems by David Hilbert [1901], which strongly influenced the development of mathematics for at least half of this century. I think with some effort we could create such a list and explain why we care about those issues, why we think that they are difficult, and how we would measure a solution. One such problem is for instance understanding children's stories. From the previous discussion, it is clear that we care about it; but it remains to be seen how we would measure the correctness of a solution. I would like see a list of standards.

Doug Skuce:

The other day I referred to *deja vu* understanding, and I just had another one, with all the psychic energy exploding in the room. This one also goes back about twenty years, when I was interested in pattern recognition. At that time, the people who were working on pattern recognition were all taking different examples from all kinds of problems. Even those that were working on, let's say, recognition of letters of the alphabet, all worked on different data that they dreamed up themselves.

Then it was the IEEE, I think, that stepped in and said, this is silly, let's get organized. Let's get some standardized sets of data, and we can all try our pattern recognition systems on the same data. Then we'll have some realistic scientific criteria for comparing them. Now, I would like to think that in a few years we could get organized to the point where we can work on reasonably agreed upon similar sets of problems, realistically chosen ones. Then, instead of everybody inventing their own examples, we would have some better way of comparing different representations to see what their strengths and weaknesses were.

In terms of stories that we might work on, I'd like to suggest that we work on the kind of stories that I struggle with every day, namely typical computer manuals and textbooks. I have to try and figure out their meaning and explain it to my students, because I know they aren't going to be able to figure it out.

Participant:

Well, the problem with introducing this kind of benchmark problem in software engineering in AI is that X will propose the problem, and lo and behold, it's the problem that their system is best at working at.

Bob Mac Gregor:

Even if you could solve that problem, I think the other problem is, if you have a benchmark, even if it's by an independent agency, AI is very good at solving specific problems. They could come up with a system pretty fast that would solve any benchmark that wasn't too complicated, too huge. But they wouldn't necessarily have solved the general problem; they just solved the benchmark.

Wlodek Zadrozny:

Well, it all depends on the situation. I can imagine a situation where the problem is posed in such a way that you have a certain set of data on which you are allowed to work, and then there comes another sequence of test stories for which your system is supposed to answer questions. And if your system can handle test data that you haven't seen before, I think you could say that it is doing more that just satisfying the benchmark.

David Gardiner:

Having worked on applications for customers in the real business world, I think that some data is better than none. Doing something like what has been suggested is not going to be a perfect solution to everything, but the larger the set of data that you have, the more likely you are to measure something real. You may as well have something, even though you may feel it's not as good as you can get.

Norm Sondheimer:

Other topics?

John Sowa:

One of the problems with these examples is that real stories are much too big and too complicated. In this workshop, we saw so many examples of Nixon the Quaker and Tweety the Penguin. There is a big gap between real stories and these tiny problems. When we get to natural language understanding, single sentences are difficult, and just moving to an entire paragraph is a major challenge. I think it would be worthwhile to select, say, ten paragraphs representing different kinds of text and challenge people to represent them.

Norm Sondheimer:

Another topic?

Alfred Kobsa:

This is a workshop on the formal aspects of *semantic* networks and for three days we've talked about various kinds of network data structures, network representations, etc. My impression is that none of us has explicitly addressed the problem of what's so specifically semantic about these network representations that justifies the notion of *semantic* networks. Quite the contrary, several speakers have hinted that this term is actually a misnomer.

We all know that semantic networks are called semantic networks for purely historical reasons. Quillian wanted to represent the meaning of English, the semantics of English words. He even wanted to define a model of how the meaning of English words gets represented in human memory. So it's the application of these networks that suggested the name, and not any special characteristics of them. My guess is that if Quillian had invented these networks for representing the rules of a baseball game, we would have called them baseball networks.

So what about changing the name of our workshop here, changing the name of the forthcoming book, changing the name of the baby? In this way we would not mislead people who are not familiar with knowledge representation to believe that there is something more semantic about semantic networks than there actually is. And we would also avoid criticism from other people in the field of knowledge representation. People in formal logic have been criticizing us for a long time that the term "semantic network" implies that there's something inherently semantic about these network structures, which there actually isn't. So what about simply calling them "network representations"?

Stuart Shapiro:

Well, you're right, it's historical. And as Len said, it means several different things, but we can trace their histories back to a common point, at least coming together at Quillian, and as John constantly reminds us, going back further into history. They are certainly network structures. I guess we agree on that. People used "associative networks" for quite a while. And "semantics" is from meaning. Schank wanted to call them "conceptual" instead. So we could just as easily have called them "conceptual networks," because they have to do with networks not of the surface terms, but of the concepts underlying them. Quillian's dissertation was titled *Semantic Memory*. I'm not sure if he used the term "semantic network" in it.

John Sowa:

Margaret Masterman used the term "semantic network" in 1961.

Stuart Shapiro:

I used the term "semantic associational memory net" in 1969. [laughter] But if you want to use something different, use something different. I don't see that arguing over the name is really relevant.

Bill Woods:

It's certainly an appropriate topic to close on.

Norm Sondheimer:

Yes, this is *deja vu*, we're out of tape, and so we have to stop.

LIST OF PARTICIPANTS

The workshop was organized in 90-minute sessions, each of which consisted of two 30-minute talks followed by two 15-minute discussion periods. Each discussion period was led by a discussant who commented on the themes of the two preceding talks and added his or her own perspective on the themes. Since everyone who participated in the workshop either presented a paper or served as a discussant, they were all active contributors who should be given credit for directly or indirectly influencing the ideas in this book. Following is a complete list of participants:

James M. Crawford, University of Texas,
David Gardiner, University of Minnesota,
Eric Grégoire, Université Catholique de Louvain,
Roger T. Hartley, New Mexico State University,
Rattikorn Hewett, Stanford Knowledge Systems Laboratory,
Graeme Hirst, University of Toronto,
Paul S. Jacobs, General Electric Research,
Alfred Kobsa, University of Saarbrücken,
Debbie Leishman, University of Calgary,
Robert MacGregor, USC Information Science Institute,
Deborah L. McGuinness, AT & T Bell Laboratories,
Bernhard Nebel, German Research Center for AI,
Peter Norvig, University of California at Berkeley,
Lenhart K. Schubert, University of Rochester,
Bart Selman, University of Toronto,
Stuart C. Shapiro, SUNY at Buffalo,

Lokendra Shastri, University of Pennsylvania,
Douglas Skuce, University of Ottawa,
Norm Sondheimer, General Electric Research,
John F. Sowa, IBM Systems Research Institute,
Lynn Andrea Stein, MIT AI Laboratory,
Richmond H. Thomason, University of Pittsburgh,
Robert Wilensky, University of California at Berkeley,
William A. Woods, Harvard University,
Wlodek Zadrozny, IBM T. J. Watson Research Center.

References

Ait-Kaci, H. 1986. An algebraic semantics approach to the effective resolution of type equations, *Theoretical Computer Science* 45:293–351.

Cardelli, L. and Wegner, P. 1985. On understanding types, data abstraction, and polymorphism, *ACM Computing Surveys* 17:471–522.

Charniak, E. 1986. A neat theory of marker passing, *Proc. Fifth National Conference on Artificial Intelligence*, Philadelphia, pp. 584–588.

Cohen, P. 1990. Methodological problems, a model-based design and analysis methodology, and an example. In *Methodologies for Intelligent Systems 5*, Ras, Z., Zemankova, M., and Emrich, M. (ed.s). North-Holland, New York.

Dick, J.P. 1987. Conceptual retrieval and case law. *Proc. First International Conference on Artificial Intelligence and Law*, Boston, May 1987, pp. 106–115.

Fawcett, B. 1985. *The Representation of Ambiguity in Opaque Contexts*, MSc thesis, published as technical report CSRI-178, Department of Computer Science, University of Toronto.

Fawcett, B. and Hirst, G. 1986. The detection and representation of ambiguities of intension and description, *Proc. 24th annual meeting, Association for Computational Linguistics*, New York, pp. 192–199.

de Groot, A.D. 1965. *Thought and Choice in Chess*, Mouton, The Hague.

Hays, D.G. 1964. Dependency theory: A formalism and some observations, *Language* 40(4):511–525.

Hendler, J. 1988. *Integrating Marker-Passing and Problem-Solving: A Spreading Activation Approach to Improved Choice in Planning*, Lawrence Erlbaum Associates, Hillsdale, NJ.

Hilbert, D. 1901. Mathematical problems, *Bulletin of the American Mathematical Society* 8:437–479.

Hirst, G. 1987. *Semantic Interpretation and the Resolution of Ambiguity*, Cambridge University Press, Cambridge.

Hirst, G. 1988. Resolving lexical ambiguity computationally with spreading activation and Polaroid Words, In *Lexical Ambiguity Resolution*, Small, S.L., Cottrell, G.W., and Tanenhaus, M.K. (ed.s), Morgan Kaufmann, San Mateo, CA, pp. 73–108.

Johnson, M. 1988. *Attribute-Value Logic and the Theory of Grammar*, CSLI Lecture Notes No. 16, Chicago University Press, Chicago.

Kasper, R. and Rounds, W. 1986. A complete logical calculus for record structures representing linguistic information, *Symposium on Logic in Computer Science*, IEEE Computer Society.

Kobsa, A. 1989. *Conceptual Hierarchies in Classical and Connectionist Architecture*, Technical Report 89-010, International Computer Science Institute, Berkeley, CA.

Lyons, D. 1989. *A Compositional Semantics for Focusing Subjuncts*, MSc thesis, published as technical report CSRI-234, Department of Computer Science, University of Toronto.

Miezitis, M. 1988. *Generating Lexical Options by Matching in a Knowledge Base*, MSc thesis, published as technical report CSRI-217, Department of Computer Science, University of Toronto.

Miezitis, M. and Hirst, G. 1989. Finding word options for a text generator, submitted for publication.

Minsky, M., ed. 1968. *Semantic Information Processing*, MIT Press, Cambridge, MA.

Newell, A. and Simon, H.A. 1972. *Human Problem Solving*, Prentice-Hall, Englewood Cliffs, NJ.

Peirce, C.S. 1878. How to make our ideas clear, *Popular Science Monthly* 12, January 1878, pp. 286–302. Reprinted in *Writings of Charles S. Peirce*, vol. 3, Indiana University Press, Bloomington, pp. 257–276.

Pollard, C. and Sag, I. Forthcoming. *Information-Based Syntax and Semantics*, vol. 2, Chicago University Press, Chicago.

Porphyry, *Isagoge et in Aristotelis Categorias Commentarium*, in *Commentaria in Aristotelem graeca* 4:1, Busse, A. (ed.), Berlin (1887).

Quillian, M.R. 1966. *Semantic Memory*, PhD Dissertation, Carnegie Institute of Technology. Abridged version in [Minsky, 1968; pp. 227–270].

Reder, L. 1983. What kind of pitcher can a catcher fill? Effects of priming in sentence comprehension, *Journal of Verbal Learning and Verbal Behavior* 22(2):189–202.

Roberts, D.D. 1973. *The Existential Graphs of Charles S. Peirce*, Mouton, The Hague.

Schank, R.C. and Tesler, L.G. 1969. A conceptual parser for natural language, *Proc. IJCAI-69*, pp. 569–578.

Selz, O. 1913. *Über die Gesetze des geordneten Denkverlaufs*, Spemann, Stuttgart.

Selz, O. 1922. *Zur Psychologie des produktiven Denkens und des Irrtums*, Friedrich Cohen, Bonn.

Shieber, S. 1986. *An Introduction to Unification-Based Approaches to Grammar*, Chicago University Press, Chicago.

Sowa, J.F. 1984. *Conceptual Structures: Information Processing in Mind and Machine*, Addison-Wesley, Reading, MA.

Tesnière, L. 1959. *Eléments de Syntaxe Structurale,* 2nd edition, Librairie C. Klincksieck, Paris, 1965.

Woods, W.A. 1975. What's in a link: Foundations for semantic networks. In *Representation and Understanding*, Bobrow, D. and Collins, A. (ed.s), Academic Press, New York.

Woods, W.A. 1987. Don't blame the tool, *Computational Intelligence* 3(3):228–237.

Zdonik, S. and Maier, D. (ed.s). 1989. *Readings in Object-Oriented Database Systems*, Morgan Kaufmann, San Mateo, CA.

1

UNDERSTANDING SUBSUMPTION AND TAXONOMY:

A Framework for Progress

W. A. Woods
(Harvard University and SUN Microsystems, Inc.)

Abstract

This chapter seeks a solid foundation for network representations of knowledge. Its goal is to clarify issues and establish a framework for progress.

The chapter analyzes the concepts of subsumption and taxonomy and synthesizes a framework that integrates and clarifies many previous approaches and goes beyond them to provide an account of abstract and partially defined concepts. The distinction between definition and assertion is reinterpreted in a framework that accommodates probabilistic and default rules as well as universal claims and abstract and partial definitions. Conceptual taxonomies in this framework are shown to be useful for indexing and organizing information and for managing the resolution of conflicting defaults.

The chapter introduces a distinction between intensional and extensional subsumption and argues for the importance of the former. It presents a classification algorithm based on intensional subsumption and shows that its typical case complexity is logarithmic in the size of the knowledge base.

1.1 INTRODUCTION

The theme I want to address in this chapter—taxonomies of structured conceptual descriptions—originated in the knowledge representation system KL-ONE [Woods and Brachman, 1978; Brachman and Schmolze, 1985]. A distinguishing characteristic of this work was the ability to automatically "classify" a structured concept with respect to a taxonomy of other concepts. That is, on the basis of its structure and the structure of concepts already in the taxonomy, a new concept could be automatically inserted into the taxonomy at the correct position. This capability has emerged as an important issue in knowledge representation [Woods, 1986]. It is one of the major innovations in knowledge representation research and one of the powerful driving themes underlying the interest in KL-ONE and related formalisms.

The operation of classification in KL-ONE stimulated a prolific investigation of systems of "terminological subsumption." Mac Gregor [this volume] and Woods and Schmolze [1991] give overviews of this research. However, despite considerable attention and progress, we still do not have an adequate understanding of structured concepts or the relationship of subsumption to description, deduction, and taxonomy. In fact, it has seemed to me that there are more open issues now than ever before—partly because of our increased understanding of the problem and partly due to the diversity of applications to which such knowledge representation systems are being put. Without a framework, it is difficult even to describe what the issues are. However, many of the issues have to do with the diversity of uses of links in semantic networks and the consequences of the semantics of those links. This chapter will examine the notions of subsumption and taxonomy and their dependence on the semantics of links. It will also provide a framework for integrating and extending the capabilities of current systems.

To establish a perspective, I will first briefly summarize the concepts of subsumption and taxonomy at an intuitive level. I will then look more closely at the notion of a concept, and introduce the notions of composite description and conceptual abstraction. This will be followed by a review of the distinction between assertional and structural links, an analysis of the semantics of assertional links, and then an analysis of the semantics of structural links in composite descriptions. Following this, I will examine in some detail the notions of subsumption and taxonomy and discuss current research in this area. I will then introduce a notion of intensional subsumption, define a classification algorithm for a version of intensional subsumption, and present timing analyses for several taxonomic operations on large knowledge bases.

1.1.1 Subsumption and Taxonomy

In virtually every semantic network formalism, there is at least one link that relates more specific concepts to more general concepts (from which generic information can be inherited). Such links have been variously named "is a," "kind of," "subset of," "member of," "subconcept of," "subkind of," "superconcept," "ako," etc. Such links are used to organize concepts into a hierarchy or some other partial ordering. I will call this structure a "taxonomy." The taxonomy is used for storing information at appropriate levels of generality and automatically making it available to more specific concepts by means of a mechanism of inheritance. More general concepts in such a partial order are said to *subsume* more specific concepts, and a more specific concept is said to *inherit* information from its subsumers.

In traditional semantic networks, the conceptual taxonomy is composed of directly asserted subsumption relations. In systems in which there are formally structured concepts, as in KL-ONE, subsumption of structured concepts can sometimes be inferred from the structures of the concepts (together with the subsumption relationships of their constituents). For example, a description

[person whose sons are professionals]

subsumes

[woman whose sons are doctors]

by virtue of its structure and the fact that [person] subsumes [woman] and [professional] subsumes [doctor]. (Throughout this chapter, I will use English descriptions in square brackets to refer to concepts.) I will refer to this kind of inferred subsumption relationship between structured concepts as *structural subsumption.*

This relationship of structural subsumption is what makes possible the operation of classification in KL-ONE. Classification is the operation of assimilating a new description into a taxonomy of existing concepts by automatically linking it directly to its most specific subsumers and the most general concepts that it in turn subsumes. This allows newly added concepts to automatically inherit appropriate information from other concepts in the network (i.e., without having to be manually placed in the correct position to do so). For example, if there are rules for behavior or attached data associated with concepts in the taxonomy, then a newly entered concept would inherit appropriate rules and data. Most other semantic networks, as well as frame-based representations and object-oriented programming systems, provide such inheritance only for concepts that are directly placed by their designers (or by specific programs) at the correct position in the taxonomy to inherit what is intended.

I will have more to say about subsumption and taxonomy in subsequent sections. First, however, we need to consider some more fundamental issues.

1.1.2 What Is a Concept?

In many semantic networks, the notion of a *concept* is primarily that of a *data structure.* In KL-ONE, an attempt was made to represent conceptual structure in a way that would reflect the structure of abstract concepts, independent of particular data structures. However, the semantics of these abstract structures were not totally clear. This was a problem, since a classification algorithm depends on an explicit understanding of the semantics of its representational elements (see [Brachman,

1983, 1985]). Although a classification algorithm was implemented in KL-ONE [Schmolze and Lipkis, 1983], it did not support all of KL-ONE's representational devices, partly due to the lack of a sufficiently clear semantics. Moreover, many users of KL-ONE used links in ways that violated the semantics intended by its designers. The need for a clearer understanding of the semantics of conceptual representation was apparent.

Many researchers, in search of a formal semantics for semantic networks, have chosen to identify the notion of a concept with the notion of a predicate in first-order logic. A significant number of researchers in the KL-ONE tradition have made this choice, e.g., Levesque and Brachman [1985]. However, there are risks of oversimplification associated with this identification, as I have argued elsewhere [Woods, 1986, 1987]. In "What's in a Link" [Woods, 1975], I argued that it is necessary to represent *intensional* concepts, in the sense in which [morning star] and [evening star] are intensionally distinct concepts, while referring to the same extension (the planet Venus). Such intensions cannot be expressed in first-order logic, nor can they be thought of as classes. For example, the concepts [prime number less than one] and [round square] both necessarily denote the empty class in all possible worlds, but are nevertheless distinct concepts. Others have also pointed out limitations of traditional predicate logic for representing natural concepts—e.g., Barwise and Perry [1983] and Hirst [1989].

Although much has been learned from theoretical investigations that identify concepts with first-order predicates, some of the confusion that currently exists seems to me to be a consequence of some resulting oversimplifications. In searching for an alternative that could provide a sound and intuitive basis for intensional concepts, I have found it useful to identify concepts with an appropriate notion of abstract description. The next section argues for this approach.

1.1.3 Concepts as Description

It is useful to think of the semantics of concepts in terms of abstract descriptions (rather than as predicates or classes) even though the notion of a description is not as well understood as that of a predicate or a class. As a starting point, we can take the idea of description as a pretheoretic notion, not immediately comparable to the theoretically well-understood notion of a predicate. However, I will attempt to put some more meat on this notion as we go along.

Initially, we can observe that a description has several aspects that go beyond the characteristics of a predicate in the predicate calculus. Specifically, where a predicate is simply true of something or not, a description has three principle characteristics, only the first of which corresponds to predicate satisfaction:

1. A description can be satisfied *by* something (in the way that a predicate is satisfied by values for its arguments). That is, a description can be true of a

thing it describes—e.g., an existing conceptualized structure can satisfy the description [ARCH]: an assembly of two upright blocks supporting a third horizontal block.

2. A description can be satisfied *in* a situation (by something that was not previously identified as an entity in the situation) and can be used to characterize the entity so recognized—e.g., the [ARCH] description can be satisfied by three blocks, resulting in the creation of a new concept for the arch composed of those blocks.
3. A description can be used as a structured plan for creating or reasoning about something that does not yet exist or may never exist—e.g., the [ARCH] description, as a structured intensional entity, can be used to determine the parts list and the assembly instructions for an arch plan, without any arches ever existing.

The notion of a description as a formal entity can provide a concrete understanding of some otherwise subtle phenomena that do not fit well in the traditional semantics of the first-order logic. For example, descriptions can provide a concrete basis for concepts of things that have various kinds of existence (or nonexistence), where classical predicate logic has difficulties (see [Hirst, 1989]). This is because a description is a conceptual entity that encodes certain characteristics of the things it could describe (whether such things exist or not). The structure of a description can entail properties in a formal way that does not necessarily require the description to be satisfied.

Descriptions, as used here, should not be thought of merely as data structures, but as *abstract conceptual entities*, independent of any particular notation for representing them. The important property is that descriptions have parts that can be analyzed and reasoned with.

1.1.4 The Structure of Descriptions

Conceptual descriptions can be divided into two kinds: *atomic* and *composite*. An atomic description consists merely of the name of an atomic category such as [mammal] or [tree]—there is no formal substructure to such a description. Such concepts are treated as primitives by most representational systems.

Many semantic networks and frame-based systems use only atomic conceptual descriptions and link them to other information by the equivalent of assertional links in order to express facts about the classes so named. Most discussions of the semantics of inheritance and default reasoning in frame-based systems take place in the context of hierarchies of primitive, atomic concepts (see, for example, the critique in [Brachman, 1985]). However, the strength of representational systems such as KL-ONE comes from an ability to deal with composite descriptions and to automatically organize them into hierarchies on the basis of their structure.

1.1.4.1 A Composite Description Schema

A *composite* conceptual description is constructed from other conceptual descriptions by means of concept-forming operators. The structure of this composition amounts to a definition of the concept, and this definition can be used to judge whether one such concept is more general or more specific than another. It is this composite definition that makes it possible to automatically organize such descriptions into a taxonomy on the basis of generality and to place a new description into the taxonomy at the correct place.

Many different notations and conventions have been used to represent composite descriptions. Almost all of them share a basic attribute:value or slot:filler structure that can be thought of as a constellation of links emerging from a central node. For the sake of discussion, I will use a notation here that attempts to capture the common elements of many such representations. The notation is simpler in some respects than that used in KL-ONE, while in other respects it is more powerful. Specifically, I will represent composite descriptions using a single concept-forming operator expressed by the schema

$$c_1 , \ldots , c_k / (r_1 : v_1) , \ldots , (r_n : v_n) : \{ p_1 , \ldots , p_t \}$$

where the c_i are *primary* conceptual descriptions, the $(r_i : v_i)$ are relational *modifiers* ("relation:value" pairs), and the p_i are *general conditions* expressed as predicates in a second-order functional calculus. As we will see, one can represent an extremely powerful range of composite descriptions using this single concept-forming operator.

Each $(r_i : v_i)$ pair can be thought of as a structural link with relational label r_i from the concept being defined to a concept v_i. Each r_i is a concept that denotes a relationship, and each v_i is a conceptual description for a value or object of that relation. Each primary concept can be thought of as equivalent to a [kind of] link from the concept being defined to the corresponding primary concept. Each general condition can be thought of as a [satisfies] link from the defined concept to a description of a predicate that it must satisfy.

Intuitively, an entity *e* satisfies a composite description of the above form if:

1. *e* can be described by each of the c_i ;
2. for each of the modifiers $m_i = r_i : v_i$ there is a concept *v* and a relationship *r* such that:

   r holds between *e* and *v*,

   r can be described by r_i, and

   v can be described by v_i ; and
3. *e* satisfies each of the general condition predicates p_i.

For example,

[person] / ([like] : [golf])

would be a composite conceptual description that describes a person who likes golf. That is, this description is satisfied by an entity if it is an instance of [person] and has a relationship described by [like] to the concept [golf]. If there are no general predications in the composite description schema, then the colon operator following the relation-value pairs can be omitted, as in the above example. If there are no modifiers, then the slash can be omitted, as in

[golfer] , [woman]

which describes a golfer that is also a woman. The degenerate case of a single primary concept with no modifiers will be considered to be the same as the primary concept.

Unlike in KL-ONE, but consistent with many of KL-ONE's successors, the relationships in the above relational modifiers can be arbitrary binary relations (such as [like]) and not just relational attributes (such as [hobby]). Note that I treat the relations r_i as a distinguished subclass of concepts. In many semantic networks and KL-ONE-like systems, relations are treated as disjoint from concepts. However, in any network with self-reflexive properties—i.e., a network with an ability to describe its own representational machinery or to make generic statements about relations—it would be necessary for the link label (i.e., the relation), as well as the linked concepts, to be represented by conceptual nodes in the network.

Notice that the above definition allows for classification and description of the relations r_i as well as value restrictions v_i. Since the relations are themselves specified by conceptual descriptions, the semantics of a relation can be defined by characterizing it in the same conceptual framework used to represent other concepts. That is, relations are a subclass of concepts and can be cataloged and organized into a taxonomy just like other concepts. This will be significant when we come to look more closely at subsumption.

The above notation generalizes the notation of KL-ONE by allowing arbitrary binary relations in positions where KL-ONE would use only generalized attributes (i.e., roles). The notation appears to be more limited than KL-ONE in having no obvious counterpart to number restrictions, role differentiation, or role modification, but this is not actually the case. As we will see below, number restrictions, role differentiation, role modification, and various quantificational capabilities can all be represented within this framework by using appropriate relation-forming operators.

1.1.5 Conceptual Abstraction

Objects described by a composite description often turn out to have additional properties that were not part of the description but are logical consequences of the description. For example, a polygon with three sides will necessarily also have three angles. Sometimes there are alternative descriptions that mutually imply each other and give rise to effectively the same concept—e.g., [polygon with three sides] and [polygon with three angles]. When this happens with the definition of some concept in mathematics, the move that is usually made is to consider the alternative definitions to be equivalent and the concept so defined to be an abstraction that in some sense fuses or merges the different definitions. That is, any of the definitions can be used, whichever is convenient, and the results will apply to the abstraction, independent of how it is described.

KL-ONE did not deal with such abstractions—nor have any of its successors. However, with a little thought, it is possible to extend the notion of description given above to handle abstractions of this kind. One need only think of abstract concepts as equivalence classes of descriptions. One way to express this is by means of a special kind of disjunction operator that takes a collection of descriptions and produces a description that is satisfied if any of its disjuncts are satisfied (like ordinary disjunction) and furthermore asserts that if any of its disjuncts are satisfied then all of them will be. This operator is equivalent to a combination of a disjunction and an equivalence statement. I will refer to this operation as *conceptual abstraction*.

It is useful to think of concepts in a semantic network as abstract descriptions in the above sense—that is, to think of a concept as an equivalence class of descriptions. For such a concept, any of its disjunctive descriptions will be sufficient to determine that something is an instance of the concept, but once an instance is so classified, it can be concluded that all of the other equivalent descriptions are satisfied as well. Thus, the concept of a triangle would consist of the conceptual abstraction of the two descriptions [polygon with three sides] and [polygon with three angles].

In KL-ONE, representing the fact that these two definitions of triangle are equivalent would require that they be merged. However, the resulting merged concept would be equivalent to the description [polygon with three sides and three angles]. This says that one can classify something as a triangle if it has both three sides and three angles. The knowledge that either of the two, less specific, original descriptions would have been sufficient is lost in the merged concept.

The triangle example shows that identifying concepts with single descriptions is too limiting. It is unable to represent certain quite typical situations. Identifying concepts with equivalence classes of descriptions allows one to deal with abstract concepts in what seems to be just the right way. It captures that fact that all of the descriptions will be satisfied if any are, and it preserves the information that any one of them will be sufficient.

One might think that formally defined concepts like [triangle] are a rare special case and that most concepts do not admit definitions in this way. While it is true that there are a great many "natural kind" concepts, like [person], which are difficult to define, there is an even larger number of concepts that can be defined in terms of these—[person with red hair], [person with no children], etc. Moreover, as I will show later, one can apply similar techniques to concepts that are only partially defined.

I will have more to say about conceptual abstraction and about partially defined concepts below. At this point, however, I want to establish a framework by looking carefully at the semantics of ordinary assertional links and then turn to the semantics of the structural links that make up composite descriptions. The semantics of the latter are quite different from those of the former. First, I will review the distinction between structural and assertional links.

1.1.6 Structural and Assertional Links

What distinguishes semantic networks from many other representations of knowledge is the use of links to both record facts and serve as associative access paths by which facts are accessible from each other. These associative paths can then support efficient algorithms for certain kinds of reasoning. Thus, the links in a semantic network are used both to express facts and to link facts together. They are also used to link individual elements that make up complex facts.

A link that is used to express a fact can be said to be an *assertional* link. Such a link, by its very existence, asserts the fact to be true. When a link is used to form a part of a larger structure that, taken as a whole, may express a fact, then the individual links making up the structure are said to be *structural* links. Occasionally a structural link may play a role in the definition of a term or concept. In this case, we can characterize the link as *definitional*. The importance of the structural/assertional distinction was raised in "What's in a Link" and illustrated by the question of whether the link structure expressed by the triple:

[telephone] [color] [black]

was to be interpreted as an assertion that telephones are black or as representing the concept of a black telephone. In the latter case, I characterized the link as *structural or definitional* [Woods, 1975], since the link formed a part of the defining structure of the concept.

The distinctions between assertional links and structural links and between definition and assertion are important, but the distinctions have often seemed subtle and confusing. I think this is partly because the distinctions are often treated as if they were mutually exclusive alternatives. Note that although these different uses of a link are distinct, it is possible for some links to simultaneously play several roles. For example, a single link might be both assertional and structural. Thus, the fact that a structural link in the concept [black telephone] also has the assertional import that all such telephones are black does not conflict with its role as a structural link. I will have more to say about definitions later.

Interestingly, while "What's in a Link" made an issue of making the distinction between assertional and structural uses of links, most subsequent work on formal conceptual structure has concentrated on the structural uses. In the meantime, many semantic networks and frame-based systems have been developed for a variety of practical purposes using primarily assertional links (often not in a principled way). There are good reasons to have assertional links in a semantic network and to distinguish them from structural links. In the next few sections, I will present a framework that can accommodate both structural and assertional links. I will first address some issues concerning the semantics of assertional links, and then turn to the semantics of structural links in composite descriptions.

1.2 SEMANTICS OF ASSERTIONAL LINKS

The prototypical use of an assertional link labeled with a relation r from a node x to a node y in a semantic network corresponds to the assertion of a relationship described by r between the object represented by x and the object represented by y. For example, the relational triple

[John] [live in] [New York]

might be a way of expressing the fact that John lives in New York.

However, many uses of assertional links in semantic networks (and their equivalents in frame systems), are not between individual concepts such as [John] and [New York], but between generic concepts such as [person] and [place]. It is not uncommon to find links in a semantic network like

[person] [live in] [place].

One might spontaneously take such a link to indicate that people live in places—i.e., every person lives in some place. However, one of the lessons of "What's in a Link" is that one must be careful to make such interpretations on the basis of a clear understanding of the semantics of the notation and not on the basis of the informal semantics implied by the names of the nodes and links.

Making the semantics explicit in the notation is especially important for examples like the one above, because the common English locutions for generic statements often have subtly different, alternative interpretations. For example, does "people live in places" mean that every person has a place to live, or that if a person lives in x, then x must be a place (or *vice versa*)? If such distinctions are not made in the representation and treated correctly by reasoning algorithms, then unexpected consequences will arise from inconsistencies between interpretations assumed by a person entering information and interpretations assumed by (the designers of) the algorithms that will operate on the information.

1.2.1 Quantificational Import

When we interpret the above triple to mean that every person lives in some place, we are effectively interpreting the subject of the link as the range of a universal quantification and the object concept as the range of an existential quantification. We might more formally express this as

every [person] [live in] some [place]

or in a "beefed up," but readable, predicate calculus notation (with typed quantifier variables):

(For every x / person)
(there is some y / place) (such that)
(x live in y)

I will call this the *AE interpretation* (using A for All and E for Exist), and one might represent it compactly as

AE [person] [live in] [place]
"every person lives in some place."

The AE interpretation of a link between two generic concepts seems to be a very common thing to say. However, it is only one possible interpretation of such a link, and it is not the only kind of thing one might want to express using links in a semantic network. Other possible interpretations of such relational triples would include:

AA [person] [need] [vitamin]
"every person needs every vitamin"
EE [person] [break] [window]
"some person breaks some window"
EA [student] [take] [course]
"some student takes every course"

Moreover, there are interpretations in which two of the elements of the link restrict the third:

VR [person] [live in] [place]
"if a person lives in y then y is a place,"
SR [person] [live in] [apartment]
"if x lives in an apartment then x is a person"

(Mnemonically, SR = Subject Restriction, VR = Value Restriction.) Note that "value" restrictions here apply to subjects and objects of arbitrary relations and not just to values of attributes. These are similar to the range and domain restrictions of many of KL-ONE's descendants, except that SR and VR are used for making assertions rather than for expressing terminological constraints.

1.2.2 Defeasible Assertion

In addition to interpretations of generic statements in terms of standard logical quantifiers, there are also interpretations as generalizations that admit exceptions. Such assertions are said to be *defeasible*. There are two paradigms for defeasible assertions—*probability* and *defaults*. The former is based on statistical concepts and provides some notion of how likely the defeasible conclusion is to be true. The latter is based on a principle that says, essentially, make the default assumption unless there is reason to believe otherwise. For our purposes, we need not make a judgment on the merits of the two paradigms. It is merely important to distinguish the defeasible sense of a link from the absolute sense. We can do this by means of typicality annotations such as

TAE [person] [live in] [house]

"typically, if x is a person then x lives in some house"

TAA [person] [like] [candy]

"typically, if x is a person and y is candy x will like y"

TVR [dog] [eat] [dog food]

"typically, if a dog eats y then y is dog food"

TSR [person] [have] [plan]

"typically, if x has a plan, then x is a person"

There are many proposals in the literature for formal systems of defeasible reasoning, for example [Shastri, 1989]. Since some of them have different capabilities, one may want to integrate several such systems into a single framework. If so, then one will need a set of typicality annotations for each such interpretation (and perhaps for their combinations). For probabilistic interpretations, there will be accompanying probability estimates or other quantitative measures of likelihood. In such cases, the typicality annotation would include the appropriate quantitative parameters.

Most frame systems use defeasible links (i.e., *slots*), and do so by interpreting all links as making defeasible claims. This, however, leaves them incapable of expressing a true universal claim if that is what is desired (see [Brachman, 1985]). Moreover, they generally do not make the quantificational distinctions illustrated above, although their implemented reasoning mechanism must necessarily assume some such interpretation. Ideally, a knowledge representation system should be able to express both universal and defeasible claims of a variety of kinds and to distinguish what is intended in each case. I will now present a framework that permits this.

1.2.3 Relation-forming Operators

We started our discussion of assertional links with a simple notion of a link between two individual concepts asserting a relationship between those two individuals. We then considered the case of links between generic concepts and found a diversity of distinct quantificational imports. Interestingly, there is a way to return to the original simple semantics of link assertions while at the same time gaining control over the diversity of quantificational interpretations. Moreover, this can be done without sacrificing a rigorous and explicit semantics for the links.

The trick is to introduce a small set of relation-forming operators that construct relations whose semantics entail a quantification over generic concepts. Consider the following example:

Define an operator AE that will apply to a relation r to produce a new relation AE [r] that can link two generic concepts. This new relation asserts about those two generic concepts that for each instance x of the first, there is an instance y in the second, such that the relation r holds between x and y. That is, for two generic concepts X and Y,

X (AE [r]) Y iff (for every x / X)
(there exists a y / Y) (such that)
$x\ r\ y$.

Similar operators can be defined for all of the other quantificational imports—including the defeasible notions of typicality. Note that in doing this, we have left first-order logic behind and are solidly in the realm of higher order logic (where one can quantify over relations and classes). This is necessary in order to treat concepts as intensional entities and not simply extensions.

By introducing relation-forming operators and using the composite relations that result, one can make quantificational assertions between generic concepts that have the same straightforward semantics as do simple relations between individuals. Such an assertion between generic concepts makes a claim equivalent to a quantification over instances of those concepts. Thus, the relation AE [live in] could be asserted between two generic concepts to assert that every instance of the first lives in some instance of the second.

1.2.4 Quantificational Tags

Quantificational relation-forming operators provide a methodology and an appropriate semantics for any desired quantificational import of a link. It will be necessary for a reasoning engine to know this quantificational import in the course of its reasoning. Thus, the quantificational import of a link should be explicitly distinguishable from the underlying (domain-specific) relation to which the quantificational operator has been applied. This could be done in any number of ways, including by making it an attribute of the relation so it can be interrogated by the reasoning algorithm. For the remainder of this chapter, I will choose to represent it as an explicit quantificational tag associated with the link. That is, the link relation can be thought of as always having two parts: a quantificational tag and an underlying domain relation. For example,

[person] AA [need] [vitamin].

By distinguishing the quantificational tag from the base relation, one can classify these two components separately and use information from the relational component independent of information from the quantificational tag. Note that these link tags themselves could be conceptualized and classified in a taxonomy, compactly summarizing those that quantify over the subject, those that quantify over the object, those that are defeasible, etc.

1.2.5 Tagging the Kind/Instance Distinction

The above examples of quantificational import cover the cases of a quantificational statement between two generic kinds. However, there are also cases in which either the subject or the object of a link is filled by a particular instance while the other is a generic. Thus we also need quantificational tags for the following distinctions (where I stands for "Individual"):

AI	"everybody likes John"
EI	"somebody likes John"
IA	"John likes everybody"
IE	"John likes somebody"
SRI	"only sport fans like John"
IVR	"John eats only vegetarian food"

To complete the paradigm, we can add the tag

II	"John likes Mary."

1.2.6 Other Relation-forming Operators

In addition to quantificational tags, there are other relation-forming operators that will be useful for making assertions and for composing composite descriptions. These include CONVERSE, which reverses the subject and object of its argument relation (like the English passive construction), and RESTRICT, an operator that restricts the objects of a relation to instances of a specified concept. These can be defined by

x (CONVERSE [r]) y iff y [r] x,
x (RESTRICT [r] [c]) y iff x [r] y and y [instance of] [c].

Examples using these operators are

[course] AE (CONVERSE [take]) [student]
"Every course was taken by some student"

[Sally] IVR (RESTRICT [friend] [male]) [married]
"Sally's male friends are all married"

The CONVERSE operator is necessary for expressing a quantificational dependency across a relation in which the order of quantifier precedence goes from object to subject rather than *vice versa*. That is, the compositions AE CONVERSE and EA CONVERSE cannot be otherwise expressed.

Another relation-forming operator, CHAIN, is used to express indirect relationships consisting of a sequence of other relations. CHAIN can be defined by

x (CHAIN [r_1] , ... , [r_n]) y iff

there is some sequence of entities x_1 , ... , x_{n-1} such that

$x\ r_1\ x_1$, $x_1\ r_2\ x_2$, ... , and $x_{n-1}\ r_n$ y.

Such chains can be used to assert constraints about entities indirectly related to a given entity without knowing or instantiating any of the intermediate concepts. For example,

[John] IE (CHAIN [mother] [sister] [son]) [golfer]
"One of John's mother's sister's sons is a golfer"

Since the result of such relational composition is itself a relation, the result can be used in assertions and in composite descriptions in any positions where a relation can be used. Such access paths were provided in KL-ONE for the special case of role sequences in structural descriptions, where they were called *role chains*, and similar structures are used in many of KL-ONE's successors.

The above account of the semantics of assertional links provides a framework within which one can integrate the representation of both assertional and structural information. It also sets a pattern for the semantics of some of the structural links to which we will now turn our attention—the links that make up a composite description.

1.3 SEMANTICS OF COMPOSITE DESCRIPTION

Links that are used to form composite descriptions have a semantics that is quite different from those of assertional links. Such links are structural rather than assertional. A single structural link need not have a self-contained semantics; rather, the entire constellation of structural links emanating from a node takes on a collective meaning as a function of its structure. In principle, one could define any number of structured-concept paradigms, whose individual links could have idiosyncratic semantic import. The composite description schema that I introduced above, however, has only three distinct kinds of links, each of which contributes in a uniform way to the semantics of the whole. The way in which the primary concepts contribute is simply the conjunction of their individual semantic constraints—that is, each instance of the composite description must satisfy each of the primary conceptual descriptions. The way in which the relational modifiers contribute (which we will discuss next) is also a simple conjunction, but somewhat more involved.

1.3.1 Relational Restrictions

Each of the relational modifiers (r_i : v_i) in the composite description schema imposes a relational constraint on possible instances of the composite description. Like assertional links, these relational modifiers can have different quantificational imports, and here also, we can express those imports by relation-forming operators that construct the appropriate quantified relation as a composition of a quantificational tag with an underlying domain-specific relation.

The semantics of three such quantificational imports are systematically related to the semantics of corresponding assertional quantifications—the AA, AE, and AI cases. The corresponding tags for relational modification (MA, ME, and MI) express the constraints that for any instance of the composite concept there must be a relation described by r_i from that instance either

1. to every instance of v_i (the MA case),
2. to some instance of v_i (the ME case), or
3. to v_i itself (the MI case).

Examples of descriptions using these three quantificational tags are:

"a student who takes every math course"

[student] / (MA [take course] : [math course])

"a student who takes some math course"

[student] / (ME [take course] : [math course])

"a student who takes Math 21"

[student] / (MI [take course] : [Math 21])

A third quantificational tag (MR) is related to the VR (value restriction) case. It imposes the constraint that every thing that is related to an instance by a relation satisfying the description r_i must satisfy the object description v_i. An example of this case would be

"a student all of whose courses are math courses"

[student] / (MR [take course] : [math course]).

Note that we have two distinct kinds of universal quantification—MA and MR. The MR case corresponds closely to value restrictions on roles in KL-ONE—it requires that every value of the role must satisfy the stated object description. The MA case states, conversely, that every instance of the specified object description must stand in the indicated relation to any instance of the concept being described. The first is universally quantifying over the value set of the role; the latter is quantifying over the instances of the value description. There is no equivalent to the MA case in KL-ONE.

Note that since an existential role restriction would be symmetric with respect to the above distinction, there is only one existential role restriction—ME. That is, the following two English descriptions are equivalent, and both are handled by the above ME case:

"a student some of whose courses are math courses"

"a student who takes some math course"

[student] / (ME [take course] : [math course])

One might argue that these two descriptions are (psychologically) intensionally distinct and only extensionally equivalent—i.e., that it takes reasoning to tell that the two descriptions are equivalent. I will not take that position here, however.

1.3.1.1 Number Restrictions

Not all semantic network systems deal with number restrictions as part of their representational machinery. However, such restrictions were formalized as a facet of roles in KL-ONE and are used in many of KL-ONE's successor systems. Like quantificational operators, number restrictions can be introduced by relation-forming operators playing the role of quantificational tags. Specifically, parameterized quantification operators ML(n) and MU(n) (for lower bound and upper bound, respectively) can express the constraints that at least n or at most n entities stand in the indicated relation—e.g.,

"a student at least n of whose courses are math courses"

[student] / (ML(n) [take course] : [math course])

"a student at most n of whose courses are math courses"

[student] / (MU(n) [take course] : [math course])

To express an exact number, one can define MQ(n) as the "conjunction" of ML(n) and MU(n):

"a student exactly n of whose courses are math courses"
[student] / (MQ(n) [take course] : [math course])

Note that the ML(1) case is equivalent to the ME case above, so a system that implements number restrictions should probably standardize on one or the other of these tags.

1.3.1.2 Negation

In order to express the absence of a property, one can define a negation operator NOT that will compose with relations, just as a quantificational tag does, to produce descriptions such as

"a student none of whose courses are math courses"
[student] / (NOT [take course] : [math course]).

If upper bound number restrictions are implemented, then this is equivalent to and could also be expressed as

"a student at most 0 of whose courses are math courses"
[student] / (MU(0) [take course] : [math course]).

1.3.2 General Conditions

In the above composite description schema, one can say a great deal using only the primary concepts and the relational modifiers. We will call such descriptions *type 1 descriptions*. With type 1 descriptions, one can say anything about a concept that does not require coordination among more than one role or relational chain. That is, one can make any unary predication about instances of the concept or the values at the ends of relations or relational chains. However, type 1 descriptions cannot state conditions that involve constraints among more than one role or relational chain at a time. Thus, one could describe

[person who likes music]

but could not describe

[boy whose mother cleans his room].

The general conditions p_i in the composite description schema provide for such coordination constraints. They consist of descriptions of predications whose arguments (roles) may themselves be "filled" by roles or role chains, interpreted to represent the sets of individuals so related to the concept being defined. For reasons of time, space, and complexity, we will not go further into the structure and consequences of general conditions in this chapter. Suffice it to say that handling role interactions is a problem for continuing research and is a significant factor in tractability and decidability of subsumption [Schmidt-Schauss, 1989].

In the remainder of this chapter, I will investigate the concepts of subsumption and taxonomy inherent in type 1 descriptions. Such descriptions already provide enough machinery to do a substantial amount of useful work. Before proceeding, however, we need to look more closely at the concept of definition.

1.4 DEFINITION

In order to build a knowledge base of any complexity, it is necessary to lay a foundation of basic concepts and define other concepts in terms of them. These defined concepts are then used to define still other concepts until a substantial knowledge system is built up from many layers of defined abstractions. To be effective, such definitions should produce new concepts that can be used as efficiently as primitive concepts—not just as abbreviations that make reading easier but have to be expanded in order to be applied. The purpose of such definitions is to hide unnecessary details—not only from a human reader but also from the inferential machinery when the details are not necessary to the inference. For example, if an assertion and a potentially matching goal both mention a concept by name, there is no reason to expand the name into its definition in order to discover the match. On the contrary, there may be combinatorially explosive reasons not to.

The status of definition in knowledge representation is not always clear. In much of the research in terminological subsumption, definition seems to have been taken as somehow synonymous with the notion of composite description. This is not an adequate view, for we may have concepts in a knowledge representation system that are defined by deductive rules in an inference system or by perceptual machinery to which the knowledge base and reasoning system has no direct access. Moreover, we may have concepts defined to be disjunctions of other concepts or by a conceptual abstraction of several descriptions. Finally, we may have concepts that are partially defined—leaving gaps between what is included and what is excluded. (I have argued elsewhere, [Woods, 1981, 1987], that certain predicates must necessarily have partial definitions and that many of our everyday concepts—especially natural kinds—have such partial definitions.)

A better way to view definition is to think of a concept as potentially having both a name and a definition (and sometimes multiple names and/or multiple definitions). An undefined primitive concept has only a name. Conversely, a pure description (such as "person with three sons") has only a definition and has no other name. Many concepts have both names and definitions—e.g., [triangle], which we previously defined as the abstraction of [polygon with three sides] and [polygon with three angles].

As discussed previously, some concepts may be defined by single descriptions, or by disjunctions of descriptions, or by abstractions of multiple descriptions. Other concepts may be defined by axioms relating them to other concepts in terms of operations of deductive inference. All of these senses of definition will fit in a framework that identifies concepts not with names or definitions but with something that can have both names and definitions as attributes.

1.4.1 Separating Necessity and Sufficiency

Traditionally, a predicate in logic or mathematics is defined by a biconditional equation specifying necessary and sufficient conditions for it to be true. The above discussion makes it clear that sometimes this is too much to expect for natural concepts. Rather, a definition should provide for separate statements of *necessary* conditions and *sufficient* conditions, so that it can accommodate the case where there are gaps between the two. This also accommodates definition by a disjunction of descriptions and by conceptual abstraction.

The notions of partial definition, disjunctive definition, and conceptual abstraction dovetail nicely with the separation of necessary and sufficient conditions. The conjunction of alternative descriptions of an abstract concept becomes a collective set of necessary conditions for the concept. Each of the separate descriptions that make up the abstraction becomes a separate sufficient condition. For example, [polygon with three sides] and [polygon with three angles] are each separately sufficient conditions for the concept whose necessary condition is [polygon with three sides and three angles]. In this case, the necessary conditions are stronger than the individual sufficient conditions.

For a disjunctive definition, on the other hand, each of the disjuncts is a separate sufficient condition, but the only necessary conditions are those that are implied by each of the individual disjuncts—e.g., some condition that they all have in common or that they disjunctively imply. In this case, the necessary conditions are generally weaker than the sufficient conditions. The strongest necessary condition for a disjunctively defined concept is the disjunction itself—that's what disjunction means.

For a partial definition, there is a gap between the coverage of the sufficient conditions and the complement of the necessary ones—that is, there may be many entities and situations that are neither ruled out nor ruled in by the definition. Such partially defined concepts are an important class of naturally occurring concepts. For example, many natural kind terms may be given such partial definitions.

The separation of necessary and sufficient conditions, although it has not been done in previous subsumption-based systems, will become important in the discussion of subsumption in Section 1.5.

1.4.2 Definitional Operators

Whether biconditional or separate statements of necessary and sufficient conditions, a definition needs to be distinguished from other conditional statements that merely happen to be true. That is, there should be distinguished operators for making definitions that are distinct from those used for assertion of (nondefinitional) truth-functional equivalence and conditional implication. For something to be a definition, it needs to be more than just a set of conditions that happen to be correlated with the extension of the intended concept. Rather, a definition must represent the intended meaning of the concept, an intent that will be the last thing to relax in the face of an apparent counterexample [Woods, 1983]. This can be illustrated by the following example.

Aristotle is reported to have once defined "human" as

"a featherless biped."

When challenged with the example of a plucked chicken, he is said to have added the qualification

"with broad flat nails."

Clearly Aristotle had an intended concept in mind and his reported definition was not faithful to it. Otherwise, he would not have added a qualification when confronted with the chicken. Had his first "definition" been his true intent, he should have judged the chicken to have become human by virtue of being plucked.

To distinguish between conditions that are part of a definition and those that are merely conditionally associated with a concept, we need some specific operators of definition. In order to deal with abstract and partial definitions, these operators must be capable of making separate statements of necessary and sufficient conditions. The following schematic notations will suffice for expressing such definitions:

<concept> [d-if] <condition>

<concept> [d-only-if] <condition>

<concept> [d-iff] <condition>

The first of these ("definitional if") covers the case of a single sufficient condition; the second ("definitional only-if") covers the case of a single necessary condition; the third ("definitional if-and-only-if") covers a full biconditional definition. The use of multiple [d-iff] links defines abstract concepts like [triangle], discussed earlier—i.e., any one of the conditions is sufficient, and all of them are necessary.

1.4.3 Expressive Power

It is now appropriate to take inventory of where we stand. The question of interest is: "What is the expressive power of the mechanism we have introduced?" Is it, for example, sufficient to express anything that can be expressed in first-order logic? Can it express things that cannot be expressed in first-order logic? The answer is that it can express more than at first appears, but the full range of expressibility of these operators is not obvious.

The basic schema for structural description is clearly conjunctive, so that arbitrary conjunctions of descriptions can be constructed. Moreover, since the nature of the sufficient condition definitional operator is inherently disjunctive, we can define a concept for any disjunction of descriptions (even though we can't use a disjunction directly in a description without first defining a concept for the disjunction). Consequently, we have the full power of conjunctions of disjunctions to arbitrary depth (intermediated by definitions).

Moreover, if we have either an upper bound number restriction or the NOT operator, then we can describe concepts that lack certain properties. Moreover, we can express any normal quantificational statement involving arguments to a binary relation. Any unary predicates can also be expressed by links from the subject to the predicate using a relation [satisfy]. Hence we have enough machinery to express directly, using assertional links and defined concepts, almost anything that one would want to express in the predicate calculus using unary and binary relations. What about the case of relations of more than two arguments?

1.4.3.1 Relations of More than Two Arguments

Any relation involving more than two arguments that would be expressed in the form $R(x_1, \ldots, x_n)$ in the predicate calculus can be described within the conceptual machinery introduced above by the description

$$R \,/\, (r_1 : x_1), \ldots, (r_n : x_n)$$

where $r_1, \ldots, r_n$ are coined names for the n argument positions in R. This involves conceptualizing the relationship expressed by R and coining named relations (roles) for the arguments or parameters of R. With this convention, any relation of more than two arguments can be expressed using a binary, link-oriented notation. This technique is quite common, and is used in relational databases, semantic networks, case grammars, frame systems, and many other knowledge representation systems. (For another approach to relations of more than one argument see [Schmolze, 1989].)

Note that this construction represents only a description of the relationship. The mere existence of such a description does not assert that the relationship is true. In order to record that such a relationship is true in the current framework, one would need to link this description to something by means of an assertional link—for example by a relation [satisfied in] to a concept for a context in which it is believed to be true. In order to use such a description as a condition of another description, one would insert it as one of the general conditions in the composite description schema.

1.4.3.2 General Quantification

We have just seen that, in spite of the focus on binary relations and conjunctive descriptions, there is sufficient power in the composite description schema and the definitional machinery to describe relationships of arbitrary degree and to express disjunction and negation.

It is not immediately clear, however, that the quantificational machinery introduced for binary relations, together with the above techniques for defining concepts, is sufficient to express all quantificational statements that one might want to express when more than two quantified variables are involved. It is an interesting open question whether by sufficient ingenuity one could express any quantificational statement using just the machinery so far.

If necessary, however, one can always take the approach followed by Shapiro and Rapaport [1987] and construct explicit descriptions of quantified statements, which are then operated on by general purpose deductive machinery.

An area of research yet to be explored is the issue of organizing general quantified statements on the basis of generality.

1.5 SUBSUMPTION

We now have sufficient machinery in place to look more closely at the issue of subsumption. As mentioned previously, subsumption is a formal relationship between pairs of conceptual descriptions that allows them to be ordered into a taxonomy on the basis of generality. I will begin with an informal introduction to the idea and then give a more formal definition.

Informally, a composite description can subsume another composite description for any combination of the following reasons (all other things being equal):

1. A primary category in one is more general than one in the other:
   [a person whose sons are doctors]
   subsumes [a woman whose sons are doctors]
2. A relational modifier in one is more general than one in the other:
   [a person whose sons are professionals]
   subsumes [a person whose sons are doctors]

3. A general condition of one is more general than one in the other:
   [a child one of whose parents cleans his room]
   subsumes [a child whose mother cleans his room]
4. The more specific description includes a category, modifier, or condition not present in the more general description:
   [a person whose sons are doctors] subsumes
   [a person whose sons are doctors and who enjoys driving]

Note that there is considerable subtlety buried in the statement of case 2—the subsumption of relational modifiers. We shall see later that depending on the semantics of the link involved—i.e., on the quantificational tag involved in the relation—we will get different effects from generalizing elements of the modifier. Generalizing an element of a relational modifier may either generalize or specialize the resulting description, depending on the quantificational tag and on whether the element being generalized is the relation or the object of the modifier. Most of this subtlety was not identified in KL-ONE and seems not to be generally appreciated. Likewise, there is considerable subtlety in case 3, but since we are restricting ourselves here to type 1 descriptions, we will not discuss case 3 here.

1.5.1 Concepts of Subsumption

Although the basic idea of one concept subsuming another seems simple and straightforward, the application of this insight in practice has been less than crystal clear. The basic idea that subsumption is used to organize a taxonomy of concept nodes to which information can be attached (linked) and inherited seems clear. Yet when one attempts to construct a system such as KL-ONE and to use it for applications, the clarity of the basic idea seems to slip away. Part of the problem is a lack of sufficient precision and/or expressive power in the semantics of the notation. The machinery I have introduced above is an attempt to address these issues. Another issue seems to be a confusion about subsumption itself.

In attempting to understand subsumption and classification, I have come to identify several distinct notions of subsumption that are important to keep straight but are not distinguished in most discussions of the topic. That is, the term *subsumption* is overloaded and has several distinct senses that are generally confused. These include:

1. *extensional subsumption*—by virtue of the meaning of the concepts, any instance of the subsumed concept must necessarily be an instance of the subsuming concept in a model-theoretic sense. That is the extension of the subsuming concept contains the extension of the subsumed concept.
2. *structural subsumption*—the subsuming concept is determined to be more general than the subsumed concept by virtue of a formally specified subsumption criterion applied to the structures of the descriptions—preferably by an

algorithm that is computationally tractable or at least more efficient than general deduction.

3. *recorded subsumption*—the more general concept is explicitly recorded as subsuming the more specific concept in a stored taxonomic structure—either directly or indirectly, i.e., either by a direct link or by the transitive closure of such links.
4. *axiomatic subsumption*—the more general concept is asserted to subsume the more specific concept as an axiom of the subject matter of the knowledge base.
5. *deduced subsumption*—the more general concept is deduced to subsume the more specific concept by deductive inference operations applied to knowledge of the domain—e.g., by a general-purpose deduction component.

The importance of the distinctions among these senses comes about in the context of using subsumption as a basis for organizing a taxonomy of conceptual descriptions. Sense 3 comes into play as the result of the taxonomic organization; sense 2 is used for testing subsumption when setting up the taxonomy or when classifying new descriptions with respect to it; and sense 1 is used only for determining the soundness and completeness of the operations of sense 2. Sense 4 provides the basis on which the definition of structural subsumption is grounded. That is, these are the base axioms of generality whose consequences are propagated to composite descriptions by the operation of structured subsumption. Sense 5 arises when there is a subsumption relationship that can be deduced from logical or theoretical constraints of the domain, but which may not follow from the criterion of structured subsumption—for example, the constraint that a polygon with three sides must also be a polygon with three angles.

Note that senses 1, 2, and 5 are all context-sensitive in that they depend on more than just the two descriptions involved—they depend on what is true in the context. For example, sense 1 depends on what constraints (logical or domain-specific) are operating to constrain the instances of the "subsumee" to be instances of the "subsumer." In sense 2, whether a composite description subsumes another depends on the subsumption relationships between their corresponding constituents, ultimately resting on the ground set of axiomatic subsumption relations on which structural subsumption is based. Sense 5, of course depends on the axiomatic base and whatever inference rules enable the reasoning system to draw its conclusions.

In organizing a conceptual taxonomy, conceptual descriptions are inserted into a taxonomic structure, generally one at a time, although possibly in batches or groups. In constructing the taxonomy, each such concept is arranged so that it has explicit subsumption links to its most specific subsuming concepts, and has explicit subsumption links pointing to it from each of its most general subsumees. Thus, except for the operations involved in testing a new description to determine its correct position in the taxonomy, the formal definitions of structural subsumption are not used in most operations on the network. The bulk of the processing for many reasoning operations consists of simple transitive closure operations on the explicitly recorded subsumption links. Failure to appreciate this fact can lead to unrealistic interpretations of the significance of some complexity results and to setting unrealistic tractability and completeness objectives for the operations of subsumption testing—see Mac Gregor [Chapter 13, this volume] in this volume, where a similar point is made.

I believe that much current confusion about what a classifier is and does results from the confusion of these conceptually distinct senses of subsumption. Specifically, an assumption that subsumption in sense 2 should be sound and complete with respect to sense 1 plays a significant role in the current profusion of intractability results (see below).

1.5.2 Research in Subsumption

Since the introduction of the idea of structural subsumption, a great deal of research has been carried out on the nature of subsumption and its relationship to the expressive power of semantic networks. For example, Levesque and Brachman [1985] showed that testing the subsumption relationship between two descriptions was more difficult for descriptions involving powerful term-forming operators than for descriptions involving less expressive operators. Since then, a number of papers have addressed computational tractability of the subsumption test for various systems of term-forming operators, e.g., [Nebel, 1988, 1989; Patel-Schneider, 1989; Schmidt-Schauss, 1989].

Much of this research has been couched in terms of a trade-off between expressive power and computational tractability of subsumption testing, identifying intractability with versions of "NP-difficulty" (NP-complete, NP-hard, co-NP-complete, etc.). This vein of research seems now to have nearly run its course, reaching the conclusion that almost everything of interest is computationally intractable in the worst case. Woods and Schmolze [1991] give a summary of this research. Although Levesque and Brachman acknowledged from the outset that worst-case performance might not be the best measure of tractability, the accumulation of evidence now seems to suggest that this is in fact the case.

In the meantime, a number of groups have used KL-ONE or KL-ONE-like systems as knowledge representation formalisms for a variety of applications. The consensus of these efforts seems to be that the trade-off of expressive power against computational tractability is a poor bargain. Experience suggests that expressive power is essential and therefore not available to trade away for efficiency. The field seems ripe for a new paradigm of research, perhaps focusing on a different criterion of efficiency or a completely different way to characterize the problem.

Surprisingly, in spite of considerable attention from researchers with a formal perspective, and the apparent simplicity and naturalness of the above examples, the semantics of terminological subsumption are still not clear. Users of such systems often find it difficult to understand the distinctions that are made by the formalists; and in many cases, the formalisms omit key features needed for practical application. Moreover, it is often not clear what the role of subsumption is and what it is useful for. In many cases it appears that subsumption plays a minor role compared to other inferential mechanisms. Perhaps it would be helpful to analyze more carefully some of the assumptions that underlie current approaches to subsumption.

1.5.3 Problems with Extensional Subsumption

In attempting to find a semantic foundation for the notion of subsumption, Levesque and Brachman [1985] adopted the notion of extensional subsumption defined above as their criterion. That is, a concept x subsumes a concept y if and only if every instance of y will necessarily be an instance of x. This definition, however, leads directly to problems of intractability if applied to a fully capable logic or semantic model because of the fundamental intractability of deduction in first-order logic. Although ideally this is the standard that one would like subsumption to achieve, it is not possible.

To avoid intractability, researchers in this paradigm, have sought to limit expressive power of descriptions in order to obtain a system that is less powerful and for which the deduction problem (in this technical sense) is more tractable. One approach has been to define subsumption extensionally in terms of consistent models of some restricted logic with limited expressive power. That is, a description x subsumes a description y if and only if in any consistent model of a suitably restricted logical system, an individual satisfying the description y will also necessarily satisfy the description x.

The fruits of this research, however, have been a collection of "tractable" systems with too little expressive power to be useful for general-purpose knowledge representation and a variety of attempts to couple such systems to more traditional deductive reasoning systems to form "hybrid systems" with complete expressive and deductive capabilities. For example, KRYPTON [Brachman et al., 1983], was one of the first systems to use a conceptual taxonomy similar to KL-ONE as the "terminological" component for a general-purpose reasoning system. In such a system, the conceptual descriptions in the taxonomy provide the inventory of terms to be used by the reasoning component, and the taxonomy provides some special-purpose inference capabilities as a function of the structure of those terms. The objective is that these specialized terminological inference capabilities should be fast and efficient, whereas the general-purpose reasoner is assumed to be slow and inefficient.

Research in such hybrid systems is ongoing, and the results are not yet conclusive. However, at a minimum, such systems must deal with a variety of subtle communication and coordination problems between the terminological component and the general reasoning component. Moreover, the standard approach of coupling a structured terminological component with a conventional, general-purpose reasoner (usually based on predicate logic) fails to exploit some potential benefits of a link-oriented knowledge network for general reasoning.

Perhaps there are other ways to look at the problem.

1.5.4 Other Perspectives

An alternative approach to defining subsumption in terms of an extensional criterion is to base subsumption directly on a more "syntactic" and "intensional" notion of purely structural subsumption. That is, one can define subsumption as a specific relationship between conceptual structures. Structural subsumption should be *sound*—i.e., every instance of the subsumed concept should be an instance of the subsumer. However, the converse need not be the case—that is, structural subsumption should entail extensional subsumption but not *vice versa*. For example, [polygon with three sides] would extensionally subsume [polygon with three angles], but there is no direct structural correspondence between the two descriptions that would imply this.

Implemented classification algorithms in the KL-ONE tradition are actually defined in terms of structural criteria. What I am proposing here is to make this kind of structural relationship the base criterion, rather than treating it as an artifact of the classification algorithm. If subsumption is defined by a structural relationship rather than a model-theoretic criterion, it can be defined to have a tractable subsumption computation—i.e., one can choose a structural subsumption relationship with a tractable computation as the definition. From this perspective, there can be different definitions of structural subsumption with different levels of ambition and different efficiency/completeness trade-offs, but without necessarily sacrificing expressibility of the individual conceptual descriptions.

One goal would be to define a criterion of structural subsumption based on an idea of *intensional* subsumption—a notion that one concept would subsume another by virtue of the structures of their meanings or *intensions*. For example, one might judge the concepts [polygon with three sides] and [polygon with three angles] to be intensionally distinct, even though they will necessarily have the same extensions in all possible worlds, because that fact does not follow directly from the structure of the descriptions but has to be deduced from the logic of the domain. If these two expressions were intensionally the same, one would argue, then a proof should not be necessary—it would suffice to examine the meanings to see that they are the same. This argument parallels the classical argument for the intensional distinctness of the concepts [morning star] and [evening star], except that here the issue is one of logical consequence rather than empirical discovery. On the same grounds, one can argue that neither the concept [polygon with three sides] nor [polygon with three angles] should intensionally subsume the other. However, both should subsume [polygon with three sides and three angles], because in this case the subsumption relationship does follow directly from the structure of the descriptions.

A criterion of intensional subsumption might turn out to be as much a psychological as a logical criterion. Subsumption in this intensional sense is a conceptual relationship, applying to abstract structured conceptual descriptions rather than to their extensions. It makes an intensional judgement about the relationship of the two descriptions (rather than a judgement about their extensions). I will have more to say about actual criteria for intensional subsumption below.

Another assumption worth questioning is that the dividing line between fast and efficient reasoning and the slower, more complete reasoning in a hybrid system should lie at the boundary between a terminological component and a general deduction engine. The general principle of increasing efficiency by replacing pattern-match⇒substitution operations with link-following algorithms has no special status for terminological facts that would not carry over to nonterminological ones. Such techniques can be just as useful for consequences that follow from domain facts as from those that follow from the definitions of terms.

In fact, one can derive just as much benefit from a subsumption relationship that follows from nondefinitional facts as from the meanings of terms. For example, it might be useful to record a deductive subsumption that the concept [president of the United States prior to 1990] is "subsumed" by the concept [man], even though this does not follow from the meanings of the terms. In early experiences with KL-ONE, there were often situations where one would have liked to perform classifications involving constraints that were merely true facts but not parts of definitions. Indeed, many users of KL-ONE deliberately or sometimes inadvertently violated the intended semantics of KL-ONE's notational structures in order to obtain the effects of such inference. Thus, it appears desirable to consider nonterminological as well as terminological subsumption.

Finally, it should be noticed that existing research on terminological subsumption has been done under the assumption of complete biconditional definitions—i.e., definitions providing complete necessary and sufficient defining conditions for their terms. The discussion above has pointed out the desirability of separating the necessary and sufficient conditions. This enables one to classify abstract concepts with multiple, independent sufficient conditions, like the concept [triangle]. Moreover, it handles partially defined concepts whose sufficient conditions and necessary conditions do not determine the outcome for all possible situations. This will allow some classification inferences with respect to many natural kind terms (which are usually treated simply as primitive concepts).

For the remainder of this discussion, for the reasons outlined above, I will use the extensional criterion of subsumption only as a criterion of soundness—abandoning any ambitions of completeness with respect to that criterion (although it is still desirable, all other things being equal, to be as complete as possible in this dimension). Instead, I will take the perspective that subsumption is defined by structural operations on conceptual descriptions and is intended to constitute a definition of intensional subsumption. Moreover, I will allow versions of subsumption that take account of assertional links that may be associated with concepts as well as their structural links. This can even be done with assertional links using defeasible quantification, producing defeasible subsumption conclusions, if desired.

Let us look more closely at the idea of structural subsumption.

1.5.5 Structural Subsumption

A good basic rule for structural subsumption is

$c_1 , \ldots , c_k / m_1 , \ldots , m_n$
subsumes
$c'_1 , \ldots , c'k' / m'_1 , \ldots , m'_{n'}$
if:
each c_i subsumes some c'_j and
each m_i subsumes some m'_j

(where a modifier $m_i = r_i : v_i$ subsumes a modifier $m'_j = r'_j : v'_j$ according to rules for relational modifier subsumption to be given shortly). As a base case, any concept c_1 subsumes another concept c_2 if they are the same, if c_1 has been asserted to subsume c_2 by an axiom, or if c_1 subsumes some concept c_3 that subsumes c_2. Recall that we are dealing only with type 1 descriptions here.

This is not the most general or the most powerful definition of subsumption that one might envision. In particular, it does not cover cases where a combination of the m'_j imply the satisfaction of some m_i where no single m'_j does. For example, the concept

"person whose limbs are hairy"

extensionally subsumes the description

"person whose arms are hairy and whose legs are hairy,"

but the given rule will not recognize this case. Nevertheless, the rule is quite useful and seems to correspond fairly well to those subsumption inferences that humans can make rapidly and without conscious effort. For the remainder of this chapter, I will use it as the criterion for intensional subsumption.

Note that any concept subsumes any composite description in which it is a primary concept, e.g.,

c_1 subsumes c_1 , c_2 / m_1 , ... , m_n.

It also follows from the definition that subsumption of composite descriptions is reflexive and transitive—i.e., any concept subsumes itself, and if *x* subsumes *y* and *y* subsumes *z*, then *x* subsumes *z*.

Subsumption relationships between conceptual descriptions can be inferred by the above subsumption rule, starting from a set of explicitly stated (axiomatic) subsumption assertions that serve as a basis. Subsumption relationships that are deduced logically, but do not follow from the application of the structural subsumption rule, can be explicitly recorded by treating them as if they were axioms (perhaps with justifications associated with them), after which further consequences of structural subsumption may follow. Such recorded relationships become efficiently usable "lemmas" that can be used directly without having to reproduce the deduction.

Typically, subsumption relationships between nodes in a conceptual taxonomy will be inferred and stored when those nodes are created, although some of them may need to be updated when new nodes are added or new subsumption relationships are asserted between existing nodes. Subsumption relationships between a newly formed description and existing concept nodes can be used to construct a corresponding new concept node and assimilate it into the taxonomy at the appropriate point.

1.5.5.1 Subsumption Between Concept Nodes

When computing a subsumption relation involving concept nodes with potentially disjunctive, partial, or multiple defining descriptions (e.g., equivalence classes of descriptions), subsumption should hold if any of the sufficient descriptions in the subsumer candidate can be inferred to subsume a description obtained by combining all of the necessary conditions of the subsumee candidate. For the purposes of this definition of structural subsumption, these necessary conditions will be only those that have been explicitly identified and linked to the concept (i.e., recorded as necessary conditions). There may be other necessary conditions that could be inferred (e.g., by general deduction) but have not been so recorded.

If the subsumee candidate is defined by an abstraction operation applied to equivalent definitions, then its necessary conditions are obtained by conjoining all of the necessary conditions of any of its defining descriptions. If the subsumee is defined by a disjunction, then its necessary conditions for the purposes of structural subsumption are those that are common to all of the disjuncts (if any) and/or those that have been explicitly identified and linked to the concept. In any case, the necessary conditions will include any necessary conditions that the subsumee candidate inherits from known subsumers—both from assertional links as well as from structural links.

Thus, for example, the description

[polygon] / MI[number of sides] : [three] ,
MI[number of angles] : [three]

would subsume the node [triangle] defined as

[triangle]
[d-iff] [polygon] / MI[number of sides] : [three]
[d-iff] [polygon] / MI[number of angles] : [three]

because it would subsume the combined description

[triangle], [polygon] / MI[number of sides] : [three] ,
MI[number of angles] : [three].

Conversely, it would also be subsumed by the node [triangle] because it is subsumed by at least one of the descriptions of that node; for example,

[polygon] / MI[number of sides] : [three].

Thus, the candidate description is equivalent to the [triangle] node because it both subsumes it and is subsumed by it. It can thus be added to that node as an (equivalent) alternative definition. One of the uses of abstract concepts is to collapse, in this way, descriptions that participate in closed loops of subsumption relationships.

In summary, to deal with the possibility of disjunctive, partial, and abstract concept nodes, where sufficient and necessary defining conditions may be different, the subsumption definition must be asymmetric in its treatment of the subsumer candidate and subsumee candidate. From the subsumer candidate it looks separately at each of its defining sufficient conditions, while from the subsumee candidate it looks at the total collection of all necessary conditions from any source—both definitional and assertional, whether locally linked or inherited.

1.5.5.2 Subsumption of Relational Modifiers

There is considerable subtlety in determining whether one relational modifier subsumes another, depending on the quantificational tags of the links. Surprisingly, when the individual cases are considered carefully, it turns out that in several cases (marked with an asterisk below), specializing an element of a relational modifier generalizes the resulting modifier (and *vice versa*). This depends on the quantificational tag and on whether the element being generalized is the relation or the object of the modifier.

A relational modifier x is more general than a corresponding modifier *y* in any of the following cases (all other things—i.e., unmentioned relations and objects—being equal):

Changing the object of the modifier:

1a. an MR object restriction in *x* is more general than that in *y*:
[a person whose sons are professionals]
subsumes [a person whose sons are doctors]

1b.* an MA object restriction in *x* is more specific than that in *y*:
[a person who takes every math course]
subsumes [a person who takes every course]

1c. an ME object restriction in *x* is more general than that in *y*:
[a person one of whose children is a professional]
subsumes [a person one of whose children is a doctor]

1d.* an MU(*n*) object restriction in *x* is more specific than that in *y*:
[a person at most *n* of whose sons are doctors] subsumes
[a person at most *n* of whose sons are professionals]

1e. an ML(*n*) object restriction in *x* is more general than that in *y*:
[a person at least *n* of whose sons are professionals]
subsumes [a person at least n of whose sons are doctors]

1f.* a NEG object restriction in *x* is more specific than that in *y*:
[a person who doesn't take any math course]
subsumes [a person who doesn't take any course]

Changing the relation of the modifier:

2a.* an MR relation in *x* is more specific than that in *y*:
[a person whose sons are doctors]
subsumes [a person whose children are doctors]

2b. an MA relation in *x* is more general than that in *y*:
[a person who takes every course]
subsumes [a person who passes every course]

2c. an ME relation in *x* is more general than that in *y*:
[a person one of whose children is a doctor]
subsumes [a person one of whose sons is a doctor]

2d.* an MU(*n*) relation in *x* is more specific than that in *y*:
[a person at most *n* of whose sons are doctors]
subsumes [a person at most *n* of whose children are doctors]

2e. an ML(*n*) relation in *x* is more general than that in *y*:
[a person at least *n* of whose children are doctors]
subsumes [a person at least *n* of whose sons are doctors]

2f.* a NEG relation in x is more specific than that in y:
[a person none of whose sons are doctors]
subsumes [a person none of whose children are doctors]

2g. an MI relation in x is more general than that in y:
[a person one of whose children is Dr. Ruth]
subsumes [a person one of whose daughters is Dr. Ruth]

Changing the tag of the modifier:

3a. an MU(n) tag in x has a larger n than that in y:
[a person with at most four children]
subsumes [a person with at most three children]

3b. an ML(n) tag in x has a smaller n than that in y:
[a person with at least two children]
subsumes [a person with at least three children]

3c. an ME tag in x matches an ML(n) tag in y with $n > 0$
[a person with children]
subsumes [a person with at least two children]

3d. an ML(n) tag in x with $n > 0$ matches an MI tag in y
and the object of y is an instance of the object of x:
[a person with a daughter who is a Doctor]
subsumes [a person whose daughter is Dr. Ruth]

Note that most of these cases follow the expected trend that generalizing an element of a description produces a more general description. However, the opposite holds for 1b, 1d, 1f, 2a, 2d, and 2f. In those cases, one obtains a more general description by specializing an element rather than generalizing it. Negated roles and upper bound number restrictions are not the only cases that have this behavior. This fact has not been generally recognized.

Note also that, in order to deal with assertional information that may be inherited by the subsumee candidate (for nonterminological subsumption as discussed above), each of the MR, MA and ME rules above would need a corresponding version with the MR, MA, and ME of the subsumee candidate replaced by VR, AA, and AE, respectively.

The above subsumption criteria generalize the subsumption criteria implemented in KL-ONE in several dimensions:

1. KL-ONE role restrictions and number restrictions apply only to generalized attributes of a concept (i.e., to roles)—not to arbitrary relations, although most formalizations of KL-ONE-like systems make this generalization from roles to relations.
2. There is no analog of the MA tag for role restrictions in KL-ONE or its successors. KL-ONE role value restrictions correspond to the MR tag. The

ML(n) and MU(n) tags are equivalent to KL-ONE number restrictions. ME and NEG were not provided separately in KL-ONE but are equivalent to ML(1) and MU(0), respectively.

3. Subsumption in the KL-ONE classifier did not deal with the case of specializing the relations in a role modifier. Although role differentiation was represented in KL-ONE, the KL-ONE classifier required role relations to be identical in its definition of role subsumption [Lipkis, 1982; Schmolze and Lipkis, 1983].

As we mentioned, this definition of structural subsumption will not draw all of the (extensional) subsumption inferences that one might like. It does, however, cover a significant range of useful cases and has a tractable computation. Note that it keeps negative conditions and positive conditions separate and does not use negation as failure. That is, if a sufficient condition for a subsumer includes a negative relation, it can only be satisfied if the subsumee has a negative condition that implies it—not by mere absence of anything contradictory. Note also that the notation allows the expression and classification of inconsistent descriptions such as [a man whose sex is not male] or [a square that is not a square], if anyone should want to create such descriptions and do something with them.

We see that, when examined closely, the notion of structural subsumption is considerably more intricate than it appears, and it depends in detail on the semantics of the links. However, when all of the details are carefully taken into account, a reasonably useful definition of intensional structural subsumption emerges with a quite powerful range of expression.

This is not intended to be the final word on structural subsumption. For example, there are extensions to the above criteria that would make subsumption more extensionally complete. However, let us now turn to the question of how subsumption is used to organize a taxonomy.

1.6 TAXONOMIC STRUCTURE

The structure that results from organizing conceptual descriptions on the basis of subsumption will be a partial ordering. If composite descriptions are allowed, it will not be a classical hierarchy (in which each concept below a single topmost concept has exactly one parent). For example, any composite description of the form

c / (r : v) , (u : v)

will have at least the parents (subsumers)

c / (r : v)
c / (u : v).

Depending on the concept-forming operators involved, the structure may be a formal lattice with respect to subsumption (that is, a partial ordering in which each pair of concepts has a unique least upper bound in the form of a most specific joint subsumer and a unique greatest lower bound in the form of a single most general common subsumee). There are advantages for this structure to be a lattice, having to do with expressive power and the detection and resolution of conflicts in inherited information. More about this shortly.

The construction of a conceptual taxonomy results in two kinds of recorded subsumption—direct (or explicit) when there is an explicit recorded subsumption link from the subsumee to the subsumer, and indirect (or implicit) when there is a transitive chain of such links. The subsumption taxonomy amounts to a compact encoding of the results of all known subsumption relationships (structural, axiomatic, and deduced). Once this taxonomy is constructed, subsumption questions involving concepts already in the taxonomy can be answered by simple transitive closure operations on the recorded subsumption links. Explicit subsumption testing based on the structure of the conceptual descriptions is done only when a new concept is classified with respect to the taxonomy.

In general, the conceptual taxonomy should include subsumption links from a given concept to all of its most specific subsumers—i.e. all of the nodes in the network that subsume it and do not subsume some intermediate node that also subsumes it. Note that this criterion applies after all cyclical subsumption relationships are collapsed into a single abstract concept so that we're talking about proper subsumption here and not the degenerate case of equivalence. Subsumption relationships that follow from these links by transitive closure need not be explicitly recorded since they can be quickly accessed by following chains of links (although they may be cached or hash coded if desired—e.g., if the speed gained is worth the space required and the cost and complexity of updating and maintaining the consistency of the cache).

1.6.1 Virtual and Explicit Taxonomies

For any collection of relations and atomic concepts, there is a rather large and combinatoric space of all possible composite descriptions that can be formed from them. Moreover, for any collection of axiomatic and deduced subsumption relationships among such concepts, there is a corresponding collection of induced structural subsumption relationships on the space of composite descriptions. This space of all descriptions, organized by the collection of all such subsumption relations, has been referred to as the "virtual taxonomy," because, although its structure is important, one never wants to make it explicit in the memory of a computer (or a person).

Whenever a reasoning agent constructs an explicit collection of concept nodes and computes and records the subsumption relationships among those concepts, the result is a subgraph of the virtual taxonomy. All of the operations of classification and deduction operate on the explicit taxonomy, and every description that is added to it is in some sense already in the virtual taxonomy (except when adding a new primitive concept or relation). Thus, classifying a new concept is, in a sense, merely making explicit a concept that already exists in the virtual taxonomy.

1.6.2 Lattice-structured Taxonomies

Whenever the concept-forming operators of a representational system include operations of conjunction and disjunction, the abstract space of potential conceptual structures will be a formal lattice. That is, any two concepts will have a common least upper bound (their disjunction) and a common greatest lower bound (their conjunction). In particular, for the system of structured concepts presented above, the resulting virtual taxonomy will be a lattice. Note, however, that it does not follow that the explicit taxonomy will be a lattice, since one might fail to make explicit some of the least upper bounds or greatest lower bounds that exist virtually.

There are some advantages to adopting a policy of making explicit the greatest lower bounds for at least certain pairs of concepts in a conceptual taxonomy. In particular, if the taxonomy is used to organize a collection of rules or assertions with defeasible inheritance, then the presence of greatest lower bound concepts can be used for detecting potential conflicts between inherited defaults. Since the greatest lower bound concept is by definition the most general concept subsumed by both parents, it follows that if any situation can occur in which information inherited from two different nodes would conflict, then all such situations are summarized by the greatest lower bound concept (i.e., all conflicting situations will be instances of the greatest lower bound).

Hence by examining the greatest lower bound concepts for all pairs of concepts that have associated rules or defeasible inheritance links, it is possible to check a taxonomy for possible conflicts without having to wait for conflicting instances to arise. Moreover, having detected a possible conflict and determined a policy for resolving it, one can then store an appropriate overriding rule or assertion at the greatest lower bound concept and thereby eliminate any possible runtime confusions. After making such additions, assuming that the a rule or value inherited from a concept overrides a comparable rule or value inherited from a more general concept, then any runtime situation will always find an appropriate nonconflicting rule or value by straightforward inheritance with no need for any runtime conflict-resolution machinery.

This technique would deal with the famous Nixon diamond conflict in the following way. (The problem is that Nixon is both a Republican and a Quaker and those two concepts have different default values for the property of being a pacifist—specifically, Quakers tend to be pacifists and Republicans do not.) Since Republicans and Quakers are not mutually inconsistent (Nixon being a demonstration of the fact), a most general common specialization—[Republican Quaker]—would be constructed and made explicit in the taxonomy. Nixon would then be classified as a Republican Quaker rather than separately as a Republican and as a Quaker.

Now, there is no *a priori* logical or philosophical principle on which to base a preference for which of the two default assumptions should take precedence in this case—correct resolution depends on specific domain knowledge—ideally, the true joint probability of Republican Quakers being pacifist. If an appropriate resolution can be obtained from a domain expert or a suitable experiment, then it would be attached to the concept [Republican Quaker] and would be inherited as the default assumption for Nixon, thereby overriding the conflicting defaults. If no such resolution can be obtained, an annotation could be made at the [Republican Quaker] concept that conflicting evidence is present and either possibility is partially supported and partially contradicted.

1.6.3 Classification

Classification is the name given to the process by which new concepts are added to an existing taxonomy and linked in at the appropriate position or by which a collection of concepts linked by some recorded subsumption relationships is expanded to include all direct subsumption relationships that can be inferred by means of the structural subsumption rule. Note that this operation is an operation on a system of concepts, unlike subsumption, which is an operation on a pair of concepts.

1.6.3.1 Classifying Generics

There are at least two circumstances under which one might want to classify generic concepts. One is to organize a relatively stable taxonomy for subsequent use in some reasoning activity. Another is to classify situations, subgoals, queries, tasks to be done, etc. in the course of some reasoning process so that the most specific applicable facts or rules can be found from a taxonomy of possibilities. This latter is an alternative to searching a database of rules for those whose patterns match the current situation, and the technique has been used in systems such as CONSUL [Mark, 1981]. In this case, the pattern parts of the rules will have been classified into the taxonomy with the rule bodies attached. The classification operation will then automatically identify the most specific matching rules. This technique not only exploits the taxonomy as an indexing structure to organize the rules for efficient retrieval, but has the advantage that it can automatically resolve conflicts as discussed above.

1.6.3.2 mss and mgs

There are two parts to the operation of classifying a new description into a taxonomy. One is to locate the most specific subsumers of that description, and the other is to locate the most general concepts that are subsumed by it (the most general subsumees). These can be performed by two separate algorithms, which I will call "mss" (for most specific subsumer) and "mgs" (for most general subsumee). Both of these algorithms operate on a composite description to classify it with respect to an explicit conceptual taxonomy. The algorithms presented here assume that all of the concepts involved as parts of the composite description have already been classified.

One version of a most specific subsumer algorithm is to start at the top of the lattice and progress downward in waves, maintaining an active list of conceptual descriptions that subsume the input and keeping track of those for whom no more specific subsumers are found. This is essentially the algorithm described by Lipkis [1982] as part of the KL-ONE classifier, except for the details of the subsumption criterion.

Note that it is not sufficient to search only below the primary concepts of the input description—there may be concepts that are incomparable with the primary concepts but nevertheless subsume the input. For example the concept

[golfer] (i.e., [person] / ([hobby] : [golf]))

should subsume the input description

[woman] / ([hobby] : [golf])

even though [golfer] does not subsume the primary concept [woman].

The corresponding most general subsumee algorithm also moves downward in waves, this time looking for concepts that are subsumed by the input. This algorithm, however, is more subtle.

Since any concept subsumed by the input will also be subsumed by (all of) its most specific subsumers, the search for subsumees can begin moving downward from the most specific subsumers found by the mss algorithm, without risk of missing any potential subsumees. In fact, the search can safely begin from any one of the mss concepts.

When a concept is encountered that is subsumed by the input, it is added to a list of candidate subsumees and is not pursued further. However, very few concepts encountered in the search can be dropped from the wavefront in this way. Each concept that is not a subsumee (presumably the normal case) will be replaced in the wavefront by all of its recorded specializations. This is because some further specialization may yet lead to a concept that is subsumed by the input. Thus, the wavefront for the mgs algorithm has a potential to grow quite large if started near the top of a large network—see below.

When the mgs search has exhausted all possibilities, then the list of candidate subsumees will become the answer after it is pruned of any candidates that are duplicates or are subsumed by other candidates and hence are not most general. This purging process can, of course, be done incrementally as new candidates are added to the list.

Note that the wavefront of the mgs search could be pruned if it were possible to tell that all specializations of a candidate are necessarily inconsistent with the input. This could be done with a system of mutual exclusion constraints among concepts. Such constraints were proposed in KL-ONE and are present in some systems. However, the exploitation of such constraints in classification is beyond the scope of this chapter.

Note also that since it is sufficient to start the mgs search from any one of the mss's, one could choose the one expected to have the fewest concepts below it, if that information were available. It would not be difficult to maintain a count for this purpose.

The above mgs algorithm is similar in spirit to the corresponding part of the KL-ONE classifier described in Lipkis [1982]. However, Lipkis observes that the algorithm can start with the most specific subsumers without observing that any one of them would be sufficient. Again, the details of the subsumption operation itself are different.

Note that the above algorithms are rough sketches of an obvious algorithm for each case. More sophisticated algorithms can and should be developed. Note also that when the potential exists for circular chains of subsumption, then these algorithms need to be supplemented or preceded by an algorithm to detect cycles of subsumption and collapse them into a single conceptual node. Similarly, complexities arise when a concept being classified is recursively involved in its own description or definition—see Nebel [Chapter 11, this volume].

1.6.3.3 The Cost of Subsumption

In the wake of Levesque and Brachman [1985], many papers have dealt with the computational complexity of various versions of the subsumption algorithm, generally concluding that subsumption is NP-hard, NP-complete, co-NP-complete, etc. Aside from the fact that worst case performance is probably not the best measure for these algorithms, a major problem is that these results address complexity in terms of the size of the individual descriptions—not the size of the overall conceptual taxonomy. Typically, however, the number of modifiers in a structured description of interest will be relatively small, while a knowledge base of interest could contain thousands or even millions of concepts. In this section we will examine the dependence of the subsumption test on the size of the knowledge base. In the next section, we will look at the more important question of the overall cost of the classification operation.

One can make the following rough estimate of the time required for the structural subsumption algorithm described above. (These are merely "back of the envelope calculations," but should give a general idea of how much time this algorithm might take. They are neither worst case, nor quite average case, but something like typical upper bounds. I will refer to them as "typical case." One would hope that clever algorithms could do better than these bounds.)

In general, the algorithm operates between concept nodes, which may have several distinct sufficient conditions and a separate set of necessary conditions and may be disjunctively defined. The algorithm will have to check each sufficient condition in the subsumer candidate against a description that combines all of the necessary conditions in the subsumee (possibly a disjunction of alternative descriptions if the concept is disjunctively defined).

If the number of separate sufficient conditions in an average concept is s, and the number of alternative disjuncts in the necessary conditions is d (both numbers are typically close to 1), then testing the structural subsumption of two concepts, on the average, would be expected to take roughly sd times the expected time to test a subsumption relationship between a pair of composite descriptions.

In testing whether one composite description subsumes another, each subsumer primary concept is potentially compared with each subsumee primary concept and each subsumer relational modifier is compared against each subsumee relational modifier. Moreover, each modifier comparison involves two comparisons of a constituent concept with another (one for the relation and one for its object).

Hence, if we assume that the average composite description has p primary concepts and m modifiers, then testing for structural subsumption between the two descriptions should take something like $(p^2 + 2m^2)$ times the expected amount of time to test a subsumption relationship between two constituent concepts.

If we assume that the constituent concepts of these description have already been classified into the taxonomy (which could be done automatically as a part of the classification algorithm), then each constituent subsumption test can be performed by simply searching the transitive closure of recorded subsumers from the subsumee candidate to see if the subsumer candidate appears above it.

The key to the complexity of this test involves assumptions about the statistical structure of the conceptual taxonomy. For most conceptual taxonomies, one can assume that the explicit taxonomy branches out from a relatively small width at the top to quite a large width at the bottom. Although it is not a tree because of the presence of multiple parents for many concepts, it will still have the basic characteristic of most classification trees in that the vast majority of its nodes will be at or near the bottom fringe and, if the structure is approximately balanced, the number of nodes in a subsumer chain above an average node will be roughly proportional to log N, where N is the total number of nodes in the structure. The constant of proportionality here has two factors—W, a measure of the "width" of the ancestor chain above a typical node due to multiple parents and B, a factor due to how much out of balance the tree is. Typical values for these numbers might be in the range of 1 to 3.

Thus checking recorded subsumption by searching the recorded subsumer chain of the subsumee would take approximately $BW \log N$ time. This could be speeded up to effectively constant time by caching all recorded subsumer pairs using hash coding techniques.

In summary, after a number of assumptions, it appears that the time required to test the subsumption of a pair of concepts whose constituents have already been classified is something like

$$ds(p^2 + 2m^2)\ BW \log N,$$

and if hashing is used, the $BW \log N$ factor can be effectively eliminated.

If the constituents were not previously classified, then the cost of their classification would have to be added to the cost of subsumption by this algorithm.

1.6.3.4 The Cost of Classification

As mentioned above, the important cost issue is not the complexity of subsumption, but the complexity of the overall classification operation. This operation not only involves a substantial number of calls for subsumption testing, but also, in order to be useful, needs to be done in a preferably sublinear time relative to the size of the knowledge base. This section will examine this cost. We will assume that the algorithm begins by recursively classifying any constituents of the input description that are themselves composite descriptions, so that each such level of classification can assume that all of its constituents have already been classified. We will then analyze the cost of one such level of classification. Hence, the overall cost of classifying a description with composite constituents will be bounded by the estimate derived below times one plus the number of composite constituents in the input description—typically a small number.

It is useful to separate the time estimates for the mss algorithm and the mgs algorithm. We will begin with the mss algorithm.

First, we should notice that, since almost all of the nodes will be near the fringe of the network, the average time will be determined by the time required to classify a node near the fringe. By the above assumptions, such a node will have approximately $BW \log N$ recorded subsumers. A key parameter for these estimates will be the downward branching ratio of the taxonomy—that is, on the average how many children (most general subsumees) does a node (that is not on the bottom fringe) have. Let's call this ratio r. Another useful parameter is the upward branching ratio—i.e., the average number of most specific subsumers a node has. Let's call this ratio u.

The search for the most specific subsumers (mss) will involve exploring something on the order of r $BW \log N$ nodes, each of which will be compared with the input. This search will result in roughly u most specific subsumers being found. Since the subsumee candidate in this case is the input description, we can dispense with the factor d for disjunctive definitions of the subsumee and thus (assuming that the input has the typical p primary concepts and m modifiers), the expected time for the mss algorithm would be something like

$$rs(p^2 + 2m^2)\ (BW \log N)^2.$$

For atypical inputs whose most specific subsumers are near the top of the taxonomy, the time required could be substantially less. (Again, with appropriate caching we could eliminate one of these factors of $BW \log N$.)

For the mgs algorithm, we will start from one of the most specific subsumers and follow its subsumees for, say, two levels, on the average (the average node is near the bottom). With a branching ratio of r, this will give something like $r(r + 1)$ concepts to be compared with the input. Since the input description will be the subsumer candidate in this case, and thus has no equivalent alternative descriptions, we can dispense with the factor s in the subsumption estimate (but keep the d this time) for a total (average) time to find the subsumee candidates of

$$r(r + 1)\ d\ BW \log N.$$

Some number of the above comparisons will produce candidate most general subsumers (mgs). It is difficult to say how many candidates would be found, but it certainly can't be more than the r(r + 1) concepts explored. Since it would then take approximately the square of the size of this candidates list to eliminate duplicates and concepts that are subsumed by other candidates, and the test here involves only recorded subsumption, the total time for pruning the candidates list cannot be more than

$$(r(r + 1))^2\ BW \log N.$$

Hence, the average time for the mgs algorithm (for an input that belongs near the bottom fringe) will be something on the order of

$$r(r + 1)(d + r(r + 1))\ BW \log N \text{ (i.e., roughly, } r^4\ BW \log N)$$

(and again, the $BW \log N$ factor could be eliminated by hashing).

Unfortunately, this mgs algorithm is not well behaved for the atypical inputs that belong near the top of the taxonomy. For such inputs, the mgs search may have to sweep through almost all of the taxonomy to find its candidates list, so there may be on the order of N comparisons with the input, rather than $r(r + 1)$. In this case, the search for subsumee candidates alone could take $N \log N$ time, and hashing only kills the log N factor here—not the factor of N. If on the order of N candidates were found (presumably an extremely rare event), eliminating those that are not most general can also be expensive. Fortunately, one can get this time down to N^2 log N (instead of the obvious N^2) by using a mark and sweep algorithm.

Thus, the mgs algorithm is unpredictable, since for atypical inputs (near the top of the taxonomy) it could easily take time proportional to N and for a (rare) worst-case node with on the order of N mgs candidates, it could take N log N. This makes the mgs algorithm suitable for maintenance operations on relatively stable taxonomies, but not for an operation that might occur in the middle of a man–machine interaction. Fortunately, this seems to fit what is needed—see below.

To obtain the improved bounds that result from hashing, we need to consider the cost of building the hash table during classification. When each concept is added, it will have on the order of BW log N concepts above it and an average of r concepts below it, so the total number of hash entries to store will be of the same order as the time required to find the mss and mgs candidates—i.e., order of log N. Hence the cache can be built without increasing the time bounds. Also, the hash table would require on the order of $N\,BW$ log N space, rather than the N^2 space that one might at first expect.

Again, these are only rough estimates. One would hope that clever algorithms could do better.

1.6.3.5 Classifying Instances

One of the purposes of having a conceptual taxonomy is to link individual instances of generic concepts to the most specific generics that they instantiate. Thus, the conceptual taxonomy serves as an organizing structure for classifying individuals and grouping them by common characteristics. This structure may be used to organize rules to execute when instances are encountered. Consequently, an important special case of classification is the operation of placing an individual under its most specific "subsumers" in the taxonomy. This operation, which was called *realization* in KL-ONE, is essentially the same as the mss algorithm above, assuming that individuals are not further specialized, and so would take on the order of $(\log N)^2$ time (or log N with hashing), with no anomalous atypical behavior.

1.6.3.6 Classifying Subgoals

Another use of a conceptual taxonomy is to organize facts and rules for retrieval during inferential processes (and for resolving conflicts among such rules). Applicable rules can be determined by classifying a description of the current situation or current subgoal with respect to the taxonomy to identify its most specific subsumers and then inheriting the rules to be applied. Once again, for this purpose, one needs only the mss part of the classification operation, since one is only interested in inheriting rules from more general concepts. Fortunately, this also avoids the problematic atypical behavior of the mgs algorithm, and can be expected to take $(\log N)^2$ time (or $\log N$ with hashing).

1.7 WHERE TO FROM HERE?

In the above discussions I have made simplifying assumptions and/or left issues unaddressed in numerous places. Most significantly, I have looked at subsumption only in the context of type 1 structural descriptions, which do not deal with role interactions—i.e., constraints between roles in a description. Moreover, for the processes I have looked at, I have presented the most obvious algorithms—algorithms that essentially directly mirror the definitions of what they are supposed to do. No deep insights have been exploited to gain efficiency. For example, in classification, no advantage is taken of what might be learned in the course of one subsumption test that might be redundant with part of another subsumption test. There are a number of important areas of future research dealing with criteria for subsumption and discovery of improved subsumption algorithms.

Moreover, I have not addressed all of the different uses to which taxonomies of structured concepts can be put. I have considered only the issues inherent in the use of such representations for organizing systems of rules or facts. The use of descriptions for recognizing objects in situations (such as recognizing sentences of English or plans in discourse or objects in visual scenes) have not been addressed. The semantics of links used for such purposes is significantly different from that of the links discussed here (which apply primarily to objects that have already been conceptualized). A general theory of subsumption and taxonomy should integrate these and other uses of descriptions.

1.7.1 Universal Expressive Power

The above algorithms constitute a benchmark of performance for subsumption and classification using conceptual descriptions with limited expressive power—i.e., descriptions that do not permit general constraints between roles. However, we have argued that application systems are not free to trade away expressive power for other benefits. Understanding the boundaries of the expressive power of these mechanisms and the consequences of extending them is an important area for further research. As mentioned earlier, the issue of organizing general quantificational assertions by a relationship of generality is an interesting open question.

One way to proceed would be to use the subsumption mechanism described here to organize a taxonomy of fully expressive descriptions, treating all of the general conditions as if they were primitive concepts and hence not comparable unless identical. This would provide a base system with complete expressive power but a noticeably incomplete criterion of structural subsumption. The resulting taxonomy would still be useful for organizing facts and rules, but could perhaps be improved by a more complete algorithm. Such improvement might include criteria for when to invoke general inference mechanisms to seek deduced subsumption relationships to extend the taxonomy. The issues associated with this approach are interesting to consider. There is no longer a trade-off of expressive power against tractability; rather, the question is how complete a given subsumption algorithm is (and how one can characterize such completeness in a comprehensible way).

1.7.2 Universal Deduction

Most knowledge representation systems in the tradition of KL-ONE have assumed that their conceptual taxonomies will be used in conjunction with relatively traditional deductive components in hybrid systems. However, this approach foregoes many possibilities for exploiting "link chasing" algorithms as part of the general deduction engine. Moreover, it limits the system's reasoning abilities to the kinds of things that can be expressed in first-order logic. Since much of the reasoning that humans do, and we would like our systems to be able to handle, is at least second order (i.e., reasoning about properties, functions, and intensional objects of belief), we need to devote more attention to viable reasoning systems that operate in these domains and to look for ways to exploit specialized inferential paradigms in general deduction.

We should not be excessively concerned about completeness results for such systems—at least not at first. We know that second-order logic is not complete, that any formal system that includes arithmetic is not complete, and that even for formally complete systems, the computational reality is that we may not be able to wait around for a complete search process to finish—even when it is guaranteed to eventually find an answer (given sufficient resources). Similarly, we need to place worst-case results in an appropriate perspective, and address more attention to typical-case results.

1.7.3 Efficient Algorithms

I have given sufficient details of the subsumption relationship and the classification process to specify fairly concretely what the job of constructing and using a taxonomy amounts to. I have also given rough sketches of some straightforward algorithms for performing the necessary operations. A major open question is whether there are algorithms that are much more effective than the ones sketched here. I suspect that there may be and that more effort devoted to the search for such algorithms would be well spent. Moreover, effort spent in looking for ways to exploit conceptual taxonomies for efficient reasoning in the deductive component is also likely to be fruitful. The role of taxonomy in reasoning is only starting to be understood, and there is a great deal yet to learn.

1.8 CONCLUSION

I have attempted to present a carefully reasoned tour of the issues involved in the formation and use of structured conceptual taxonomies. I argue that the basis for understanding such systems should be a suitable theory of conceptual description rather than interpreting such structures as notational variants of the predicate calculus. I also argue that careful attention to the semantics of links is essential for developing adequately expressive conceptual descriptions and for understanding the subsumption relationships among them. A general mechanism of quantificational tags, interpreted as relation-forming operators, is introduced for expressing the quantificational import of both assertional and structural links. In addition, machinery is introduced to deal with abstract concepts having multiple equivalent descriptions. The result is a framework that integrates assertional and definitional knowledge and can accommodate probabilistic information and default values as well as absolute universals and definitions.

The framework presented goes beyond the capabilities of previous taxonomic knowledge representation systems in a number of dimensions. First, it combines techniques from traditional frame-based systems using defeasible inheritance with the structural subsumption techniques of KL-ONE and its successors. Previously these two traditions seemed fundamentally incompatible, since the latter is based on definitions that do not admit exceptions, while the former is based on exceptions that preclude formal definition. Second, this framework generalizes the notion of definition used in the latter systems to deal with abstract and partially defined concepts by separating necessary and sufficient conditions.

Unlike most systems in these traditions, the current framework does not impose any specific ontological assumptions about the nature of individuality or individual concepts. (The consequences of this are the topic of another paper in progress.) The current framework allows concepts to be both generic and individual at the same time (e.g., generic concepts can have instances and can also themselves be instances of other abstract concepts, allowing systems that have models of their own concepts). Moreover, this framework can allow specialization of individual descriptions, a capability ruled out in most such systems but found desirable in a number of applications.

The general notion of subsumption is shown to involve several distinct, more specific kinds of subsumption, and the operation of classification is shown to involve different kinds of subsumption at different points in the process. It is shown that with careful attention to semantic details, one can formalize a powerful system of conceptual description and define a formal relation of structural subsumption with respect to it that is both well defined and tractable. One can use conceptual taxonomies based on this definition to organize facts and rules for efficient retrieval and for managing conflicting defaults.

This chapter introduces a distinction between intensional and extensional subsumption, argues for the importance of the former, and analyzes the typical-case complexity for a restricted form of intensional subsumption. It criticizes previous tractability research in the KL-ONE tradition for focusing on worst-case behavior, addressing an unrealistic goal of completeness, neglecting the issue of knowledge base size, and focusing on subsumption rather than classification. It argues that the primary tractability concern is not the cost of subsumption, but the cost of classification into a large taxonomy. A classification algorithm based on intensional subsumption is presented and is argued to have a typical-case complexity that is logarithmic in the size of the knowledge base.

Finally, some areas for further research are identified. The chapter lays a foundation for understanding subsumption and taxonomy and proposes a framework within which to view and compare various systems. It establishes a benchmark of capability and enough detail to see where gaps in our understanding remain. The issues discussed are intended to set the stage for further progress.

ACKNOWLEDGMENTS

My thanks to the following people who read earlier drafts: Dave Albert, Ron Brachman, Jon Christensen, Scott Decatur, Barbara Grosz, Tom Hancock, Harry Lewis, Joe Marks, Jim Schmolze, Stu Shieber, Candy Sidner, John Sowa, and Marc Vilain. This research was supported in part by a grant from the Kapor Family Foundation.

References

Barwise, J. and Perry, J. 1983. *Situations and Attitudes*. MIT Press, Cambridge, MA.

Brachman, R.J. 1983. What IS-A is and isn't: An analysis of taxonomic links in semantic networks, *IEEE Computer*, 16(10):30–36.

———. 1985. I lied about the trees, *The AI Magazine*, VI(3):80–93.

Brachman, R.J. and Schmolze, J.G. 1985. An overview of the KL-ONE knowledge representation system, *Cognitive Science* 9(2):171–216.

Brachman, R.J., Fikes, R.E., and Levesque, H.J. 1983. KRYPTON: A functional approach to knowledge representation, *IEEE Computer*, 16(10):67–73.

Hirst, G. 1989. Ontological assumptions in knowledge representation. In *Proceedings of the First International Conference on Principles of Knowledge Representation and Reasoning*, Brachman, R.J., Levesque, H.J., and Reiter, R. (ed.s), pp. 157–169. Morgan Kaufmann Publishers, San Mateo, CA.

Levesque, H.J. and Brachman, R.J. 1985. A fundamental tradeoff in knowledge representation and reasoning (revised version). In *Readings in Knowledge Representation*, Brachman, R.J. and Levesque, H.J. (ed.s). Morgan Kaufmann Publishers, San Mateo, CA.

Lipkis, T. 1982. A KL-ONE classifier. In *Proceedings of the 1981 KL-ONE Workshop*, BBN Technical Report No. 4842, Schmolze, J.G. and Brachman, R.J. (ed.s), pp. 128–145. Bolt Beranek and Newman Inc., Cambridge, MA.

Mac Gregor, R. 1991. The evolving technology of classification-based knowledge representation systems. This volume.

Mark, W. 1981. Representation and inference in the consul system. In *Proceedings of the Seventh International Joint Conference on Artificial Intelligence*, Vancouver, BC. IJCAI proceedings are available from Morgan Kaufmann Publishers, San Mateo, CA.

Nebel, B. 1988. Computational complexity of terminological reasoning in BACK, *Artificial Intelligence*, 34(3):371–383.

———. 1989. Terminological reasoning is inherently intractable, *Artificial Intelligence*, 43(2):235–249. Also available as IWBS Report 82, Wissenschaftliches Zentrum, IBM Deutschland GmbH, October, 1989.

———. 1991. Terminological cycles: semantics and computational properties. This volume.

Patel-Schneider, P.F. 1989. Undecidability of subsumption in NIKL, *Artificial Intelligence*, 39(2):263–272.

Schmidt-Schauss, M. 1989. Subsumption in KL-ONE is undecidable. In *Proceedings of the First International Conference on Principles of Knowledge Representation and Reasoning*, Brachman, R.J., Levesque, H.J., and Reiter, R. (ed.s), pp 421–431. Morgan Kaufmann Publishers, San Mateo, CA.

Schmolze, J.G. and Lipkis, T.A. 1983. Classification in the KL-ONE knowledge representation system. In *Proceedings of the Eighth International Joint Conference on Artificial Intelligence*, Karlsruhe, W. Germany.

Schmolze, J.G. 1989. Terminological knowledge representation systems supporting n-ary terms. In *Proceedings of the First International Conference on Principles of Knowledge Representation and Reasoning*, Brachman, R.J., Levesque, H.J., and Reiter, R. (ed.s), pp 432–443. Morgan Kaufmann Publishers, San Mateo, CA.

Shapiro, S.C. and Rapaport, W.J. 1987. SNePS considered as a fully intensional propositional semantic network. In *The Knowledge Frontier: Essays in the Representation of Knowledge*, Nick Cercone and Gordon McCalla (ed.s.). Springer-Verlag, New York.

Shastri, L. 1989. Default reasoning in semantic networks: A formalization of recognition and inheritance, *Artificial Intelligence*, 39(3):331–392.

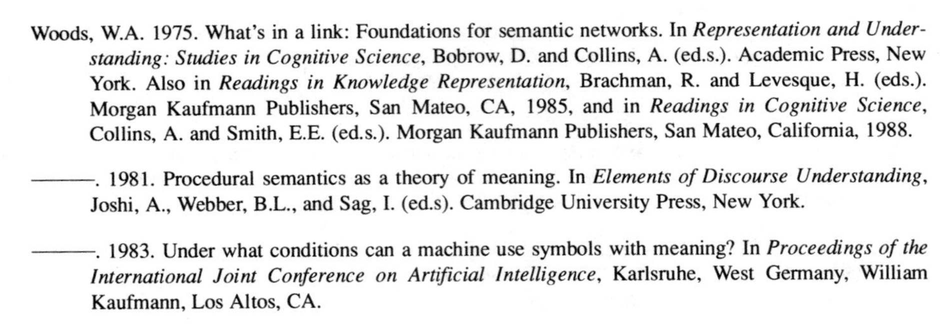

Woods, W.A. 1975. What's in a link: Foundations for semantic networks. In *Representation and Understanding: Studies in Cognitive Science*, Bobrow, D. and Collins, A. (ed.s.). Academic Press, New York. Also in *Readings in Knowledge Representation*, Brachman, R. and Levesque, H. (eds.). Morgan Kaufmann Publishers, San Mateo, CA, 1985, and in *Readings in Cognitive Science*, Collins, A. and Smith, E.E. (ed.s.). Morgan Kaufmann Publishers, San Mateo, California, 1988.

———. 1981. Procedural semantics as a theory of meaning. In *Elements of Discourse Understanding*, Joshi, A., Webber, B.L., and Sag, I. (ed.s). Cambridge University Press, New York.

———. 1983. Under what conditions can a machine use symbols with meaning? In *Proceedings of the International Joint Conference on Artificial Intelligence*, Karlsruhe, West Germany, William Kaufmann, Los Altos, CA.

———. 1986. Important issues in knowledge representation. In *Proceedings of the IEEE*, 74(10).

———. 1987. Don't blame the tool. *Computational Intelligence*, 3(3):228–237.

Woods, W.A. and Brachman, R.J. 1978. *Research in Natural Language Understanding*, Quarterly Technical Progress Report No. 1, 1 September 1977 to 30 November 1977, Tech. Report No. 3,742, Bolt Beranek and Newman, Cambridge, MA.

Woods, W.A. and Schmolze, J.G. 1991. The KL-ONE family. *Computers & Mathematics with Applications*, Special Issue on Semantic Networks in Artificial Intelligence, (forthcoming).

2

SEMANTIC NETS ARE IN THE EYE OF THE BEHOLDER

Lenhart K. Schubert
(University of Rochester)

Abstract

The term "semantic nets," in its broadest sense, has become virtually meaningless. It is applied to systems which, as a class, lack distinctive representational and computational properties *vis à vis* other knowledge representation (KR) schemes. This terminological problem is not due to lack of substance or coherence of work done under the semantic net banner. Rather, it is due to convergence of the major KR schemes: the representational and computational strategies employed in semantic net systems are abstractly equivalent to those employed in virtually *all* state-of-the-art systems incorporating a substantial propositional knowledge base, whether they are described as logic-based, frame-based, rule-based, or something else. In particular, I will argue that using a graph-theoretic propositional representation does not automatically distinguish it from others: even sets of predicate calculus (PC) formulas, abstractly viewed, are graphs. Nor is "proximity-based" inference (using graph-theoretic distance) automatically distinctive, since even resolution strategies (with reasonable indexing schemes) are proximity based in the abstract; nor is hierarchic property inheritance any longer distinctive, given its availability in state-of-the-art logic-based, frame-based, and rule-based systems. So I urge some more restrictive, and hence more meaningful use of the term "semantic nets" than is the current practice.

2.1 INTRODUCTION

In artificial intelligence (AI), as in any science, ideas do not evolve linearly. There is no universally shared terminology, let alone a universally assimilated body of knowledge, which is augmented step-by-step by the "advances" we (as practitioners) announce. Rather, ideas tend to emerge and evolve in variant forms in many places, in more or less parallel fashion.

On the face of it, this parallelism is wasteful, but it has compelling causes. For one thing, too much is being written for any of us to read, so naturally we fragment into colonies that are internally cohesive, but only loosely integrated with each other. It is often faster to rediscover something within the framework of one's colony than to glean it from the writings of another. For another, our numbers are legion and our sources of inspiration widely shared—so if a good idea occurs to one of us, it is apt to occur to many. Since ideas are our livelihood, we are disposed to emphasize differences—however superficial—rather than similarities, and jealously defend our terminological niches. Besides, we may argue, evolution thrives on diversity.

However, in the evolution of a set of related scientific notions, there is a time to explore diverse alternatives—and later, a time to consolidate ideas, discarding artificial distinctions and inconsistent terminology. It seems to me that the time for such a consolidation and redefinition has arrived in the area of KR. In particular, I want to argue that the term "semantic nets" has become virtually meaningless, at least in its broadest sense. (By the same token, questions can also be raised about "frame-based systems," "rule-based systems," and various other KR terms, but I would like to focus on what I know best.) It no longer signifies an objectively distinguishable species in the KR taxonomy. *All* KR schemes I have lately encountered, which aspire to cope with a large, general propositional knowledge base, qualify as semantic nets, appropriately viewed. However, their designers often don't view them that way, preferring such terms as "frame-based system," "semantic database," "blackboard," or some neologism. The choice of KR terminology seems to be more a matter of intellectual affiliation than one of substance.

More specifically, I will argue that semantic nets fail to be distinctive in the way they (1) represent propositions, (2) cluster information for access, (3) handle property inheritance, and (4) handle general inference. In other words, they lack distinctive representational properties (i.e., 1) and distinctive computational properties (i.e., 2–4). Certain propagation mechanisms, notably "spreading activation," "intersection search," or "inference propagation" have sometimes been regarded as earmarks of semantic nets, but since most extant semantic nets lack such mechanisms, they cannot be considered criterial in current usage. One way of reinvigorating the term, I will suggest, would be to restrict it to just such active networks. Another would be to reserve it for certain specialized representations (such as taxonomic and temporal graphs) that use graph-theoretic notions in an essential, nontrivial way.

2.2 REPRESENTATIONAL PROPERTIES OF SEMANTIC NETS

By the representational, as opposed to computational, properties of semantic nets, I mean those aspects of their structure that are interpretable as *denoting* something in the domain: individuals, properties, relations, magnitudes, facts, states of affairs, and so on. With respect to these representational properties, semantic nets have often been called "notational variants" of logic (or rather, of various logics). In a certain sense, I concur; but what exactly does this mean?

Let us note at once that the term "notational" is prejudicial: it suggests that we are concerned with notations on paper (or display screens), whereas my concern here is with *information structures in computers*. These two notions of representation *are* related; for instance, sets of predicate logic expressions on paper and node-and-link diagrams (of the right type) would appear to be expressively equivalent just in case their corresponding computer realizations are expressively equivalent. Furthermore, it is hard to *write* about propositional representations in computers without resorting to some notation like bracketed expressions or diagrams on paper. However, if we blur the distinction between these two notions of representation, we are apt to get tangled up in questions that are not at issue here: for instance, whether node-and-link drawings provide more perspicuous propositional representations than bracketed expressions.

So in what follows, all references to propositional representations or "notations" are to be understood as references to information structures in computers. This does not mean, of course, that we are concerned with machine-oriented, hardware-level information structures, but rather with structures at some appropriate level of abstraction, such as the level of symbolic expressions or graphs.

A propositional representation (in computers as well as on paper) has two parts: a syntax and a semantics. (There is usually an associated *calculus* as well, for establishing new propositions from given ones, but that is a computational matter.) Suppose that two representations admit transformations from each to the other, such that any syntactically well-formed knowledge set (for lack of a better word) in one representation is effectively mapped into a well-formed knowledge set in the other, and furthermore, the original knowledge set and its transform are semantically equivalent. (Accept for the moment that this last notion can be made precise—I will elaborate shortly.) Then we have two effectively interchangeable representations, enabling us to express exactly the same things. Can we therefore regard them as "notational" variants (more exactly, *structural* variants)?

It may be felt that this is not quite enough. After all, there seems to be a similar correspondence between, say, programs of a universal Turing machine (i.e., tape expressions describing some other, or the same, Turing machine) and LISP programs. There are effective (in fact, primitive recursive) mappings from each to the other, such that each program and its transform have exactly the same partial recursive function as extension (or the same class of partial recursive functions, if we allow for different ways of interpreting inputs and outputs as numbers or other abstract objects.) Yet the two representations may be so wildly different, and so lacking in any *structural* resemblance, that we would hesitate to call them mere "notational variants" of each other. (When we talk about a notational variant of LISP, we might be thinking of something like Interlisp, but hardly universal Turing machine programs!)

However, there's more to the transformations from nets to sets of formulas, and the reverse, than mere effectiveness: they can be chosen to be *isomorphisms* with certain special properties. These special properties pertain to the *meaningful expressions* (meaningful parts) making up two corresponding knowledge sets. Specifically, such an isomorphism maps the atomic and compound expressions of one formalism to those of the other in a way that

1. associates with each interpretable atomic expression of one knowledge set an interpretable atomic expression of the transformed knowledge set which admits exactly the *same* interpretations (such as individuals in the domain of discourse, sets or relations over such individuals, intensions, properties, or what have you); and
2. preserves semantically significant structural features of compound expressions (such as the subexpression relation and subexpression ordering).

Such an isomorphism induces a very strong semantic correspondence: the two knowledge sets have the same "valuations," and hence the same models. By a valuation of a knowledge set I mean an assignment of semantic values to all of its meaningful expressions (parts), beginning with admissible interpretations of its interpretable atomic expressions and continuing with values for compound expressions determined in accordance with the semantic rules of the formalism (in logic, the rules for interpreting functional expressions, atomic formulas, logically compound formulas, and quantified formulas). A model of a knowledge set is a valuation that renders its "top-level" proposition-denoting expressions true.

Let me illustrate. Besides clarifying some of the preceding notions and claims, the illustration will serve to allay the following sort of skepticism, which experienced network theorists may by now feel: How can there be an *isomorphism* between nets and sets of formulas when one of the clearest intuitions about nets is that they introduce just *one* node for each distinct entity, whereas sets of formulas duplicate individual tokens with prodigal abandon? The answer contained in the illustration is that we need not view sets of formulas in terms of the distinct tokens they contain, but rather we can view them in terms of the distinct *expressions* they contain, however many occurrences (tokens) of those expressions there may be.

The illustration may strike the reader as a sort of extended pun—and so it is. I will define a particular, "bare bones" type of semantic net called an *s-net*, serving as a propositional representation but devoid of any specific access structures or other computational features. This type of net is so closely related to logic that I will not need to construct an explicit isomorphism from one to the other. In fact it *is* logic (first-order predicate calculus (FOPC) to be exact) but couched in terms that make it appear to be a net (a directed, acyclic, labeled graph). Thus from a purely representational perspective, formulas—appropriately viewed—*are* nets.

To define s-nets, we begin with *vertices*, defined as the following types of expressions:

constant vertices	$c_1, c_2, \ldots$
variable vertices	$x_1, x_2, \ldots$
function vertices	$f^1_1, f^1_2, \ldots, f^2_1, f^2_2, \ldots$
	(intuitively, the upper index indicates adicity)
predicate vertices	$P^1_1, P^1_2, \ldots, P^2_1, P^2_2, \ldots$
quantifier vertices	$\forall, \exists$
operator vertices	$\vee, \wedge, \sim, \supset$

In the following i, n are any positive integers.

term vertex: any constant or variable vertex, or any expression of form $(f^n_i\ t_1 \ldots t_n)$ where $t_1, \ldots, t_n$ are term vertices.

propositional vertex: any expression of form $(P^n_i\ t_1 \ldots t_n)$ where $t_1, \ldots, t_n$ are term vertices; or any expression of form $(Q\ x\ R)$ where Q is a quantifier vertex, x is a variable vertex, and R is a propositional vertex; or any expression of form $(\vee\ R\ S)$, $(\wedge\ R\ S)$, $(\sim R)$, or $(\supset R\ S)$, where R and S are propositional vertices.

We use labeled-edge terminology to describe the relation between an expression and its immediate (ordered) constituents. In a vertex V of form $(O\ V_1 \ldots V_n)$ (where necessarily O is a function, predicate, quantifier, or operator vertex), we say that there is a labeled directed edge (V, O, OP) from vertex V to vertex O and a labeled directed edge (V, V_i, i) from vertex V to vertex V_i for $i = 1, \ldots, n$.

Finally, we define an s-net as a finite set of propositional vertices.

It is patently obvious that an s-net is just a set of FOPC formulas, in a slightly altered terminological guise. Yet an s-net also meets the minimal intuitive requirement for a semantic net, that of being a graphical structure (with vertices capable of representing things, concepts, and propositions, and edges supplying the "glue" that binds together the parts of functional concepts and propositions).

Theorem The vertices and edges of an s-net form a directed, acyclic labeled graph without isolated vertices.

Proof Briefly, this follows from the fact that the "proper subexpression" relation is irreflexive, and atomic vertices occur only as constituents of nonatomic ones. In more detail, a directed labeled graph is any triple of sets $\{V_1,..., V_n\}$, $\{E_1,..., E_m\}$, $\{L_1,..., L_l\}$, where each E_i $(1 \leq i \leq m)$ is a triple (V_j, V_k, L) such that $1 \leq j,k \leq n$ and $L \in \{L_1,..., L_l\}$. Obviously the vertex set, edge set, and label set $\{OP, 1,..., N\}$ where N is the smallest integer ≥ 2 such that every function vertex f_i^n and predicate vertex P_i^n in the s-net has $n \leq N$, form a directed labeled graph.

An acyclic graph is one not containing a closed path, i.e., a subset of edges $\{(V_{j_1}, V_{j_2}, L_{l_1}), (V_{j_2}, V_{j_3}, L_{l_2}),..., (V_{j_s}, V_{j_{s+1}}, L_{l_s})\}$, $(s \geq 1)$, such that $j_1 = j_{s+1}$. In an s-net, edges correspond to the "immediate subexpression" relation. Paths, therefore, correspond to the "proper subexpression" relation (not necessarily immediate). Hence if an s-net contained a closed path, it would contain an expression that has itself as a proper subexpression—an obvious impossibility.

An isolated vertex of a graph is one that does not occur in any edge. Clearly, an s-net has no isolated vertices, since each immediate subexpression of each non-atomic vertex is by definition not isolated (i.e., it occurs in the edge from the embedding vertex to it), and atomic vertices occur only as subexpressions of non-atomic ones (ultimately, of the propositional vertices comprising the s-net). □

Our sample isomorphism, then, is just the identity map from FOPC expressions to s-net vertices (or *vice versa*), these being one and the same thing. The claim about semantic equivalence (admitting the same valuations) is also trivially true as long as we agree to interpret s-net vertices just as we would logical expressions (which they are).

Of course, demonstrating isomorphism/equivalence for s-nets and FOPC doesn't demonstrate it for any of the many subspecies of nets and their putative logical counterparts. But at least it indicates how to proceed. A few further remarks are in order. S-nets are similar (in terms of representational properties) to the sorts of nets proposed by Shapiro [1971], Rumelhart et al., [1972], Schubert [1976], and many later schemes. In particular, there are explicit proposition nodes (vertices), and edge labels serve essentially to indicate argument order (though they may be chosen to remind us of uniformities across predicates: SUBJ, OBJ, and the like). Another popular type of net uses edges themselves as representations of binary predications—the labels being predicate symbols and thus freely interpretable (e.g., [Winston, 1970; Deliyanni and Kowalski, 1979; Nilsson, 1980]). Here we naturally need a slightly different strategy for demonstrating the desired sort of isomorphism/equivalence. For instance, we might define a "propositional edge" as an expression of form $(P\ t_1\ t_2)$ where P is an edge label (drawn from a set of labels interpretable as binary relations) and t_1, t_2 are term vertices. A (bare bones) semantic net of this type would ultimately be defined as just a set of propositional edges—these entail the presence of the vertices they connect.

Also, many semantic net theorists have taken as their basic binary relations the "instance" relation between objects or events and their types, the "isa" relation between subtypes and supertypes, and case relations such as "agent-of," "object-of," "recipient-of," etc., tying participants in events to those events. This particular viewpoint appears to present no special obstacles to the sort of equivalence construction I have indicated. Even if its proponents were to deny that relationships such as (*agent-of John Kissing-event1*) can be formally evaluated in the manner of logical predications, it is hard to conceive of any alternative formal method of evaluation that would not, thereby, also provide an alternative formal semantics of binary predicate logic, and thus make the equivalence go through under that semantics.

Closely related to the notion of case relations is the frame-based notion of *slots* or *roles* associated with a concept, such as the parts of a thing or the participants in a situation. As [Hayes, 1979] points out, roles can be viewed as relations or Skolem functions, and as such are logically unproblematic. However, one representational feature of frames emphasized by Minsky [1975] is that they supply *default* characteristics for the object types they describe and their frame slots (roles). So, for instance, elephants are gray and have a rope-like tail by default, though specific exceptions (such as a white elephant with a deformed tail or none at all) are permitted. (Much the same idea lies at the heart of *prototype* theory.) Are the network (or frame) representations of defaults beyond the pale of logic and thus a counterexample to the claimed representational equivalence?

Well again, the answer is that if we can find a formal way of making sense of defaults in role-structured nets (or frames), we'll also have a way of doing so for a linearized, "logical" representation of those defaults. There is nothing magical about drawing an arc labeled DEFAULT-V from the COLOR slot for the TYPICAL-ELEPHANT to GRAY, instead of writing down DEFAULT-V(COLOR(TYPICAL-ELEPHANT)) = GRAY. However, there *is* something slightly magical about drawing *conclusions* from either of these representations without being able to say under what conditions "Elephants are typically gray" is *true* (which, as a matter of fact, it is). A good deal of effort is being devoted in AI and in linguistic semantics to this profound semantic puzzle. If and when this effort succeeds, we will also know what the correct net/logic mapping for default characterizations is.

In general, there is finicky work to be done in finding just the right logics to serve as isomorphic images of various network formalisms. For instance, the formalism in Schubert [1976] contains quantifier and operator scope conventions that generalize Skolem dependencies in a way that is not entirely trivial to map isomorphically into an ordinary logical format. More interestingly, it is easy to define network syntax so as to permit cycles, which, on a "subexpression" interpretation of network edges, cannot occur in an ordinary logical syntax. However, one can extend ordinary logical syntax in the following way. Introduce a set of *formula labels* p_1, p_2, ..., where the last element of each formula is to be a formula label (i.e., this last element comes immediately after the usual constituents of the formula). Thus, for instance, we write (*loves John Mary* p_1) rather than (*loves John Mary*). Labels of otherwise distinct formulas must also be distinct, and labels of otherwise identical formulas must also be identical. Furthermore, in forming any compound formula, the labels of the embedded formulas must be used in place of the formulas themselves. Thus we write

$(\wedge\ p_1\ p_3\ p_4)$, (*loves John Mary* p_1), (*loves Mary John* p_2), $(\sim p_2\ p_3)$

instead of

($\wedge$ (*loves John Mary*) ($\sim$ (*loves Mary John*))).

Formulas are regarded as asserted only if their labels do not occur elsewhere. Thus, only p_4 above is regarded as asserted. It is easy to see how to formally interpret formulas of this new type, as long as there is no cyclic reference to formula labels. However, consider the following pair:

($\supset$ *true* p_1 p_2), $(\sim p_1\ p_1)$

Here p_2 is asserted; it says that truth implies p_1 (assuming *true* is an atomic formula interpreted as truth), and so asserts p_1. But p_1 says that p_1 is not the case, and so denies itself. Thus, we have a paradox.

This extended logic models potentially cyclic semantic nets in an obvious way, and reflects the potential for paradox in such nets. Again, however, this does not create any problem for isomorphism between nets and logic. Rather, it creates a problem for the semantics of *both* nets and the corresponding logic. Any formal semantics successfully addressing this problem in one formalism will immediately address it in the other, as well. (The non-well-founded set theory of [Aczel, 1986] or the truth-revision theory of [Gupta, 1987] may perhaps provide a basis for a solution.)

2.3 COMPUTATIONAL PROPERTIES AND A STATE-OF-THE-ART SYSTEM

The clustering of properties around concepts, and the incorporation of inheritance hierarchies, have often been held up as the most significant features of semantic nets; and so they are. The trouble, from a terminological standpoint, is that neither of these features is at this stage still distinctive of semantic nets. On the contrary, both have been more or less universally incorporated into *all* KR formalisms designed to cope with substantial bodies of propositional knowledge.

Frames, in particular, encode clusters of information about entities and are standardly organized into inheritance hierarchies. As well, inheritance hierarchies have been integrated into databases, expert system shells, and PROLOG extensions. Similarly, the clustering of information about entities has been a ubiquitous theme in intelligent system design, even in systems that no one would call net-based or frame-based. For instance, Fahlman's block-stacking program relied heavily on packets of knowledge associated with particular geometric shapes [Fahlman, 1974], and Coles's question-answering system accessed groups of logical formulas clustered around the physical laws that constituted its domain of discourse [Coles, 1972].

But, one might ask, isn't the key property of semantic nets ultimately how they exploit property clustering and hierarchies to control inference? And isn't the distinctive characteristic of inference, so controlled, that it combines information at an accessed propositional vertex with information at *neighboring* (or at least *nearby*) vertices, rather than with arbitrarily remote ones?

In the first place (I would reply), thinking of inference propagation in the above sort of way is as familiar to frame folks as it is to net folks, and to miscellaneous other folks with no admitted semantic net loyalties. So this sort of proximity-based control of inference does not distinguish nets—at least not anymore. Secondly, and more importantly, I would claim that *any* reasonable way of controlling inference, even if formulated by a logician with a distaste for nodes and links, will inevitably be "proximity-based," on the kind of view of formula sets as s-nets outlined earlier. Again, it's all a matter of how you "picture" the structure of expressions.

Consider, for instance, a simple resolution step such as

(~ (*loves John x*)) versus (*loves John Mary*),

where the first literal might be the "denial clause" formed in an attempt to deduce an answer to the question "Whom does John love?" On an s-net view of the two formulas, this amounts to a "graph-based inference" involving three closely linked propositional vertices; namely, those for (~ (*loves John x*)), (*loves John x*), and (*loves John Mary*), where the first two are linked via a pair of edges labeled "*OP*" and "1," and the last two are linked via edges labeled "*OP*" and "1" to common destinations "*loves*" and "*John*" respectively. Indeed, a reasonable and obvious way of organizing formulas for this kind of resolution inference is to hash index them on combinations of a predicate name with an argument name. Thus (*loves John Mary*) would be indexed under (*loves, John*) and (*loves, Mary*). But this storage organization essentially associates various *properties*, such as "love-properties," with various *concepts*, such as *John* and *Mary*—and this is regarded as a crucial feature of semantic net organization! The same point applies, for instance, to property inheritance. A logical view of the inference that

(*color Clyde gray*)

for instance, based on

(*elephant Clyde*), ($\forall$ x ($\supset$ (*elephant x*) (*color x gray*)))

would again involve "nearby" s-net vertices, and might well be facilitated by the previous sort of hash indexing under (predicate, argument) pairs such as (*elephant, Clyde*), (*elephant*, \$), (*color*, \$), and (*color, gray*), with an inference strategy that pays special attention to "type predications" such as (*elephant Clyde*), accessing information about the type via index (*elephant*, \$). ("\$" is here used as a uniform variable token, for hash purposes.) This strategy can be improved on (e.g., [deHaan and Schubert, 1986]), but whether one regards the improved strategy as a logical inference strategy or a semantic net strategy is purely a matter of terminological preference.

These issues have been very much on my mind in the choice of terminology for describing ECOLOGIC, an inferential knowledge base recently implemented at the University of Alberta (see [Schubert and Hwang, 1989, 1990]). The system is intended to support a general narrative-understanding and question-answering system. (ECO derives from English **CO**nversation, and LOGIC from the system's logical soul.) The logic is intensional, probabilistic (allowing unreliable generalizations and degrees of belief), and rather close to English surface structure. Here, for instance, is the preliminary unscoped translation and a disambiguated translation with explicit episodic variables of a "donkey sentence" (compare [Sowa, Chapter 4, this volume]:

Every farmer who owns a donkey beats it

$(pres\ [<\forall\ \lambda\ x\ [[x\ farmer] \wedge (pres\ [x\ owns < \exists\ donkey>])> (Gn\ (beat\ it))])$

$$
\begin{aligned}
&(\exists\ e_1\text{:}\ [e_1 at\text{-}about\ Now_1]\\
&\qquad [(\forall x\text{:}\ [[x\ farmer] \wedge (\exists e_2\text{:}\ [e_2\ at\text{-}about\ Now_1]\\
&\qquad\qquad\qquad\qquad (\exists y\text{:}[y\ donkey]\ [[x\ owns\ y]{*}{*}e_2]))]\\
&\qquad\qquad [x\ (Gn\ (beat\ y))])^{**}e_1])
\end{aligned}
$$

("**" symbolizes the *characterization* relation between a sentence intension and an episode; *Gn* is a "gnomic" or "habitual" operator; and occurrences of variables outside the scopes of their existential quantifiers function essentially like *reference markers* in discourse representation theory.) ECOLOGIC incorporates many features of its predecessor, ECONET, which we still hesitantly termed a semantic net: a concept-centered, topic-oriented retrieval mechanism, type and topic hierarchies, and a general goal-directed inference mechanism aided by several "specialists" that short-circuit temporal, taxonomic, set and number inferences [Miller and Schubert, 1988]. In addition it performs input-driven inference, working out the probable consequeces and explanations of logical-form inputs. Both systems are able to infer answers to questions such as "Did the wolf eat a person?" and "Does Grandmother live in a shoe?" based on a simplified, logically encoded version of *Little Red Riding Hood.* The new system, however, also anticipates that Little Red Riding Hood is probably in danger when she meets the wolf and makes many other inferences spontaneously that could previously be obtained only in goal-directed fashion.

Though the "semantic competence" of our most recent system thus improves over our previous ones, we now generally avoid the term "semantic net." Already in the design of ECONET, we ceased drawing our propositions as graphs; in the new, enriched syntax (admitting restricted quantification, lambda abstraction, and nominalization, among other things), it would be even less helpful to replace the logical notation by swirling lines. This seemingly insignificant fact greatly diminished our disposition to think in semantic net terms. Perhaps the last straw was the fact that input-driven inference can be quite effectively implemented by hash table methods of the sort mentioned above—an access method not particularly indebted to semantic net theory.

2.4 WHAT'S LEFT?

To say that semantic nets, in the broadest sense, lack distinctive representational and computational properties is not to say that the term should be expunged from the AI lexicon. There *are* some promising, and quite familiar, directions for useful redeployment of the term.

One possibility, which I discussed in [Schubert, 1976], is to reserve "semantic nets" for the graphical *depictions* of propositional information we find helpful in conceiving or explaining certain inferential processes. (As such, they would be viewed as analogous to Venn diagrams in set theory.) However, I doubt that many people are ready to think of semantic nets as mere pictures, however strongly they may feel about the advantages of node-and-link diagrams or nested boxes. That is why I set aside the diagrammatic aspect from the outset. A better possibility is to reserve the term for propositional representations that, like Quillian's original networks, make essential use of *spreading activation* or similar propagation processes for inference or understanding. This use may be compatible with some of the current work in neural nets (inasmuch as this work also depends on concept-to-concept signal propagation). A third possibility is to reserve it for special-purpose graphical structures and their associated inference mechanisms, such as taxonomic hierarchies, parts hierarchies, or time graphs. These have, of course, proved very useful as enhancements to general propositional inference systems.

With regard to this last possibility, I need to emphasize two things. First, a representation is *graphical* in the sense I intend only if it uses graph-theoretic notions in an essential, nontrivial way. The mere possibility of depicting a representation in node-link form does not, in itself, demonstrate that the representation is intrinsically graphical; nor does the use of an inference strategy that prefers to combine closely linked facts necessarily show this; whereas systematic reliance on formally defined distance metrics or topological properties (connectivity, cycles, classes of paths, etc.) for inference (deduction, analogy, associative retrieval, etc.) may indeed do so.

Second, I need to emphasize the distinction between graph-based auxiliary representations on the one hand, and the larger, more general inference systems that *incorporate* them on the other. If we were to call a representation a semantic net merely because it *incorporates* a taxonomic subsystem (say, to support property inheritance), we would revert precisely to the practice I am decrying! The point is that a taxonomic (or temporal, etc.) reasoner that makes *essential* use of *nontrivial* graph-theoretic properties is, on account of that, a member of an important and objectively distinguishable species of knowledge representation. A system that merely incorporates some such special reasoner is, nowadays, a system like any other.

ACKNOWLEDGMENTS

I am grateful for the helpful and provocative comments (in the best sense of the word) on the manuscript by Roger Hartley, Alfred Kobsa, John Sowa, and (at the Catalina workshop) Bill Woods. The research was supported by operating grant A8818 of the Natural Sciences and Engineering Research Council of Canada, by the Boeing Company under Purchase Contracts W-278258 and W-288104, and ONR/DARPA Research Contract No. N00014-82-K-0193.

References

Aczel, P. 1986. *Lectures on Non-Well Founded Sets*. CSLI, Stanford, CA.

Coles, L.S. 1972. *Techniques for Information Retrieval Using an Inferential Question Answering System with Natural Language Input*. SRI Tech. Rep., SRI International, Menlo Park, CA.

deHaan, J., and Schubert, L.K. 1986. Inference in a topically organized semantic net. *Proceedings of AAAI-86*, pp. 334–338. AAAI, Menlo Park, CA.

Deliyanni, A., and Kowalski, R. 1979. Logic and semantic networks. *CACM* 22:184–192.

Fahlman, S.E. 1974. A planning system for robot construction tasks. *Artificial Intelligence* 5:1–49.

Gupta, A. 1987. The meaning of truth. In *New Directions in Semantics*, E. LePore (ed.), Academic Press, New York, pp. 453–480.

Hayes, P.J. 1979. The logic of frames. *Frame Conceptions and Text Understanding*, In D. Metzing (ed.), de Gruyter, Berlin, pp. 46–61. Also in *Readings in Artificial Intelligence*, B.L. Webber and N.J. Nilsson (eds.), Morgan Kaufmann Publishers, San Mateo, CA, 1981, pp. 451–458.

Hendrix, G.G. 1973. Language processing via canonical verbs and semantic models. *Adv. Papers of IJCAI-73*, pp. 262–269. Proceeings of the IJCAI conferences are available from Morgan Kaufmann Publishers, San Mateo, CA.

Miller, S.A., and Schubert, L.K. 1988. Using specialists to accelerate general reasoning. *Proceedings of AAAI-88*, Aug. 21–26, St. Paul, MN. AAAI, Menlo Park, CA, pp. 161–165.

Minsky, M. 1975. A framework for representing knowledge. In *The Psychology of Computer Vision*, P.H. Winston (ed.), McGraw-Hill, New York, pp. 211–277.

Nilsson, N.J. 1980. *Principles of Artificial Intelligence.* Morgan Kaufmann Publishers, San Mateo, CA.

Rumelhart, D., Lindsay, P., and Norman, D. 1972. A process model for long term memory. In *Organization of Memory*, E. Tulving and W. Donaldson (eds.), Academic Press, New York, pp. 198–221.

Schubert, L.K. 1976. Extending the expressive power of semantic nets, *Artificial Intelligence* 7:163–198.

Schubert, L.K., and Hwang, C.-H. 1989. An episodic knowledge representation for narrative texts. *Proceedings of the First International Conference on Principles of Knowledge Representation and Reasoning* (KR-89), May 15–18, 1989, Toronto, Canada. Morgan Kaufmann Publishers, San Mateo, CA, pp. 444–458.

———, 1990. *An Episodic Knowledge Representation for Narrative Texts.* Tech. Rep. 345, Department of Computer Science, U. of Rochester. (This substantially elaborates the KR-89 version.)

Shapiro, S.C. 1971. A net structure for semantic information storage, deduction, and retrieval. *Adv. Papers of IJCAI-71*, pp. 512–523. Proceeings of the IJCAI conferences are available from Morgan Kaufmann Publishers, San Mateo, CA.

Winston, P. 1970. *Learning Structural Descriptions from Examples*, Ph.D. Thesis, MIT, MAC-TR-76, Cambridge, MA.

3

WHY SEMANTIC NETWORKS?

Lokendra Shastri
(University of Pennsylvania)

Abstract

It is often asserted that semantic networks, are mere notational variants of other well-defined and "standard" representation languages. Yet semantic networks seem to have a substantial following and a special appeal of their own. What makes semantic networks special, and why has so much research effort been devoted to developing network-based knowledge representation languages? In this chapter we attempt to answer this question from the perspective of *computational effectiveness*. We argue that a knowledge representation language must not only be characterized in terms of its representational adequacy but also in terms of its computational effectiveness. Furthermore, a computationally effective knowledge representation framework must explicate the relationship between the nature of representation, the effectiveness of certain inferences and the computational architecture in which the computations/inferences are performed. Semantic networks, or graph-based representation formulations are examples of such knowledge representation frameworks. In particular, semantic networks—realized as massively parallel networks—may provide the appropriate framework for modeling reflexive reasoning—reasoning that we can perform rapidly, effortlessly, and without conscious effort.

3.1 INTRODUCTION

It is often asserted that semantic networks, are mere notational variants of some well-defined and "standard" representation language such as the first-order predicate calculus [Schubert, 1991]. Yet semantic networks seem to have a substantial following and a special appeal of their own. What makes semantic networks special, and why has so much research effort been devoted to developing network-based knowledge representation languages [Findler, 1979; Sowa, 1991]. In this chapter we attempt to answer this question from the perspective of *computational effectiveness*.

In general it is possible to translate a semantic network into a nongraphical language and *vice versa*. For example, several translations of semantic networks into the first-order predicate calculus (FOPC) have been proposed (see [Hayes, 1979; Charniak, 1981]).[1] On the other hand, one can replace the linear notation of FOPC by a two-dimensional graphical notation without in any way changing its semantics and expressive power [Schubert, 1991]. It is also possible to define graphical representation languages that are more expressive than FOPC [Sowa, 1991]. The richer expressive power of such a language, however, cannot be ascribed to its graphical *form*. With some ingenuity one can always translate such a graphical notation into a complex linear one, without in any way affecting the semantics and expressive power of the underlying representation language. Thus the class of semantic network languages cannot be differentiated from the class of non-semantic network languages solely on the basis of their representational adequacy.

But should we characterize a knowledge representation language solely by its expressiveness? We argue that we should not. We believe that a knowledge representation language must not only be characterized in terms of its representational adequacy but also in terms of its *computational effectiveness*: A knowledge representation framework should not merely prescribe how individual pieces of information ought to be represented, but it should also specify how the totality of information ought to be structured and organized so that relevant information may be retrieved and appropriate inferences drawn with requisite efficiency. We elaborate on this below.

1. The notion of a *representation* is meaningful only in the context of the computations and *operations* it is expected to support. Consequently, the specification of any knowledge representation framework must include a specification of the retrieval and inferential operations it intends to support.
2. Any computational model of intelligence must be *effective*; i.e., *it should explain how an agent may perform certain tasks within a specified time*

[1] Most semantic network formulations explicitly deal with defaults, exceptions, and conflicting information. The direct translation of semantic networks into FOPC cannot capture these aspects of knowledge and more sophisticated translations based on various nonmonotonic logics and probability theory (to name a few) are required. This issue, though extremely important, is orthogonal to the point we wish to make in this chapter, and hence, is not discussed further. For a detailed discussion refer to [Shastri, 1988, 1989].

frame.[2] Consequently, a knowledge representation framework is relevant to AI only if it can be *realized* as a physical system that can compute a desired subclass of inference within an appropriate time scale [Shastri, 1988; Levesque, 1988].

3. In view of (2), the specification referred to in (1) must also specify the limits of acceptable performance for the retrieval and inference operations the representation is expected to support. Hence both, a specification of the operations that a representation must support and the time frame within which these operations must be performed together constitute the full specification of a representation framework.[3]

We wish to argue that semantic networks are extremely significant if we consider this broad and more appropriate characterization of a knowledge representation framework. Semantic networks are the product of the insight that a representation language must *explicate* and *vividify* the intimate and *symbiotic* relationship between the nature of representation, the effectiveness of inference, and ultimately, the computational architecture in which the associated computations are situated.

3.2 REFLEXIVE REASONING

Research in artificial intelligence has made it abundantly clear that tremendous inferential activity underlies even the most commonplace intelligent behavior that humans carry out effortlessly and with remarkable speed.[4] For example, language understanding—a task that we perform effortlessly most of the time—requires solving several subtasks such as disambiguating word senses, parsing, resolving anaphoric references, imposing selectional restrictions, recognizing speaker's plans, and performing various predictive and explanatory inferences.

To underscore the extreme efficiency with which certain inferences need to be drawn in order to support intelligent behavior, let us label such inferences *reflexive*. Later in this section we characterize reflexive reasoning in terms of its time complexity but informally, reflexive reasoning involves inferences that we humans draw effortlessly, without deliberation and within a fraction of a second—it is as if

---

[2] By "effective" we do not mean "terminating," but rather "terminating within a specified time frame." We deliberately avoid the use of the work "efficient" as it has a rather weak connotation in AI (see Section 3.2).

[3] Incidently, such a specification also provides the design constraints and the criteria for evaluating a representation framework.

[4] Once again, the *nature* of inference is not an issue here, and we include in its scope deduction, probabilistic inference, default reasoning, analogical reasoning, etc.

these inferences are a *reflex* response of our cognitive apparatus. Hence the name reflexive reasoning.[5]

The following example illustrates the richness of reflexive inference (this example is based on [Schubert, 1989]). Consider a person reading a variation of the Little Red Riding Hood (LRRH) story in which the wolf intends to eat LRRH in the woods. The reader is at the point in the story where the wolf, who has followed LRRH into the woods, is about to attack her. The next sentence reads: "The wolf heard some woodcutters nearby and so he decided to wait." It seems reasonable to claim that the reader will understand this sentence spontaneously and without deliberate thought. However, a careful analysis of this sentence makes it apparent that even though the reader does not become aware of it, understanding this sentence requires fairly elaborate reasoning. This reasoning may (very) informally be described as follows (the "rules" are in parentheses): To eat LRRH the wolf will have to approach her (because to eat something you have to be near it); if the wolf approaches LRRH she will scream (because a child is scared by an approaching wild animal); if LRRH screams, the woodcutters will hear her (because a loud noise can be heard at a distance and screaming generates a loud noise); if the woodcutters hear the scream they will know that a child is in danger (because a child's screaming suggests that the child is in danger); the woodcutters will come to the location of the scream (because people want to protect children in danger and in part, this involves determining the source of the danger); when the woodcutters see the wolf they will try to prevent it from attacking LRRH (because people want to protect children); in doing so the woodcutters may hurt the wolf (preventing an animal from attacking a child may involve physical force...); so the wolf will decide to wait (the wolf does not want to get hurt).

One might quibble about specific details, but clearly, something equivalent to the above chain of reasoning must be taking place during the understanding of the sentence in question. So the moral we wish to draw from the above story is:

- Cognitive agents can perform systematic reasoning extremely fast, i.e., reflexively.
- Such reasoning can be quite elaborate and involve chains of inference. In particular, it cannot be characterized as mere retrieval or table lookup.
- Reflexive reasoning is pervasive in cognitive activity. Arguably, a significant fraction of the reasoning carried out by human agents during language understanding and commonsense reasoning is reflexive in nature.

---

[5] Reflexive reasoning may be contrasted with *reflective* reasoning, i.e., reasoning that requires reflection and conscious thought.

3.2.1 Time Complexity of Reflexive Reasoning

In evaluating the effectiveness of reflexive reasoning it must be remembered that such reasoning takes place with reference to a vast body of knowledge. We believe that a conservative estimate of the number of "rules" and "facts" required to encode all relevant aspects of the domain of common sense will easily run into the tens of million—perhaps even more.[6] Given a knowledge base of this size and given that an agent can perform reflexive reasoning within fractions of a second, what should be a reasonable *upper bound* on the running time of an inference algorithm for performing such reasoning? We think that this can be no more than *sublinear* in $|KB|$, the size of the knowledge base. In fact we believe that reflexive reasoning may be characterized as a process that occurs in time that is *independent* of $|KB|$ and is only proportional to the length of the shortest chain of inference leading to the conclusion.

The time constraints on reflexive reasoning mentioned above introduce a very strong notion of computational effectiveness and should be contrasted with the existing trend in the field of knowledge representation and reasoning where inference algorithms that are *polynomial* in the size of the knowledge base are considered acceptable [Levesque, 1988]. We believe that any polynomial time inference algorithm—even if it is only a low-order polynomial—will be inadequate for meeting the tight time constraint imposed by reflexive reasoning.

3.3 RELATING STRUCTURE AND INFERENCE— A CASE FOR SEMANTIC NETS

Perhaps the most important step in tackling the problem of effective inference, and reflexive inference in particular, is to recognize that

> the *syntactic structure* (i.e., the *form*) of an *effective* representation must directly *mirror* the *inferential structure* of the knowledge it encodes.

This requires that the syntax of the representation language should be fairly rich and include primitives that allow the explicit encoding of the inferential structure of a body of knowledge.

---

[6] The choice of terminology is not critical here and the reader may replace "rules" and "facts" by scripts, schemas, frames, constraints, or whatever might happen to be the reader's favorite way of describing a chunk of knowledge.

Semantic networks have precisely the above characteristic—as do frame languages and inheritance hierarchies [Quillian, 1968; Minsky, 1975; Fahlman, 1979; Shapiro, 1979].[7]

A representation that naturally provides the requisite coupling between the syntactic structure of the representation and the inferential structure of domain knowledge is a graph whose nodes correspond to "units" of information (constants, predicates, concepts, properties, features, frames, or whatever) and whose arcs correspond to inferential dependencies between these units. Adopting such a graphical representation has the interesting consequence that *inference* reduces to a traversal of a physically instantiated graph (also see [Hartley and Coombs, 1991]). The organization of concepts in a *IS-A* hierarchy using *IS-A* links to capture the transitivity of subclass–superclass relationship is an excellent case in point. In an *IS-A* hierarchy, the subclass–superclass relationship is explicitly represented using dedicated *IS-A* links that allow the system to compute the transitive closure of these relations. The use of dedicated links reduces the problem of applying the transitivity rule: $\forall x, y, z\ IS\text{-}A(x, y) \wedge IS\text{-}A(y,z) \Rightarrow IS\text{-}A(x, z)$, to a problem of link traversal.

Reducing inference to graph traversal does not in itself solve the problem of effectiveness because searching arbitrary graphs is a costly operation. However, once we identify inference with graph search it becomes possible to relate the *effectiveness* of the inference process (search) with the *structural properties* of the representation (graph). For instance, searching a tree or a directed acyclic graph (DAG) is cheaper than searching a general graph—especially if the search can be performed in parallel (see Section 3.4). This suggests that computational effectiveness may be achieved if our representation maps the domain knowledge into a graph with the following property:

> Portions of the graph that are relevant to the solution of a reflexive inference problem are trees or DAGs.

The *direct* relationship between the structural properties of the representation and the effectiveness of inference also underscores the significance of choosing appropriate representational primitives. An appropriate choice of primitives would impart the required structural properties to the graph encoding the domain knowledge, and hence, lead to effective inference. Within this approach, answers to questions such as: "Should our epistemological primitives be undifferentiated predicates or should we distinguish between 'concepts,' 'relations,' and 'attributes'?" and "Should we use a typed (sorted) logic or not?," depend on—and follow directly

[7] Levesque's notion of "vividness" [Levesque, 1988] also captures this characteristic to some extent.} Below we argue that coupling the form of the representation language and the inferential structure of domain knowledge leads to a computational account of reflexive inference.

from—a detailed specification of the types of inferences that need to be computed reflexively.

To illustrate how the choice of representational primitives affects the structural properties of a representation consider two different ways of representing the following knowledge:

- Persons are nonpacifists,
- Republicans and Quakers are persons,
- Quakers are pacifists, and Republicans are nonpacifists.

First consider a "class-only" system in which everything is expressed in terms of monadic predicates. Next consider a "class-property system" that makes a distinction between classes (concepts) and properties. These two representations are illustrated in Figure 3.1. Notice how the second representation leads to a DAG whereas the first one does not. This is significant because it illustrates that depending on the choice of representational primitives, the same underlying knowledge may either lead to an acyclic structure that is amenable to effective inference, or a cyclic one that is not.[8] Distinguishing between classes and properties allows a class-property system to organize information along several "dimensions," namely, the *subclass–superclass* relation and the various *property-attachment* relations. By projecting the graph along specific dimension(s) one can selectively focus on different sorts of knowledge. This makes it possible to map a larger class of problems into acyclic structures. The above example is meant to illustrate the general observation that choosing a different set of epistemological primitives can change the structural properties of the representation in ways that may have a significant impact on computational efficiency.

Structural constraints required for supporting reflexive inference may not be as stringent as they might appear. This is because the complete graph need not satisfy these constraints, only subgraphs relevant for solving particular problems need do so. A concrete example of this may be found in the massively parallel realization of semantic networks described in [Shastri, 1988]. There it is shown that property inheritance may be computed extremely efficiently—in time proportional to the depth of the conceptual structure—provided the following requirement is satisfied:

> In order to inherit the value of a property *P* of a concept *C* effectively, concepts that lie *above* *C* and that have information about *P* attached to them, must form a tree.

---

[8] Note however, that the two representations are not equivalent, and we are glossing over a number of differences such as treatment of negation, quantification, and necessary versus default properties. In particular, the class-only representation explicitly encodes that pacifists are people and pacifist and nonpacifist are mutually exclusive. This information is not expressed in the class-property representation shown in Figure 3.1.

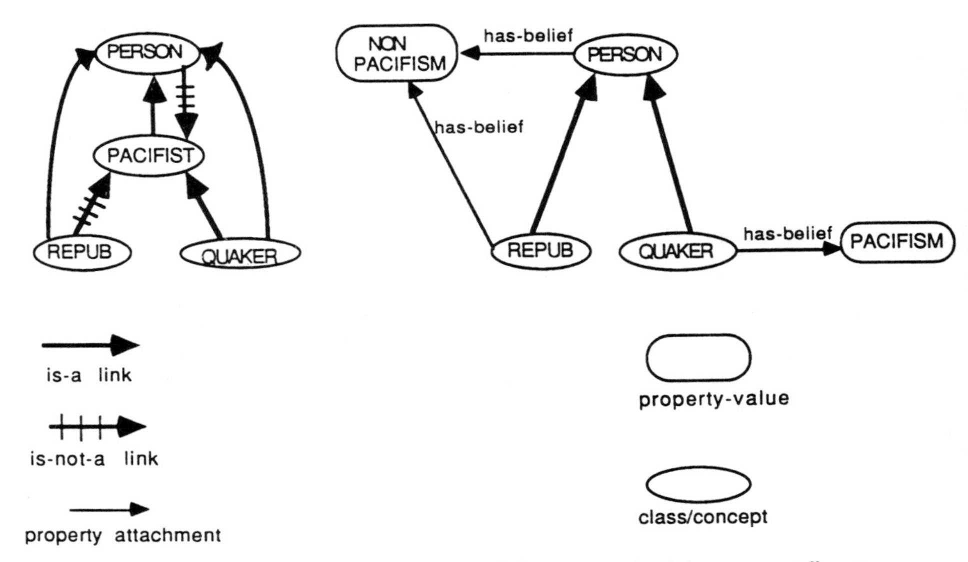

Figure 3.1: Two representations : A "class-only" system and a "class-property" system

In general, information about every property is not attached to every concept and, hence, the above constraint may be satisfied for a large class of inheritance queries even though the complete *IS-A* hierarchy may not be a tree. As an example, consider the *IS-A* hierarchy shown in Figure 3.2. Assume that the property has-belief—with values pacifist and nonpacifist—applies to the concepts shown in Figure 3.2 and that information pertaining to this property is attached to concepts enclosed in a dark box. Even though the concepts form a tangled *IS-A* hierarchy, the inheritance question: "Is Dick a pacifist or a nonpacifist?" can be answered efficiently because the relevant portion of the graph—consisting of all concepts that lie above DICK and that have information about the property has-belief attached to them—forms a tree (see Figure 3.3).

We have argued above that within a graphical framework, a concern for effective inference translates into constraints on the structural properties of the graph. We also pointed out that these constraints need not be satisfied by the graph as a whole and it suffices that only subgraphs relevant for solving individual problems satisfy the constraints. This raises two questions: (1) Who enforces the constraints on the structure of the graph? and (2) What happens if the subgraph corresponding to a given problem does not satisfy the constraint? The second question has a simple answer—if the subgraph corresponding to a particular problem does not satisfy the constraints, the system cannot answer the question in an effective man-

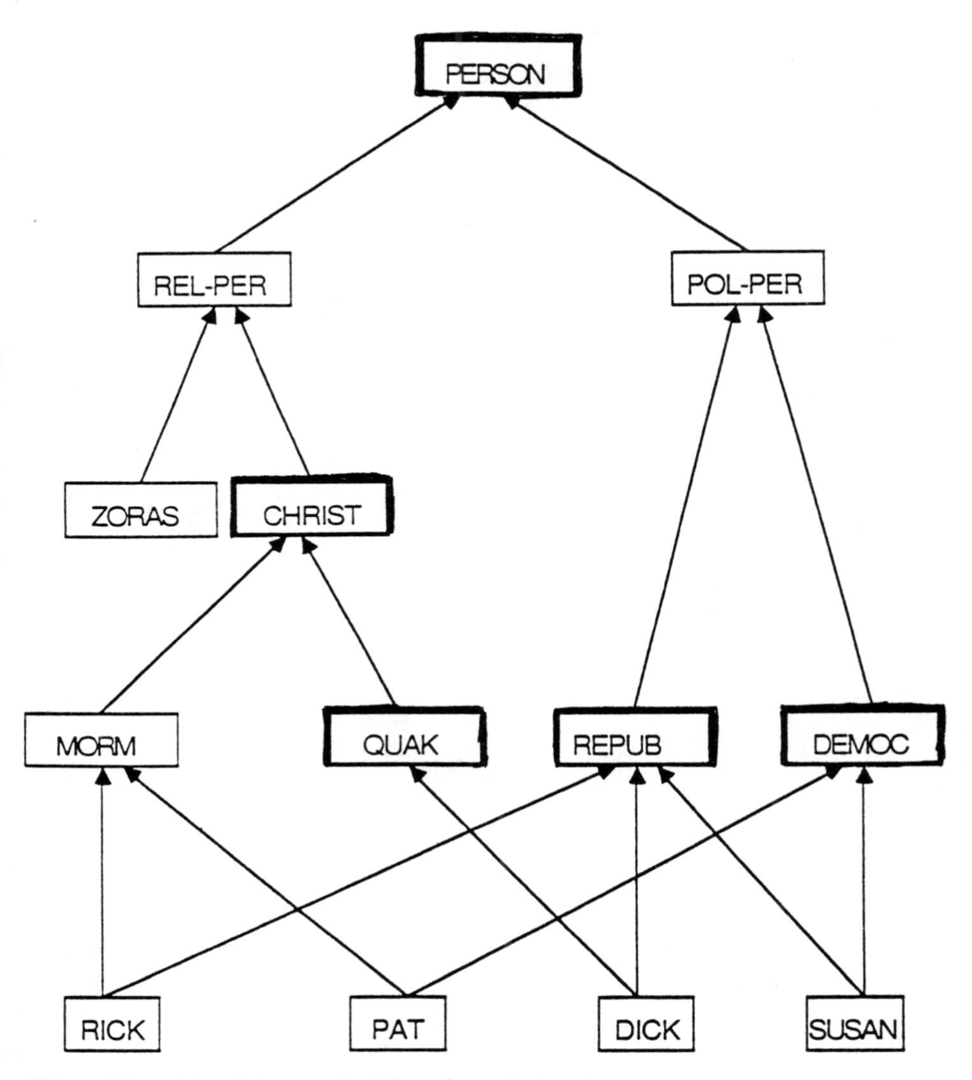

Figure 3.2: A tangled conceptual hierarchy

ner. This is exactly what we should expect because complexity theory tells us that any effective reasoning system has to be a *limited inference* system: It can only solve a limited class of problems efficiently. The issues raised by the first question are more involved and relate to knowledge acquisition, concept formation, and learning in general. It is envisaged that the proposed graphs (semantic networks)

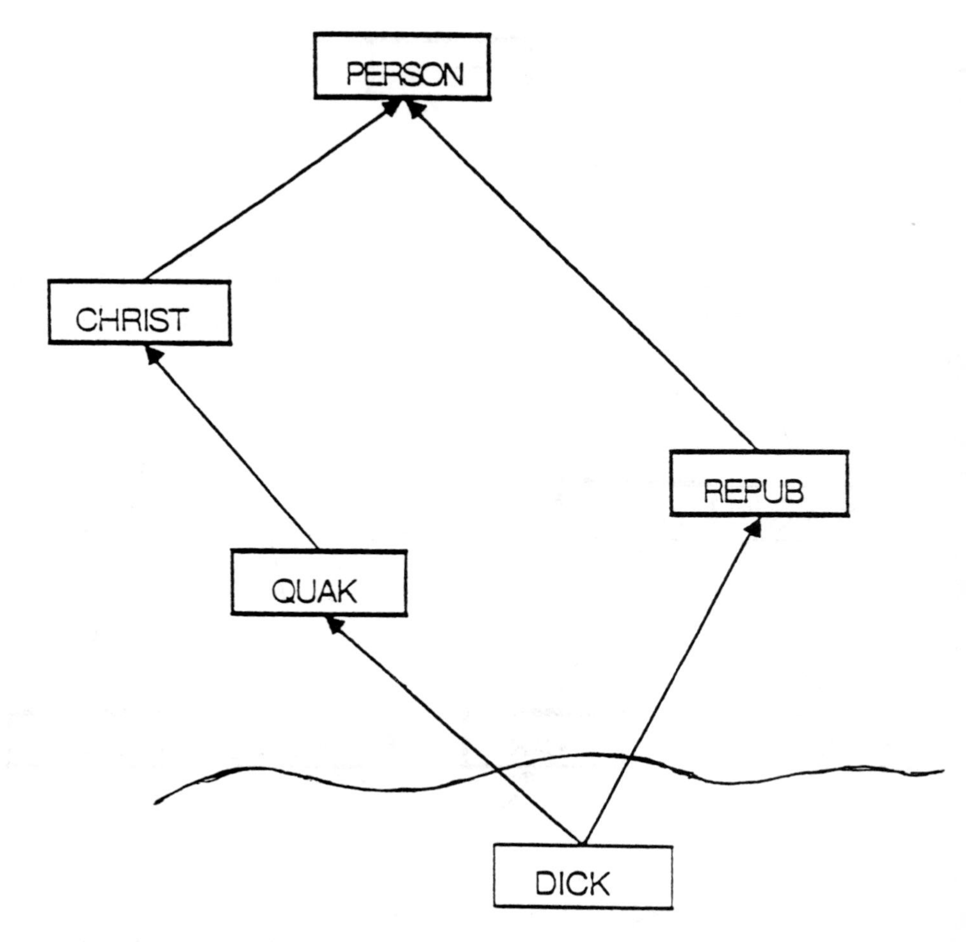

Figure 3.3: The subgraph relevant to the inheritance problem: Is Dick a pacifist or a non-pacifist?

would be the result of a systematic knowledge acquisition/learning process that would be predisposed to creating conceptual structures that satisfy the appropriate constraints—at least for an interesting subclass of problems. Work in the area of concept formation already has this general flavor; in the course of assimilating new data, concept formation algorithms posit new concepts if doing so makes it possible to use the new data effectively in predicting attributes of entities. (Also see Section 3.5.3).

3.4 SEMANTIC NETWORKS LEND THEMSELVES TO PARALLELISM

Once we identify inference with graph search the significance of architecture also becomes obvious. Consider searching a DAG with n nodes. A serial search algorithm will take $O(n)$ steps to complete the search. However, if we assume that each node is a (simple) processor that can directly communicate with all its neighbors then the graph search will only take time equal to the *diameter* of the graph. It seems reasonable to assume that in most cases, the diameter of the network will be *logarithmic* in the size of the knowledge base, and, hence, the parallel search will be sublinear in the size of the graph. For example, in the context of inheritance and recognition in a semantic network, the diameter of the network corresponds to the number of levels in the conceptual hierarchy and is typically logarithmic in the number of concepts in the knowledge base.

Based on the above observation the development of a physical system capable of performing reflexive inference might involve

- mapping domain knowledge onto a graph whose nodes correspond to "units" of information and arcs to inferential dependencies between these units.
- mapping the graph onto a parallel machine by assigning a processor to each node and creating a hardwired link for each arc.
- making appropriate epistemological and ontological choices so that the projection of the graph with respect to a reflexive query (i.e., the subgraph relevant to solving the query) is always such that the answer to the query can be computed in a sweep of information flow through the parallel machine.

One can trace the beginnings of such an "inference propagation" system to Quillian's model of semantic memory [Quillian, 1968] as well as Fahlman's NETL [Fahlman, 1979] and Shapiro's SNePs [Shapiro, 1979]. Two recent examples of such systems are the massively parallel semantic network described in [Shastri, 1988] and the massively parallel rule-based reasoning system reported in [Shastri and Ajjanagadde, 1990]. These systems are described in brief in the following sections. Both these systems are instances of structured connectionist systems [Feldman and Ballard, 1982]. In the present context it suffices to say that the nodes and links in these systems obey certain biologically motivated computational constraints: Each node is assumed to be a very simple processor that has no local memory except for a level of activation (*potential*). A node communicates with the rest of the network by transmitting a simple scalar value to all its neighbors. The output transmitted by a node is closely related to its potential, which in turn is a simple function of the node's present potential and the inputs it is receiving from its neighboring nodes. In addition to being biologically plausible, connectionist models correspond to an interesting massively parallel architecture—one in which all connections are hardwired, messages are only scalar quantities, and there is no central controller. These features entail that, in principle, the routing cost and the decoding and encoding costs (in other words, the communication overhead) in such systems is minimal.

3.5 A CONNECTIONIST SEMANTIC MEMORY

Reasoning that may be characterized as *inheritance* and *recognition* (classification) within a semantic network plays a central role in language understanding, visual recognition, and commonsense reasoning. Inheritance and recognition are also significant because humans can perform these inferences effortlessly and extremely fast—to wit language understanding in real time.

A massively parallel (connectionist) semantic network that can solve the inheritance and recognition problems with the desired degree of efficiency has been proposed in [Shastri, 1988]. This work prescribes a mapping from a formal specification at the knowledge level to a connectionist network that can solve an interesting class of inheritance as well as recognition problems in time proportional to the *depth* of the conceptual hierarchy. As the response time is only proportional to the depth of the hierarchy, the system scales gracefully and can deal with very large knowledge bases. The number of simple processors required to realize a semantic network is only linear in the number of concepts, *IS-A* relationships, properties, and property-values being encoded. In addition to achieving efficient performance, the connectionist semantic network has the following characteristics:

- Attempts at formalizing inheritance and recognition in semantic networks have been confounded by the presence of conflicting property-values among related concepts, which gives rise to the problems of exceptions and multiple inheritance during inheritance, and partial matching during recognition. Several formalizations of inheritance hierarchies have been proposed but none of them offer a uniform treatment of multiple inheritance and recognition. The suggested approach leads to an evidential formalization of conceptual knowledge and provides a principled treatment of exceptions, multiple inheritance, and recognition based on best/partial match.
- The work results in the identification of constraints on the conceptual structure that lead to efficient solutions. One of these constraints was mentioned earlier in Section 3.3. (The constraint specified that in order to inherit the value of some property *P* of a concept *C* effectively, concepts that lie *above C* and that have information about *P* attached to them, must form a tree.) Another constraint imposes a uniformity requirement on property value attachments in the conceptual structure and suggests that the conceptual hierarchy must comprise several alternate "views" of the underlying concepts if information about property values is to be used efficiently during recognition.

A detailed description of the system is beyond the scope of this paper and may be found in [Shastri, 1988]. A brief description of the representation language follows.

3.5.1 An Evidential Representation Language

The knowledge in the semantic memory is expressed in terms of a partially ordered set of concepts (i.e., a *IS-A* hierarchy of concepts) together with a partial specification of the property values of these concepts.

The set of concepts is referred to as *CSET*, the partial ordering as <<, and the information about property values of a concept is specified using the distribution function δ, where, $\delta(C, P)$ specifies how instances of C are distributed with respect to the values of property P. For example, δ(*APPLE, has-color)* may be {*RED* = 60, *GREEN* = 55, *YELLOW* = 23...}. Note that δ is only a partial mapping. In terms of a traditional representation language, knowing $\delta(C, P)$ amounts to knowing—explicitly—the values of P associated with C. For convenience we also make use of the # notation. Thus, $\#C[P, V]$ equals the number of instances of C that are observed by the agent to have the value V for property P. For example, given the above specification of δ(*APPLE, has-color*), *#APPLE[has-color, RED]* = 60. The # notation may be generalized so that $\#C[P_1, V_1][P_2, V_2]...[P_n, V_n]$ = the number of instances of C observed to have the value V_1 for property P_1, ... and value V_n for property P_n.

In terms of the above notation, the inheritance and recognition problems may be stated as follows:

Inheritance Given a concept C, a property P, and a set of property values $X = \{V_1, V_2,...V_n\}$, find a V_i that is the most likely value of property P for concept C. In other words, find V_i such that the most likely value of $\#C[P, V_i]$ equals or exceeds the most likely value of $\#C[P, V_j]$ for any other V_j in X. The inheritance problem: C = *BIRD*, P = *mode-of-transportation*, and X = {*FLY, SWIM, WALK*}, may be paraphrased as: Is the mode of transportation of a bird most likely to be flying, swimming, or walking?

The formal problem specification suggests that a set of possible property values has to be specified explicitly. This has been done only to emphasize that the system computes the *relative* likelihood of possible property values. The system, however, can deal with inheritance questions where the range of property values is implicit in inheritance query. Thus it is acceptable to say "What is the most likely color of an Apple," because the potential set of values is the set of all color values.

Recognition: Given a set of concepts, $Z = \{C_1, C_2,...C_n\}$, and a description consisting of a set of property value pairs, i.e., $DESCR = \{[P_1, V_1], [P_2, V_2] ,...[P_m,V_m]\}$, find a C_i such that relative to the concepts specified in Z, C_i is the most likely concept described by *DESCR*. In other words, find C_i such that the most likely value of $\#C_i\ [P_1, V_1], [P_2, V_2] ,...[P_m, V_m]$ exceeds the most likely value of $\#C_j\ [P_1, V_1], [P_2, V_2],...[P_m, V_m]$ for any other C_j. If Z = {*APPLE, GRAPE*}, *DESCR* = {[*has-color, RED*], [*has-taste, SWEET*]} then the recognition problem may be paraphrased as: "Is something red in color and sweet in taste more likely to be an apple or a grape?"

The proposed system solves such *inheritance* and *recognition* problems in time proportional to the depth of the conceptual hierarchy provided the constraints specified below (Section 3.5.3) are satisfied.

3.5.2 Some Aspects of the Representation Language

Partial nature of knowledge: The agent's knowledge is partial with respect to its experience; *it does not store all the information that it observes.* The agent's knowledge of the distribution mapping δ is partial. Specifically, the agent may record $\delta(C, P)$ only if this information is useful in solving inheritance and recognition tasks that are of significance to the agent.

Probabilistic as well as exemplar representation: The language supports a probabilistic as well as an exemplar-based description of concepts: $\delta(C, P)$'s encode probabilistic information about concepts whereas instances encode exemplars of their parent concepts.

Multiple and default property values: For a concept C and a property P, $\delta(C, P)$'s allow the agent to specify multiple values for the same property together with information that indicates the relative likelihood of occurrence of these values.

Only property values may be exceptional, but not IS-A links: A concept is either an instance or subtype of another concept or it is not; the << relation specifies this unequivocally. The notion of exceptions applies only to property values, and even here exceptions do not entail "cancellation" or "blocking" of properties. This leads to a clear semantics of conceptual taxonomies. Problems arising from allowing exceptions to *IS-A* links are discussed in [Brachman, 1985].

Necessary properties are a special case of default ones: The evidential representation of property values suggested here subsumes the nonevidential case. Properties correspond to roles or slots. Consequently, δ may be taken as a specification of role values or slot fillers in a frame-based language with the distinction that the specification of $\delta(C, P)$ also includes the quantities $\#C[P,V]$. But if the domain is extremely well behaved and generalizations such as

$\forall x C(x) \Rightarrow P(x,V_1)$

i.e., all instances of C have the value V_1 for property P.

may be made, then δ reduces to a nonevidential specification of a property value and may be expressed as $\delta(C, P) = V_1$, or equivalently as $P(C, V_1)$, which is the FOPC version of property value specification.

Only relative frequencies are required: Although we have used absolute numbers to specify the distributions and the size of concepts, *an agent need only deal with ratios of such frequencies*. These ratios appear as weights on links in a connectionist realization. What is significant is that these weights may be computed based on purely *local* interactions between nodes in the connectionist network using a Hebbian synaptic weight change rule [Hebb, 1949].

3.5.3 Constraints on the Conceptual Structure

The following terms will be used in stating the constraints:

Relevance: Given a concept C and a property P, a concept B is relevant to C with respect to P, if and only if (1) $C << B$ (i.e, B lies "above" C in the partial ordering); (2) $\delta(B, P)$ is known (i.e., distribution of instances of B with respect to values of property P is known); and (3) there exists no other concept A between C and B for which $\delta(A, P)$ is known.

Projection: Given a concept C and a property P, $CSET/C, P$, the projection of $CSET$ with respect to C and P, is defined to be the set of all concepts X_i such that $C << X_i$ and $\delta(X_i, P)$ is known. (i.e., the projection $CSET/C, P$ is the set of all concepts above C whose distribution with respect to the property values of P is known.)

The first constraint on the conceptual structure restricts the nature of the partial ordering of concepts. This restriction is predicated by the nature of property-value attachment in the conceptual structure.

Constraint 1: The conceptual structure must be such that the ordering induced by $<<$ on the projection $CSET/C, P$ results in a tree.

The above constraint does not require that all concepts be organized as a tree. It only requires that given any property P, all concepts that have values of property P explicitly associated with them should form a tree.

Before we state the second constraint we describe a particular conceptual structure that allows this constraint to be expressed in a relatively simple manner. The proposed conceptual structure also (trivially) satisfies constraint 1 mentioned above.

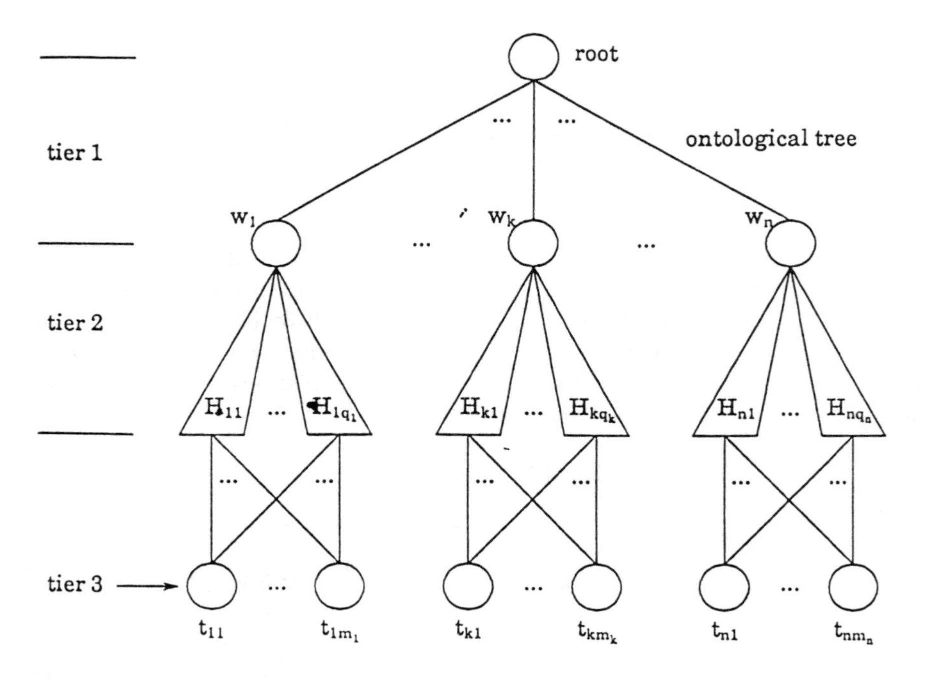

Figure 3.4: The multiple views organization

In the proposed scheme (see Figure 3.4), concepts are organized in a three-tier structure. The topmost tier consists of a pure taxonomy that classifies the domain concepts into several distinct ontological categories. Such categories are derived using the principle of predicability [Keil, 1979; Sommers, 1965], which says that different sorts of things have different sorts of properties applicable to them, and one may classify things according to the predicates that apply, or do not apply, to them. Sommers has argued that ontological categories should form a strict taxonomy. The third or the lowest tier of the conceptual structure consists of instances. The second tier consists of a number of taxonomies called *views*. The root of a view is a leaf of the ontological tree, and the leaves of a view are instances. Multiple views may be defined with the same leaf of the ontological tree as their root and therefore, there may be multiple views that have the same instance as one of their leaves. Thus instances may have multiple parents; however, each parent must lie in a distinct view. The above organization offers advantages permitted by tangled hierarchies by allowing instances to have multiple parents, but retains certain tree-like characteristics that helps in simplifying the interactions between information represented in the conceptual structure and eventually leads to a parallelizable solution.

Constraint 2: If $\delta(C_i, P)$—i.e., the distribution of instances of C_i with respect to property P—is known for some concept C_i situated in view H, then for every token T_j situated under H, there must exist a concept B_j in H that is relevant to T_j with respect to P.

Constraint 2 requires that if information about some property is stored within a view then such information must be stored at a sufficient number of concepts (sufficient in the sense specified in the constraint). This constraint also suggests that if a property value (or a cluster of property values) can be used to discriminate among a set of instances but is of no special significance as far as members outside this set are considered, then the learning or concept-formation system must define a distinct view over this set of instances so that information about this property value may be used efficiently during recognition.

If either of the constraints mentioned above is violated, the system will produce anomalous results. These and other issues are discussed at length in [Shastri, 1988, 1989].

3.6 BEYOND *IS-A* HIERARCHIES: REPRESENTING FIRST-ORDER RULES AND FACTS

If we suppress the evidential aspects of the semantic network described above then it is possible to characterize its expressive power as follows. The network represents rules of the form

$$\forall(x)\ P(x) \Rightarrow Q(x)$$

and

$$\forall(x)\ P(x) \Rightarrow Q(x, a)$$

The first of these rules represents the *IS-A* relationship and the second the property values associated with concepts. A representation system, however, must be expressive enough to encode *systematic* and *abstract* knowledge about structured and composite entities; i.e., it must be expressive enough to encode facts and rules involving *n-ary* predicates.

In recent work with Venkat Ajjanagadde, we have proposed a system that can represent first-order *rules* and *facts* and perform a limited but broad class of deductive inferences with extreme efficiency [Shastri and Ajjanagadde, 1990].

The system consists of a network of simple processing elements that operate without a central controller and communicate via simple 1-bit messages. Rules in the system are assumed to be sentences of the form

$$\forall x_1, ..., x_m\ [P_1(...) \wedge P_2(...)... \wedge P_n(...) \Rightarrow \exists\ z_1, ...\ z_l\ Q(...)]$$

The arguments of P_i's are elements of $\{x_1, x_2, ...\ x_m\}$. An argument of Q is either an element of $\{x_1, x_2, ...\ x_m\}$, or an element of $\{z_1, z_2, ...\ z_l\}$, or a constant. It is required that any variable occurring in multiple argument positions in the antecedent of a rule must also appear in its consequent.

Facts are assumed to be partial or complete instantiations of predicates. Thus facts are atomic formulas of the form $P(t_1, t_2\ ...\ t_k)$ where t_i's are either constants or distinct existentially quantified variables. The system may also be extended so that the t_i's may refer to concepts in a *IS-A* hierarchy.

A query has the same form as a fact: It is a partially or fully instantiated predicate where the uninstantiated arguments are assumed to be existentially quantified. Observe that a query, all of whose arguments are bound to constants, corresponds to the *yes–no* question: "Does the query follow from the rules and facts encoded in the system?" A query with existentially quantified variables, however, has several interpretations. For example, the query $P(a, x)$, where a is a constant and x is an existentially quantified argument, may be viewed as the *yes–no* query: "Does $P(a, x)$ follow from the rules and facts for some value of x?" Alternately this query may be viewed as the *wh*-query: "For what values of x does $P(a, x)$ follow from the rules and facts in the system?"

Some examples of rules and facts are given below. Table 3.1 lists some queries, their interpretation(s), and their answer(s).

Rules:

1. $\forall x, y, z\ [give(x, y, z) \Rightarrow own(y, z)]$
2. $\forall y, z\ [buy(y, z) \Rightarrow own(y, z)]$
3. $\forall y, z\ [own(y, z) \Rightarrow can\text{-}sell(y, z)]$
4. $\forall x\ [omnipresent(x) \Rightarrow \forall y, t\ present(x, y, t)]$
5. $\forall x, y\ [born(x, y) \Rightarrow \exists t\ present(x, y, t)]$
6. $\forall x\ [triangle(x) \Rightarrow number\text{-}of\text{-}sides(x, 3)]$
7. $\forall x, y\ [sibling(x, y) \wedge born\text{-}together(x, y) \Rightarrow twins(x, y)]$

Facts:

1. *give(John, Mary, Book*1);	John gave Mary Book1.
2. *give(x, Susan, Ball*2);	Someone gave Susan Ball2.
3. *buy(John, z)*;	John bought something.

4. *own*(*Mary*, *Ball*1); Mary owns Ball1.
5. *omnipresent*(*x*); There exists someone who is omnipresent.
6. *triangle*(*A*3); A3 is a triangle.
7. *sibling*(*Susan*, *Mary*); Susan and Mary are siblings.
8. *born-together*(*Susan*, *Mary*); Susan and Mary were born at the same time.

If the conditions specified in Section 3.6.3 are met, the system answers *yes* to all *yes–no* queries that follow from the encoded rules and facts in time proportional to the *length* of the *shortest* derivation of the query. The system obeys the closed world assumption and produces a *no* answer in time proportional to *d*, where *d* equals the diameter of the inferential dependency graph associated with the rulebase (see Section 3.3). *wh*-queries are also answered in time proportional to *d*. Finally, the *space* complexity of the system is just *linear* in $|KB|$.

Table 3.1: Interpretation of some queries and their answers

Query	Yes–No-Form (Answer)	Wh-Form (Answer)
own(*Mary*, *Ball*1)	Does Mary own Ball1?	—
can-sell(*Mary*, *Book*1)	Can Mary sell Book1? (yes)	—
can-sell(*Mary*, *x*)	Can Mary sell something? (yes)	What can Mary sell? (Book1, Ball1)
own(*x*, *y*)	Does someone own something? (yes)	Who owns something? (Susan, Mary, John) What is owned by someone? (Book1, Ball1, Ball2)
can-sell(*John*, *x*)	Can John sell something? (yes)	What can John sell?
present(*x*, *Northpole*, 1/1/89)	Was someone present at northpole on 1/1/89? (yes)	Who was present at northpole on 1/1/89? (There was someone; but, don't know who)
number-of-sides(*A*3, 4)	Does A3 have 4 sides? (no)	—
can-sell(*Mary*, *Ball*2)	Can Mary sell Ball2? (no)	—
twins(*Susan*, *Mary*)	Are Mary and Susan twins? (yes)	—

3.6.1 Network Encoding—Explicit Representation of the Inferential Structure

Conceptually, the proposed encoding of the knowledge base amounts to creating a directed *inferential dependency* graph wherein the inferential dependencies between the antecedent and consequent predicates together with the correspondence between arguments of these predicates are represented explicitly. Thus each predicate and each predicate argument is represented by a distinct node in the graph, and a rule is represented by linking nodes denoting the arguments of the consequent predicate to nodes denoting the appropriate arguments of the antecedent predicate. Nodes denoting the antecedent and consequent predicates are also linked. Facts are small networks attached to their respective predicates nodes.

Figure 3.5 illustrates the nature of the network encoding by depicting how the following knowledge is encoded. For simplicity we only describe the realization of single antecedent rules without constants and existentially quantified variables in the consequent.

- $\forall x, y, z\ [give(x, y, z) \Rightarrow own(y, z)]$
- $\forall x, y\ [buy(x, y) \Rightarrow own(x, y)]$
- $\forall x, y\ [own(x, y) \Rightarrow can\text{-}sell(x, y)]$
- $give(John, Mary, Book1)$
- $buy(John, x)$
- $own(Mary, Ball1)$

The encoding shown in Figure 3.5 makes use two types of nodes, namely, ρ-btu nodes (depicted as circles) and τ-and nodes (depicted as pentagons). The computational behavior of these nodes is as follows.

A ρ-btu is a phase-sensitive binary threshold unit. When such a node becomes active, it produces an oscillatory output in the form of a pulse train that has a period π and pulse width ω. The timing (or the *phase*) of the pulse train produced by a ρ-btu node is precisely governed by the phase of the input to the node. A τ-and node acts like a *temporal and* node. Such a node also oscillates with the same frequency as a ρ-btu node except that it becomes active only if it receives *uninterrupted* activation over a whole period of oscillation. Furthermore, the width of the pulses produced by a τ-and node equals π. The implementation parameter Ω that governs the maximum number of distinct entities that may participate in the derivation of a *yes–no* query equals ω / π (assume integer divide).

The output pulse of a node propagates along every link emanating from the node. The encoding also makes use of *inhibitory modifiers*. An inhibitory modifier is a link that impinges on and inhibits another link. Thus a pulse propagating along an inhibitory modifier will block the propagation of a pulse propagating along the

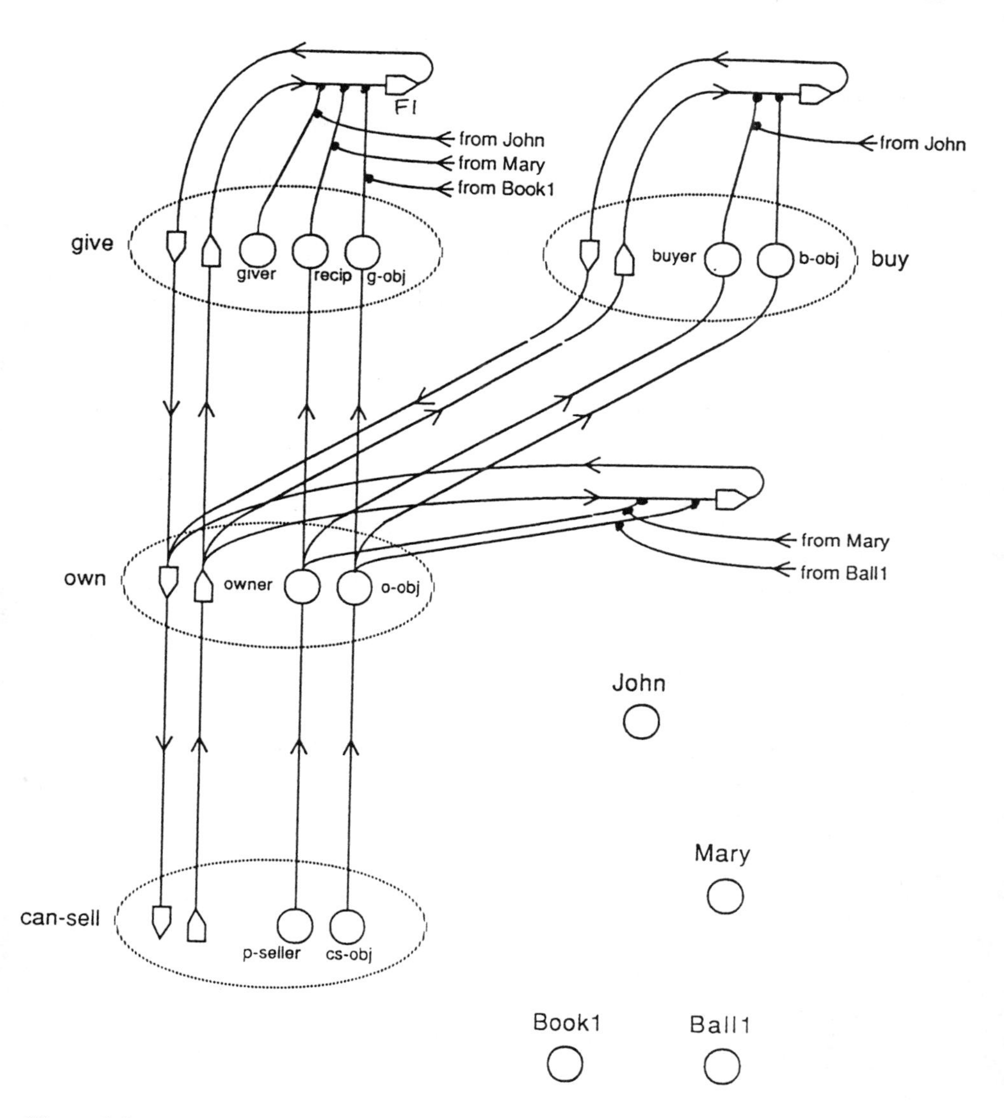

Figure 3.5: An example encoding of rules and facts

link it impinges upon. In Figure 3.5, inhibitory modifiers are shown as links ending in dark blobs.

Each constant in the domain is encoded by a ρ-node. An n-ary predicate is encoded by a pair of τ-and nodes and n ρ-btu nodes, one for each of the n arguments. One of the τ-and nodes is referred to as the *enabler* and the other as the *collector*. As a matter of convention, an *enabler* always points upwards and is named *e:[predicate-name]*. A *collector* always points downwards and is named *c:[predicate-name]*.

A rule is encoded by connecting the *collector* of the antecedent predicate to the *collector* of the consequent predicate, the *enabler* of the consequent predicate to the *enabler* of the antecedent predicate, and by connecting the argument nodes of the consequent predicate to the argument nodes of the antecedent predicate in accordance with the correspondence between these arguments specified in the rule (refer to Figure 3.5.)

A fact is encoded using a τ-and node that receives an input from the enabler of the associated predicate. This input is modified by inhibitory modifiers from the argument nodes of the associated predicate. If an argument is bound to a constant in the fact then the modifier from such an argument node is in turn modified by an inhibitory modifier from the appropriate constant node. The output of the τ-and node is connected to the *collector* of the associated predicate (refer to the encoding of the fact *give(John, Mary, Book1)* and *buy(John, x)* in Figure 3.5.)

A rule with conjunctive predicates in the antecedent, i.e., a rule of the form $P_1(...) \wedge P_2(...) \wedge \ldots P_m(...) \Rightarrow Q(...)$, is encoded using an additional τ-and node that has a threshold of m. The outputs of the *collector* nodes of $P_1, \ldots, P_m$ are connected to this node which in turn is connected to the *collector* of Q. This additional node becomes active if and only if it receives inputs from the *collector* nodes of all the m antecedent predicates. The interconnections between the argument nodes of the antecedent and consequent predicates remain unchanged.

The encoding of rules and facts described in the previous section assumes that constants or existentially quantified variables do not appear in the consequent of a rule. It also assumes that the same variable does not occur in multiple argument positions in the consequent of a rule. The encoding of such rules can be carried out by very simple mechanisms that involve detecting whether appropriate nodes are firing in synchrony or not. A complete description may be found in [Shastri and Ajjanagadde, 1990].

The number of nodes required to encode a knowledge base (i.e., the space complexity) is only *linear* in $|KB|$. Specifically, the number of nodes required are $O(r + f + a + c)$, where r is the number of rules, f is the number of facts, a is the total number of predicate arguments and c is the number of constants in the domain. The number of links required is also only linear in $|KB|$. Specifically, the number of links required is $O(r1 + f1)$, where $r1$ is the number of rules weighted by the number of predicate arguments occurring in each rule, and $f1$ is the number of facts weighted by the number of arguments in the predicate associated with each fact.

3.6.2 Reasoning Process: An Example

In the proposed system, reasoning is the transient but systematic propagation of *rhythmic* patterns of activation, where each *phase* in the rhythmic pattern corresponds to an object involved in the reasoning process, where variable bindings are represented as the *in-phase* firing of appropriate nodes, where facts are subnetworks that act as temporal pattern matchers, and where rules are interconnection patterns that cause the propagation and transformation of rhythmic patterns of activation. A detailed explanation of the encoding and the computations performed by nodes in the network are beyond the scope of this paper but may be found in [Shastri and Ajjanagadde, 1990].

Figure 3.6 illustrates how the system processes the question *can-sell*(*Mary*, *Book*1) (i.e., "Can Mary sell Book1"). This query is posed to the system by providing inputs to the constants *Mary* and *Book*1, the arguments *p-seller*, *cs-obj* and *e:can-sell* (the *enabler* of the query predicate *csn-sell*) as shown. Notice that *Mary* and *p-seller* receive *in-phase* activation and so do *Book*1 and *cs-obj*. The eventual activation of *c:can-sell*, the *collector* of the query predicate *can-sell*, indicates that the answer to the query is *yes*.

In terms of the inferential dependency graph, the reasoning process process corresponds to a *parallel* breadth-first traversal of a directed graph and the encoding allows any number of rules to apply in parallel. It also follows that the time taken to generate a chain of inference will be independent of the total number of rules and facts and will just be equal to $l * \pi$ where l equals the *length* of the chain of inference and π equals the period of oscillation of the nodes. As indicated earlier, the creation and propagation of variable bindings during reasoning is achieved by phase-locked oscillation of appropriate argument and filler nodes.

3.6.3 Combining a Rulebase with an *IS-A* Hierarchy

The reasoning system described above can be combined with an *IS-A* hierarchy. Such an interface allows *terms* in the rules and facts to be any concept (type/instance) in the *IS-A* hierarchy and also allows for the expression of type constraints on variables occurring in rules. An example of an interaction between the rule-base and the *IS-A* hierarchy is depicted in Figure 3.7. The networks encodes the following knowledge:

- $\forall x, y$ [*preys-on*(x, y) $\Rightarrow$ *scared-of*(y, x)]
- *preys-on*(*Cat*, *Bird*)

and the *IS-A* relationships:

is-a(*Bird*, *Animal*)	*is-a*(*Cat*, *Animal*)
is-a(*Robin*, *Bird*)	*is-a*(*Canary*, *Bird*)
is-a(*Tweety*, *Canary*)	*is-a*(*Chirpy*, *Robin*)
is-a(*Sylvester*, *Cat*)	

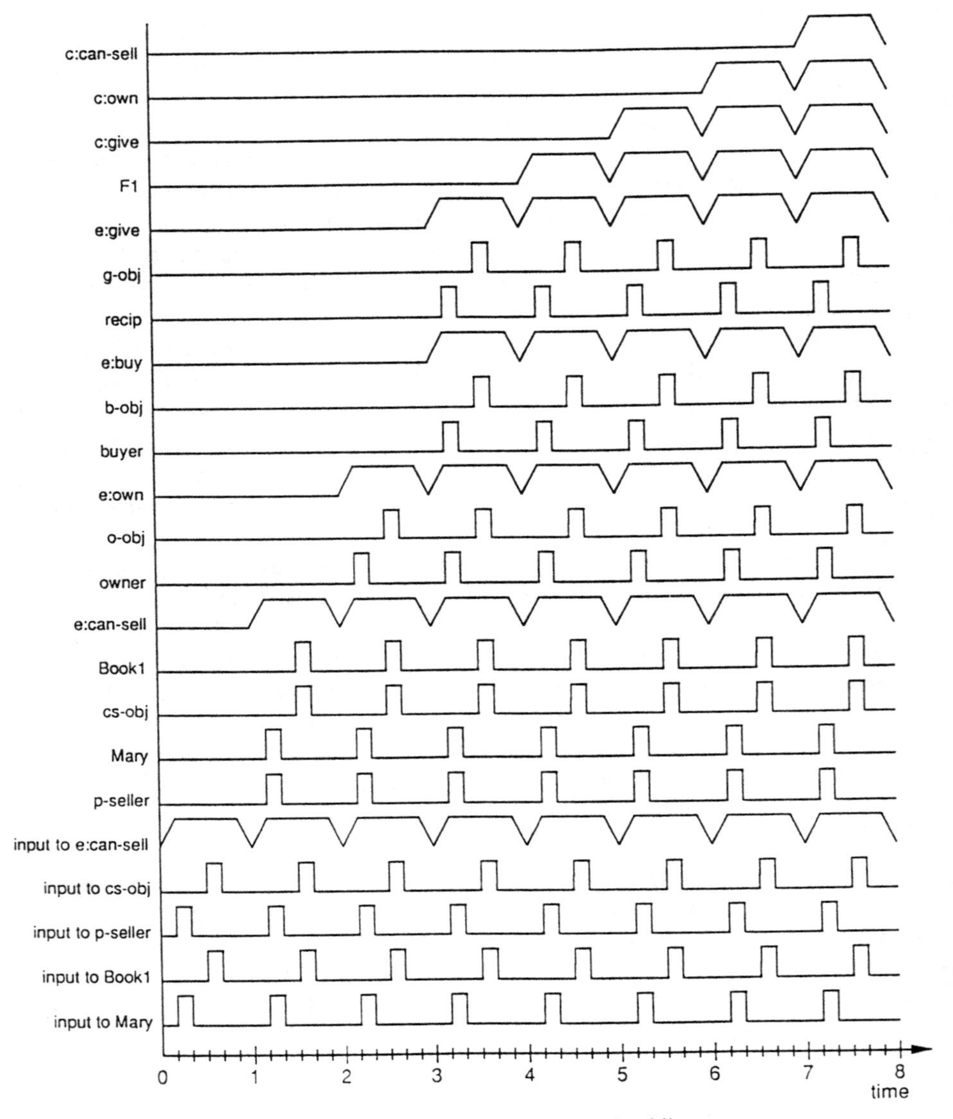

Figure 3.6: Activation trace for the query *can-sell(Mary, Book1)*

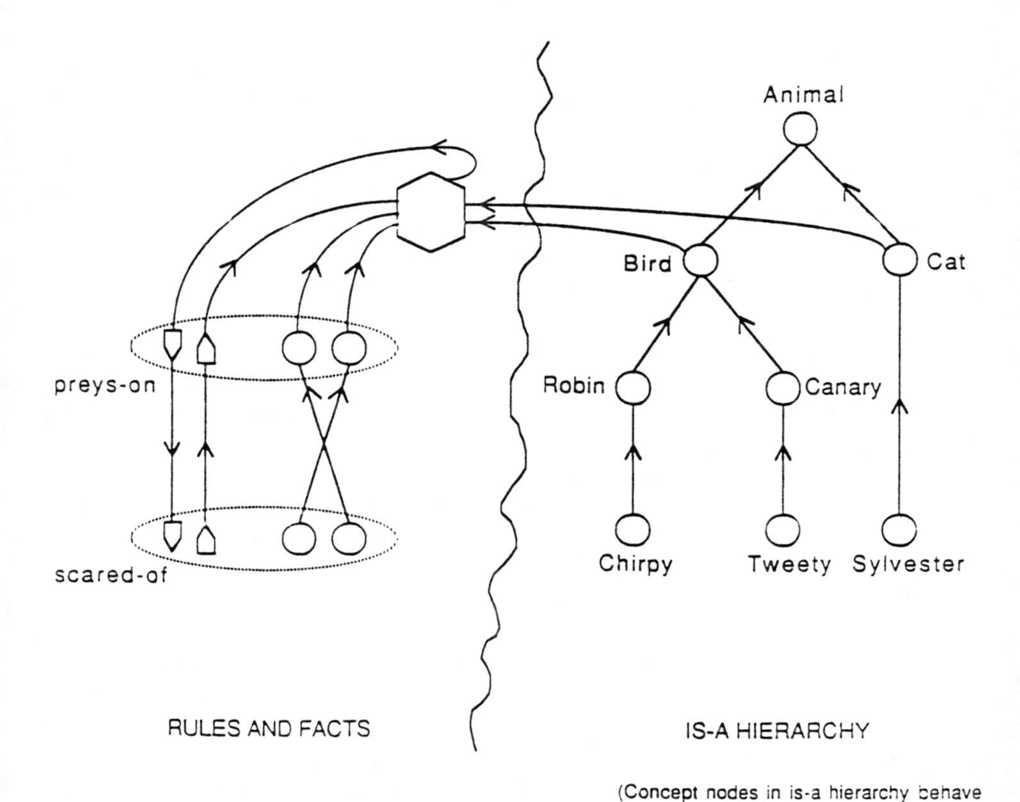

Figure 3.7: Interaction between a rule-based reasoner and an *IS-A* hierarchy (conceptual hierarchy). The rule component encodes the rule $\forall x, y\ preys\text{-}on(x, y) \Rightarrow scared\text{-}of(y, x)$ and the fact *preys-on*(*Cat*, *Bird*).

The system can answer queries such as

- *preys-on*(*Sylvester*, *Tweety*)
- *scared-of*(*Tweety*, *Sylvester*)
- *scared-of*(*x*, *Sylvester*); Is someone scared of Sylvester?
- *preys-on*(*Cat*, *Bird*)
- *scared-of*(*Bird*, *Cat*); Are birds scared of cats?

The time taken to answer the queries is again proportional to the length of the shortest derivation.

3.6.4 Constraints on Rules and Derivations

The first constraint on the backward reasoning system is that only a bounded number of argument bindings may be specified in a query. This bound is given by π / ω, where π, and ω are the period of oscillation of the nodes and the spike width of the ρ-btu nodes respectively. A biologically, as well as psychologically, plausible estimate of this bound appears to be about seven.

A second constraint is that a variable occurring in multiple argument positions in the *antecedent* of a rule that participates in the derivation of a query, should get bound during the reasoning process (recall that the form of rules encoded the system guarantees that any such variable also occurs in the consequent). This condition rules out reasoning that requires generating specific cases and testing them one by one, in other words, it rules out the computation of relational *joins*. Given that in designing this system, we were primarily concerned with modeling *reflexive* reasoning, this restriction is very reasonable.

In a restricted and simple version of the system (the one illustrated in Figure 3.5), any given predicate may only be instantiated once during the process of answering a query. This restriction only applies to dynamic or "runtime" instantiations of inferred facts pertaining to the same predicate. Any number of long-term facts pertaining to a predicate may be encoded in the network. The above restriction may be relaxed using a more elaborate encoding scheme so that a predicate may be instantiated at most a bounded number of times. We conjecture that any given episode of reflexive reasoning does not require the same predicate to be dynamically instantiated more than k times, where a psychologically plausible value of k may be as low as three to five (observe that k greater than 1 allows for bounded recursion). Thus this limitation of the reasoning system also seems well motivated.

3.6.5 Extensions

The reasoning and expressive power of the system described above can be increased by allowing a limited use of function terms in rules. This extension is described in [Ajjanagadde, 1990]. Finally by using the strength of activation (the amplitude of the output pulse) and weighted links (as was done in realizing the system described in Section 3.5) the proposed system can be extended to encode evidential/probabilistic rules.

3.7 CONCLUSION

A knowledge representation language must not only be characterized in terms of its representational adequacy but also in terms of its *computational effectiveness*. Furthermore, a computationally effective representation language must explicate the relationship between the nature of representation, the effectiveness of certain inferences, and the computational architecture in which the computations/inferences are performed. Semantic networks, or graph-based representation formulations are examples of such representation languages. The two reasoning systems described in this chapter are examples of computationally effective reasoning systems that result from pursuing the graph-based approach outlined in Sections 3.3 and 3.4. These systems perform a limited class of inference with extreme efficiency by virtue of (1) the explicit representation of the inferential dependencies in the body of knowledge they encode, and (2) the mapping of such a representation onto massively parallel architecture.

ACKNOWLEDGMENTS

I would like to thank Lynn Stein and James Crawford for their valuable suggestions. This work was supported by NSF grants IRI 88-05465, MCS-8219196-CER, MCS-83-05211, DARPA grants N00014-85-K-0018 and N00014-85-K-0807, and ARO grant ARO-DAA29-84-9-0027.

References

Ajjanagade, V. 1990. Reasoning with function symbols in a connectionist system. In *Proceedings of the Cognitive Science Society Meeting.*

Brachman, R.J. 1985. I lied about the trees. *AI Magazine*, 6(3):80–93.

Charniak, E. 1981. A common representation for problem solving and language comprehension information. *Artificial Intelligence*, 16: 225–255.

Fahlman, S.E. 1979. *NETL: A System for Representing and Using Real-World Knowledge.* The MIT Press, Cambridge, MA.

Feldman, A. and Ballard, D.H. 1982. Connectionist models and their properties. *Cognitive Science*, 6(3):205–254.

Findler, N.V. (ed.). 1979. *Associative Networks: Representation and Use of Knowledge by Computers.* Academic Press, New York.

Hartley, R.T. and Coombs, M.J. 1991. Reasoning with graphs. Chapter 16, this volume.

Hayes, P.J. 1979. The logic of frames. In *Frame Conception and Text Understanding*, Metzing, D. (ed.), pp. 46–61. Walter de Gruyter, Berlin.

Hebb, D.O. 1949. *The Organization of Behavior*. Wiley, New York.

Keil, F.C. 1979. *Semantic and Conceptual Development.* Harvard University Press, Cambridge, MA.

Levesque, H.J. 1988. Logic and the complexity of reasoning. *Journal of Philosophical Logic*, 17:335–389.

Minsky, M.A. 1975. A framework for representing knowledge. In *The Psychology of Vision*, Winston, P.H. (ed.). McGraw-Hill, New York.

Quillian R.M. 1968. Semantic Memory. In *Semantic Information Processing*, Minsky, M.A. (ed.). The MIT Press, Cambridge, MA, 1968.

Schubert, L.K. 1989. An episodic knowledge representation for narrative texts. In *Proceedings of KR-89*. Toronto, May.

Schubert, L.K 1991. Semantic nets are in the eye of the beholder, Chapter 2, this volume.

Shapiro, S.C. 1979. The SNePs semantic network processing system. In *Associative Networks: Representation and Use of Knowledge by Computers*, Findler, N.V. (ed.), pp. 179–203. Academic Press, New York.

Shastri, L. 1988. *Semantic Networks: An Evidential Formulation and its Connectionist Realization.* Morgan Kaufmann Publishers, San Mateo, CA, copublished with Pitman, London.

———. 1989. Default reasoning in semantic network: A formalization of recognition and inheritance. *Artificial Intelligence*, 69(3):331–392.

Shastri, L. and Ajjanagadde, V. 1990. *From Simple Associations to Systematic Reasoning: A Connectionist Representation of Rules, Variables and Dynamic Bindings*. Technical Report MS-CIS-90-05. Department of Computer and Information Science, University of Pennsylvania.

Sowa, J. 1991. Toward the expressive power of natural language. Chapter 5, this volume.

Sommers, F. 1965. Predicability. In *Philosophy in America*. Black, M. (ed.). Cornell University Press, Ithaca, NY.

Thorpe, S.J. and Imbert, M. 1988. Biological constraints on connectionist modelling. In *Connectionism in Perspective*, Pfeiffer, R. (ed). Springer.

4

CABLES, PATHS, AND "SUBCONSCIOUS" REASONING IN PROPOSITIONAL SEMANTIC NETWORKS

Stuart C. Shapiro
(State University of New York, Buffalo)

4.1 INTRODUCTION

In this chapter, I will discuss two aspects of SNePS propositional semantic networks [Maida and Shapiro, 1982; Morgado, 1986; Shapiro 1979; Shapiro and Rapaport, 1987]—cables and paths that distinguish them as formalisms for the representation of knowledge. I will also discuss a kind of inference sanctioned by each one—reduction inference and path-based inference, respectively—and the integration of these two kinds of inference into a kind of "subconscious" reasoning.

Informally, a semantic network is a labeled, directed acyclic graph in which nodes represent entities and labeled arcs represent binary relations between entities. A *propositional* semantic network is a semantic network in which every proposition represented in the network is represented by a node, rather than by an arc. We will refer to a node that represents a proposition as a *propositional node*. Isolated nodes are not allowed in a semantic network, and since a semantic network is a variety of relational graph, it does not make sense to have two arcs with the same label emanate from the same node and terminate at the same node. However, there is no restriction forbidding several arcs with the same label from emanating from the same node if they terminate in different nodes. Informally, we will call a set of such arcs a *cable*. (We will formalize this below.)

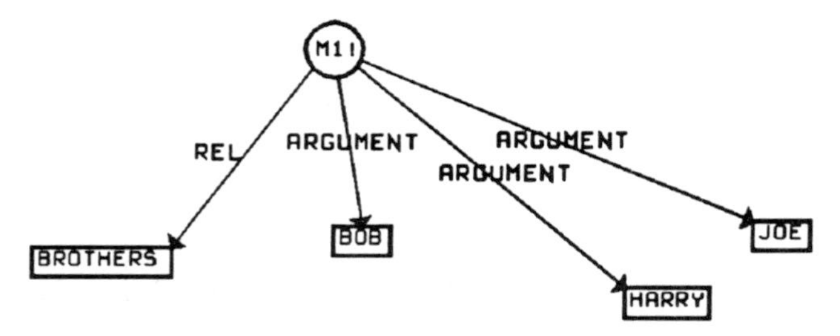

Figure 4.1: A SNePS network representing the proposition that Bob, Joe, and Harry are brothers. The proposition node `M1!` has two cables emanating from it, one consisting of the `REL` arc and the node it goes to, the other consisting of the `ARGUMENT` arcs and the nodes they go to.

A propositional node, therefore, may have a set of cables emanating from it. Each cable represents an argument position of the proposition represented by the propositional node, the label associated with each cable is the keyword that identifies the argument position, and the nodes of each label are the arguments in that position. A proposition with multiple arguments in a single position is not a situation that occurs in the standard syntax of predicate logic. For example, Figure 4.1 shows a diagram of a SNePS network in which `M1!` is a propositional node from which emanate two cables: a cable consisting of one `REL` arc going to the node `BROTHERS` and a cable consisting of three `ARGUMENT` arcs going to the nodes `BOB`, `JOE`, and `HARRY`. As discussed in [Shapiro, 1986], `M1!` is intended to represent the proposition that Bob, Joe, and Harry are brothers. In this proposition, the order in which "Bob," "Joe," and "Harry" appear is entirely arbitrary—they are really in the same argument position relative to the relation "are brothers," and this is captured by putting the nodes that represent them in the same cable from the node `M1!`.

Path-based inference [Shapiro, 1978; Srihari, 1981] involves the inferring of an arc between two nodes from the existence of a path of arcs between the same two nodes. Since this inference ignores the other arcs emanating from the starting node, it corresponds to an inference rule that ignores the arity of the atomic propositions. This, also, is not a situation that can occur in the standard syntax of predicate logic.

We might consider the labels of semantic network arcs to be binary predicates and the nodes to be individual constants. Then an arc in the network corresponds to a ground atomic formula in which the label-predicate is applied to the two node-individual constants. A cable is then just the set of all such atomic formulas for which the predicate and the first argument are the same. The semantics of a network is then derived by taking all the atomic formulas conjunctively, and path-based inference rules are straightforward conditionals. This translation actually gives us a model of the network, rather than another syntax for the same network. The differences include:

- In the atomic predicate version, there is nothing to prevent the situation from occurring in which there are two individual constants, n_1 and n_2 such that $\forall(P, x)[P(n_1, x) \Leftrightarrow P(n_2, x)]$. As we shall see below, this conflicts with the Uniqueness Principle and cannot occur in a SNePS network the way SNePS networks are defined in this chapter.
- In the atomic predicate version, there is nothing to prevent one from adding a new formula $P(n_1, n_2)$ to the database at any time even though there are already formulas whose first arguments are n_1. As we shall see below, this is severely restricted in SNePS.

Nevertheless, the atomic predicate model does suggest that a cable, as a conjunction of formulas, should imply a proper subset of itself. So, for example, node `M1!` of Figure 4.1 implies that Bob and Harry are brothers, that Bob and Joe are brothers, and that Harry and Joe are brothers.[1] We will adopt a version of this kind of inference, calling it *reduction inference*, in such a way that it does not conflict with the Uniqueness Principle. Reduction inference may involve a kind of arity reduction and so is intimately tied up with path-based inference.

4.2 A MOTIVATING EXAMPLE

Figure 4.2 shows a small SNePS network containing the information that Rover is a dog, and that dogs are animals. What each node is supposed to represent is shown in Table 4.1.

If we want inheritance of classes to be handled by path-based inference, we could give SNePS a path-based inference rule that would sanction the inference of a `CLASS` arc from `M1!` to `ANIMAL`. This past sentence, however, is informal. The attempt to formalize path-based inference raises the following issues and questions.

Table 4.1

ROVER	Rover
DOG	the class of dogs
ANIMAL	the class of animals
M1!	the proposition that Rover is a dog
M2!	the proposition that dogs are animals

[1] For the reason that it does not imply that Bob and Bob, Harry and Harry, and Joe and Joe are brothers, see [Shapiro, 1986].

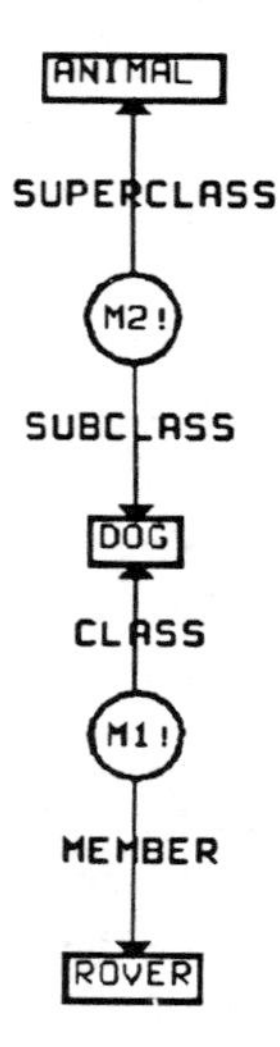

Figure 4.2: A SNePS network containing the information that Rover is a dog, and that dogs are animals

- We would want the system whose "knowledge base" is shown in Figure 4.2 to act as if it had already stored the information that Rover is an animal; i.e., the network shown in Figure 4.2 already contains that information. In what way is this so?
- SNePS does not allow a user to add a new arc coming out of an existing node, because that would change the entity represented by the node into another entity. Is this not being done by the inference of a new `CLASS` arc emanating from `M1!`?
- One might answer the latter question "No" because that arc (in some sense to be determined by answering the first point above) already exists in the network. But that raises the question of what the structure of node `M1!` actually is, and what the relationship is among the three nodes shown in Table 4.2?[2]

By the Uniqueness Principle, they should be different nodes and should represent different entities. So which one appears in Figure 4.3, and what is the relationship among them?

---

[2] The name of a propositional node is of the form M*n*, where *n* is some integer. A "!" is appended to the name to indicate that the proposition represented by the node is asserted (taken to be true) in the network. However, the "!" does not affect the identity of the node, nor the proposition it represents.

Table 4.2

Node	with **MEMBER** arc to	and with **CLASS** arc to
$M1_1$	ROVER	DOG
$M1_2$	ROVER	ANIMAL
$M1_3$	ROVER	{DOG, ANIMAL}

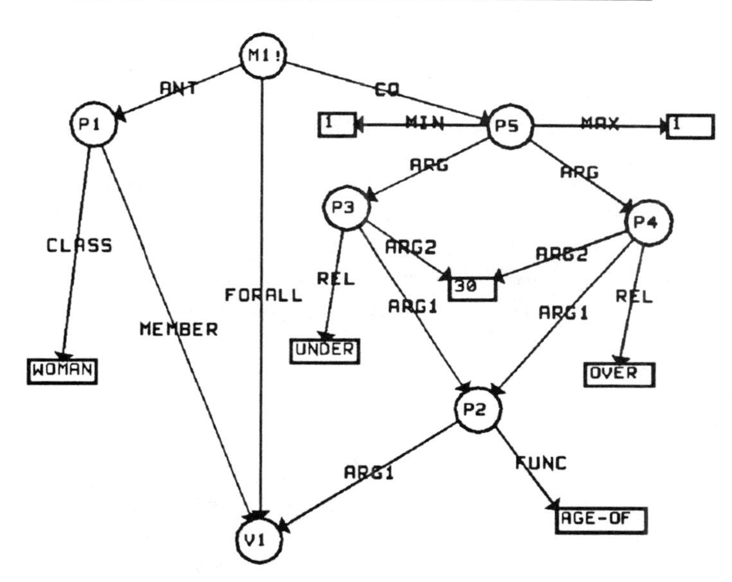

Figure 4.3: A SNePS network expressing the node-based inference rule that every woman is either under 30 or over 30

In this chapter, we will develop the following answers:

- $M1_1$, $M1_2$ and $M1_3$ are different nodes and represent different entities.
- $M1_1$ and $M1_2$ are *reductions* of $M1_3$ and are implied by it by reduction inference.
- The network of Figure 4.3 contains $M1_1$ explicitly and, given the path-based inference rule, "virtually" contains $M1_2$ and $M1_3$.

4.3 NODE-BASED INFERENCE

It should not be inferred from anything in this paper that the only kinds of inference SNePS supports are reduction inference and path-based inference, although those are the only two that will be discussed here in any detail. SNePS also supports node-based inference [Shapiro, 1978]. Figure 4.3 shows a SNePS network

Table 4.3

V1	An arbitrary woman, v_1
P1	The proposition that v_1 is a woman.
P2	The age of v_1.
P3	The proposition that v_1 is under 30 years old.
P4	The proposition that v_1 is over 30 years old.
P5	The proposition that v_1 is either under 30 or over 30 (not both).
M1!	The rule that every woman is either under 30 or over 30.

expressing the node-based inference rule that every woman is either under 30 or over 30, taken from the presentation in [Martins and Shapiro, 1988] of the logic puzzle, "The Woman Freeman Will Marry" from [Summers, 1972, p. 6].

What the principal nodes of Figure 4.3 are intended to represent are shown in the Table 4.3. The logic that SNePS supports for node-based inference is discussed in [Martins and Shapiro, 1988].

4.4 THE AGENT

I will present the semantics of SNePS networks in terms of an "agent." The agent has beliefs and performs actions (see [Morgado and Shapiro, 1985]). Such an agent is (a model of) a cognitive agent [Shapiro and Rapaport, 1987].

Among the actions the agent can perform is the new believing of a previously not believed proposition. Rather than having the agent be logically omniscient [Hintikka, 1975] (i.e., believe all the logical consequents of its beliefs) at any time, the agent will believe only those logical consequents of its beliefs that it has come to believe by "consciously" performing the act of believing them, or those it has come to believe by thinking of them after already "subconsciously" believing them.

4.5 THE DOMAIN OF INTERPRETATION

SNePS nodes are terms of a formal language. The interpretation of a node is an object in the domain of interpretation, $\mathcal{D}$. In this chapter, the members of $\mathcal{D}$ will be called "entities": "A being; esp., a thing which has reality and distinctness of being either in fact or for thought" [Merriam-Webster, 1961, p. 275]. Every SNePS node denotes an entity. If n is a SNePS node, $[\![n]\!]$ will denote the entity represented by n.

In our recent work with SNePS, we distinguish four types of entities: individuals, propositions, acts, and rules. Propositions are characterized by being the kind of entities an agent may or may not believe. Acts (see [Shapiro, 1988; Shapiro et al. 1990]) are characterized by being the kind of entities an agent may or may not intend to perform. Rules are, in some ways, like both propositions and acts. In order for a rule to "fire," it must be believed, the agent must intend to apply it, and its (appropriate) antecedents must be believed. When a rule fires, the agent forms the intention of believing its consequents. Intending to apply a rule is what is called "activating" a rule in [Shapiro, 1987].

Individuals include everything that is neither a proposition nor an act; i.e., that is neither the kind of entity that can be believed, nor the kind of entity that an agent could intend to perform. Thus, individuals include not only traditional individuals, but also classes, properties, relations, etc.

SNePS nodes are typed according to the type of entities they represent. Thus, there are four types of nodes: individual nodes, proposition nodes, act nodes, and rule nodes. As research proceeds, there may be a need to distinguish other types of entities, but at this time propositions, acts, rules, and individuals are the only types we have found a need for.

In this chapter, I will only discuss individual and proposition nodes. When the need arises, I will refer to SNePS restricted to individual and proposition nodes as $SNePS_P$ (for propositional SNePS).

4.6 METAPREDICATES

In formalizing SNePS, we need a set of metapredicates. These will not necessarily be represented in SNePS, although if the agent, itself, were engaged in the appropriate philosophical reflection, it could conceive of them. The metapredicates we will need include *Conceive*, *Believe*, and =. Others will be introduced below.

Letting n, n_1, and n_2 be metavariables ranging over nodes, and p be a metavariable ranging over proposition nodes, the semantics of the metapredicates listed above are:

> *Conceive*(n) means that the node n is actually constructed in the SNePs network, and that the agent has conceived of, or thought of, or thought about $[\![n]\!]$. *Conceive* is similar to, but different from Fagin and Halpern's [1987] awareness functions. They gloss $A_i\phi$ as, " 'i is aware of ϕ,' 'i is able to figure out the truth of ϕ,' or even (when reasoning about knowledge bases) 'i is able to compute the truth of ϕ within time T.' " Here, *Conceive*(n) may be true without the agent's being able to figure out the truth of $[\![n]\!]$.
>
> *Believe*(p) means that the agent believes the proposition $[\![p]\!]$. (In which case, we say that p is an *asserted* node.)
>
> $n_1 = n_2$ means that n_1 and n_2 are the same, identical, node.

Only conceived of entities may be believed. This is captured in the following axiom.

Axiom 1 $Believe(p) \Rightarrow Conceive(p)$

4.7 ARCS AND RELATIONS

SNePS nodes are connected to each other by labeled, directed arcs. The labels are drawn from the set of *SNePS relations*, which can be added to by the user of SNePS in the design of a particular agent. Isolated nodes cannot be constructed in SNePS; neither can cycles of arcs.

4.8 TYPES OF NODES

Besides the categorization of nodes into individual nodes and proposition nodes, nodes can also be categorized into base nodes and molecular nodes. The two categorizations of nodes are orthogonal, so there are four types of nodes. As a heuristic aid to understanding, base nodes approximately correspond to individual constants in a standard predicate logic and molecular nodes to sentences and functional terms. However, remember that all nodes are terms in SNePS.

4.8.1 Base Nodes

Base nodes have no arcs emanating from them. Each base node represents some entity of the appropriate type. An individual base node represents an individual entity, and a propositional base node represents a proposition. No two base nodes represent the same entity. This is the Uniqueness Principle of Maida and Shapiro [1982] for base nodes.

Axiom 2 Contrapositive of Uniqueness Principle $n_1 \neq n_2 \Rightarrow [[n_1]] \neq [[n_2]]$[3]

4.8.2 Molecular Nodes

Informally, a molecular node has one or more labeled, directed arcs emanating from it, each labeled by a relation in the set of SNePS relations, and each going to another node. Two or more arcs may go from one node to one other node, as long as each arc is labeled with a different label.

In this chapter, we will formally define molecular nodes using the cableset approach of Morgado [1986].

[3] Note that "=" is overloaded to represent both identity of nodes and of entities.

Definition 1 A **wire** is an ordered pair $\langle r, n\rangle$, where r is a SNePS relation, and n is a SNePS node. We will let the metavariables $w, w_1, w_2, \ldots$ range over wires.

Definition 2 A **cable** is an ordered pair $\langle r, ns\rangle$, where r is a SNePS relation, and ns is a nonempty set of SNePS node. We will let the metavariables $c, c_1, c_2, \ldots$ range over cables.

Definition 3 A **cableset** is a nonempty set of cables, $\{\langle r_1, ns_1\rangle, \ldots, \langle r_k, ns_k\rangle\}$, such that $r_i = r_j \Leftrightarrow i = j$. We will let the metavariables $cs, cs_1, cs_2, \ldots$ range over cablesets.

Definition 4 Every cableset is a SNePS **node**. Every SNePS_P **node** is either a base node or a cableset.[4]

Definition 5 A **molecular node** is a cableset.

Definition 6 We will overload the **membership** relation "$\in$" so that $x \in s$ holds just under the following conditions:

- If x is any object and s is a set of such objects, then $\in$ has its usual meaning. (Note that this situation obtains if x is a cable and s is a cableset.)
- If x is a wire, $\langle r_1, n\rangle$, and s is a cable, $\langle r_2, ns\rangle$, then $x \in s \Leftrightarrow r_1 = r_2 \wedge n \in ns$.
- If x is a wire and s is a cableset, then $x \in s \Leftrightarrow \exists(c)[c \in s \wedge x \in c]$.
- If x is a wire or a cable and s is a base node, then $x \notin s$.

Definition 7 An **nrn-path** from the node n_1 to the node n_{k+1} is a sequence, $n_1, r_1, \ldots, nk, r_k, n_{k+1}$ where the ni are nodes, the r_i are SNePS relations, and for each i, $\langle \mathrm{r_i}, n_{i+1}\rangle$ is a wire in n_i. We say that the nrn-path $n_1, r_1, \ldots, nk, r_k, n_{k+1}$ goes through ni, $1 \leq i \leq k$.

Definition 8 A node n_1 **dominates** a node n_2 just in case there is an nrn-path from n_1 to n_2.

The use of *sets* of cables and *sets* of nodes is significant, e.g.,

$$\{\langle r_1, \{n_1, n_2\}\rangle, \langle r_2, \{n_3, n_4\}\rangle\} = \{\langle r_2, \{n_4, n_3\}\rangle, \langle r_1, \{n_2, n_1\}\rangle\}.$$

However, a node and a proper subset of it are different nodes, and if two nodes differ only in that one contains the cable $\langle r, ns_1\rangle$ while the other contains the cable $\langle r, ns_2\rangle$ and the sets ns_1 and ns_2 are different, then the two nodes are nonidentical nodes. Notice that this means that it makes no sense to add a new arc emanating

---

[4] Full SNePS also contains variable nodes.

Table 4.4

Node Name	Cableset
$M1_1$	{⟨MEMBER, {ROVER}⟩, ⟨CLASS, {DOG}⟩}
$M1_2$	{⟨MEMBER, {ROVER}⟩, ⟨CLASS, {ANIMAL}⟩}
$M1_3$	{⟨MEMBER, {ROVER}⟩, ⟨CLASS, {DOG, ANIMAL}⟩}

from an existing node (i.e., a new wire to a node, while having it remain the same node). Also notice that a node is determined by the arcs emanating from it, not by the arcs pointing into it.

4.8.2.1 Examples

M1! in Figure 4.1 is the cableset {⟨REL, {BROTHERS}⟩, ⟨ARGUMENT, {BOB, HARRY, JOE}⟩}, one of whose wires is ⟨ ARGUMENT, HARRY⟩.

In Figure 4.2, M1! is the cableset {⟨MEMBER, {ROVER}⟩, ⟨CLASS, {DOG}⟩}, and M2! is the cableset {⟨SUBCLASS, {DOG}⟩, ⟨SUPERCLASS, {ANIMAL}⟩}.

$M1_1$, $M1_2$ and $M1_3$ of Table 4.2 are the cablesets shown in the Table 4.4. It is, therefore, clear that they are different nodes, and represent different entities.

4.8.3 Reduction

The relation between a node and a proper subset of it is captured by the *Reduce* metapredicate:

> *Reduce*(cs_1, cs_2) means that the set of wires in cs_2 is a subset of the set of wires in cs_1. If *Reduce*(cs_1, cs_2), we will say that cs_2 is a *reduction* of cs_1.

This definition is formalized in:

Axiom 3 $Reduce(cs_1, cs_2) \Leftrightarrow \forall(w)[w \in cs_2 \Rightarrow w \in cs_1]$

Recall that a node, even a cableset, may not actually be built in the SNePS network, so it is possible that there is some node n for which *Conceive*(n) is false. However, a cableset cannot be in the network unless every node it dominates is in the network.

Axiom 4 $\langle r, n\rangle \in cs \wedge Conceive(cs) \Rightarrow Conceive(n)$

Molecular nodes may represent either individuals or propositions. Which one a given node represents depends on, and is determined by, the set of relations in the node.[5] Propositional molecular nodes roughly correspond to formulas in standard predicate logic, while individual molecular nodes (which we sometimes call "structured individuals") roughly correspond to functional terms. (Since propositional molecular nodes are also terms, they both roughly correspond to functional terms.) Like their counterparts, nodes get their semantics from the user—the person who designs a particular SNePS agent. The semantics also depends on the set of relations in the node, which, therefore roughly corresponds to a predicate or function. The Uniqueness Principle for molecular nodes is enforced by virtue of the fact that different nodes *are* different nodes and represent different entities.

As examples we will use in the rest of this chapter, in SNePS/CASSIE [Shapiro and Rapaport, 1987], `member`, `class`, `subclass`, and `superclass` are SNePS relations, and the semantics given for SNePS/CASSIE nodes include[6] (paraphrased):

- a node of the form $\{\langle \texttt{member}, \{i_1\}\rangle, \langle \texttt{class}, \{i_2\}\rangle\}$ represents the proposition that the entity $[\![i_1]\!]$ is a member of the class $[\![i_2]\!]$.
- a node of the form $\{\langle \texttt{subclass}, \{i_3\}\rangle, \langle \texttt{superclass}, \{i_4\}\rangle\}$ represents the proposition that the class $[\![i_3]\!]$ is a subclass of the class $[\![i_4]\!]$.

4.9 PATH-BASED INFERENCE AND VIRTUAL BELIEF

Although different nodes represent different entities, an asserted node may give rise to several beliefs depending on the rest of the network it is connected with. Informally, *path-based* inference [Shapiro, 1978; Srihari, 1981] is a means of inferring a virtual arc from a node n to a node m when there is a certain path from n to m. For example, using the relations mentioned above, we may specify the inheritance of class membership with the SNePS User Language (SNePSUL) command,

```
(define-path class
  (compose class (kstar (compose subclass- ! superclass))))
```

Informally, this says that a virtual `class` arc may be inferred from a node n to a node m whenever a path of arcs consisting of a `class` arc, followed by zero or more occurrences of the path consisting of a `subclass` arc (followed backwards) followed by a `superclass` arc goes from n to m, as long as each `superclass` arc

---

[5] SNePS, as currently implemented, does not actually type nodes as representing individuals or propositions, but a node can be so characterized, as stated, as long as the user supplies a consistent semantics to various sets of relations.

[6] This representation of classification hierarchies is simplistic, but will serve the purposes of the present paper. For a more sophisticated representation of classification hierarchies, see [Peters and Shapiro, 1987].

emanates from an asserted node (one representing a believed proposition). There are 12 path formation operators like `compose` and `kstar` in SNePSUL including `converse`, `kplus`, `or`, and `and`. Path-based reasoning was described in [Shapiro, 1978] as being a kind of "subconscious" reasoning. This is captured in the formalization of path-based reasoning which follows.

In the remainder of this section, metavariables

r will range over SNePS relations;
w will range over wires;
p will range over paths;
$m, m_1, m_2, \ldots$ will range over propositional molecular nodes;
$n, n_1, n_2, \ldots$ will range over nodes.

Additional metapredicates we will need are:

Pbr(r, p) means that the path based inference rule `(define-path r p)` has been entered into the system.

HavePath(m, p, n) means that the path p is in the network going from m to n, both of which are built in the network. See the appendix for a formal definition of the syntax of paths and a formal, inductive definition of *HavePath*.

Vbelieve(m) means that the agent acts as if it believes $[\![m]\!]$, although *Conceive*(m) is not necessarily true. *Vbelieve* (for *Virtual belief*) is a kind of subconscious belief that captures the notion of the agent's believing a proposition $[\![p]\!]$ even though p is not constructed in the network.[7]

Definition 9 We will extend the notion of $\cup$ so that for a node cs and a wire w, $cs \cup w$ will be the node that contains all wires that cs contains, plus w also.

The following axioms specify when *Vbelieve*(m) holds:
First, a proposition that is believed is also subconsciously believed.

Axiom 5 $Believe(m) \Rightarrow Vbelieve(m)$

Second, if a virtual r arc may be inferred as going from a node m, denoting a subconsciously believed proposition, to a node n from a path-based inference rule entered into the system, then the proposition $[\![(m \cup \langle r, n\rangle)]\!]$ is subconsciously believed, even though its node is not necessarily in the network.

---

[7] *Vbelieve* is a kind of implicit belief, but it is not as powerful as Levesque's implicit belief predicate L [Levesque, 1984]. $L\alpha$ is true whenever α logically follows from the agent's explicit or implicit beliefs, but as will be seen, *Vbelieve*(m) is true only when m follows from explicitly believed propositions, conceived of entities, and explicitly entered path-based inference rules.

Axiom 6 $Vbelieve(m) \wedge Pbr(r, p) \wedge HavePath(m, p, n) \Rightarrow Vbelieve(m \cup \langle r, n \rangle)$

Third, the agent subconsciously believes propositions denoted by reductions of nodes that denote subconsciously believed nodes.

Axiom 7 $VBelieve(m_1) \wedge Reduce(m_1, m_2) \Rightarrow Vbelieve(m_2)$

A subconscious belief in some proposition can lead to a conscious belief in the proposition if the agent conceives of the proposition:

Axiom 8 $Vbelieve(m) \wedge Conceive(m) \Rightarrow Believe(m)$

Let $Pbclosure(n, m)$ mean that n contains all the wires in m and all the virtual wires that can be inferred to be in m by virtue of path-based inference rules:

Axiom 9

$$
\begin{aligned}
& Pbclosure(m_1, m_2) \Leftrightarrow \\
& \qquad Reduce(m_1, m_2) \\
& \wedge \forall(r, p)\,[Pbr(r, p) \wedge HavePath(m_2,p,m_3) \\
& \qquad \Rightarrow \langle \mathrm{r}, m_3 \rangle \in m_1] \\
& \wedge \forall(w)[w \in m_1 \Rightarrow w \in m_2 \vee \exists(r, p)[Pbr(\mathrm{r}, p) \wedge HavePath(m_2, \mathrm{p}, m_3) \\
& \qquad \wedge w = \langle r, m_3 \rangle]\,]
\end{aligned}
$$

If the agent believes (at least subconsciously) a proposition, it will subconsciously believe the proposition represented by the *Pbclosure* of the node that represents that proposition.

Lemma 1 $Vbelieve(m_1) \wedge Pbclosure(m_2, m_1) \Rightarrow Vbelieve(m_2)$

Proof: Follows by induction from axioms 6 and 9.

If the agent conceives of a proposition represented by a reduction of the *Pbclosure* of an asserted node, the agent will believe that proposition:

Theorem 1 $Believe(m_1) \wedge Pbclosure(m_2, m_1) \wedge Reduce(m_2, m_3) \wedge Conceive(m_3) \Rightarrow Believe(m_3)$

Proof: Follows from axiom 5, lemma 1, axiom 7, and axiom 8.

This theorem captures the notion of subconscious reasoning in SNePS. Propositions that are derived on the basis of reduction and path-based inference are essentially "already" represented in the network "embedded" in the nodes that have been explicitly built and asserted. This subconscious reasoning contrasts with the "conscious" reasoning performed on the basis of node-based inference rules [Shapiro, 1978]. For an up-to-date presentation of node-based inference in SNePS, see [Martins and Shapiro, 1988].

As an example of subconscious reasoning, assume again the SNePS relations `member`, `class`, `subclass`, and `superclass`, and the path-based inference rule shown above. Then,

{⟨ member, {rover, snoopy}⟩, ⟨class, {dog, male}⟩}

represents the proposition that ⟦rover⟧ and ⟦snoopy⟧ are ⟦dog⟧s and ⟦male⟧s, and {⟨ subclass, {dog}⟩, ⟨superclass, {animal}⟩} represents the proposition that ⟦dog⟧s are ⟦animal⟧s. In that case, belief in the two propositions:

⟦{⟨ member, {rover, snoopy}⟩, ⟨class, {dog, male}⟩}⟧
⟦{⟨ subclass, {dog}⟩, ⟨superclass, {animal}⟩}⟧

entails belief in any of the following (different) propositions that the agent conceives of:

⟦{⟨ member, {rover}⟩, ⟨class, {dog}⟩}⟧,
⟦{⟨ member, {rover}⟩, ⟨class, {male}⟩}⟧,
⟦{⟨ member, {rover}⟩, ⟨class, {animal}⟩}⟧,
⟦{⟨ member, {snoopy}⟩, ⟨class, {dog}⟩}⟧,
⟦{⟨ member, {snoopy}⟩, ⟨class, {male}⟩}⟧,
⟦{⟨ member, {snoopy}⟩, ⟨class, {animal}⟩}⟧.

Example Run

The following is the output of an interaction with SNePS 2.0, edited only to eliminate extra blank lines and the list of nodes returned by the `describe` command, and to add comments (in italics). The SNePSUL prompt is "*". `build` is the command to construct a node in the network, and thereby to make the agent conceive of the entity represented by the built node. `assert` builds a node and makes it asserted, thereby causing the agent to believe the proposition represented by the node. `describe` is a command to print a LISP-like description of a node, so the reader can see its cableset. Symbols of the form M*n*, where *n* is an integer, are the names of the nodes. SNePS prints the names of asserted nodes with "!" appended, and does not append "!" to the names of unasserted nodes. The fact that a previously unbuilt node is asserted as soon as it is built shows that it was already *Vbelieved* before it was *Conceived of*.

declare the relations to be used.

```
*(define member class subclass superclass)
(MEMBER CLASS SUBCLASS SUPERCLASS)
CPU time : 0.25
```

```
*(define-path class
   (compose class (kstar (compose subclass- ! superclass))))
CLASS implied by the path
(COMPOSE CLASS (KSTAR (COMPOSE SUBCLASS- ! SUPERCLASS)))
CLASS-implied by the path
(COMPOSE (KSTAR (COMPOSE SUPERCLASS- ! SUBCLASS)) CLASS-)
CPU time : 0.30

*(describe (build subclass dog superclass animal))
(M1 (SUBCLASS DOG) (SUPERCLASS ANIMAL)) ; M1 is built,
CPU time : 0.10                          ; but not asserted.

; order of cables doesn't matter.
(describe (assert superclass animal subclass dog))
(M1! (SUBCLASS DOG) (SUPERCLASS ANIMAL)) ; This is M1 again,
CPU time : 0.10                           ; now asserted.

*(describe (assert member (rover snoopy) class (dog male)))
(M2! (CLASS DOG MALE) (MEMBER ROVER SNOOPY)) ; built and
CPU time : 0.12                               ; asserted.

*(describe (build member rover class dog))
(M3! (CLASS DOG) (MEMBER ROVER))  ; A restriction of M2!,
CPU time : 0.05                   ; therefore asserted

*(describe (build member rover class male))
(M4! (CLASS MALE) (MEMBER ROVER)) ; A restriction of M2!,
CPU time : 0.07                   ; therefore asserted

*(describe (build member rover class animal))
(M5! (CLASS ANIMAL) (MEMBER ROVER))
       ; restriction of Pbclosure of M2!, therefore asserted
CPU time : 0.07

*(describe (build member snoopy class dog))
(M6! (CLASS DOG) (MEMBER SNOOPY))
CPU time : 0.10

*(describe (build member snoopy class male))
(M7! (CLASS MALE) (MEMBER SNOOPY))
CPU time : 0.08

*(describe (build member snoopy class animal))
(M8! (CLASS ANIMAL) (MEMBER SNOOPY))
CPU time : 0.08
```

4.10 CONCLUDING REMARKS

The definition of SNePS molecular nodes as cablesets captures the notion that a new arc (wire) cannot be added as emanating from an already existing node. It makes it clear that this would amount to changing the denotation of the node. Instead, a new wire joined to an old node makes a new node that is related to the old one by the reduction relation. Similarly, if one contemplates a node without one or more of its wires, one is contemplating a new node that is a reduction of the old one. The propositions denoted by a node and a reduction of it are related by reduction inference, which is one kind of "subconscious" inference supported by SNePS. Path-based inference is another kind of "subconscious" inference that justifies belief in a proposition when a reduction is already believed and the "extra" wires can be inferred from path-based inference rules and paths in the network. The set of propositions subconsciously believed by the SNePS agent is the set denoted by the set of nodes that could be gotten by path-based closure of asserted nodes followed by reduction. These nodes are "virtually" or "implicitly" in the net, and need be made explicit only when there is a specific reason (such as the user asks about one, or explicitly builds one).

Although analogs of reduction inference and path-based inference could be defined on knowledge representation formalisms other than propositional semantic networks, they most naturally arose from, and are most easily understood in terms of these networks.

ACKNOWLEDGMENTS

The development of the theory and implementation of SNePS has been carried out over the years with the help of the members of SNeRG, the SNePS Research Group of SUNY at Buffalo. Their collaboration is gratefully acknowledged. I am also grateful for comments on earlier versions of this paper made by SNeRG members and by the other participants of the Workshop on Formal Aspects of Semantic Networks, particularly Robert Wilensky.

This work was supported in part by the National Science Foundation under Grant IRI-8610517, and in part by the Air Force Systems Command, Rome Air Development Center, Griffiss Air Force Base, New York 13441–5700, and the Air Force Office of Scientific Research, Bolling AFB DC 20332 under Contract No. F30602–85-C-0008, which supported the Northeast Artificial Intelligence Consortium (NAIC).

APPENDIX: FORMAL SYNTAX OF PATHS

Below is a formal syntax of all the paths available in SNePS, and a formal, inductive definition of the *HavePathL* metapredicate. In the axioms for *HavePathL*, metavariables: r will range over SNePS relations; w will range over wires; $p, p_1, p_2, \ldots$ will range over paths; $m, m_1, m_2, \ldots$ will range over cablesets; $n, n_1, n_2, \ldots$ will range over nodes; $i, i_1, i_2, \ldots$ will range over nonnegative integers. *HavePathL* is related to *HavePath* as shown by the following axiom:

Axiom 10 $HavePath(m, p, n) \Leftrightarrow \exists (i) HavePathL(m, p, n, i)$

The syntax of paths with the axioms for *HavePathL* are:

unitpath ::= *relation*
If the wire $\langle r, n\rangle$ is in the cableset m, then r is a unitpath from m to n.

unitpath ::= *relation–*
If the wire $\langle r, n\rangle$ is in the cableset m, then $r-$ is a unitpath from n to m.

path ::= *unitpath*
$\langle r, n\rangle \in \mathrm{m} \wedge Conceive(m) \Leftrightarrow HavePathL(m, r, n, 1)$
$\langle r, n\rangle \in m \wedge Conceive(m) \Leftrightarrow HavePathL(n, r-, m, 1)$

path ::= (`converse` *path*)
$HavePathL(m, p, n, i) \Leftrightarrow HavePathL(n, (\texttt{converse}\ p), m, i)$

path ::= (`compose` *path* [`!`] *path**)
$\exists(m_2)[HavePathL(m_1, p_1, m_2, i_1) \wedge HavePathL(m_2, p_2, m_3, i_2)]$
$\Leftrightarrow HavePathL(m_1, (\texttt{compose}\ p_1\ p_2), m_3, i_1 + i_2)$
$\exists(m_2)[HavePathL(m_1, p_1, m_2, i_1) \wedge Believe(m_2) \wedge HavePathL(m_2, p_2, m_3, i_2)]$
$\Leftrightarrow HavePathL(m_1, (\texttt{compose}\ p_1\ !\ p_2), m_3, i_1 + i_2)$
$\exists(m_2)[HavePathL(m_1, p_1, m_2, i_1)$
$\wedge HavePathL(m_2, (\texttt{compose}\ p_2 \ldots p_k), m_3, i_2)]$
$\Leftrightarrow HavePathL(m_1, (\texttt{compose}\ p_1\ p_2 \ldots p_k), m_3, i_1 + i_2)$
$\exists(m_2)[HavePathL(m_1, p_1, m_2, i_1) \wedge Believe(m_2)$
$\wedge HavePathL(m_2, (\texttt{compose}\ p_2 \ldots p_k), m_3, i_2)]$
$\Leftrightarrow HavePathL(m_1, (\texttt{compose}\ p_1\ !\ p_2 \ldots p_k), m_3, i_1 + i_2)$

path ::= (`kstar` *path*)
$HavePathL(m_1, (\texttt{kstar}\ \mathrm{p}), m_1, 0)$
$\exists(m_2)[HavePathL(m_1, p, m_2, i_1) \wedge HavePathL(m_2, (\texttt{kstar}\ \mathrm{p}), m_3, i_2)]$
$\Leftrightarrow HavePathL(m_1, (\texttt{kstar}\ \mathrm{p}), m_3, i_1 + i_2)$

path ::= (kplus *path*)
$HavePathL(m_1, p, m_2, i) \Leftrightarrow HavePathL(m_1, (\texttt{kplus}\ p), m_2, i)$
$\exists(m_2)[HavePathL(m_1, p, m_2, i_1) \wedge HavePathL(m_2, (\texttt{kplus}\ p), m_3, i_2)$
$\Leftrightarrow HavePathL(m_1, (\texttt{kplus}\ p), m_3, i_1 + i_2)$

path ::= (or {*path*}^*)
$HavePathL(m_1, p_1, m_2, i_1) \vee HavePathL(m_1, p_2, m_2, i_2) \Leftrightarrow HavePathL(m_1, (\texttt{or}\ p_1\ p_2), m_2, \min(i_1, i_2))$
$HavePathL(m_1, p_1, m_2, i_1) \vee HavePathL(m_1, (\texttt{or}\ p_2 \ldots p_k), m_2, i_2)]$
$\Leftrightarrow HavePathL(m_1, (\texttt{or}\ p_1\ p_2 \ldots p_k), m_2, \min(i_1, i_2))$

path ::= (and {*path*}^*)
$HavePathL(m_1, p_1, m_2, i_1) \wedge HavePathL(m_1, p_2, m_2, i_2) \Leftrightarrow HavePathL(m_1, (\texttt{and}\ p_1\ p_2), m_2, max(i_1, i_2))$
$HavePathL(m_1, p_1, m_2, i_1) \wedge HavePathL(m_1, (\texttt{and}\ p_2 \ldots p_k), m_2, i_2)]$
$\Leftrightarrow HavePathL(m_1, (\texttt{and}\ p_1\ p_2 \ldots p_k), m_2, \max(i_1, i_2))$

path ::= (not *path*)
$\neg HavePath(m_1, p, m_2) \Leftrightarrow HavePathL(m_1, (\texttt{not}\ p), m_2, 0)$

path ::= (relative-complement *path path*)
$HavePathL(m_1, p_1, m_2, i) \wedge \neg HavePath(m_1, p_2, m_2)$
$\Leftrightarrow HavePathL(m_1, (\texttt{relative-complement}\ p_1\ p_2), m_2, i)$

path ::= (irreflexive-restrict *path*)
$HavePathL(m_1, p, m_2, i) \wedge m_1 \neq m_2$
$\Leftrightarrow HavePathL(m_1, (\texttt{irreflexive-restrict}\ p), m_2, i)$

path ::= (*domain-restrict* (*path node*) *path*)
$HavePath(m_1, p_1, m_2) \wedge HavePathL(m_1, p_2, m_3, i)$
$\Leftrightarrow HavePathL(m_1, (\texttt{domain-restrict}\ (p_1\ m_2)\ p_2), m_3, i)$

path ::= (range-restrict *path* (*path node*))
$HavePathL(m_1, p_1, m_2, i) \wedge HavePath(m_2, p_2, m_3)$
$\Leftrightarrow HavePathL(m_1, (\texttt{range-restrict}\ p_1\ (p_2\ m_3)), m_2, i)$

path ::= (exception *path path*)
$HavePathL(m_1, p_1, m_2, i_1) \wedge \neg(i_2)[i_2 \leq i_1 \wedge HavePathL(m_1, p_2, m_2, i_2)]$
$\Leftrightarrow HavePathL(m_1, (\texttt{exception}\ p_1\ p_2), m_2, i_1)$

References

Fagin, R. and J.Y. Halpern. 1987. Belief, awareness, and limited reasoning. *Artificial Intelligence*, 34(1):39–76.

Hintikka, J. 1975. Impossible possible worlds vindicated. *Journal of Philosophical Logic*, 4:475–484.

Levesque, H.J. 1984. A logic of implicit and explicit belief. In *Proceedings of the National Conference on Artificial Intelligence*, pp. 198–202. Morgan Kaufmann Publishers, San Mateo, CA.

Maida, A.S. and S.C. Shapiro. 1982. Intensional concepts in propositional semantic networks. *Cognitive Science*, 6(4):291–330. Reprinted in *Readings in Knowledge Representation*, R.J. Brachman and H.J. Levesque (ed.s), Morgan Kaufmann Publishers, San Mateo, CA, 1985, 170–189.

Martins, J.P. and S.C. Shapiro. 1988. A model for belief revision. *Artificial Intelligence*, 35:25–79.

Merriam-Webster. 1961. *Webster's New Collegiate Dictionary*. G. and C. Merriam Co., Springfield, MA.

Morgado, E.J.M. 1986. *Semantic Networks as Abstract Data Types*. Ph.D. thesis, Technical Report 86–19, Department of Computer Science, SUNY at Buffalo, Buffalo, NY.

Morgado, E.J.M. and S.C. Shapiro. 1985. Believing and acting: A study of meta-knowledge and meta-reasoning. In *Proceedings of EPIA*-85 "Encontro Portugues de Inteligencia Artificial," pp. 138–154, Oporto, Portugal.

Peters, S.L. and S.C. Shapiro. 1987. A representation for natural category systems. In *Proceedings of the Tenth International Joint Conference on Artificial Intelligence*, pp. 140–146. Morgan Kaufmann Publishers, San Mateo, CA.

Shapiro, S.C. 1978. Path-based and node-based inference in semantic networks. In *Tinlap-2: Theoretical Issues in Natural Languages Processing*, D.L. Waltz (ed.), pp. 219–225. ACM, New York.

———. 1979. The SNePS semantic network processing system. In *Associative Networks: The Representation and Use of Knowledge by Computers*, N.V. Findler (ed.). Academic Press, New York, pp. 179–203.

———. 1986. Symmetric relations, intensional individuals, and variable binding. *Proceedings of the IEEE*, 74(10):1354–1363.

———. 1987. Processing, bottom-up and top-down. In *Encyclopedia of Artificial Intelligence*, S.C. Shapiro (ed.). John Wiley and Sons, New York, pp. 779–785.

———. 1988. Representing plans and acts. In *Proceedings of the Third Annual Workshop on Conceptual Graphs*. AAAI, Menlo Park, CA, pp. 3.2.7-1–3.2.7-6.

Shapiro, S.C., D. Kumar, and S. Ali. 1990. A propositional network approach to plans and plan recognition. In *Proceedings of the 1988 Workshop on Plan Recognition*, A. Maier (ed.).

Shapiro, S.C. and W. J. Rapaport. 1987. SNePS considered as a fully intensional propositional semantic network. In *The Knowledge Frontier*, N. Cercone and G. McCalla (ed.s). Springer-Verlag, New York, pp. 263–315.

Srihari, R. 1981. Combining path-based and node-based reasoning in SNePS. Technical Report 183, Department of Computer Science, SUNY at Buffalo, Buffalo, NY.

Summers, G. 1972. *Test Your Logic*. Dover, New York.

5

TOWARD THE EXPRESSIVE POWER OF NATURAL LANGUAGE

John F. Sowa
(IBM Systems Research)

Abstract

The structure of a knowledge representation language depends critically on its ultimate goal. For conceptual graphs, the goal is a system of logic that can express the propositional content of sentences in natural language in as simple and direct a manner as possible. Since there are still many unsolved problems in semantics, the system of conceptual graphs must continue to evolve to accommodate new research. But the central core of the system is stable, and new features have fit into place in a smooth way. This chapter discusses the main features of conceptual graphs, their use in semantics, and their relationship to the predicate calculus. For most sentences in ordinary language, the mapping to conceptual graphs is shorter, simpler, and more direct than the mapping to predicate calculus. For some aspects of language, especially context dependencies, predicate calculus has no way to represent them, but conceptual graphs can represent them in a principled way.

5.1 REPRESENTING SEMANTIC STRUCTURES

Conceptual graphs are a system of logic for representing natural language semantics. Unlike the predicate calculus, which was designed for studies in the foundations of mathematics, conceptual graphs were designed to simplify the mapping to and from natural languages. They are based on a graph notation for logic first developed by the philosopher and logician C. S. Peirce [1882]. He observed that the relationship of a cat on a mat is more explicitly shown by a graph such as

```
CAT - ON - MAT
```

than by a formula in predicate calculus

```
(∃x)(∃y)(cat(x) ∧ mat(y) ∧ on(x,y)).
```

Whereas the graph shows the connections directly, the variables x and y force the eye to scan back and forth across the formula to determine how the pieces are related. Furthermore, the formula introduces two conjunctions where neither the English sentence nor the graph has any. A sorted predicate calculus can simplify the formula by tagging each variable with a sort or type label:

```
(∃x:cat)(∃y:mat)on(x,y).
```

This is more concise than the ordinary predicate calculus, but it is still more complicated than the graph. Conceptual graphs are derived from Peirce's graphs, but with boxes or square brackets around the concept nodes and circles or parentheses around the relation nodes; the arcs have arrows to distinguish the first and second arguments:

```
[CAT]→(ON)→[MAT].
```

Although Peirce's early graphs were simple, they were not general enough to represent all of logic. In 1883, he continued to develop his linear notation for logic, which, with minor modifications, evolved into the modern predicate calculus. But in 1897, he discovered how to extend the graphs to represent all of first-order logic; later, he extended them to modal and higher order logic as well. His system, called *existential graphs*, forms the logical foundation for conceptual graphs.

Since both conceptual graphs and the predicate calculus are systems of logic, they both have a model-theoretic semantics that defines the truth values of propositions. Those truth values are preserved by the *formula operator* φ, which translates conceptual graphs to formulas in the predicate calculus. But preservation of truth value is a weak kind of equivalence: the graphs and the formulas are structurally very different, and conceptual graphs that have context-dependent features cannot be translated directly to the predicate calculus. Consider the mapping from language to conceptual graphs and then via φ to predicate calculus:

```
Natural language ⇒ Conceptual graphs ⇒ Predicate calculus
```

Since the meaning of a sentence depends heavily on background knowledge, the first arrow cannot be completely formalized. The second arrow, however, corresponds to the operator φ, which is a formally defined function from conceptual graphs to the predicate calculus. Conceptual graphs simplify the nonformalized first stage by providing direct correspondences for the semantic features of natural languages. The function φ, which implements the second stage, must make some complex structural transformations to generate a formula. For certain features, such as plural nouns, the mapping by φ is nontrivial. For context-dependent features, φ is undefined until the contextual references have been resolved.

As an example of the two mappings, consider the sentence *A lady is dancing.* The corresponding conceptual graph would be

```
[LADY]←(AGNT)←[DANCE].
```

This graph has a concept of type DANCE linked by the agent relation (AGNT) to a concept of type LADY. The operator φ translates this graph to the following formula in predicate calculus:

```
(∃x)(∃y)(lady(x) ∧ dance(y) ∧ agnt(y,x)).
```

When φ translates a graph to a formula, it assigns variables to the concept nodes; in this case, x is assigned to [LADY] and y to [DANCE]. The existential quantifier ∃ is the default quantifier on each variable. Conceptual relations map to predicates, where the arrow pointing towards the relation is the first argument and the arrow pointing away is the second argument. For relations with more than two arguments, the arcs are numbered.

The formula for the lady dancing would have been slightly simpler if the verb had been represented by a relation instead of a concept. Conceptual graphs permit such a representation:

```
[LADY]←(DANCING).
```

Then φ would translate this graph into a simpler formula:

```
(∃x)(lady(x) ∧ dancing(x)).
```

But the relation DANCING can be defined in terms of DANCE by means of a λ-expression:

```
DANCING = (λx) [PERSON: *x]←(AGNT)←[DANCE].
```

This statement defines DANCING by a graph with a parameter x that refers to a person who is the agent of a dance. By the rules of λ-conversion, the relation DANCING may be expanded to recover the concept DANCE. Conversely, a graph with DANCE may be contracted to the relation DANCING. The concept form is usually more convenient for mapping to and from natural languages. For example, the sentence *A lady is dancing gracefully* contains an adverb *gracefully*, whose concept can be attached by the manner relation (MANR) to the concept node:

```
[LADY]←(AGNT)←[DANCE]→ (MANR)→[GRACEFUL].
```

When translated to the predicate calculus, this graph implies that there exists an instance of dancing whose manner is an instance of gracefulness or grace. This rich ontology of nominalized actions and properties is also necessary to represent verbs and adjectives that are converted to nouns, as in the example *I saw a lady dancing; her dance lasted 60 seconds*. The participle *dancing* and the noun *dance* are each represented by a concept of type DANCE. To show that the two concepts refer to the same activity, they are linked by a dotted line, called a *coreference link*.

Plural nouns require only a single extra letter in English, but they require complex circumlocutions in predicate calculus. Consider the sentence *Nine ladies are dancing*. The corresponding conceptual graph would be

```
[LADY: {*}@9]←(AGNT)←[DANCE].
```

In this graph, the LADY concept has a *plural referent*, represented by the symbol {*}. It indicates some unspecified elements of type LADY, and the qualifier @9 indicates that there are 9 of them. Those 9 ladies are linked by the AGNT relation to a concept of type DANCE. The operator φ translates this graph to the following formula:

```
(∃S)(set(S) ∧ count(S,9) ∧
    (∀x∈S)(∃y)(lady(x) ∧ dance(y) ∧ agnt(y,x))).
```

As this example illustrates, the conceptual graph with three nodes is comparable in complexity to the four-word English sentence, but the formula generated by φ is considerably more complex. When φ is applied to a concept with a plural referent, it must assign two quantified variables: one variable *S* for the set of ladies, and another variable *x* that ranges over the elements of *S*. In the default mapping by φ, the quantifier (∃y) on the dance *y* is placed within the scope of the quantifier (∀x) on the ladies. Therefore, each lady may be dancing a separate dance, or they may all be dancing the same dance. The distributive interpretation, where each lady is dancing separately, and the collective interpretation, where they are all dancing the same dance, are discussed in Section 5.6.

Since natural languages are highly context dependent and predicate calculus makes no provision for context, many sentences cannot be translated directly to predicate calculus. Conceptual graphs accommodate contextual dependencies with *indexical referents* marked by the symbol #. The basic indexical word is the definite article *the*, as in the following conceptual graph for the sentence *The cat is on the mat*:

```
[CAT: #]→(ON)→[MAT: #].
```

For this graph, the φ operator is undefined because the predicate calculus has nothing that corresponds to #. Before φ can be applied, the two # referents must be resolved by searching through the current context to find appropriate referents. If the current cat is named Yojo and the current mat has serial number #81649, each # marker can be resolved to a constant:

```
[CAT: Yojo]→(ON)→[MAT: #81649].
```

Now φ can translate this graph to a formula:

```
cat(Yojo) ∧ mat(#81649) ∧ on(Yojo,#81649).
```

The # marker indicates a definite reference to an entity that is known contextually, but not yet resolved in the current graph. When the correct referent is found, its serial number is appended to the # symbol, as in #81649. The search rules for resolving # markers can be adapted from *discourse representation theory* [Kamp, 1981a,b], since the contexts in conceptual graphs are isomorphic to Kamp's DR structures.

Other indexicals can be defined by expressions that contain the article *the*: the pronoun *I* refers to the person who is speaking, and *you* refers to the person who is being addressed. Tenses are also indexicals that refer to the speech time, the time of the situation under discussion, and for compound tenses, some other reference time in the past or future. To simplify the mapping from language to conceptual graphs, common indexical terms have short abbreviations: the pronouns *I* and *you* are represented by [PERSON: #I] and [PERSON: #you]; *here* and *now* are represented by [PLACE: #here] and [TIME: #now]. The past tense can be represented by a monadic relation (PAST), which applies to the situation under discussion; it is defined in terms of the speech time of the current context, represented by #s-time:

```
PAST = (λx) [SITUATION: *x]→(PTIM)→ [TIME]→(SUCC)→[TIME: #s-time].
```

This λ-expression defines PAST as a relation that applies to a situation x that occurs at a point in time (PTIM), which is some time that has a successor, which is the time #s-time. The specific referents for the # symbols are resolved by a search through the current context or nest of contexts. As a result of the search, the # symbols are replaced by conventional variables or constants, and the graphs can then be mapped to the predicate calculus.

Although conceptual graphs are primarily a semantic representation, syntax is important for many applications, especially machine translation. For such applications, *syntactic annotations* may be added to the concept and relation nodes, separated from the semantic information by a semicolon. The participle *dancing*, for example, may be represented by the concept [DANCE; prtp] and the noun *dance* by [DANCE; n]. As another example, the English pronoun *it* and the German pronoun *es* make definite references, but with no restrictions on the concept type. Logically, they are both represented as [⊤: #], where ⊤ is the most general type at the top of the type lattice. The two pronouns differ, however, in their gender restrictions: the English *it* refers to something nonhuman while the German *es* refers to something of neuter gender, which may be human, as in *Kind* [child] or *Mädchen* [girl]. To show the distinction, the English *it* is represented as [⊤ : #; nonhuman], and the German *es* as [⊤: #; neuter]. The syntactic annotations, which are discussed further in Section 5.7, are ignored by φ in the mapping to predicate calculus; but they are important in the mapping to and from natural language.

This section has summarized the basic features of conceptual graphs: concepts, relations, λ-expressions for definitions, and the referent field for names, quantifiers, plurals, and indexicals. Only one more feature is needed for a complete system of logic: the nested contexts described in Section 5.2. This small number of features, which can be combined in all possible ways, forms a rich semantic for-

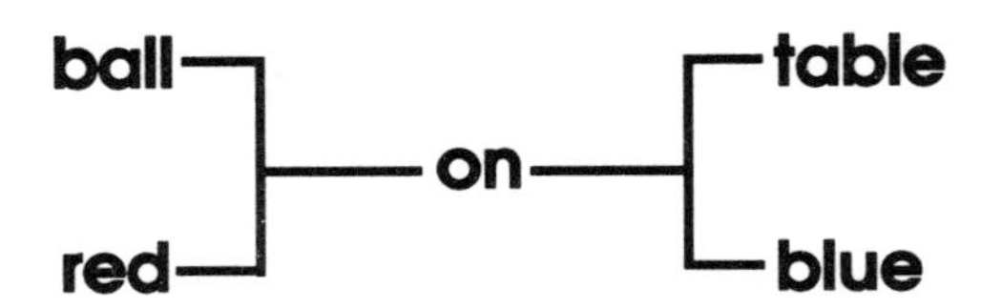

Figure 5.1: A graph for "A red ball is on a blue table"

malism. The remaining sections of this chapter show how it is used to represent definitions and taxonomies, generalized quantifiers, plural referents, syntactic annotations, and related issues in semantics. Since each of these topics is complex enough to fill a book by itself, there is no room here to cover them in depth. For more detail, see the book *Conceptual Structures* and some more recent papers [Sowa, 1988, 1990, forthcoming; Sowa and Way, 1986].

5.2 NESTED CONTEXTS

A context is represented by a concept with one or more conceptual graphs nested inside the referent field. Linguistically, contexts reflect the nesting of clauses in language; logically, they derive from Peirce's existential graphs. As an example of a graph without contexts, Figure 5.1 shows a graph for the sentence *A red ball is on a blue table*, using Peirce's conventions of 1882.

In both Peirce's early graphs and his later existential graphs, he represented an existential quantifier with a set of linked bars, which he called a *line of identity*. In Figure 5.1, there are two lines of identity: one represents a red ball x and the other a blue table y. Figure 5.1 may be translated to the following formula:

```
(∃x) (∃y) (ball(x) ∧ red(x) ∧ table(y) ∧ blue(y) ∧ on(x,y)).
```

Figure 5.1 is reminiscent of many AI networks that can represent conjunction and existential quantifiers, but not negation, disjunction, implication, or universal quantifiers. Peirce experimented with various ways of marking negations on the bars and the relations, but none of them gave him a complete system of first-order logic. Meanwhile, his linear notation, which was fully developed by 1883, was equivalent to the modern predicate calculus, but with the symbols Π_x for $(\forall x)$ and Σ_x for $(\exists x)$.

In 1896, Peirce discovered a general way to represent negation in his graphs. The crucial innovation was the introduction of ovals to enclose negated contexts. That convention gave him a complete system of first-order logic with negation, conjunction, and existential quantification as the primitives. Although his system of 1882 also had those primitives, it could only negate a single bar or relation; it could not negate an arbitrary structure. The ability to negate any graph or conjunction of graphs makes it possible to define the universal quantifier and all Boolean opera-

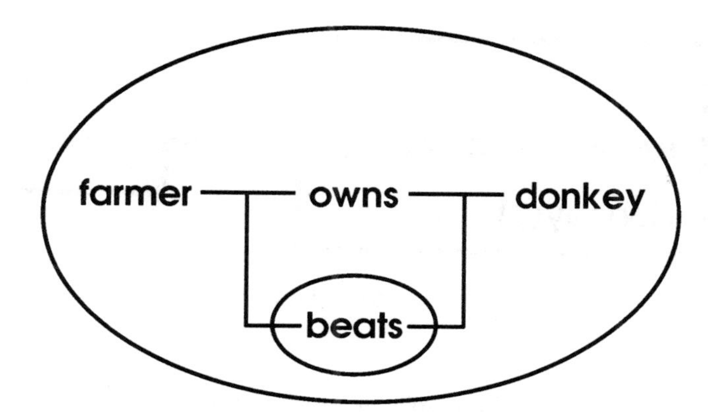

Figure 5.2: Existential graph for "If a farmer owns a donkey, then he beats it"

tors. Using Peirce's conventions of 1896, Figure 5.2 shows a graph for the sentence *If a farmer owns a donkey, then he beats it.*

In Figure 5.2, the nest of two ovals represents *if-then*, since $\sim(p \wedge \sim q)$ is equivalent to $(p \supset q)$. The *if*-oval contains one line of identity for the farmer and one for the donkey, both of which extend into the *then*-oval. Figure 5.2 may be translated to the following formula in predicate calculus:

$$\sim (\exists x)(\exists y)(\mathrm{farmer}(x) \wedge \mathrm{donkey}(y) \wedge \mathrm{owns}(x,y) \wedge \sim \mathrm{beats}(x,y)).$$

With the symbol $\supset$ for *if-then*, this formula may also be written

$$(\forall x)(\forall y)((\mathrm{farmer}(x) \wedge \mathrm{donkey}(y) \wedge \mathrm{owns}(x,y)) \supset \mathrm{beats}(x,y)).$$

Besides introducing the notation, Peirce stated complete rules of inference for reasoning with the graphs. His rules led to short, simple proofs that had a strong affinity with Gentzen's later rules for natural deduction. In 1906, Peirce introduced colored contexts to represent modalities, such as possibility, necessity, obligation, and intention.

In the predicate calculus, the operator $\supset$ interacts with quantifiers in a peculiar way. If the previous formula with $\supset$ were translated into English, the result would be decidedly odd:

> *For all* x *and all* y, *if* x *is a farmer and* y *is a donkey and* x *owns* y, *then* x *beats* y.

The existential quantifiers on *a farmer* and *a donkey* inside the if-clause become universal quantifiers in front of the formula. To express such features more naturally, Kamp developed a systematic treatment of contexts and a different way of representing implication. Remarkably, Kamp's discourse representation struc-

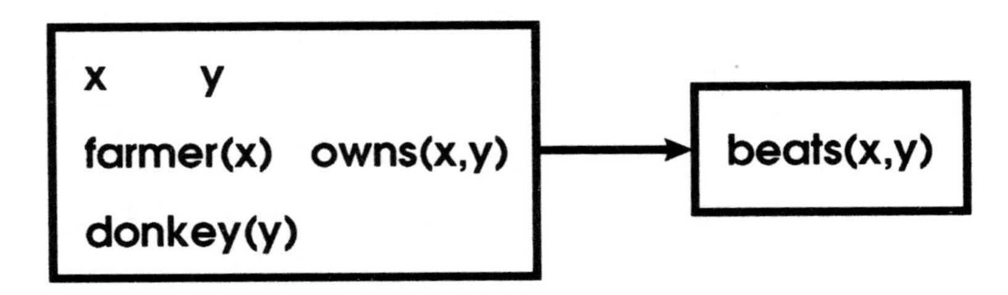

Figure 5.3: If a farmer owns a donkey, then he beats it

tures (DRS) turn out to be isomorphic to Peirce's graphs. Figure 5.3 shows the DR structure that corresponds to Peirce's Figure 5.2.

In Figure 5.3, the variables x and y represent *discourse referents*, which correspond to existentially quantified variables. The two boxes are contexts, and the arrow represents implication. Kamp's implication does not correspond to the symbol $\supset$ in predicate calculus, since Kamp makes the additional assumption that variables in the consequent are within the scope of discourse referents in the antecedent; the predicate calculus form with $\supset$ does not allow that interpretation. There is no space in this chapter to summarize all of Kamp's examples and arguments, but the important point to note is that his DR structures are isomorphic to Peirce's graphs. Kamp's search rules for resolving anaphora correspond to a search through Peirce's contexts from the inner contexts outward.

Whereas Peirce used links to represent existential quantifiers, conceptual graphs associate quantification with the concept nodes. To say that a farmer owns a donkey, Peirce represented the verb by a relation. That representation is possible in a conceptual graph:

```
[FARMER]→(OWNS)→[DONKEY].
```

The standard mapping from language to conceptual graphs, however, represents the verb by a concept:

```
[FARMER]→(STAT)→[OWN]→ (PTNT)→[DONKEY].
```

Since *own* is a stative verb, the farmer isn't the agent of owning; instead, the farmer is in the state (STAT) of owning, and the donkey is the patient (PTNT) of owning.

As in Peirce's graphs, implication in conceptual graphs is represented by a nest of two negative contexts. Instead of ovals, boxes marked with the symbol $\neg$ are used to represent negative contexts. The concepts [FARMER] and [DONKEY] occur only in the *if*-context. To show references to those concepts in the *then*-context, two concepts of type $\top$ (the top of the type lattice) are shown in that context.

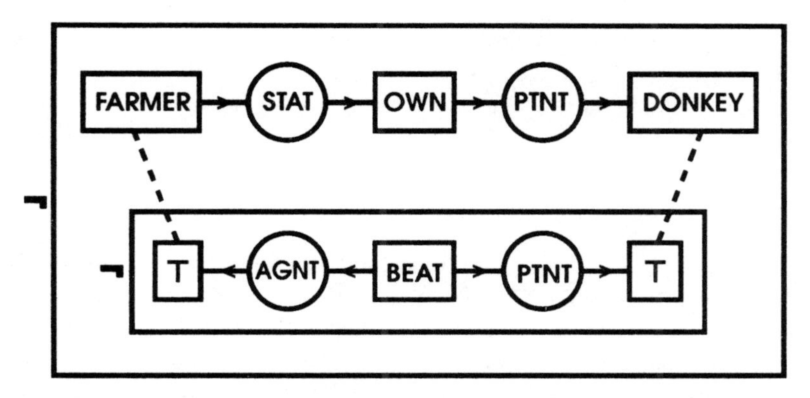

Figure 5.4: Conceptual graph for "If a farmer owns a donkey, then he beats it"

They are linked by dotted lines, called *coreference links*, to the concepts [FARMER] and [DONKEY]. Figure 5.4 is the resulting graph.

Concepts of type ⊤ correspond to pronouns in natural language. Since ⊤ is the universal type, it may be coreferent with any concept of any type. In the linear form, coreference links are represented by variables like **x* and **y*. The concept [⊤] becomes [⊤: *x], which may be abbreviated as [*x]. Figure 5.4 then becomes

```
¬ [FARMER: *x]→(STAT)→[OWN]→(PTNT)→[DONKEY: *y]
    ¬[ [*x]←(AGNT)←[BEAT]→(PTNT)→[*y]]].
```

To improve readability, the symbols IF and THEN may be introduced as synonyms for the negative context markers ¬ [, and the period at the end would represent the two closing brackets]]. The result is the following graph:

```
IF  [FARMER: *x]→(STAT)→[OWN]→(PTNT)→[DONKEY: *y]
THEN  [*x]←(AGNT)←[BEAT]→(PTNT)→[*y].
```

This linear form can be read directly as an English sentence:

If a farmer x *owns a donkey* y, *then* x *beats* y.

As in Peirce's graphs and in Kamp's DR structures, existential quantifiers in natural language correspond to existential quantifiers in conceptual graphs. Because of the isomorphism between Kamp's contexts, Peirce's contexts, and conceptual graph contexts, Kamp's rules for resolving discourse referents can be used for resolving # referents in conceptual graphs.

Peirce introduced contexts as a special primitive. In conceptual graphs, they are assumed to be concepts. Like any other concepts, they can have attached conceptual relations, and they also have their own type label, which is sometimes omitted from the diagram for conciseness. The conceptual graphs nested inside a context are the referent of that concept. Yet in a strict sense, a conceptual graph can only occur as a literal in the referent field of a concept of type GRAPH. The following concept has type GRAPH and a conceptual graph as a referent:

```
[GRAPH: [PERSON: Mary]←(AGNT)←[MARRY]→(PTNT)→[SAILOR]].
```

This graph happens to state the proposition that Mary is marrying a sailor. But when the type label is GRAPH, the meaning is irrelevant, and the nested graph is simply treated as a literal; in effect, the graph is "quoted" so that one can make further assertions about it. One kind of assertion about a graph is to say that it states a proposition. The following conceptual graph uses the relation STMT (statement) to say that there exists a proposition with that graph as its statement:

```
[PROPOSITION]→(STMT)→[GRAPH:
    [PERSON: Mary]←(AGNT)←[MARRY]→(PTNT)→[SAILOR]].
```

A situation can be described by a proposition, which in turn can be stated by a graph:

```
[SITUATION]→(DSCR)→[PROPOSITION]→(STMT)→[GRAPH:
    [PERSON: Mary]←(AGNT)←[MARRY]→(PTNT)→[SAILOR]].
```

For conciseness, a conceptual graph may be written directly in the referent field of a concept of type PROPOSITION or SITUATION. That option is an abbreviation similar to a type coercion in a programming language. When a conceptual graph is the referent of a concept of type PROPOSITION, it represents the proposition stated by the graph. When it is the referent of a concept of type SITUATION, it represents the situation described by the proposition stated by the graph. This is an example of the distinction between use and mention: when a conceptual graph is the referent of a concept of type GRAPH, it is merely being mentioned; when it is the referent of a concept of type PROPOSITION or SITUATION, it is being used to state a proposition or describe a situation. As an example, Figure 5.5 shows a graph for the sentence *Tom believes that Mary wants to marry a sailor*.

In Figure 5.5, BELIEVE and WANT are states that have experiencers (EXPR) rather than agents. What Tom believes is a proposition, but what Mary wants is a situation. In general, negation, modalities, and the patients of verbs like *think* and *know* are linked to contexts of type PROPOSITION; times, locations, and the patients of verbs like *want* and *fear* are linked to contexts of type SITUATION. Whatever the types of the contexts, however, the way they are nested determines the scope of quantifiers. In Figure 5.5, the existential quantifier on SAILOR is

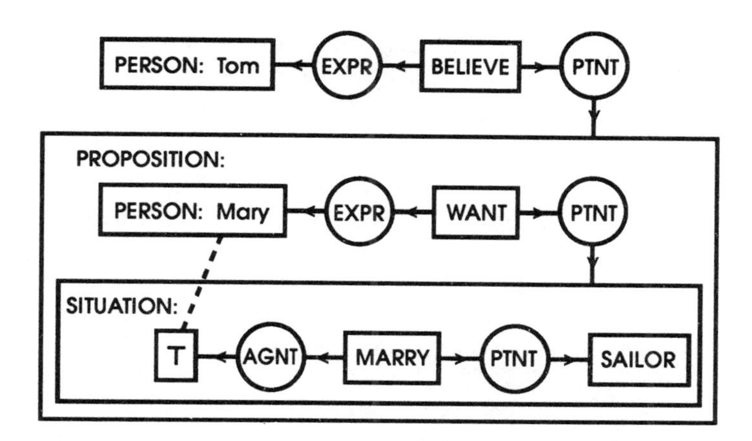

Figure 5.5: A nested proposition containing a nested situation

inside the situation of Mary's want, which is existentially quantified inside Tom's belief. Following is the linear form:

```
[PERSON: Tom]←(EXPR)←[BELIEVE]→(PTNT)→[PROPOSITION:
    [PERSON: Mary*x]←(EXPR)←[WANT]→(PTNT)→[SITUATION:
        [*x]←(AGNT)←[MARRY]→(PTNT)→[SAILOR] ]].
```

As this example illustrates, the linear form is quite readable for simple graphs, but the box and circle diagrams are better for showing the nesting of contexts.

5.3 DEFINITIONS AND TAXONOMIES

As a system of logic, conceptual graphs normally assert propositions. Some semantic networks described in this book are primarily definitional systems for building taxonomies: they provide ways of defining new concepts and ordering them in a hierarchy of types and subtypes. Conceptual graphs also support definitions, but they do so by λ-abstractions over the assertions:

- **Definitions:** If $(\exists x)p(x)$ is a proposition, the quantifier $\exists$ may be replaced with the Greek letter λ in order to specify x as a formal parameter. The resulting expression $(\lambda x)p(x)$ defines a type P; the instances of P include the original x and all other x's for which p(x) is true.
- **Subtypes:** If $(\lambda x)p(x)$ defines a type P and $(\lambda x)q(x)$ defines a type Q, then Q is a subtype of P if and only if for all x, q(x) implies p(x).

- **Inheritance:** If a(x) is an attribute that is true for all instances of type P, then a(x) is true for all instances of any subtype of P. This fact follows from the definition of subtype and the rules of inference in logic.

By this method, a type system with inheritance can be defined over any system of logic. In effect, the type hierarchy is a precompiled system of implications, and inheritance is a fast inference rule that takes advantage of the compiled structures. The method was applied to conceptual graphs by Sowa [1979], and it is presented in detail in Sections 3.5 and 3.6 of *Conceptual Structures* [Sowa, 1984]. By theorem 3.6.10 in that book, the place of any concept type in the hierarchy is determined by its definition. The theory is compatible with the taxonomic systems discussed elsewhere in this book, any of which could be adapted to manage the type hierarchy and compute inheritance for a conceptual graph system.

The method of λ-abstraction can be used to define both concept types and relations: some conceptual graph forms the body of the definition, and λ specifies one or more concepts in the graph as formal parameters. The following λ-expression defines PET-CAT as a type of CAT that is owned by some person:

```
PET-CAT = (λx) [CAT: *x]←(PTNT)←[OWN]←(STAT)←[PERSON].
```

The variable **x* marks the concept [CAT] as the parameter. The type of that concept is called the *genus*, which then becomes a supertype of the newly defined type. In this example, the genus type CAT is a supertype of PET-CAT. The equal sign in the definition shows that the type label is a synonym for the λ-expression that defines the type. Any occurrence of the type label PET-CAT could be replaced by the λ-expression.

In the definition of PET-CAT, the new property of being owned by a person is added to the property of being a cat. Such a definition uses conjunction as the only Boolean operator. Some definitional systems do not allow any other Boolean operators in the definitions. That restriction simplifies the reasoning process, but it limits the expressive power of the language. The definition of PENNILESS, for example, requires a negation:

```
PENNILESS = (λx) [STATE: *x]←(STAT)←[PERSON: *y]
  ¬[ [*y]→(POSS)→[PENNY]].
```

This definition says that PENNILESS is a state *x* of a person *y*, where it is false that *y* has possession (POSS) of a penny. Systems that prohibit such definitions ensure that the reasoning process is fast, but they make it impossible to define many kinds of concepts. Since conceptual graphs are designed to represent anything in natural language, they must allow negations in definitions.

Besides negations, other logical operators and contexts may be needed in a definition. Certain Mexican dialects, for example, make a distinction between a *difunto*, a deceased person who was married at the time of death, and an *angelito*, a deceased person who was not married at the time of death [El Guindi, 1986]. The definition for the concept type DIFUNTO would require a relation WHEN linking two situations:

```
DIFUNTO = (λx) [PERSON: *x]→(STAT)→[DEAD]
   [SITUATION: [*x]→(STAT)→[MARRIED]]→(WHEN)→
      [SITUATION: [*x]←(PTNT)←[DIE]].
```

By this definition, a difunto is a person *x* in state dead, where *x* was in a situation of being married when a situation occurred in which *x* died. The definition of *angelito* is similar, but with a negation inside the first situation:

```
ANGELITO = (λx) [PERSON: *x]→(STAT)→[DEAD]
   [SITUATION: ¬ [[*x]→(STAT)→[MARRIED]]]→(WHEN)→
      [SITUATION: [*x]←(PTNT)←[DIE]].
```

In reasoning by inheritance, both DIFUNTO and ANGELITO could be treated as simple subtypes of DEAD-PERSON, and the details inside the definition could be ignored. But to determine whether a particular individual was a *difunto* or an *angelito*, the details could be recovered by expanding the λ-expression.

New types of conceptual relations can also be defined by λ-abstraction. The relation WHEN in the previous examples could be defined by the following graph:

```
WHEN = (λx,y)
   [SITUATION: *x]→(PTIM)→ [TIME]←(PTIM)←[SITUATION: *y].
```

In this definition, WHEN has two formal parameters *x* and *y*; each of them refers to a situation that occurs at the same point in time (PTIM). Any occurrence of the relation WHEN in a graph could be replaced by the sequence of concepts and relations between [*x] and [*y]. The graph in the definition of DIFUNTO could be expanded to the following:

```
[SITUATION: [*x]→(STAT)→[MARRIED]] →(PTIM)→[TIME]-
   (PTIM)←[SITUATION: [*x]←(PTNT)←[DIE]].
```

This graph says that *x* is in the state married at some point in time, which is the same time that *x* dies. Since the graph is too long to fit on one line, the hyphen shows that the relation attached to [TIME] is continued on the next line.

Frame systems allow hyphenated attributes like COUNTRY-OF-RESIDENCE. Such attributes could be defined as two-place relations in conceptual graphs:

```
COUNTRY-OF-RESIDENCE = (λx,y)
   [PERSON: *x]→(STAT)→[LIVE]→(IN)→[COUNTRY: *y].
```

This definition has two formal parameters *x* and *y*, where the person *x* is in the state of live in a country *y*. With this definition, the relation (COUNTRY-OF-RESI-

DENCE) could be used in conceptual graphs in the same way as the attribute in a frame system. But whenever the details are relevant, the definition could be expanded to recover the implicit concepts and relations.

5.4 MAPPING LANGUAGE TO CONCEPTUAL GRAPHS

One of the most difficult problems in mapping language to logic is the selection of predicates for representing each semantic feature. Since pure predicate calculus has no built-in primitives, it is perfectly general, but it offers the student no guidelines for applying it. The great mismatch between English and predicate calculus even leads professors into making careless mistakes. One textbook gave the following formula for the sentence *You can fool some of the people all of the time*:

```
(∃x)(∀t)(person(x) ∧ time(t) ∧ canfool(x,t)).
```

This formula makes the common mistake of using ∧ instead of ⊃ with a universal quantifier. It thereby implies that everything is a time: (∀t)time(t). The author should have written

```
(∃x)(person(x) ∧ (∀t)(time(t) ⊃ canfool(x,t))).
```

Besides the mistake, the formula has the rather odd predicate canfool(x,t), which supposedly means "You can fool *x* at time *t*." That predicate is an attempt to gloss over two features of ordinary language that cannot be represented in first-order logic: the indexical *you* and the modal auxiliary *can*. The formula also ignores the difference between the plural *people* and the singular *person*. For this example, the singular form is permissible, but it evades the problem of mapping plural nouns to sets.

Like predicate calculus, conceptual graphs are a formal system with a minimum of built-in features. But besides the formalism, the system also includes relations, structures, and guidelines for representing sentences in natural language. The basic principle is that content words map to concept nodes, and function words like prepositions and conjunctions map to relation nodes. That principle is a good first approximation, but languages have many syntactic features that have to be considered. Following are some finer distinctions:

- Ordinary nouns, verbs, adjectives, and adverbs map to type labels in a concept node:

  lady ⇒ `[LADY]`, *dance* ⇒ `[DANCE]`, *happy* ⇒ `[HAPPY]`.

- Proper names map to the referent field of a concept whose type field specifies the type:

  Yojo ⇒ `[CAT: Yojo]`, *White House* ⇒ `[BUILDING: White House]`.

- The symbol # with optional qualifiers is used in the referent field for contextually defined references:

  the cat ⇒ `[CAT: #]`, *this* ⇒ `[⊤: #this]`.

- Plural nouns are represented by the plural referent {*} followed by an optional count:

  nine ladies ⇒ `[LADY: {*}@9]`.

- Modal auxiliaries like *can* or *must* map to conceptual relations like PSBL (possibility) or OBLG (obligation) attached to a context enclosing the graph for the sentence or clause. The sentence *Tom can go* becomes

  ```
  (PSBL)→[PROPOSITION: [PERSON: Tom]←(AGNT)←[GO]].
  ```

- Verb tenses and aspects map to relations like PAST or PROG (progressive). Those relations are defined in terms of more primitive relations like DUR (duration), PTIM (point in time), and SUCC (successor) as well as contextually defined reference times like #now and #s-time. The sentence *Tom went* becomes

  ```
  (PAST)→[SITUATION: [PERSON: Tom]← (AGNT)←[GO]].
  ```

  The contexts may be nested to any depth. *Tom couldn't go* leads to three nested contexts:

  ```
  (PAST)→[ ¬[ (PSBL)→[ [PERSON: Tom]←(AGNT)←[GO]]]].
  ```

  As abbreviations, the type labels SITUATION and PROPOSITION may be omitted from the contexts, since they are implied by the types of the relations. As a further abbreviation, the relation ¬ PSBL could be defined as a combination of the relations ¬ and PSBL.

- The verb *be* when used as an auxiliary affects the voice or aspect; when used as a main verb, it shows a coreference link between concepts. The sentence *Mary is the teacher* becomes

  ```
  [PERSON: Mary]- - -[TEACHER: #].
  ```

  The dotted line linking two concept nodes shows that they are coreferent; i.e., they refer to the same individual. In the linear notation, dotted lines may be replaced by variables:

  ```
  [PERSON: Mary*x] [TEACHER: #*x].
  ```

- The verb *have* when used as an auxiliary also affects the tense; when used as a main verb, it may map to various relations such as PART (have as part) or POSS (possession). The sentence *The car has an engine* becomes

  ```
  [CAR: #]→(PART)→[ENGINE].
  ```

Note: in the standard mnemonic for remembering the directions of the arrows, the arrow pointing towards the circle is read "has a" and the arrow pointing away is read "which is a"; therefore, the relation itself is called PART, not HASPART.

- Case endings in inflected languages and word order in languages without inflections map to *case relations* or *thematic roles* like AGNT (agent), PTNT (patient), INST (instrument), RCPT (recipient), and RSLT (result). The sentence *I sent a book to Fred by mail* becomes

```
(PAST)→[SITUATION: [SEND]-
                        (AGNT)→[PERSON: #I]
                        (PTNT)→[BOOK]
                        (RCPT)→[PERSON: Fred]
                        (INST)→[MAIL]].
```

  Since the [SEND] concept has four relations attached to it, the linearized form of the graph cannot be written in a straight line. Therefore, the hyphen after [SEND] shows that the relations are continued on separate lines.

- Conjunctions like *when* or *because* map to relations that link contexts containing the graphs that represent the clauses. The sentence *Tom came after you left* is represented by the following graph:

```
(PAST)→[[PERSON: Tom]←(AGNT)←[COME]]→(AFTR)→[
               [PERSON: #you]←(AGNT)←[LEAVE]].
```

  Time relations like AFTR (after) and WHEN link situations, but ERGO (therefore) links propositions. To simplify the diagrams, the type labels SITUATION and PROPOSITION may be omitted when they are implied by the attached relations.

- Restrictive relative clauses map to λ-expressions that go to the type field of a concept. Examples of this construction are shown in Section 5.5.

This list illustrates the mapping from English to conceptual graphs, but much more detail would be necessary for a comprehensive treatment of all the semantic features. Among other things, this discussion has not addressed lexical ambiguities, such as the question of mapping *must* to OBLG for obligation or NECS for necessity. Ambiguities are discussed in more detail by Sowa [1988, forthcoming]; computer implementation is discussed by Sowa and Way [1986].

To illustrate the semantic features, the graph in Figure 5.6 represents the sentence *You can fool some of the people all of the time*. The graph could also be read *There exist some people, and at any time, it is possible for you to fool them.* These two sentences map to the same graph, but they differ in emphasis. Such distinctions are not part of the propositional content of the graph, but they can be represented by the syntactic annotations discussed in Section 5.7. Since the original

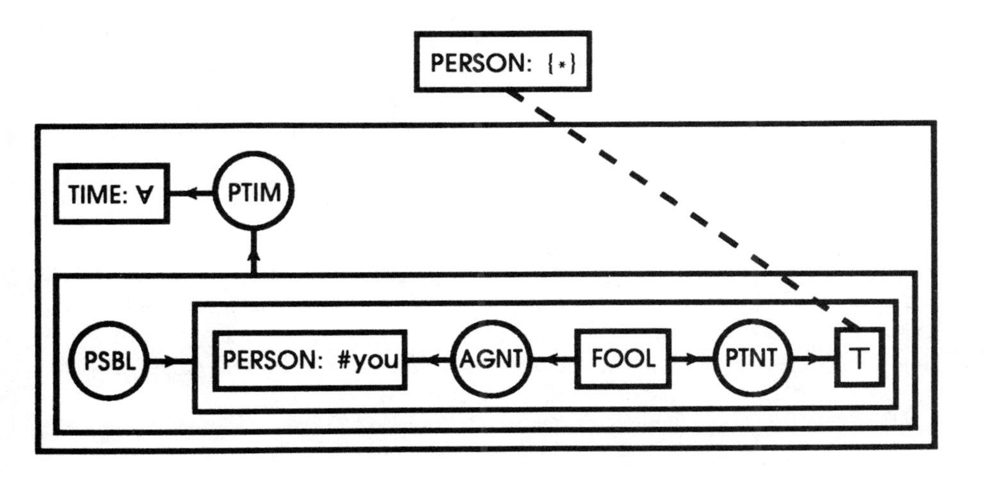

Figure 5.6: Conceptual graph for "You can fool some of the people all of the time"

sentence had four content words *you, fool, people*, and *time*, the corresponding graph has one concept node for each of those words plus an extra concept [⊤] to show the coreference across different contexts. Note that the pronoun *you* in this example could be interpreted as a way of saying *anyone*. If the listener in the current context is undefined, the indexical #you could not be resolved; it would therefore behave like a free variable in predicate calculus, which would have the effect of a universal quantifier. The graph could also be written in the following linear form:

```
[PERSON: {*}*x]
[ [TIME: ∀ ]←(PTIM)←[SITUATION: (PSBL)→[PROPOSITION:
    [PERSON: #you]←(AGNT)←[FOOL]→(PTNT)→[*x] ]]].
```

In predicate calculus, the linear order of the formula is used to show the scope of quantifiers. In conceptual graphs, however, the scope is determined by the *precedence* of each quantifier: the universal quantifier ∀ normally takes precedence over the existential quantifiers in the same context. For the graph in Figure 5.6, the concept [PERSON: {*}] is outside the scope of the ∀, since it is outside the context that contains the concept [TIME: ∀]. This graph cannot be translated to predicate calculus since it contains the indexical #you. But if it were written in a predicate calculus style, it would look something like the following:

```
(∃x)(set(x) ∧ (∀y)(y∈x ⊃ (person(y) ∧ (∀t)(time(t) ⊃
   ptim(◊(∃z)(fool(z) ∧ person(#you) ∧ agnt(z,#you) ∧
      ptnt(z,y)),t))))).
```

This formula is more complex than the example in the logic book, but it comes closer to capturing all the features expressed in the sentence. It further illustrates the point that conceptual graphs require fewer symbols than the predicate calculus, even though many of the symbols in the formula are single characters like $\wedge$, $\in$, and $\Diamond$.

5.5 GENERALIZED QUANTIFIERS

In natural languages, quantification has three parts: a *quantifier*, a *restrictor*, and a *scope*. The quantifier may be a word like *every* or a phrase like *almost all.* The restrictor determines the domain over which quantification ranges. It can be a single word like *elephant* in the sentence *Every elephant has a long nose*, or it can be a phrase like *shiny new penny* in the sentence *Place every shiny new penny in the box*. The scope is the context over which the quantification extends; it may be a phrase, a sentence, or even an entire paragraph. The quantifier, the restrictor, and the scope make up the *tripartite structure* of quantification. In standard predicate calculus, quantification has a much simpler structure. It only has two quantifiers, the universal $\forall$ and the existential $\exists$. It also lacks a restrictor: a quantifier like $(\forall x)$ allows the variable x to range over anything in the domain of discourse. *Sorted logic* provides a limited number of *sorts* that restrict the variable, but natural language allows arbitrarily complex expressions as restrictors.

In conceptual graphs, the three parts are shown explicitly. The quantifier itself goes into the referent field of a concept, the restrictor goes into the type field, and the scope is the entire context in which the quantifier occurs. For a simple quantifying phrase like *every farmer*, the restrictor is just the type label in the concept [FARMER: ∀]. With restrictive relative clauses, however, the modifying clause goes in a λ-expression in the type field. In the sentence *Every farmer who owns a donkey beats it*, the phrase *farmer who owns a donkey* is the restrictor that defines the subtype of farmer from which the quantifier selects, and the entire sentence is the scope of the quantification. To represent quantification over that subtype, a λ-expression could be used to define a new type DONKEY-FARMER:

```
DONKEY-FARMER = (λx) [FARMER: *x]→(STAT)→[OWN]→(PTNT)→[DONKEY].
```

With this definition, the type DONKEY-FARMER represents the subtype of FARMER distinguished by the property of owning a donkey. Then the sentence *Every farmer who owns a donkey beats it* could be represented by the following graph:

```
[DONKEY-FARMER: ∀]←(AGNT)←[BEAT]→(PTNT)→[⊤: #; nonhuman].
```

There are two problems with this representation: first, it is undesirable to define a special subtype for every restrictive relative clause; second, the concept [⊤: #], which represents the pronoun *it*, has no explicit antecedent in the context. A better solution is to put the λ-expression for the relative clause directly in the type field of the concept:

```
[(λx) [FARMER: *x]→(STAT)→[OWN]→(PTNT)→[DONKEY]: ∀]-
          (AGNT)←[BEAT]→(PTNT)→[⊤: #; nonhuman].
```

There is now a potential antecedent for *it* nested inside the type field. Before that referent can be resolved, the ∀ quantifier must be reduced to an existential, according to the definition for ∀ given by Sowa [1984]; then the λ-expression can be expanded. The first step leads to an IF-THEN form:

```
IF    [(λx) [FARMER: *x]→(STAT)→ [OWN]→(PTNT)→[DONKEY]: *y]
THEN  [*y]←(AGNT)←[BEAT]→(PTNT)→[⊤: #; nonhuman].
```

Since the concept in the IF clause now has a simple existential quantifier as its referent, the λ-expression can be expanded:

```
IF    [FARMER: *y]→(STAT)→[OWN]→(PTNT)→[DONKEY]
THEN  [*y]←(AGNT)←[BEAT]→(PTNT)→[⊤: #; nonhuman].
```

This graph has the same structure as Figure 5.5, and Kamp's rules for resolving anaphora, can be applied to resolve the indexical # to the concept [DONKEY]. The result is the following graph, which may be read *If a farmer* y *owns a donkey* z, *then* y *beats* z:

```
IF    [FARMER: *y]→(STAT)→[OWN]→(PTNT)→[DONKEY: *z]
THEN  [*y]←(AGNT)←[BEAT]→(PTNT)→[*z].
```

Plurals in natural languages are generalized quantifiers, and conceptual graphs represent them in the same way as other quantifiers. As examples, consider the next three sentences:

Every elephant that performs in a circus earns money.

Some elephants that perform in a circus earn money.

Many elephants that perform in a circus earn money.

These sentences have similar syntax, and the corresponding conceptual graphs represent them in parallel ways. Following is the graph for *every elephant*:

```
[(λx) [ELEPHANT: *x]←(AGNT)←[PERFORM]→(IN)→[CIRCUS]: ∀]-
     (BENF)←[EARN]→(PTNT)→[MONEY].
```

The BENF relation indicates that the elephants are the beneficiaries of the earning. When this graph is translated to the predicate calculus, the restrictor becomes the antecedent of an implication:

```
(∀x)(∀y)(∀z)((elephant(x) ∧ perform(y) ∧ circus(z)
     ∧ agnt(y,x) ∧ in(y,z))
     ⊃ (∃u)(∃v)(earn(u) ∧ money(v) ∧ benf(u,x) ∧ ptnt(u,v)).
```

The plural referent {*} is a kind of generalized quantifier that goes in the same field as ∀ . Following is the graph for *some elephants*:

```
[(λx)[ELEPHANT: *x]←(AGNT)←[PERFORM]→(IN)→[CIRCUS]: {*}]-
     (BENF)←[EARN]→(PTNT)→[MONEY].
```

This graph is structurally similar to the previous one, but the formula in predicate calculus is quite different:

```
(∃S)(set(S) ∧ (∀x∈S)(∃y)(∃z)(∃u)(∃v)(elephant(x)
    ∧ perform(y) ∧ circus(z) ∧ agnt(y,x) ∧ in(y,z) ∧
    ∧ earn(u) ∧ money(v) ∧ benf(u,x) ∧ ptnt(u,v))).
```

The quantifying word *many* behaves syntactically like *some*, but it has no counterpart in the standard predicate calculus. In conceptual graphs, it is represented by the symbol @many:

```
[(λx)[ELEPHANT: *x]←(AGNT)←[PERFORM]→(IN) →[CIRCUS]: {*}@many]-
     (BENF)←[EARN]→(PTNT)→[MONEY].
```

Semantically, a graph with the quantifier @many has denotation **true** if a large number of entities that satisfy the λ-expression (elephants that perform in a circus) also satisfy the conditions of the attached subgraph (earn money). But what is considered a large number depends on the type: a group of many ants is likely to have more members than a group of many elephants. For further discussion of such quantifiers, see Benthem and ter Meulen [1985] and Gärdenfors [1987].

The indexical referent #, which derives from definite articles and other contextual references, also behaves like a generalized quantifier. As examples, consider the next three sentences:

John is eating the cake.

John is the one who is eating the cake.

The cake is what John is eating.

After the definite references are resolved, all three sentences would express the same proposition, but they differ in their presuppositions. They all presuppose the existence of a cake in the current context, but the second and third sentences make other presuppositions as well. The first sentence has a simple conceptual graph:

```
[PERSON: John]←(AGNT)←[EAT]→(PTNT)→[CAKE: #].
```

The second sentence presupposes that the listener also knows that someone is eating the cake. It adds the information that John is the culprit:

```
[PERSON: John*x]
[(λy) [PERSON: *y]←(AGNT)←[EAT]→(PTNT)→[CAKE: #]: #*x].
```

The variable *$*x$* indicates a coreference link between the individual concept for John and the concept of the one who is eating the cake. The first step in resolving the reference is to search for a concept of some person eating cake and mark that concept with the variable *$*x$*. Then all three concepts marked with *$*x$* could be joined, and the λ-expression could be eliminated. The third sentence presupposes that the listener knows that John is eating something. It adds the information that the cake is coreferent with what John is eating:

```
[CAKE: #*x]
[(λy) [PERSON: John]←(AGNT)←[EAT]→(PTNT)→[*y]: #*x].
```

Two concepts in this graph are marked with the symbol #*x. Resolving these references requires two separate searches for previous discourse referents: one for the cake, and one for something that John is eating. When these referents have been found, four concepts will have been marked with *x. All four of them could then be joined, and the λ-expression could finally be expanded.

5.6 PLURAL REFERENTS

Plural referents in conceptual graphs can be represented by sets, but sets allow constructions that never occur in ordinary language. Set theory, for example, distinguishes the individual John from a singleton set {John} whose only element is John, a singleton set {{John}} whose only element is {John}, or an infinite number of other sets of sets whose only content is John nested within varying numbers of braces. Many logicians from Frege to Quine have found this aspect of set theory highly suspect: in the real world, there are no marks that distinguish John from any of those sets that contain him. To avoid the suspect constructions, several alternatives to set theory have been developed: Lesniewski's mereology [Luschei, 1962], Goodman's calculus of individuals [1972], and Bunt's theory of ensembles [1985]. All these systems obey Goodman's principle: "No distinction of entities without distinction of content." That slogan also holds for the normal use of plurals in natural language. Ideally, a system that obeys Goodman's principle should be used to define plural referents in conceptual graphs. Yet this chapter will use set theory, primarily because of its greater familiarity. Constructions with nested sets, however, will be avoided.

In predicate calculus, every plural noun phrase requires two quantified variables: one that represents a set, and one that ranges over the elements of the set. Those quantifiers may interact with other quantifiers in complex ways. As an example, consider the sentence *Every trailer truck has 18 wheels*. The universal quantifier for *every trailer truck* has precedence over the existential quantifier for the set of wheels. Following is the conceptual graph:

```
[TRAILER-TRUCK: ∀]→(PART)→[WHEEL: {*}@18].
```

As before, the symbol {*} represents some unspecified entities of type WHEEL, and the operator @18 says that there are 18 of them. The operator φ maps this graph to the following formula:

```
(∀x)(trailer-truck(x) ⊃ (∃S)(set(S) ∧ count(S,18) ∧
    (∀y∈S)(wheel(y) ∧ part(x,y))).
```

This formula has three quantifiers: a universal quantifier (∀x) that ranges over trailer trucks, an existential quantifier (∃ S) for a set of wheels for each *x*, and a universal quantifier (∀y) that ranges over wheels in S. In this case, the universal quantifier over trailer trucks includes the other two quantifiers in its scope.

For the trailer-truck example, the quantifiers for the set of wheels had narrower scope than the quantifier over trailer trucks. But sometimes the quantifiers associated with a plural noun have wider scope than the quantifiers for other things in the sentence. In such cases, they are said to *distribute* over the other things. To show the scope of quantifiers, the plural referent {*} may have a prefix that shows a distributive or a collective interpretation:

- **Distributive:** Dist{*} is the distributive symbol that implies the widest scope for the quantifiers associated with the set. Each element of the set participates separately in the pattern of relationships expressed by the sentence.
- **Collective:** Col{*} is the collective symbol that implies the narrowest scope for the quantifiers associated with the set. All the elements of the set participate together in the relationships expressed in the sentence.
- **Default:** {*} makes the least commitment; it is consistent with either the collective or the distributive interpretations and other states intermediate between them.

The symbol {*} is called a *generic plural* because it gives no indication of which individuals it contains. A specific plural like *Bill and Mary* would be represented {Bill, Mary}, and a partially specified plural like *Bill, Mary, and others* would be represented {Bill, Mary, *}. All of these forms may occur in the referent field of a concept with a prefix like Dist and a numeric count, as in [PERSON: Dist{Bill, Mary, *}@5], which would represent five persons distributively including Bill, Mary, and others.

For the sentence *Nine ladies are dancing*, the default representation gives no indication of whether the ladies are dancing the same dance or separate dances. But the sentence *Nine ladies are each dancing* suggests that they are dancing separately. Therefore, the prefix Dist with the plural referent indicates that interpretation:

```
[LADY: Dist{*}@9]←(AGNT)←[DANCE].
```

This graph indicates that the ladies distribute over the dances: for each lady there is an instance of dancing that is different from the dances by all the other ladies. That condition is difficult to state with only the quantifiers ∃ and ∀. To represent such relationships succinctly, Whitehead and Russell [1910] introduced the symbols E! and E!! as operators on classes; for each of those operators, it is possible to define a corresponding quantifier ∃! or ∃!!. Kleene [1952] introduced ∃ ! by the following definition:

```
(∃!x)P(x)  ≡  (∃x)(P(x)  ∧  (∀y)(P(y)  ⊃  x=y)).
```

The quantifier ∃! indicates that there exists one and only one object that satisfies the condition. But for the distributive interpretation of plurals, the ∃!! quantifier is needed to show that for each lady *x*, there is a dance *y* that is different from the dance for any other lady. That quantifier is defined by the following formula:

```
(∀x)(∃!!y)P(x,y)  ≡
    (∀x)(∃y)(P(x,y)  ∧  (∀z)(P(x,z)  ⊃  y=z)  ∧  (∀w)(P(w,y)  ⊃  x=w)).
```

This definition takes into account the dependency of *y* on *x*. If *y* depends on several variables x_1, x_2, ..., the definition can be generalized by treating *x* and *w* as vectors of variables.

Using the ∃!! quantifier, the φ operator can generate the following formula for the ladies dancing distributively:

```
(∃S)(set(S)  ∧  count(S,9)  ∧
    (∀x∈S)(∃!!y)(lady(x)  ∧  dance(y)  ∧  agnt(y,x))).
```

In this formula, (∃y) has been replaced by (∃!!y). It indicates that for each lady *x*, there is a separate dance *y*. To represent *Nine ladies are dancing together*, the prefix Col indicates a collective interpretation:

```
[LADY: Col{*}@9]←(AGNT)←[DANCE].
```

The prefix Col causes the quantifiers for the set to have narrower scope than the quantifier for the dance:

```
(∃y)(dance(y)  ∧  (∃S)(set(S)  ∧  count(S,9)  ∧
    (∀x∈S)(lady(x)  ∧  agnt(y,x)))).
```

In these examples, the different interpretations are represented by local changes to the graph, but the φ operator causes those local changes to propagate throughout the formula. The default reading that there may or may not be a separate instance of dancing for each lady is consistent with either the distributive or the collective reading. But the distributive and collective readings are inconsistent with one another.

With two plural nouns in the same sentence, the number of interactions between quantifiers increases further. Consider the sentence *Five blocks are supported by three pyramids*. From background knowledge about the fact that pyramids have pointed tops, a person could assume that the pyramids must be used collectively to support the blocks. Nothing is implied, however, about the number of blocks supported by each group of three pyramids. Following is the conceptual graph for that sentence:

```
[BLOCK: {*}@5]←(PTNT)←[SUPPORT]→(INST)→[PYRAMID: Col{*}@3].
```

This graph says that five blocks are the patient of support and three blocks collectively are the instrument of support. The operator φ maps this graph to a formula that shows the scope of quantifiers explicitly:

```
(∃S)(set(S) ∧ count(S,5) ∧ (∀x∈S)(block(x) ∧
   (∃T)(set(T) ∧ count(T,3) ∧ (∃z)(support(z) ∧
      (∀y∈T)(pyramid(y) ∧ ptnt(z,x) ∧ inst(z,y)))))).
```

This formula says that there exists a set *S* of five blocks, and for each *x* in *S*, there is a set of three pyramids and an instance *z* of support, where the block is the patient of support and each of the three pyramids is the instrument of support. In this formula, the universal quantifier on blocks (∀x) has wide scope, including the existential quantifier on the instances of support and the quantifiers on the pyramids. The universal quantifier on pyramids (∀y) has the narrowest scope. This formula permits, but does not require the instance of supporting and the set of pyramids to be different for each block.

The distributive interpretation requires a unique instance of supporting and set of pyramids for each block. In English, it may be represented by the word *each* in the sentence *Five blocks are each supported by three pyramids.* That word is represented by the prefix Dist in the conceptual graph:

```
[BLOCK: Dist{*}@5]←(PTNT)←[SUPPORT]→(INST) →[PYRAMID: Col{*}@3].
```

The formula for the distributive interpretation has two slight changes from the default; it uses the quantifiers ∃ !!T and ∃ !!z instead of the simple existentials:

```
(∃S)(set(S) ∧ count(S,5) ∧ (∀x∈S)(block(x) ∧
      (∃!!T)(set(T) ∧ count(T,3) ∧ (∃!!z)(support(z) ∧
            (∀y∈T)(pyramid(y) ∧ ptnt(z,x) ∧ inst(z,y)))))).
```

Whereas the default formula allows multiple blocks to share the same set of pyramids and instance of support, the quantifiers ∃!!T and ∃!!z require each block to have its own set of pyramids *T* and instance of support *z*. This formula implies that there are exactly 5 × 3 or 15 pyramids.

The collective interpretation implies that all the blocks collectively are supported by one set of three pyramids, also acting collectively. In English, it is suggested by the word *all* in the sentence *Five blocks are all supported by three pyramids.* The conceptual graph has the prefix Col for both the blocks and the pyramids:

```
[BLOCK: Col{*}@5]←(PTNT)←[SUPPORT]→(INST) →[PYRAMID: Col{*}@3].
```

In the corresponding formula, the quantifier ∀x over blocks and the quantifier ∀y over pyramids both have the narrowest scope:

```
(∃z)(support(z) ∧ (∃S)(set(S) ∧ count(S,5) ∧
   (∃T)(set(T) ∧ count(T,3) ∧ (∀x∈S)(block(x) ∧
      (∀y∈T)(pyramid(y) ∧ ptnt(z,x) ∧ inst(z,y)))))).
```

This formula shows a single instance of support *z*, where all the blocks are the patient of *z* and all the pyramids are the instrument of *z*. It implies that there are exactly three pyramids.

The distributive interpretation, which implies 15 pyramids, is inconsistent with the collective interpretation, which implies three pyramids. Both of them, however, are consistent with the default, which allows 3, 6, 9, 12, or 15 pyramids. In general, the default makes the weakest assumption: it is implied by either the distributive or the collective assumptions. When English sentences are mapped to conceptual graphs, the default symbol may be inserted in the referent field for any plural noun. As the representation is refined, the prefixes Col or Dist may be added. Sometimes the prefixes are determined by explicit words like *each, all*, or *together*. But sometimes background knowledge must be used, such as the knowledge that the pointed top of a pyramid cannot support a block by itself and three of them must be used collectively.

As these examples show, the formulas in predicate calculus are considerably more complex than the sentences in English. Furthermore, a local change in one word can cause a global rearrangement of the entire formula. In the English sentence, the noun phrase *five blocks* occurs at the beginning of the sentence, and the noun phrase *three pyramids* occurs at the end. But in the corresponding formula, the variables *S* and *x* for the first noun phrase are inextricably intermingled with the variables *T* and *y* for the second noun phrase.

In conceptual graphs, quantification is specified by concept nodes rather than operators placed in front of a formula or subformula. This difference makes it possible for an entire noun phrase together with all of its implicit or explicit quantifiers to be mapped to a single concept. A semantic interpreter that maps English to conceptual graphs can keep all the information about the phrase *five blocks* in one concept node and all the information about *three pyramids* in another node. Consequently, the mapping from English to the graphs is more direct, and the scattering of information takes place in a separate stage when conceptual graphs are translated to predicate calculus.

The importance of notation can best be appreciated by comparisons with other systems, such as Montague grammar. Link [1987], for example, gave the following formula as "a Montague-style translation" of the distributive interpretation of *Three men lifted a piano*:

$3\ men\ \mathbf{U}\ \lambda P\ \exists x\ [(3\ men)'(x) \wedge P(x)]$
$^{D}(lifted\ a\ piano)\ \mathbf{U}\ ^{D}\lambda y\ \exists z[piano'(z) \wedge lifted'(y,z)]$

This formula contains a great many symbols that are derived from the sentence by a complex process. By contrast, the corresponding conceptual graph has nearly a one-to-one mapping from the original sentence.

```
[MAN: Dist{*}@3]←(AGNT)←[LIFT]→(PTNT)→[PIANO].
```

The conceptual graph captures all the nuances of the Montague notation, and it is just as formally defined. There are many unsolved linguistic problems in representing plurals, and neither notation can solve them by itself. But conceptual graphs provide a more tractable tool for analyzing and representing them, both for linguistic theory and for the practical tasks of knowledge engineering.

5.7 SYNTACTIC ANNOTATIONS

Since conceptual graphs are a form of logic, they only represent the propositional content of a sentence; syntactic features of the original are lost. As an example, the sentences *The cat ate the fish* and *The fish was eaten by the cat* would both be represented by the same graph:

```
(PAST)→[SITUATION: [CAT: #]←(AGNT) ←[EAT]→(PTNT) →[FISH: #]].
```

This form captures the logical relationships, but it loses information about the emphasis. For language generation, further information is needed to determine which concept should become the subject. If eating happened to be the main topic, the graph might even be expressed as the phrase *The eating of the fish by the cat.*

To preserve syntactic nuances, research groups who have been using conceptual graphs often add *syntactic annotations* that are not included in the propositional content [Fargues et al., 1986; Velardi et al., 1988]. With annotations, the graph could be written

```
(PAST; v-infl)→[SITUATION:
     [CAT: #; n]←(AGNT; subj)←[EAT; v]→(PTNT; obj) →[FISH: #; n]].
```

The annotation "v-infl" indicates that the past tense was specified in a verb inflection; "n" and "v" indicate parts of speech; and "subj" and "obj" indicate that the relations AGNT and PTNT were expressed syntactically as subject and object. When the conceptual graph is translated to predicate calculus by φ, everything following the semicolons would be ignored. But the extra syntactic information could be used to reconstruct the original sentence. If the same information were stated with a gerund, *the eating of the fish by the cat*, the annotations would be completely different:

```
[CAT: #; n]←(AGNT; by)←[EAT: #; gerund] →(PTNT; of) →[FISH: #; n].
```

The annotations show that [EAT] was expressed as a gerund, and the relations AGNT and PTNT were expressed by the prepositions *by* and *of*.

Syntactic functions like subject and object are language dependent. For languages with similar syntax, such as Spanish and Italian or Swedish and Danish, the subject in the source language almost always corresponds to the subject in the target language. Even for languages like French and English, there are usually enough similarities to allow the same concept to be expressed as the subject in both languages. But for languages as different as Japanese and English, the parse trees are so different that the syntactic categories are unreliable as guides to the proper form of expression. As an example, consider the following Japanese sentence:

```
Kare  wa      shitte   iru   rashii.
He    (topic) knowing  be    seems.
```

This sentence could be interpreted as the following conceptual graph:

```
[SEEM]→(PTNT)→[SITUATION: [MALE: #]→(STAT)→[KNOW]].
```

This graph might then be expressed by any of the following English sentences:

It seems that he knows.

Apparently, he knows.

He seems to know.

All three of them express the same proposition, but each with a very different syntax. To indicate preferences, the conceptual graph could be annotated with information from the original sentence. The Japanese postposition *wa* marks *kare* as the topic, and the focus is *rashii* (which in Japanese is an adjective, not a verb). The corresponding concepts would have the annotations "topic" and "focus":

```
[SEEM; focus]→(PTNT)→[SITUATION: [MALE: #; topic]→(STAT)
    →[KNOW]].
```

When English is generated from this graph, the topic could be raised from the embedded context to make *he* the main subject. Since [SEEM] is marked as the focus, the language generator would also make it the main verb instead of an adverb like *apparently*. The preferred sentence would therefore be *He seems to know*.

Sometimes a sentence could be unambiguous syntactically, but it might not contain sufficient information to determine the conceptual relations. As an example, consider the following sentence:

It broke the window.

The pronoun *it* is the subject of the verb *broke*, but the conceptual relation cannot be determined until the referent of *it* has been resolved. If *it* refers to a dog, then the dog would be the agent of breaking; but if *it* refers to a baseball, then the baseball would be the instrument of breaking. In the initial stage of parsing the sentence, the syntactic annotation could be written in the relation node, but the relation type would be left unspecified:

```
[⊤: #; nonhuman]←(; subj)←[BREAK; v]→(PTNT; obj)→[ΩΙΝΔΟΩ: #].
```

Metonymy and ellipsis are two linguistic phenomena where the conceptual relations are often unknown, at least in the initial parsing stage. As an example of metonymy, consider the sentence *The White House announced the budget*. Syntactically, *White House* is the subject of *announce*, but semantic constraints rule out the building as a possible agent of the concept ANNOUNCE. Therefore, the semantic interpreter could construct a graph with "subj" as the syntactic annotation, but with the conceptual relation unspecified:

```
[BUILDING: White House]←(; subj)←[ANNOUNCE]→(PTNT) →[BUDGET: #].
```

After constructing this graph in the parsing stage, the semantic interpreter might search for background knowledge about the White House, discovering that many people work there who make announcements. It could therefore construct the following λ-expression to define a possible relation between an act and a building:

```
(λx,y) [ACT: *x]→(AGNT)→[PERSON]→(LOC)→[BUILDING: *y].
```

This definition relates an act *x* whose agent is a person located in a building *y*. The entire λ-expression could then be inserted just before the semicolon of the undefined relation:

```
[BUILDING: White House]→(
   (λx,y) [ACT: *x]→(AGNT)→[PERSON]→(LOC)→[BUILDING: *y];
      subj)←[ANNOUNCE]→(PTNT)→[BUDGET: #].
```

When the λ-expression is expanded, the concept marked by x (the first parameter) is joined to the concept with the arrow pointing towards the relation; and the concept marked by *y* (the second parameter) is joined to the concept with the arrow pointing away from the relation. The syntactic annotation "subj" must be dropped, since no single relation in the expansion exactly corresponds to the original subject of the sentence.

```
[BUILDING: White House]←(LOC)←[PERSON]←(AGNT)←[ANNOUNCE]-
   (PTNT)→[BUDGET: #].
```

This graph represents the expanded sentence *A person at the White House announced the budget*. The option of omitting the conceptual relation in cases of metonymy or ellipsis allows certain decisions to be deferred until additional information is obtained from the context or from background knowledge.

Ellipsis requires both syntax and semantics to reconstruct the missing information. Following is an example discussed by Prüst and Scha [1990]:

An American flag is hanging in front of every house.
So is a Canadian one.

This example is difficult to handle because the order of the quantifiers in English is the reverse of the order in predicate calculus. The universal quantifier for *every house* must contain the existential quantifier for *an American flag* within its scope. Furthermore, the result of expanding the ellipsis must have the same quantifier scope whether the second sentence is expressed *So is a Canadian one* or *A Canadian one is too*. The first sentence corresponds to the following formula:

```
(∀x:house) (∃y:flag) (∃z:hang) (american(y) ∧ ptnt(z,y)
 ∧ frontof(z,x)).
```

To resolve the ellipsis, information scattered through all parts of the formula must be retrieved and reassembled. Conceptual graphs, however, keep closely related information together; it is not necessary to tear a graph apart to show scope of quantifiers, since scope is determined by the precedence of the quantifiers, not by their linear order. Following are the graphs with their syntactic annotations:

```
[AMERICAN]←(ATTR)←[FLAG]←(PTNT; subj)←[HANG; v]→ (FRNT)→[HOUSE:∀].
[CANADIAN]←(ATTR)←[; type-anaphor]←(; subj) ←[; v, ellipsis].
```

Whereas the pronoun *it* refers to the same individual as its antecedent, the pronoun *one* refers to another individual of the same type. Therefore, the annotation "type-anaphor" specifies that the type label is copied from the antecedent, in this case [FLAG]. For verb-phrase anaphora, the annotation "ellipsis" would cause the system to unify the missing parts of the second graph with the corresponding parts of the first graph. As a result, PTNT would fill in the missing relation; HANG would become the type label for the verb node; and the attached subgraph→(FRNT)→[HOUSE: ∀] would be copied as well:

```
[CANADIAN]←(ATTR)←[FLAG]← (PTNT; subj)←[HANG; v]→
 [FRNT)→[HOUSE:∀].
```

In this graph, the rules for precedence of quantifiers would correctly include the existential quantifier on FLAG within the scope of the universal quantifier on HOUSE. Yet sometimes the existential quantifier may take precedence over the universal, as in the following sentence:

Some American flag was carried to every house.

This sentence says that there is a single flag for all of the houses. The existential quantifier for *some* must have higher precedence than the universal quantifier for *every*. To delimit the scope of the ∀ quantifier, a separate context box could be used to enclose the subgraph containing ∀ :

```
[AMERICAN]←(ATTR)←[FLAG: *x]
[[*x]←(PTNT; subj)←[CARRY; v]→ (DEST)→[HOUSE: ∀ ]].
```

In this graph, the flag is outside the scope of the ∀ quantifier, but the concept [CARRY] is within the scope of ∀, indicating a possibly separate act of carrying for each house. In some cases, however, the extra context boxes might block the resolution of ellipses by graph matching. Therefore, a syntactic annotation such as [FLAG; high-precedence] could be used to override the default precedence levels, at least until ellipses and related phenomena are resolved.

Since conceptual graphs are primarily a semantic representation, the choice of syntactic annotations depends on the theory of grammar that has been adopted, and it may also depend on the parsing strategy. In Chomsky's GB theory, for example, the notion of *c-command* is important for resolving pronoun references. If those references can be resolved before the conceptual graph is constructed, then the graph would contain coreference links that show the correct references. But if the resolution depends on further semantic or contextual information, the decision may be delayed until after the graph is constructed, and the c-command relationships would have to be shown with syntactic annotations. Normally, concept nodes are annotated with syntactic categories such as noun or verb, while relation nodes are annotated with syntactic functions such as subject or object; discourse features such as topic or focus or even more elaborate cross references might also be included. But a definitive catalog of annotations must depend on the particular syntactic theory.

5.8 MAPPING TO PREDICATE CALCULUS

Since conceptual graphs form a complete system of logic with their own rules of inference and model-theoretic semantics [Sowa, 1984], there is no need to map them to any other version of logic. Yet the definition of the φ operator that maps conceptual graphs to predicate calculus is interesting for several reasons: it explicitly shows the structural differences between the two systems; it enables theoretical advances made with one system to be adapted to the other; and it allows programs that use one system to interact with programs based on the other. The mapping by φ, however, loses information: it cannot represent context dependencies or syntactic annotations; it also maps plural referents into sets rather than a more congenial system such as mereology.

To simplify the definition of φ, it is convenient to break it down into several stages. The first stage partitions the conceptual graph into multiple contexts, in each of which there is only one kind of quantifier. The second stage starts from the outermost context and works inward, translating the graphs in each context to formulas in a sorted predicate calculus, using λ-expressions for defining new sorts whenever a λ-expression occurs in the type field of a context. Finally, the third stage translates the sorted predicate calculus to an unsorted form. As an example, consider the graph for *Every trailer truck has 18 wheels*:

```
[TRAILER-TRUCK:∀]→(PART)→[WHEEL: {*}@18].
```

The first step is to note that the ∀ quantifier has precedence over {*}. Therefore, the concept with that quantifier is placed in the outer context, and another context box is drawn around the rest of the graph:

```
[TRAILER-TRUCK: ∀*x]
[  [*x]→(PART)→[WHEEL:  {*}@18]].
```

When the graph is split in this way, a coreference link must be drawn between the concept in the outer context and the node [*x] that serves as a place holder in the inner context. This partitioned graph may be read *For every trailer truck x, x has 18 wheels.* The next step is to translate this graph to a sorted predicate calculus, working from the outermost context inward. A separate variable must be assigned to each quantifier. All the relations in each context are mapped to predicates with the same number of arguments, and they are linked by conjunctions:

```
(∀x:trailer-truck)
    (∀y∈{*}@18:wheel)part(x,y).
```

The third step is to expand the sort expressions according to appropriate rules for each type of quantifier (except for generalized quantifiers like @many, which cannot be translated further):

```
(∀x)(trailer-truck(x) ⊃ (∃S)(set(S) ∧ count(S,18) ∧
     (∀y∈S)(wheel(y) ∧ part(x,y)))).
```

Following are some observations about the translation process:

1. Ellipses, anaphora, and other phenomena that depend on syntactic annotations should be resolved before the φ operator is applied. Any annotations that change the quantifier precedence should be replaced by contexts that explicitly delimit the quantifier scope.
2. After all surface-related features have been resolved, the syntactic annotations may be erased: in concept and relation nodes, everything from the semicolon to the closing bracket or parenthesis is treated as a comment.
3. There is a precedence ranking for quantifiers: universals take precedence over existentials, and plural existentials take precedence over simple existentials.
4. A plural referent always results in two quantifiers: the outer one (which could be existential or universal) governs the set as a whole, and the inner one is a universal quantifier that ranges over the elements of the set.
5. The prefixes Dist and Col on plural referents affect the precedence of the two quantifiers for the set and its elements: Col lowers the precedence relative to

other quantifiers in the context; Dist raises the precedence, and it forces lower precedence existentials to switch from $\exists$ to $\exists$!! quantifiers.

6. Nested contexts limit the scope of quantifiers in the same way as parentheses in predicate calculus. But within a single context, all of the quantifiers can be ordered according to their precedence.
7. If the type field of a concept is a λ-expression $(\lambda x)g(x)$ where g is a conceptual graph, then the sort expression in the sorted predicate calculus is $(\lambda x)\varphi g(x)$.
8. When the sorted predicate calculus is translated to the unsorted formula, a universal quantifier of the form $(\forall x{:}t)p(x)$ expands to the form $(\forall x)(t(x) \supset p(x))$, and an existential quantifier $(\exists x{:}t)p(x)$ expands to $(\exists x)(t(x) \wedge p(x))$.
9. After the translation to the unsorted predicate calculus, an application of a λ-expression $(\lambda y)t(y)(x)$ may be converted to $t(x)$.

As this discussion shows, the mapping from conceptual graphs to predicate calculus is nontrivial. Conceptual graphs have been designed to simplify the mapping to and from natural languages; but since natural languages do not map smoothly to predicate calculus, much of the complexity appears in the definition of φ. This complexity is one more illustration of the unnaturalness of the predicate calculus as a semantic representation for natural language.

ACKNOWLEDGMENTS

The theory of conceptual graphs evolved over the years with contributions from a great many people. But the presentation in this chapter benefited from comments and discussions with Aaron Broadwell, Mike Gunther, Noi Hewett, Graeme Hirst, David Johnson, John Justeson, Shalom Lappin, Paula Newman, Remko Scha, Len Schubert, and Doug Skuce.

References

Benthem, J. van, and ter Meulen, A. (ed.s). 1985. *Generalized Quantifiers in Natural Language*. Foris Publications, Dordrecht.

Bunt, H. 1985. *Mass Terms and Model-Theoretic Semantics*. Cambridge University Press, Cambridge.

El Guindi, F. 1986. *The Myth of Ritual*, University of Arizona Press, Tucson.

Fargues, J., Landau, M-C., Duguord, A., and Catach, L. 1986. Conceptual graphs for semantics and knowledge processing, *IBM Journal of Research and Development* 30(1):70–79.

Gärdenfors, P. (ed.). 1987. *Generalized Quantifiers*, D. Reidel Publishing Co., Dordrecht.

Goodman, N. 1972. *Problems and Projects*. Bobbs-Merrill Co., New York.

Kamp, H. 1981a. Events, discourse representations, and temporal references, *Languages* 64:39–64.

———. 1981b. A theory of truth and semantic representation. In *Formal Methods in the Study of Language*, Groenendijk, J.A.G., Janssen, T.M.V., and Stokhof, M.B.J. (ed.s.), pp. 277–322. Mathematical Centre Tracts, Amsterdam.

Kleene, S.C. 1952. *Introduction to Metamathematics*. D. Van Nostrand Co., Princeton.

Link, G. 1987. Generalized quantifiers and plurals. In [Gärdenfors, 1987; pp. 151–180].

Luschei, E.C. 1962. *The Logical Systems of Lesniewski*. North-Holland Publishing Co., Amsterdam.

Peirce, C.S. 1882. Letter, Peirce to O.H. Mitchell. In *Writings of Charles S. Peirce*, vol. 4, pp. 394–399. Indiana University Press, Bloomington, IN.

———. 1897–1906. Manuscripts on existential graphs. Some are reprinted in *Collected Papers of Charles Sanders Peirce*, Burks, A.W. (ed.), vol. 4, pp. 320–410. Harvard University Press, Cambridge, MA; others are summarized by [Roberts, 1973].

Prüst, H., and Scha, R. 1990. A discourse approach to verb-phrase anaphora. In *Proceedings of ECAI 90*, pp. 528–530.

Roberts, D.D. 1973. *The Existential Graphs of Charles S. Peirce*. Mouton, The Hague.

Sowa, J.F. 1979. Definitional mechanisms for conceptual graphs, *Graph Grammars and their Application to Computer Science and Biology*, Claus, V., Ehrig, H., and Rozenberg, G. (ed.s), pp. 426–439. Springer-Verlag, Berlin.

———. 1984. *Conceptual Structures: Information Processing in Mind and Machine*. Addison-Wesley, Reading, MA.

———. Using a lexicon of canonical graphs in a semantic interpreter. In *Relational Models of the Lexicon*, Evens, M. (ed.). Cambridge University Press, pp. 113–137.

———. 1990. Definitional mechanisms for restructuring knowledge bases. In *Methodologies for Intelligent Systems 5*, Ras, Z.W. (ed.). North-Holland Publishing Co., New York.

———. Forthcoming. Lexical structures and conceptual structures. In *Semantics in the Lexicon*, Pustejovsky, J. (ed.), to be published by Kluwer.

Sowa, J.F., and Way, E.C. 1986. Implementing a semantic interpreter using conceptual graphs, *IBM Journal of Research and Development* 30(1):57–69.

Velardi, P., Pazienza, M.T., and DeGiovanetti, M. 1988. Conceptual graphs for the analysis and generation of sentences, *IBM Journal of Research and Development* 32(2):251–267.

Whitehead, A.N. and Russell, B. 1910. *Principia Mathematica*. Cambridge University Press, Cambridge (second edition 1925).

6

SENTENCES, SITUATIONS, AND PROPOSITIONS

Robert Wilensky
(University of California, Berkeley)

Abstract

Sentences are about situations. How to represent the situations that sentences describe is an important problem for AI. In particular, it is useful for a representation to provide entities corresponding to individual situations, and to be able to represent facts about a situation separately from stating that something is a situation of a particular field.

Most semantic network formalisms seem to achieve one of these criteria at the expense of the other. However, it is possible to achieve both criteria by extending the usual ontology of situations. Such an extended ontology poses a number of questions about the representation of situations corresponding to sentences designating states, about the representation of situations corresponding to sentences involving logical connectives, about the propositional objects, and the equality of situations and of propositions. Some of the implications entailed in resolving these questions are surprising. For example, a proper treatment of propositional objects seems to eliminate the need for intensions *per se*.

6.1 INTRODUCTION

The relation between sentences and what they describe is an important theoretical and practical representational issue. This issue comprises two primary components: an ontological issue about what the major classes of entities to be represented are, and a formal issue of how best to represent them. Some semantic network systems make a point of providing entities corresponding to propositions, and some provide entities corresponding to situations, although the distinction between the two is sometimes confused. Both propositions and situations are useful, but for quite different purposes. Also, the representation of situations and propositions can be done in various ways, some of which have important representational advantages.

Situations on the whole have been relatively neglected. When they are provided at all, the ontology of situations has generally been too limited. One way to overcome these limitations is to introduce an operator that associates a situation with any logical sentence, as advocated by Schubert and Hwang [1989]. Unfortunately, such an approach appears to introduce serious difficulties.

Instead, I suggest that the best solution is simply to extend the usual ontology of situations somewhat, while maintaining a separate set of entities that correspond to propositions. The components of this proposal are by and large familiar. However, considering them together gives a somewhat novel picture. For example, it seems that the notion of intensions becomes unnecessary. Some of the implications of an extended ontology of situations are explored, including the relation of propositions to situations and the notion of equality of situations.

6.2 BACKGROUND

In this section I review some of the issues that have been used to motivate certain representational choices. I believe most of this material is well known. However, I review and elaborate on it here to emphasize what is at stake in these representational decisions, and what problems remain with various approaches currently in use.

Many theories of natural language presume that sentences describe events, states, or processes. (Events, states, and processes have been collectively called *eventualities* by Bach [1983]; the term *situation* has also become popular in this context [Barwise and Perry, 1983]. I will use the latter term informally here as a superordinate category encompassing actions, events, states, processes, and whatever else sentences may refer to, but without importing any particular theoretical baggage.) For both theoretical and practical reasons, it is useful to conceive of situations as entities to which one may refer or about which one may say things. On the other hand, sentences are purported to have a logical form of a predicate-argument nature, with the matrix verb serving as the predicate and its complements specifying the arguments. However, this logical form is propositional, and does not readily provide an entity to designate the underlying situation.

For example, consider a simple sentence like the following:

(1) Jan gave Lynn a cigar.

The logical form commonly attributed to (1) is some variant of the following:

(2) Give(jan,lynn,cigar1)

(where temporal information and the facts that "jan" and "lynn" are people and "cigar1" a cigar are ignored for the time being). Now suppose (1) were followed by

(3) This made Terry furious.

We would like some way to say that the pronoun "this" refers to the event described in (1). However, there is no readily apparent way of expressing this fact given the representation of (1) as (2). The problem is that while (2) expresses the logical structure of the sentence, it does not provide any object designating the reported event. We might be tempted to have the predicate corresponding to the verb "make" take a proposition as an argument, and then represent (3) as the following:

(4) Make(Give(jan,lynn,cigar1),furious)

But this approach doesn't help, because we have no way of asserting that this was the same event as the one described in (1), and not some other, albeit similar, occurrence.

A second motivation for having entities corresponding to situations is to capture important generalizations across varying linguistic forms. For example, consider the following utterance:

(5) Jan giving Lynn a cigar made Terry furious.

Here the phrase *Jan giving Lynn a cigar* has a quite similar content to that of (1). However, the stance of a speaker using this sentence to its content is different: Both sentences describe an event of Jan giving Lynn a cigar, while the speaker of (1) is asserting the occurrence of the event, and that of (5) presupposing it (or, as Schubert et al., [1979] would say, the *propositional content* is the same, while the *pragmatic aspects* differ). Whatever representation we choose should make this similarity of content apparent, while allowing us to express the difference in attitude taken toward this event.

This need becomes even more apparent when we consider lexical nouns that encode events [Parsons, 1985]. Some nouns, like "punch" and "destruction," seem to describe the same events as certain verbs, e.g., "punch" "destroy." This claim is supported by the observation that sentences like the following appear to have the same truth conditions, if we adjust for presupposition:

(6) The Romans destroyed the city, resulting in much grief.

(7) The destruction of the city by the Romans resulted in much grief.

Whatever meaning difference one can discern between the noun and the verb does not appear to be attributable to a difference in the events they encode. Hence the representational reflex of attributing a predicate to a verb and an argument position to a complement would pave over a crucial and obvious generalization.

A third argument for representing the designatum of a sentence as an entity is a corollary of the first two. Namely, there are often a number of different things to say about a situation, and we need some way of saying only some of them and of saying additional things about that situation later on. In particular, elements of a sentence frequently specify the time, place, and manner of a situation, as well as its modality and the speaker's attitude toward the situation. Some of these may be thought of as higher order predicates. However, such an approach is problematic in some cases.

In particular, consider the problems that arise from distinguishing adjuncts from complements. Many proposals attribute argument positions to a predicate in accordance with the complement structure of the verb associated with that predicate; adjuncts are dealt with in some other manner. Thus, in (1) above, we presumed that the predicate corresponding to the verb "give" is a three-place predicate because this use of the verb takes three complements. However, suppose we had continued the sentence with "in New York." Since this phrase is an adjunct, we would not have provided an argument position for it. Indeed, such a solution would not easily be possible, since an arbitrary number of such adjuncts can be present. Moreover, the adjunct seems to predicate something about the whole event, rather than constitute a component of it, as was the case for the complements.

We can accommodate such adjuncts into the representation by introducing a higher order "in" predicate, one of whose arguments would be the predication describing the entire situation (or, alternatively, the application of some functional operator to this formula, denoting the situation) and the other, the location. However, this proposal is awkward for many reasons, not the least of which is that we would then have at least two semantically unmotivated but formally distinct "in" predicates, one of which applies to formulas, and the other to individuals (compare [Shapiro, 1971b]).

The situation is compounded by cases in which the adjunct does not appear to apply to the entire situation. For example, consider the following sentences:

(8a) Jan stumbled into the room.

(8b) Jan threw up in the sink.

(8c) Jan bled on a shirt.

(8d) Jan sliced the salami onto the bread.

Note first that treating the prepositional phrases as complements appears untenable. If we did so, then we must make one of two assumptions: We could assume that each verb corresponds to a predicate with one more argument than had been obvious, and that this argument is omitted most of the time. However, this proposal would lead to the wrong analysis of at least some cases; for example, Jan stumbling doesn't require that Jan stumbled directionally. Alternatively, we can assume that each verb corresponds to several different predicates (e.g., "bleed" and "bleed-directionally," and "throw-up," and "throw-up-directionally"). But this proposal requires a gratuitous meaning postulate to sanction the inference from the $n + 1$-place predicate to the n-place predicate (e.g., to sanction "Jan bled" from "Jan bled on a shirt"). Both alternatives seem unmotivated, at best.

Thus, we must consider the prepositional phrases in (8) to be adjuncts. However, if adjuncts are not to be incorporated in the associated predicate, we are left in the following situation. We can once again attempt to treat the adjunct as a higher order predicate. For example, we might represent (8c) as the following:

(9) Onto(Bleed(jan),shirt1)

But then prepositions like "into" and "onto" get a radically different treatment when they are complements from when they are adjuncts, even when there is no semantic justification for doing so. This situation is worse than the case above in which the prepositional phrase modified the whole sentence, because here, there is presumably no difference at all in meaning between the use of the prepositional phrase in sentences like (8d) and those in which it is a complement, such as the following:

(10) Jan threw the ball onto the roof.

In sum, when the distinction between being a complement and an adjunct does not correspond to a distinction in meaning, but is merely a fact about whether or not a verb happens to subcategorize for a particular type of constituent, then the difference should not be reflected in the underlying logical form. But doing so appears to be problematic if the designatum of the matrix verb and complements are thought to correspond to a predication.

Note that a version of this problem applies whenever we have the quite common case of a verb that can describe the same situation with several different complement structures. For example, consider the following sentences:

(11a) Jan opened the jar.

(11b) Jan opened the lid (to the jar).

(12a) Jan tied the string.

(12b) Jan tied a knot (in the string).

If we proposed having a predicate-per-valence description, we would once again require a meaning postulate to recognize that the (a) sentences follow from the (b) sentences. Thus, one goal of whatever representation we adopt should be to do without an additional postulate when the inference is analytic.

Before going on, note that the various problems just presented are essentially invariant with the other choices one can make about representation. For example, if one believes that the meaning of "give" should be decomposed into primitives, and that only the latter can appear in the description of events, then all the same problems persist.

6.3 PROPOSED SOLUTIONS

To summarize, the problem is to determine what representations we can use for the situations described by utterances so that proper generalizations can be captured. In particular, the grammatical form of lexical items should not have an undue influence, lest we should be incapable of capturing generalizations that hold between various parts of speech or about terms that admit various complements and adjuncts.

6.3.1 Situation-based Approaches

A well-known solution to some of the problems mentioned above was proposed by Reichenbach [1947] and elaborated by Davidson [1969, 1980). Basically, this solution amounts to postulating another argument for every event predicate. According to this account, the logical form of (1) includes not (2) but rather

(13) Exists x (Give(jan,lynn,cigar1,x))

where *x* is construed as an event. We will discuss extending this sort of analysis to states below, but for the time being we will assume that such an extension is straightforward.

This particular formalism can be characterized as "situation based" and "predicate based." By situation based, I mean that the system provided entities corresponding to individual situations (e.g., the variable in (13)). By "predicate based," I mean that the situations are specified by altering each domain predicate in some fashion, in this case, by the inclusion of an additional argument. An example of a use of such a notation is [Hobbs, 1986].

It is the situation-based character of the formalism that provides a solution to some of the concerns voiced above. If we skolemize (13) to produce a constant x1, say, then we have our unique referent. We could postulate that the logical form corresponding to (3), with the referent of the pronoun established, was not (4) but rather the following:

(14) Make(x1,furious)

Similarly, *Jan giving Lynn a cigar* might be represented as x1 with the same formula predicated about it as in (13). In other words, the "giving" event described in (1) and (5) has the same logical form, although (1) asserts that this event transpired while (5) presumes it.

Also, it is trivial to add in first-order format information about the event. For example, specifying the proper time might be done by something like the following:

(15) Before(x1,NOW)

Similarly, the logical form of verbal adjuncts is easy to accommodate in such a formalism. For example, the sentence

(16) Jan gave Lynn a cigar in New York.

might be construed as follows:

(17) Exists x (Give(jan,lynn,cigar1,x) & In(x,newyork))

6.3.2 Aspectualized Representations

These last two observations point to some degree of arbitrariness in deciding on the argument structure of various predicates, to which the situation-based notation offers an attractive solution. Instead of having to predetermine a fixed number of arguments for a given predicate, we assume that each predicate has only one argument—namely, the situation. Other aspects of the situation (for example, if it is an action, who its actor is) are added by additional predications completely analogously to the way time and location were added above. In this formulation, (1) is given the logical structure

(18) Exists x (Give(x) & Agent(jan,x) & Patient(cigar1,x)
& Recipient(lynn,x))

In (18), the argument positions of the main predicate are exchanged for a set of two-place predicates. This style of representation is called *slot-assertion notation* by Charniak and McDermott [1985]. Indeed, one may view the use of these predicates as a notational variant that allows us to make a predication with a variable number of arguments (with more than one possibly being in the same argument "position"). I will use the informal term *aspectual* [Wilensky, 1986] for any two-place predicate introduced into a representation for the purpose of separating the assertion of an aspect of a situation from the assertion that something is a particular kind of situation. Aspectuals are meant to include the arcs of some semantic network systems (in particular, those arcs emanating from nodes denoting situations) and the slots of most frame-based systems.

The particular aspectuals used in the example above are the familiar relations imported from case theory. But nothing in our argument depends on the choice of these predicates, although one must eventually specify a set that is appropriate for the particular situation involved. Some theories assume only a small set of quite general aspectuals; others prefer a much larger set that depends on the situation, for example, *Giver*, *Givee*, *Given* for *Give* situations. We make no commitment here and use whatever aspectuals are useful for expository purposes.

With this representation, verbal complements can now be given the same logical treatment as verbal adjuncts: Both are represented by predication using aspectuals; e.g., extending (18) to incorporate "in New York" involves adding a predication that looks formally identical to those corresponding to the complements.

Representations for nonsentential verbal adjuncts can be given analogously. For example, (8c) above could be represented as the following:

(19) Exists x,y,z (Bleed(x) & Experiencer(jan,x) & Patient(y,x) & Blood(y)
& Onto(y,z) & Shirt(z))

Representing the adjunct requires only the addition of the last two predications, and the representation of the sentence without the adjunct is identical to (19) without these predications.[1]

Thus, such a notation allows us to represent adjuncts and complements in a logical structure that captures what is being expressed, as opposed to how these elements are packaged into the language. The latter difference is maintained in the grammar, where it belongs, but not in the logical form.

Note also that the resulting notation treats situations analogously to physical objects, persons, etc. For example, had our representation of (1) been more elaborate, and included information about the nature of the entities corresponding to the noun phrases in the sentence, it might have been more like the following:

(20) Exists x,jan,lynn,cigar1
(Give(x) & Agent(jan,x) & Person(jan)
& Patient(cigar1,x) & Cigar(cigar1)
& Recipient(lynn,x) & Person(lynn))

Here *Person(jan)* denotes the fact that Jan is a person analogously to *Give(x)* denoting that *x* is a giving event. In both cases we would have to make further predications to express additional facts about the nature of the entities. For example, we would need an additional predication to express that the first name of the person Jan is "Jan," just as we needed an additional predication to express that the patient of the giving event was a cigar.

---

[1] One might argue for a more elaborate analysis of "onto" both for (8c) and (10). For example, another plausible analysis is that there are events described by the sentences (bleeding and throwing, respectively) and that these caused additional events (blood moving onto a shirt and a ball moving onto a roof). The important point is that parallel analyses are available for the two sentences using either analysis.

This uniformity is particularly important in capturing the unity of a preposition like "in," when we have the intuition that the same spatial meaning is being used regardless of the arguments. Thus, the representation of the phrase *the pen in the box* can make use of exactly the same "in" as that of *The pen broke in the box.* Both have the following logical form

(21) In(x,box1)

where *x* is alternatively a pen, or the event of a pen breaking.

Finally, the analytic inferences involving verbs with different valence structures can be handled appropriately. We specify the structure of the underlying event by specifying the set of aspectuals it accommodates. Verbs with multiple valences hence may specify the same event but supply the arguments to different aspectuals. An event-class corresponding to the verb "open," for example, might have aspectuals for the object constituting a barrier or container, the object moved to create the opening, etc. Then the representations for "open the jar" and "open the lid" could be identical except for the aspectuals that the uses of the verb specify; i.e., the first would relate an opening event to a jar via a "containing-object" aspectual, and the second would relate an opening event to a lid via a "object-moved" aspectual. Similarly, in the case of optional complements, when a complement is omitted, the representation is identical except for the omission of a predication using the corresponding aspectual.

Note that the key property of the representation that solves many problems for us is that it is amenable to "aspectualization," i.e., we can predicate different aspects of a situation separately. A situation-based, predicate-based system does not necessarily have this property, as we noticed when a predicate provides argument positions corresponding to complements. However, a situation-based, predicate-based system in which domain predicates take only situations as arguments is aspectualized. Henceforth, when I refer to predicate-based representations, I will assume they are aspectualized, unless otherwise noted.

6.3.3 Category-based Approaches

Another way to have representations that are amenable to aspectualization is to have within one's system entities corresponding to categories, including categories for situation types, e.g., *Giving* and *Event,* as well as *Person* and *Book.* We would also introduce a predicate, say AIO (**A**n **I**ndividual **O**f) relating an individual to a category it belongs to. Then, instead of (20) we would have the following:

(22) Exists x,jan,lynn,cigar1
    (AIO(x,Giving) & Agent(jan,x) & AIO(jan,Person)
        & Patient(cigar1,x) & AIO(cigar1,Cigar)
        & Recipient(lynn,x) & AIO(lynn,Person))

Such formulas, or perhaps, the skolemized versions of them, can be viewed as the basis for many semantic network and "frame-based" systems, in particular, of all those formalisms that have some explicit relation meaning "an individual of." I will call a proposal in which there are individuals corresponding to categories of situations a *category-based* representation.[2] I would construe Simmons [1973], Rumelhart et al. [1972], Hendrix [1975], Schank [1973], Bobrow and Winograd [1977], Roberts and Goldstein [1977] and Brachman [1979] as all adopting category-based schemes of some sort.

This classification is akin to what Israel [1983] calls *inheritance-based networks*. However, the above systems vary in the degree to which inheritance *per se* is prominent in them; for example, inheritance is rather conscientiously avoided in Conceptual Dependency [Schank, 1973], while it is quite prominent in KRL [Bobrow and Winograd, 1977] and KL-ONE [Brachman, 1979]. What all these systems do have in common is the idea of an individual of a category corresponding to a situation type.

One advantage of category-based representations is the availability of categories for predication. For example, the representation for a classic sentence like *The Saber-toothed tiger is extinct* could involve a reference to the concept *Saber-toothed-tiger*. However, I will not make a substantial case here for the advantages of category-based over predicate-based representation, except to note that an aspectualized representation seems inherent in the category-based representation, whereas a predicate-based approach must be tailored to have this property.

Some semantic networks make a habit of providing categories, but no individuals corresponding to situations. Rather, in these formalisms, the emphasis is on nodes representing propositions. For example, Cercone [1975], Schubert et al., [1979] and especially Shapiro [1979] fall into this category. Such systems are sometimes called *propositional semantic networks*, although this term seems to be used to emphasize the point that, in such a system, every accessible assertion is a node [Maida and Shapiro, 1985], rather than as a contrast between systems that have nodes for propositions versus those that have nodes for situations. To be sure, such systems are not necessarily hostile to the inclusion of individuals corresponding to situations; they just do not make a commitment to provide such individuals. While having individuals corresponding to propositions is a useful idea we will

---

[2] Allen [1987] interprets the categories of semantic networks as corresponding to logical predicates rather than to individuals. Perhaps this is because the semantics of the terms corresponding to categories might be problematic for some, who like to interpret formulas over models that somehow correspond to the world (what I have called a *direct correspondence* theory [Wilensky, 1986]). In this case, *Giving*, etc., probably have to be construed as sets. However, semantic network theorists (e.g., Maida and Shapiro [1985]) often prefer to interpret formulas with respect to some normative cognitive agent (a *cognitive correspondence theory*). In this case, *Giving* is supposed to be the concept of giving; each individual of such a category denotes a conception of an individual event; the actual events, etc., are generally not designated at all.

return to later, it does not address the problem of providing referents for situational anaphora.

Note that propositional and situation-based representations will often use the same labels for arcs, but with a quite different semantics. For example, Shapiro [1971a), Schubert et al. [1979] and Shapiro [1979] use arc labels as uninterpreted syntactic markers. Thus, in SNePS [Shapiro, 1979], one can have a node representing the proposition in *John loves Mary*, and relate this node to nodes for John and Mary using arcs labels "Agent" and "Object," respectively. However, propositions do not have agents or objects, so the arc "Agent" is simply an indicator of the first argument of the predication represented by the node. This fact is clearer in Schubert et al. [1979], in which the corresponding arcs would be simply be labeled "A" and "B." I do not regard such uninterpreted arcs as aspectuals.

In sum, *situation-based* representations provide situations as part of the meaning of utterances; *propositional representations* provide propositions. Only situation-based representations address the problem of providing referents for situational anaphora. *Predicate-based* systems introduce situations into the notation by providing argument positions for situations in various predicates; *category-based* systems introduce situations by providing objects corresponding to categories and a predicate or some other apparatus that one can use to specify that some entity is an individual of a category or a type of situation. Furthermore, it is convenient if our representation is *aspectualized*, i.e., if we can separate the assertion that something is a situation from other facts about that situation, such as which roles are played by which participants. Both situation-based and propositional representations come in aspectualized and nonaspectualized varieties, although category-based situational representations seem to be naturally aspectualized. Also, the aspectuals of aspectualized propositional representations are just syntactic markers for argument positions of a relation, while the aspectuals of situation-based notations encode relations between situations and participants.

6.4 A PROBLEM

Situation-based representations provide objects corresponding to situations; these are convenient when subsequent utterances refer to previously mentioned events. However, an important characteristic of situation-based proposals is that their vocabulary is generally *lexically determined*. That is, the vocabulary of predicates or categories is approximately that of the word senses of the various verbs, etc., recognized as designating situations. However, as Schubert and Hwang [1989] point out, such representations do not yield an object for sentences involving logical operators or quantifiers, but only for atomic formulas. They give as an example the following sentence:

(23) Everyone looked at Mary.

They note that standard situation-based representations would provide no object for the event described by this sentence, even though such an event may be referred to subsequently, if followed, for example, by a sentence like (3) above:

(3) This made Terry furious.

Schubert and Hwang propose a solution to this problem in the form of *episodic logic*, in which symbols designating situations are related to propositions capturing the logical structure of the sentence via connectives introduced just for this purpose. In particular, the connective "**" relates a proposition to a situation it "characterizes." For example, (23) would be represented[3] as

(24) Exists e1 (**(All x (Person(x) → Look-at(x,mary)),e1))

Here "e1" is the situation with characterization "Everyone looked at Mary." This gives us a handle on the entire situation, just as the word-style representations did on events requiring only atomic formulas. For example, we can represent the following sentence

(25) This made her blush.

as describing the situation

(26) Exists e2 (Cause(e1,e2) & **(Blush(mary),e2))

allowing the scope of the existential in (24) to extend a bit further than the parenthesis would ordinarily allow.

Schubert and Hwang also propose a more fundamental operator, "*," that is used to relate a situation to a partial description. To illustrate the significance of characterizing versus partial descriptions, they note that, if it were everyone looking at Mary *derisively* that made her blush, then (24) with "**" replaced with "*" would still be true, even though (23) together with (25) would not be.

I call Schubert and Hwang's proposal a *proposition-based situation* proposal. That is, they define situations as objects that correspond to logical propositions. Note that what I am calling a proposition-based situation solution has little to do with what has sometimes been called a *propositional semantic network*, which Maida and Shapiro [1985] describe as a network "in which *every* assertion that can be stored or accessed ... is ... represented by a node." Rather, I use the term to refer to proposals in which situations are defined by an operator that relates them to a logical formula.

---

[3] These authors use the terms "event," "situation," and "episode" interchangeably. Also, I have omitted temporal information here which the authors include in their analyses. Finally, Schubert and Hwang use an infix notation I have eschewed for uniformity's sake.

Schubert and Hwang's proposal is very attractive because it allows one to have situational objects corresponding to arbitrary propositions. However, it is not unproblematic. First, while it provides a way to refer to the entire situation, it does not provide a way to refer to its individual components. For example, in (24), each individual looking action is not readily accessible. This is problematic for several reasons. One is that there is no obvious way to specify case relations as in (20). That is, we cannot explicitly represent the fact that Mary was the patient of any number of individual looking actions. Another problem is that there is no obvious way to relate one of these individual events to the entire situation. For example, if (23) were followed by

(27) and someone looked at her derisively

then how do we express the fact that the event underlying (27) is not unrelated to the event described in (23)?

We are also back to a system in which complements and adjuncts are treated quite differently. Schubert and Hwang represent verbal complements as arguments to the corresponding predicate, but they advocate having temporal modifiers that take episodes as arguments. Thus, they use

(28) Before(e1,NOW)

to express the fact that episode e1 occurred in the past. And, as in the example above, causal relations hold between episodes. But then the representational implications of being a complement versus an adjunct, and all the associated problems discussed above and conveniently eliminated by either predicate- or category-based representations are reintroduced. That is, the representation is not aspectualized.

Even worse, it is not clear that the semantics of "**" and "*" can be made coherent. In particular, what it means to "characterize" a situation seems problematic. Schubert suggests[4] that the situation described by

(29) Looking down the barrel of the gun, John fired the gun.

is characterized by the representation corresponding to the main clause, but not by the representation corresponding to the dependent clause. However, the same would then presumably apply to a sentence like the following:

(30) John fired his gun looking down the barrel.

But this sentence could be followed with

---

[4] Personal communication. Schubert and Hwang have revised their ideas considerably since the initial publication of their 1989 paper. In particular, "**" now means "completely describes," i.e., that everything else one an say about an event completely described by a proposition is entailed by that proposition. This proposal is somewhat similar to one I propose below *re* equality of situations. However, I believe that the other difficulties of proposition-based situation representations, except perhaps the difficulty involving causation, are still problematic for this new proposal.

(31) This enabled him to focus clearly on the target.

This sentence is problematic since we have no event characterized by "looking down the barrel," and only such events are supposed to be the bearers of useful causal information.

Indeed, the whole purpose of introducing the notion of characterizing an event seems to be to avoid the annoying problem of figuring out, when one event is predicated to cause another, what is really being asserted to have caused what, since an indefinite number of predications might apply to the two events, but most of these are not presumed to describe factors that have any causal role. However, there appears to be no in-principle basis for deciding whether a predication is characterizing or not. In any case, events or situations are entities in the world, so their characterization couldn't matter with respect to causality.

The power of a proposition-based situation representation may also be problematic. In particular, it raises the question of how in principle we decide what gets reified. For example, that event e1 causes event e2 was itself not reified above. But this seems to be a perfectly good situation. Of course, Schubert and Hwang's notation makes it easy to express this fact:

(32) Exists e3 (*(Cause(e1,e2),e3))

But when are such expressions meaningful? For example, consider what would it mean to say something like the following:

(33) Exists e (*(Time(e1,NOW),e))

We can paraphrase (33) as *The situation of event e1 occurring at the present*. But it is not clear what situation in the world *e* can be referring to. That is, if situations are in the world, then it wouldn't be meaningful to distinguish an event, which occurs at a certain time, and the situation of that event occurring at a certain time.

Part of the difficulty here may be that Schubert and Hwang's notation is intended to be situational, but the objects associated with formulas are better interpreted as propositions rather than as events. That is, what the notation really allows us to do is to tag propositions for subsequent reference. But propositions and events are quite different. Hence a number of problems arise; for example, the need to identify which of the multiple propositions that can be given the same identifier are implicated in causal relations and the like. I will elaborate on this point below.

Some of these problems might be superficial. For example, the problem of describing situations so that causal relations between them can be handled using Schubert and Hwang's representation might be circumvented as follows. We drop the notion of characterization altogether, and define a new predicate, say "Reason-for." Using this predicate, we could express the meaning of the sentence

(34) Everyone looked at Mary, causing her to blush.

by the formula

(35) Exists e1,e2 (*(All x (Person(x) → Look-at(x,mary)),e1) &
*(Blush(mary),e2) &
Cause(e1,e2) &
Reason-for(Cause(e1,e2),
*(All x (Person(x) → Look-at(x,mary),e1))))

That is, we separate the fact that one event caused another from the reason that it caused it (in this case that it was a certain category of event). In general, depending on one's theory of causation, the details of the description of the reason might vary. Using such a representation, we can harmlessly assert that one event caused another, but we would have to rely on the additional information in the "Reason-for" predication to determine how the causation related to various facts that were known about these events.

Similarly, while the representation does not make explicit facts like the relationship of individual looking events to the overall situation, it is still possible to add this information. However, the other difficulties appear to be intrinsic. In particular, it does not appear to be possible to reaspectualize the representation. For example, the episodic logic representation of

(36) Jan looked at Lynn.

would be

(37) Exists e (*(look-at(jan,lynn),e)).

Now, suppose we tried to regain an aspectualized form by removing arguments from "look-at" and moving them to aspectual predications of *e*. Doing so would yield the following form:

(38) Exists e (*(look-at(),e) & Experiencer(jan,e) & Patient(lynn,e))

But this is essentially a category-based notation, with predicates of no arguments substituting for categories and the operator "*" having the corresponding semantics to the predicate *AIO*. (I explore the implications of this observation below.) Moreover, * has lost its ability to relate an arbitrary proposition to an event; should we try to quantify over experiencers, as was the case in the original sentence (23), we would no longer have an object that corresponds to the whole event.

Another possibility along this line would be to have both predicate- or category-based situations *and* proposition-based situations within the same representation. That is, we could have both entities that are predicated to be situations via a first-order predicate, plus an entities that are related to formulas via an operator. Indeed, Moore [1989] makes just such a proposal. In his proposal, however, events and situations are different objects. Simply put, events consist of lots (typically an infinitude) of different situations. Moore's primary motivation for introducing such an ontology is to accommodate linguistic data about the interpretation of adverbs. In particular, he is concerned with accounting for the observation that, while many manner adverbs have both sentential and predicate readings with verbs that denote events, they typically do not have both readings with the copula. For example, the following sentences show a predicate and sentential interpretation of the same adverb:

(39) John sang strangely.

(40) Strangely, John sang.

However, only the sentential reading is available with the copula:

(41) Strangely, John was at the party.

(42) *John was at the party strangely.

Moore's explanation for this phenomenon is that event verbs have both events and situations as part of their denotation, while the copula has only the situation. Specifically, he proposes that "John sang" be given the following logical form:

(43) Exists s (Fact(s,Exists e (Sing(john,e))))

Fact, like Schubert and Hwang's "*" operator, relates situations to arbitrary formulas. (Moore restricts his discussion to adverbs whose sentential interpretation is factive, hence the terminology.) Then the remainder of (39) and (40) is expressed by stating *Strange(e)* and *Strange(s)*, respectively. Strange events are supposed to be interpreted as strange in manner, while strange situations are to be interpreted as strange in that they occurred. On the other hand, "John was at the party" might get expressed as the following:

(44) Exists s (Fact(s,At(john,party)))

Since there is no event, there is only the situation available for predication. And predicating *Strange* of *s* here yields the appropriate sentential interpretation.

There are many problems with Moore's argument, however. First of all, there are numerous counterexamples to the claim that with adverbs, the copula only allows sentential interpretation. The best examples involve so-called "tough" adjectives. For example:

(45) The problem was surprisingly hard.

(46) Surprisingly, the problem was hard.

In (45), it is the degree of difficulty of the problem that is surprising, whereas in (46), we are surprised to find that the problem was difficult at all.[5]

Indeed, predicate rather than sentential modification is common with the copula, even if both with the same adverb is rare:

(47) The light was on brightly.

(48) The book was on the shelf precariously.

Note that both of these sentences are amenable to subsequent, factive, sentential modification by other adverbs:

(47) Strangely, the light was on brightly.

(48) Curiously, the book was on the shelf precariously.

However, Moore's analysis would seem to predict that such examples would not occur.

The inability of some adverbs to serve as manner adverbs with the copula (and other stative verbs) most likely falls out of specific facts about meanings of the terms, as opposed to general ontological issues involving situations versus events. Thus, it is not that there is no event/situation distinction with respect to sentences with the copula; rather, the state described by the utterance and various adverbs, e.g., "being at" and "strangely," are just generally semantically incompatible. Presumably, reasons such as this also explain why "loudly," etc., only has a predicate-modifying reading and "probably," etc., only a sentential one. (See [Ernst, 1984, 1986]) for a compelling analysis of such phenomena.)

A second problem with Moore's analysis is the difficulty of giving a coherent interpretation to predicates associated with adverbs this way—e.g., how do we give the semantics to the predicate *Strange* so that it means one thing when said of an event and another thing when said of a situation? Namely, *Strange* of an event is supposed to mean "strange in manner," and *Strange* of a situation is supposed to mean "strange in that it happened," but it is not clear where this semantics comes from. That is, Moore's proposal appears to simply sweep the manner/sentential distinction under the rug.

Indeed, a fundamental ontological distinction between event and situation seems unwarranted and is certainly not justified by linguistic evidence. States and events seem to be two kinds of situations, and while they have different properties, they do not require and should not entail thoroughly distinct representational devices.

---

[5] One might object that the adverb modifies the adjective here, and not the verb, as is the case for event verbs. However, this is exactly what one would expect from the copula; moreover, the adverb modifies the underlying predication (i.e., *Hard(problem1)*) analogously to the way we have postulated a predicate adverb would modify the underlying predication of an event-verb sentence.

In sum, the prospect of using both predicate- or category-based situations and proposition-based situations within a single notational system seems dim. A pure proposition-based situation analysis leaves us with the problems of not being able to represent the individual events of a complex event like that described by (23) and with an unaspectualized representation that reintroduces many nasty problems, such as adjunct/complement asymmetry.

6.5 A SOLUTION

I propose one solution to the problem of how best to represent situations, which I term an ontological solution, because it gets around the problem Schubert and Hwang pointed out by hypothesizing more kinds of entities. In particular, we posit entities for the situations corresponding to sentences involving logical connectives or quantifiers. For example, recall sentence (23) above:

(23) Everyone looked at Mary.

Let us posit that this sentence corresponds to a situation class called *Complex-event*. *Complex-event* has exactly the same status as a category like *Giving*. However, it is amenable to any number of "subevent" predications. Then (23) could have the following characterization:

(49) Exist c1 (AIO(c1,Complex-event) &
All x (AIO(x,Person) → Exists l (AIO(l,Looking-at) &
Actor(x,l) &
Patient(mary,l)) &
Sub-event(l,c1)))

That is, there is a complex event that has a subevent corresponding to each individual's looking action. Each of these actions has the standard case structure. We can refer to the entire complex-event by referring to *c1*, while preserving the desirable structure of the individual component actions. Note that it is relatively easy now to say that one of these looking actions is derisive, say, simply by creating a description of an individual event having this property, and assertion that it is a subevent of *c1*.

One appealing aspect of this proposal is that it captures some of aspects of the underlying events that one would want independently. That is, that events like *c1* are composed of individual subevents is a fact that is useful for any number of purposes. Therefore, relying on such an ontology for a solution to the situation-as-entity problem is not simply gratuitous. Also, the same particular category, *Complex-event*, would be used to represent sentences involving many other quantifiers, such as "many," "most," or "almost all," should a suitable analysis of these quantifiers be given.

One perhaps less appealing aspect of the proposal is that it at least opens the door to having ontological categories duplicating various logical connectives. For example, consider the following sentence:

(50) John didn't go to New York.

The representation for (50) might be the following:

(51) Exists n,e (AIO(n,Non-event) &
negated-event(e,n) &
AIO(e,Going) &
Actor(john,e) &
Destination(newyork,e))

Here *n* denotes the non-event of John going to New York.

Having situations that are "non-events" may seem ontologically suspect (compare [Hobbs, 1985] and [Hirst, 1989]). However, that such situations are plausible is suggested by the fact that (50) could be followed by

(52) This caused the firm to lose an important customer.

That is, non-events seem to be as referable and as causally culpable as "real" events.

In contrast, note that there does not appear to be a need to have disjunctive situations. For example, consider the following sentence:

(53) Either John went to New York or Bill went to Pittsburgh.

Presumably, if (53) is followed with (52), it is not some disjunctive situation *per se* that caused the loss, but one of the two disjuncts. That is, we would have to interpret these events as either John's going to New York or Bill's going to Pittsburgh having caused the firm to lose an important customer. Therefore, we are not compelled to enter such a category of situations into our ontology, at least by our current arguments.

Note that a somewhat different reading is available if (53) is followed by

(54) This infuriated Mary.

There is an interpretation of (54) in which Mary's infuriation depends only on her having learned the disjunction, and not on her learning of one *or* the other event. I take this as evidence of the need for propositional rather than situational objects, which are discussed further below.

Such extended ontologies are not new, but there appears to have been confusion over what they are ontologies of. For example, Hendrix [1975] has categories like "Negations," "Implications," and "Disjunctions" and has nodes (actually, "supernodes" denoting spaces in his partitioned semantic network notation) that are predicated to be individuals of this category. However, these categories, unlike those associated with more basic sentences, are explicitly categories of propositions. Thus, two very different notions seem to be conflated here. *John owns a car* gives rise to a node that is an individual "Owning" situation, but *John doesn't own a car* and *Everyone owns a car* yield nodes that are individual propositions; they are not situations at all. In effect, Hendrix has changed from a situation-based representation to a propositional one in midstream. Moreover, the ontology of situations is not extended to cover those situations corresponding to the more complex logical forms. While Hendrix is clear that his categories are categories of propositions, his lack of comment on the transition may indicate that the difference is not much appreciated. In this instance, Hendrix appears to build on prior confusion, such as that in Woods ([1975] p. 57), which construes individual nodes in case-based representations as standing for both assertions of facts and instances of events.

Note also that propositional networks, i.e., networks in which the emphasis is on representing as nodes the propositions underlying an utterance, can easily provide representations for the content of logically complex sentences. But in such systems the representations are of course propositional rather than situational, and what distinctions there might be between different kinds of propositions has a rather different role. For example, Schubert et al. [1979] and Shapiro [1979] provide representations for utterances containing logical operators, and in Shapiro in particular it is clear that these involve nodes denoting the logical propositions. Thus in SNePS [Shapiro, 1979], all sentences involving logical operators are classified as *deduction rules* and yield corresponding *rule nodes* in the notation. So *John loves Mary* would correspond to an (ordinary) assertion node, while *John does not love Mary* would correspond to a rule node. But nothing appears to hang on this distinction. Rule nodes just correspond to nonatomic logical sentences (i.e., *John does not love Mary* is no more a "rule" than *John loves Mary* is). Of course, an inference mechanism would make different inferences based on the nature of an assertion, but only as one would expect from the logical interpretation of these nodes.

In sum, the ontological solution seems to be a plausible remedy for the problems of reifying events corresponding to nonatomic sentences, while preserving an aspectualized representation. Having a richer ontology raises the issue of which logical forms correspond to situations, but it seems that this can be satisfactorily handled on a case-by-case basis. However, several potential problems arise from this approach. These are quite general issues, having to do with reifying states, with reifying propositions, and with when two events should be considered the same event. I now look at each problem in turn.

6.5.1 Reifying States

We have just seen how a modest extension of the kinds of situations we are willing to entertain solves the problem of representing the designatum of certain sentences. However, most of the examples we have examined so far have either been events or notions derivative of events, specifically, non-events and complex events. Probably the most significant class of omissions is that of stative situations, or states.

As the critique of Moore's proposal above suggests, it seems quite reasonable to consider states on par with events as a subclass of situations. If we follow the ontological solution to the reification of situations, we should analyze sentences denoting states as instances of state categories. For example, consider how we should represent the content of the following sentence:

(55) Jan owns a book.

Using a category-based representation, we would posit a category denoting the concept of being the owner of some possession and represent (55) as the following:

(56) Exists o (AIO(o,Owning) & Owner(jan,o) & Object(book1,o))

There is a serious issue that such representations raise, however. This is the question of just which entities constitute states. There are several ways in which this question manifests itself. One is that virtually any relation seems to be a plausible candidate for the state of that relation holding. Hence there is a potential for infinite regress of states. Another is that all the domain predicates denoting states are no longer predicates in the proposed logical form. This is counterintuitive.

Let us consider the first problem. Note that, in (56), we propose a relation *Owner* holding between the state of ownership and an individual person. However, one might further propose that the content of this aspectual predication, Jan's being the owner of an owning state, is also a feasible state; at least, we have not yet articulated a principle to rule out this possibility. Hence, we might want to further reify this state, for example, by replacing the aspectual above with the following:

(57) Exists a (AIO(a,Being-owner) & Owner-of-being-owner(jan,a)
& Owning-of-being-owner(o,a)

Here *Being-owner* denotes the state of being the owner of some state of ownership. We can continue reifying such proposals as long as we like, proposing state objects that are less and less intuitive. (This issue is discussed in Shapiro [1979] and Norvig [1987]).

Of course, we need not start with the representation of a state for such a proposal to arise; we could just as well have proposed a state like being the agent of an action, etc. It is simply representing states as objects, and a liberal notion of what may be a state, that allows the problem to arise.

The point here is not to recommend representations like (57), but merely to recognize that they are notational possibilities we cannot in principle rule out. Indeed, perhaps the best way to deal with such potential representations is not to attempt to rule them out in principle, but rather, propose that they are simply empirically unmotivated. That is, having a term *Owning* but not a term *Being-owner* is a claim about the particular ontology employed by a conceptual system; the choice of state terminology amounts to an empirical claim that English speakers have the first concept (i.e., being the owner of a state of ownership) but not the second (being the person in a state of being the owner of an ownership state).

We might even want to propose that representations like (57) are appropriate should one conceptualize a situation in a peculiar fashion. That is, one *could* conceivably think about the state of being the owner of an owning event (as opposed to simply being the owner of an owning event). In such a case, (57) would be the appropriate representation. However, this state is difficult to express in natural language, and seems to occur rarely, if at all, because it is not particularly useful for anything; thus, the ordinary interpretations of most natural language utterances does not entail this particular conceptualization.

The second problem with representations such as (56) is that they have a counterintuitive consequence. As an illustration, consider how we might represent a simple utterance such as a proper name. For example, consider how we should represent the utterance "Jan," as it occurs as part of some larger utterance. Assuming we believe that this is just the first name of a person, we might include the following in our representation:

(58) Exists jan (AIO(jan,Person) & first-name(jan,"Jan"))

However, as per our previous arguments, if the expression "Jan" has the same content as expressions like

(59) The person named Jan

(60) That person is named Jan.

and differs only in the stance of the speaker, then the logical form of the content of these utterances should be the same. Moreover, (60) is most clearly a state, and therefore has a logical form we would render as

(61) Exists jan,s (AIO(jan,Person) & AIO(s,First-name-state)
& First-name-state-holder(jan,s)
& First-name-state-name("jan",s))

That is, *s* is the state of some person being named "Jan." Thus (60) and the simple utterance "Jan" must also have this structure. Moreover, we should eschew predicates like *first-name* in (58) in favor of categories like *First-name-state* for exactly the same reason we eschewed predicates like *Give* in favor of categories like *Giving*.

Following this line of reasoning to its logical extreme, all our beloved, prototypical predicates, e.g., *Tall, Sweet, Red* are no longer predicates in the analysis, but instead are replaced by the likes of *Tall-state*, *Sweet-state*, and *Red-state*, plus some associated aspectuals. There is nothing immoral about doing so, but the consequences should be fully appreciated. In particular, facts involving such concepts are a bit more awkward to write down, and one is tempted to revert to a shorthand in which predicates like *Tall* (and indeed, *Give*) reappear as a notational convenience, to be replaced in the actual representation by the more fundamental *Tall-state* and *Giving*.

While the resulting analysis is somewhat awkward to work with, I note that the problems that motivated us to this solution in the case of verbs expressing events also appear in the adjectival cases. First, we might want to refer to situations involving such states just as we would to those involving events. Second, such an approach levels linguistic distinctions that probably do not have conceptual import. For example, we normally express height and weight in English with quite different grammatical forms:

(62) John is six feet tall.

(63) John weighs 190 pounds.

(62) and (63) have parallel paraphrases in "The height of John is six feet" and "The weight of John is 190 pounds," and we probably do not wish to attribute much cognitive significance to the fact that we have no verb for height parallel to "weigh," or that the adjective "heavy" cannot be used analogously to "tall" for the expression of weight. Of course, this is just an argument for having a canonical representation for such utterances, which the ontological approach easily admits. In particular, we would represent (62) and (63) as situations that are instances of *Height-state* and *Weight-state* categories, respectively, with analogous aspectuals.

Also, with adjectives like "tall" or "taller," we have the issue of optional complements versus adjuncts. Thus, while "tall" is often thought of as a one-place predicate, many analysts (e.g., [Bierwisch, 1987]) have noted that the logical structure of the predicate makes recourse to a group whose height establishes a norm with which the predicate contrasts its subject. That is, "tall" is really a two-place predicate whose second argument is some contrast group. Indeed, this argument may be specified by a prepositional phrase:

(64) John is tall for a 7 year old.

When such information is omitted, it is presumably inferred pragmatically. Similarly, comparatives like "taller" can often be used without specifying a complement, as in

(65) I would like America to be a kinder, gentler nation.

The comparatives may also allow an additional argument, as in:

(66) John is taller than Bill by two inches.

Thus, while it is possible to describe "tall" as a two-place predicate (one of whose arguments in rarely expressed) and "taller" as a three-place predicate (two of whose arguments are typically expressed but with complex omissibility criteria), doing so is not appealing. Using arguments analogous to those about event verbs, representing the content of these sentences as objects, with aspectuals to be asserted as needed, is a compelling alternative.[6]

Of course, we have still not addressed the issue of exactly what constitutes an event. For example, one can imagine that a category like *Non-event* qualifies for statehood; alternatively, one can imagine a scheme in which this is not a state, but is simply its own kind of situation (perhaps dominated by a category like *Non-situation*). While some stand eventually needs to be taken on such issues, the details of categorization do not appear to have any substantive bearing on the other issues at hand, and hence are not dealt with here.

6.5.2 Generic Facts and "Frames"

At this point, it is useful to look at how some general facts about events might be represented using the ontological approach. Suppose we want to represent some facts about robberies. Let us assume that robberies have agents who rob victims of some goods, using some weapon. Suppose that we also want to represent the fact that possessing the weapon is necessary for performing the action.

To represent

(67) Jan robbed Lynn of 20 using a gun,

we might state the following:

---

[6] It is interesting that one cannot say, "John is tall by two inches," even if we knew exactly the height norm of the contrast group. I speculate that the reason for this is that, unlike "taller," "tall" does not have in its logical structure an aspectual specifying the quantity corresponding to the difference in height. Similarly, adverbs like "much" might apply to quantities, and hence to "taller," but not to "tall." A more thorough analysis of such issues cannot be presented here.

(68) Exists r (AIO(r,Robbery)
& Robber(jan,r)
& Victim(lynn,r)
& Loot(20,r)
& Enforcer(gun1,r))

Such a representation is easy to depict as an network with the relations shown as links and the constants (including the skolemized version of the variable) as nodes. It is equally obvious how to depict the relations as slots and the other entities as frames. Also, we can easily represent the event of Jan possessing the gun, and predicate that this state is a precondition for event *r* above. However, many frame and semantic network systems either lack the means for representing more general facts, or must resort to awkward (and generally too limited) notations. For example, Conceptual Dependency [Schank, 1973] and Simmons's networks [Simmons, 1973] provide nice analyses of individual sentences but no obvious formalism for general facts.

However, a simple logical notation suffices. Here is the general structure of robbery, including the constraints on role-fillers and the fact about having the gun being a precondition:

(69) Forall r (AIO(r,Robbery) →
Exists a,o,v,w,h,p
(AIO(a,Person) & Robber(a,r)
& AIO(o,Phys-obj) & Loot(o,r)
& AIO(v,Person) & Victim(v,r)
& AIO(w,Weapon) & Enforcer(w,r)
& AIO(h,Possessing) & Possesser(a,h) & Possession(w,h)
& AIO(p,Precondition) & Pre-action(r,p) & Pre-state(h,p)))

One can view the handling of quantifiers in partitioned semantic networks [Hendrix, 1975] as advocating such a representation, and Hayes [1985] notes that such logical representations are generally adequate for representing frames. In general, the scoping of the quantifiers in (69) is the default for most semantic network and frame systems that do not specify them explicitly (e.g., Bobrow and Winograd [1977], Lenat and Guha [1988], Brachman [1979]). That is, the interpretation we are to give to there being a "name" slot in a "person" frame is that each person has some name. The advantage of having explicit quantifiers is that many concepts do not conform to this quantificational structure. For example, if we believe that an anti-Semite is someone who hates Jews, then those nonquantificational notations have difficulty expressing this concept: The standard frame-like notation would mean that every anti-Semite hates some Jew, which may be true, but is not the fact to be expressed. However, with a general quantificational capability at hand, such concepts are not problematic.

Note that we have not included many other facts about robberies. For example, we have not mentioned the essential fact that a robbery is an action involving the use of force or threat to procure goods. Making these assertions requires the inclusion of standard hierarchical information, for example, that a robbery is a kind of action. There are any number of ways of adding this information, but since doing so interacts with the issue of when two events are the same, we shall discuss both issues together below.

6.5.3 A Note on Aspectuals

The reader may have noted that some of the aspectuals we have posited thus far are quite similar to the motivating English words, while others appear to be rather different. For example, while the aspectual *Agent* relates an individual to an action, as the English word suggests, the aspectual *Owner* relates an individual to a state, not to an object owned, as does the English word. That is, we can say "the owner of that car," but do not ordinarily say "the owner of that owning."

Now, it is not the case that these English words are supposed to be directly related to similarly named aspectuals. Indeed, the words "owner" and "agent" should refer to concepts that are further defined in relation to the categories *Owing* and *Action* and their associated aspectuals. (Doing so is one way to give a "frame semantics" to certain words, as advocated by Fillmore [1982].) For example, we can say that the *category Agent* (as opposed to the aspectual of the same name) applies to individuals in the *Agent* aspectual relation to individual *Actions*, and that the *category Owner* applies to individuals in the *Owner* aspectual relation to individual *Ownings*. But we still have not explained why we talk of actors of actions and owners of object, but not owners of ownings.

However, I suspect that this apparent asymmetry is actually rather superficial. Consider for example how we might use the preposition "of" to express any number of relations between and among objects participating in situations. Thus, we can speak of "the victim of a robbery," "the victim of a robber," "the robber of a victim," "the robber of the jewelry," "the loot of the victim," and perhaps "the robber of that robbery." One analysis of this phenomenon is to construe words like "robber" as meaning "an individual in a *Robber* relation to a robbery event." We must then also construe "of" generously enough to include the relationship between such individuals to other individuals in aspectual relations to situations (e.g., "victim of the robber"), as well as the relationship of such individuals to situations themselves (e.g., "victim of that robbery"). The peculiarity of phrases like "the owner of that ownership" is then attributed to the rarity of the direct expression of the state of owning something *per se*.

Note that I am positing no relations in the underlying logical form that hold directly between the individuals that participate in aspectual relations of the same situation. For example, there is no *Owner-owned* predicate that might hold between an owner and a possession; having such a predicate would be equivalent to adopting the nonaspectualized predicate-based representation that we have eschewed. (That is, it is the same as having a predicate *Owns* that holds been owner and possession.) Similarly, a *Robber-victim* predicate, while not identical to reintroducing a predicate like *Rob*, would be a step in this direction and a step away from an aspectualized format. Arguing as we did in the previous section, we cannot rule out having a *Robber-victim* state, which is some relation to a *Robbery* event, but we can take the position that such states are neither necessary nor appropriate for representing the way events like robberies are normally conceptualized.

6.5.4 Propositions and Situations

Thus far I have emphasized the importance of situational objects. I have suggested that such objects have received less attention in semantic network research than they are due; occasionally, they have even been confused with propositions. Propositions, on the other hand, have been given rather prominent treatment. What role remains for them?

Adding a full ontology of situations does not seem to reduce the need for propositional objects. There are at least two arguments for their existence. One is the need for propositional anaphora, the other is the familiar arguments about referential opacity. However, when situational and propositional objects are considered together, the demands on propositional objects change considerably.

Let us first look at situations corresponding to verbs of propositional attitude. For example, suppose we want to represent sentences like the following:

(70) Lynn knows that Jan went to New York.

Presumably, we will represent a "knowing" similarly to any other state, namely, as an object with aspectuals designating the knower and the known. However, what kind of object can be known? While it may be tempting to believe this to be a situation, this cannot be so. A situation is just the wrong kind of entity to be known or believed, just as a person or physical object cannot be known or believed (in the pertinent sense). More formally, if we tried using situations for this purpose, exactly what is known or believed about the situation becomes difficult to determine. For example, suppose we represented (70) as involving the following:

(71) AIO(k1,Knowing) & Knower(lynn,k1) & Known(g1)
& AIO(g1,Going) & Goer(jan,g1) & Destination(newyork,g1)

Then the standard issues of referential opacity would appear. In particular, there are apt to be other predications about the situation referred to by g1, and we would normally not want to attribute all of them to the knower. For example, if we knew about Jan's going to New York that Jan left from San Francisco, but we don't know whether Lynn knows this particular fact, then it is awkward at best to state this fact without also falsely implying that Lynn was aware of it. That is, there might be another event term, *g2*, denoting Jan's going from San Francisco to New York, but which denotes the same event as does g1 above; i.e., *g1* = *g2*. Since the facts about *g1* are not in any special context (they are simply facts about an event), an agent to which we attribute all these beliefs could infer, correctly, that the origin of *g1* is San Francisco. This inference is correct because the origin of that event *is* San Francisco. But then (71) would no longer state what it is supposed to state.

Intuitively, what we want is some way to delineate just those propositions about *g1* that appear in (71). One possibility is to do what Maida and Shapiro [1985] propose, which is to interpret terms like *g1* intensionally, and not to substitute equals for equals as a basic reasoning rule. However, we have reasons to be discussed below for rejecting this notion of intension altogether. But in any case, even Maida and Shapiro assume that the object propositional attitudes is a proposition. Thus, we introduce proper propositional objects. One way to do so is simply to put the proposition "in-line." Then, in place of (71) we would have the following:

(72) AIO(k1,Knowing)
& Knower(lynn,k1)
& Known(AIO(g1,Going) & Goer(jan,g1) & Destination(newyork,g1))

Since the known here is a proposition, and is in a context involving propositional attitude, anything else we may come to believe about *g1* would not affect the meaning of (72).

This argument demonstrates the utility of propositions, but not of propositional objects. However, objects corresponding to propositions can be justified on a basis similar to that we have been using for situations. In particular, pronouns can refer back to the propositional content of an utterance as well as the situation such a proposition describes. For example, consider following

(73) Jan went to New York.

with

(74) This took five hours.

versus

(75) Lynn knew this.

In the first case, "this" presumably refers to the event, which has a duration, and not the proposition, which doesn't. However, in the second case, "this" refers to the proposition, not the event. Therefore, one would have needed to posited a proposition associated with (73), as well as a situation.

Moreover, one needs a way to represent unknown propositions. That is, in a sentence like *Jan told Lynn something, but Lynn couldn't remember it* we would like to represent what Jan told Lynn as a proposition whose content is unavailable to us. Perhaps later on, we would want to refer back to this proposition, and specify what its content is. This would also be the preferred treatment of (75) above: We might want to initially state that Lynn knew some (contextually uniquely determinable) proposition; only when the referent has been determined would this proposition be identified as the contents of (73).

Thus, it seems that we need propositional objects as well as situational ones. Let us introduce the operator *Prop* for this purpose. For example, using *Prop* we can offer the following notation for (70):

(76) AIO(k1,Knowing) & Knower(lynn,k1) & Known(p1)
& Prop(p1,AIO(g1,Going) & Goer(jan,g1) & Destination(newyork,g1))

Here *p1* designates the proposition that Jan went to New York.

If we knew that Lynn knew something, but we didn't know what, we would say the following:

(77) AIO(k1,Knowing) & Knower(lynn,k1) & Known(p1))

Later on, we can use *Prop* to unproblematically assert the content of *p1*.

Prop is syntactically identical to *Fact* or "**." However, *Prop* is to be interpreted as associating an individual with a proposition, rather than with a situation, which, as was suggested in our critique of Schubert and Hwang's proposal, is probably a better interpretation of proposition-based situation notations.

It seems that considering both situations and propositions together eases the representation burden that is sometimes overextended to each one. Note that as a reification of propositions, rather than situations, proposition-based situation proposals are no longer problematic. Unlike situations, propositions are completely bounded in extent and are thus identical given the same content. That is, there is only one proposition that Jan went to New York, and that Jan went to New York is its entire contents; however, the event of Jan's going to New York might have any number of other components.

Also, the problem of what predicates should apply to situations in a proposition-based situation notation does not arise if we consider these items propositions. For example, situations can be implicated in causality, and hence need to be the arguments of predicates like *cause*. Propositions, on the other hand, don't cause much to happen in the world; therefore, they can be restricted to a few types of situations, namely, those situations of propositional attitude (and, of course, the operator *Prop*). A case in point is (53) and (54) above:

(53) Either John went to New York or Bill went to Pittsburgh.

(54) This infuriated Mary.

Here the referent of "this" could be interpreted as the proposition expressed in (53) (or perhaps, Mary's learning of this proposition), rather than a situation described in (53). Also, we can avoid troublesome potential circularities by simply recognizing that predications involving *Prop* are not predications within the domain of discourse, and hence, are not amenable to further predication of *Prop*.

6.5.5 Intensional Representations and the Equivalence of Situations

The preceding discussion took an extensional view of situational objects. This implicitly raises the general issue of whether intensions need to be represented at all. In intensional semantic networks, e.g., Maida and Shapiro [1985], much is made of the view that no two distinct nodes are equal and that referential opacity is the norm. However, with propositional objects, it seems that all needs for intensions in the representation can be eliminated. That is, it is perfectly acceptable to assume that situational and other individuals refer to objects in the world, and that nothing in our system corresponds to an intension.

One motivation for intensional representations (e.g., [Woods, 1975]) and [Maida and Shapiro, 1985]) is that without them, it is not possible to represent sentences like *Jan knows that the Morning Star is the Evening Star*. This is because such a representation would only have one node representing the extension, about which it is predicated that the object was both the Morning Star and the Evening Star. But in fact, with propositions in our notation, this is not the case. Here is one possible way to represent exactly this sentence without intensions:

(78) AIO(k1,Knowing) & Knower(jan,k1) & Known(p1)
  & Prop(p1, AIO(m1,Star) & Named(m1,"Morningstar")
    & AIO(e1,Star) & Named(e1,"Eveningstar")
    & =(e1,m1))

That is, Jan knows that something called the Morning Star and something called the Evening Star are the same thing. (I should have used a stative form instead of the predicate *Named* (and indeed, instead of the predicate "=") to be consistent with previous analyses, but I did not do so for the sake of clarity.)

Propositional contexts are considered referentially opaque, but elsewhere we can freely substitute equals for equals and arrive at truth conditionally equivalent formulas.

One might argue about whether the right facts are included in the proposition proposed in (78). Actually, this famous example is rather defective, since what is meant by the intension of a proper name, especially one that is an interpretable phrase, is problematic, or at least, subject to a number of distinct interpretations.

There are at several ways in which we might wish to modify (78), but none of them affect the force of the argument. For example, we might include "more meaning" in the propositional content, e.g., facts like the Evening Star is the first star seen in the evening. While I would argue against such an account, this proposal simply amounts to having other conjuncts in the propositional content and does not affect the utility of the proposal.

Another set of modifications involves the degree to which we recognize this utterance to have achieved successful reference. The representation in (78) does not show how an agent might have understood this utterance as referring to objects with which it is already familiar. For example, it might be the case that the agent hearing (78) interprets both "the Evening Star" and "the Morning Star" as referring to the same object, the planet Venus. However, we could provide this interpretation by adding to (78) =(*e1,venus*) and =(*m1,venus*)" (not as part of the proposition, of course, but as other top-level conjuncts), where *venus* is a node having many other facts predicated about it. Once again, the representation has all the desired properties.

Alternatively, we might believe that some linguistic expressions refer more directly than this analysis would indicate. For example, in a given discourse, whenever the word "Jan" is used referentially, we might translate each use directly to the same constant, say *jan*, rather than produce a new constant for each occurrence, each of which, when it is determined to be the same as some previous *jan*, would at that point be declared equal to such a node, and perhaps merged with it. In the domain at hand, a corresponding example might be an interpretation of the sentence

(79) The Evening Star is Venus.

in which "Venus" is being used referentially, while "the Evening Star" is interpreted as a name; i.e., a paraphrase of (79) would be something like "The so-called 'Evening Star' is actually Venus." Moreover, if (79) were the object of Jan's belief, say, then the propositional object itself would contain a mention of *venus*, i.e., the same constant used by the agent to designate the extension is predicated to be part of someone else's belief. Thus, we would have the following:

(80) AIO(k1,Knowing) & Knower(jan,k1) & Known(p1)
& Prop(p1, AIO(e1,Star) & Named(e1,"Eveningstar") & =(el,venus))

The complication here is to figure out what it means to postulate sharing an extension with someone else. In particular, the question arises as to what (80) implies about what Jan knowns about *venus*.

The answer to this question sanctioned by the representation alone is "nothing much." All we have said is that Jan knows that the star named the Evening Star is the same as some object, but we have not said what Jan knows about this object. The broader answer to this question, though, is whatever is sanctioned by appropriate inferential processes. For example, if almost everyone knows that *venus* is called "Venus," or that it is the second planet from the sun, then it is reasonable to assume that Jan knows this too, unless this assumption is contraindicated.

The issue here is really a very general one having little to do with the particulars of the proposed representation. The issue arises any time a term is used both within and without a referential opaque context, which happens even in intensional networks like that of Maida and Shapiro [1985]. The broader issue is the relation between mutual belief and successful reference. There is of course much to say about this issue (e.g., see [Fauconnier, 1985] and [Sperber and Wilson, 1986]). I note only that any number of proposals are compatible with the suggestions made above, none of which require objects representing intensions.

We are able to do without intensions here because we are willing to provide "redundant" information in the proposition. Thus, rather than have an intension for the Evening Star, we simply specify the propositional content of "a star named 'the Evening Star' ," and associate this content with a term. We may already know that "venus" is also known as "the Evening Star," so a very similar fact is already in the knowledge base. However, this redundancy seems to correspond to a rather intuitive interpretation of the information the sentence is actually conveying.

If intensions are not needed to deal with referentially opaque contexts, perhaps they are still required for "roles." For example, a sentence like

(81) The president is elected [every four years].

is not true of the person occupying the president role, but rather, seems to be true of the president role itself. That such roles are intensions is explicit in KL-ONE [Brachman, 1978]. However, once again, intensions appear to be unnecessary. This time, the solution is ontological. If we assume that we have categories like "President," then utterances such as (81) are treated by quantifying over individuals of such categories. Thus, it is simply true of all individual "President"s that they are elected. In this sense "the president" is treated analogously to "the dog" in *The dog has a tail.* Of course, any individual president might be represented by an (extensional) object about which many other things are true, but such facts will not be true of individuals of "President" *per se.*

Another justification of intensions has to do with enabling agents to reason about nonexistent objects [Woods, 1975]. However, this objection to extensions can also be eliminated if extensions are construed in a cognitive correspondence sense. That is, when I say that *venus* denotes the planet Venus, I mean that it denotes some cognitive agent's idea of the referent in the world, rather than any actual object *per se.* Such objects are part of what Jackendoff [1983] calls the *projected world.* Thus, we are not making any commitment to objective truth or reality by considering these objects as extensions. I believe this interpretation comes closest to capturing the intuition that there are objects to which linguistic expressions refer, even if these objects are not actual or real, and that it is preferable to denying that such objects have mental representations, but rather, that there are only many different descriptions which are known to be coreferential.

The same reasoning applies directly to situations. The only caution is about when it is correct to identify two events. It is perhaps useful to distinguish two cases. First, there is the case in which one situation is logically entailed by the other. Consider for example the representation of hierarchical information. As suggested above, suppose we want to assert that robberies are actions, with the robber the actor and the loot the object. One way to represent this information is to simply predicate these additional facts about the variable *r* in (69) that ranges over robberies. That is, we could include the following predicates within the scope of the variables of (69):

(82) AIO(r,Action) & Actor(a,r) & Object(o,r)

An alternative is to specify a new situation, and declare it to be coreferential with r:

(83) Exists action (AIO(action,Action) & Actor(a,action) & Object(o,action))
& =(action,r)

(83) is supposed to be within the scope of the universal quantifier of (69), so it means that, for every robbery event, there is an action involving the robber and the loot of that robbery, and in fact, this action is the same event as the robbery.

(Note that in any case, we are postulating very abstract categories like *Action*. Categories like *State*, *Event*, and *Situation*, etc., would also be included in the knowledge base. The knowledge base would also specify that each individual State or Event is also an individual *Situation*, etc., however we decide to express such information.)

This case seems harmless enough. On the other hand, consider the case in which one of the two events does not necessarily entail that other. For example, suppose that I have replaced a pipe under my sink, and that this replacement fixed a problem with my sink. In this case, we could say that one event, described as replacing a pipe, is coreferential with another event, that of fixing my sink. Suppose we attempt to represent this situation with a single entity, *e1*. Then we would say something like the following:

(84) AIO(e1,Replacing) & Replacer(rw,e1) & Replaced(oldpipe,e1) &
Replacement(newpipe,e1) & AIO(e1,Fixing) & Fixer(rw,e1) &
Fixed(sink,e1)

Let us suppose further that both the replacer and the fixer are agents, and that both the thing replaced and the thing fixed are objects. That is, we can infer (85) from the first set of conjuncts of (84) and (86) from the second:

(85) AIO(e1,Action) & Agent(rw,e1) & Object(oldpipe,e1)

(86) AIO(e1,Action) & Agent(rw,e1) & Object(sink,e1)

But, if (85) and (86) are both true, we have lost some crucial information; we no longer know which aspectuals go with which event category. In particular, if we make the usual assumption that actions have unique objects, one can infer that I replaced my sink with a new pipe, which is simply false. (A version of this problem appears in Parsons [1985]).

It is probably undesirable to abandon the assumption of actions having unique objects, since then actions may have any number of objects, only one of which is qualified to be grammaticalized as a syntactic object. The better solution, it would seem, is to deny the coextensive nature of these events. We would say instead that there was a fixing event, *f1*, say, and a replacing event, *r1*, and that the latter "comprised" the former, or that some other such intimate but nonidentifying relation holds between them. Determining the correct vocabulary of such situational relations is an important open problem.

Finally, I note in passing that while Maida and Shapiro [1985] emphasize that their network is intensional and propositional, i.e., that it has nodes for propositions, it doesn't make sense to consider the propositional nodes themselves as intensional. That is, there is only one proposition corresponding to *John loves Mary*, and if two nodes were created denoting this content, they would be equal, and, moreover, mutually substitutable in all contexts. The same could not be said for the other nodes of such a system.

6.6 SUMMARY

I began by acknowledging the virtues of predicate- and category-based representations, in particular, their amenability to aspectualization, but accepting Schubert and Hwang's point about such representations being limited to reifying situations described only by atomic sentences in the logic. However, we found that their proposition-based situation proposal, while overcoming this difficulty, results in an apparently unaspectualizable representation, and hence reintroduces a number of problems, some of which predicate- and category-based representations address, plus some additional problems of its own. I abandoned hope of resolving these difficulties, and instead, sought to extend the category-based solution.

The extension is first an ontological one, in that it introduces situations corresponding to the logical forms for which category-based solutions would not otherwise apply. The problems Schubert and Hwang illuminate can thereby be resolved while maintaining category-based advantages.

The second aspect of the extension is to allow propositional objects. These are needed primarily to deal with problems of referential opacity and for propositional anaphora. Having propositions as objects in the system eliminates the need for any kind of intension altogether.

While the proposal is primarily a way of maintaining aspectualization, this necessary virtue yields a rather cumbersome representation. In particular, what used to be a simple predication now requires a variable or a constant and a number of predications; also, every utterance has both a propositional and situational object associated with it. However, this inelegance appears to be the price one has to pay for the features crucial for an adequate representation.

ACKNOWLEDGMENTS

This research was sponsored by the Defense Advanced Research Projects Agency (DOD), monitored by Space and Naval Warfare Systems Command under Contract N00039-88-C-0292 and by the Office of Naval Research, under Contract N00014-89-J-3205. I would like to thank Peter Norvig, Pat Hayes, Len Schubert, and Laura Michaelis for helpful comments that contributed to this work. Nigel Ward, Paul Jacobs, and Stuart Shapiro suggested many corrections and improvements on a previous draft of this work.

References

Allen, J. 1987. *Natural Language Understanding*. Benjamin/Cummings, Menlo Park, CA.

Bach, E. 1983. On Time, tense and aspect: An essay in English metaphysics. In *Meaning Use and Interpretation*, R. Bauerle, C. Schwarze & A. von Stechnow (eds.). de Gruyter, New York.

Barwise, J. and Perry, J. 1983. *Situations and Attitudes*. Bradford Books, MIT Press, Cambridge, MA.

Bierwisch, M. 1986. Some aspects of semantic form in natural language. In *Language and Artificial Intelligence*, M. Nagao (ed.). Elsevier Science Publishers B. V., North Holland, Amsterdam, The Netherlands.

Bobrow, D.G. and Winograd, T. 1977. An overview of KRL, a knowledge representation language. *Cognitive Science*, 1(1).

Brachman, R.J. 1978 Structure inheritance networks. In *Research in Natural Language Understanding*, W.A. Woods and R.J. Brachman. Quarterly Progress Report No. 1, BBN Report No. 3,742. Bolt Beranek & Newman, Cambridge, MA.

———. 1979. On the Epistemological Status of Semantic Networks. In *Associative Networks: Representation and Use of Knowledge by Computers*, N.V. Findler (ed.). Academic Press, New York.

Cercone, N. 1975. *Representing Natural Language in Extended Semantic Networks*. Technical Report TR75-11, Department of Computer Science, University of Alberta, Edmonton, Albert, Canada.

Charniak, E. and McDermott, D. 1985. *Introduction to Artificial Intelligence.* Addison-Wesley Publishing Company, Reading, MA.

Davidson, D. 1969. The individuation of events. In *Essays in Honor of Carl G. Hempel*, N. Rescher et al., (ed.). Reidel, Dordrecht, Holland, pp. 216–234.

———. 1980. *Essays on Actions and Events*. Clarendon Press, Oxford.

Ernst, T. 1984. *Toward an Integrated Theory of Adverb Position in English.* Indiana University Linguistics Club, Bloomington, IN.

———. 1986. *Manner Adverbs and the Sentence/Predicate Distinction.* MS, The Ohio State University.

Fauconnier, G. 1985. *Mental Spaces.* Mit Press, Cambridge, MA.

Fillmore, C. 1982. Frame semantics. In *Linguistics in the Morning Calm*, Hanshin Press, Seoul, Korea.

Hayes, Patrick J. 1985. The logic of frames. In *Readings in Knowledge Representation*, R.J. Brachman and H. J. Levesque (eds.). Morgan Kaufmann Publishers, San Mateo, CA.

Hayes, Philip J. 1977. On semantic networks, frames, and associations. In the *Proceedings of the Fifth International Joint Conference on Artificial Intelligence.* IJCAI proceedings are available from Morgan Kaufmann Publishers, San Mateo, CA.

Hendrix, G.G. 1975. Expanding the utility of semantic networks through partitioning. In the *Proceedings of the Fourth Joint International Conference on Artificial Intelligence.* IJCAI proceedings are available from Morgan Kaufmann Publishers, San Mateo, CA.

Hirst, G. 1989. Ontological assumptions in knowledge representation. In the *Proceedings of the First International Conference on Principles of Knowledge Representation and Reasoning*, Toronto, Canada. Morgan Kaufmann Publishers, San Mateo, CA.

Hobbs, J.R. 1985. Ontological promiscuity. In the *Proceedings of the 23rd Annual Meeting of the Association for Computational Linguistics*, Chicago, IL.

———. 1986. Overview of the Tacitus project. *Computational Linguistics*, 12(3).

Israel, D. 1983. Interpreting network formalisms. In *Computational Linguistics*, N. Cercone (ed.). Pergamon Press, Oxford.

Jackendoff, R. 1983. *Semantics and Cognition.* The MIT Press, Cambridge, MA.

Lenat, D. and Guha, R.V. 1988. *The World According to CYC*. MCC Technical Report No. ACA-AI-300-88.

Maida, A.S. and Shapiro, S.C. 1985. Intensional concepts in propositional semantic networks. In *Readings in Knowledge Representation*, R.J. Brachman and H.J. Levesque (eds.). Morgan Kaufmann Publishers, San Mateo, CA.

Moore, R.C. 1989. *Events, Situations, and Adverbs*. Unpublished manuscript, SRI International.

Norvig, P. *A Unified Theory of Inference for Text Understanding*. Ph.D. Thesis, University of California, Berkeley. Technical Report No. UCB/CSD 87/339, 1987.

Parsons, T. 1985. Underlying events in the logical analysis of English. In *Actions and Events: Perspectives on the Philosophy of Donald Davidson*, E. LePore and B.P. McLaughlin (eds.). Basil Blackwell.

Reichenbach, H. 1947. *Elements of Symbolic Logic*. The Free Press, New York.

Roberts, R.B. and Goldstein, I.P. 1977. *The FRL Manual*. Technical Report AIM-408, MIT Artificial Intelligence Laboratory.

Rumelhart, D.E., Lindsay, P.H., and Norman, D.A. 1972. A process model of long-term memory. In *Organization of Memory*, E. Tulving and W. Donaldson (eds.). Academic Press: New York.

Schank, R.C. 1973. Identification of conceptualizations underlying natural language. In *Computer Models of Thought and Language*, Schank, R. C. & Colby, K. M. (eds.). W.H. Freeman and Company, San Francisco, CA.

Schubert, L.K. and Hwang, C.H. 1989. An episodic knowledge representation for narrative texts. In *Proceedings of the First International Conference on Principles of Knowledge Representation and Reasoning*, R.J. Brachman, H.J. Levesque and R. Reiter (eds.). Morgan Kaufmann Publishers, San Mateo, CA, pp. 444–458.

Schubert, L.K., Goebel, R.R., and Cercone, N.J. 1979. Structure and organization of a semantic net. In *Associative Networks: Representation and Use of Knowledge by Computers*, N. V. Findler (ed.). Academic Press, New York

Shapiro, S.C. 1971a. A net structure for semantic information storage, deduction, and retrieval. In *Proceedings of the Second International Joint Conference on Artificial Intelligence*. IJCAI proceedings are available from Morgan Kaufmann Publishers, San Mateo, CA.

———. 1971b. *The MIND System: a data structure for semantic information processing*. R-837-PR, The Rand Corporation, Santa Monica, CA.

———. 1979. The SNePS semantic network processing system. In *Associative Networks: Representation and Use of Knowledge by Computers*, N. V. Findler (ed.). Academic Press, New York.

Shapiro, S.C. and Rapaport, W.J. 1983. SNePS considered as a fully intensional propositional semantic network. In *Proceedings of the Fifth National Conference on Artificial Intelligence*, AAAI, Menlo Park, CA, pp. 278–283.

Simmons, R.F. 1973. Semantic networks: Their computation and uses for understanding English sentences. In *Computer Models of Thought and Language*, Schank, R.C. and Colby, K.M. (eds.). W. H. Freeman and Company, San Francisco, CA.

Sperber, D. and Wilson, D. 1986. *Relevance*. Harvard University Press, Cambridge, MA.

Wilensky, R. 1986. Knowledge representation—a critique and a proposal. In *Experience, Memory, and Reasoning*, Kolodner, J.L., and Riesbeck, C.K. (eds.). Lawrence Erlbaum Associates. Hillsdale, NJ.

Woods, W.A. 1975. What's in a link: Foundations for semantic networks. In *Representation and Understanding: Studies in Cognitive Science*, D.G. Bobrow and A. Collins (eds.). Academic Press, New York.

PART II

FORMAL ANALYSES

The original name for the Catalina workshop was "Formal Aspects of Semantic Networks." That name was dropped as the title of this book, since many of the chapters did not use formal methods. The six chapters in Part II, however, are closest in spirit to the original theme. These chapters use formal methods in logic and mathematics to analyze the structure of semantic networks, the methods of reasoning with them, and their computational complexity.

SURVEY OF CHAPTERS

The first three chapters analyze path-based methods for reasoning about inheritance in semantic networks. Rich Thomason came to this subject from his background in logic and formal semantics, and David Touretzky spent several years analyzing informal systems such as NETL and developing a semantically motivated, implementation-independent theory of them. In Chapter 7, Thomason and Touretzky address the problems of relational reasoning in such systems. They show that complete reasoning is beyond their capacity and that further research, theoretical as well as experimental, is necessary. In Chapter 8, Lynn Stein addresses resolving the ambiguities caused by conflicting exceptions, which is a serious issue in nonmonotonic reasoning. Path-based approaches have been popular, since they preserve the structures that guide the preferences for one interpretation over another; but those approaches have not had a satisfactory model-theoretic semantics. In her approach, Stein considers the possible extensions of an ambiguous hierarchy and thereby generates a model-theoretic interpretation that preserves the path-based topology. In Chapter 9, Bart Selman and Hector Levesque pursue some issues raised by Touretzky's earlier work on inheritance. They show that the general case of inheritance is NP-hard and therefore computationally intractable. Even the hardware implementations proposed for NETL could not make such computations efficient. Despite the complexity of the general case, Selman and Levesque also find several tractable variants. In analyzing various definitions of inheritance, they show which combinations of features affect the tractability of the associated reasoning.

The last three chapters of Part II address logical issues concerning the representational power of semantic networks and the reasoning upon them. In Chapter 10, James Crawford and Benjamin Kuipers develop a system of logic called Access-Limited Logic (ALL), which is designed to be efficient for the kinds of reasoning supported by a semantic network. They show that ALL is not complete in the sense that it can prove everything that is provable from a knowledge base, but they propose an interesting alternative, called *Socratic completeness*: everything provable can be proved as long as the interlocutor asks an appropriate sequence of leading questions. In Chapter 11, Bernhard Nebel addresses a problem that plagues almost every large dictionary: circular definitions of concepts that are defined directly or indirectly in terms of themselves. Such definitions include recursive definitions, which are logically correct, but computationally problematical. Nebel analyzes various approaches to defining their semantics and the implications of each approach for computational complexity and decidability. In Chapter 12, Wlodek Zadrozny analyzes the logical properties of several different graph formalisms, including the conceptual graphs by John Sowa, the higraphs by David Harel, and his own approach to a three-level semantics. He analyzes the ways in which the graph structure can assist or support reasoning in each of these systems. As a test for the adequacy of a formalism, he proposes the capacity to offer new tools, which he believes is a more quantifiable criterion than fidelity to intuitions.

7

INHERITANCE THEORY AND NETWORKS WITH ROLES

Richmond H. Thomason
(University of Pittsburgh)

David S. Touretzky
(Carnegie Mellon University)

Abstract

We present a formalization of monotonic inheritance nerworks with roles. Roles (like the role *father*) are partial functions from individuals to individuals and figure in universal-existential statements like "every person has a father." The networks we consider also permit relational statements such as "every person's father loves that person's mother," and equality statements among roles and individuals. Restricted networks of this sort are less expressive than first-order logic; like all inheritance systems, they constitute a sort of weak logic founded on path-based reasoning. On the other hand, their rules of inference and resulting proofs are substantially more complex than what one finds in simple IS-A hierarchies; the latter use purely linear proof sequences. We show all that query answering in networks with roles corresponds to parsing a fragment of the network with a context-free grammar whose nonterminals are inference rules and whose terminals are links. Proofs in these systems, although still path-based, take the form of trees rather than chains.

7.1 LOGIC AND NETWORK FORMALISMS

This volume is a testimony to the ubiquity of network-based formalisms in applied knowledge representation. Of course, declarative knowledge bases for intelligent systems differ widely in detail. But at a very general level most of the ones that have been successfully deployed in reasonably large applications depend heavily on network organization and inheritance reasoning. There is a taxonomy, and there are algorithms that transfer information from more to less general concepts in the taxonomy.

Applied systems have to work; and the reasons for the success of this knowledge representation strategy are practical. In particular, systems organized on these principles are *buildable* and *usable* on the scale required for most expert tasks. The taxonomic organization provides a modularity and "picture-ability" that facilitates entering and checking knowledge, and—whether or not the problems are sound or tractable—this organization also supports algorithms that seem in practice to provide reasonable reasoning performance.

Most often, these netlike formalisms are "uninterpreted," in that they are not accompanied by a precise interpretation, in Tarskian model-theoretic terms.

It is easy to miss the significance of uninterpretedness. If it is taken to be an accusation, as a criticism of some applied system, the accusation seems to assume that radically different and competing goals—formal clarity and useful applicability—can somehow be reconciled. Practically minded people may then dismiss the criticism as irrelevant, while theoretically minded people may use it as an excuse to dismiss many applied systems. The effect is an altogether harmful estrangement of theory and application in knowledge representation.

We feel that the point should be understood more as a challenge to logicians than as a threat to networks. An *uninterpreted* system needn't be *uninterpretable*. Providing an interpretation is a job for a logician. The process of trying to do this job may or may not lead to specific criticisms, depending on the details. The situation is similar in many ways to the case of natural language semantics. Languages like English don't have a model-theoretic semantics. This could be taken to show either that logic is irrelevant to natural language, or that these languages are hopelessly confused. These alternative conclusions in fact do correspond roughly to philosophical positions that were adopted earlier in this century. More recently, though, the task of providing such a semantics for suitably expressive fragments of natural languages has come to be accepted by linguists and logicians as a research field in its own right. Despite many difficult and unsolved problems, this work has helped to illuminate our understanding of both model theory and of linguistic meaning.[1]

Until this century was well underway, the formalisms used by mathematicians were also "uninterpreted," and were justified by considerations that, like their utility in axiomatizing mathematical reasoning, were in part practical. The historical process that led to the emergence of modern logic began with foundational prob-

[1] The remainder of this section elaborates the above paragraph, with reference to the history of logic. It can be skipped by readers who want to get on to details about networks.

lems that made some mathematicians feel that the reasoning processes they employed were not sufficiently well understood. It was only long after formalized languages had been developed, and provided with axioms and rules, that it was felt that this process needed to be supplemented with a semantic definition of validity. (In fact, many logicians resisted this process because model-theoretic techniques were felt to be insufficiently constructive.)

The success of semantic ideas depended in large part on their plausibility and mathematical power. The model theoretic definition of validity matched exactly the leading proof-theoretic notion of logical consequence and also provided a powerful basis for establishing metatheoretic results.

Without a prior formalization of mathematical proof, this success story would have been impossible. A general definition of proof provided the antecedent concepts and problems to which model theory could be applied. Proof theory was never outmoded and replaced by model theory—it still remains an active, independent area of logic.[2]

"Model theoretically uninterpreted" does not mean "unintelligible"; model theory is not the only way to make sense of reasoning. Mathematical logic has been successful in part because it has been able to provide independent ways of thinking about reasoning. This applies not only to the two-valued intuitions concerning "classical" systems of logic, but to other logical systems as well. Intuitionistic logic, for instance, has a well-developed proof theory, and model-theoretic interpretations that differ markedly from the classical interpretation. Similar results have been obtained for other, more exotic logics.

The absence of a model-theoretic interpretation, then, is not so much a criticism of a proof-theoretic formalism, as a challenge to logicians. Some systems of logic (e.g., some of the modal logics formalized by C.I. Lewis) have never been provided with satisfactory model-theoretic interpretations. But in many cases in which a well-motivated proof theory has been presented, it has been possible to match it with an equally well-motivated model theory. In other cases, the task of providing a model theory has in turn clarified the proof-theoretic situation, and inspired changes in it; in some cases, there are proofs that a consequence relation cannot be axiomatized at all.

In the case of network formalisms, the logical challenge is greater, since they are designed with practical constraints in mind. These constraints may compete with theoretical clarity. This means that a certain amount of work may be needed on the theory of reasoning before model theory can be invoked. The project of [Hayes, 1979], of interpreting a network *language* in model-theoretic terms, is really not of much interest, except as a preliminary exercise. The model-theoretic

---

[2] See [Curry, 1963], and the more recent survey in [Barwise, 1977; Part D: "Proof Theory and Constructive Mathematics"].

enterprise needs a theory of reasoning on which to work, not just a language. We can easily interpret the *language* of intuitionistic logic using classical models—in fact, the language is the same as that of classical logic. But this interpretation is not well motivated, since it validates inferences that from the intuitionistic standpoint are invalid. Without good, informal intuitions about valid inference, or formalized proof procedures, or implemented reasoning algorithms, we have nothing to guarantee that the model theory is appropriate.

In interpreting networks, then, the first challenge is to articulate the intuitions about reasoning and present them in a suitable format (one that is relatively independent of irrelevant implementation details). The second challenge is to seek appropriate model-theoretic interpretations, and to show that they meet technical criteria of adequacy, such as soundness and, if possible, completeness.[3] The final challenge is to demonstrate that the process of formalization and model-theoretic interpretation has a practical point—that it helps us to understand network formalisms better, and that this improved understanding actually serves the applied purposes of knowledge representation.

7.2 OVERVIEW OF INHERITANCE THEORY

Fahlman's NETL project, carried out at MIT during the late 1970s, is the starting point for the research presented here. Though, of course, many of the ideas Fahlman brought together in the NETL system derive from earlier work, the combination was new. And though it proved very difficult to advance NETL directly, the ideas have influenced later work in many directions. On the technological side, it inspired the "connection machine." And the later work in inheritance theory that worked backward, toward theoretical foundations for network formalisms, was inspired by Fahlman's more informal treatment of knowledge representation issues.

Fahlman's dissertation [Fahlman, 1979] is visionary in concentrating on a central, critical problem and suggesting how resources from many areas of computer science could be mobilized to solve it. The task Fahlman targets is the efficient, intelligent retrieval of knowledge from massive amounts of stored information. The strategic significance of this problem for AI, and its difficulty, is uncontroversial.

Fahlman's solution features graph-like structures as the representation language and inheritance as the central reasoning mechanism. In showing how to organize knowledge in the NETL formalism, Fahlman developed a pictorial notation that proved to be very useful in presenting examples of reasoning problems and working out algorithms for solving them. He argues, through case-by-case

[3] Other criteria, especially *modularity*, have been suggested in connection with the logical interpretation of nonmonotonic inheritance networks. See, for instance, [Etherington, 1988; p. 102].

presentation of many examples, that the reasoning algorithms required for a wide variety of knowledge representation purposes can be carried out by *parallel marker propagation algorithms*. These are low polynomial in time complexity when simulated by serial processors, and *extremely* fast if they are performed by truly parallel processors,[4] and he speculates in some detail on the engineering problems involved in building a NETL machine.

Touretzky's 1986 dissertation began the process of providing theoretical foundations for Fahlman's ideas. Fahlman's net language is comprehensive in its expressive coverage. Therefore, Touretzky adopts a strategy of focusing on "fragments" of NETL, and providing general, implementation-independent definitions of the consequence relation between a NETL fragment and the conclusions that it yields. The consequences of these general definitions can then be explored; in particular, questions of soundness can be dealt with.

In their appeal to the graph-like structure of networks and to Fahlman's diagram conventions, Touretzky's inheritance definitions are much more pictorial in flavor than the traditional definitions of proofs in logic. But they closely resemble these accounts in many ways. There is a strong analogy between the notion of a *proof*, which in logic is a tree-like array of formulas, and that of a *path*, which in Touretzky's work is usually a sequence of linked nodes in a network. Just as in logic the existence of a proof using only certain premises justifies a conclusion from these premises, in inheritance theory the existence of a path through a network justifies a conclusion supported by the network.

Touretzky concentrates mainly on the problem of multiple inheritance with exceptions. He shows that Fahlman's shortest-path algorithms are unsound for this case, but that a more sophisticated definition using "inferential distance," or specificity of information, yields an algorithm that seems intuitive and that still can be implemented using efficient parallel marker propagation algorithms.

Touretzky's theoretical analysis provides many insights into the workings of inheritance algorithms. For instance, the work shows that nonmonotonic networks must in general be acyclic in order to yield sensible inheritance definitions.

Much of Touretzky's study is devoted to implementation issues. By providing a characterization of inheritance problems, his general inheritance definitions enable a theoretical analysis of the relevant algorithms. Improving on Fahlman's techniques, Touretzky develops general methods for showing that inheritance definitions can be implemented using parallel marker propagation. Subsequent work, and, in particular [Selman and Levesque, 1989], has shown that implementation issues are subtler, and the danger of intractability is greater, than Touretzky

---

[4] Fahlman suggested an architecture in which one processor was allocated to each node and link of the net. In these machines, all processors respond to global commands from a superprocessor. Transitive closure algorithms run in time linear in the depth of the graph.

assumed in his 1984 work. Some natural inheritance problems turn out to be intractable—and so presumably cannot be efficiently implemented even in parallel.

The published intractability results all depend heavily on the treatment of exceptions, and so might create the expectation that intractability, when it is present, is related to nonmonotonicity. But the problems we will discuss later in this chapter suggest that there may also be natural monotonic inheritance problems that have a polynomial time complexity that is uncomfortably large. There may even be intractable monotonic inheritance problems.

More recently, a group of logically minded collaborators joined Touretzky in a long-term project devoted to the theoretical analyses of semantic networks.[5] Like [Touretzky, 1986], most of the later research concentrates on issues concerning nonmonotonic inheritance in "network fragments" that are very limited in expressive power. Most of the analyses apply to nonmonotonic networks[6] that only have IS-A and IS-NOT-A links, though in some cases these links may either be strict or defeasible. Thus, the work has been come to be seen as closely connected to research in nonmonotonic reasoning, where it provides a rich source of reasoning and representation problems, and a sort of "bridge discipline" that can relate the general logical approaches to nonmonotonic reasoning to applied formalisms.

However, a general theoretical approach to network formalisms and path-based reasoning has also emerged from this work. This general theory of inheritance has no intrinsic connection to nonmonotonic reasoning. Monotonic networks are investigated in [Thomason et al., 1986] and [Thomason, 1989], and even in fairly restricted cases have turned out to be more complex and interesting than might have been supposed.

7.3 CHARACTERIZING NETS IN GENERAL

Choosing different type styles for network items (as opposed, say, to syntactic logical items, or elements of models), helps with topic management. When notation is wanted for network items, we will generally use bold italics. In particular, we will use $\boldsymbol{a}$, $\boldsymbol{b}$, $\boldsymbol{c}$, ... for individuals, $\boldsymbol{p}$, $\boldsymbol{q}$, $\boldsymbol{r}$, ... for kinds, and $\boldsymbol{x}$, $\boldsymbol{y}$, $\boldsymbol{z}$, ... for nodes in general, either individuals or kinds.

At a very abstract level, a *net* Γ consists of the following components.

---

[5] The main figures in the LINKUP project group are J.F. Horty, R.H. Thomason, and D.S. Touretzky. John Aronis, Bob Carpenter, and Charles Cross have collaborated. See the reference section of this paper for project results. We gratefully acknowledge support from the National Science Foundation.

[6] A network is *monotonic* if adding information to it never loses conseqences, and it is *nonmonotonic* if it isn't monotonic. More precisely, a set Γ of links with support relation $\rhd$ is monotonic if whenever $\Gamma \rhd \boldsymbol{A}$ and $\Gamma \subseteq \Delta$, then $\Delta \rhd \boldsymbol{A}$.

- A set $\boldsymbol{I}$ (= $\boldsymbol{I}(\Gamma)$) of *individuals;*
- A disjoint set $\boldsymbol{K}$ (= $\boldsymbol{K}(\Gamma)$) of *kinds*;
- A set ***L-types*** of *link types*;
- A set ***WF-links***(Γ) of "well-formed links;"
- A set ***KB***(Γ) of "known links," that is, links that are part of the knowledge base of Γ;
- A set ***Q-types***(Γ) of *query types*;
- A *support* relation $\triangleright$ between ***KB***(Γ) and the query types of Γ. '$\Gamma \triangleright \boldsymbol{A}$' means that the network Γ supports the conclusion $\boldsymbol{A}$.

In general, the link types will be determined by the expressivity of the network. To have any inheritance at all there should be IS-A links. But often other sorts of links may be included: IS-NOT-A links, relational links, etc. In general, link types will not only affect algorithms but will play a crucial part in the network's informal interpretation. Links are usually represented using arrows, which may or may not be decorated with type labels; $\Rightarrow$, for example, is a monotonic IS-A link connecting concepts $\boldsymbol{p}$ and $\boldsymbol{q}$.[7] Formally, though, we can think of a link as a triple $\langle \theta, \boldsymbol{x}, \boldsymbol{y} \rangle$, where θ is the link type. The link $\boldsymbol{p} \Rightarrow \boldsymbol{q}$, for instance, is really the triple $\langle \mathrm{IS}, \boldsymbol{p}, \boldsymbol{q} \rangle$.

The set ***WF-links***(Γ) of well-formed links over Γ is obtained by imposing syntactic constraints on the set of all possible links involving elements of Γ. (For instance, it is natural to require that for $\boldsymbol{x} \Rightarrow \boldsymbol{y}$ to be well-formed, $\boldsymbol{y}$ must be a kind.) The set ***Q-types***(Γ) represents the possible queries over Γ. Since units of information are stored in networks in the form of links, well-formed links represent the allowable data inputs to a network; queries, on the other hand, represent allowable data outputs.

In simple cases, the allowable data inputs and outputs are the same; there will be no important differences between the query language of a net and its set of well-formed links. In others, there may be well-formed links that do not correspond to queries, or queries that correspond not to simple links, but to certain combinations of links. For instance, there might be conjunctive queries, even though there are no conjunctive links, or (in cases where closed-world reasoning is allowed) there might be negative queries but no negative links.

We expect that the support relation associated with a network will be determined from its knowledge base by general rules, much like the inferential rules of a logic. Thus, we can group networks according to *logical category*; networks belonging to the same logical category share the same grammar and inheritance

---

[7] Single-shafted arrows are reserved for nonmonotonic, or defeasible links; double-shafted arrows denote strict links. In this chapter, all the examples we will consider will be monotonic.

definition; their link types and well-formedness constraints are the same, and they share the same rules determining how the network will compute answers to queries from its knowledge base. But the individuals, the kinds, and the connections in linguistically similar nets may differ.

Inheritance theory deals with nets at the level of logical category—the theory is concerned with general characteristics of networks that share a certain syntax and inference strategy. [Horty et al., 1987b], for instance, describes networks involving only defeasible IS-A and IS-NOT-A links, and employing a "bottom up, skeptical" reasoning strategy in calculating multiple inheritance with exceptions. This paper will discuss monotonic networks involving IS-A and IS-NOT-A links, as well as links standing for identity, relations, and roles.

The most distinctive characteristic of the network approach to reasoning is that answering a query depends on the existence of a path involving the parts of the query, a path that can then be found using algorithms like Fahlman's parallel marker propagation procedures. The task of defining support and investigating its properties, then, leads us to concentrate on defining the paths through a net that correspond to correct reasoning patterns given the hypotheses in the net's knowledge base—the paths that are *permitted* by the net. In the theory of network-based reasoning, all inquiry into support tends to lead to detailed questions about the permitted paths.

The inferential structure of a network Γ, then, consists of the following additional elements.[8]

- A set ***WF-paths***(Γ) of structures composed of well-formed links of Γ, the paths that are well-formed in Γ;
- An assignment to each path in ***WF-paths***(Γ) of an associated query type in ***Q-types***(Γ);
- A subset ***OK-paths***(Γ) of ***WF-paths***(Γ)—the paths that are inferentially correct in Γ.

We then say that a net Γ supports a conclusion $\boldsymbol{A}$, $\Gamma \rhd \boldsymbol{A}$, if Γ permits a path whose query type is $\boldsymbol{A}$.

A simple example may help to fix these ideas. Let's suppose that we have only IS-A link types, and that a link $\boldsymbol{x} \Rightarrow \boldsymbol{y}$ is well formed if and only if $\boldsymbol{y}$ is a kind. All queries over Γ have the form IS$(\boldsymbol{x},\boldsymbol{p})$, where $\boldsymbol{x}$ is any node of Γ (individual or kind) and $\boldsymbol{p}$ is a kind of Γ. In this simple case, a well-formed path is simply any sequence of well-formed links. Such a path corresponds to the query type IS$(\boldsymbol{x},\boldsymbol{p})$, where $\boldsymbol{x}$ is the tail of its first and $\boldsymbol{p}$ the head of its last link. Finally, a path π is permitted by Γ if it has the form

---

[8] This is a simplified characterization that has to be generalized to accommodate cases in which there can be "multiple extensions."

$$\langle x_0 \Rightarrow x_1, x_1 \Rightarrow x_2, \ldots, x_{n-1} \Rightarrow x_n \rangle,$$

where each component link $x_i \Rightarrow x_{i+1}$ of π belongs to $\boldsymbol{KB}(\Gamma)$.

Here, support is determined simply by computing the transitive closure of a set of IS-A links. A simple depth-first serial algorithm of complexity $O(m)$, where m is the number of links in the net, performs the required computation.[9] In Fahlman's parallel architecture, the computation is linear in the "height" of the net—that is, in the length of the longest permitted path.[10] Even in very large-scale knowledge representation algorithms, one would expect this to be bounded by a fairly low constant, say 20.

In this simple example, paths are just connected sequences of links, and there is a direct and natural connection to the "spreading activation" idea of parallel marker propagation algorithms, in which inferential processes spread through links to other nodes. In more complex cases, however, it may be necessary to think of paths as organized into parts according to some sort of syntactic structure, or necessary to deal with configurations of links that are not linear. We will discuss such a case later in this paper.

7.4 THE TOPIC

The remainder of this paper will concentrate on issues that arise in accounting for roles and "dependent relations" in inheritance theory. This case was discussed informally in [Fahlman, 1979]. On the other hand, virtually every usable applied network or frame-based representation incorporates roles, and supports the sort of "structure copying" relational inheritance that is described, for instance, on pages 263–268 of Winston's textbook [Winston, 1974].[11]

Despite the ubiquity of roles and dependent relations in applications, almost no theoretical attention has been devoted to the investigation of related network formalisms and analysis of the appropriate accompanying algorithms. Theoretical work on the treatment of role inheritance seems to have been confined to studies like [Hayes, 1979] and [Nilsson, 1980; pp. 370–378], which present translations of the network formalism into first-order logic.

---

[9] See [Aho et al., 1974] and [Guerreiro et al., 1990].

[10] Actually, in the length of the longest "shortest path between two nodes." This needn't be the same as the longest path, when multiple inheritance is permitted and Γ is a directed acyclic graph.

[11] The idea of structure copying is described in more detail in Section 7.5, below.

But, as we argued above, a logical translation of a network language is premature without an analysis of the network as an independent reasoning module. Without such an analysis, we have no guarantee that the logical interpretation is a match for the network. Such a translation can help to fix the interpretation of network formalisms and to specify algorithms.

There are several reasons we need a careful preliminary analysis of network reasoning before promoting a logical interpretation. A logical interpretation is incorrect unless it not only delivers valid translations of inferences that are validated by the network it interprets, but provides *invalid* interpretations of those that are invalidated by the network.[12]

On this criterion, we have argued in [Thomason et al., 1986] that classical logic is inappropriate for interpreting even monotonic path-based reasoning systems. Also, logical formalisms are in general much more expressively powerful than networks. Since inheritance networks are expected to be relatively tractable, one would hope that they would turn out to correspond to relatively constrained logics—certainly, more tractable than full first-order logic, or even than propositional logic. But the only way to discover the appropriate logical fragment is first to work out a definition of inheritance in the appropriate network, then to show that this definition is equivalent to logical consequence in some logical translation.

Formulating this translation and proving soundness and completeness is itself a major theoretical task, which presupposes the project discussed here. We will occasionally use logical translations of the inheritance formalism to clarify the interpretation; but this use of the translation apparatus will be entirely informal. We'll concentrate on formulating the inheritance theory and explaining the major results that need to be established about it.

This chapter is intended as a generally readable presentation for nonspecialists. This creates some expository problems, since we will be trying to present the ideas behind complex issues that have only recently been worked out and that have not yet even been discussed in print. We will compromise here by stressing the general motivating ideas and leaving out most of the technical details.

7.5 ROLES AND DEPENDENCE: INFORMAL MOTIVATION

In addition to a basic IS-A hierarchy, many semantic network formalisms provide a way to define dependent individuals called "roles" that correspond roughly to natural language possessives and that support limited sorts of quantificational reasoning. For example, the ***father*** role might be attached to the individual

---

[12] An interpretation according to which *every* argument is valid is automatically sound, but trivial. An interpretation of intuitionistic logic that makes every classical argument valid is sound, but fails to respect the motivation of the logic.

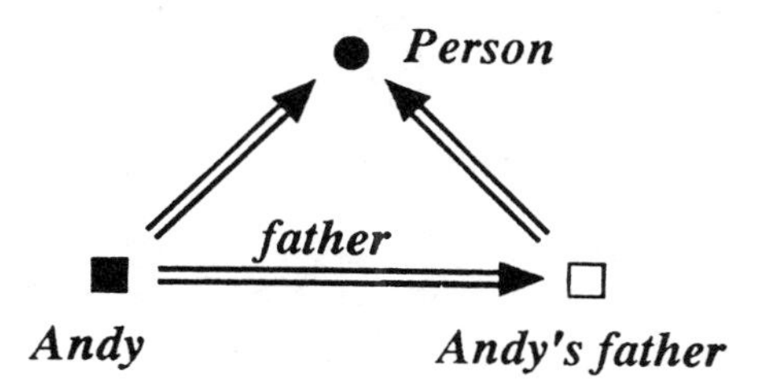

Figure 7.1: Roles attached to individuals

Andy, as in the following simple net, which also contains the information that Andy and his father are persons.

In Figure 7.1, individual nodes are square and kind nodes are round. Note that roles are realized as *link types*, not as nodes. The interpretation of the role link in Figure 7.1 is that Andy has a father; thus, a link involving the role *f* can be thought of as a "HAS-AN-*f*" link.

Each role attachment also automatically creates a node (in our example, the node labeled ***Andy's father***) that then serves as a locus of information about the corresponding role filler. (Thus, the information that Andy's father is a person is represented by the IS-A link between ***Andy's father*** and ***Person***.) We will call such role-created nodes *dependent*; thus, in this diagram the node labeled ***Andy*** is independent, and the one labeled ***Andy's father*** is dependent. In the figure, the independent node is shown as solid, while the dependent node is shown in outline.

Roles may lead from dependent nodes to other dependent nodes. But, if role cycles are disallowed (a constraint we will impose on nets) and nets are finite, then given a dependent node ***x*** we will eventually be able to locate an independent node from which ***x*** can be obtained by a series of role links. We can call this node an *ancestor* of ***x***.[13] In Figure 7.1, the node labeled ***Andy*** is an ancestor of the one labeled ***Andy's father***.

It is very helpful, both in providing a theoretical analysis of these nets and in interpreting them informally, to distinguish sharply between dependent and independent nodes, where (by definition) a dependent node is one that is created by a

[13] Given other constraints we will impose, we will also have uniqueness, so that we can actually speak of *the* ancestor of an arbitrary node.

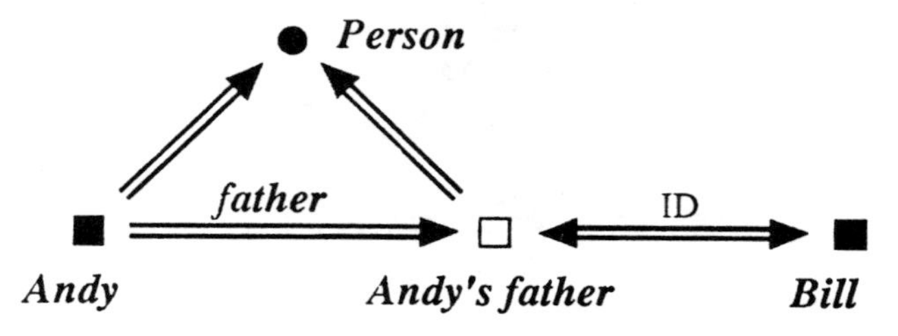

Figure 7.2: Dependent roles and identity

role attachment.[14] Thus, if Bill is Andy's father, we insist on representing this by an identity link, as in Figure 7.2, rather than by pointing a role link directly at ***Bill***.

From this net we will be able to infer that Bill is a person by means of inheritance rules for identity. This is very similar to the situation in logic or mathematics, where one doesn't try to represent the identity of *fa* and *b* by somehow identifying the notations or names '*fa*' and '*b*', but rather by asserting the identity '$fa = b$'. The fact that we require a distinction between two network representations of the same object could perhaps be useful in cases where intensionality is needed.[15] But our insistence on the notational distinction doesn't mean that we are associating an intensional interpretation of some sort with our nets; in fact, our rules for identity will validate a rule of replacement of identicals with identicals. In this sense, the logic associated with the network will be extensional.

Of course, the true power of roles is only realized when we also allow them to attach to kinds, as in Figure 7.3. Attaching the role ***father*** to the kind ***Person*** signifies that a partial function is defined on all instances of this kind—that is, it means that each person has a father. This role attachment creates a *dependent kind*, the node labeled ***Person's father***). Following through on our notational conventions, this node is shown as an unfilled circle in Figure 7.3.

The representation of roles that we will develop here is based on [Fahlman, 1979] rather than on the more familiar KL-ONE tradition of [Brachman and Schmolze, 1985]. If we remember that we are confining ourselves to *single-valued* roles (sometimes called "attributes" in KL-ONE terminology) there are, of course, many similarities, since we are dealing with the same underlying notion—that of a

---

[14] One way of seeing why this might be important is to notice the logical difference between the two IS-A links in Figure 7.1. The one between ***Andy*** and ***Person*** is represented by Pa, while the one between ***Andy's father*** and ***Person*** is represented by $\exists x[x = fa \wedge Px]$. The former predication is direct, whereas the latter is asserted through pointers to a.

[15] For instance, in an application in which we wanted to represent the information that Carol doesn't know whether Bill is Andy's father.

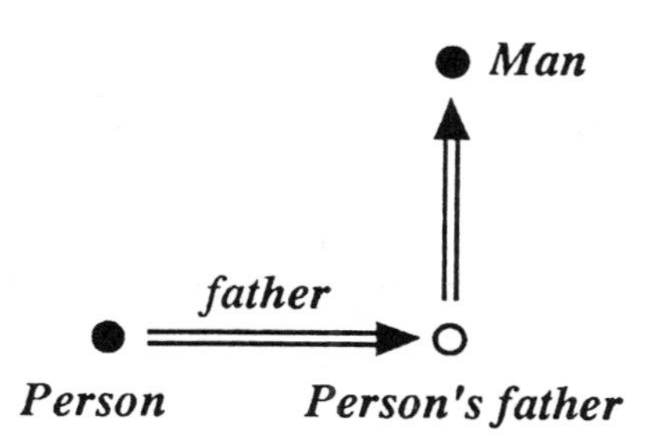

Figure 7.3: Roles attached to kinds

function. But there are some differences. Most importantly, there is nothing in KL-ONE representations that corresponds directly to our notion of a dependent node. Such differences explain why the pictorial conventions we have adopted are somewhat different from others that have been used for diagramming networks with roles, and in particular from those of KL-ONE.

One good way to think of a dependent node, say ***Person's father*** in Figure 7.3, is as a representation of the generic person's father. But of course, Platonic objects like these are less scientific (or at least, less well understood) than logical representations. If we want first-order interpretations of net formalisms with roles, it is probably best not to think of a dependent kind as standing for any concept at all, but as a sort of peg on which to hang information about the independent concept from which it derives. Thus, the formalization of the information in the role link in Figure 7.3 is $\forall x[Px \rightarrow M(fx)]$. This formula doesn't contain an explicit representation, such as $\lambda x \exists y[Py \wedge Fy = x]$, of the class of things that are fathers of people.

Using lambda abstraction, we can represent the IS-A link in Figure 7.3 as a subsumption between two class terms:

$$\lambda x \exists y[Py \wedge fy = x] \ \forall \ \lambda x\, Mx.$$

In this formula we have a logical unit, the term $\lambda x \exists y[Py \wedge fy = x]$, which represents the set of things that are fathers of some person and which does correspond to the dependent node ***Person's father***. But if we take relational links into account, it turns out that this idea is seriously flawed. It misrepresents the logic of dependent nodes as they figure in inheritance systems.

Thus, suppose that we introduce a ***Loves*** relation into the network, and use it to link the dependent node ***Person's father*** to the role node ***Person's mother***. We also create an individual, Andy, and stipulate explicitly that Andy has a father and a mother. We want to be able to conclude from this configuration that Andy's father loves Andy's mother, even though no explicit link connects the two dependent nodes attached to ***Andy***. See Figure 7.4.

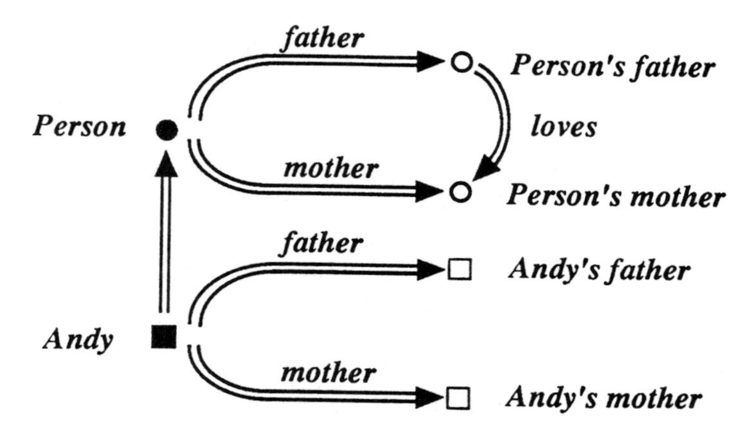

Figure 7.4: Correct inference from dependent relations

Now contrast this with the net in Figure 7.5, containing the information that Bob is a person's father and Carol is a person's mother, and that people's fathers love their mothers. (We understand this last clause in the sense that is equivalent to 'A person's father loves that person's mother.') Here, we definitely do *not* want to infer that Bob loves Carol; we could only do this if we knew that Carol is a person's mother and Bob *that same person's* father—for instance, if we had an identity link between ***Carol*** and ***Andy's mother*** and one between ***Bob*** and ***Andy's father***.

For this reason, we can't interpret relational links between dependent kinds, such as the ***Loves*** link in Figure 7.5, as having the natural class-term interpretation:

$\check{R}(\lambda x \exists y[Py \wedge fy = x], \lambda x \exists y[Py \wedge my = x])$,
where $\check{R}(Q_1,Q_2) =_{df} \forall x \forall y[[Q_1 x \wedge Q_2 y] \Rightarrow R(x,y)]$.

This would be equivalent to treating dependent relational links as universal relational links. Such links are worth studying;[16] but to use them here would be to confuse *People's fathers love their mothers* with *People's fathers love people's mothers*. A more general argument (which we won't give here) shows that *any* logical interpretation that assigns class terms to dependent nodes won't capture the proper relational inferences.

The simplest way to think of dependent nodes so as to get the inferences correct is as *syncategorematic*: Though they have no meaningful logical interpreta-

[16] See [Touretzky, 1986] and [Thomason, 1989].

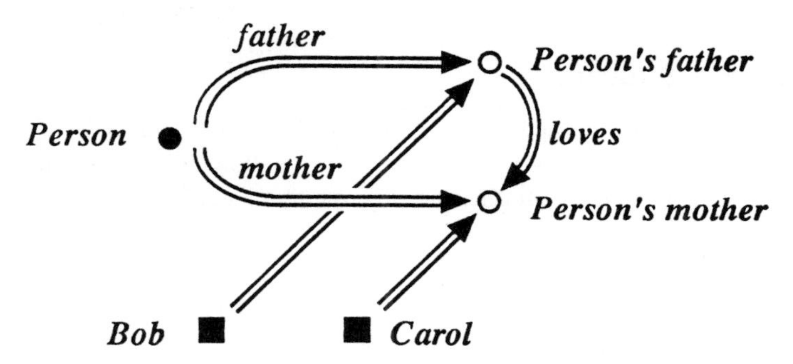

Figure 7.5: Incorrect inference from dependent relations

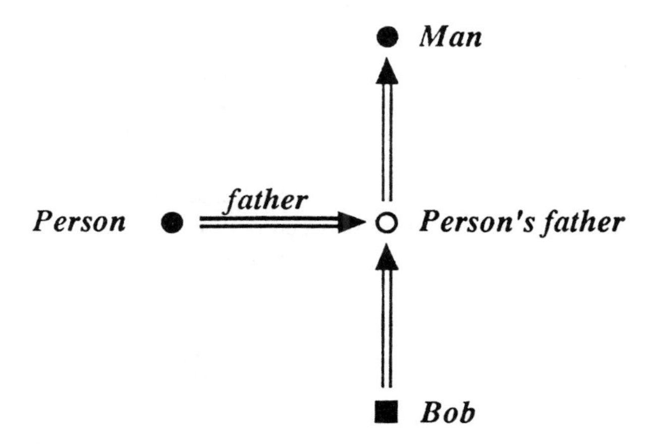

Figure 7.6: IS-A links and dependent kinds

tion in themselves, they do contribute to the meaning of larger units in which they occur. In Figure 7.6, for instance, the lower IS-A link is interpreted

$$\exists x[Px \wedge fx = b],$$

and the higher IS-A link is interpreted

$$\forall x\ [Px \rightarrow \exists y[y = fx] \wedge Mfx].$$

Finally, returning to Figure 7.5, the relational link is interpreted

$$\forall x\ [Px \rightarrow \exists y[y = fx] \wedge \exists z[z = mx] \wedge R(fx,mx)].$$

7.6 CHARACTERIZING NETS WITH ROLES AND RELATIONS

7.6.1 Network Structure

The link types of the nets we will study include IS-A and IS-NOT-A, as well as types that are generated by underlying sets of relations and roles; we treat identity as a relation. To begin with, then, we assume that a net Γ involves:

- A set ***Rels***(Γ) of *relations;* and
- A set ***Roles***(Γ) of *roles.*

We use $\boldsymbol{R}$, $\boldsymbol{S}$ for relations and $\boldsymbol{f}$, $\boldsymbol{g}$, $\boldsymbol{h}$ for simple roles.

It will be important for semantic purposes to distinguish between the way relations act on kinds and the way they act on individuals; thus, for each relation $\boldsymbol{R}$ there will be a *generic* link type $\tilde{\boldsymbol{R}}$ as well as a *specific* link type $\boldsymbol{R}$. This may sound over complicated, but we are trying to develop a notation that will accommodate several types of generic relations, such as unrestricted universal–universal relations, like *Squares have more sides than triangles.* In later applications we will need a notation that mentions the underlying relation as well as the way in which the relation is deployed in a generic link; we'll use $\boldsymbol{R}$ for the relation, $\check{\boldsymbol{R}}$ for universal relational links, and $\tilde{\boldsymbol{R}}$ for dependent generic relational links. Otherwise, we would not be able to represent the difference between propositions like *People are younger than their fathers* and *People are younger than people's fathers.*

To provide for identity, we will assume that relations for identity and difference are among the relations in ***Rels***(Γ).

Our nets will therefore have the following link types: IS, $\overline{\text{IS}}$, $\boldsymbol{R}$ for $\boldsymbol{R} \in \boldsymbol{Rels}$, $\tilde{\boldsymbol{R}}$ for $\boldsymbol{R} \in \boldsymbol{Rels}$, $\boldsymbol{f}$ for $\boldsymbol{f} \in \boldsymbol{Roles} \cup \{\boldsymbol{i}\}$, ID, $\widetilde{\text{ID}}$, and $\overline{\text{ID}}$.[17]

The first two types are called *the sortal types.* The role $\boldsymbol{i}$ is a designated element that is not already in ***Roles***; we use $\boldsymbol{i}$ to represent the role type of the identity role, "self."

We use the following notation for links.

1. $\boldsymbol{x} \Rightarrow \boldsymbol{y}$ for an IS-A link $\langle \text{IS}, \boldsymbol{x}, \boldsymbol{y} \rangle$.
2. $\boldsymbol{x} \Leftrightarrow \boldsymbol{y}$ for a specific identity link $\langle \text{ID}, \boldsymbol{x}, \boldsymbol{y} \rangle$.
3. $x \not\Rightarrow \boldsymbol{y}$ for an IS–NOT link $\langle \overline{\text{IS}}, \boldsymbol{x}, \boldsymbol{y} \rangle$
4. $x \overset{\boldsymbol{R}}{\Rightarrow} \boldsymbol{y}$ for a relational link $\langle \boldsymbol{R}, \boldsymbol{x}, \boldsymbol{y} \rangle$.
5. $x \overset{\tilde{\boldsymbol{R}}}{\Rightarrow} y$ for a dependent generic relational link $\langle \tilde{\boldsymbol{R}}, \boldsymbol{x}, \boldsymbol{y} \rangle$.

---

[17] We have not included a link type for generic negated identities in this presentation. To keep things slightly simpler, negative relational links (except for specific negated identities) are also omitted. But adding them to the language does not seem to cause any special difficulties.

6. $z \overset{\overline{ID}}{\Leftrightarrow}$ for a dependent generic identity link $\langle \overset{\overline{ID}}{\Leftrightarrow}, \boldsymbol{y}, \boldsymbol{z} \rangle$.
7. $\boldsymbol{x} \overset{f}{\Rightarrow} \boldsymbol{y}$ for a role link $\langle \boldsymbol{f}, \boldsymbol{x}, \boldsymbol{y} \rangle$.

In our nets, a link is well-formed only if it meets the following conditions.

[Constraint 1.] If the link type is sortal, the head is a kind;

[Constraint 2.] If the link type is ID or $\overline{\text{ID}}$, the head and tail are both individuals;

[Constraint 3.] If the link type is nonsortal, the head and tail are either both individuals or both kinds; and in particular;

[Constraint 4.] If the link type is a specific relation, the head and tail are both individuals, and if the link type is a dependent generic relation, the head and tail are both kinds.

Thus, $\langle \text{IS}, \boldsymbol{a}, \boldsymbol{b} \rangle$, $\langle \boldsymbol{R}, \boldsymbol{a}, \boldsymbol{p} \rangle$, and $\langle \boldsymbol{f}, \boldsymbol{a}, \boldsymbol{p} \rangle$ are all disallowed as ill-formed links.

The sense of these conditions is that, while the subject of an IS-A proposition can be either an individual or a kind, the predicate must be a kind; thus, our representation treats IS-A propositions like *Clyde is an elephant* and *Elephants are grey things* as fundamentally different in form from specific identity propositions like *Clyde is Jumbo's father.*[18]

Also, we disallow relational statements that mix individuals and kinds;

$$\boldsymbol{a} \overset{\tilde{\boldsymbol{R}}}{\Rightarrow} \boldsymbol{p} \text{ and } \boldsymbol{p} \overset{\tilde{\boldsymbol{R}}}{\Rightarrow} \boldsymbol{a}$$

are both ill-formed.[19] Finally, the restriction on roles tells us that if ***elephant*** is a kind, then ***elephant's trunk*** is a kind; and if ***Clyde*** is an individual, then ***Clyde's trunk*** must also be an individual. As long as we assume that there is a difference between kinds on the one hand and classes and the like on the other, so that classes

---

[18] This distinction is borrowed from the usual practice in logic. But, since inheritance through identity links is very similar to inheritance through IS-A links, it is not at all necessary to make this distinction in inheritance formalisms. In fact, the predicational and identity forms are collapsed in [Thomason, 1989]. In analyzing roles, though, as we will do in this paper, it simplifies things to make the distinction.

[19] Both of these are ruled out on categorial grounds; a dependent generic relation can neither be induced by an individual nor induce a dependent node that is an individual. Of course, we may well want to mix kinds and individuals in relational propositions; for instance, we may want to say something like *Numbers are divisible by 1.* But this would be a universal relational link rather than a dependent generic relational link.

are best thought of as *individuals* that can contain other individuals as members, this restriction makes sense.[20]

We will discuss the queries associated with these nets, as well as paths and support, in later sections.

7.6.2 Composite Roles

$\boldsymbol{F}$, $\boldsymbol{G}$, $\boldsymbol{H}$, $\boldsymbol{J}$ range over *composite roles*. These should be thought of as composite functions generated from simple roles. We represent composite roles as strings of simple roles; the identity role $\boldsymbol{i}$ counts as a simple role. We also allow the empty list $\varnothing$ as a (trivial) composite role.

Where $\boldsymbol{F} = \boldsymbol{f}_1 \ldots \boldsymbol{f}_n$ is a composite role and for all i, where $1 < i \leq n$, either

$$\boldsymbol{x}_{i-1} \overset{f_i}{\Rightarrow} \boldsymbol{x}_i \in \boldsymbol{KB}(\Gamma) \text{ or } \boldsymbol{f}_i = \boldsymbol{i} \text{ and } \boldsymbol{x}_i = \boldsymbol{x}_{i-1},$$

we will say that $\boldsymbol{x}_n$ is a *dependent of* $\boldsymbol{x}_0$ (in $\boldsymbol{KB}(\Gamma)$), and in fact will say that

$$\boldsymbol{x}_n = \boldsymbol{F}(\boldsymbol{x}_0).$$

It will follow from well-formedness constraints that $\boldsymbol{F}(\boldsymbol{x})$ is unique if it is defined. A node that depends only on itself as a dependent is *independent*. A node that is not independent is *dependent*.

7.6.3 Further Well-Formedness Constraints on Nets

[Constraint 5.] There are no nontrivial *role cycles*. That is, if $\boldsymbol{FfG}(\boldsymbol{x})$ is defined (where $\boldsymbol{F}$ and $\boldsymbol{G}$ are possibly null) and $\boldsymbol{f} \neq \boldsymbol{i}$, then $\boldsymbol{FfG}(\boldsymbol{x}) \neq \boldsymbol{x}$.[21]

Since our logical interpretation of a dependent node $\boldsymbol{x}$ presupposes an ancestor, role cycles are disallowed by our interpretation. Unless they were restricted in some way, such cycles could also undermine the algorithms for reasoning about roles.

[Constraint 6.] A role value can be the value of only one role. That is, if $\boldsymbol{x} \overset{f}{\Rightarrow} \boldsymbol{y} \in \boldsymbol{KB}(\Gamma)$ and $z \overset{g}{\Rightarrow} \boldsymbol{y} \in \boldsymbol{KB}(\Gamma)$ then $\boldsymbol{f} = \boldsymbol{g}$ and $\boldsymbol{x} = z$. (It will follow from the rules below that if $\boldsymbol{x}$ is a node of Γ, then $\boldsymbol{x} \overset{i}{\Rightarrow} \boldsymbol{x}$ is permitted by Γ. But this path does not count as cyclic by the above definition.)

---

[20] Such a distinction at the logical level, between what is predicational (like 'associate' in 'They associate together') and what is nominal (like 'association' in 'Their association lasted a long time', has a long history in modern logic, going back to Frege; it can also be motivated by considerations having to do with the workings of natural languages.

[21] The use of '≠' in this condition is metalinguistic; the condition requires that $\boldsymbol{FfG}(\boldsymbol{x})$ and $\boldsymbol{x}$ must be different nodes. But we do allow identity relations (both specific and generic) to link $\boldsymbol{FfG}(\boldsymbol{x})$ and $\boldsymbol{x}$ under the conditions of this constraint.

This constraint is largely a matter of convenience; for purposes of analysis it is easier to represent a value of two functions by creating two nodes representing the function value and declaring them to be identical. This policy would also have some value in correcting misidentifications, and in applications in which intensionality is important.

[Constraint 7.] A role can have only one value. That is, if $\boldsymbol{x} \overset{f}{\Rightarrow} \boldsymbol{y} \in \boldsymbol{KB}(\Gamma)$ and $\boldsymbol{x} \overset{f}{\Rightarrow} \boldsymbol{y} \in \boldsymbol{KB}(\Gamma)$ then $\boldsymbol{y} = z$.

This constraint is an obvious limitation on the ability of our net formalism to deal with roles as they are used in knowledge representation applications, since it prohibits multiple role fillers. Part of our motivation for this constraint is the need to make simplifying assumptions that will allow us to develop a theory of the network algorithms; as we will see, even with this restriction the analysis is quite complex. The assumption also simplifies the logical picture; whereas functions whose values are individuals are routinely included in the apparatus of first-order logic, we do not see how to treat functions whose values are *sets* naturally in a first-order setting. Finally, we believe that the best way to implement multiple role fillers may well be to add types of sets and of numbers to the inheritance network, together with simple special-purpose algorithms for processing these types, and to treat multiple roles as set-valued single roles. In this way, multiple roles could be accommodated even while respecting Constraint 7.

It follows from our constraints that every node depends on exactly one independent node.

7.6.4 More Motivation: Roles and Virtual Structure

If we omit the roles attached to ***Andy*** in Figure 7.4, we can still infer that Andy's father loves Andy's mother, even though no special role information attaches to ***Andy***. See Figure 7.7.

Here the IS-A link between ***Andy*** and ***Person*** creates implicit or virtual ***father*** and ***mother*** roles attached to ***Andy***. Obviously, we want the inheritance mechanism to include these roles, so that not only derived *links* can be implicit in a net, but also derived *dependent nodes*.[22]

It is natural to deal with this problem by automatically creating the inferred dependent nodes, and letting information about them be inherited. This idea is illustrated in Figures 7.8–7.10, where a net Γ_1 is presented, and enlarged to form a

[22] In [Fahlman, 1979], IS-A links are called "virtual copy" links because they serve as the backbone for this sort of role inheritance. Likewise, KL-ONE "inheritance cables" are so named because they allow rich collections of structural information to be inherited via the IS-A hierarchy.

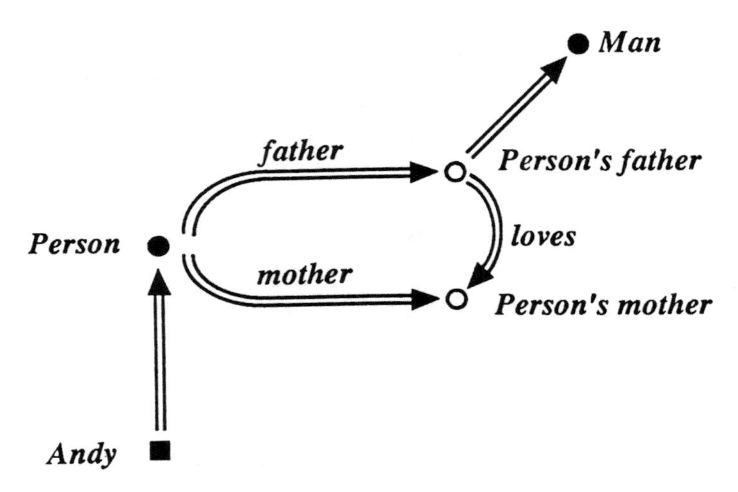

Figure 7.7: Virtual dependent nodes

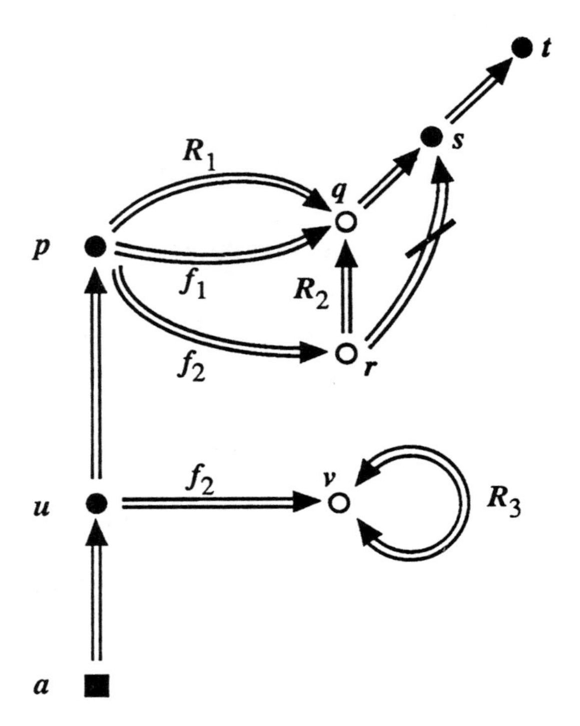

Figure 7.8: A presented net Γ_1

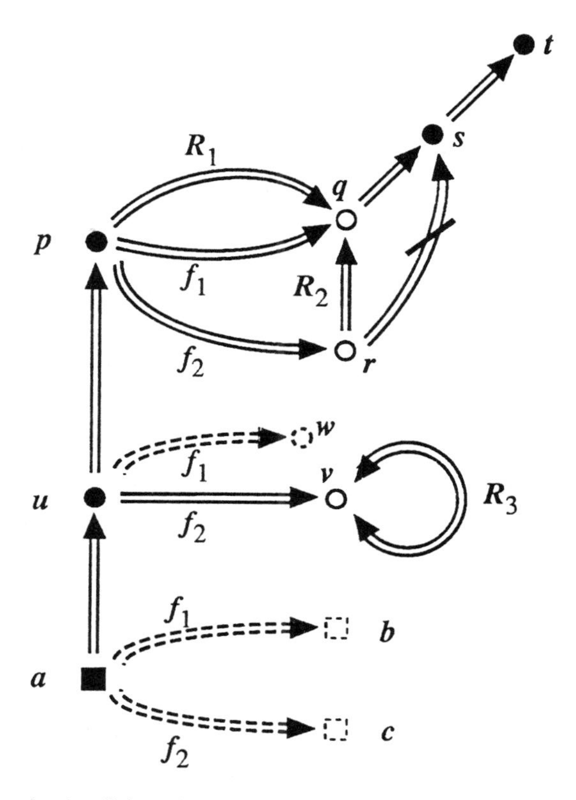

Figure 7.9: Creating implicit nodes in Γ_1 yields Γ_2

net Γ_2. Created nodes in Γ_2 and Γ_3 are shown in dotted outline. Inherited information is shown in Γ_3 by dotted links.

But this idea is more complex than it seems at first glance: There is a recursion concealed in it. To see this, notice that IS-A paths may themselves depend on virtual role links, as in the abstract network in Figure 7.11. Here we can only copy a $\boldsymbol{g}$ role onto a dependent node $\boldsymbol{f(a)}$ after we have created $\boldsymbol{f(a)}$ and used this to derive an IS-A path between $\boldsymbol{f(a)}$ and $\boldsymbol{q}$.

But there is a fundamental obstacle to turning the idea of creating explicit copies into an algorithm—the new structures that are created may be unbounded, so the process of creation will never end. This can happen even in well-motivated and simple examples such as Figure 7.12.

Thus, in developing inheritance algorithms for roles, it is absolutely crucial to carry through to virtual nodes the basic motivation of inheritance. That is, it is

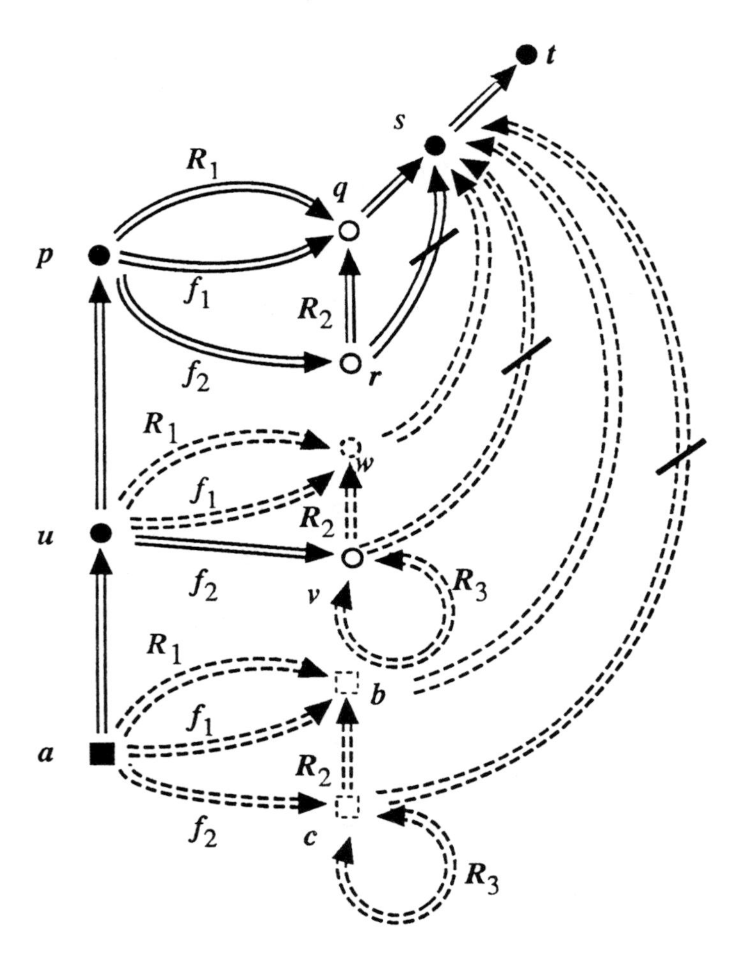

Figure 7.10: Showing inherited links in Γ_2 yields Γ_3

crucial to keep implicit information implicit and to create no structure in addition to what is given in the originally presented net.[23] Nevertheless, the intuition behind the "structure copying" idea remains useful as a *specification* of what the inheritance algorithm should deliver: One of our main results shows that an algorithm that creates no new structure is equivalent to simple inheritance in the (possibly

[23] This basic idea is well motivated in [Fahlman, 1979].

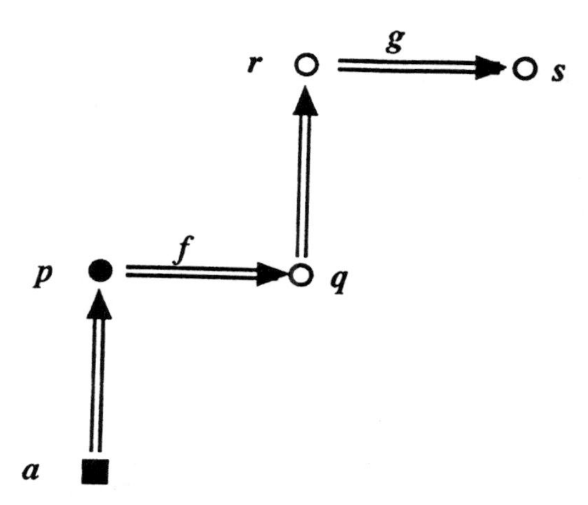

Figure 7.11: IS-A paths derived through virtual roles

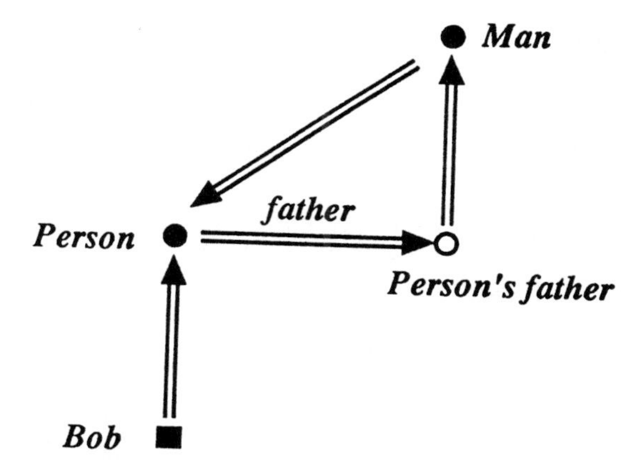

Figure 7.12: IS-A links and dependent kinds

infinite) net obtained by systematically adding derived nodes and links to the original net.

7.6.5 Paths and Configurations

In previous presentations of inheritance theory, *paths* have played a central role. It is paths that mediate between a net and the conclusions that it supports; and the main results of a theory of inheritance will follow from the "inheritance definition" that characterizes inductively the set of paths permitted by a network or permitted by an extension of a network.

In the simplest cases, it is possible to think of the proof-like arrangements of nodes that permit conclusions as simple sequences of nodes; this is what leads to the term 'path'. But as we consider more expressive nets, this simple picture of things becomes harder to maintain. The general principle at work here is that the more expressive the representation system, the harder it is to maintain a visually simple and attractive picture of how concepts are related by proofs in the system.[24] Thus, at one extreme we have visually simple systems like that of [Thomason et al., 1986] and [Horty et al., 1987a]; these systems are severely limited in expressivity, since they only allow IS-A and IS-NOT-A links. At another extreme are full-scale systems like first-order logic, in which it would be a hopeless task to diagram the possible arrangements of concepts in proofs in any visually perspicuous way.

In trying to extend the expressivity of nets, we strain both the visual appeal of "proofs" and the efficiency of proof techniques. However, it seems that inheritance theories can hold up well under the strain of even quite powerful expressive extensions. Though paths become harder to diagram and inheritance algorithms more computationally demanding, the situation is by no means hopeless.

One effect of the tension caused by enhanced expressivity is the need for a more general notion of path, and for a more careful examination of the mechanisms for defining the paths that are permitted by a net.

First, we will need to provide some way of parsing node sequences into subunits. In the role formalism that we will be developing in this chapter, this need is illustrated by a simple sort of inference that was proposed by the nineteenth century logician Augustus de Morgan as a challenge to traditional logic:

Horses are animals.

Therefore, horses' heads are animals' heads.

In terms of our role formalism, this corresponds to the need for a derived IS-A link between ***horse's head*** and ***animal's head*** in Figure 7.13. But such configurations can iterate. Obviously, to trace derived IS-A paths in such structures, such as the path from ***Horse's Head's Size*** to ***Animal's Head's Size*** in Figure 7.14, we will have to parse the roles as we traverse the path, in exactly the same way that we would have to parse a context free language. Thus, we want to think of paths not as unstructured sequences of links, but as *parsed link sequences*, in which certain subsequences are assigned a query type, exactly as phrases of a context-free grammar are assigned a grammatical category in parse trees or labeled bracketings.

---

24 (This is not quite the same as Brachman and Levesque's well-known trade-off between efficiency and expressivity, since visual appeal is not exactly the same as efficiency; but it is a similar trade-off.)

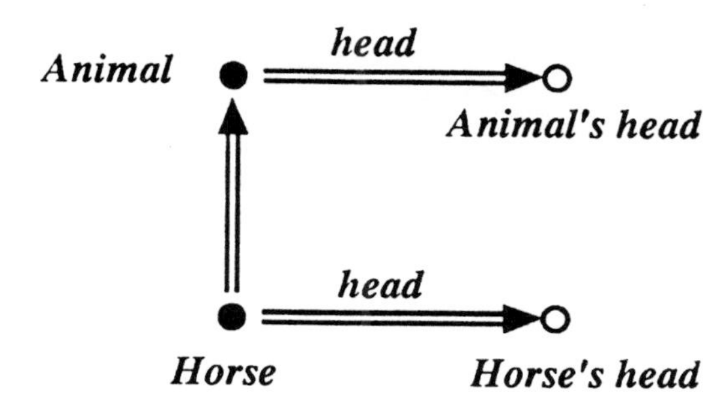

Figure 7.13: Simple IS-A paths through roles

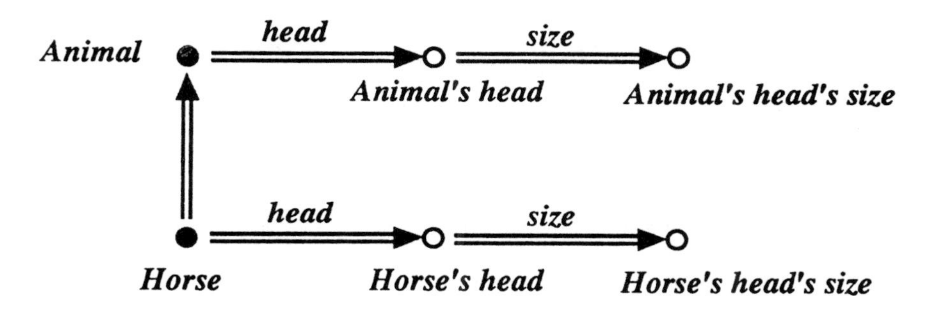

Figure 7.14: Simple IS-A paths through complex roles

Secondly, this application forces us to depart from a strictly linear conception of paths. For instance, it's easy to see that it will be hard to fit the relational conclusion in Figure 7.4 with a linear path from ***Andy's father*** to ***Andy's mother***. The natural diagram of this inference forks at the top and the bottom. And Figure 7.15 illustrates an even more extreme case of nonlinearity.

This net should support the conclusion ID(***b***, ***c***). Even though a role link labeled with ***h*** is not explicitly attached to ***a***, we should be able to derive the conclusion that ***a***'s ***f*** and ***a***'s ***g*** are identical by inheritance, using transitivity of identity.

For reasons such as these, the idea that reasons for conclusions are paths, which are linear sequences of links, or even parsed linear sequences, has to be generalized when roles are present to allow for more complex, nonlinear arrangements of links. We call these larger arrangements *configurations*. Our formal models of configurations have changed several times; at the moment, we think of configurations as structures involving a finite set of nodes together with other components, which may be either paths or nodes. Configurations can in general be

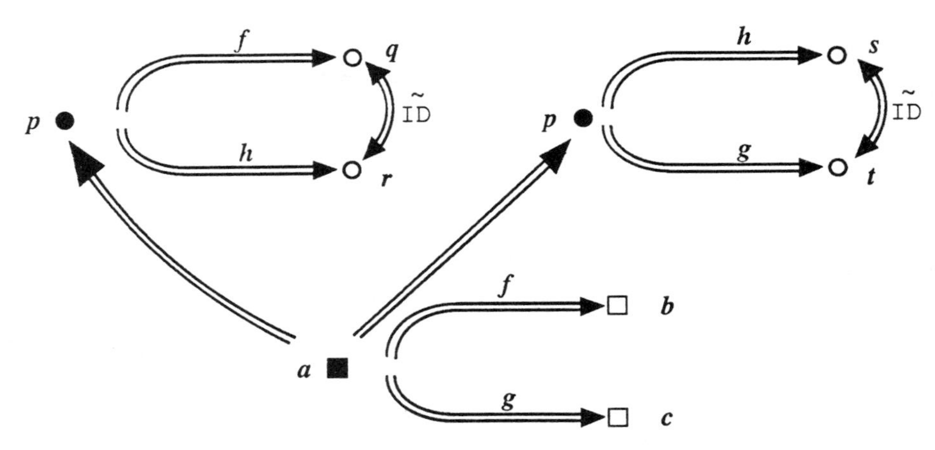

Figure 7.15: Nonlinear reasoning

diagrammed as directed graphs whose vertices are nodes and whose edges are paths. Since we are avoiding technical details in this chapter, this is all we will need to say about configurations.

7.6.6 Trouble for Parallel Marker Solutions?

These reflections show pretty clearly that things are more complicated than Fahlman assumed in his dissertation. If markers not only have to move from one node to another but have to keep track of a potentially unbounded stack of roles that have been traversed, it is difficult to see how the subsumption algorithm can be calculated in Falhman's architecture, in which the storage of each processor is limited by a small constant.[25]

---

[25]This can be turned into a proof that subsumption with roles is beyond the capacity of NETL-style parallel marker propagation algorithms. The point is that, whereas the markers of a NETL machine are limited by a constant bound, there is no limit to the number of roles that can occur in a net. Even if we restrict ourselves to nets with only one role, *f*, a NETL machine doesn't have enough markers to distinguish between all iterations of *f*, e.g., *f*, *ff*, etc. Thus, although NETL machines can deal with some types of proofs of unbounded length, namely those involving transitive closures over a small number of link types, they cannot deal with proofs that involving an unbounded number of link types. Even if the NETL formalism were extended to provide an unbounded number of markers, the global-broadcast nature of the machine would still force it to examine one type of path at a time. The model cannot, for example, propagate marker 1 across ***f*** links and marker 2 across ***g*** links simultaneously. So the combinatorial explosion from examining potentially lengthy compound paths is not eliminated by the marker propagation technique, in the way that the explosion of paths through a graph composed of IS-A links is.

Moreover, since this is a *subsumption* problem, one of Fahlman's basic assumptions is undercut—that the essence of inheritance is taking a transitive closure of IS-A links. This makes it much more difficult to be confident *a priori* of the efficiency of inheritance reasoning. For instance, the depth of inheritance chains is no longer bounded by the chaining of basic taxonomic IS-A links. We also have to add the effects of role traversals. This throws considerable doubt on an argument one often hears for the efficiency of inheritance reasoning. The idea is that inheritance will be very fast in the applications one encounters in practice, because nets corresponding to real-life knowledge bases will tend to be broad and bushy. This argument depends on Fahlman's assumption that the maximum depth of subsumption chains is bounded by the chaining of basic IS-A links. From this assumption, it would indeed follow that the inheritance depth of realistic examples would be bounded by a comfortably small constant, say 20. But we have shown that Fahlman's assumption does *not* hold when roles are taken into account. In these cases, subsumption chains of considerable complexity could be hidden in those bushes!

We do not believe these reflections create insuperable problems for the NETL program, though we do feel that they illustrate well the value of a theoretical analysis of inheritance during the design stage and show that the success of a NETL style representation system would be difficult to predict without experimentation. It would certainly be possible to build a NETL machine that could approximate correct reasoning with roles up to a certain bounded role depth; if role depth is sharply limited in typical applications, this might well be a successful strategy. We could also experiment with the use of parallel marker propagation algorithms as a way to limit and guide serial techniques for proof search.

7.6.7 Queries

We now turn to the question of the queries that are associated with our networks. The fact that roles create virtual nodes means that the queries have to be more general than the well-formed links. In Figure 7.11, for instance, we need to be able to ask whether ***a***'s ***f*** is a ***q***, despite the fact that there is no node in the net corresponding to ***a***'s ***f***. This is a meaningful query for the net, one that will certainly be needed in applications. Also, in this same net, the query "is ***a***'s ***f***'s ***g*** a ***p***'s ***f***'s ***g***?" is also meaningful. (A corresponding example in English might be "Is Andy's father's mother a person's father's mother?") To solve this problem, we will have to allow composite roles to appear as parameters in queries. Thus, IS(***fg***, ***a***, ***fg***, ***p***) will count as a query.

A query has the general form θ(***F***, ***x***, ***G***, ***y***), where 'θ' ranges over nonrole link types; thus, IS(***fg***, ***x***, ***h***, ***p***) is a query if ***f***, ***g***, and ***h*** are roles, ***x*** is a node, and ***p*** is a kind; it means that the function ***fg*** is defined for ***x*** and ***h*** is defined for ***p***, and that any value of the former function is also a value of the latter. Because we count the

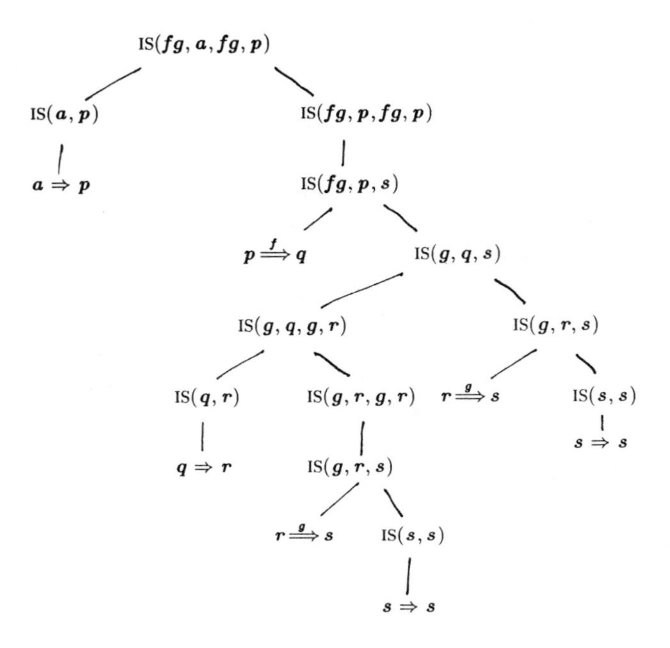

Figure 7.16: Proof that ***a***'s ***fg*** is a ***p***'s ***fg***

empty list ∅ as a (trivial) composite role, IS(∅, ***x***, ***g***, ***p***), IS(***f***, ***x***, ∅, ***p***), and IS(∅, ***x***, ∅, ***p***) count as queries. We can drop ∅ as an argument to queries; so IS(∅, ***x***, ∅, ***p***) can be rewritten as IS(***x***, ***p***). Similarly, if ***R*** is a relation, ***a*** and ***b*** are individuals, and ***f*** and ***g*** are roles, then ***R***(***a***, ***b***), ***R***(***f***, ***a***, ***b***), and ***R***(***f***, ***a***, ***g***, ***b***) are queries.

7.7 CONTEXT-FREE RULES FOR ROLES

Our definition of support brings together a number of ideas. We will reinterpret queries as the categories of a context-free grammar. We can think of these rules as analogous to the rules of a linguistic grammar. From this point of view, they generate certain sequences of links—the links that can be traced left to right through the terminal elements of a derivation. The derivation itself will provide a parse of this path, organizing it according to units that correspond to the categories of the grammar—that is, to queries.

Equally well, we can think of the rules as rules of proof, which show how the root query is justified by seeking justifications of other queries that eventually terminate in basic links of the net.

7.7.1 Sample Proof

To illustrate the general idea, we will provide a simple example of a proof using the rules of the "path grammar" system that we will define later in this section.

Figure 7.16 is a proof of the query IS($\boldsymbol{fg}$, $\boldsymbol{a}$, $\boldsymbol{fg}$, $\boldsymbol{p}$) relative to the net of Figure 7.11. The rules of proof of our system are all instances of the rule schemes presented below; ultimately, these rules would have to be justified by a logical interpretation and soundness proof, but they can also be explained intuitively. We will explain selected examples of the rules and will provide general techniques that should enable interested readers to understand the rest.

7.7.2 Presentation of All the Rules

In presenting the rules, we use context-free grammar notation; $\Rrightarrow_\Gamma$ means that a category can be expanded to a series of categories relative to the net Γ. These rules generate trees; since a tree that ends in terminal strings is also a proof of its root category relative to Γ, $\Rrightarrow_\Gamma$ can also be read "can be derived from." The rules below are schemes that are instantiated by roles (simple and composite), nodes, and link types, subject to any *ad hoc* restrictions attached to them on the spot.

Nonlexical Rules

Basic rules for sortal categories

1. IS($\boldsymbol{F}, \boldsymbol{p}, \boldsymbol{F}, \boldsymbol{p}$) $\Rrightarrow_\Gamma$ IS($\boldsymbol{F}, \boldsymbol{p}, \boldsymbol{q}$)
   Note: this rule is needed because we are thinking of roles as *partial* functions. We want to be able to prove IS($\boldsymbol{F}, \boldsymbol{p}, \boldsymbol{F}, \boldsymbol{p}$) if and only if the role $\boldsymbol{F}$ is defined for all $\boldsymbol{p}$s. This will follow if we can prove that $\boldsymbol{p}$'s $\boldsymbol{F}$s have any property at all, i.e., if we can prove IS($\boldsymbol{F}, \boldsymbol{p}, \boldsymbol{q}$) for any $\boldsymbol{q}$. "Existential presuppositions" figure in a similar way on many of the rules below.
2. IS($\boldsymbol{F}, \boldsymbol{x}, \boldsymbol{G}, \boldsymbol{p}$) $\Rrightarrow_\Gamma$ IS($\boldsymbol{F}, \boldsymbol{x}, \boldsymbol{H}, \boldsymbol{q}$) IS($\boldsymbol{H}, \boldsymbol{q}, \boldsymbol{G}, \boldsymbol{p}$)
3. $\overline{\text{IS}}$($\boldsymbol{F}, \boldsymbol{x}, \boldsymbol{G}, \boldsymbol{p}$) $\Rrightarrow_\Gamma$ IS($\boldsymbol{F}, \boldsymbol{x}, \boldsymbol{H}, \boldsymbol{q}$) $\overline{\text{IS}}$($\boldsymbol{H}, \boldsymbol{q}, \boldsymbol{G}, \boldsymbol{p}$)
4. $\overline{\text{IS}}$($\boldsymbol{F}, \boldsymbol{x}, \boldsymbol{G}, \boldsymbol{p}$) $\Rrightarrow_\Gamma$ IS($\boldsymbol{G}, \boldsymbol{p}, \boldsymbol{H}, \boldsymbol{q}$) $\overline{\text{IS}}$($\boldsymbol{F}, \boldsymbol{x}, \boldsymbol{H}, \boldsymbol{q}$)

Rules for identity (Here, and in general, θ ranges over all nonrole link-types.)

5. ID($\boldsymbol{F}, \boldsymbol{a}, \boldsymbol{F}, \boldsymbol{a}$) $\Rrightarrow_\Gamma$ IS($\boldsymbol{F}, \boldsymbol{a}, \boldsymbol{p}$)
6. ID($\boldsymbol{F}, \boldsymbol{a}, \boldsymbol{F}, \boldsymbol{a}$) $\Rrightarrow_\Gamma$ IS($\boldsymbol{F}, \boldsymbol{a}, \boldsymbol{G}, \boldsymbol{b}$)
7. θ($\boldsymbol{F}, \boldsymbol{a}, \boldsymbol{G}, \boldsymbol{x}$) $\Rrightarrow_\Gamma$ ID($\boldsymbol{F}, \boldsymbol{a}, \boldsymbol{H}, \boldsymbol{b}$) θ($\boldsymbol{H}, \boldsymbol{b}, \boldsymbol{G}, \boldsymbol{x}$)
8. θ($\boldsymbol{F}, \boldsymbol{a}, \boldsymbol{G}, \boldsymbol{b}$) $\Rrightarrow_\Gamma$ ID($\boldsymbol{G}, \boldsymbol{b}, \boldsymbol{H}, \boldsymbol{c}$) θ($\boldsymbol{F}, \boldsymbol{a}, \boldsymbol{H}, \boldsymbol{c}$)
9. ID($\boldsymbol{F}, \boldsymbol{a}, \boldsymbol{G}, \boldsymbol{b}$) $\Rrightarrow_\Gamma$ ID($\boldsymbol{G}, \boldsymbol{b}, \boldsymbol{F}, \boldsymbol{a}$)

10. $\mathrm{ID}(\boldsymbol{F}, \boldsymbol{a}, \boldsymbol{GH}, \boldsymbol{b}) \;\Rrightarrow_{\Gamma}\; \mathrm{ID}(\boldsymbol{G}, \boldsymbol{b}, \boldsymbol{J}, \boldsymbol{c}) \quad \mathrm{ID}(\boldsymbol{JH}, \boldsymbol{c}, \boldsymbol{F}, \boldsymbol{a})$

Rule for dependent sortals

11. $\mathrm{IS}(\boldsymbol{FH}, \boldsymbol{x}, \boldsymbol{GH}, \boldsymbol{p}) \;\Rrightarrow_{\Gamma}\; \mathrm{IS}(\boldsymbol{F}, \boldsymbol{x}, \boldsymbol{G}, \boldsymbol{p}) \quad \mathrm{IS}(\boldsymbol{GH}, \boldsymbol{p}, \boldsymbol{GH}, \boldsymbol{p})$

Rules for dependent generic relations

12. $\tilde{R}(\boldsymbol{F}, \boldsymbol{p}, \boldsymbol{G}, \boldsymbol{p}) \;\Rrightarrow_{\Gamma}\; \mathrm{IS}(\boldsymbol{p}, \boldsymbol{q}) \quad \tilde{R}(\boldsymbol{F}, \boldsymbol{q}, \boldsymbol{G}, \boldsymbol{q})$
13. $\tilde{R}(\boldsymbol{F}, \boldsymbol{a}, \boldsymbol{G}, \boldsymbol{a}) \;\Rrightarrow_{\Gamma}\; \mathrm{IS}(\boldsymbol{a}, \boldsymbol{p}) \quad \tilde{R}(\boldsymbol{F}, \boldsymbol{p}, \boldsymbol{G}, \boldsymbol{p})$

Rules for dependent generic identity

14. $\theta(\boldsymbol{F}, \boldsymbol{p}, \boldsymbol{G}, \boldsymbol{q}) \;\Rrightarrow_{\Gamma}\; \widetilde{\mathrm{ID}}(\boldsymbol{F}, \boldsymbol{p}, \boldsymbol{H}, \boldsymbol{r}) \quad \theta(\boldsymbol{H}, \boldsymbol{r}, \boldsymbol{G}, \boldsymbol{q})$
15. $\theta(\boldsymbol{F}, \boldsymbol{p}, \boldsymbol{G}, \boldsymbol{q}) \;\Rrightarrow_{\Gamma}\; \widetilde{\mathrm{ID}}(\boldsymbol{G}, \boldsymbol{q}, \boldsymbol{H}, \boldsymbol{r}) \quad \theta(\boldsymbol{F}, \boldsymbol{p}, \boldsymbol{H}, \boldsymbol{r})$
16. $\widetilde{\mathrm{ID}}(\boldsymbol{F}, \boldsymbol{p}, \boldsymbol{F}, \boldsymbol{p}) \;\Rrightarrow_{\Gamma}\; \mathrm{IS}(\boldsymbol{F}, \boldsymbol{p}, \boldsymbol{F}, \boldsymbol{p})$
17. $\widetilde{\mathrm{ID}}(\boldsymbol{F}, \boldsymbol{p}, \boldsymbol{G}, \boldsymbol{q}) \;\Rrightarrow_{\Gamma}\; \widetilde{\mathrm{ID}}(\boldsymbol{G}, \boldsymbol{q}, \boldsymbol{F}, \boldsymbol{p})$
18. $\widetilde{\mathrm{ID}}(\boldsymbol{F}, \boldsymbol{p}, \boldsymbol{GH}, \boldsymbol{q}) \;\Rrightarrow_{\Gamma}\; \widetilde{\mathrm{ID}}(\boldsymbol{G}, \boldsymbol{q}, \boldsymbol{J}, \boldsymbol{r}) \quad \widetilde{\mathrm{ID}}(\boldsymbol{JH}, \boldsymbol{r}, \boldsymbol{F}, \boldsymbol{p})$

Lambda rules

19. $\theta(\boldsymbol{F}, \boldsymbol{x}, \boldsymbol{G}, \boldsymbol{y}) \;\Rrightarrow_{\Gamma}\; z \stackrel{f}{\hookrightarrow} \boldsymbol{x} \quad \theta(\boldsymbol{fF}, z, \boldsymbol{G}, \boldsymbol{y})$
20. $\theta(\boldsymbol{F}, \boldsymbol{x}, \boldsymbol{G}, \boldsymbol{y}) \;\Rrightarrow_{\Gamma}\; z \stackrel{g}{\hookrightarrow} \boldsymbol{y} \quad \theta(\boldsymbol{F}, \boldsymbol{x}, \boldsymbol{gG}, z)$
21. $\theta(\boldsymbol{fF}, \boldsymbol{x}, \boldsymbol{G}, \boldsymbol{y}) \;\Rrightarrow_{\Gamma}\; \boldsymbol{x} \stackrel{f}{\hookrightarrow} z \quad \theta(\boldsymbol{F}, z, \boldsymbol{G}, \boldsymbol{y})$
22. $\theta(\boldsymbol{F}, \boldsymbol{x}, \boldsymbol{gG}, \boldsymbol{y}) \;\Rrightarrow_{\Gamma}\; \boldsymbol{y} \stackrel{g}{\hookrightarrow} z \quad \theta(\boldsymbol{F}, \boldsymbol{x}, \boldsymbol{G}, z)$

Rule for the identity role

23. $\theta(\boldsymbol{F}, \boldsymbol{x}, \boldsymbol{G}, \boldsymbol{y}) \;\Rrightarrow_{\Gamma}\; \theta(\boldsymbol{F}', \boldsymbol{x}, \boldsymbol{G}', \boldsymbol{y})$ where $\boldsymbol{F} \cong \boldsymbol{F}'$ and $\boldsymbol{G} \cong \boldsymbol{G}'$

    Note: $\boldsymbol{F} \cong \boldsymbol{F}'$ iff it is possible to transform $\boldsymbol{F}$ into $\boldsymbol{F}'$ by a series of additions and deletions of occurrences of identity roles $\boldsymbol{i}$.

Lexical Rules

24. $\mathrm{IS}(\boldsymbol{x}, \boldsymbol{p}) \;\Rrightarrow_{\Gamma}\; \boldsymbol{x} \Rightarrow \boldsymbol{p}$ iff $\boldsymbol{x} = \boldsymbol{p}$ or $\boldsymbol{x} \Rightarrow \boldsymbol{p} \in \boldsymbol{KB}(\Gamma)$
25. $\overline{\mathrm{IS}}(\boldsymbol{x}, \boldsymbol{p}) \;\Rrightarrow_{\Gamma}\; \boldsymbol{x} \not\Rightarrow \boldsymbol{p}$ iff $\boldsymbol{x} \not\Leftarrow \boldsymbol{p} \in \boldsymbol{KB}(\Gamma)$ or $\boldsymbol{p} \not\Rightarrow \boldsymbol{x} \in \boldsymbol{KB}(\Gamma)$.
26. $\mathrm{ID}(\boldsymbol{a}, \boldsymbol{b}) \;\Rrightarrow_{\Gamma}\; \boldsymbol{a} \Leftrightarrow \boldsymbol{b}$ iff $\boldsymbol{a} \Leftrightarrow \boldsymbol{b} \in \boldsymbol{KB}(\Gamma)$ or $\boldsymbol{b} \Leftrightarrow \boldsymbol{a} \in \boldsymbol{KB}(\Gamma)$ or $\boldsymbol{a} = \boldsymbol{b}$.
27. $\widetilde{\mathrm{ID}}(\boldsymbol{p}, \boldsymbol{q}) \;\Rrightarrow_{\Gamma}\; \boldsymbol{p} \stackrel{\mathbb{ID}}{\Leftrightarrow} \boldsymbol{q}$ iff $\boldsymbol{p} \stackrel{\mathbb{ID}}{\Leftrightarrow} \boldsymbol{q} \in \boldsymbol{KB}(\Gamma)$ or $\boldsymbol{q} \stackrel{\mathbb{ID}}{\Leftrightarrow} \boldsymbol{p} \in \boldsymbol{KB}(\Gamma)$ or $\boldsymbol{p} = \boldsymbol{q}$.
28. $\tilde{R}(\boldsymbol{p}, \boldsymbol{q}) \;\Rrightarrow_{\Gamma}\; \boldsymbol{p} \stackrel{R}{\Rightarrow} \boldsymbol{q}$ iff $\boldsymbol{p} \stackrel{R}{\Rightarrow} \boldsymbol{q} \in \boldsymbol{KB}(\Gamma)$
28. *Convention for role links:* a link $\boldsymbol{x} \stackrel{f}{\hookrightarrow} \boldsymbol{y}$ is terminal relative to $\boldsymbol{KB}(\Gamma)$ if $\boldsymbol{x} \stackrel{f}{\hookrightarrow} \boldsymbol{y} \in \boldsymbol{KB}(\Gamma)$ or $\boldsymbol{f} = \boldsymbol{i}$ and $\boldsymbol{x} = \boldsymbol{y}$.

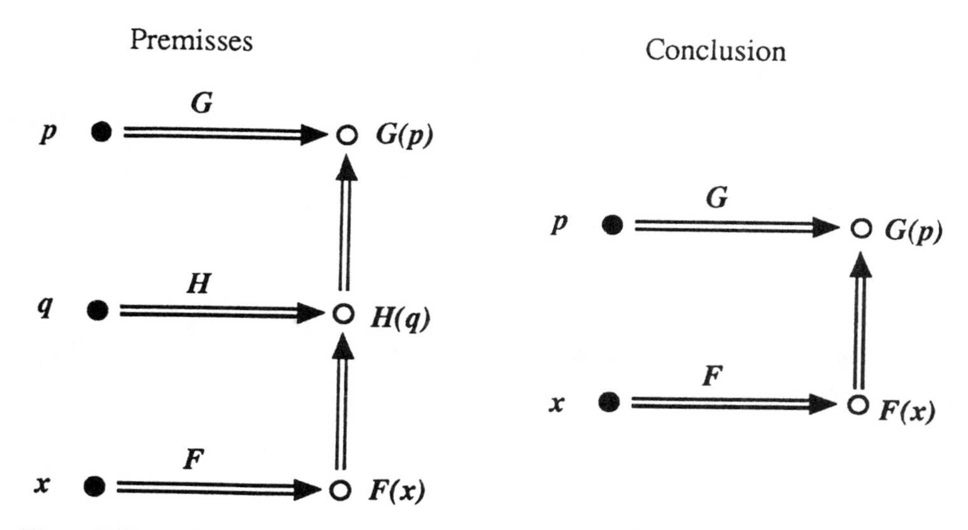

Figure 7.17: Diagram of rule 2. *Explanation:* This rule is just chaining along IS-A links.

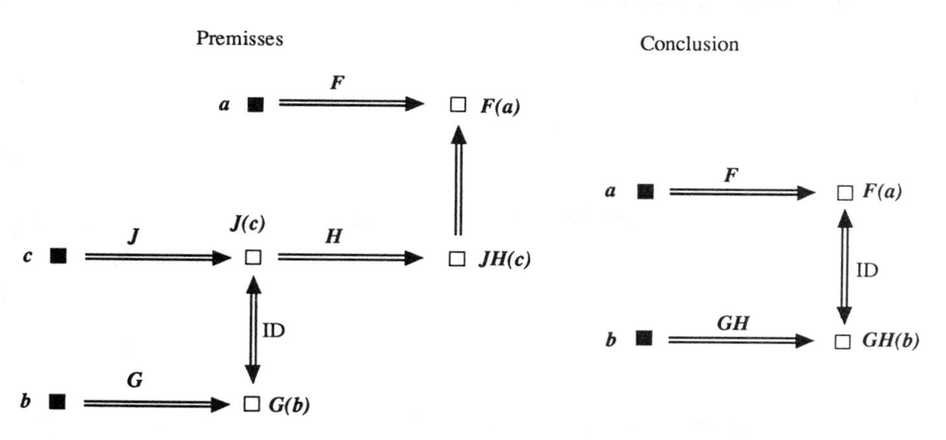

Figure 7.18: Diagram of rule 10. *Explanation:* This rule enables us to prove that corresponding roles of individuals shown to be identical are also identical, when these roles have been shown to exist.

7.7.3 Explanation of Selected Rules

To interpret a rule relative to the network formalism, draw a diagram of the premises and conclusion of the rule in which roles are represented explicitly. That is, if F, x appears in a rule, an arc is drawn from x to $F(x)$. The validity of the inference should then be evident by inspecting the picture. We will present four examples–see Figures 7.17 through 7.20.

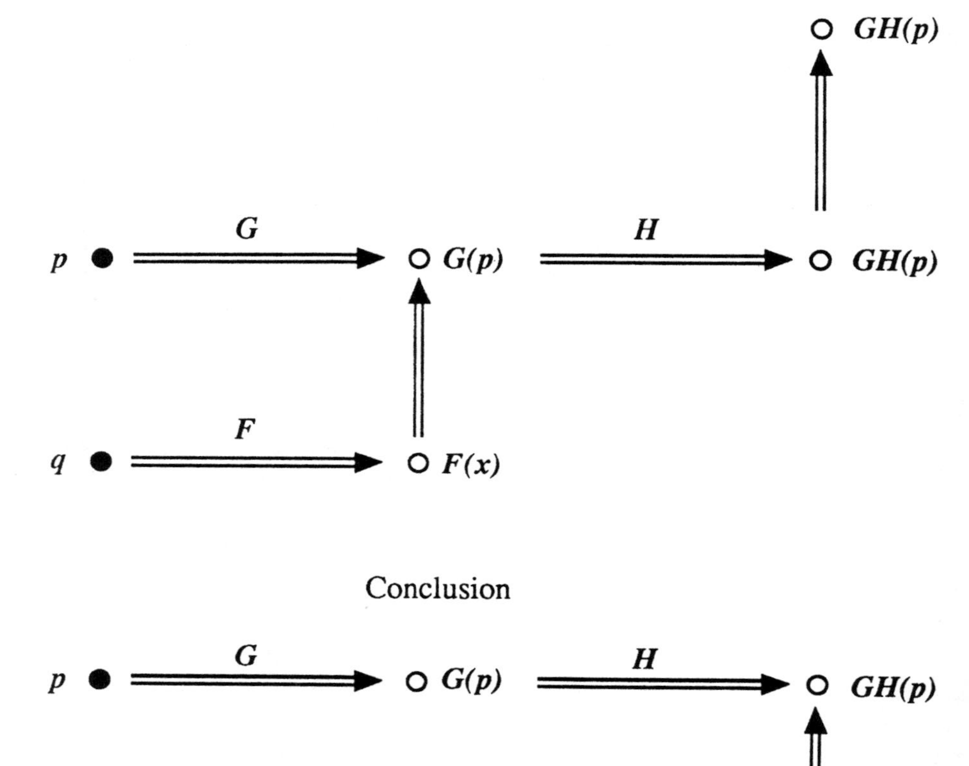

Figure 7.19: Diagram of rule 11. *Explanation:* This rule enables us to prove that a virtual node $FH(x)$ is subsumed by $GH(p)$ whenever $G(p)$ subsumes $F(x)$ and the role GH is implicitly defined for p.

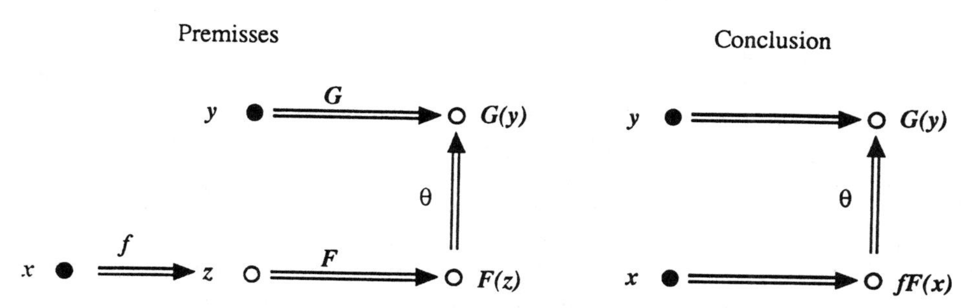

Figure 7.20: Diagram of rule 21. *Explanation:* This can be thought of as a rule of lambda abstraction, in which information about how f applies x is obtained from information about the node $f(x)$ (namely, the node z).

7.8 FURTHER WORK

The inheritance definition that we have formulated using a context-free "path grammar" is only a beginning. It is necessary to show that the rules of Section 7.7 are inferentially adequate, and to investigate the complexity of the associated algorithms.

All of these results depend on a normal form theorem for the system—a demonstration that each possible proof corresponds to a specific configuration made up of links from a net. For instance, though the rules we presented were context-free, technically they do not correspond to a context-free grammar, since the number of rules is infinite. (Note that many rules contain parameters ranging over compound roles and that the set of compound roles will always be infinite.)

Using a normal form theorem (which we will not even state here) we can show that a query over Γ of the form IS($\boldsymbol{F}$, $\boldsymbol{x}$, $\boldsymbol{H}$, $\boldsymbol{q}$) (a query about a subsumption relation in Γ) can always be associated with a context-free grammar. Though increasingly complex queries may force us to use larger sets of rules, each single query about subsumption can be settled using only a finite set of rules.[26]

This establishes the decidability of subsumption, but—because the ruleset associated with a query could grow as an exponential function of the size of the query—it does not automatically show that subsumption is tractable. In fact, we do not yet know whether support, or even subsumption, is tractable for the full system. However, there are tractability results for subsystems. In particular, [Guerreiro et al., 1990] shows that the case with only IS-A and role links, and queries of the form IS(x, p) has complexity $O(n\, r(\log r) + n^2 r + n^3)$, where n is the number of

---

[26] The result that we have proved in detail applies only to networks containing no generic identity links. We believe that the method extends to the general case.

nodes in the net and r is the number of roles. The method of proof in that paper can be extended to larger fragments of the entire system of rules. The chief reason we are not yet sure about the entire system is generalized identity. When generalized identity is present, the network configurations underlying support are much more difficult to analyze and may as far as we know be intractable.

However this turns out, it is largely, we feel, a matter of theoretical interest. The complexity issues are already sufficiently clear for practical purposes. We already showed, in Section 7.6.6, that parallel marker propagation algorithms will not provide an efficient means of resolving simple inheritance questions involving roles. Assuming that the bound of [Guerreiro et al., 1990] for a very simple case is near optimal, we are dealing with theoretical complexity that is at best a more than linear polynomial function of the *total size* of the network. We therefore have no theoretical guarantee that a complete reasoning strategy will perform properly in very large knowledge bases. (We are convinced by Fahlman's arguments that inheritance mechanisms should perform more or less instantaneously in such knowledge bases.)

Whether or not the full system is tractable, it could not be implemented for use in applied knowledge representation without an extended period of experimentation and testing with large knowledge bases. We believe that Fahlman's parallel algorithms, perhaps in combination with other reasoning techniques, might turn out to work very well in such cases.

In quite another direction, the inferential adequacy of the rules needs to be established. This involves showing them sound and complete with respect to a translation into a model-theoretically interpreted logic. Here, the situation is much the same as with tractability, and for the same reasons—both tractability and completeness depend on normal form configuration results. With respect to a translation into a four-valued logic, similar to that presented in [Thomason, 1989] for an inheritance system with universal relations, we have shown some subsystems of the rules sound and complete but have not yet extended the completeness results to the full system.

7.9 CONCLUSIONS

We have tried to make a case here for a useful, productive role for theory in network-based systems. If they are used properly, logical techniques can provide a way of testing and elaborating informal accounts of these systems. Whether or not the informal ideas are confirmed or disconfirmed (and our case study of Fahlman's ideas suggests that both can happen), the result is useful and can actually advance the process of system building.

We also believe that this sort of research can be a source of new and interesting ideas for logic. Weak systems of logic that use path-based methods of reaching conclusions are interesting from a theoretical point of view and—probably because these systems are too expressively weak to carry out nontrivial mathematical reasoning—had not been studied by logicians until the work in inheritance theory described in Section 7.2.

This relationship between logic and network-based systems seems to promise a productive and beneficial working arrangement, for both applied AI and logic. Certainly, this would be a much healthier arrangement than the use of logic as a kind of blunt instrument for beating on systems builders.

Furthermore, as we argued above in Section 7.8, though logical analysis can be very illuminating in the design stage, it does not provide a substitute for an extensive program of experimental testing of a system that may use either incomplete algorithms or special heuristics. We believe that this methodology is one of the most promising ways to obtain knowledge representation technology that is both usable and well understood from a theoretical point of view.

ACKNOWLEDGMENTS

This material is based on work supported by the National Science Foundation under grant No. IST-8700705 (Logical Foundations for Inheritance and Knowledge Update). We are grateful to Lynn Stein for comments.

References

Aho, A., Hopcroft, J., and Ullman, J. 1974. *The Design and Analysis of Computer Algorithms.* Addison-Wesley, Reading MA.

Barwise, J. (ed.). 1977. *Handbook of Mathematical Logic.* North-Holland, Amsterdam.

Brachman, R. and Schmolze, J. 1985. An overview of the KL-ONE knowledge representation system. *Cognitive Science* 9:191–216.

Curry, H. 1963. *Foundations of Mathematical Logic.* McGraw-Hill, New York.

Etherington, D. 1988. *Reasoning with Incomplete Information.* Morgan Kaufmann Publishers, San Mateo, CA.

Fahlman, S. 1979. *NETL: A System for Representing and Using Real-World Knowledge.* MIT Press, Cambridge, MA.

de T. Guerreiro, R.A., Hemerly, A., and Shoham, Y. 1990. On the complexity of monotonic inheritance with roles. In *AAAI-90: Proceedings of the Ninth National Conference on Artificial Intelligence.* AAAI, Menlo Park, CA.

Hayes, P. 1979. The logic of frames. *Frame Conceptions and Text Understanding*, Metzing, D. (ed.). Walter de Gruyter and & Co., pp. 46–61.

Horty, J. and Thomason, R. 1988. Mixing strict and defeasible inheritance. In *AAAI-88: Proceedings of the Seventh National Conference on Artificial Intelligence*, Volume 2, pp. 427–432. AAAI, Manlo Park, CA.

———. 1990. Boolean extensions of inheritance networks. *AAAI-90: Proceedings of the Ninth National Conference on Artificial Intelligence*. AAAI, Menlo Park, CA.

Horty, J., Thomason, R., and Touretzky, D. 1987a. *A Skeptical Theory of Inheritance in Nonmonotonic Semantic Nets*. Technical Report No. CMU-CS-87–175. Department of Computer Science, Carnegie Mellon University. Forthcoming in *Artificial Intelligence*.

———. 1987b. A skeptical theory of inheritance in nonmonotonic semantic nets. In *AAAI-87: Proceedings of the Sixth National Conference on Artificial Intelligence*, Volume 2, pp. 358–363. AAAI, Menlo Park, CA.

Nilsson, N.J. 1980. *Principles of Artificial Intelligence*. Morgan Kaufmann Publishing, San Mateo, CA.

Selman, B. and Levesque, H.J. 1989. The tractability of path-based inheritance. In *Proceedings of IJCAI-89*, pp. 1140–1145. Morgan Kaufmann Publishers, San Mateo, CA.

Thomason, R. 1989. Completeness proofs for monotonic nets with relations and identity. In *Methodologies for Intelligent Systems (Proceedings of the Fourth International Symposium on Methodologies for Intelligent Systems*), Ras, Z. et al. (ed.s.), pp. 523–532. North-Holland, Amsterdam.

Thomason, R., Horty, J., and Touretzky, D. 1986. *A Calculus for Inheritance in Monotonic Semantic Nets*. Technical Report No. CMU-CS-86–138. Department of Computer Science, Carnegie Mellon University.

———. 1987. A calculus for inheritance in monotonic semantic nets. In *Methodologies for Intelligent Systems (Proceedings of the Second International Symposium on Methodologies for Intelligent Systems)*, Ras, Z. and Zemankova, M. (eds.), pp. 280–287. North-Holland, Amsterdam.

Touretzky, D. 1986. *The Mathematics of Inheritance Systems*. Morgan Kaufmann Publishers, San Mateo, CA copublished with Pitman, London.

Touretzky, D. and Thomason, R. 1988. Nonmonotonic inheritance and generic reflexives. In *AAAI-88: Proceedings of the Seventh National Conference on Artificial Intelligence*, Volume 2, pp. 433–438. Morgan Kaufmann Publishers, San Mateo, CA.

Touretzky, D., Horty, J., and Thomason, R. 1987. A clash of intuitions: the current state of nonmonotionic multiple inheritance systems. In *Proceedings of IJCAI-87*, pp. 476–482. Morgan Kaufmann Publishers, San Mateo, CA.

———. Forthcoming. *Issues in the Design of Nonmonotonic Multiple Inheritance Systems*. Forthcoming Technical Report, Computer Science Department, Carnegie Mellon University.

Winston, P. 1984. *Artificial Intelligence*, Second edition. Addison-Wesley, Reading, MA.

8

EXTENSIONS AS POSSIBLE WORLDS

Lynn Andrea Stein
(Massachusetts Institute of Technology)

Abstract

This chapter presents a model-theoretic, path-based semantics for inheritance. Ambiguous inheritance hierarchies have multiple credulous extensions corresponding to their various possible disambiguations. Each of these extensions represents an unambiguous possible world-state and has a straightforward model-theoretic interpretation. Specificity can be seen as a preference over these multiple extensions; it is a path-based criterion for resolving certain types of inheritance ambiguity.

8.1 INTRODUCTION

Previous attempts to define consequence for inheritance hierarchies with exceptions have fallen into two major approaches: translational and path-based. Translational approaches, including those of [McCarthy, 1986; Etherington, 1988; Przymusinska and Gelfond, 1988; Bacchus, 1989; Boutilier, 1989; Krishnaprasad et al., 1989], provide traditional model-theoretic semantics for a hierarchy by encoding the hierarchy in some existing logic. While this results in a well-behaved semantics, the translation process itself loses the path-based nature and topological relations of the original hierarchy. It is our belief that the particular topology of an inheritance hierarchy is crucial to its interpretation,[1] and translational approaches that confound explicit edges of the hierarchy with derived conclusions cannot preserve this topology.

---

[1] For example, most definitions of preemption make the subtle distinction between redundant and preempting paths based solely on fine topological distinctions.

In contrast, path-based approaches such as those of [Sandewall, 1986; Touretzky, 1986; Horty et al., 1987; Geffner and Verma, 1989] preserve precisely the fundamental nature of topology in inheritance; unfortunately, no previous path-based approach has led to a model-theoretic characterization of the conclusions of an inheritance hierarchy. Path-based approaches characterize the supported paths and inferences in much the same way that proof-theoretic approaches to logic define proofs and provability. Though they furnish some insight into reasoning over networks, they don't provide a model-theoretic semantics.

Finally, every previous approach to inheritance reasoning contains a fixed ambiguity-resolving (preemption) strategy. Although the selection of an appropriate preemption strategy is still a subject for debate in the inheritance literature (see, e.g., [Touretzky et al., 1987]), every existing system assumes some single, fixed strategy. This makes principled analyses of preemption strategies at a theoretical level impossible. As a result, most so-called "comparisons of inheritance theories" are in reality *ad hoc* comparisons of system performances on selected examples.

This chapter describes a path-based approach to inheritance that reduces hierarchies to their credulous extensions—unambiguous possible interpretations. Since extensions are also hierarchies, and since the reduction to a set of extensions is purely path-based, this approach takes seriously the primacy of topology in inheritance reasoning. However, these credulous extensions are unambiguous, and it is straightforward to provide a model-theoretic semantics for any single credulous extension. Thus, we reduce an ambiguous hierarchy to its space of credulous extensions—possible world-states—and then describe these world-states in terms of traditional model-theoretic semantics. Unlike translational approaches, we do not rely on a logic as an intermediary; unlike past path-based approaches, we *do* obtain a model-theoretic interpretation as an end result. Further, while we describe only one particular flavor of inheritance here, this approach is more generally applicable; indeed it can be used to provide semantics for—and comparisons among—most of the flavors of inheritance described by [Touretzky et al., 1987]. In [Stein, 1990a, 1990b], we replicate these results for other inheritance theories.

8.2 HIERARCHIES AS BELIEF SPACES

In this section, we present an intuitive interpretation of inheritance hierarchies. In later sections, we give formal definitions of these ideas; here, we hope to motivate that more formal work by answering the question of "what we mean" when we draw an inheritance hierarchy. Regrettably, most previous theories of inheritance omit such a statement of intents, and the lack of such an intuitive semantics has been one of the criticisms leveled against the entire inheritance endeavor.

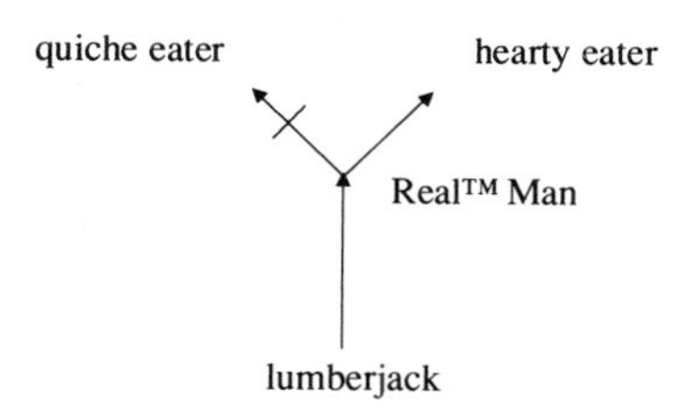

Figure 8.1: A simple inheritance hierarchy

Our interpretation of inheritance hierarchies is relatively simple. Each arc in an inheritance hierarchy represents an atomic assertion in the knowledge base of some reasoning agent—what this agent "believes," if you will.[2] Since this chapter deals exclusively with defeasible inheritance, it is possible that an arc in the hierarchy—an atomic belief—is mistaken. For example, in Figure 8.1 *lumberjacks* might not, in fact, be *Real™ men*; nonetheless, in this agent's world-model, each of these atomic assertions holds.[3]

Reachability, or transitivity-by-default, poses a second constraint on the agent's world models. This constraint arises when we try to apply an atomic assertion—*Real™ men* are *hearty eaters*—to some other class or individual—*lumberjacks*, or *Joe* the *Real™ man*. The fact that *Joe* may be a picky eater does *not* defeat either the assertion that *Joe* is a *Real™ man*, or the assertion that *Real™ men* are generally *hearty eaters*; it merely makes *Joe* an atypical *Real™ man*. In the absence of conflicting information, the world-model of our reasoner is constrained so that subclasses and individuals are *typical* of their superclasses.

Finally, we address the issue of conflicting assertions. Figure 8.2 gives a taxonomic hierarchy that poses seemingly contradictory constraints on our domain model. Certainly, it cannot be the case that platypuses are both mammals and nonmammals! Here, as in any case involving ambiguity, the answer is that atomic links *directly* constrain the domain model but derived paths do not. That is, in our domain model, *platypuses* are (generally) both *egg-layers* and *furry*; *egg-layers* are not typically *mammals*; and *furry animals* are usually *mammals*. But this does not

---

[2] We put the word "believes" in quotation marks to emphasize that we are not proposing that edges of an inheritance hierarchy follow any realistic epistemology; rather, we find the term belief, when removed from that formal context, to be suggestive of the kind of tentative assertion about the world we wish to describe.

[3] The exception to this is the case in which the knowledge base contains both the atomic assertion that a (defeasibly) is an x, and the atomic assertion that a (defeasibly) is not an x. Here, there are (at least) two possibilities: The reasoner's beliefs may be ambiguous, or they may be (locally) inconsistent. We opt for the ambiguity interpretation (see below).

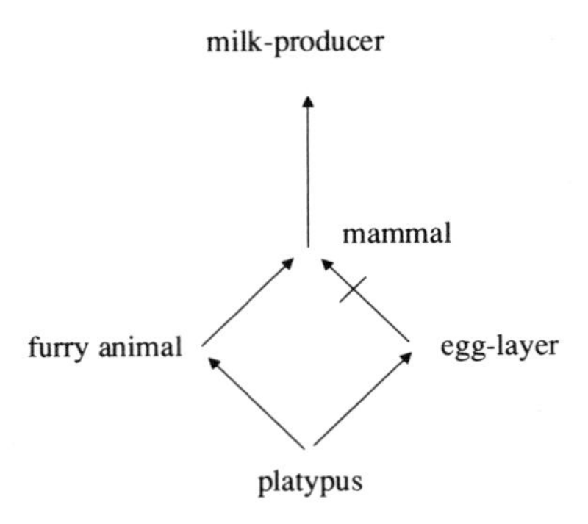

Figure 8.2: Is a *platypus* a *mammal*?

tell us whether *platypuses* are *mammals*. In fact, there are two domain models consistent with this inheritance hierarchy: one in which *platypuses* are *mammals* and the other in which they are not. The hierarchy provides only the information that we are in one of these two models; based on the information obtained by the reasoner so far, we can't distinguish which of these two models we're actually in.

We can actually make this seemingly vague information quite useful. For example, if we know that most *mammals* are *warm-blooded*, we can conclude that *if* the domain is such that *platypuses are mammals*, they're likely to be *warm-blooded*. We still can't classify *platypuses*, but we can reason within each of the several possible domain models. Further, in some cases we can use the topology of the hierarchy to resolve these ambiguities.

Consider the hierarchy in Figure 8.3, where *blue whales* are both *aquatic* and *mammalian*. Strictly speaking, this hierarchy might be viewed as ambiguous. But *specificity* provides a disambiguating preference. If we were reasoning about *whales*, this conflict would be easily resolved: The assertion that *whales* are *aquatic* is explicit, and therefore blocks the derived assertion (through *mammals*) that *whales* are not *aquatic*. In the case of *blue whales*, we can resolve this ambiguity by resorting to arguments about specificity. Because *blue whales* are *mammals* only by virtue of being *whales*, information about *whales* is more specific to *blue whales* than information about *mammals*, and the reasoner prefers to believe that the actual world-state is one in which *blue whales* are *aquatic*. For this reason, although it's *consistent* that *blue whales* not be *aquatic*—it's all derived information, after all—we prefer domain models in which the properties of *whales* override the properties of *mammals* animals, and *blue whales* are *aquatic*.

In this context, the restriction that subclasses override superclasses induces a *preference relation* on domain models. Many ambiguity-resolving heuristics that have been applied to inheritance hierarchies (e.g., inferential distance, shortest path, local inconsistency elimination, on- and off-path preemption) can be viewed

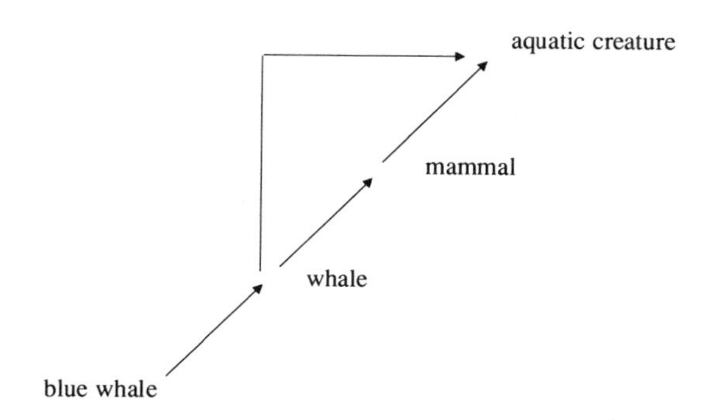

Figure 8.3: A blue whale *is* a mammal

in this way. Since domain models are unambiguous, they have straightforward model-theoretic semantics. An inheritance theory translates the constraints of the inheritance hierarchy into preferences over these domain models. In the remainder of this chapter, we describe a semantics for inheritance hierarchies based on this framework.

8.3 HIERARCHIES, AMBIGUITY, AND CREDULOUS EXTENSIONS

This section presents formal definitions of inheritance hierarchies, paths, and credulous extensions. The approach described here is upward reasoning; that is, inheritance reasons about the properties of some particular object, rather than about the set of objects possessing some particular property. The ramifications of this type of inheritance are discussed by Touretzky et al. [1987]; some complexity concerns are described by Levesque and Selman [1989].

An *inheritance hierarchy* $\Gamma = \langle V_\Gamma, E_\Gamma \rangle$ is a directed acyclic graph with positive and negative edges, intended to denote "is-a" and "is-not-a" respectively. We write a positive edge from a to x as $a \cdot x$, and a negative edge $a \cdot \neg x$. The notation $a \cdot s_1 \cdot s_2$ abbreviates the sequence of edges $\{a \cdot s_1, s_1 \cdot s_2\}$; $s_1 \cdots s_n$ abbreviates $\{s_1 \cdot s_2, s_2 \cdot s_3, \cdots s_{n-1} \cdot s_n\}$. We call a sequence of positive edges $a \cdot s_1 \cdots s_n \cdot x$ ($n \geq 0$), a *positive path*, and a sequence of positive edges followed by a single negative edge $a \cdot s_1 \cdots s_n \cdot \neg x$ ($n \geq 0$) a *negative path*.

A path, or *argument*, $a \cdot s_1 \cdots s_n \cdot (\neg)x$ supports the inference "a is (not) an x." We use the notation $\alpha \rightarrow x$ (resp., $a \not\rightarrow x$) to stand for this inference, or conclusion, independent of the path through which it is derived. One inference—e.g., $a \rightarrow x$—may have many supporting arguments—$a \cdot s_1 \cdots s_n \cdot x$, $a \cdot t_1 \cdots t_m \cdot x$, etc.

Given an inheritance hierarchy $\Gamma = \langle V_\Gamma, E_\Gamma \rangle$ with nodes $a, x \in V_\Gamma$, we say that x is *reachable from a* (alternately, a-reachable) if there is some path $a \cdot s_1 \cdots s_n \cdot (\neg)x$ in E_Γ. If the final edge is positive—$s_n \cdot x$—we say that x is *positively*

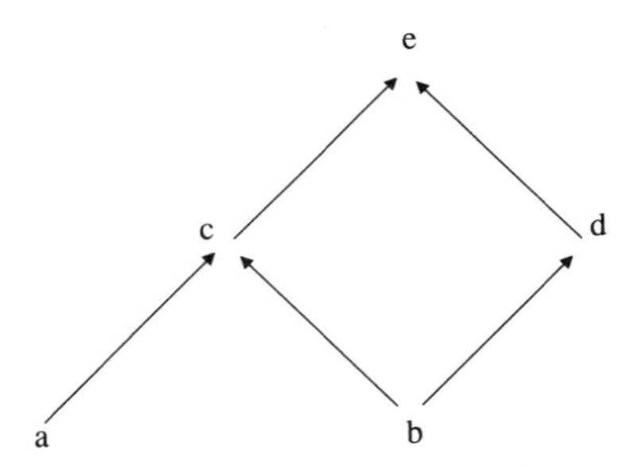

Figure 8.4: A hierarchy is ambiguous with respect to a focus node

reachable from a; similarly, $s_n \cdot \neg x$ and *negatively a-reachable*. By extension, we say that an *edge* $s \cdot (\neg)x$ is reachable from a if s is *positively a-reachable*, and a path $s_1 \cdots s_n \cdot (\neg)x$ is reachable from a if every edge on that path is a-reachable. We say that a hierarchy Γ is *a-connected* if every node in V_Γ and every edge in E_Γ is reachable from a. When reasoning about an inheritance hierarchy with respect to a particular node, we call that node the *focus node*.

Ambiguity arises when two paths conflict. Formally, an inheritance hierarchy Γ is *ambiguous* with respect to a node a if there is some node $x \in V_\Gamma$ such that both $a \cdot s_1 \cdots s_n \cdot x$ and $a \cdot t_1 \cdots t_m \cdot \neg x$ are in E_Γ. In this case, we say that the ambiguity is *at x*. Ambiguity is always relative to a focus node: For example, the hierarchy in Figure 8.4, Γ_4, is unambiguous with respect to a but ambiguous with respect to b (at e).

An inheritance hierarchy Γ *supports a path* $a \cdot s_1 \cdots s_n \cdot (\neg)x$, written $\Gamma \rhd a \cdot s_1 \cdots s_n \cdot (\neg)x$, if the corresponding sequence of edges $a \cdot s_1 \cdots sn \cdot (\neg)x$ is in E_Γ *and it is admissible* according to specificity. Admissibility is intended to capture the intuitive preferences contained in hierarchies like the one in Figure 8.3, and a path is inadmissible just in case there is a stronger counterargument. We discuss admissibility further, and give formal definitions, in Section 8.5. Γ *supports an inference* $a \rightarrow x$ (resp, $a \not\rightarrow x$) if it supports some corresponding path. For simplicity, we also allow the degenerate path a, with the corresponding inference $a \rightarrow a$.

A credulous extension corresponds to a possible 'world-state,' or domain model. Formally, a *credulous extension* of an inheritance hierarchy Γ with respect to a node a is a maximal unambiguous a-connected subhierarchy of Γ with respect to a: if X_a^Γ is a credulous extension of Γ with respect to a, then for every edge

$$v \cdot (\neg)x \in E_\Gamma - E_{X_a^\Gamma},$$

adding $v \cdot (\neg)x$ to X_a^Γ would make X_a^Γ unambiguous or not a-connected. An example of several credulous extensions—and some nonextensions—for the hierarchy of Figure 8.2 is given in Figure 8.5. If X_a^Γ is a credulous extension of Γ with respect to

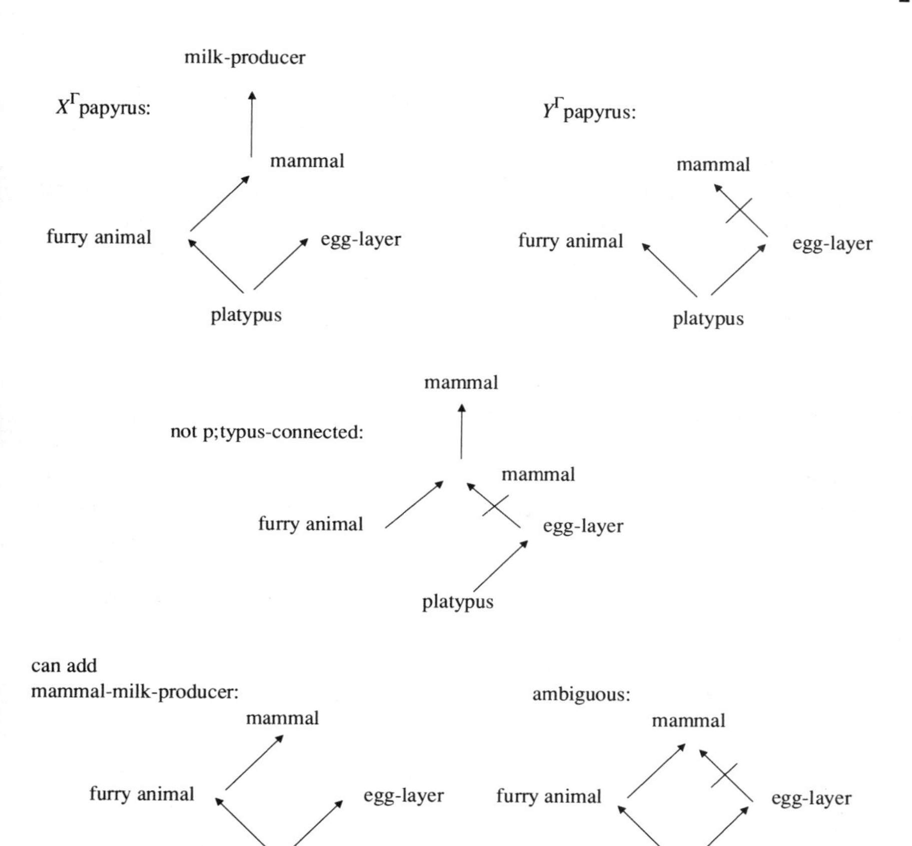

Figure 8.5: Some extensions and nonextensions of Figure 8.2

a, a is called the *focus node* of X^{Γ}_{a}. If an extension $X^{\Gamma}_{a} \rhd a \rightarrow x$, x is *true in* X^{Γ}_{a}; similarly $a \not\rightarrow x$ and *false in* X^{Γ}_{a}.

8.4 FROM CREDULOUS EXTENSIONS TO MODELS

A domain model is represented formally by a credulous extension. Since each credulous extension is unambiguous, credulous extensions have straightforward model-theoretic semantics. Providing semantics for a single, unambiguous domain model is the topic of this section. If X^{Γ}_{a} is a credulous extension of Γ with respect to a, it supports a fixed, consistent set of conclusions with respect to a: $X^{\Gamma}_{a} \rhd a \rightarrow x$ iff x is positively a-reachable in X^{Γ}_{a}, and $X^{\Gamma}_{a} \rhd a \not\rightarrow x$ iff x is negatively a-reachable in

X_a^Γ (i.e., if x is a-reachable but not positively a-reachable). Consider some a-reachable node x in X_a^Γ. Since x is a-reachable, there is some path $a \cdot s_1 \cdots s_n (\neg) \cdot x$ in X_a^Γ, so X_a^Γ contains an argument that a is (or is not) an x. But what about counterarguments? If there were a counterargument—say, $a \cdot t_1 \cdots t_m \cdot \neg s_i$, for some s_i, or $a \cdot t_1 \cdots t_m \cdot (\neg)x$—then X_a^Γ would be ambiguous with respect to a (at s_i, or at x). But X_a^Γ is a credulous extension of Γ with respect to a, so it cannot be ambiguous with respect to a, and no such counterargument can exist.[4]

As a result, we can translate the graph-based extension into a logical theory, and use traditional semantics on that theory. Recall that earlier we argued against translational approaches to semantics, because they lose topological information. Also, translational approaches generally provide less than satisfactory means of dealing with ambiguities, and even these means are fixed properties of either the translation procedure or the target logic itself. In this case, however, the path-based and ambiguity-resolving aspects of the semantics are independent of this translation—they are part of the task of *selecting* a preferred set of credulous extensions in the first place. (So far, we have largely ignored this question, but we will address it in detail in Section 8.5.) Once we *have* a credulous extension, we've settled on an unambiguous domain-state, and we can safely use classical logic to provide a model-theoretic semantics.

The translation procedure that we use is a naive one: We simply replace the edges of the credulous extension with material implications. For every vertex

$$x \in V_{X_a^\Gamma},$$

we create a unique propositional variable $\hat{x}$. $\widehat{X_a^\Gamma}$ the theory (in the propositional calculus) given by

$$\hat{a} \wedge \bigwedge_{x \cdot y \in E_{X_a^\Gamma}} (\hat{x} \supset \hat{y}) \wedge \bigwedge_{x \cdot \neg y \in E_{X_a^\Gamma}} (\hat{x} \supset \sim\hat{y})$$

(where $\wedge$, $\supset$, and $\sim$ are propositional conjunction, material implication, and negation, respectively). Since X_a^Γ is acyclic and unambiguous, $\widehat{X_a^\Gamma}$ is consistent and has a model.

---

[4] The definition of $\rhd$ is: $\Gamma \rhd a \to x$ if $a \cdot s_1 \cdots s_n \cdot x \in E_\Gamma$ *and it is admissible* (resp., $a \not\to x$ and $a \cdot s_1 \cdots s_n \cdot \neg x$). Admissibility, which we discuss in Section 8.5, below, is intended to deal with ambiguity-resolving heuristics. The absence of counterarguments in credulous extensions means that all paths in a credulous extension are admissible. A few inheritance theories, like [Bacchus, 1989], use more restricted forms of path concatenation. These restrictions would not fit well in the definition of admissibility; however, they would fit naturally in the definition of reachability. With an appropriately modified definition of reachability, the semantics provided here would apply to these inheritance theories as well.

The path-based interpretation of inheritance in credulous extensions is straightforward. As stated above, any path in a credulous extension is admissible. The propositional theory corresponding to a credulous extension provides both classical proof-theoretic and model-theoretic semantics to complement this path-based interpretation:

Theorem 1 (Semantics for Extensions) Let Γ be an inheritance hierarchy, with a, $x \in V_\Gamma$. Let X_a^Γ be a credulous extension of Γ with respect to a, and let $\hat{X}_a^\Gamma$ be the propositional theory corresponding to X_a^Γ. The following are equivalent:

1. $X_a^\Gamma \rhd a \rightarrow x$ (resp., $a \not\rightarrow x$).
2. x is positively a-reachable in X_a^Γ (resp., negatively a-reachable).
3. $\hat{X}_a^\Gamma \vdash \hat{x}$ (resp., $\sim \hat{x}$).
4. $\hat{X}_a^\Gamma \models \hat{x}$ (resp., $\sim \hat{x}$).

This approach to semantics for credulous extensions *is* translational. However, it is not subject to the criticisms of translational approaches that we describe above, precisely because it provides translations *only* for credulous extensions—*unambiguous* subhierarchies—and not for a hierarchy as a whole. Thus, it does not rely on the translation procedure or the underlying logic for ambiguity-resolution strategies. All ambiguity-resolution is done in *selecting* some preferred subset of the credulous extensions. Once the set of preferred credulous extensions—or possible interpretations—for a hierarchy has been established, the semantics for any single extension are straightforward. In the next section, we discuss the problem of deriving the appropriate (preferred) set of credulous extensions for a hierarchy.

8.5 SPECIFICITY

In Section 8.4, we described a semantics for individual credulous extensions. In order to provide semantics for general inheritance hierarchies, we must describe the set of credulous extensions that correspond to the interpretations of the hierarchy. In particular, we are interested in the *preferred* credulous extensions—those extensions corresponding to intuitively appealing states of the world.

In this section, we describe a *specificity criterion*, or preemption strategy, that makes choices among certain competing paths. The idea of a specificity criterion dates from [Etherington and Reiter, 1983] and [Touretzky, 1986]. Since then, many definitions of specificity have appeared in the literature, but all operate on the same underlying principle: More specific information is likely to be more accurate. For example, in Figure 8.3, information about *whales* is more specific to *blue whales* than information about *mammals*, so we can infer that *blue whales* are *aquatic*. The particular definition of specificity presented here was first described in [Stein,

1989] and has the advantage of being computable in polynomial time. In [Stein, 1990a, 1990b], we discuss other specificity criteria.

This definition of specificity is *on-path* and *upward*. On-path means that a path is preempted only if one of its member nodes is involved in a counterargument. In contrast, some preemption strategies also allow a path to be preempted by a counterargument originating with a node *off* the path. Upward inheritance reasons about the properties of a particular object, rather than the objects possessing a particular property. Our definition most closely resembles an upward version of [Touretzky, 1986].

We define specificity recursively. As with credulous extensions, specificity is *relative* to a focus node. Certainly, if we are reasoning about a and the explicit assertion $a \cdot x \in E_\Gamma$, then $a \rightarrow x$—that is, both the path, and the inference "a is an x"—are acceptable in Γ; similarly with $a \cdot \neg x$ and $a \not\rightarrow x$.[5] But what about derived inferences?

> Consider a generic edge. The edge $v \cdot (\neg)x$ is admissible in Γ with respect to a if there is some path $a \cdot s_1 \cdots s_n \cdot v$, $(n \geq 0)$, in E_Γ, and
>
> 1. none of the edges of $a \cdot s_1 \cdots s_n \cdot v$ is redundant in Γ with respect to a;
> 2. each of the edges of $a \cdot s_1 \cdots s_n \cdot v$ is admissible in Γ with respect to a; and
> 3. no intermediate node $a, s_1, \ldots s_n$ is a preemptor of $v \cdot (\neg)x$.
>
> A *path is admissible* in Γ with respect to a if every edge in that path is admissible, and no edge except possibly the last is redundant in Γ with respect to a.[6]
>
> A node s is a *preemptor* of $v \cdot x$ (resp., $v \cdot \neg x$) if $s \cdot \neg x$ (resp., $s \cdot x$) is admissible in Γ with respect to a.

Although the definitions of admissible and redundant edges are mutually dependent, they are not circular. Because the hierarchy is acyclic, it can be ordered topologically, and the definition of support for a path from a to x depends only on the redundancy of nodes strictly topologically earlier than x. With this definition of admissibility, the "proof-theoretic" path-based notion of *supports* ($\triangleright$) is complete.

---

[5] Actually, even this apparently simple case may have an exception, if both $a \cdot x$ and $a \cdot \neg x$. We choose to regard such a hierarchy as ambiguous with respect to a at x.

[6] The difficulties caused by redundant links were noted by Touretzky [1986]: in Figure 8.3, if we were to add an edge from *blue whale* to *mammal*, this should not change the interpretation of the hierarchy. That is because this additional information is redundant—*blue whales* are typically *mammals* even without that link. However, if that edge is not excluded, there will be a path *blue whale* $\cdot$ *mammal* $\cdot$ $\neg$*aquatic* for which no intermediate node has a positive edge to *aquatic*. Clearly, this is not the intended meaning here (or, indeed, in any network of this form, since the "whale" node is always more specific than the "mammal" node).

We use this definition of specificity to select the set of *preferred* extensions—possible world-states that accord with the intuitive interpretation of the inheritance hierarchy:

Let X_a^Γ and Y_a^Γ be two credulous extensions of an inheritance hierarchy Γ with respect to focus node a. Then *specificity* prefers X_a^Γ to Y_a^Γ ($X_a^\Gamma \leq Y_a^\Gamma$) if there are some nodes v and x such that

1. X_a^Γ and Y_a^Γ agree on all edges whose end points topologically precede x in any topological sort,
2. The edge $v \cdot (\neg)x$ is inadmissible in Γ with respect to a.
3. $s_1, \ldots s_n, Y_a^\Gamma \rhd a \cdot s_1 \cdots s_n \cdot v \cdot (\neg)x$, and
4. $X_a^\Gamma \not\rhd a \cdot s_1 \cdots s_n \cdot v \cdot (\neg)x$

If a credulous extension is minimal under this preorder—i.e., no other extension is preferred to it—we call it a *preferred extension* of the hierarchy:

$\mathcal{P}ref(\Gamma, a) = \{X_a^\Gamma \mid \forall Y_a^\Gamma, Y_a^\Gamma \not\leq X_a^\Gamma\}$

If we examine a hierarchy, Γ, from the perspective of a particular node, a, specificity provides a means of pruning the hierarchy—removing those edges that have been preempted. We call this subhierarchy Σ_a^Γ, the *specificity extension* of Γ with respect to a. For example, the specificity extensions of the hierarchies in Figure 8.3 with respect to *blue whale* are shown in Figure 8.6. The definition of specificity above always yields a unique specificity extension for a hierarchy with respect to a focus node. The following algorithm computes the specificity extension of an inheritance hierarchy in polynomial time:

Compute—Specificity—Extension

Let Γ be an inheritance hierarchy.

Sort the nodes of Γ topologically

For each focus node a ; Σ_a^Γ will be the *specificity*

  $\Sigma_a^\Gamma := \Gamma$; *extension* of Γ with respect to a.

  For each node x reachable from a in Σ_a^Γ, in topological order

    ; from a to ...

    For each edge $v \cdot (\neg)x \in E_{\Sigma_a^\Gamma}$, in reverse topological order

      ; check if $v \cdot (\neg)x$ is admissible in Γ

      Let $\Gamma^* = \Sigma_\alpha^\Gamma - \{q \mid q$ is a preemptor of $v \cdot (\neg)x$ in $\Sigma_\alpha^\Gamma\}$

      If Γ^* no longer contains a positive path from a to v,

        then remove the edge $v \cdot (\neg)x$ from Σ_α^Γ

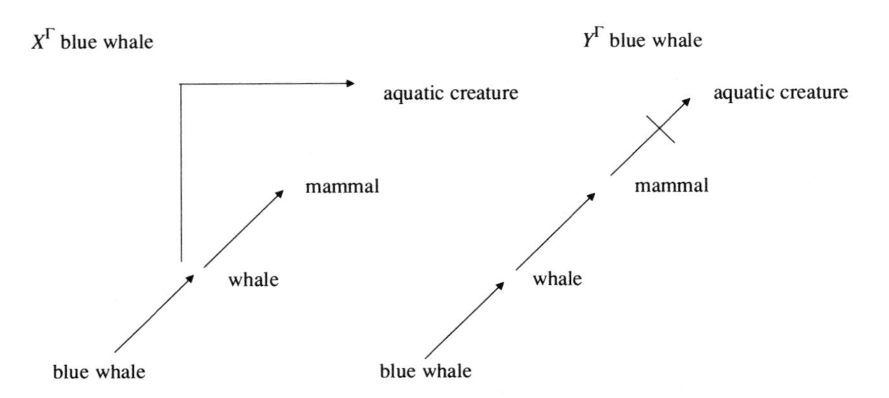

Figure 8.6: Specificity extensions for the hierarchies of Figure 8.3 with respect to *blue whale*

For each remaining positive edge $p \cdot$ x
  ; check if $p \cdot\ x$ is redundant in Γ
  If Σ_a^Γ contains a path $p \cdot q_1 \cdots q_n \cdot x$ $(n \geq 1)$
    such that there is no negative path through
      admissible edges from a to any of q_i, x, in Σ_a^Γ
    then mark the edge $p \cdot$ x as redundant

Once we've eliminated redundant and preempted edges, semantic interpretation of the hierarchy is trivial: Support—admissible reachability—becomes simple reachability. Similarly, we need not restrict ourselves to the preferred credulous extensions of the specificity extension—if an inference is supported by any credulous extension of the specificity extension, it is supported by a preferred credulous extension.

Theorem 2 (Semantics for Specificity Extension) Let Γ be an inheritance hierarchy, with $a,x \in V_\Gamma$, and let Σ_a^Γ be the specificity extension of Γ with respect to a. Then the following are equivalent:

1. $\Sigma_a^\Gamma \rhd a \rightarrow x$ (resp., $a \not\rightarrow x$).
2. x is positively a-reachable in Σ_a^Γ (resp., negatively a-reachable).
3. There is an extension $X_a^{\Sigma_a^\Gamma}$ of Σ_a^Γ with respect to a, such that $X_a^{\Sigma_a^\Gamma} \rhd a \rightarrow x$ (resp., $a \not\rightarrow x$).

Not all of the ambiguities in an inheritance hierarchy are susceptible to specificity. For example, "diamond" ambiguities such as the platypus diamond of Figure

8.2 cannot be resolved using any preemption technique. For this reason, Σ_a^Γ may still contain ambiguities and may yield several credulous extensions with respect to a. These credulous extensions are the possible world-states consistent with the specificity criterion and are a subset of the possible world-states delimited by Γ—the credulous extensions of Γ with respect to a. As theorem 3 below demonstrates, the inferences supported by Σ_a^Γ are the inferences supported by the *preferred* extensions of Γ with respect to a, according to the preference induced by specificity.

8.6 SOUNDNESS AND COMPLETENESS

The following theorem states the equivalence of the various definitions of inheritance given throughout this paper. The equivalence of conditions 2 and 3 provides a soundness and completeness theorem for the preferential semantics of Sections 8.4 and 8.5 with respect to the path-based semantics of Section 8.3. The equivalence of these conditions to 4 gives a proof of correctness for the algorithm for computing the specificity extension given in Section 8.5.

Theorem 3 (Semantics for Inheritance Hierarchies) Let Γ be an inheritance hierarchy, with $a, x \in V_\Gamma$. Let $\mathcal{Pref}(\Gamma, a) \subseteq \{{}_iX_a^\Gamma\}_i$ be the set of preferred extensions of Γ with respect to a, and let Σ_a^Γ be the specificity extension of Γ with respect to a. Then the following are equivalent:

1. $\Gamma \rhd a \rightarrow x$ (resp., $a \not\rightarrow x$).
2. There is an admissible (in Γ with respect to a) positive path $a \cdot s_1 \cdots s_n \cdot x \in E_\Gamma$ (resp., negative path $a \cdots s_1 \cdots s_n \cdots \neg$ x).
3. There is a preferred extension $X_a^\Gamma \in \mathcal{Pref}(\Gamma, a)$ such that $X_a^\Gamma \rhd a \rightarrow x$ (resp., $a \not\rightarrow x$).
   a. x is positively a-reachable in X_a^Γ (resp., negatively a-reachable).
   b. $\hat{X}_a^\Gamma \vdash \hat{x}$ (resp., $\sim \hat{x}$).
   c. $\hat{X}_a^\Gamma \models \hat{x}$ (resp., $\sim \hat{x}$).
4. $\Sigma_a^\Gamma \rhd a \rightarrow x$ (resp., $a \not\rightarrow x$).
   a. x is positively a-reachable in Σ_a^Γ (resp., negatively a-reachable).
   b. There is an extension $X_a^{\Sigma_a^\Gamma}$ of Σ_a^Γ with respect to a, such that $X_a^{\Sigma_a^\Gamma} \rhd a \rightarrow x$ (resp., $a \not\rightarrow x$).
   i. x is positively a-reachable in $X_a^{\Sigma_a^\Gamma}$ (resp., negatively a-reachable).
   ii. $\hat{X}_a^{\Sigma_a^\Gamma} \vdash$ (resp., $\sim \hat{x}$).
   iii. $\hat{X}_a^{\Sigma_a^\Gamma} \models \hat{x}$ (resp., $\sim \hat{x}$).

Proofs of all of the theorems in this chapter, and further discussion of many of these points, may be found in [Stein, 1990a, 1990b].

ACKNOWLEDGMENTS

This paper is based on a talk presented at the Catalina Workshop on Formal Aspects of Semantic Networks in February, 1989. I would like to thank the participants of that workshop for their comments, discussions, and insights. Rich Thomason and Lokendra Shastri additionally made many helpful suggestions regarding the revision of this paper. (This work was completed while the author was a graduate student at Brown University. She was supported by an IBM Graduate Fellowship.)

References

Bacchus, F. 1989. A modest, but semantically well founded, inheritance reasoner. In *IJCAI-89*, pp. 1104–1109. IJCAI proceedings are available from Morgan Kaufmann Publishers, San Mateo, CA.

Boutilier, C. 1989. A semantical approach to stable inheritance reasoning. In *IJCAI-89*, pp. 1134–1139. IJCAI proceedings are available from Morgan Kaufmann Publishers, San Mateo, CA.

Etherington, D.W. and Reiter, R. 1983. On inheritance hierarchies with exceptions. In *Proceedings of the National Conference on Artificial Intelligence*, pp. 104–108. AAAI, Menlo Park, CA.

Etherington, D.W. 1988. *Reasoning with Incomplete Information.* Morgan Kaufmann Publishers, San Mateo, CA.

Geffner, H. and Verma, T. Inheritance = chaining + defeat. In *ISMIS-89* .

Horty, J.F., Thomason, R.H., and Touretzky, D.S. 1987. A skeptical theory of inheritance in nonmonotonic semantic networks. In *Proceedings of the Sixth National Conference on Artificial Intelligence*, pp. 358–363. AAAI, Menlo Park, CA.

Proceedings of the Eleventh International Joint Conference on Artificial Intelligence. 1989. IJCAI proceedings are available from Morgan Kaufmann Publishers, San Mateo, CA.

Proceedings of the Fourth International Symposium on Methodologies for Intelligent Systems, 1989.

Krishnaprasad, T., Kifer, M., and Warren, D.S. 1989. On the declarative semantics of inheritance networks. In *IJCAI-89*, pp. 1098–11103. IJCAI proceedings are available from Morgan Kaufmann Publishers, San Mateo, CA.

McCarthy, J. 1986. Applications of circumscription to formalizing common-sense knowledge. *Artificial Intelligence*, 28:89–116.

Przymusinska, H. and Gelfond, M. 1988. *Inheritance Hierarchies and Autoepistemic Logic*. Technical report, Computer Science Department, University of Texas at El Paso.

Sandewall, E. 1986. Non-monotonic inference rules for multiple inheritance with exceptions. *Proceedings of the IEEE*, 74:1345–1353.

Selman, B. and Levesque, H. 1989. The tractability of path-based inheritance. In *IJCAI-89*, pp. 1140–1145. IJCAI proceedings are available from Morgan Kaufmann Publishers, San Mateo, CA.

Stein, L.A. 1989. Skeptical inheritance: Computing the intersection of credulous extensions. In *IJCAI-89*. IJCAI proceedings are available from Morgan Kaufmann Publishers, San Mateo, CA.

———. 1990. *A Preference-based Approach To Inheritance*. Technical report, Department of Computer Science, Brown University, Providence, RI.

———. 1990. *Resolving Ambiguity in Nonmonotonic Reasoning*. Ph.D. thesis, Department of Computer Science, Brown University, Providence, R.I.

Touretzky, D.S., Horty, J.F. and Thomason, R.H. 1987. A clash of intuitions: The current state of nonmonotonic multiple inheritance systems. In *Proceedings of the Tenth International Joint Conference on Artificial Intelligence*, pp. 476–482. IJCAI proceedings are available from Morgan Kaufmann Publishers, San Mateo, CA.

Touretzky, D.S. 1986. *The Mathematics of Inheritance Systems*. Morgan Kaufmann Publishers, San Mateo, CA, copublished with Pitman, London.

9

THE TRACTABILITY OF PATH-BASED INHERITANCE[1]

Bart Selman and Hector J. Levesque
(University of Toronto)

Abstract

Touretzky [1984] proposed a formalism for nonmonotonic multiple inheritance reasoning that is sound in the presence of ambiguities and redundant links. We show that Touretzky's inheritance notion is NP-hard, and thus, provided $P \neq NP$, computationally intractable. This result holds even when one only considers unambiguous, totally acyclic inheritance networks. A direct consequence of this result is that the conditioning strategy proposed by Touretzky to allow for fast parallel inference is also intractable. Therefore, it follows that nonmonotonic multiple inheritance hierarchies, although compact representations, may not allow for efficient retrieval of information as has been suggested in attempts to use such hierarchies, e.g., in NETL [Fahlman, 1979]. We also analyze the influence of various design choices made by Touretzky. We show that all versions of downward (coupled) inheritance, i.e., on-path or off-path preemption and skeptical or credulous reasoning, are intractable. However, tractability can be achieved when using upward (decoupled) inheritance. Thus, the main source of intractability in path-based inheritance formalisms is the downward (coupled) reasoning.

---

[1] This a revised version of a paper that appeared in the *Proceedings of IJCAI-89*, Detroit, MI, [1989] 1140–45. Used by permission of the International Joint Conferences on Artificial Intelligence, Inc.; copies of this and other IJCAI Proceedings are available from Morgan Kaufmann Publishers, Inc., PO Box 50490, Palo Alto, CA 94303, U.S.A.

9.1 INTRODUCTION

Since the early semantic networks of Quillian [1968], inheritance hierarchies have been used to provide a compact representation and efficient reasoning mechanism for certain kinds of taxonomic information. One problem that has plagued these systems is that of *exceptions* (or cancellation) in non-tree hierarchies. Early attempts to systematically deal with this issue, such as that of NETL [Fahlman, 1979], were later shown to be unsound in the presence of redundant links and ambiguities [Reiter and Criscuolo, 1983; Touretzky, 1984]. The first comprehensive definition that appeared to solve these problems was that of Touretzky [1984]. Since then, other equally sound schemes have been proposed [Sandewall, 1986; Horty et al., 1987]. But despite a decade of study, with increasingly subtle examples and counterexamples being considered, consensus has yet to emerge regarding the proper treatment of multiple inheritance with cancellations.

From a knowledge representation standpoint, part of the problem is that there are tremendous subtleties in reasoning with propositions that admit exceptions, such as "Birds fly" [Brachman, 1985]. Not surprisingly, the research on inheritance systems mentioned above has not attempted to settle the larger logical and semantic issues associated with defeasible reasoning. Rather, the argument has been that inheritance systems need to conform to a set of special intuitions involving paths through hierarchies. We therefore call such systems *path-based inheritance systems* and contrast them with the more general *nonmonotonic reasoning systems* [Reiter, 1987]. The latter approach attempts to establish a logical account of defeasible reasoning (using, for example, autoepistemic, circumscriptive, conditional, or default logic), and somehow absorb hierarchies and inheritance as a special case. While the nonmonotonic systems tend to be more principled and semantically motivated on the whole, they have yet to be applied successfully to problems as intricate as those considered by the path-based approaches.

But if there are indeed irreducible intuitions about inheritance and paths through hierarchies, these intuitions are sometimes in conflict and can give rise to different inheritance systems [Touretzky et al., 1987]. How then to choose among the competing systems, especially since there is no independent semantic characterization that adequately covers the phenomena in question? While we do not claim to have an answer to this question, we do propose here a *criterion* that should be taken into account when comparing systems. What we will show is that there can be a significant difference in the *computational tractability* of inheritance depending on fine points of the definition used. In other words, two accounts of inheritance that cover by and large the same territory, differing only in certain complex cases, may nonetheless be quite different in their overall computational demands.

The main technical result of this paper is that the definition of inheritance proposed by Touretzky[2] is inherently NP-hard, and remains so even for totally acyclic unambiguous networks. Thus there cannot be an algorithm that correctly determines if one node is inheritable from another that runs in time that is polynomial in the size of the network.[3] An immediate consequence of this is that the conditioning of a network, which Touretzky proposes to allow for fast parallel inference, is itself computationally intractable. This suggests that a Touretzky inheritance procedure cannot run unsupervised, unless the network can be restricted in form or in size.

But the news is not all bad. We also show that there are plausible variants of the Touretzky definition that are indeed tractable. Among these is the definition proposed by Horty et al. [1987], who first exhibited a polynomial algorithm for computing inheritance. We extend this work and demonstrate which parts of the definition are responsible for making inheritance tractable.

Again, we do not wish to claim that the tractability of inheritance implies the *correctness* of the definition; but it is certainly one issue among many that needs to be taken into account in resolving differences among competing accounts.

In the next section, we consider the precise definition of several forms of path-based inheritance. In the subsequent section, we examine the complexity of inheritance, and which combination of features in the definition affect the tractability of the associated reasoning. In the final section, we summarize our results and discuss directions for future research.

9.2 PATH-BASED INHERITANCE SYSTEMS

For our purposes, an inheritance network consists of a finite set N of objects called *nodes* denoted with lowercase letters x, y, z, and a set Γ of *edges*, defined as follows:

---

[2] When speaking of "Touretzky's definition of inheritance" or "Touretzky's inheritance system," we are referring to the system defined in Touretzky [1984].

[3] For the purpose of this paper, and to keep the provisos to a minimum, we assume that $P \neq NP$.

Definition: Edge
An edge is an element of $N \times \{0,1\} \times N$, that is, any ordered pair of nodes and a 0–1 value called its *polarity*. Edges with a 0 are called *negative* and those with a 1 are called *positive*. We draw positive edges as $x \rightarrow y$ and negative edges as $x \not\rightarrow y$.

Intuitively, the nodes of a network are intended to stand for concepts or properties such as "bird," "penguin," "Tweety," or "flies." Edges, on the other hand, stand for statements: A positive edge $x \rightarrow y$ stands for the statement "an x is normally a y," while the corresponding negative edge represents the statement "an x is normally not a y."[4] Path-based inheritance is concerned with the logic of statements of this type only.[5] The goal is to define what it means for a new edge $x \rightarrow$ y (or $x \not\rightarrow y$) to be inferable from a given set of edges Γ. To do so, we use the notion of a path.

Definition: Path
A path in Γ is a sequence of edges in Γ from nodes x_0 to x_1 to ... to x_{n-1} to x_n where $n \geq 1$ and the first $n - 1$ edges are positive.[6] *The polarity* of a path is the polarity of the final edge. The nodes x_0 and x_n are called the *start point* and *end point* of the path. The edge formed by taking the start and end points and the polarity of a path we call the *conclusion* supported by the path. This conclusion need not be an element of Γ. We will let lowercase Greek letters stand for paths and draw them $x_0 \rightarrow x_1 \rightarrow \ldots x_n$.

It is tempting to define the set of edges that are inferrable from a network Γ directly as the set of all conclusions supported by at least one path formed by edges in Γ. The complication is that a path may be invalidated in one of two ways: It may be contradicted by other paths (in which case neither path wins) or it may be preempted by a more specific path (in which case the more specific path wins).

For the following definitions, we will let Φ be any set of paths, σ be any path $x_0 \rightarrow x_1 \rightarrow \ldots x_n$, going through nodes $x_0, x_1, \ldots x_n$, and x be any node.

Definition: Contradiction
σ is *contradicted in* Φ iff there is path in Φ with the same start and end points as σ, but of opposite polarity.

---

[4] In the case where x is a property, instead of "an x," this should read "something with property x." This also applies to y as a property. When x denotes an individual concept, instead of "an x is normally," the phrase "x is" should be used. The case with y as an individual concept never arises.

[5] Touretzky also defines "no-conclusion" edges. Such edges are not often used in practice, and therefore we will ignore them here in order to simplify our definitions. Note that these edges cannot decrease the complexity of the inheritance reasoning.

[6] So every edge in a network is a path.

So for example, the path $x_0 \rightarrow x_1 \rightarrow x_2$ is contradicted by the path $x_0 \rightarrow x_3 \rightarrow x_4 \rightarrow x_5 \not\rightarrow x_2$ since the start and end points are the same but the final edge is of opposite polarity.

For preemption, the idea is that a path is preempted by an edge of opposite polarity from an intermediate of the path. We will consider two definitions of intermediate.

Definition: On-path intermediate
x is an *on-path intermediate of* σ in Φ iff for some $i \leq n$, either $x = x_i$ or Φ contains a positive path $\gamma = x_0 \rightarrow \ldots \rightarrow x_{i-1} \rightarrow y_0 \rightarrow \ldots \rightarrow y_m \rightarrow x_i$ with $x = y_j$ for some $j \leq m$. (Note that σ and γ must be identical up to node x_{i-1}.)

Definition: Off-path intermediate
x is an *off-path intermediate of* σ in Φ iff there is a positive path γ in Φ from x_0 to x_{n-1} that contains x. (Note that σ and γ can be completely disjoint except for the nodes x_0 and x_{n-1}.)

Definition: Preemption (off-path or on-path)
σ is *preempted in* Φ iff there is a node x that is an intermediate of σ in Φ, and an edge in Φ of the opposite polarity of σ from x to x_n.

For example, consider the set of paths $\Phi = \{ C \rightarrow re \rightarrow e, e \rightarrow g, re \not\rightarrow g \}$, where C, re, e, and g respectively denote "Clyde," "royal elephant," "elephant," and "gray." Figure 1(a) gives the underlying inheritance network. (The figure contains an additional node Ae, which will be discussed below.) The path $C \rightarrow re \rightarrow e \rightarrow g$ would be on-path preempted in Φ by the edge $re \not\rightarrow g$, since re is an on-path intermediate of the path.[7] It would also be off-path preempted by the same edge. On the other hand, the path $C \rightarrow Ae \rightarrow e \rightarrow g$, where Ae denotes "African elephant," would only be off-path preempted in Φ.

Contradiction and preemption tell us how a path in a network may be invalidated. But once a path is invalidated, other paths that contain it may be invalidated also. So in determining inheritable paths, we must only consider paths that are formed by linking together those paths that have not been ruled out. As it turns out, there are two ways to concatenate paths.

Definition: Upward concatenation
σ is an *upward concatenation of paths in* Φ iff the last edge of σ is in Φ and the path consisting of all but the last edge of σ is also in Φ.

---

[7] Royal elephant is a subclass of elephant; therefore, information associated with it should override information associated with the elephant class. This is precisely what is captured by preemption.

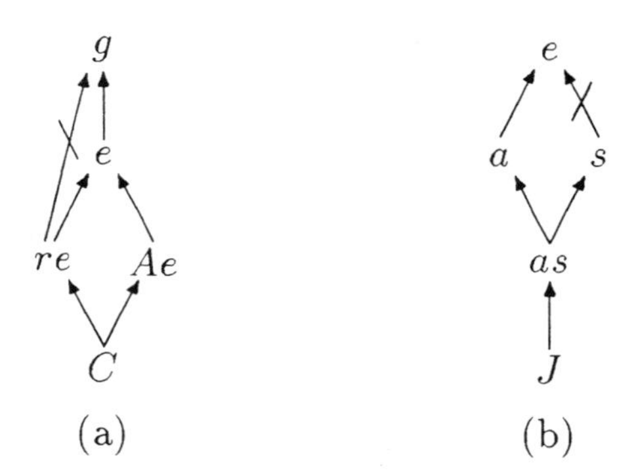

Figure 9.1: Examples of preemption and path concatenation. Arrows with a cross bar denote negative edges, the other arrows denote positive edges.

Definition: Downward concatenation
σ is a *downward concatenation of paths in* Φ iff the path consisting of all but the first edge of σ is in Φ and the path consisting of all but the last edge of σ is also in Φ.

The latter form of concatenation was originally called *double chaining* in Touretzky [1984]. Here we opt for the more recent terminology used in Touretzky et al. [1987]. The definition of inheritance based on upward concatenation that we will consider leads to so-called decoupled inheritance, as opposed to the coupled inheritance when using downward path concatenation.

To illustrate the difference between the two forms of concatenation, consider the following set of paths $\Phi = \{ J \rightarrow as \rightarrow a,\ as \rightarrow s \not\rightarrow e,\ a \rightarrow e \}$, where J, as, s, a, and e respectively denote "Jill," "adult student," "student," "adult," and "employed." The underlying inheritance network is given in Figure 1(b). The path $J \rightarrow as \rightarrow a \rightarrow e$ can now be formed by upward path concatenation. This path supports the conclusion $J \rightarrow e$, while $as \rightarrow s \not\rightarrow e$ in Φ supports $as \not\rightarrow e$. So, in this case, Jill and the class of adult students differ w.r.t. the property "employed." In general, when there is no coupling between the properties of a class and the properties of its superclasses, one speaks of decoupled inheritance. But with downward path concatenation the path $J \rightarrow as \rightarrow a \rightarrow e$ cannot be obtained from the paths in Φ. To do so, one would also need $as \rightarrow a \rightarrow e$ which, in fact, is contradicted in Φ by $as \rightarrow s \not\rightarrow e$. So, in this case, there is a coupling between the properties that Jill can inherit and those inherited by the class of adult students.

We now define the inheritable paths.

Definition: Inheritable path (on-path and off-path, downward and upward)
σ is *inheritable in* Φ iff

a. σ is a concatenation of paths in Φ;

b. σ is not contradicted in Φ;

c. σ is not preempted in Φ.

Intuitively, the paths that are inheritable in Φ are those that are inferrable from but not invalidated by Φ. But where does this set Φ come from? There are different ways of choosing a set Φ. We first consider Touretzky's definition of so called *credulous* inheritance reasoning. In this approach, Φ is chosen to be the least set of paths whose edges are those of Γ and closed under inheritance. We call such sets *credulous grounded extensions.*[8]

Definition: Credulous grounded extension
Φ is a *credulous grounded extension of a set of edges* Γ iff

a. $\Gamma \subseteq \Phi$;

b. For all σ, $\sigma \in \Phi - \Gamma$ iff σ is inheritable in Φ.

Unfortunately, there need not be a unique credulous grounded extension for a given set Γ; that is a network can be *ambiguous*. Inheritance reasoners allowing for multiple extensions, such as Touretzky's, are called *credulous reasoners* because they explore the various alternatives in different extensions. Instead of allowing for multiple extensions, Horty et al. [1987] propose a form of *skeptical* inheritance in which at most one grounded extension is generated. In this form of inheritance a unique extension is inductively constructed by including paths that are inheritable only if a path with the same start and end point but of opposite polarity could not be inherited. The induction is based on the degree of a path:

Definition: Degree
Given a set of edges Γ, the degree of a path with start point x and end point y is the length of the longest path in Γ from x to y (ignoring the polarity of the edges).

Horty et al. restrict their definition of skeptical inheritance to acyclic networks:

Definition: Acyclic
A set of edges Γ is *acyclic* iff the graph formed by the elements of Γ is acyclic.[9]

We can now state the definition of skeptical inheritance as follows:

---

[8] These were called *grounded expansions* in Touretzky [1984].

[9] Touretzky [1984] speaks of *totally acyclic*, as distinguished from *IS-A acyclic* networks in which the graph formed by only the positive edges is required to be acyclic.

Definition: Skeptical grounded extension
Φ is a *skeptical grounded extension of a set of edges* Γ iff $\Phi = \bigcup_{i=1}^{\infty} \phi_i$ where ϕ_i is defined as follows:

a. $\phi_1 = \Gamma$;
b. ϕ_{i+1} contains the paths in ϕ_i and each path σ of degree $i + 1$ with the following properties:
   - σ can be obtained by concatenation of two paths in ϕ_i;[10]
   - there neither exists an edge in ϕ_i nor a path inheritable in ϕ_i with the same start and end point as σ but of opposite polarity.

What we ultimately care about is the conclusions (that is, the edges defined by the start and end points) supported by the paths in a grounded extension of a network. So, we define:

Definition: Conclusion set
A set of edges is a *conclusion set* for Γ iff for some grounded extension Φ, the edges are all the conclusions supported by the elements of Φ.

The inheritance problem, then, is this:

Definition: Inheritance problem
Given an acyclic network Γ, find a conclusion set of Γ.

Note that we are really talking about eight inheritance problems here according to whether we consider off-path or on-path preemption, upward or downward path concatenation, and skeptical or credulous reasoning. Touretzky's definition, for example, would be classified as on-path, downward, and credulous, while Horty's version is off-path, upward, and skeptical.

For skeptical reasoners one sometimes defines the inheritance problem more narrowly: Determine whether a certain conclusion is supported by the (unique) extension of an acyclic network [Horty et al., 1987]. It is important to note when a network is unambiguous or when skeptical reasoning is desired, the computational complexity of this inference task is essentially the same as that of the inheritance problem defined above, since after at most a polynomial number of queries, one can determine the conclusion set (for a network containing n concepts one has to consider at most $n\,(n-1)$ possible conclusions).

We now consider the computational difficulty of the inheritance problem.

---

[10] The perhaps more natural condition "σ is inheritable in ϕ_i" leads to a different notion of skeptical inheritance. We use the condition given above for compatibility with Horty et al. [1987]. Under this definition, the credulous grounded extension of an unambiguous inheritance network need not be identical to its skeptical grounded extension [Selman and Levesque, 1990].

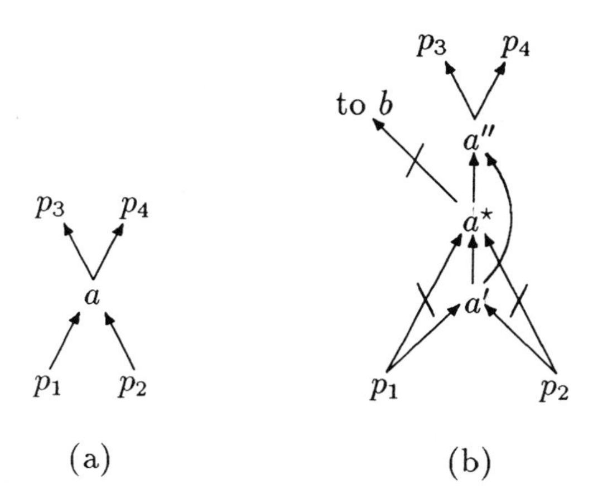

Figure 9.2 Construction used in proof of theorem 1. Arrows with a cross bar denote negative links, the other arrows denote positive links.

9.3 COMPUTATIONAL COMPLEXITY

The following theorem shows that for Touretzky's inheritance notion there is no polynomial algorithm that takes as input an acyclic network Γ and finds a conclusion set of Γ.

Theorem 1 The inheritance problem for on-path, downward, credulous inheritance [Touretzky, 1984] is NP-hard.

The proof of this theorem is based on a reduction from the NP-complete decision problem *path with forbidden pairs* (or PWFP) defined by Gabow, Maheshwari, and Osterweil [1976]. An instance of PWFP consists of a directed graph $G = (V, E)$, specified vertices $s, t \in V$, and a collection $C = \{(a_1, b_1),\ldots,(a_n, b_n)\}$ of pairs of vertices from V. The question is: Does there exist a path from s to t in G that contains at most one vertex from each pair in C? This problem remains NP-complete even if we only consider acyclic graphs and all pairs in C are disjoint. Consider an instance of this restricted version of PWFP. Without loss of generality, we may assume that each forbidden pair (a_i, b_i) is such that there does not exist a path from b_i to a_i in C.

We now construct an acyclic network Γ from this instance of PWFP. First, we include every edge of G as a positive edge of Γ. Then for every node a that is the first element of a forbidden pair in C, we replace a in Γ by the network shown in Figure 9.2.

Figure 9.2(a) shows a node a from the forbidden pair (a, b) with all of its neighbors in G, and 9.2(b) shows the structure in Γ that replaces a: Two additional nodes (for a total of three) and $n + 4$ additional edges must be included, where n is the number of edges pointing to a in G. Note that of the three new nodes, the middle one a^* is linked to b by a negative edge. Since G is acyclic and the forbidden pairs are such that there is no path from b_i to a_i for any pair in C, it follows that Γ is an acyclic network. Moreover, Γ is such that given an arbitrary on-path, downward, credulous conclusion set C of Γ, there is a path in G from s to t containing at most one vertex from each forbidden pair iff the conclusion $s \rightarrow t$ is in C.[11]

Now, consider an algorithm that takes as input an instance of PWFP, constructs (in polynomial time) an acyclic network Γ as outlined above, then finds an on-path, downward, credulous conclusion set C of Γ, and, finally, returns "yes" if $s \rightarrow t \in C$, and and "no" otherwise. Such an algorithm returns "yes" iff there exists a path from s to t in G containing at most one node from each forbidden pair; but if finding a conclusion set can be done in polynomial time, the overall algorithm will run in polynomial time. Since PWFP is NP-hard, the inheritance problem for on-path, downward, credulous reasoning must be NP-hard too.

The construction shown in Figure 9.2 exploits various properties of inheritance reasoning in general, and Touretzky's notion specifically. Firstly, we rely on preemption since preemption prevents inheritance of a path from s to t going through a'' and b (corresponding to a path through a and b in G) because of the negative edge between a^* and b.[12] Secondly, we use *quasi-redundant* edges [Touretzky, 1984, p. 10; Horty et al., 1987, Techn. Report, p. 21]. The edge $a' \rightarrow a''$ is an example of a quasi-redundant edge, since this edge is strictly redundant for concluding $a' \rightarrow a''$; however, to be able to conclude, for example, $p_1 \rightarrow a''$, the edge is essential (so it allows us to have a path from s to t through p_1 and a'' in a grounded extension, corresponding to a path from s to t via p_1 and a in G). Thirdly, the reduction relies on coupled inheritance; we will see below that decoupled (upward) reasoning allows for polynomial time inheritance.

A direct consequence of theorem 1 is that the conditioning of a network as proposed in Touretzky [1984], to enable fast parallel inference, is also intractable. Conditioning is a process of adding edges to an inheritance network in such a way that a parallel marker-passing procedure can subsequently be used to draw conclusions in time proportional to the height of the inheritance network.

We show in Selman and Levesque [1990] that the inheritance network Γ used in the above reduction is unambiguous. Thus, it follows that even when we restrict ourselves to unambiguous acyclic networks the inheritance problem based on Touretzky's notion of inheritance is intractable. Note that it also follows that deter-

[11] We prove this property of Γ in Selman and Levesque [1990].

[12] Downward concatenation is also relevant here.

mining whether an unambiguous acyclic network supports a particular conclusion is NP-hard.

Recently, Geffner and Verma [1989] used a variation of our reduction to show that reasoning based on their definition of defeasible inheritance is NP-hard. Thus, the technique given above may prove to be useful in determining the complexity of future proposals for path-based inheritance reasoners.

We will now consider the influence of the various design choices made in [Touretzky, 1984; Horty et al., 1987] on the computational complexity of the inheritance reasoning. Our results are summarized in the following theorem:

Theorem 2 The computational complexity of the inheritance problem for the various choices between off-path or on-path, upward or downward path concatenation, and skeptical or credulous reasoning is as given in Table 9.1 (P stands for doable in polynomial time).

Clearly the choice between off-path or on-path preemption and between skeptical or credulous inheritance does not change the complexity of inheritance reasoning. However, when we consider upward (decoupled) inheritance, we do obtain tractability. The latter finding generalizes the tractability result obtained by Horty et al. [1987] for their off-path, upward, skeptical inheritance reasoner. The NP-hardness results are proved by showing that the various design choices do not affect the correctness of the above reduction when dealing with downward path concatenation. Details are given in Selman and Levesque [1990], which also contains polynomial algorithms for the tractable cases.

To summarize, theorem 2 clearly shows that the type of path concatenation (upward or downward) is the determining factor in the complexity of the reasoning. This distinction corresponds to the difference between decoupled and coupled reasoning. It should be noted though, that in formalisms with substantially different definitions of preemption or grounded extension, other factors may also influence the complexity of the reasoning.

A further understanding of the complexity issues underlying inheritance reasoning can be obtained by considering the polynomial algorithms for upward inheritance. These algorithms iteratively construct a conclusion set. The main difficulty

Table 9.1

	Skeptical		**Credulous**	
	Off-path	*On-path*	*Off-path*	*On-path*
Down	NP-hard	NP-hard	NP-hard	NP-hard
Up	P	P	P	P

in adding a new conclusion to the set arises from having to determine whether the path that supports this conclusion is preempted or not. So, we have to search for intermediates, which requires access to the set of *paths* in the underlying grounded extension. At worst, one would have to keep track of the full extension obtained so far (which can be of exponential size). But for upward inheritance it is sufficient to keep track of the current conclusion set, since one can rederive in polynomial time any particular path in the underlying extension, and thus, search for intermediates efficiently.

To summarize, theorem 2 clearly shows that it is the method of concatenating paths together in the definition of inheritability that is the main source of intractability: If we require that a path of length n be composed from two paths of length $n - 1$, the overall inheritance problem is intractable; but if we allow a path of length n to be formed from a path of length $n - 1$ and a final edge, the overall inheritance problem is tractable.[13] This is surprising since the problem is to come up with a conclusion set, and there is no requirement that paths be explicitly calculated one way or another. It is a mistake, in other words, to think of downward and upward concatenation as specifications of procedures to follow in calculating conclusion sets, where the former is less efficient than the latter. Rather, the issue is more like whether or not an algorithm that searches for a conclusion set needs to explicitly store the set of paths in the corresponding grounded extension. An algorithm that needs to keep track of all those paths is necessarily exponential since a grounded extension may contain exponentially many (in the number of concepts in the inheritance network) paths. The polynomial algorithms for upward inheritance iteratively construct a conclusion set extension, and, while doing so, only store a polynomial amount of information about the extension.

As a final topic, we will consider *goal-directed* inheritance. Note that so far we have considered the complexity of finding any arbitrary conclusion set given an inheritance hierarchy. In some situations, however, it might be wasteful to generate the entire conclusion set, and moreover, one might be interested in an extension that supports some particular conclusion (or set of conclusions). We therefore define the problem of goal-directed inheritance reasoning: given an inheritance network Γ and a conclusion $x \rightarrow y$ (or $x \not\rightarrow y$), does there exists an extension of Γ supporting $x \rightarrow y$ (or $x \not\rightarrow y$)? [14]

When a network is unambiguous or when skeptical reasoning is desired, the computational complexity of this inference task is essentially the same as that of

---

[13] Left open by this theorem is what happens if we allow a path of length n to be formed from an *initial* edge and a path of length $n - 1$.

[14] In Selman and Levesque [1990] we also discuss the related extension completion problem: Given a network and a conclusion c, find an conclusion set containing c. Clearly, this problem is at least as hard as the associated decision problem given above.

searching for a conclusion set; since, on the one hand, after finding the unique conclusion set, it is trivial to determine whether it contains a certain conclusion, and, on the other hand, after at most a polynomial number of queries, one can determine the conclusion set (for a network containing n concepts one has to consider at most $2n(n-1)$ possible conclusions). Moreover, our reduction from PWFP shows that goal-directed inheritance for on-path and off-path, credulous, downward inheritance is NP-hard, just like the problem of finding an extension. (Consider the query: Does the constructed network have an extension that supports the conclusion $s \rightarrow t$?) The following theorem, however, shows that goal-directed reasoning is strictly more difficult than searching for an arbitrary conclusion set.[15]

Theorem 3 Goal-directed, on-path, upward, credulous inheritance is NP-hard.

The proof of this theorem is again based on a reduction from PWFP [Selman and Levesque, 1990]. For this reduction, it is essential for the constructed network to be ambiguous. This theorem reveals some of the extra difficulties in inheritance reasoning due to ambiguities, although these difficulties do not arise when searching for an arbitrary conclusion set, as shown by theorem 2. The complexity of goal-directed, off-path, upward, credulous inheritance remains an open problem.

9.4 CONCLUSIONS

We have shown that path-based inheritance reasoning as defined in Touretzky [1984] is NP-hard, even when restricted to acyclic unambiguous networks. Moreover, the versions of this form of inheritance that use skeptical reasoning and off-path preemption are also intractable. Thus, while Touretzky [1984] showed that inheritance networks can be conditioned to allow for correct and efficient retrieval of information (time $O(log(n))$ for n concepts) such as in NETL [Fahlman, 1979], our results demonstrate that this conditioning procedure itself is intractable when based on downward (coupled) inheritance. However, our other complexity results, generalizing the tractability result obtained by Horty et al. [1987], also suggest that the various forms of upward (decoupled) inheritance can be used to achieve tractability. It follows that the main source of intractability in these path-based inheritance formalisms is the downward (coupled) inheritance reasoning.

One possible direction for future research is to consider further restrictions on the form of inheritance networks that would allow for a polynomial inference

---

[15] Kautz and Selman [1989] show that goal-directed reasoning for default logic is also strictly harder than generating an arbitrary extension.

mechanism based on downward inheritance.[16] One candidate we have already begun to explore is inheritance restricted to completely balanced hierarchies. Such hierarchies have a maximum depth of $O(log(n))$, where n is the total number of concepts in the hierarchy. Such a restriction seems quite reasonable, given that taxonomic hierarchies will often be "shallow." However, we have found a reduction from the small-clique problem[17] to downward inheritance reasoning with such networks. This result indicates that Touretzky's inheritance notion restricted to balanced hierarchies is most likely still intractable (i.e., not polynomial). See Selman and Levesque [1990] for a more detailed discussion of these issues.

ACKNOWLEDGMENTS

This work was supported in part by a Government of Ontario Scholarship to the first author, and a grant to the second from the Natural Sciences and Engineering Research Council of Canada. We would like to thank David Etherington for pointing out to us that the complexity of inferential distance was unknown. We also would like to thank Sue Becker, Jim des Rivières, Russ Greiner, Jeff Horty, Gerhard Lakemeyer, Bernhard Nebel, Peter Patel-Schneider, Lokendra Shastri, Rich Thomason, David Touretzky, Wlodek Zadrozny, and the anonymous referees for providing useful comments.

References

Brachman, R.J. 1985. I lied about the trees (or, defaults and definitions in knowledge representation). *The AI Magazine* **6**(3):80–93.

Fahlman, S.E. 1979. *NETL: A System for Representing and Using Real-World Knowledge*. MIT Press, Cambridge, MA.

Gabow, H.N., Maheshwari S.N, and Osterweil L. 1976. On two problems in the generation of program test paths. *IEEE Trans. Software Engineering*, pp. 227–231.

Geffner, H. and Verma, T. 1989. *Inheritance = Chaining + Defeat*. Technical report TR-129, Department of Computer Science, University of California, Los Angeles, CA.

Horty, J.F., Thomason, R.H., and Touretzky, D.S. 1987. A skeptical theory of inheritance in nonmonotonic semantic nets. *Proceedings of AAAI-87*. AAAI, Menlo Park, CA. More complete version:

[16] Shastri [1988] gives various conditions under which the inheritance problem in his evidential framework is solvable in time polynomial in the depth of the IS-A hierarchy.

[17] Given a graph G with n vertices, does G contain a clique of size $log(n)$? [Karchmer, 1989; Megiddo and Vishkin 1988].

technical report CMU-CS-87-175, Department of Computer Science, Carnegie Mellon University, Pittsburgh, PA, 1987.

Haugh, B.A. 1988. Tractable theories of multiple defeasible inheritance. *Proceedings of AAAI-88*. AAAI, Menlo Park, CA, pp. 421–426.

Karchmer, M. 1989. Personal communication.

Kautz, H.A. and Selman, B. 1989. Hard problems for simple default logics. *Proceedings of the First International Conference on Principles of Knowledge Representation and Reasoning,* Toronto, Ont., Canada. Morgan Kaufmann Publishers, San Mateo, CA.

Megiddo, N. and Vishkin, U. 1988. On finding a minimum dominating set in a tournament. *Theoretical Computer Science*, 61:307—316.

Quillian, M. 1968. Semantic memory. In *Semantic Information Processing*, M. Minsky (ed.). MIT Press, Cambridge, MA, pp. 216–70.

Reiter R. 1987. Nonmonotonic reasoning. *Annual Reviews of Computer Science*. Annual Reviews, Palo Alto, CA.

Reiter, R. and Criscuolo, G. 1983. Some representational issues in default reasoning. *Computers* and *Mathematics with Applications*, (Special Issue on Computational Linguistics), 9(1):1–13.

Sandewall, E. 1986. Nonmonotonic inference rules for multiple inheritance with exceptions. *Proceedings of the IEEE*, 74:81–132.

Selman, B. and Levesque, H.J. 1990. *The Tractability of Path-Based Inheritance*. Technical Report, Department of Computer Science, University of Toronto, Toronto, Ont., Canada.

Shastri, L. 1988. *Semantic Nets: An Evidential Formalization and Its Connectionist Realization*. Morgan Kaufmann Publishers, San Mateo, CA, copublished with Pitman, London.

Touretzky, D.S. 1984. *The Mathematics of Inheritance Systems*. Report CMU-CS-84-136, Department of Computer Science, Carnegie Mellon University, Pittsburgh, PA, 1984; also Morgan Kaufmann Publishers, San Mateo, CA copublished with Pitman, London, 1986.

Touretzky, D.S., Horty, J.F., and Thomason, R.H. 1987. A clash of intuitions: The current state of nonmonotonic multiple inheritance systems. In *Proceedings IJCAI-87*, Milan, Italy, pp. 476–482. IJCAI proceedings are available from Morgan Kaufmann Publishers, San Mateo, CA.

10

ALL: Formalizing Access-Limited Reasoning

J. M. Crawford and Benjamin Kuipers
(The University of Texas, Austin)

Abstract

Access-limited logic (ALL) is a language for knowledge representation that formalizes the access limitations inherent in a network-structured knowledge base. Where a classical deductive method or logic programming language would retrieve all assertions that satisfy a given pattern, an access-limited logic retrieves all assertions reachable by following an available access path. The complexity of inference is thus independent of the size of the knowledge base and depends only on its local connectivity. Access-limited logic, though incomplete, still has a well-defined semantics and a weakened form of completeness, *Socratic completeness*, which guarantees that for any query that is a logical consequence of the knowledge base, there exists a series of queries after which the original query will succeed. This chapter presents an overview of ALL, and sketches the proofs of its Socratic completeness and polynomial time complexity.

10.1 INTRODUCTION

It has long been a guiding principle in work on semantic networks that by imposing a network structure on large knowledge bases one can increase the efficiency of reasoning. Intuitively, in a semantic network related concepts are located "close together" in the network and thus search and inference can be guided by the structure of the knowledge base. However, formalisms for semantic networks have generally treated the semantic network notation as a variant of predicate calculus and have regarded the access limitations inherent in a network as an extra-logical indexing mechanisms. In *access-limited logic* (ALL) we incorporate these access limitations directly into the logic. One benefit of this approach is that we can assess the impact of access limitations on the completeness and complexity of reasoning. ALL is, in fact, not complete, but it is *Socratically complete*—that is, for any query that is a logical consequence of the knowledge base, there exists a series of queries after which the original query will succeed. Further, the complexity of inference in ALL is independent of the size of a knowledge base and depends only on the size of the accessible portion of the knowledge base.

Reasoning is hard. If a knowledge representation language is as expressive as first-order predicate calculus, then the problem of deciding what an agent implicitly knows (i.e., what an agent could logically deduce from its knowledge) is unsolvable [Boolos and Jeffrey, 1980]. Thus a sound and decidable knowledge representation and reasoning system must either give up expressive power or use a weak inference system with an incomplete set of deduction rules or artificial resource limits (e.g., bounds on the number of applications of *modus ponens*). However, such inference systems tend to be difficult to describe semantically and tend to place unnatural limits on an agent's reasoning ability [Levesque, 1986].

As an example of nontrivial inference, consider the following problem (from [Wylie, 1957]):

> In a certain bank the positions of cashier, manager, and teller are held by Brown, Jones and Smith, though not necessarily respectively. The teller, who was an only child, earns the least. Smith, who married Brown's sister, earns more than the manager. What position does each man fill?

A person looking at such a problem cannot come up with a solution immediately (though the positions follow from a fairly small amount of commonsense knowledge about families, partial orders, and coreference). A certain amount of conscious thought is required; one has to ask just the right questions. Similarly, we do not expect our knowledge representation system to be able to solve such a problem immediately, since intuitively we expect it to be able to reason only about as well as a person could reason without conscious thought. We do, however, expect it to be able to solve such a problem after being given an appropriate set of leading questions. If we ask:

1. If Smith were the manager then how could he earn more than the manager?
2. If Smith were the teller then how could he earn more than the manager?
3. If Brown were the teller then how could he have a sister?

then we can see immediately that Smith must be the cashier, Brown the manager, and Jones the teller. Similarly, a knowledge representation system, after being asked by the user (or heuristically generating) such a series of questions should be able to determine which man holds which position. We have translated this problem into ALL and given it (along with appropriate commonsense knowledge) to our

LISP implementation, Algernon. Inference in Algernon is incomplete, and Algernon initially fails to solve the problem. However, after we ask it the questions given above, it is able to determine which position each man fills.

More abstractly, ALL has an important property we call *Socratic completeness*[1]—for any query of a proposition that is a consequence (in predicate calculus) of the knowledge base, there exists a preliminary query after which the original query will succeed. ALL also has a more technical weakened completeness property, which we call *partitional completeness*. Roughly, partitional completeness says that if all facts and rules needed to prove a query are located "close enough" (see Section 10.3) to the query, then it will succeed immediately.

The rest of this chapter is organized as follows. In Section 10.2 we discuss our general approach to knowledge representation. Section 10.3 gives an overview of the formalization of ALL, and the proofs of Socratic and partitional completeness. We outline the argument for the polynomial time complexity of ALL in Section 10.4. In Section 10.5 we briefly discuss related work, and Section 10.6 is our conclusion.

10.2 OVERVIEW OF ACCESS-LIMITED LOGIC

In the broadest sense, the study of knowledge representation is the study of how to represent knowledge in such a way that the knowledge can be used by a machine. From this vague definition we can conclude that a knowledge representation system must have the following properties:

1. It must have a reasonably compact syntax.
2. It must have a well-defined semantics so that one can say precisely what is being represented.
3. It must have sufficient expressive power to represent human knowledge.
4. It must have an efficient, powerful, and understandable reasoning mechanism.
5. It must be usable to build large knowledge bases.

It has proved difficult, however, to achieve the third and fourth properties simultaneously.

Our approach in ALL begins with the well-known mapping between atomic propositions in predicate calculus and slots in frames; the atomic proposition that the object a stands in relation r to the object b can be written logically as $r(a,b)$ or expressed, in frames, by including object b in the r slot of object a [Hayes, 1979].

---

[1] We have since discovered that the idea of *Socratic completeness* is also used in [Powers, 1978] where it is referred to as *Socratic adequacy*.

$r(a,b) \equiv$

```
a:
    r:
        values: { ... b ... }
```

We refer to the pair $\langle a,r \rangle$ as a *frame-slot*. Thus $r(a,b)$ is equivalent to saying that the value b is in the frame-slot $\langle a,r \rangle$. The frames *directly accessible* from a frame-slot are those that appear in the frame-slot.[2] Extending this idea, we define an *access path*, in a network of frames, as a sequence of frames such that each is directly accessible from a frame-slot of its predecessor. It is useful to generalize this definition and allow access paths to branch on all values in the frame-slots. A sequence of propositions defines an access path if any variable appearing as the first argument to a proposition has appeared previously in the sequence (operationally, this means that retrieval always accesses a known frame-slot). For example, "John's parent's sister" can be expressed in ALL as the path:

$(parent(John, x), sister(x, y))$

This defines an access path from the frame for *John* to the frames for *John*'s parents (found by looking in the frame-slot $\langle John, parent \rangle$), to *John*'s parents' sisters.

From access paths we build the inference rules of ALL. A rule is always associated with a particular slot in the network. Backward-chaining *if-needed* rules are written in the form: $\beta \leftarrow \alpha$ (the structure of α and β is discussed in more detail in Section 10.3.2.3) and applied when a value for the slot is needed. Forward-chaining *if-added* rules are written in the form: $\alpha \rightarrow \beta$ and applied when a new value for the slot is inserted. In either case the antecedent of a rule must define an access path (beginning with the slot the rule is associated with). For example, using the access path above we can write the if-needed rule:

$aunt(John, y) \leftarrow parent(John, x), sister(x, y)$

But we *cannot* write the (logically equivalent) rule:

$aunt(John, y) \leftarrow sister(x, y), parent(John, x),$

since the antecedent does not define an access path.[3]

---

[2] Slots in ALL contain only frames and rules (defined below).

[3] The restriction to access paths limits the syntax of ALL but is not a fundamental limit on its expressive power since one could always add a new constant and make it the first argument to every predicate. This would amount to making the entire knowledge base a single frame.

Where a classical deductive method or logic-programming language would retrieve all known assertions that satisfy a given pattern, an access-limited logic retrieves all assertions reachable by following an available access path. The use of access paths alone, however, is insufficient to guarantee computational tractability in very large knowledge bases. The evaluation of a path can cause an explosive back-chaining of rules, which can spread throughout the knowledge base. To prevent this, ALL introduces a second form of access limitation. The knowledge base in ALL is divided up into partitions and back-chaining is not allowed across partitions—facts in other partitions are simply retrieved. When used together, these two kinds of access limitations can limit the complexity of inference to a polynomial function of the size of the portion of the knowledge base accessible from the local partition.

10.3 THE LOGICAL COHERENCE OF ALL

A price must be paid for the efficiency of access limitations. Inference in ALL is weaker than inference in predicate calculus, since only locally accessible facts and rules can be used in deductions. However, logical coherence does not necessarily require completeness. Rather it is an informally defined collection of desirable formal properties. We have proven that a dialect of ALL has the following properties of a logically coherent knowledge representation system:

- ALL has a well-defined syntax and proof theory.
- The semantics of ALL can be defined by a purely syntactic mapping of ALL knowledge bases, queries and assertions to predicate calculus.
- In terms of this mapping, inference in ALL is sound, Socratically complete, and partitionally complete.

These properties are stated more precisely in theorems 1–3, which follow.

We view these formal properties as necessary but not sufficient conditions for logical coherence. There remains, at least, the less formal claim that knowledge can be organized cleanly into partitions. This claim is discussed further in Sections 10.3.4.2 and 10.6.2.

The rest of this section sketches the formal development of ALL. The full account can be found in [Crawford and Kuipers, 1990]. Our formal work in ALL generally lags several months behind our implementation work and the results presented here only formalize a part of ALL. Specifically, our current formalism does not allow negation or quantification (though our LISP implementation supports both—see Section 10.6).

10.3.1 Basic Notation

In the metatheory of ALL we use the following notation. Quantified expressions are written in the form:

$$(\langle Quantifier \rangle\ \langle Variable \rangle : \langle Range \rangle : \langle Expression \rangle).$$

Thus, for example:

$$(\forall x : pred_1(x) : pred_2(x))$$

is read "For all x such that $pred_1(x)$, $pred_2(x)$." Similarly:

$$(\cup x : pred(x) : foo(x))$$

(where *foo* is a set-valued function) denotes the union, over all x such that $pred(x)$, of $foo(x)$.

We delineate lists with the usual ( ) and notate the empty list by *nil*. If α is a list then:

- $head(\alpha)$ is the first element in α.
- $rest(\alpha)$ is all but the first element in α.

We define $append(\alpha_1,\alpha_2)$ to be the result of appending the list α_1 to the beginning of the list α_2.

10.3.2 Syntax of ALL

The syntax of ALL is quite similar to the syntax of logic programming. Accordingly we develop the syntax of ALL generally following the notation in [Apt, 1988].

10.3.2.1 Alphabets, Terms, and Propositions

The *alphabet* of an access-limited logic consists of countably infinite sets of variables, constants, and relations, the connectives $\leftarrow$ and $\rightarrow$, and the operators *query* and *assert*. A *term* is a constant or a variable. $r(t_1,\ldots,t_n)$ is a *proposition* iff r is an n-ary relation and all t_i are terms. [4] A *fact* is a proposition such that all t_i are constants. For a term, proposition, or list of propositions, α:

- $vars(\alpha)$ is the set of variables appearing in α.
- $relations(\alpha)$ is the set of relations appearing in α.
- $constants(\alpha)$ is the set of constants appearing in α.

If $vars(\alpha) = \emptyset$ then α is *ground*. (So a ground proposition is a fact).

---

[4] n place relations cause no problems in ALL. Intuitively, $r(t_1,\ldots,t_n)$ corresponds to putting the value $(t_2,\ldots,t_n)$ in the r slot of t_1.

10.3.2.2 Access Paths

An *access path* (or simply a *path*) is a pair $\langle V,\alpha\rangle$ where α is a list of propositions and V is a set of variables. In general the first argument to each proposition in α must have occurred previously in α. The variables in V are exceptions to this rule and may occur as the first argument to propositions without having occurred previously in α. The need for such exceptions will become apparent when rules are defined below. If $V = \{\ \}$ then we omit it and say α is a path. A path of length one is a *primitive* path.

10.3.2.3 Rules

Assume $r(t_1,\ldots,t_n)$ is a proposition and α is a nonempty list of propositions. $r(t_1,\ldots,t_n) \leftarrow \alpha$ is an *if-needed rule* iff both of the following hold:

1. Either t_1 is a constant and α is a path, or t_1 is a variable and $\langle\{t_1\},\alpha\rangle$ is a path.
2. $vars(\{t_1,\ldots,t_n\}) \subset vars(\alpha)$.

Intuitively, the first restriction ensures that when the rule is "fired" (i.e., when the consequent of the rule has been unified against a primitive path), the antecedent is an access path. The second restriction ensures that any substitution that grounds the antecedent of a rule also grounds its consequent.

If $\rho = r(t_1,\ldots,t_n) \leftarrow \alpha$ is an if-needed rule, we use the accessor functions: $Key(\rho) = r(t_1,\ldots,t_n)$, $Conseq(\rho) = r(t_1,\ldots,t_n)$, and $Ant(\rho) = \alpha$. Intuitively, the *Key* of a rule is the proposition under which the rule is indexed in the knowledge base.

Assume $r(t_1,\ldots,t_n)$ is a proposition and α is a nonempty list of propositions. $\alpha \rightarrow r(t_1,\ldots,t_n)$ is an *if-added rule* iff both of the following hold:

1. $\langle vars(head(\alpha)),\alpha\rangle$ is a path.
2. $vars(\{t_1,\ldots,t_n\}) \subset vars(\alpha)$.

As for if-needed rules, the first restriction ensures that when the rule is "fired" (i.e., when the head of the antecedent of the rule has been unified against a fact being added to the knowledge base), the antecedent is an access path. The second restriction again ensures that any substitution that grounds the antecedent of a rule, also grounds its consequent.

If $\rho = \alpha \rightarrow \mathrm{r}(t_1,\ldots,t_n)$ is an if-added rule, we again use the accessor functions: $Key(\rho) = head(\alpha)$, $Conseq(\rho) = r(t_1,\ldots,t_n)$, and $Ant(\rho) = \alpha$.

10.3.2.4 Knowledge Bases

If S is a set then $s_1,\ldots,s_n$ is a *partitioning* of S iff:

- $(\forall i : 0 \le i \le n : s_i \subset S)$, and
- $(\cup\, i : 1 \le i \le n : s_i) = S$

A *Knowledge Base*, K, is a six-tuple $\langle C, R, Nr, Ar, F, P \rangle$ where:

C = A set of constants.
R = A set of relations.
Nr = A set of if-needed rules such that
$(\forall \rho : \rho \in Nr : constants(\rho) \subset C \wedge relations(\rho) \subset R)$.
Ar = A set of if-added rules such that
$(\forall \rho : \rho \in Ar : constants(\rho) \subset C \wedge relations(\rho) \subset R)$.
F = A set of facts such that $(\forall f : f \in F : constants(f) \subset C \wedge relations(f) \subset R)$.
P = A partitioning of $C \times R$.

If $K = \langle C, R, Nr, Ar, F, P, A \rangle$ is a knowledge base and α is a proposition, list of propositions, or a rule, then α is *allowed* in K iff $constants(\alpha) \subset C \wedge relations(\alpha) \subset R$. Finally, the members of P are referred to as the *partitions* of K.

Unless otherwise specified a knowledge base K_i should be understood to have components $\langle C, R, Nr, Ar_i, F_i, \rangle$. (We subscript Ar and F because, as will be seen, they are the two components that change when operations are performed.)

10.3.2.5 Operations and Formulas

If α is a path then $query(\alpha)$ is a *query*. If α is a primitive path then $query(\alpha)$ is a *primitive* query. If f is a fact then $assert(f)$ is an *assertion* (assertions of paths are not currently allowed). Any query or assertion is an *operation*, and any assertion or primitive query is a *primitive* operation. If $O = query(\alpha)$ or $O = assert(\alpha)$ is an operation and α is allowed in a knowledge base K, then O is *allowed* in K. If an operation O is allowed in a knowledge base K, then $O(K)$ is an ALL *formula*.

10.3.3 Mapping ALL to Predicate Calculus

We define the semantics of ALL by mapping ALL knowledge bases, assertions, and queries to (first-order) predicate calculus. An alternative approach would be to define a model theory for ALL, in terms of which ALL is complete. This could be done, but we believe that (since the model theory of predicate calculus is well understood) mapping to predicate calculus and appropriately weakening the notion of completeness gives a more perspicuous picture of the semantics of ALL. Further, we believe that consistency and Socratic completeness relative to predicate calculus (or perhaps an appropriate nonmonotonic logic) are necessary properties for any knowledge representation system.

Mapping ALL to predicate calculus is straightforward. Propositions do not change at all. Paths become conjunctions. Rules become implications with all variables universally quantified. Knowledge bases become the conjunction of their rules and facts. We notate the predicate calculus equivalent of an ALL object, a, by $\mathcal{PC}(a)$.

10.3.4 Knowledge Theory

The knowledge theory of ALL defines the values of ALL formulas by defining the action of ALL operations (i.e., queries and assertions). Intuitively, the assertion of a fact *f*, adds *f* to a knowledge base and returns the resultant knowledge base (i.e., the knowledge base after *f* is added, all applicable if-added rules are applied, and all if-added rules are closed (see Section 10.3.4.5)). A query of q returns the substitutions needed to make q true in the knowledge base. It also returns a new knowledge base (since processing the query may change the knowledge base by invoking rules).

10.3.4.1 Substitutions

A *substitution* is a finite mapping from variables to terms:

$$\theta = \{v_1/t_1, \ldots, v_n/t_n\}$$

where the v_i $(1 \le i \le n)$ are distinct variables. If all t_i $(1 \le i \le n)$ are constants then θ is *ground*. Let the variables in the alphabet (see Section 10.3.2.1) be V. A substitution θ is a *renaming* iff it is a bijection (i.e., a 1 : 1 onto mapping) from V to V.

If e is an expression and θ is a substitution then $e\theta$ is the result of applying θ to e (simultaneously replacing each occurrence in e of the variables in $\{v_1, \ldots, v_n\}$ with the corresponding term).

If there exists a substitution ζ such that $\eta = \theta \circ \zeta$ then θ is *more general* than η. Intuitively, if θ is more general than η, then θ does strictly "less work" than η. A *unifier* of two primitive propositions q_1 and q_2, is a substitution θ such that $q_1\theta = q_2\theta$. The *most general unifier* of two primitive propositions q_1 and q_2 is a unifier θ of q_1 and q_2 such that for any other unifier η of q_1 and q_2, θ is more general than η. A unifier θ of q_1 and q_2 is *relevant* iff it binds only variables in q_1 and q_2, and it maps to only variables in q_1 and q_2. We notate the most general, relevant unifier of q_1 and q_2 as $mgru(q_1,q_2)$.[5] It has been shown in [Apt, 1988] that any unifiable propositions have a most general, relevant unifier.

10.3.4.2 The Partitions of ALL Operations

Intuitively, a partition of K corresponds to a part of the knowledge base that is somehow semantically cohesive and distinct from the rest of the knowledge base. Facts and rules are often thought of as being "in" partitions and operations are thought of as "taking place" in subsets of $C \times R$ (unions of partitions). The intuition behind this comes from the frame view of ALL knowledge bases. Recall that ALL

---

[5] The use of most general, relevant unifiers (instead of just most general unifiers) is necessary for technical reasons. The basic problem with most general unifiers is that one can compose a most general unifier with an arbitrary renaming and the result is still a most general unifier.

constants can be thought of as frames, and relations as slots in these frames (e.g., the fact $r(c_1,c_2)$ is equivalent to having the value c_2 in the r slot of the frame c_1). Thus a pair $\langle r,c \rangle$ can be thought of as a particular slot in a particular frame in the knowledge base. Recall that we refer to such a pair as a *frame-slot*. Partitions are thus sets of frame-slots. Further, note that any primitive path α (by the definition of a path) must reference exactly one frame-slot and thus can be said to be "in" a partition. In fact, since partitions can overlap, it can be in several partitions and any operation on α is performed "in" the subset of $C \times R$ formed by taking the union of these partitions. Intuitively, this union defines the rules that are available to the operation.

More formally, if K is a knowledge base and $\alpha = r(c,t_1,\ldots,t_n)$ is a primitive path (i.e., c a constant and all t_i, $1 \le i \le n$, are terms) and p is a subset of $C \times R$ (e.g., a partition or the union of several partitions) then $\alpha \in p$ iff $\langle c,r \rangle \in p$. If $P = \{p_1,\ldots,p_n\}$[6] and $O = query(\alpha)$ or $O = assert(\alpha)$ then the union of partitions for O is:

$$par_K(O) = (\cup i : 1 \le i \le n \wedge \alpha \in p_i : p_i)$$

10.3.4.3 The Domain and Range of ALL Operations

Any given sets C, R, Nr, P define a finite set of possible knowledge bases KB (differing only in facts and if-added rules) and an infinite set of ground substitutions Θ (binding variables in the alphabet to constants in C).[7] For any operation O allowed in the knowledge bases in KB (note that an operation allowed in any knowledge base in KB is allowed in all knowledge bases in KB):

$$O : KB \rightarrow 2^{\Theta} \times KB. \qquad (1)$$

We notate these returned values with pairs: ⟨'Set of Substitutions', 'Knowledge Base'⟩ and use *sub* and *kb* as accessors on the first and second components respectively.

10.3.4.4 The Values of ALL Operations

Defining the values of ALL operations is primarily a matter of formalizing the action of forward- and backward-chaining rules. We use the following basic notation for knowledge bases and substitutions:

If K_1 and K_2 are knowledge bases (differing only in their facts and if-added rules), then:

---

[6] Recall that a knowledge base K is understood to have components $\langle C, R, Nr, Ar, F, P \rangle$. Thus P is the set of partitions of K.

[7] Technically, we should write $KB_{C,R,Nr,P}$ and $\Theta_{C,R,Nr,P}$, but we generally omit the subscripts since they are clear from context.

$$K_1 \cup K_2 = \langle C, R, Nr, Ar_1 \cup Ar_2, F_1 \cup F_2, P\rangle.$$

If further, f is a fact allowed in K_1 then:

$$K_1 + f = \langle C, R, Nr, Ar_1, F_1 \cup \{f\}, P\rangle,$$

and $f \in K_1$ iff $f \in F_1$. If θ and η are substitutions then $\theta \circ \eta$ notates θ followed by η. If further, Θ_1 is a set of substitutions then $\eta \circ \Theta_1 = \{\eta \circ \theta_1 \mid \theta_1 \in \Theta_1\}$.

For a primitive operation O, we define $O_n(K,p)$ to be the result of the operation O on the knowledge base K, in some subset of $C \times R$, p, with rule chaining cut off at depth n. A certain amount of technical care is required to formalize O_n (as it requires carefully defining forward and backward rule chaining). Details of the definition are given in the appendix to this chapter.

We define O to be the union over all n of O_n (in the partition of O). The idea here is to cause O to be a fixed point of rule applications. We will eventually show (in Section 10.4) that there is always an n after which increasing the depth of rule chaining does not affect the result. Thus, intuitively, O chains just far enough so that chaining any further would have no effect (one advantage of this approach is that recursive rules (e.g., rules of form $q \leftarrow q$) do not cause problems in ALL (or its LISP implementation)).

It will be important that the knowledge bases resulting from ALL operations are "closed." We guarantee this by applying the function *closure* to the knowledge base that is to be returned. Closed knowledge bases and *closure* are discussed in the next subsection (10.3.4.5).

We thus define:

$$O(K) = closure((\cup n : n > 0 : O_n(K, par_K(O))))$$

The result of a nonprimitive operation can then be defined in terms of the results of its constituent primitive operations. If O is nonprimitive then it must be a query (see Section 10.3.2.5). Assume $O = query(\alpha)$ for some path α. Further, assume $q = head(\alpha)$, and $\alpha' = rest(\alpha)$, then:

If $sub(query(q)(K)) = \{\ \}$ (i.e., $query(q)$ "failed"):

$$O(K) = \langle\{\ \}, K\rangle$$

else ($query(q)$ succeeded so we branch on all resultant substitutions and union the results):

$$\begin{aligned} O(K) = closure((\cup\theta \in sub(query(q)(K)) ::\\ \langle\theta \circ sub(query(\alpha'\,\theta)(K)),\\ kb(query(q)(K)) \cup kb(query(\alpha'\,\theta)(K))\rangle)) \end{aligned} \quad (2)$$

Figure 10.1 shows a query on a simple knowledge base.

Assume K is a knowledge base such that:

$$C = \{c\}$$
$$R = \{r_1, r_2\}$$
$$Nr = \{r_1(c,x) \leftarrow r_2(c,x)\}$$
$$Ar = \{\ \}$$
$$F = \{r_2(c,c)\}$$
$$P = \{\{\langle c,r_1\rangle, \langle c,r_2\rangle\}\}$$

Consider $query(r_1(c,x))(K)$ (where x is a variable). This is a primitive operation and $par_K(r_1(c,x)) = \{\langle c,r_1\rangle, \langle c,r_2\rangle\}$, so we must first compute:

$$query_0(r_1(c,x))(K, \{\langle c,r_1\rangle, \langle c,r_2\rangle\})$$

Rule back-chaining is cut off at depth zero so no rules apply, and

$$query_0(r_1(c,x))(K, \{\langle c,r_1\rangle, \langle c,r_2\rangle\}) = \langle\{\ \},K\rangle$$

(an empty list of substitutions is returned, since there is no known value of x for which the query succeeds). However, when we calculate

$$query_1(r_1(c,x))(K, \{\langle c,r_1\rangle, \langle c,r_2\rangle\}),$$

the if-needed rule applies and

$$query_1(r_1(c,x))(K, \{\langle c,r_1\rangle, \langle c,r_2\rangle\}) = \langle\{\{x/c\}\}, K + r_1(c,c)\rangle$$

($\{x/c\}$ binds x to c). As n is increased further there are no other rules to apply so

$$query(r_1(c,x))(K) = \langle\{\{x/c\}\}, K + r_1(c,c)\rangle.$$

Figure 10.1: A query on a simple knowledge base

10.3.4.5 The Problem of If-Added Incompleteness

In ALL, the application of an if-added rule is triggered by the assertion of a fact that matches the *Key* of the rule. One problem with this approach is that, if one is not careful, rules, whose antecedents are entailed by the knowledge base, may never fire. Such a case is shown in the Figure 10.2.

Our solution to this problem is to "close" the if-added rules in the knowledge base. Intuitively this means that for any fact f and any if-added rule $\alpha \rightarrow q$, if there is some substitution $\theta = mgru(f, head(\alpha))$, then we add to the knowledge base the rule $rest(\alpha)\theta \rightarrow q\theta$. For a knowledge base K, we notate by $closure(K)$, the knowledge base formed by closing all the if-added rules in K. We also use the shorthand $closure(\langle K,\Lambda\rangle)$ for $\langle closure(K),\Lambda\rangle$.

Assume K is a knowledge base such that:

$$C = \{c\}$$
$$R = \{r_1, r_2, r_3\}$$
$$Nr = \{\ \}$$
$$Ar = \{r_1(x,x), r_2(x,x) \rightarrow r_3(x,x)\}$$
$$F = \{r_1(c,c)\}$$
$$P = \{\{\langle c,r_1\rangle, \langle c,r_2\rangle, \langle c,r_3\rangle\}\}$$

Assume that we define $closure(K) = K$. Consider $assert(r_2(c,c))(K)$. After this operation both $r_1(c,c)$ and $r_2(c,c)$ will be facts in the knowledge base. However, $query(r_3(c,c))(K)$ will fail. The rule $r_1(x,x), r_2(x,x) \rightarrow r_3(x,x)$ never applies because $r_1(c,c)$ was added before $r_2(c,c)$.

Figure 10.2: An example of if-added incompleteness

Consider the example in Figure 10.2. Note that the initial knowledge base is not closed, since it includes the rule $r_1(x,x), r_2(x,x) \rightarrow r_3(x,x)$ and the fact $r_1(c,c)$, but not the rule $r_2(c,c) \rightarrow r_3(c,c)$. Further, if we consider $assert(r_2(c,c))(closure(K))$, then the resultant knowledge base does include $r_3(c,c)$.

10.3.4.6 Implementation Note

There are three important differences between the formal definitions of ALL operations given here and our LISP implementation. First, in the formalism, when an operation branches (e.g., when several rules are applied or when the evaluation of a path branches on several possible instantiations of its variables) the branches are computed separately ("in parallel") and the results are unioned together. In our implementation the branches are computed serially (i.e., one rule is applied and then the next rule is applied in the resultant knowledge base).[8] There are two advantages of the formalization presented here over a "serial" formalization. First, the complexity analysis is considerably simplified; and second, the formalism given here would also apply to a parallel implementation of ALL.

The second difference is that our implementation supports limits on the accessibility of rules, which have been omitted (for simplicity) from the current formal-

---

[8] Since ALL operations are monotonic, the serial implementation returns knowledge bases that are supersets of those given by the formalism. Hence, our completeness results carry over to the serial case.

ization. In our implementation, a rule can be "associated" with a frame f_0, and only accessed from frames known to be in an *isa* relation with f_0. Intuitively, such rules apply only to members of the set f_0.[9]

Our implementation of *closure* demonstrates a useful application of rules associated with sets. One might worry that closing a knowledge base might add a large number of if-added rules and thus slow the system (since we have to try to unify against all of them). However, we associate these if-added rules with very small sets (sets of size one), and they are thus ignored except when they are needed. Consider a rule added in the closing of a knowledge base. It must be of form $rest(\alpha)\theta \rightarrow q\theta$. It follows from the definition of if-added rules that $rest(\alpha)\theta$ must be a path. This implies that $head(rest(\alpha))$ must be of form $r(c,t_1,\ldots,t_n)$. Thus (in our implementation) we simply associate this rule with a set consisting of the single element (frame) c (creating such a set if it does not exist).

The third difference is also related to our implementation of *closure*. Consider an assertion of a fact f. This assertion may trigger an if-added rule that asserts a fact f' into a partition p' which is disjoint from the partitions of f. In our implementation, f' is queued (in p') and any if-added rules for f' are not applied until "attention" is drawn to p' (by some operation in p'). This ensures that the complexity of an operation is a function only of the rules in its partitions. We have not yet incorporated the notion of "queueing" assertions into our formalism. Thus facts are closed with respect to all if-added rules in the knowledge base, and the complexity of an operation (as will be seen in Section 10.4) is a function of the set of all if-added rules in the knowledge base.

10.3.5 Soundness

Soundness is often intuitively thought of as "You can't derive a contradiction." Soundness requires that the substitutions returned by a query must be semantic consequences of the old knowledge base.[10] The requirements on the new knowledge base are more subtle. Soundness intuitively requires that propositions do not suddenly become true, or, in model theoretic terms, that models are not suddenly lost. Thus any model of the new knowledge base must also be a model of the old knowledge base (and in an assertion a model of the formula being asserted):

---

[9] Such access limitations can be formalized. The key idea is that when a rule associated with a set is translated to predicate calculus (see Section 10.3.3) one must prepend an appropriate *isa* relation to its antecedent. It should be possible to show that the completeness results carry over (some care must be taken, however, when defining the *closure* of a knowledge base with respect to an *isa* relation).

[10] More precisely, for any query of a path α, if θ is returned then $\mathcal{PC}(\alpha\theta)$ must be a consequence of the knowledge base.

Theorem 1 [Soundness of ALL] For any knowledge base K, any path α allowed in K, and any fact f allowed in K:

1. $(\forall \theta \in \Theta : \theta \in sub(query(\alpha)(K)) : \mathcal{PC}(K) \models \mathcal{PC}(\alpha\theta))$
2. $\mathcal{PC}(K) \models \mathcal{PC}(kb(query(\alpha)(K)))$
3. $(\mathcal{PC}(K) \wedge \mathcal{PC}(f)) \models \mathcal{PC}(kb(assert(f)(K)))$

Proof (sketch): The proof of soundness is primarily a matter of carefully working through the definition of O. One inducts on n to show, for all n, that O_n is sound. One can then induct on the length of α to show that O is sound.

10.3.6 Completeness

Completeness can be thought of as "Any true fact is derivable." Thus completeness requires that all substitutions that are semantic consequences of the old knowledge base are returned by query. Completeness also requires that true facts do not suddenly become false. In model theoretic terms this means that we do not gain models. Thus any model of the old knowledge base must also be a model of the new knowledge base. Note that the requirements for completeness are essentially the requirements for consistency with their implications reversed:

Conjecture 1 [Completeness of ALL] For any knowledge base K, any path α allowed in K, and any fact f allowed in K, let Θ_α be the set of all ground substitutions binding all and only variables in α. Then:

1. $(\forall \theta \in \Theta_\alpha : \mathcal{PC}(K) \models \mathcal{PC}(\alpha\theta) : \theta \in sub(query(\alpha)(K)))$
2. $\mathcal{PC}(kb(query(\alpha)(K)) \models \mathcal{PC}(K)$
3. $\mathcal{PC}(kb(assert(f)(K))) \models (\mathcal{PC}(K) \wedge \mathcal{PC}(f))$

Unfortunately, part one of this conjecture is false. In some cases, rules necessary for a query to succeed cannot be accessed. Two such cases are shown in Figures 10.3 and 10.4.

Notice, however, that in the example in Figure 10.3:

$$query(r_3(c,x))(kb(query(r_1(c,x))(K)))$$

would succeed since $r_3(c,c)$ is added to $kb(query(r_1(c,x))(K))$ by the if-added rule $r_1(c,x) \rightarrow r_3(c,x)$. Similarly, in Figure 10.4,

$$query(r_1(c,x))(kb(query(r_2(c,x))(K)))$$

succeeds. This suggests the idea behind *Socratic completeness*. Informally, the Socratic completeness theorem says that for any query of α "should" succeed in a knowledge base, there exists a series of preliminary queries, Γ, after which a query of α will succeed. We also show a second type of weakened completeness result,

Assume $K = \langle C, R, Nr, Ar, F, P \rangle$ is a knowledge base such that:

$$C = \{c\}$$
$$R = \{r_1, r_2, r_3\}$$
$$Nr = \{r_1(c,x) \leftarrow r_2(c,x)\}$$
$$Ar = \{r_1(c,x) \rightarrow r_3(c,x)\}$$
$$F = \{r_2(c,c)\}$$
$$P = \{\{\langle c,r_1\rangle, \langle c,r_2\rangle, \langle c,r_3 \rangle\}\}$$

Consider *query*($r_3(c,x)$)(K). This query must fail since it matches no facts in F and there are no *if-needed* rules for $r_3(c,x)$. But, any model of $\mathcal{PC}(K)$ must be a model of $\mathcal{PC}(r_3(c,c))$ (by the two rules and the fact that $r_2(c,c)$ is in F). Hence, inference in ALL is not complete.

Figure 10.3: A form of incompleteness in ALL

Assume $K = \langle C, R, Nr, Ar, F, P \rangle$ is a knowledge base such that:

$$C = \{c\}$$
$$R = \{r_1, r_2, r_3\}$$
$$Nr = \{r_1(c,x) \leftarrow r_2(c,x), r_2(c,x) \leftarrow r_3(c,x)\}$$
$$Ar = \{\ \}$$
$$F = \{r_3(c,c)\}$$
$$P = \{\{\langle c,r_1\rangle\}, \{\langle c,r_2\rangle,\langle c,r_3\rangle\}\}$$

Consider *query*($r_1(c,x)$)(K). This query must fail since the only rule for $r_1(c,x)$ depends on $r_2(c,x)$, which matches no facts in F and is not in $par_K(r_1(c,x))$ (so no rules for $r_2(c,x)$ fire). But, any model of $\mathcal{PC}(K)$ must be a model of $\mathcal{PC}(r_1(c,c))$ (by the two rules and the fact that $r_3(c,c)$ is in F).

Figure 10.4: Another form of incompleteness in ALL

partitional completeness. Partitional completeness says that if all information needed to process a query can be located by the if-needed rules in the partitions of the query, then the query will succeed.

10.3.6.1 Socratic Completeness

To state the Socratic completeness theorem we need a shorthand for the result of a series of queries:

If Γ is a series of paths allowed in a knowledge base K then let:

$$query(nil)(K) = K \tag{3}$$
$$query(\Gamma)(K) = query(head(\Gamma))(kb(query(rest(\Gamma)((K))) \tag{4}$$

Theorem 2 [Socratic Completeness] For any knowledge base K, any path α allowed in K, and any fact f allowed in K, let Θ_α be the set of all ground substitutions binding all and only variables in α. Then:

1. $(\forall\theta \in \Theta_\alpha : \mathcal{PC}(K) \models \mathcal{PC}(\alpha\theta)$
   $: (\exists\Gamma : \Gamma$ *a series of paths allowed in* $\mathrm{K} : \theta \in sub(query(\alpha)$
   $(kb(query(\Gamma)(K))))))$
2. $\mathcal{PC}(kb(query(\alpha)(K))) \models \mathcal{PC}(K)$
3. $\mathcal{PC}(kb(assert(f)(K))) \models (\mathcal{PC}(K) \wedge \mathcal{PC}(f))$

Proof (sketch): Parts 2 and 3 follow relatively easily from the definitions of $\mathcal{O}$, and $\mathcal{PC}$. Part 1 is shown by induction on the length of α. The tricky part is the base case. We map K to an equivalent logic program $\mathcal{LP}(K)$. One can then show that for any rule in K which would apply on the next iteration of $T_{\mathcal{LP}(K)}$ (where T is the immediate consequence operator in logic programming—see [Crawford and Kuipers, 1990] or [Apt, 1988]) there exists a path in ALL the query of which will cause the rule to fire (this result would not hold for if-added rules if we did not close our knowledge bases—see Section 10.3.4.5). We know from the study of logic programming (see [Apt, 1988]) that "completeness" with respect to the immediate consequence operator is sufficient to guarantee completeness.

10.3.6.2 Partitional Completeness

Intuitively, partitional completeness says that if all information needed to prove a query is located "close enough" to the query then the query will succeed. Formally "close enough" will mean that the information is reachable using only if-needed rules in the partitions of the query. In order to state the partitional completeness theorem, we first have to define which rules in the knowledge base are considered "part" of which partitions. A rule is considered a part of a partition if it could be triggered by queries to, and assertions into, the frame-slots in that partition. Counterintuitively, partitions limit access to *rules* not facts. When we speak of a fact as being in a partition, we mean that the fact is queried (or asserted) using the rules in that partition. Theoretically a rule could access facts in every partition of the knowledge base; it is the use of access paths, not partitions, that limits access to facts.

If K is a knowledge base, $p \subset C \times R$, and S is a set of rules from K, then $S\backslash_p$, the restriction of S to p, is given by:

$$S\backslash_p = \{\rho\theta \mid \rho \in S \wedge Key(\rho) = r(t_1,\ldots,t_n) \wedge ((t_1 \text{ a constant} \wedge \theta = \varnothing \wedge \langle t_1,r\rangle \in p) \vee (t_1 \text{ a variable} \wedge (\exists c \in C : \langle c,r\rangle \in p : \theta = \{t_1/c\})))\}.$$

Intuitively, $S\backslash_p$ is the restriction of S to only the rules in p. The knowledge base K with its rules restricted to only the if-needed rules in $p \subset C \times R$ is given by:

$$K\backslash_p = \langle C, R, Nr\backslash_p, \varnothing, F, \{p\}\rangle. \quad (5)$$

Note that $K\backslash_p$ is never computed (in the definition of ALL formula or in our LISP implementation of ALL); it is only a formal object used to state the partitional completeness theorem.

Theorem 3 [Partitional Completeness] For any knowledge base K and any primitive path q allowed in K, let Θ_q be the set of all ground substitutions binding all and only variables in q, then:

$$(\forall\theta \in \Theta_q : \mathcal{PC}(K\backslash_{par_k(q)}) \models \mathcal{PC}(q\theta) : \theta \in sub(query(q)(K)))$$

Proof (sketch): The proof of this theorem again relies on results from the study of logic programming. Let $ground(q)$ be the set of all variable free instantiations of q. Further, for any logic program pg, and any set of facts I, let:

$$T_{pg} \uparrow 0(I) = I$$
$$T_{pg} \uparrow (n+1)(I) = T_{pg}(T_{pg} \uparrow n(I))$$

The key lemma is that for any $p \subset C \times R$, and for all $n > 0$:

$$ground(q) \cap T_{\mathcal{LP}(K\backslash p)} \uparrow n(\varnothing) \subset kb(query_n(q)(K,p))$$

Intuitively, this says that if a fact is an instantiation of q, and is in the knowledge base produced by n iterations of the immediate consequence operator, then it is in the knowledge base produced by $query_n(q)$. From this lemma the result again follows by the observation (from the study of logic programming, see [Apt, 1988]) that "completeness" with respect to the immediate consequence operator is sufficient to guarantee completeness.

10.4 COMPLEXITY

In this section we show that a primitive ALL operation can be computed in time polynomial in the size of the portion of the knowledge base accessible to it. We focus on primitive operations since nonprimitive operations are defined as sequences of primitive operations (equation (2)).

To discuss the complexity of ALL it is useful to return to the view of an ALL knowledge base as a collection of frames and slots. This view was introduced in Section 10.1 and discussed further in Section 10.3.4.2. The basic idea is that constants are thought of as *frames*, and relations are thought of as *slots*. The fact $r(c_1,c_2)$ is equivalent to putting c_2 in the r slot of the frame c_1. Recall that if c is a frame and r is a slot, then we refer to the pair $\langle c,r \rangle$ as a *frame-slot*. Recall also that partitions are simply collections of frame-slots.

The definition of the accessible portion of a knowledge base is fairly technical and is given in [Crawford and Kuipers, 1990]. In this section we simply give the intuitions behind the definition.

For a knowledge base K, and $p \subset C \times R$ we first define $rules(p) = Ar \cup Nr\backslash_p$. Now, consider a primitive operation O allowed in a knowledge base K, and assume $O = query(q)$ or $O = assert(q)$. We define the $reach_n(q,p)$ to include all frame-slots that can be accessed in the calculation of O_n in p, with rule back-chaining cut off at depth n, and $change_n(q,p)$ to include all frame-slots that can be changed in the calculation of O_n in p (with rule back-chaining cut off at depth n). We define $frames_n(q,p)$ to include all *frames* that O_n can access (with rule back-chaining cut off at depth n). $frames_n(q,p)$ includes the frames appearing in frame-slots in $reach_n(q,p)$, plus the frames appearing explicitly in rules in $rules(p)$ or in q itself. Finally, we define $closure_{f\&r}(O)$ to include all facts and rules that could potentially be added to the knowledge base by O.

We define $ops_n(O)$ to include all operations that O_n "potentially depends on." These include all queries of frame-slots in $reach_n(q,par_K(O))$ and all assertions (of frames in $frames_n(q,par_K(O))$) into frame-slots in $change_n(q,par_K(O))$ (some amount of care is required to prove that *ops* includes all the assertions and queries which O_n depends on—for details (and a formal definition of "the set of all operations which O depends on") see [Crawford and Kuipers, 1990]).

We then define:

$$reach(q,p) = (\bigcup n : n > 0 : reach_n(q,p)) \tag{6}$$

$$change(q,p) = (\bigcup n : n > 0 : change_n(q,p)) \tag{7}$$

$$frames(q,p) = (\bigcup n : n > 0 : frames_n(q,p)) \tag{8}$$

$$ops(O) = (\bigcup n : n > 0 : ops_n(O)). \tag{9}$$

Figures 10.5 and 10.6 show *reach*, *change*, and *ops* for two simple queries.

Theorem 4 If $O = query(q)$ or $O = assert(q)$ is a primitive operation allowed in a closed knowledge base K then let:

Recall the knowledge base, K, from Figure 10.1:

$$C = \{c\}$$
$$R = \{r_1, r_2\}$$
$$Nr = \{r_1(c,x) \leftarrow r_2(c,x)\}$$
$$Ar = \{\ \}$$
$$F = \{r_2(c,c)\}$$
$$P = \{\{\langle c,r_1\rangle, \langle c,r_2\rangle\}\}$$

Consider $O = query(r_1(c,x))$ (where x is a variable). Let $q = r_1(c,x)$ and $p = par_K(O)$, then:

$$reach_0(q,p) = \{\langle c,r_1\rangle\}$$
$$reach_1(q,p) = \{\langle c,r_1\rangle, \langle c,r_2\rangle\}$$
$$reach_2(q,p) = \{\langle c,r_1\rangle, \langle c,r_2\rangle\}$$
$$reach_n(q,p) = \{\langle c,r_1\rangle, \langle c,r_2\rangle\}$$
$$reach(q,p) = \{\langle c,r_1\rangle, \langle c,r_2\rangle\}$$

Thus:

$$change(q,p) = \{\langle c,r_1\rangle\}$$
$$ops\ (O) = \{query(r_1(c,x)), query(r_2(c,x)), query(r_1(c,c)), query(r_2(c,c)), assert(r_1(c,c))\}$$

Figure 10.5: The accessible frame-slots and dependent operations for a simple query

$$nops(O) = |\ ops(O)\ | \tag{10}$$
$$nfr(O) = |\ frames(q,par_K(O))\ | \tag{11}$$
$$nrules(O) = |\ rules(par_K(O))\ | \tag{12}$$

Finally, let ma be the maximum arity of any relation in R, $mvars(O)$ be the maximum number of variables in any rule in $rules(par_k(O))$, and len be the maximum length of the antecedent of any rule in $rules(par_K(O))$. $O(K)$ can be computed in time of order:

$$len^5 \times nops(O)^2 \times nrules(O)^5 \times nfr(O)^{5\ mvars(O)\ +\ ma}.$$

Proof (sketch): O is defined as an infinite union of O_n's thus it is not obvious how it can be computed. However, one can show that if there is an n at which all the operations that O "depends on" (i.e., all operations in $ops(O)$) return the same value they returned at $n - 1$, then $O(K) = O_n(K, par_K(O))$.

One can further show that such an n exists and can compute a bound for it. Consider the vector of all operations in $ops(O)$. There are:

$$nops(O)$$

Recall the knowledge base, K, from Figure 10.4:

$$C = \{c\}$$
$$R = \{r_1,r_2,r_3\}$$
$$Nr = \{r_1(c,x) \leftarrow r_2(c,x), r_2(c,x) \leftarrow r_3(c,x)\}$$
$$Ar = \{\ \}$$
$$F = \{r_3(c,c)\}$$
$$P = \{\{\langle c,r_1\rangle\}, \langle c,r_2\rangle,\langle c,r_3\rangle\}\}$$

Consider $O = query(r_1(c,x))$ (where x is a variable). Let $q = r_1(c,x)$ and $p = par_K(O)$, then:

$$reach_0(q,p) = \{\langle c,r_1\rangle\}$$
$$reach_1(q,p) = \{\langle c,r_1\rangle, \langle c,r_2\rangle\}$$
$$reach_2(q,p) = \{\langle c,r_1\rangle, \langle c,r_2\rangle\}$$
$$reach_n(q,p) = \{\langle c,r_1\rangle, \langle c,r_2\rangle\}$$
$$reach(q,p) = \{\langle c,r_1\rangle, \langle c,r_2\rangle\}$$

Thus:

$$change(q,p) = \{\langle c,r_1\rangle\}$$
$$ops(O) = \{query(r_1(c,x)), query(r_2(c,x)), query(r_1(c,c)), query(r_2(c,c)), assert(r_1(c,c))\}$$

Figure 10.6: The accessible frame-slots and dependent operations for a query in a knowledge base with two partitions

such operations. As we increase n the knowledge bases returned by these operations may not shrink. Further, if we ever reach a point where none of them grow, then we can quit. Any ALL operation can only add a fact or complete an if-added rule (there are no operations, for example, that create an entirely new frame). The facts and rules that can be added must be in the set $closure_{f\&r}(O)$, and one can show that the size of this set is bounded by

$$len \times nrules(O) \times nfr(O)^{mvars(O)}.$$

Each iteration may increase at worst one knowledge base in the set of knowledge bases returned by the operations in $ops(O)$. Thus if n is greater than or equal to

$$nops(O) \times len \times nrules(O) \times nfr(O)^{mvars(O)}$$

then all knowledge bases must be "full."

Thus it only remains to find the time to calculate the result of a primitive operation O_n given the results of all operations O'_{n-1}. We may have to apply at most

$$nrules(O)$$

rules. Each rule may branch on all values in $frames(q,par_K(O))$ for all variables. Thus we may have

$$nfr(O)^{mvars(O)}$$

branches (the results of which must be unioned together). Finding the result of each branch involves taking at most *len* unions and closures. There are thus order:

$$len$$

unions and closures per branch. Each union is done on a knowledge base of form $K + S$ where S is of size $|\, closure_{f\&r}(O)\, |$ or smaller. Thus each union can be done in time of order:

$$len \times nrules(O) \times nfr(O)^{mvars(O)}$$

Finally, one can show that each closure can be computed in time:

$$len^2 \times nrules(O)^2 \times nfr(O)^{2mvars(O) + ma}$$

Multiplying these bounds together gives the time bound in the theorem.

10.5 RELATED WORK

ALL draws from several diverse fields. We attempt only to sketch in general terms the fields from which it draws and discuss a few particularly relevant past approaches.

ALL draws from semantic networks [Brachman et al., 1983; Bobrow and Winograd, 1977; Findler, 1979; Quillian, 1967; Shapiro, 1989; Vilain, 1985] the intuition that retrieval and reasoning can be guided and limited by the structure of the network. This has long been a key intuition behind semantic networks: "...the knowledge required to perform an intellectual task generally lies in the semantic vicinity of the concepts involved in the task." [Schubert et al., 1979]. In particular, ALL draws from semantic networks its frame-based data structures [Minsky, 1975] and the idea of access paths. Our use of access paths is closely related to previous work on path-based inference. Path-based inference can be traced back (at least) to [Raphael, 1968] and later to [Schwarcz et al., 1970] and [Shapiro and Woodmansee, 1969]. A good discussion of path-based and node-based inference (both of which are partially subsumed by inference in ALL and would be totally subsumed if ALL supported full quantification—see Section 10.6.4) is given in [Shapiro, 1978].

One difference between ALL and much recent, careful work on knowledge representation is that ALL (along with first-order logic and the original work on semantic networks) allows the knowledge base designer to name the relations used in the knowledge base. After Woods's influential "What's in a Link" paper [Woods, 1975], many knowledge representation languages restricted the allowable relations to a small set, which were given a precise syntax and semantics [Brachman, 1979; Shapiro, 1989]. Our approach in ALL is to define our semantics by "borrowing" the model theory of predicate calculus (by mapping ALL knowledge bases to statements in predicate calculus and proving consistency and weakened completeness results) and to allow relations to be given any names. The *meanings* of the relations are thus restricted only by the contents of the knowledge base (as in predicate calculus).

ALL also differs from past formal work on semantic networks in that it uses a single, general-purpose retrieval/reasoning mechanism that is guided by the structure of the network. Past work has generally used the structure of the network only for special-purpose reasoning (spreading activation, classification, etc.), and has relied on a first-order logic theorem prover [Brachman et al., 1983; Schubert et al., 1983] or a weaker deduction system [Levesque, 1984; Patel-Schneider, 1985; Vilain, 1985] for general reasoning.

A notable exception to this generalization is the recent work of de Haan and Schubert [Schubert et al., 1979; de Haan and Schubert, 1986]. ALL and the networks of Schubert share several features including the use of access limitations to guide reasoning. The most obvious way to use the structure of a semantic network to limit access would be to perform deduction with facts not more than a few (say, two) nodes away in the network. The problem with this strategy is that some nodes (e.g., the node for your spouse) may have a large number of links, many of which are irrelevant to the problem at hand. The solution used in ECOSYSTEM is to maintain a taxonomy of knowledge and use this taxonomy to guide reasoning [de Haan and Schubert, 1986]. The difference in ALL is that access is limited to known *access paths*, which access facts many nodes away in the network, but do so in a controlled fashion. Thus in ALL it is the structure of the knowledge itself (or more specifically the structure of the access paths in the rules) that controls access and reasoning.

Another relevant line of research is the work on *vivid* knowledge bases [Etherington et al., 1989]. A vivid knowledge base "... trades accuracy for speed ..." [Etherington et al., 1989] by constructing a complete database of ground facts, from statements in a more expressive language. This approach has some of the same goals as ALL—particularly in the area of efficiency—but takes a much different approach and makes different trade-offs. At a very high level, the principal differences are:

- ALL represents all the knowledge that has been asserted (though not all of it may be accessible at a given time), while a vivid knowledge base is an approximation of the asserted knowledge (thus weakened completeness results such as Socratic completeness do not hold for vivid reasoning).
- To obtain increased efficiency, ALL trades completeness for speed, while a vivid approach trades both consistency and completeness for speed.

The design of the inference mechanism in ALL has been heavily influenced by logic programming. In fact any function-free logic program (without negation) can be written in ALL. Further, the notation and results from the proof of the completeness of logic programming [Apt, 1988; Lloyd, 1984] have been used extensively in the completeness proofs for ALL. In a sense, our use of access paths is a strategy for ordering conjunctive queries and as such is related to the more elaborate approach given in [Smith and Genesereth, 1985]. In fact, if one follows a discipline of avoiding frame-slots containing a large number of frames[11] then the use of access paths enforces an ordering on conjunctive queries much like that discussed in [Smith and Genesereth, 1985].

10.6 CONCLUSION

Given a knowledge representation system with a model theory and a knowledge base, one may divide the set of all possible queries in several ways. For example, one can distinguish the queries that succeed from those that fail. If this set is exactly equal to the set of all queries that are model-theoretic consequences of the knowledge base, then the knowledge representation system is consistent and complete. In ALL we divide the set of all queries into three subsets:

- those that succeed immediately.
- those that will succeed after some appropriate series of preliminary queries.
- those that will never succeed (without additional assertions).

Socratic completeness gives a precise characterization of the second and third sets—the second set is equal to the set of all queries that are model-theoretic consequences of the knowledge base, and the third set is equal to the set of all queries that are not model-theoretic consequences. Partitional completeness gives a partial characterization of the first set—a query will succeed immediately if all the information needed to prove it is located "close enough" to the query in the knowledge base.

10.6.1 About Socratic Completeness

One of the questions asked about our work[12] was "What good is Socratic completeness when Socrates is dead?" Meaning that the hard part of reasoning has simply been pushed off to the problem of posing the right questions. The first

---

[11] For example, if the set *things* is very large, then one would like to avoid filling the slot *members* with all the members of *things*—rather, the preferred representation in ALL for "*f* is a *thing*" would be to put *things* in the *isa* slot of *f*.

[12] By Rich Thomason at the 1989 Workshop on Formal Aspects of Semantic Networks.

answer to this question is that in a system with the expressive power of first-order logic, the incomputability never goes away: Our approach decomposes the problem of reasoning into two parts: the (tractable) problem of computing the results of queries and the (intractable) problem of deciding what queries to ask. Past work has made other divisions—e.g., the T-box and A-box of [Brachman et al., 1983]. The second answer is that our goal is to develop a knowledge representation system with *understandable* inferential power. To this end, Socratic completeness is a necessary (but not yet sufficient) property. Socratic completeness guarantees that there is some hope of eventually finding the right questions (by guaranteeing that the questions exist).

These answers suggest two directions for future work: first, encoding (in the knowledge base) commonsense knowledge about what general types of queries are useful for solving common types of complex reasoning problems; and second, identifying other weakened completeness properties, which, like partitional completeness, indicate which queries will immediately succeed.

Socratic completeness is also a step toward a formal specification of what inferential power a knowledge representation system should provide. Due to its intractability, full logical completeness is too strong a specification but provides an upper bound in the search for an appropriate specification. Socratic completeness is a fairly weak specification but is arguably a necessary property. Thus it provides a lower bound on the space of appropriate specifications.

10.6.2 About Partitional Completeness

Partitioning the knowledge base is not a new idea. Minsky's original proposal [Minsky, 1975] for frames envisioned a structure on the knowledge base consisting of groups of related frames. Hayes's "Naive Physics Manifesto" [Hayes, 1985] also viewed commonsense knowledge as consisting of clusters of closely related concepts, loosely related to each other. Closer to the implementation level, blackboard architectures [Hayes-Roth, 1985] also group inference methods into weakly interacting partitions. While these intuitions about the modularity of knowledge are persuasive, it must be admitted that it has not yet been empirically demonstrated that the contents of large-scale commonsense knowledge bases divide naturally into partitions.

If we accept the intuition that knowledge can be meaningfully divided into partitions (or perhaps before we commit to accepting this intuition), we would like to know what effect partitions have on reasoning. Intuitively, one would expect that the rules in the partition of a query would somehow be more easily accessible to the query. The partitional completeness theorem gives a partial formalization of this intuition, by saying that if a query is a logical consequence of the if-needed rules in its partitions, then the query will succeed immediately. The theorem also gives us an empirical way to test a partitioning of a large knowledge base—if simple queries depend on many rules in other partitions (and thus require many preliminary queries before they succeed) then the partitions are not well chosen.

10.6.3 About the Complexity Results

The expression given in theorem 4 for the complexity of inference in ALL involves too many variables to be easily comprehended. In a "typical" knowledge base one might expect that:

$$nrules(O) \approx nfr(O) \quad (13)$$
$$nops(O) \approx nfr(O)^{ma} \quad (14)$$

Let $n = nfr(O)$. If we further assume that *len* is small, then ALL operations can be computed in time of order:

$$n^{3ma + 5 + 5mvars(O)}$$

Certainly a tighter bound could be computed (with somewhat more work). In general we have found that our examples run much faster than the worst-case bound. However, the complexity analysis is still a useful exercise. Our implementation of ALL originally used an algorithm that was exponential in the worst case. Replacing it with an algorithm similar to the one given here greatly improved its runtime. Further, the complexity result gives some guidance in the design of knowledge bases. For example, it suggests that while the length of rules makes little difference, rules with many variables should be avoided.

10.6.4 Implementing ALL

Our LISP implementation of ALL is considerably more powerful than the formalism presented in this paper and can express definite descriptions, full negation, some types of defaults, and quantification. Beyond simple examples of forward- and backward-chaining we have investigated some standard examples of default inheritance (essentially implementing the inferential distance rule of Touretzky [1986]), the Yale shooting problem [Hanks and McDermott, 1986], several examples that involve reasoning about sets of similar objects, and some examples of reasoning from quantified information (e.g., from "Every man loves a woman" conclude that there must be some woman that *George* loves). We have also solved the bank problem mentioned in the introduction. Our most recent work involves the use of ALL to express the ideas of Qualitative Process Theory [Forbus, 1984]. The result [Crawford et al., 1990] is a system that compiles qualitative descriptions of physical situations into qualitative differential equations that can be simulated by QSIM [Kuipers, 1986].[13]

---

[13] This is joint work with Adam Farquhar.

Ultimately we are working toward a formal theory that has the expressive power of predicate calculus, and is consistent and Socratically complete, but is still computationally tractable. It is straightforward to add to ALL the ability to express full classic negation (i.e., not negation by failure), but then inference in ALL (using rules alone) is no longer Socratically complete. We are currently working to formalize in ALL the notion of reasoning by *reductio ad absurdum* (used in our implementation). Reasoning by *reductio ad absurdum* involves adding assumptions to the knowledge base and then reasoning about their consequences (and if the consequences of an assumption include "false" concluding the negation of the assumption). We believe that such a mechanism will allow Socratically complete reasoning in the presence of classic negation. Further, the queries determine what assumptions are made, so the complexity of ALL should still be polynomial (though some hard problems may require an exponential number of preliminary queries).

There is also no way to express existential quantification in our current formalism. We have incorporated definite descriptions, which define a type of existential quantification, into the implementation of ALL, but their formalization is not straightforward (as they do not seem to translate naturally into predicate calculus). Our most recent work has been on adding to the implementation the ability to represent, and do some kinds of reasoning with, arbitrarily nested quantified expressions. Our approach to nested quantification is based on the idea of arbitrary objects [Fine, 1985]. One may, for example, reason about a large class of objects by reasoning about an "arbitrary object" having the properties common to all objects in the group. Future papers will discuss this work in more detail.

ACKNOWLEDGMENTS

The authors would like to thank Len Schubert, Rich Thomason, and Charles Petrie for careful readings and useful comments on various versions and drafts of this paper.

This work has taken place in the Qualitative Reasoning Group at the Artificial Intelligence Laboratory, The University of Texas at Austin. Research of the Qualitative Reasoning Group is supported, in part, by NSF grants IRI-8602665, IRI-8905494, and IRI-8904454, by NASA grants NAG 2-507 and NAG 9-200, and by the Texas Advanced Research Program under grant No. 003658-175. J.M. Crawford is supported in part by a fellowship from GTE.

APPENDIX—FORMAL DEFINITION OF O_n

In this appendix we give the formal definition of O_n. This amounts to defining with great care the familiar behavior of forward- and backward-chaining rules in a knowledge base. This is a nontrivial exercise, but it is necessary in order to carefully prove the theorems. Further, a careful formulation of forward- and backward-chaining reveals at least one interesting and unexpected problem—the problem of if-added incompleteness discussed in Section 10.3.4.5.

For any n, and any operation O allowed in the knowledge bases of KB:

$$O_n : KB \times 2^{C \times R} \Rightarrow 2^{\Theta} \times KB. \tag{15}$$

We define O_n in the following three cases. In all cases assume K is a knowledge base, α a (nonempty) path allowed in K, q a primitive path allowed in K, f a fact allowed in K, and p a subset of $C \times R$. We use the shorthand:

$$lookup(q)(K) = \{\theta \in \Theta \mid (\exists f \in K :: \theta = mgru(q,f))\}. \tag{16}$$

Case 1: Base case: O is a primitive operation, and $O \notin p$ or $n = 0$.

If $O = query(q)$ then

$$O_n(K,p) = \langle lookup(q)(K), K\rangle \tag{17}$$

else $O = assert(f)$ and

$$O_n(K,p) = \langle\{\{\ \}\},closure(K + f)\rangle. \tag{18}$$

Case 2: O is a primitive operation, $n > 0$, and $O \in p$.

First we find the rules that apply. Let η be a renaming that maps variables in rules in Nr to variables not used in O or K. (This must be possible since the alphabet contains a countably infinite number of variables.)

If $O = query(q)$ then:

$$R = \{\rho\eta\theta \mid \rho \in Nr \wedge \theta = mgru(Key(\rho)\eta,q)\} \tag{19}$$

Else, $O = assert(f)$ and:

$$R = \{\rho\theta \mid \rho \in Ar \wedge \theta = mgru(Key(\rho), f\ )\} \tag{20}$$

If $R = \varnothing$ then let:

$$K' = kb(O_{n-1}(K,p)) \tag{21}$$

Otherwise, we apply the rules and union the results. Applying a rule consists of querying its antecedent and then asserting its consequent. The consequent is asserted with all substitutions under which the antecedent succeeds.

If $O = query(q)$ then:

$$\begin{aligned} K' = closure(\cup\rho \in R ::\ & kb(query_{n-1}(Ant(\rho))(K,p)) \cup \\ & (\cup\theta \in sub(query_{n-1}(Ant(\rho))(K,p)) :: \\ & kb(assert_{n-1}(Conseq(\rho\theta))(K,p)))) \end{aligned} \tag{22}$$

$$O_n(K,p) = \langle lookup\ (q)(K'), K'\rangle \tag{23}$$

Else, $O = assert(f)$ and:

$$K' = closure(\cup\rho \in R :: kb(query_{n-1}(Ant(\rho))(K+f,p)) \cup (\cup\theta \in sub(query_{n-1}(Ant(\rho))(K+f,p)) :: kb(assert_{n-1}(Conseq(\rho\theta))(K+f,p)))) \quad (24)$$

$$O_n(K,p) = \langle\{\{\ \}\}, K'\rangle \quad (25)$$

Case 3: Nonprimitive queries. O = query(α) where α a path of length greater than 1. Assume $head(\alpha) = q$, and $rest(\alpha) = \alpha'$. If $sub(query_n(q)(K,p)) = \{\ \}$ (i.e., $query_n(q)$ "failed"):

$$O_n(K,p) = \langle\{\ \}, K\rangle \quad (26)$$

else ($query_n(q)$ succeeded so we branch on all resultant substitutions and union the results):

$$O_n(K,p) = closure((\cup\theta \in sub(query_n(q)(K,p)) :: \langle\theta \circ sub(query_n(\alpha'\theta)(K,p)), kb(query_n(q)(K,p)) \cup kb(query_n(\alpha'\theta)(K,p))\rangle)) \quad (27)$$

References

Allen, J.F., Giuliano, M., and Frisch A.M. 1984. *The HORNE Reasoning System.* Technical Report 126, Computer Science Department, University of Rochester, Rochester NY.

Apt, Krzysztof, R. 1988. *Introduction to Logic Programming* (revised and extended version). Technical Report TR-87-35, Department of Computer Science, University of Texas at Austin, Austin Texas. To appear in *Handbook of Theoretical Computer Science*, (J. van Leeuwen, Managing Editor), North-Holland.

Bobrow, D.G. and Winograd, T. 1977. An overview of KRL, a knowledge representation language. Cogntive Science 1(1):3–46. (Reprinted in [Brachman and Levesque, 1985, pp. 263–285].)

Boolos, G.S., and Jeffrey, R.C. 1980. *Computability and Logic.* Cambridge University Press, New York.

Brachman, R.J. 1977. What's in a concept: structural foundations for semantic networks. *International Journal of Man–Machine Studies* 9:127–152.

———. 1979. On the epistemological status of semantic networks. In *Associative Networks: Representation and Use of Knowledge by Computer*, N.V. Findler (ed.). Academic Press, New York. (Reprinted in [Brachman and Levesque, 1985, pp. 191–215].)

Brachman, R.J. and Levesque, H.J. *Readings in Knowledge Representation*, Morgan Kaufmann Publishers, San Mateo, California, 1985.

Brachman, R.J., Fikes, R.E., and Levesque, H.J. 1983. *Krypton: A Functional Approach to Knowledge Representation.* FLAIR Technical Report No. 16, Fairchild Laboratory for Artificial Intelligence

Research, Palo Alto, CA (revised version in *IEEE Computer* 16(10):67–73. (Reprinted in [Brachman and Levesque, 1985, pp. 412–429].)

Crawford, J.M., and Kuipers, B. 1989. Towards a theory of access-limited logic for knowledge representation. *Proceedings of the First International Conference on Principles of Knowledge Representation and Reasoning*. Morgan Kaufmann Publishers, San Mateo, CA.

———, Towards a Formalization of Access Limited Logic. Technical Report AI TR-90-133, University of Texas at Austin, 1990.

Crawford, J., Farquhar, A., and Kuipers, B. 1990. QPC: A compiler from physical models into qualitative differential equations. *AAAI-90*. AAAI, Menlo Park, CA.

Daniel, G., and Winograd, T. 1977. An overview of KRL, a knowledge representation language. *Cognitive Science* 1(1):3–46. (Reprinted in [Brachman and Levesque, 1985, pp. 263–285].)

Etherington, D.W., Borgida, A., Brachman, R.J., and Kautz, H. 1989. Vivid knowledge and tractable reasoning: preliminary report. *IJCAI-89*, pp. 1146–1152. IJCAI proceedings are available from Morgan Kaufmann Publishers, San Mateo, CA.

Ronald F. and Halpern, J.Y. 1988. Belief, awareness, and limited reasoning. *Artificial Intelligence*, 34:39–76.

Findler, N.V. 1979. *Associative Networks: Representation and Use of Knowledge by Computer*. Academic Press, New York.

Fine, K. 1985. *Reasoning With Arbitrary Objects*, Aristotelian Society Series, Volume 3. Basil Blackwell, Oxford.

Forbus, K.D. 1984. Qualitative process theory. *Artificial Intelligence*, 24:85–168.

de Haan, J., and Schubert, L.K. 1986. Inference in a topically organized semantic net. *AAAI-86*, pp. 334–338. AAAI, Menlo Park, CA.

Hanks, S., and McDermott, D. 1986. Default reasoning, nonmonotonic logics, and the frame problem. *AAAI-86*, pp. 328–333. AAAI, Menlo Park, CA.

Hayes, P.J. 1985. The second naive physics manifesto. In *Formal Theories of the Commonsense World*, Hobbs, J.R. and Moore, R.C. (ed.s). Ablex Publishing Co., New Jersey, pp. 18–30.

———. 1979. The logic of frames. In *Frame Conceptions and Text Understanding*, D. Metzing (ed.). Walter de Gruyter and Co., Berlin, pp. 46–61. (Reprinted in [Brachman and Levesque, 1985, pp. 288–295].)

Hayes-Roth, B. 1985. A blackboard architecture for control. *Artificial Intelligence Journal*, 26:251–321.

Hintikka, J. 1962. *Knowledge and Belief.* Cornell University Press, Ithaca, New York.

Kay, M. 1973. The MIND system. In *Natural Language Processing*, R. Rustin (ed.). Algorithmics Press, New York.

Kuipers, B.J. 1978. Modeling spatial knowledge. *Cognitive Science* **2**:129–153.

———. 1979. On representing commonsense knowledge. In *Associative Networks: Representation and Use of Knowledge by Computer*, N.V. Findler (ed.). Academic Press, New York.

———, 1986. Qualitative simulation. *Artificial Intelligence*, 29:289–338.

Lenat, D., Prakash, M., and Shepard, M. 1986. CYC: Using common sense knowledge to overcome brittleness and knowledge acquisition bottlenecks. *AI Magazine* VI(4).

Levesque, H.J. 1986. Knowledge representation and reasoning. In *Annual Reviews of Computer Science* 1:255–87. Annual Reviews Inc, Palo Alto, CA.

———. 1984. A logic of implicit and explicit belief, *AAAI-84*, pp. 198–202 AAAI, Menlo Park, CA..

Lloyd, J.W. 1984. *Foundations of Logic Programming*, Springer-Verlag, New York.

McCarthy, J. 1987. Generality in artificial intelligence. *CACM* 30:1030–1035.

Minsky, M. 1975. A framework for representing knowledge. In *The Psychology of Computer Vision*, P.H. Winston (ed.). McGraw-Hill, New York. (A later version reprinted in [Brachman and Levesque, 1985, pp. 246–262].)

Moore, R. 1979. *Reasoning about Knowledge and Action*, MIT Ph.D. thesis.

Palamidessi, C. 1989. *Algebraic Properties of Idempotent Substitutions*. University of Pisa, manuscript.

Patel-Schneider, P. 1985. A decidable first-order logic for knowledge representation. *IJCAI-85*. IJCAI proceedings are available from Morgan Kaufmann Publishers, San Mateo, CA.

Powers, L.H. 1978. Knowledge by deduction. *The Philosophical Review*, LXXXVII, No. 3, pp. 337–371.

Quillian, M.R. 1967. Word concepts: A theory and simulation of some basic semantic capabilities. *Behavioral Science* 12:410–430. (Reprinted in [Brachman and Levesque, 1985, pp. 98–118].)

Raphael, B. 1968. SIR: semantic information retrieval. In *Semantic Information Processing*, M. Minsky (ed.). MIT Press, Cambridge, MA., pp. 33–145.

Shapiro, S.C. 1978. Path-based and node-based inference in semantic networks. *Tinlap-2: Theoretical Issues in Natural Languages Processing*, D. Waltz (ed.). ACM, New York, pp. 219–225.

Shapiro, S.C. and the SNePS Implementation Group. 1989. *SNePS-2 User's Manual*. Department of Computer Science, SUNY at Buffalo.

Shapiro, S.C. and Woodmansee, G.H. 1969. A net structure based relational question answerer: description and examples. *IJCAI-69*, pp. 325–346. IJCAI proceedings are available from Morgan Kaufmann Publishers, San Mateo, CA.

Schubert, L.K., Goebel, R.G. and Cercone, N.J. 1979. The structure and organization of a semantic net for comprehension and inference. In *Associative Networks: Representation and Use of Knowledge by Computer*, N.V. Findler (ed.). Academic Press, New York, pp. 121–175.

Schubert, L.K., Papalaskaris, M.A., and Taugher, J. 1983. Determining type, part, color, and time relationships. *IEEE Computer*, 16(10):53–60.

Schubert, L.K., and Hwang C.H. 1989. An episodic knowledge representation for narrative texts. *Proceedings of the First International Conference on Principles of Knowledge Representation and Reasoning*. Morgan Kaufmann Publishers, San Mateo, CA.

Schwarcz, R.M., Burger, J.F., and Simmons, R.F. 1970. A deductive question-answerer for natural language inference. *CACM* 13(3):167–183.

Smith, D.E., and Genesereth, M.R. 1985. Ordering conjunctive queries. *Artificial Intelligence*, 26: 171–215.

Touretzky, D.S. 1986. *The Mathematics of Inheritance Systems.* Morgan Kaufmann Publishers, San Mateo, CA, copublished with Pitman, London.

Treitel, R. and Genesereth, M.R. 1987. Choosing directions for rules. *Journal of Automated Reasoning* 3:395–431.

Vilain, M. 1985. The restricted language architecture of a hybrid representation system. *IJCAI-85*, pp. 547–551. IJCAI proceedings are available from Morgan Kaufmann Publishers, San Mateo, CA.

Woods, W. 1975. What's in a link: foundations for semantic networks. In *Representation and Understanding: Studies in Cognitive Science*, Bobrow, D. and Collins, A. (ed.). Academic, New York, pp. 35–82.

Wylie, C.R., Jr. 1957. *101 Puzzles in Thought and Logic*. Dover Publications Inc, Mineola, New York.

11

TERMINOLOGICAL CYCLES:

Semantics and Computational Properties

Bernhard Nebel
(German Research Center for Artificial Intelligence)

Abstract

Terminological knowledge representation formalisms are intended to capture the analytic relationships between terms of a vocabulary intended to describe a domain. A term whose definition refers, either directly or indirectly, to the term itself presents a problem for most terminological representation systems because it is not obvious whether such a term is meaningful, nor how it could be handled by a knowledge representation system in a satisfying manner. After some examples of intuitively sound terminological cycles are given, different formal semantics are investigated and evaluated with respect to the examples. As it turns out, none of the different styles of semantics seems to be completely satisfying for all purposes. Finally, consequences in terms of computational complexity and decidability are discussed.

11.1 INTRODUCTION

When trying to represent an expert's knowledge about a sufficiently complex domain we have to account for the vocabulary used in this domain [Brachman and Levesque, 1982; Swartout and Neches, 1986]. This is exactly the purpose of *terminological knowledge representation formalisms*, which have their roots in *structural inheritance networks* [Brachman, 1979]. The main building blocks of such representation formalisms are *concepts* and *roles* [Brachman and Schmolze, 1985], similar to generic frames and slots in frame systems and to type nodes and links in semantic networks. In contrast to frame systems and semantic networks, however, it is possible to *define* concepts by specifying *necessary and sufficient* conditions, while in semantic networks and frame systems only *necessary* conditions can be specified.

The most important reasoning task in such a context is the determination of *subsumption* between concepts, i.e., whether all *instances* of a concept are necessarily instances of the other concept. This kind of reasoning can be employed to support such diverse applications as information retrieval [Patel-Schneider et al., 1984], explainable expert systems [Neches et al., 1985], natural language processing [Webber and Bobrow, 1980; Sondheimer and Nebel, 1986], and computer configuration [Owsnicki-Klewe, 1988].

Based on these ideas, a number of system were built, e.g., KANDOR [Patel-Schneider, 1984], KL-TWO [Vilain, 1985; Schmolze, 1989], KRYPTON [Brachman et al., 1985], MESON [Edelmann and Owsnicki, 1986], BACK [von Luck et al, 1987; Nebel and von Luck, 1988], LOOM [Mac Gregor, 1988]; CLASSIC [Brachman et al., 1989; Borgida et al., 1989], and SB-ONE [Kobsa, 1989], and the formal properties of these systems were investigated [Schmolze and Israel, 1983; Brachman and Levesque, 1984; Patel-Schneider, 1986; Levesque and Brachman, 1987; Nebel, 1988; Schild, 1988; Patel-Schneider, 1989a; Patel-Schneider, 1989b; Schmidt-Schauß, 1989; Schmidt-Schauß and Smolka, 1990; Nebel and Smolka, 1990; Nebel, 1990; Hollunder et al., 1990].

When studying the above-mentioned papers, one notes that *terminological cycles* are usually ignored or explicitly excluded. Terminological cycles arise when a concept is defined by referring directly or indirectly to itself (which amounts to a loop in the network depicting the terminological knowledge base) as in the (informal) definition of the concept `Human` below:

> a `Human` is defined as
> a `Mammal` with
> exactly 2 `parents` and
> all `parents` are `Humans`

Such a definition obviously violates the plausible idea that the meaning of a concept "can be completely understood in terms of the meaning of its parts and the way these are composed" [Schmolze and Brachman, 1982; p. 11]. In trying to understand the meaning of `Human`, we inevitably end up trying to figure out what the meaning of `Human` could be. Additionally, the *subsumption algorithms* usually employed (see e.g., [Schmolze and Israel, 1983; Brachman and Schmolze, 1985]) would end up in an infinite loop on such definitions. For these reasons terminological cycles have been excluded in theoretical investigations and practical terminological knowledge representation systems.

This exclusion would be justified if terminological cycles were not useful in this style of knowledge representation. However, experience with terminological knowledge representation systems in applications show that terminological cycles are used regularly [Kaczmarek et al., 1986, p. 982]. Also, envisioning a system that views a terminological knowledge base as an abstract entity that can be changed incrementally (as described in [Nebel, 1989]), terminological cycles can be easily created and either have to be detected and rejected by the system—which makes the system specification overly complex and hard to understand by a user—or the system has to accept them as legal constructions. In addition, a decision to prohibit the use of terminological cycles should not be based on the fact that we do not understand the meaning or do not know the inference algorithms, but it should be based on an understanding of terminological cycles and justified by arguments concerning semantics and/or computational properties. For these reasons it seems worthwhile to analyze the semantic and algorithmic nature of terminological cycles.

The rest of this chapter is organized as follows. A small and simple terminological formalism is formally introduced in Section 11.2. In Section 11.3, a brief description of possible kinds of terminological cycles is given, and the intuitive semantics of them are discussed. Based on that, Section 11.4 presents three different styles of semantics, namely: *descriptive semantics*, *least fixpoint semantics*, and *greatest fixpoint semantics* that are evaluated with respect to the examples. As it turns out, there is no obvious "winner." There are good arguments for the descriptive semantics and equally good arguments for the greatest fixpoint semantics. In fact, which one to choose seems to be a matter of the intended purpose. In Section 11.5, algorithmic consequences are discussed using results presented in [Nebel, 1990] and [Baader, 1990]. Finally, we will show that depending on the expressiveness of the underlying terminological formalism, terminological cycles can lead to severe computational problems, namely, to undecidability of subsumption.

11.2 A FRAMEWORK FOR REPRESENTING TERMINOLOGICAL KNOWLEDGE

In order to have something to build on, we need a concrete terminological knowledge representation formalism. In this chapter, a small terminological formalism—called $\mathcal{TLN}$[1], which is a subformalism of almost all the formalisms used in the systems quoted above[2]—will be used to investigate the nature of terminological cycles.

The basic building blocks of our formalism are a set **R** of *atomic roles* (denoted by *R*) and a set **A** of *atomic concepts* (denoted by *A* and *B*). We will assume that there are always two predefined concepts (which are also elements of

---

[1] It is the formalism $\mathcal{TL}$ introduced in [Nebel, 1990] extended by number restrictions.

[2] The only exception is KRYPTON.

A), namely, $\top$ intended to denote everything, and $\bot$ which denotes nothing. Using these *atomic terms*, the set **D** of *concept descriptions* (denoted by C and D) is defined by the following abstract syntax rule:

C, D	$\rightarrow$	A	*atomic concept*
	|	$C \sqcap D$	*concept conjunction*
	|	$\forall R: C$	*value restriction*
	|	$\exists^{\geq n} R$	*minimum restriction*
	|	$\exists^{\leq n} R$	*maximum restriction*

Intuitively, a concept description is intended to denote all *objects* that fulfill the description. For instance, the concept description

`Human` $\sqcap$ `Female` $\sqcap \exists^{\geq 1}$ `child` $\sqcap \forall$ `child`: (`Human` $\sqcap$ `Female`)

denotes the set of all `Female Humans` that have at least one `child` and whose `children` are all `Female Humans`; i.e., this expression denotes all mothers that have only daughters.

The formal meaning is given by a model-theoretic interpretation $I = \langle \mathcal{D}, [\![\cdot]\!]^I \rangle$, where $\mathcal{D}$ is an arbitrary set, the *domain*, and $[\![\cdot]\!]^I$ is a function, the *interpretation function*, that maps atomic concepts to subsets of $\mathcal{D}$ and atomic roles to total functions from $\mathcal{D}$ to $2^{\mathcal{D}}$ [Brachman and Levesque, 1984]. The predefined concepts $\top$ and $\bot$ have the fixed interpretation $\mathcal{D}$ and $\emptyset$, respectively. The set $[\![R]\!]^I(d)$ will be called the *role-filler set* of role R for object d. The *denotation of concept descriptions* is defined inductively by[3]

$$
\begin{aligned}
[\![C \sqcap D]\!]^I &= [\![C]\!]^I \cap [\![D]\!]^I \\
[\![\forall R: C]\!]^I &= \{d \in \mathcal{D} \mid [\![R]\!]^I(d) \subseteq [\![C]\!]^I\} \\
[\![\exists^{\geq n} R]\!]^I &= \{d \in \mathcal{D} \mid \| [\![R]\!]^I(d) \| \geq n\} \\
[\![\exists^{\leq n} R]\!]^I &= \{d \in \mathcal{D} \mid \| [\![R]\!]^I(d) \| \leq n\}.
\end{aligned}
$$

Since we are not only interested in forming a variety of concept descriptions, but also in defining new concepts, the notion of a *terminology* will be used, which allows us to assign the meaning of concept descriptions to atomic concepts. Formally, a *terminology* T is a total function T: $\mathbf{A} \rightarrow \mathbf{D}$, where $T(A)$ is the concept description defining the meaning of A or, if A is *primitive in the terminology*, $T(A) = A$.[4] In the following, we will use $\mathbf{A_p}$ for the set of atomic concepts that are primitive in a terminology (which are sometimes denoted by P and Q) and $\mathbf{A_n}$ for

---

[3] The expression $\|S\|$ denotes the cardinality of a set.

[4] Note that this definition of primitiveness is the same as in KRYPTON [Brachman et al., 1985] and different from the notion of a *primitive concept* in KL-ONE [Brachman and Schmolze, 1985]. However, this does not affect the formal expressiveness of the representation language [Nebel, 1989].

the set of nonprimitive atomic concepts. For $\top$ and $\perp$, we assume $\top, \perp \notin \mathbf{A_n} \cup \mathbf{A_p}$. Furthermore, we will use the expression $|C|$ when referring to the *size of the concept description C*, which is defined as the number of operators and atomic terms appearing in C, and we will use $|T|$ to denote the *size of a terminology*, which is defined as $\Sigma_{A \in \mathbf{An}} |T(A)|$.

The intended meaning of a terminology is the restriction of all possible interpretations to those that have identical denotations for atomic concepts and their defining concept descriptions. Formally, an interpretation I is a *model of T* iff

$$[[A]]^I = [[T(A)]]^I \textit{ for all } A \in \mathbf{A}.$$

Now we can formalize the notion of *subsumption* between concepts, which was informally introduced in Section 11.1. *C is subsumed by D in the terminology T*, written $C \leq_T D$, under the following condition:

$$C \leq_T D \textit{ iff } [[C]]^I \subseteq [[D]]^I \textit{ for all models } I \text{ of } T.$$

Giving an example, in the terminology

$$T(\texttt{Woman}) = \texttt{Human} \sqcap \texttt{Female} \quad (1)$$
$$T(\texttt{Mother-of-daughters}) = \texttt{Woman} \sqcap \exists^{\geq 1} \texttt{child} \sqcap \forall \texttt{child: Woman} \quad (2)$$
$$T(\texttt{Parent}) = \texttt{Human} \sqcap \exists^{\geq 1} \texttt{child} \sqcap \forall \texttt{child: Human}, \quad (3)$$

`Mother-of-daughters` is subsumed by `Parent` because every `Mother-of-daughters` is a `Parent` in any model of the terminology.

Similarly to subsumption, *equivalence of concepts in a terminology*, written $C \approx_T D$, is defined by

$$C \approx_T D \textit{ iff } [[C]]^I = [[D]]^I \textit{ for all models } I \textit{ of } T.$$

Finally, a concept C is called *incoherent in a terminology T* iff $C \approx_T \perp$.

Because of the set-theoretic semantics, incoherence and equivalence can be reduced to subsumption in $O(n)$ time, and subsumption can be reduced to equivalence in $O(n)$ time, where n is the size of the concept descriptions.

Proposition 1 Let T be a $\mathcal{TLN}$-terminology, and let C and D be concept descriptions. Then

$$C \approx_T D \textit{ iff } (C \leq_T D \textit{ and } D \leq_T C),$$
$$C \approx_T \perp \textit{ iff } C \leq_T \perp,$$
$$C \leq_T D \textit{ iff } C \approx_T C \sqcap D.$$

For the sake of simplicity, we will sometimes consider terminologies such that the second argument in each value restriction is an atomic concept. Such terminologies will be called *normalized terminologies*.[5] Since any terminology can be transformed into such a form (by introducing at most $|T|$ auxiliary nonprimitive atomic concepts) without changing the denotations of the original terms, this assumption does not affect generality.

Although everything defined so far makes perfect sense, there is usually an additional syntactic restriction enforced on the form of terminologies. As pointed out in Section 11.1, the common intuition about terminologies is that concept definitions are "well-founded," i.e., that there are no terminological cycles such as the one presented in the beginning. Formally, a *terminological cycle* can be defined as follows. An atomic concept A *directly uses* another atomic concept B iff the expression $T(A)$ contains B. An atomic concept A_0 *uses* A_n iff there is a chain $A_0, A_1, \dots A_n$ such that A_i directly uses A_{i+1}, $0 \leq i \leq n-1$. Finally, it will be said that a terminology T contains a *terminological cycle* iff some atomic concept uses itself.

The advantage of the acyclicity restriction is that the meaning of a concept can be understood in terms of the meaning of the atomic terms used in the defining description and the way these are composed. This is mirrored on a model-theoretic level by the fact that models of a terminology can be constructed inductively from *initial partial interpretations* that assign denotations to primitive concepts and roles only. Such initial partial interpretations will be denoted by $\breve{I}$.

Proposition 2 Given a terminology T without terminological cycles, any initial partial interpretation $\breve{I}$ can be uniquely extended to a model of T.

Proof sketch: By induction on the depth of a terminology (see [Nebel, 1990, lemma 1]).

From an algorithmic point of view, this means that subsumption determination in an acyclic terminology can be reduced to subsumption determination over concept descriptions, i.e., assuming that all atomic concepts are primitive (see [Nebel, 1990, theorem 1]). This is done by expanding all nonprimitive concepts in an expression until it contains only primitive atomic concepts—which cannot be done if the terminology contains cycles.

11.3 IN DEFENSE OF TERMINOLOGICAL CYCLES

Basically, there are two kinds of terminological cycles—one which is obviously meaningful and another one which does not seem to make sense. An example of the latter kind of terminological cycles is the following terminology introducing the concepts `Male-Human` and `Man`:

---

[5] Note that all the example terminologies in this chapter are normalized.

$$T(\texttt{Man}) = \texttt{Human} \sqcap \texttt{Male-Human} \tag{4}$$
$$T(\texttt{Male-Human}) = \texttt{Human} \sqcap \texttt{Man}. \tag{5}$$

These definitions suggest that Man is a specialization of Male-Human and *vice versa*, which seems to be rather weird and violates the idea that all concepts in a terminology can be ordered hierarchically.

In general, such cycles will be called *component cycles* and the concepts involved are called *component-circular concepts*. Formally, an atomic concept A_0 *uses* A_n *as a component* iff there is a chain of atomic concepts $A_0, A_1, \ldots A_n, n > 0$, *such that each* A_i directly uses A_{i+1}, and A_{i+1} appears outside of the scope of any $\forall$ expression in $T(A_i)$, for $0 \leq i \leq n - 1$. A concept A is *component-circular* iff A uses itself as a component.

We might simply prohibit the use of such cycles. However, if we view a terminological knowledge base as an abstract object on which some modification operations can be carried out as sketched in Section 11.1, we have to take special care to detect and reject operations intended to introduce cycles. This makes the specification of such a system complicated and clumsy. Therefore, if the semantics of the representation language could give us a sensible answer as to what such "definitions" could possibly mean, this would be much more elegant.

Besides the meaningless kind of cycles, there are cycles that are obviously meaningful and often appear when modeling a domain. For instance, the description of recursive structures, e.g., binary trees, requires that we can use terminological cycles:

$$T(\texttt{Binary-tree}) = \texttt{Tree} \sqcap \exists^{\leq 2}\texttt{branch} \sqcap \forall\,\texttt{branch}: \texttt{Binary-tree}. \tag{6}$$

The intuition behind this terminology is obviously that the concept Binary-Trees should describe tree-structured objects of degree two. For instance, consider the following initial partial interpretation, which is depicted in Figure 11.1:

$$\begin{aligned}
\mathcal{D} &= \{a,b,c,d,e,f,g,h\} \\
[[\texttt{Tree}]]^{\breve{I}} &= \mathcal{D} \\
[[\texttt{branch}]]^{\breve{I}} &= \begin{cases} \mathrm{a} \mapsto \{b,c\} \\ \mathrm{b} \mapsto \emptyset \\ \mathrm{c} \mapsto \{d\} \\ \mathrm{d} \mapsto \emptyset \\ \mathrm{e} \mapsto \{f,g\} \\ \mathrm{f} \mapsto \{h\} \\ \mathrm{g} \mapsto \{h\}. \end{cases}
\end{aligned}$$

Extending $\breve{I}$ to a model I of the terminology given by (6), one notes that $\{a,b,c,d\}$ is a subset of the denotation of Binary-tree, as expected. Furthermore,

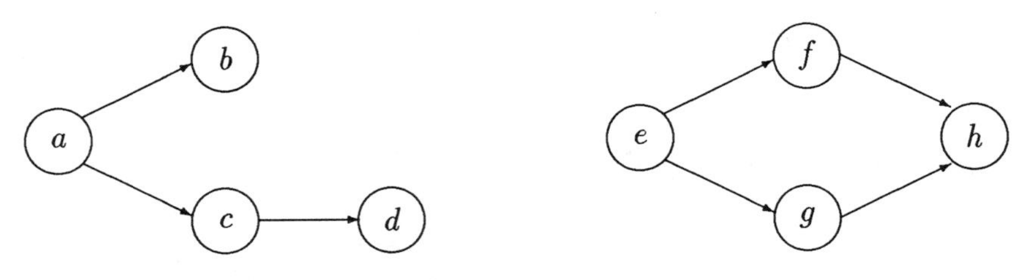

Figure 11.1: Some object structures intended by the definition of `Binary-tree`] (Arrows denote `branch` relationships, circles denote elements of the denotation of `Tree`)

also $\{e,f,g,h\}$ must be a subset of $[\![$`Binary-tree`$]\!]^I$, i.e., the terminology also permits object structures that are directed acyclic graphs.

Concepts such as `Binary-tree` will be called *restriction-circular concepts.* Formally, an atomic concept is *restriction-circular* iff it uses itself, and it is not *component circular*. Furthermore, assuming a normalized terminology T, it will be said that an atomic concept B can be *directly reached by a role R* from A iff B appears in a value restriction of $T(A)$. The atomic concept B *can be reached by a role chain* $W = R_1\, R_2 \ldots R_m$ *from* A iff

1. $m = 1$ and B can be directly reached by R_1 from A, or
2. A directly uses a concept A' outside of any value restriction and B can be reached by W from A', or
3. a concept A' can be reached by R_1 and B can be reached by $R_2 \ldots R_m$ from A'.

Finally, A is said to be *restriction-circular over the role chain W* iff A can be reached by W from A. For instance, `Binary-tree` is restriction-circular over the chain consisting of the one role "`branch`." Note that if there is one such role chain W, then there there are infinitely many such role chains, e.g., W^n, $n > 0$.

Another example of a restriction-circular concept, which at first sight seems to be similar, is `Human` as informally defined in Section 11.1:

$$T(\texttt{Human}) = \texttt{Mammal} \sqcap \exists^{\geq 2}\texttt{parent} \sqcap \exists^{\leq 2}\texttt{parent} \sqcap \forall\,\texttt{parent:}\ \texttt{Human}. \qquad (7)$$

However, in this case, we are not aiming at describing finite structures but infinite ones as in Figure 11.2, which depicts a finite subset of an infinite interpretation where the circles denote elements of the denotation of `Human` and `Mammal`, solid arrows denote `parent` relationships, and the dashed arrows indicate that the tree extends infinitely to the right.

This kind of concept definition might raise the question of the origin of human beings. Because of space limitations, however, we will not discuss this subject further. From a formal of view, one notes that if all domain elements are in the denotation of `Mammal` and `Human`, then this interpretation is a model of the

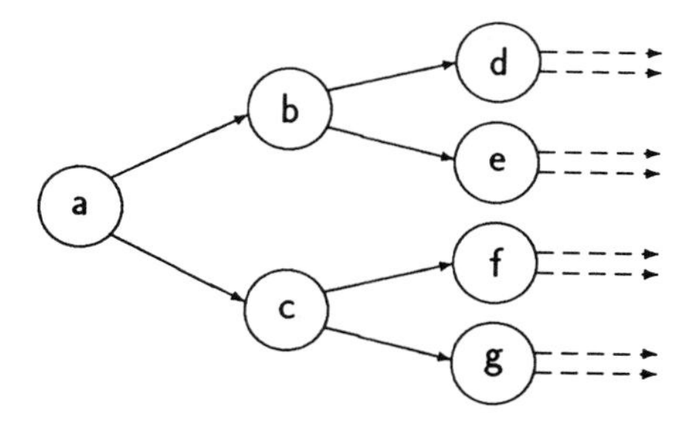

Figure 11.2: Object structures intended by the definition of `Human`. (Arrows indicate `parent` relationships and circles denote elements of the denotation of `Mammal` and `Human`.)

terminology (7). However, there is another model with the same initial partial interpretation such that $[\![\mathtt{Human}]\!]^I$ is empty.

For a commonsense view of the world, at least, the definition seems reasonable. I even believe that the conditions on `Human` are necessary and sufficient! This sounds a little strange at first but can be defended by the argument that an entity can be recognized as a `Human` when the entity has two `parents` known to be `Humans`.

A third kind of terminological cycle stresses the idea that it may be impossible to define a concept by referring to already-defined terms but possible to define two concepts by referring each to the other. In other words, we are aiming at describing circular object structures:

$$T(\mathtt{Car}) = \mathtt{Vehicle} \sqcap \forall\, \mathtt{engine\text{-}part}: \mathtt{Car\text{-}engine} \sqcap \exists^{\geq 1}\, \mathtt{engine\text{-}part} \quad (8)$$

$$T(\mathtt{Car\text{-}engine}) = \mathtt{Engine} \sqcap \forall\, \mathtt{is\text{-}engine\text{-}of}: \mathtt{Car} \sqcap \exists^{\geq 1}\, \mathtt{is\text{-}engine\text{-}of}. \quad (9)$$

Some conceivable object structures are depicted in Figure 11.3, where simple circles denote `Car` objects, double circles denote `Car-engine` objects, simple arrows denote `engine-part` relationships, and double arrows denote `is-car-engine-of` relationships. Note, however, that object structures are possible which do not follow this pattern, e.g., infinite chains of `Car` objects and `Car-engine` objects connected by the appropriate relationships.[6]

Such concept definitions are obviously not "well-founded," and I know that if I would really insist that this example is reasonable and has to be part of any knowledge engineer's basic skills in modeling terminological knowledge, then I

---

[6] Inverse roles are necessary to avoid such structures.

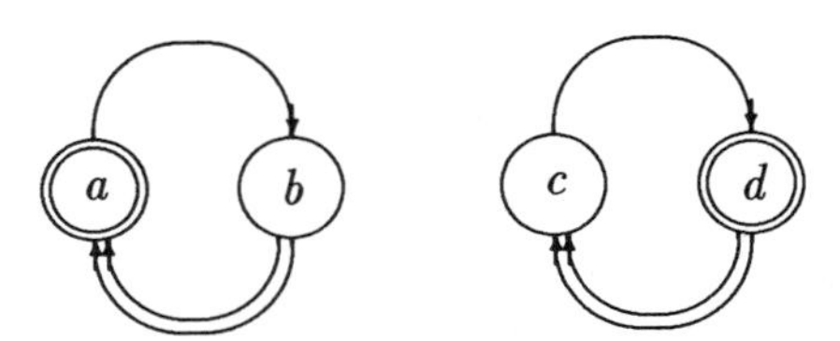

Figure 11.3: Object structures intended by the definition of `Car-engine` and `Car`. (Simple circles denote `Car` objects, double circles denote `Car-engine` objects, simple arrows denote `engine-part` relationships, and double arrows denote `is-car-engine-of` relationships.)

probably would lose some credibility. Therefore, I will defend this kind of terminological modeling only with a pragmatic argument.

Terminological cycles such as the one in (8) and (9) can be exploited in *hybrid representation systems*, which consists of an *assertional* and a *terminological component* [Brachman and Levesque, 1982]. For instance, if it is known that the object `a` is a `Car`, and a role filler of the `engine-part` role for object `a` is the object `b`, then we can conclude that object `b` must be a `Car-engine`. Obviously, this game also works the other way around. Thus, this kind of cycle permits a special and interesting mode of hybrid reasoning.

Depending on the expressiveness of the terminological formalism, there can be similar kinds of terminological cycles involving roles. Furthermore, we may have cycles such that the meaning of a role depends on a concept, which in turn uses the role in its definition. We will ignore these cases here, however.

11.4 WHAT'S IN A TERMINOLOGICAL CYCLE?

We have seen in Section 11.2 that the meaning of defined concepts can be completely derived from the meaning of primitive concepts, roles, and the various concept-forming operators (see proposition 2) provided the terminology is acyclic. If we continue to use the semantics specified in Section 11.2 (which will be called *descriptive semantics* in the following) in the presence of terminological cycles, we lose this nice property.

Using the `Binary-tree` example, for instance (see (6)), we note that for some initial partial interpretations, there is more than one extension of the initial interpretation to a model of T. Consider the following $\breve{I}$:

$$\begin{aligned} \mathcal{D} &= \{a,b,c\} \\ [[\texttt{Tree}]]^{\breve{I}} &= \{a,b,c\} \end{aligned}$$

$$[\![\texttt{branch}]\!]^{\breve{I}} = \begin{cases} a \mapsto \emptyset \\ b \mapsto \{c\} \\ c \mapsto \{b\}. \end{cases}$$

Now, there are two possible models, I and $\mathcal{J}$, extending $\breve{I}$:

$[\![\texttt{Binary-tree}]\!]^{I} = \{a\}$
$[\![\texttt{Binary-tree}]\!]^{\mathcal{J}} = \{a,b,c\}$.

Since this seems to violate the ideas spelled out in Section 11.1, one idea could be to use only one particular model extending a given initial partial interpretation, which is in some sense "canonical"—provided such a model is always identifiable. Whether one uses this approach or the descriptive semantics is a matter of the models one considers as plausible and the subsumption relationships one wants to have.

11.4.1 Fixpoint Models

In order to explore these ideas, we will characterize models as fixpoints of a certain operator on interpretations. The set of interpretations (over a given terminology T with fixed $\mathbf{A}$ and $\mathbf{R}$) that have identical interpretations of roles and primitive concepts, i.e., all interpretations with the same initial partial part $\breve{I}$, will be denoted by $\Psi_{\breve{I}}$. Furthermore, Γ shall be a function mapping interpretations to interpretations (for a given terminology T) as follows:

$\Gamma\colon \Psi_{\breve{I}} \rightarrow \Psi_{\breve{I}}$
$\Gamma\colon I \mapsto \mathcal{J}$

such that

$[\![A]\!]^{\mathcal{J}} = [\![T(A)]\!]^{I}$
$[\![R]\!]^{\mathcal{J}} = [\![R]\!]^{I}$.

A fixed point of Γ, i.e., an interpretation I with the property $\Gamma(I) = I$, is clearly a model of the terminology T according to the definition in Section 11.2, which will be called *admissible model*.

Least or greatest fixpoint models (*lfp*- and *gfp*-models for short) would fulfill the requirement of being "canonical" in the sense mentioned above. In order to define *lfp*- and *gfp*-models, however, we need an ordering on $\Psi_{\breve{I}}$. A straightforward and intuitively plausible ordering is the component-wise set-inclusion relation over the denotation of nonprimitive atomic concepts, written $\sqsubseteq$:

$I \sqsubseteq \mathcal{J}$ *iff* $[\![A]\!]^{I} \subseteq [\![A]\!]^{\mathcal{J}}$ *for all* $A \in \mathbf{A_n}$, $I, \mathcal{J} \in \Psi_{\breve{I}}$.

Obviously, $(\Psi_{\breve{I}}, \sqsubseteq)$ is a partial ordering which forms together with component-wise union as the least upper bound ($\sqcup$) a complete lattice. Thus, it seems reasonable that it is possible to apply Tarski's [1955] fixpoint theorem, which says that for a complete lattice L (with $\perp_L$ as the least element) and for any *monotone* function $f: L \to L$ (i.e., for all $x,y \in L : f(x) \sqsubseteq f(y)$ if $x \sqsubseteq y$)

1. the set of fixed points of f is nonempty and forms a complete lattice,
2. if f is *continuous* (i.e., for any totally ordered set $X \subseteq L : f(\bigsqcup X) = \bigsqcup f(X)$), then the least fixed point of f is equal to $\bigsqcup_{n=0}^{\infty} f^n(\perp_L)$.

As a matter of fact, the basic condition of the theorem can be easily verified.

Proposition 3 Given a terminology T and an initial partial interpretation $\breve{I}$, Γ is monotone on $\Psi_{\breve{I}}$.

Proof: By structural induction on the definition of the denotation of concept descriptions.

Furthermore, we get the intuitive result that the set of *lfp*- and *gfp*-models is identical with the set of admissible models when the terminology is acyclic.

Proposition 4 Let T be a terminology without terminological cycles. Then I is an admissible model iff it is a *lfp*-model and a *gfp*-model.

Proof: Immediate by proposition 2 and the fact that all admissible models are fixed points of Γ.

Similarly to subsumption w.r.t. descriptive semantics as defined in Section 11.2, we define *lfp*-subsumption, written $\leq_T^{lfp}$, and *gfp*-subsumption, written $\leq_T^{gfp}$, by

$$C \leq_T^{lfp} D \text{ iff } [\![C]\!]^I \subseteq [\![D]\!]^I \text{ for all lfp-models } I \text{ of } T,$$
$$C \leq_T^{gfp} D \text{ iff } [\![C]\!]^I \subseteq [\![D]\!]^I \text{ for all gfp-models } I \text{ of } T.$$

For concept equivalence w.r.t to *lfp*- and *gfp*-semantics we will use a similar notation.

Although we know by monotonicity of Γ on $\Psi_{\breve{I}}$ and Tarski's fixpoint theorem that the least and greatest fixpoint exist, it is not possible to generate the least fixed point by an ordinary fixpoint iteration. The reason is that Γ is not a continuous function because the denotation of $(\forall R\colon C)$ can depend on infinitely many elements in $\mathcal{D}$. Thus, we could either use transfinite fixpoint iteration (see [Lloyd, 1984, p. 29])[7] or we could restrict our attention to models with finite role-filler sets, which will be called roleset finite. Indeed, this restriction does not change subsumption relationships, and, furthermore, such models seem to be more plausible.

[7] An example of noncontinuity can be found in [Baader, 1990].

Lemma 1 $C \preceq_T^{lfp} D$ iff $[[C]]^I \subseteq [[D]]^I$ *for all roleset-finite lfp-models* I.

Proof: The "only if" direction is obvious. For the "if" direction let I be any admissible model of a normalized terminology T. Assume that for some $d \in \mathcal{D}$ the set $[[R]]^I(d)$ is infinite. Then there exists another model $\mathcal{J}$ of T that is identical with I except that $[[R]]^{\mathcal{J}}(d)$ is a finite subset of $[[R]]^I(d)$ which satisfies or violates all value, minimum, and maximum restrictions for all defined concepts and all sub-expressions of C and D which were originally satisfied or violated, for the element d.

Assume that I is a *lfp*-model, i.e., the smallest model extending the initial, partial interpretation $\breve{I}$. Now, we will show that $\mathcal{J}$ is the smallest model extending the initial partial interpretation $\breve{\mathcal{J}}$. Assuming otherwise, i.e., that there is a model $\mathscr{J}$ that extends $\breve{\mathcal{J}}$ and that is smaller than $\mathcal{J}$, leads to the conclusion that for some $e \in \mathcal{D}$ and some concept C: $e \notin [[C]]\mathscr{J}$ but $e \in [[C]]\mathcal{J}$. Since $\breve{\mathcal{J}}$ and $\breve{I}$ differ only in role-filler sets of d, d must be such an element. However, since we preserved all value, minimum, and maximum restrictions, it follows that there is a model $\mathcal{I}'$ which extends $\breve{I}$ such that $d \notin [[C]]\mathcal{I}'$, i.e., $\mathcal{I}'$ is smaller than I—a contradiction of the assumption. Thus, if I was a *lfp*-model, then $\mathcal{J}$ is a *lfp*-model, as well.

Since d was chosen arbitrarily, the arguments above apply to the entire domain. Hence, if there is an arbitrary *lfp*-model I, then there exists a roleset-finite *lfp*-model $\mathcal{J}$ with identical denotations for all $A \in \mathbf{A}$ and for given C and D. Thus, subsumption is identical.

For this set of roleset-finite interpretations, denoted by Ψ_I^f, the desired property of Γ can be easily proven.

Proposition 5 Given a terminology T and an initial partial interpretation $\breve{I}$, Γ is continuous on Ψ_I^f.

Proof: Let Φ be a totally ordered subset of Ψ_I^f. By monotonicity we know $\bigsqcup \Gamma(\Phi)$**P** $\Gamma(\bigsqcup \Phi)$. For the other direction let $I = \Gamma(\bigsqcup \Phi)$, $\mathcal{J} = \bigsqcup \Phi$, and assume $d \in [[A]]^I$. The reason for $d \in [[A]]^I$ is that there is a finite subset F of $\mathcal{D}$ such that for all $e \in F : e \in [[B]]^{\mathcal{J}}$ for some atomic concepts $B \in \mathbf{A}$ and $e \in [[R]]^{\mathcal{J}}(d)$ for some atomic roles $R \in \mathbf{R}$. Since Φ is totally ordered, there must be $\mathscr{J} \in \Phi$ with the same property. Hence, $d \in [[A]]^{\bigsqcup \Gamma(\Phi)}$, i.e., $\bigsqcup \Gamma(\Phi)$ **P** $\Gamma(\bigsqcup \Phi)$.

11.4.2 Least Fixpoint Semantics

When there is choice between different fixed points, the least one is usually the most "attractive" one—it is the fixed point that makes the fewest "commitments." For instance, in semantics of programming languages, we are usually interested in the least fixed point because in the space of functions the least fixed point corresponds to the partial function giving results for terminating computations and being undefined for nonterminating computations. In our case, an *lfp*-model amounts to something similar. It is the least model contained in all admissible models. Furthermore, for roleset-finite *lfp*-models, the semantics is highly constructive. For a given initial partial interpretation, we have $d \in [\![C]\!]^I$ for the *lfp*-model $I \in \Psi_I^f$ iff there exists some finite approximation $\mathcal{J} = \bigsqcup_{n=0}^{i} \Gamma(\bot_\Psi)$ such that $d \in [\![C]\!]^{\mathcal{J}}$, where $\bot_\Psi$ denotes the least element of Ψ_I^f.

For these reasons, *lfp*-semantics might seem to be the most plausible one to choose. Before we do so, however, the *lfp*-semantics should be evaluated against the intuitions spelled out in Section 11.3.

The first kind of cycles, the component cycles, are treated in way which seems to be reasonable.

Proposition 6 If A is a component-circular concept in a terminology T, then $A \approx_T^{lfp} \bot$.

Proof: Let $\mathbf{C}_c$ be the maximal set of nonprimitive atomic concepts that use A as a component and are used by A as a component at the same time. All concepts in $\mathbf{C}_c$ are obviously component-circular (and it is the greatest such set containing A).

Now note that if all $B \in \mathbf{C}_c$ have an empty denotation in an interpretation I, this holds for $\Gamma(I)$ as well. Thus, there exists no natural number i such that $\mathcal{J} = \bigsqcup \Gamma^i_{n=0} \bot_\Psi$ and $[\![B]\!]^{\mathcal{J}} \neq \varnothing$ for any $B \in \mathbf{C}_c$. Thus, for any *lfp*-model I of T: $[\![B]\!]^I = [\![\bot]\!]^I$ for all $B \in \mathbf{C}_c$.

This means we could eliminate these cycles by defining all component-circular concepts as $\bot$ without changing the meaning of the terminology.

Corollary 1 If the terminology T contains component cycles, then there exists a terminology T' that does not contain component cycles and

I is a lfp-model of T iff I is a lfp-model of T'.

It should be obvious that the other type of terminological cycles, the restriction cycle, is more complicated. In particular, we can describe object structures that cannot be described by acyclic terminologies, and, hence, such cycles cannot be eliminated from a terminology.

In order to describe the effect of these cycles, the denotation of role chains (as introduced in Section 11.3) has to be defined. Let $W = R_1\ R_2\ \ldots\ R_m$. Then the denotation of W is defined as the functional composition $[\![W]\!]^I = [\![R_m]\!]^I \circ \ldots \circ [\![R_2]\!]^I \circ [\![R_1]\!]^I$. The expression $|W|$ will be used to denote the length of a role chain.

Proposition 7 Let A be a restriction-circular concept that is circular over the role-chains $W_1, \ldots, W_j, \ldots$ in a terminology T. Then for all roleset-finite *lfp*-models I of

T: If $d \in [[A]]^I$, then there exists a natural number $n > 0$ such that $[[W_j]]^I(d) = \emptyset$ for all role chains with $|W_j| \geq n$.

Proof: Assume that $[[W_j]]^I(d) \neq \emptyset$ for all role chains regardless of their length. By induction over the construction of the least fixed point it follows that for all natural numbers m: for $\mathcal{J} = \bigsqcup_{i=0}^{m} \Gamma^i(\bot_\Psi)$, we have $d \notin [[A]]^{\mathcal{J}}$, and, hence, $d \notin [[A]]^I$ for any *lfp*-model I of T.

Applying proposition 7 to the `Binary-tree` example (see (6)), we see that we get neither circular binary trees nor trees with infinite depth, which matches nicely with the intuition. However, this also means that we do not get the structure we would have expected in the cases of `Human` (see (7)) and `Car` (see (8) and (9)). Even worse, the denotations of `Human` and `Car` are empty in all *lfp*-models, as can be easily deduced from the next corollary.

Corollary 2 Let $A_0\ A_1\ \ldots\ A_n$, where $A_0 = A_n$, be a restriction cycle such that A_0 is circular over $P = R_1\ \ldots\ R_m$, and let $A_{i_1}\ \ldots\ A_{i_m}$ be the concepts such that A_{ij+1} is directly reached by R_j from A_{ij}. If all expressions $T(A_{ij})$ contain a minimum restriction on R_j, then $A_i \approx^{lfp}_{T} \bot$, for $0 \leq i \leq n$.

We could take the observation that humans and cars do not exist as a deep truth (of which nobody was aware), or, taking a more pragmatic view, as an indication that *lfp*-semantics might be not the right choice.

11.4.3 Greatest Fixpoint Semantics

Using *gfp*-semantics obviously avoids the cruel consequences concerning the existence of the reader, the author, and the cars they possess. However, there are other shortcomings. First of all, it is not as constructive as *lfp*-semantics.[8] Second, it violates one intuition spelled out in Section 11.3. Elaborating on the `Human` example, we could define the concept `Horse` in the same way:

$$T(\texttt{Human}) = \texttt{Mammal} \sqcap \exists^{\geq 2}\, \texttt{parent} \sqcap \exists^{\leq 2}\, \texttt{parent} \sqcap \forall\, \texttt{parent}: \texttt{Human} \quad (10)$$

$$T(\texttt{Horse}) = \texttt{Mammal} \sqcap \exists^{\geq 2}\, \texttt{parent} \sqcap \exists^{\leq 2}\, \texttt{parent} \sqcap \forall\, \texttt{parent}: \texttt{Horse}. \quad (11)$$

As is easy to see, $[[\texttt{Human}]]^I = [[\texttt{Horse}]]^I$ for all *gfp*-models because assuming that the denotations are different leads to the conclusion that there is another fixpoint that is greater and has identical denotations for `Human` and `Horse`. That means we have to give up the intuition that (10) defines the concept `Human`. One should add a primitive atomic concept, say `Humanness`, to the definition of `Human`

---

[8] In [Baader, 1990], however, it is shown that Γ is "downward continuous" on $\Psi_{\check{I}}$, which means that any element in the complement of a concept denotation is not contained in some finite approximation of the greatest fixed point denotation of this concept.

in order to distinguish Human from other Mammals with two parents. As a consequence it follows that under *gfp*-semantics the condition that ones parents are human beings is not sufficient for proving that one is a human being as well—a way of reasoning that could be nicely exploited when assertional knowledge is represented as well.

Now that we have an idea what *gfp*-semantics does to restriction-circular concepts, it seems worthwhile to analyze component-circular concepts.

Proposition 8 Let A be a component-circular concept and let $\mathbf{C}_c$ be the largest set of concepts that use A as a component and are used by A as a component. Let $D(A)$ be a concept description identical to $T(A)$ except that all occurrences of concepts from $\mathbf{C}_c$ that do not appear in value restrictions are replaced by $\top$. Then for all $B \in \mathbf{C}_c$: $B \approx_T^{gfp} \sqcap_{A \in \mathbf{C}_c} D(A)$.

Proof: First of all, note that all concepts in $\mathbf{C}_c$ must have the same denotation. Second, since enlarging the denotation of one concept, enlarges the entire interpretation, all concepts in $\mathbf{C}_c$ must have the greatest possible denotation, which is just $\sqcap_{A \in \mathbf{C}_c} D(A)$.

Although this result is less satisfying than proposition 6, it is, of course, tolerable because we are not much interested in component-circular concepts. Furthermore, it shows that under *gfp*-semantics, such cycles can be easily eliminated, as well.

Corollary 3 If the terminology T contains component cycles, then there exists a terminology T' that does not contain component cycles and

I is a gfp-model of T iff I is a gfp-model of T'.

11.4.4 Descriptive Semantics

Finally, descriptive semantics should be briefly characterized. This style of semantics—which is similar to the ordinary semantics of first-order logic—does not lead to equivalence of Humans and Horses because we can think of infinite or circular object structures that satisfy the terminology (10)–(11) without making the denotations of Human and Horse identical. This means on one hand that we can indeed recognize somebody as a Human if and only if her two parents are Humans without being committed to conclude that she is a Horse, as well. On the other hand, the definition does not determine a unique interpretation for given initial, partial interpretations of primitive concepts and roles, which leads to the fact that for data-type-like concepts such as Binary-tree and Ternary-tree expected subsumption relations are missed.

T(`Binary-tree`) = `Tree` $\sqcap \exists^{\leq 2}$ `branch` $\sqcap \forall$ `branch: Binary-tree` (12)
T(`Ternary-tree`) = `Tree` $\sqcap \exists^{\leq 3}$ `branch` $\sqcap \forall$ `branch: Ternary-tree` (13)

Although `Binary-tree` $\leq_T$ `Ternary-tree` is something everybody would expect, descriptive semantics does not support this subsumption relationships because models may contain infinite and circular object structures. However, it should be noted that a hybrid reasoner would classify any (finite) tree-structured object that can be classified as `Binary-tree` as a `Ternary-tree` as well.

In some sense, descriptive semantics seems to assign more importance to *concept names* of circular concepts. Restriction-circular concepts are very similar to primitive concepts in that they can "choose" their denotation. However, since the denotation of these concepts is not completely unconstrained, there are some very subtle relations between such concepts, which will be analyzed in the next section. For component-circular concepts the picture is clearer. We get again the result that such cycles are superfluous and that they can be eliminated without changing the meaning of the terminology.

Proposition 9 Assume as in proposition 8 a component-circular concept A, the largest set of component-circular concepts $\mathbf{C_c}$ that contains A, and $D(A)$ as identical to $T(A)$ except that all concepts occurring in $\mathbf{C_c}$ that appear outside of value restrictions are replaced by $\top$. Then for all $B, B' \in \mathbf{C_c}$:

1. $B \approx_T B'$,
2. $B \leq_T \sqcap_{A \in \mathbf{C_c}} D(A)$,
3. $C \leq_T B$ iff $C \approx_T \bot$ or C uses B as a component.

Proof: The first property follows immediately from the definition of a model in Section 11.2, and the second property is a direct consequence of proposition 8. Furthermore, the "if" direction of the third property is obvious. For the "only if" direction assume that $C \leq_T B$, but C does not use B and $C \not\approx_T \bot$. Let $\mathcal{I}$ be a model such that $[[C]]^{\mathcal{I}} \neq \emptyset$ and $[[C]]^{\mathcal{I}} \subseteq [[B]]^{\mathcal{I}}$. Let $d \in [[C]]^{\mathcal{I}}$. Now extend the model $\mathcal{I}$ to an interpretation $\mathcal{I}'$ with domain $\mathcal{D}' = \mathcal{D} \cup \{d'\}$ such that for all $e \in \mathcal{D}$: $e \in [[R]]^{\mathcal{I}'}(d')$ iff $e \in [[R]]^{\mathcal{I}}(d)$ and $d' \in [[A]]^{\mathcal{I}'}$ iff $d \in [[A]]^{\mathcal{I}}$, for all $R \in \mathbf{R}$ and all $A \in \mathbf{A}$. As can be easily verified, $\mathcal{I}'$ is a model again. Removing d' from $[[B]]^{\mathcal{I}'}$ and from all denotations of concepts that use B as a component leads to another interpretation $\mathcal{J}$, which is again a model. $\mathcal{J}$ does not satisfy our assumption, however.

This means, a set of component circular concepts behaves as if a unique, fresh, primitive concept is used in the definition of all of them. As a matter of fact, we can transform the terminology into such a form without changing "relevant parts" of the models. Let $\mathcal{I}|_X$ denote the restriction of an interpretation to a certain set X of concepts and roles.

Corollary 4 If the terminology T over **A** and **R** contains component cycles, then there exists a terminology T' over **A**′ and **R**, where $\mathbf{A} \subseteq \mathbf{A}'$, such that for every admissible model I of T there exists an admissible model I' of T', and *vice versa*, with $I|_{(\mathbf{A} \cup \mathbf{R})} = I'|_{(\mathbf{A} \cup \mathbf{R})}$, and T' does not contain a component cycle.

Proof: Let $\mathbf{C}_c$ and $D(A)$ be defined as in proposition 9. Let $\mathtt{P} \notin \mathbf{A}$ and $\mathbf{A}' = \mathbf{A} \cup \{\mathtt{P}\}$. Let T' be a terminology defined as follows:

$$T'(A) = \begin{cases} \mathtt{P} & \textit{if } A = \mathtt{P}, \mathtt{P} \\ \mathtt{P} \quad \sqcap \sqcap_{B \in \mathbf{C}_c} D(B) & \textit{if } A \in \mathbf{C}_c, \\ T(A) & \textit{otherwise}. \end{cases}$$

If I is a model of T, then we obtain a model I' of T' by setting $[[X]]^{I'} = [[X]]^{I}$ for all $X \in \mathbf{A} \cup \mathbf{R}$ and $[[\mathtt{P}]]^{I'} = [[B]]^{I}$, for some $B \in \mathbf{C}_c$.

Let I' be a model of T'. Restricting I' to $\mathbf{A} \cup \mathbf{R}$, we get an interpretation I. To show that I is a model of T, we have to verify that all equations $[[A]]^{I} = [[T(A)]]^{I}$ are satisfied. This is trivially true for all concepts $A \notin \mathbf{C}_c$. For the concepts in $\mathbf{C}_c$, the definition can be written as $T(A) = D(A) \sqcap B$ for some $B \in \mathbf{C}_c$. Since $[[A]]^{I'} = [[B]]^{I'}$ and $[[A]]^{I'} \subseteq [[D(A)]]^{I'}$, we know $[[A]]^{I} = [[T(A)]]^{I}$ for all $A \in \mathbf{C}_c$.

Thus, removing component cycles iteratively, we can obtain a terminology T' with the desired property.

11.4.5 Comparing the Different Styles of Semantics

First of all, the different styles of semantics shall be characterized in terms of the induced subsumption relation. It is obvious that subsumption w.r.t. descriptive semantics implies *lfp*- and *gfp*-subsumption because in the former case, more models, i.e., all fixpoints, have to be considered. Furthermore, since *lfp*-semantics tends to force denotations of circular concepts to the empty set, which leads to the fact that `Human` and `Car` are identical, we know that *lfp*-subsumption does not imply *gfp*-subsumption. The converse, however, seems to be plausible—but does not hold. Because of proposition 7, we know that a restriction-circular concept cannot be *lfp*-equivalent to $\top$, but there are restriction-circular concepts that are *gfp*-equivalent to $\top$, for instance, $T(A) = \forall R{:}\, A$.

When evaluating the three styles of semantics against the intuitions spelled out in Section 11.3, it is obvious that *lfp*-semantics is a loser since it forces us to conclude that a number of examples that are intuitively plausible are in fact incoherent. There is no such clear judgement for the remaining two styles, however. Although, at first sight, *gfp*-semantics seems to be the more plausible one, there are a number of good arguments for the descriptive semantics, as well. Greatest fixpoint semantics has on the positive side that

- it supports subsumption relationships one would expect between "structurally similar concepts,"[9] such as the one between `Binary-tree` and `Ternary-tree`;
- it extends an initial partial interpretation to a unique model similar to the acyclic case, i.e., it generalizes the idea of determining the meaning of a concept in terms of the meaning of its parts and the way these are composed.

On the negative side, we find that *gfp*-semantics does not permit a special mode of hybrid reasoning where we conclude the humanness of an object from the humanness of the parents—without some unacceptable consequences. A more serious argument against *gfp*-semantics is that it cannot be generalized to more powerful terminological languages. For instance, if roles can be defined in terms of concepts,[10] Γ is not monotone any longer. The reason is that increasing role denotations leads to smaller concept denotations in the general case.

When considering descriptive semantics, we can conclude that

- by not forcing structurally similar concepts to be equivalent, hybrid reasoning might be better supported,
- it is the conceptually most straightforward generalization of the standard semantics, and
- it can be applied to arbitrary terminological languages.

On the other hand, conditions for subsumption w.r.t. descriptive semantics are conceptually more complicated than *gfp*-semantics, as we will see below.

All in all, I believe there are no conclusive arguments yet. However, by having explored the space of reasonable alternatives, we know now what the implications are—to a certain extent.

11.5 REASONING WITH TERMINOLOGICAL CYCLES

As mentioned in Section 11.1, there are two main reasons terminological cycles are usually omitted. One is the unclear semantics, and the other one is the problem cycles create for subsumption algorithms—a problem we will tackle in this section. Based on results presented in [Nebel, 1990] and [Baader, 1990], it will be shown that subsumption in *general terminologies* that may contain cycles is more difficult than subsumption in acyclic ones. For this purpose, we will concentrate on an even smaller terminological language, called $\mathcal{TL}$, that does not contain minimum and maximum restrictions. Although it seems to be straightforward to

---

[9] This somewhat vague notion will become more precise in the next section.

[10] The `restrict` operator of the language $\mathcal{FL}$ described in [Levesque and Brachman, 1987], for example, can be used for this purpose.

generalize the results obtained for $\mathcal{TLN}$, they cannot be generalized to arbitrarily powerful terminological languages, which is shown by giving an example of a terminological language for which subsumption is decidable in the acyclic case but undecidable when terminological cycles are permitted.

Usually subsumption algorithms are specified over concept descriptions only, assuming that all atomic concepts are primitive (see, for instance, [Levesque and Brachman, 1987; Patel-Schneider, 1989a; Schmidt-Schauß and Smolka, 1990; Hollunder et al., 1990]). This is sufficient as long as the terminology is acyclic because in this case we can expand all nonprimitive concepts by their definitions until the concept descriptions contain only primitive atomic concepts.[11]

In [Nebel, 1990] it was shown that another perspective on subsumption determination in terminologies is possible when considering terminological languages containing only value restrictions and concept conjunctions, namely, to view acyclic terminologies as acyclic *nondeterministic finite state automata* (NDFA). Under this view it turns out that concept equivalence is reducible to automaton equivalence. Similarly, concept subsumption is reducible to inclusion of the languages accepted by the automata.

11.5.1 Viewing Terminologies as Automata

Restricting our attention to a terminological language containing only concept conjunction and value restriction, a normalized terminology T can be viewed as a set of NDFAs

$$\mathcal{A}_{\langle T,A,S\rangle} = (\mathbf{R}, \mathbf{A}, \delta, A, S),$$

where $A \in \mathbf{A}$, $S \subseteq \mathbf{A_p} \cup \{\bot\}$, and

1. $\mathbf{R}$ is the set of *input symbols*,
2. $\mathbf{A}$ is the set of *states*
3. A is the *initial state*,
4. S is the set of *final states*, and
5. the *transition function* δ: $\mathbf{A} \times (\mathbf{R} \cup \{\varepsilon\}) \to 2^{\mathbf{A}}$, where ε is the empty word, is defined as follows. If $P \in \mathbf{A_p} \cup \{\top\}$ then $\delta(P, R) = \emptyset$ for all $R \in \mathbf{R}$. Similarly, for the empty word ε we set $\delta(P, \varepsilon) = \emptyset$. Furthermore, $\delta(\bot, R) = \mathbf{A_p} \cup \{\bot\}$, for all $R \in \mathbf{R} \cup \{\varepsilon\}$. For all nonprimitive concepts $A \in \mathbf{A_n}$, we set $B \in \delta(A, R)$ if and only if $T(A)$ contains a subexpression of the form $\forall R$: B and $B \in \delta(A, \varepsilon)$ if and only if $T(A)$ contains the atomic concept B outside of a value restriction.

[11] Note that these expanded concept descriptions may have a size exponential in the size of the original terminology, however.

A word W is called the *label* of a path from A_0 to A_n iff there is a sequence of states A_0, A_1, ..., A_n, and there is an associated sequence of symbols $R_0, \ldots, R_{n-1}$, where $R_i \in \mathbf{R} \cup \{\varepsilon\}$, such that $R_0 R_1 \ldots R_{n-1} = W$ and $A_{i+1} \in \delta(A_i, R_i)$. Note that by construction of the NDFAs it follows that a label W of a path from A_0 to A_n is a role chain such that A_n can be reached by W from A_0 in T, with the addition that if $\perp$ can be reached by a role chain W from a concept A, then A can reach $\perp$ and all primitive concepts by all role chains of the form $W\mathbf{R}^*$.

The word W is *accepted by* $\mathcal{A}$ iff W is a label of a path from the initial state to one of the final states. The set of all words accepted by $\mathcal{A}$ is called the *language accepted by* $\mathcal{A}$, written $\mathcal{L}(\mathcal{A})$. For $\mathcal{L}(\mathcal{A}_{\langle T,A,S\rangle})$ we will also write $\mathcal{L}(T,A,S)$. Based on this view, subsumption of concepts reduces to inclusion of languages accepted by the associated NDFAs.

Theorem 1 Let T be an acyclic $\mathcal{TL}$-terminology with $A, B \in \mathbf{A}$. Then

$$A \leq_T B \text{ iff } \mathcal{L}(T,A,\{P\}) \supseteq \mathcal{L}(T,B,\{P\}) \textit{ for all } P \in \mathbf{A_p} \cup \{\perp\}.$$

Proof sketch: The proof follows by generalizing the proof of theorem 2 in [Nebel, 1990]. Note that in order to decide inclusion of languages for the automata $\mathcal{A}_{\langle T,A,S\rangle}$ generated from acyclic terminologies it suffices to consider only words up to a length of $\|\mathbf{A_n}\|$.

Intuitively, this theorem says that the set of constraints of the form $\forall W$: P ($P \in \mathbf{A_p} \cup \{\perp\}$) that an instance of a concept has to obey is the same as the set of words the corresponding automata with final state P recognize. This reduction has a number of important consequences. For instance, it can be used to show that concept subsumption in acyclic $\mathcal{TL}$-terminologies is more difficult than perceived, namely, of the same complexity as the equivalence problem for NDFAs that accept finite languages, which is a co-NP-complete problem [Garey and Johnson, 1979, p. 265].

Corollary 5 Concept subsumption in acyclic $\mathcal{TL}$-terminologies is co-NP-complete.

Proof: Note that $C \leq_T D$ can be reduced to subsumption of atomic concepts in polynomial time by adding appropriate definitions to the terminology, and by theorem 1 this problem can be reduced to a language inclusion problem, i.e., subsumption is in co-NP. Since by employing theorem 1, automaton equivalence for acyclic automata can be polynomially reduced to concept equivalence in acyclic terminologies, which can be reduced in polynomial time to subsumption (proposition 1), subsumption is co-NP-hard.

This means subsumption in acyclic terminologies is co-NP-hard for all terminological formalisms considered so far—even when subsumption determination over concept descriptions is polynomial. However, subsumption determination in acyclic terminologies seems to be fairly efficient in almost all cases occurring in practice [Nebel, 1990].

Additionally, theorem 1 shows that instead of expanding definitions and determining subsumption over concept descriptions, it is also possible to transform the terminology into a form corresponding to a deterministic automaton for which equivalence and subsumption can be decided in polynomial time—which is often more efficient than the former strategy.[12] Finally, it provides us with a tool that can be used to characterize subsumption in cyclic terminologies.

11.5.2 Subsumption in General Terminologies

Since component cycles can be removed from a terminology without changing the meaning of any concept (see corollaries 1, 3, and 4), and since this can be obviously done in polynomial time, let us assume in the following that there are no such cycles.[13] This means we have to consider only restriction cycles.

In trying to generalize the view spelled out above, one notes that in general terminologies it is not enough to consider only finite role chains, but infinite role chains are also important (see proposition 7). In order to capture this formally, let $\mathcal{U}(T,A,\emptyset)$ be the set of all (infinite) labels of infinite paths starting at the initial state A. Furthermore, sometimes even the atomic concepts may play a role, as is highlighted by the "`Tree`" terminology (12)–(13)). Formalizing this aspect, let $AW_0BW_1BW_2\ldots$ denote the infinite path starting at A which reaches B infinitely often where W_j are nonempty labels from A to B for $j = 0$ and from B to B for $j > 0$.

Based on the view spelled out above, Baader [1990] analyzed subsumption in general $\mathcal{TL}$-terminologies and characterized subsumption as follows.[14]

Theorem 2 Let T be a general $\mathcal{TL}$-terminology, and let A, B be two atomic concepts. Then

$$A \preceq_T^{gfp} B \text{ iff}$$
$$\mathcal{L}(T,A,\{P\}) \supseteq \mathcal{L}(T,B,\{P\}) \text{ for all } P \in \mathbf{A_p} \cup \{\bot\}.$$

---

[12] As a matter of fact, this technique is used in most implemented terminological representation systems. See, for instance, the informal description of the first implemented terminological reasoning component in KL-ONE [Lipkis, 1982].

[13] Note that component cycles correspond to ε-cycles in the associated automata.

[14] In [Baader, 1990], also ε-cycles are covered, which we eliminated beforehand.

$A \preceq_T^{lfp} B$ iff

1. $\mathcal{L}(T,A,\{P\}) \supseteq \mathcal{L}(T,B,\{P\})$ for all $P \in \mathbf{A_p} \cup \{\bot\}$ and
2. $\mathcal{U}(T,A,\varnothing) \supseteq \mathcal{U}(T,B,\varnothing)$.

$A \preceq_T B$ iff

1. $\mathcal{L}(T,A,\{P\}) \supseteq \mathcal{L}(T,B,\{P\})$ for all $P \in \mathbf{A_p} \cup \{\bot\}$ and
2. for all infinite paths $B\ W_0\ B'W_1B'W_2 \ldots$ there is a natural number $k \geq 0$ such that $W_0W_1\ldots W_k$ is a label of a path from A to B' or to $\bot$.

Proof: Generalize the proofs in [Baader, 1990] to cover $\bot$.

A consequence of this result is that *gfp*-subsumption and *lfp*-subsumption in general terminologies is more difficult than subsumption in acyclic terminologies—from a theoretical point of view.

Corollary 6 Concept subsumption w.r.t. *lfp*- and *gfp*-semantics in general $\mathcal{TL}$-terminologies is PSPACE-complete.

Proof: Since the PSPACE-complete problem of deciding language inclusion for general NDFAs and the problem of deciding concept subsumption for general $\mathcal{TL}$-terminologies are interreducible for *gfp*-semantics, *gfp*-subsumption is PSPACE-complete. For a proof of PSPACE-completeness of *lfp*-subsumption see [Baader, 1990].

Additionally, it shows that *gfp*-semantics has indeed the conceptually easiest characterization. Furthermore, it leads directly to deterministic algorithms for *gfp*-subsumption determination in general $\mathcal{TL}$-terminologies, namely, a transformation of the NDFA corresponding to the terminology to a deterministic automaton, on which language inclusion can be decided in polynomial time. In general, the set of states that can be reached by the initial state increases exponentially when transforming a nondeterministic into an equivalent deterministic automaton. However, I expect that this behavior occurs rather seldomly in the context of terminologies because terminologies are usually formulated in a way such that the corresponding NDFA is "almost" deterministic.

Unfortunately, descriptive semantics does not lead to such a straightforward result. In [Baader, 1990] it is shown that subsumption w.r.t. descriptive semantics can be reduced to an inclusion problem for a class of languages containing infinite words (languages accepted by Büchi automata).

An alternative characterization in terms of the *structure* of automata can be given when the corresponding *deterministic* automaton (DFA) is considered.[15] Let

[15] A DFA has no ε-transitions, and the transition function does not map states and symbols to sets of states but to single states.

$\mathcal{A}_{\langle T,A,S\rangle} = (\mathbf{R}, \mathbf{A}, \delta, A, S)$ be a NDFA as defined above. Then $\hat{\mathcal{A}}_{\langle T,A,\hat{S}\rangle} = (\mathbf{R}, \hat{\mathbf{A}}, \hat{\delta}, A, \hat{S})$ shall denote the corresponding DFA, which can be created using the *subset construction* (see, e.g., [Lewis and Papadimitriou, 1981, p.59]). Each state $X \in \hat{\mathbf{A}}$ is a subset of the states in the NDFA, where singletons are identified with elements.

For notational convenience, $\hat{\delta}^*$ will be used to denote the canonical extension of the transition function $\hat{\delta}$ to words, i.e., $\hat{\delta}^*(X, \varepsilon) = X$ and $\hat{\delta}^*(X, RW) = \hat{\delta}^*(\hat{\delta}(X,R),W)$.

Using these assumptions, concept equivalence for descriptive semantics can be characterized in terms of language equivalence and the structure of the DFA.[16] Informally, two concepts A and B are equivalent if and only if the corresponding automatons accept the same language, and there are not two different cycles with identical labels in the DFAs such that one is reachable from A by a word W and the other one is reachable by the same word W from B.

Proposition 10 Let T be a general $\mathcal{TL}$-terminology. Then $A \approx_T B$ iff

1. $\mathcal{L}(T, A, \{P\}) = \mathcal{L}(T, B, \{P\})$ for all P $\mathbf{A_P} \cup \{\bot\}$ and
2. for all words $W \in \mathbf{R}^*$, if $X = \hat{\delta}^*(A,W)$, $Y = \hat{\delta}^*(B,W)$, and $X \neq Y$, then there is no word $V \in \mathbf{R}^+$ such that $X = \hat{\delta}^*(X,V)$ and $Y = \hat{\delta}^*(Y,V)$.

Proof: For the "if" direction assume that the concepts are not equivalent. By theorem 2, either the languages of the automata are not identical—which violates the first condition in the proposition—or there exists w.l.g. an infinite path in in the NDFA of the form $AW_1\, B'\, W_2\, B' \ldots$ such that for no $k \geq 0$ there is a label $W_1\, W_2 \ldots W_k$ of a path from B to B'.

Note that for a path of the above form in the NDFA starting at A there is a corresponding path in the DFA with the same label and there is at least one state $Z \in \hat{\mathbf{A}}$ that appears infinitely often and $B' \in Z$, i.e., there is an infinite path $AV_1ZV_2Z \ldots$ in the DFA. Starting at B in the DFA, we have a similar path and a sequence of states $Z_1, Z_2, \ldots$ such that $BV_1Z_1V_2Z_2 \ldots$. Since there are only finitely many states in the DFA, we know that there are i,j such that $Z_i = Z_j$. Assuming that $Z = Z_i = Z_j$ would result in the conclusion that there is a number $k \geq 0$ s.t. there is a path $BW_1W_2 \ldots W_kB'$ in the NDFA, which contradicts our assumption. Assuming that $Z \neq Z_i$ violates the second condition in the proposition. Hence, if the concepts are not equivalent, then one of the conditions will be violated.

For the "only if" direction assume that the concepts are equivalent, but one of the conditions is violated. If the first condition is violated, then by theorem 2, the concepts cannot be equivalent. If the second condition is violated, then there are words W, V and states $X,Y \in \hat{\mathbf{A}}$ such that the condition is violated. Without loss of

[16] Note that it is not possible to describe concept subsumption in terms of the structure of the DFA.

generality, let us assume $X - Y \neq \emptyset$. Choose one element B' in $X - Y$ such that there is path $B'V^nB'$ in the NDFA, for some $n > 0$. Such an element exists because of the following reasons. Since $X = \hat{\delta}^*(X,V)$, each element in X must be reachable in the NDFA by V from some element in X. Assuming that there is no state $B' \in X - Y$ s.t. $B'V^nB'$ is a path in the NDFA leads to the conclusion that some elements in $X - Y$ must be reachable in the NDFA by V from some elements in $Y \cap X$. This, however, means $Y \neq \hat{\delta}^*(Y,V)$.

Finally, using the chosen state B', it is possible to find an infinite path of the form $AWB'V^nB'V^n$... in the NDFA such that there is no natural number k with $BWV^n\ B'$. Thus, the concepts cannot be equivalent by theorem 2.

This observation leads to a PSPACE decision procedure for equivalence (and, thus, subsumption) of concepts w.r.t. to descriptive semantics.[17]

Corollary 7 Concept subsumption w.r.t. to descriptive semantics in general $\mathcal{TL}$-terminologies is in PSPACE.

Proof: Guessing two words W,V and two sets of states $S,S' \subseteq \mathbf{A}$, we can verify in polynomial space that the the second condition in proposition 10 is violated. Since the first condition can be checked in polynomial space, as well, concept equivalence is in PSPACE. Since concept equivalence and subsumption are interreducible in linear time, concept subsumption is also in PSPACE.

It is by no means obvious, however, whether subsumption w.r.t. descriptive semantics is PSPACE-complete or easier.

11.5.3 Terminological Cycles in More Powerful Languages

After having now an idea what subsumption algorithms for general terminologies look like and how difficult subsumption determination can be, there is the natural question of how to extend this result to more powerful terminological languages.

In [Nebel, 1989], a slightly more powerful language was analyzed with respect to terminological cycles. This language contains $\mathcal{TLN}$ plus subroles and negation of primitive concepts. It was shown that subsumption w.r.t. descriptive semantics is still decidable for this formalism by using an argument to the effect that it is always possible to consider only models up to a certain finite size in order to decide subsumption. Generalizing this argument, it seems possible to prove decidability for other languages. There are, of course, limits. In order to demonstrate where these limits are, $\mathcal{TL}$ will be extended in a way such that it captures an

---

[17] The same result follows from the reduction to inclusion of languages accepted Büchi automatons [Baader, 1990].

essential subset of the terminological language used in the CLASSIC system [Brachman et al., 1989; Borgida et al., 1989].

Let us assume a set **F** of *single-valued roles*, also called *features*[18] in the following, (denoted by f) that is a subset of **R**. The interpretation of these features is constrained by

$$\| [\![f]\!]^I(d) \| \leq 1 \textit{ for all } d \in \mathcal{D} \textit{ and all } f \in \mathbf{F},$$

Chains of features are denoted by v and w. These are interpreted in the same way as role-chains (see Section 11.4.2). Finally, we define a new description-forming operator $v \downarrow w$, called *coreference constraint*, intended to denote all elements such that the role filler of v is identical to the role filler of w, formally:

$$[\![v \downarrow w]\!]^I = \{d \in \mathcal{D} | \, [\![v]\!]^I(d) = [\![w]\!]^I(d)\}$$

Adding this operator to $\mathcal{TL}$ results in a terminological language—we will call $\mathcal{TLC}$—with a very interesting property. Subsumption over concept descriptions in acyclic $\mathcal{TLC}$-terminologies is decidable,[19] but if terminological cycles come into play, subsumption becomes undecidable.

The claim above will be shown by reducing the word problem in Thue systems to subsumption in general $\mathcal{TLC}$-terminologies using the same proof technique as in [Schmidt-Schauß, 1989] and [Smolka, 1989]. A *Thue system* is a finite set of unordered pairs $\mathcal{S} = \{\{v_i, w_i\}\}$, where v_i and w_i are words over an alphabet **F**. Two words $v, w \in \mathbf{F}^*$ are *interderivable in one step*, written $v \overset{\mathcal{S}}{\leftrightarrow} w$, iff

$$v = xv_jy \textit{ and } w = xw_jy \textit{ for some } \{v_j, w_j\} \in \mathcal{S}$$

Two words v,w are *interderivable* iff they are related by the transitive, reflexive closure of $\overset{\mathcal{S}}{\leftrightarrow}$, which will be denoted by $\overset{\mathcal{S}}{\Leftrightarrow}$. Note that $\overset{\mathcal{S}}{\Leftrightarrow}$ is an equivalence relation on $\mathbf{F}^*$. The *word problem in Thue systems* is the problem to decide whether $v \overset{\mathcal{S}}{\Leftrightarrow} w$. It is well known that this problem is undecidable (see e.g., [Lewis and Papadimitriou, 1981; Section 6.4]).

Lemma 2 Let $\mathcal{S} = \{\{v_i, w_i\}\}$ be a Thue system over an alphabet $\mathbf{F} = \{f_j\}$, and let T be the following $\mathcal{TLC}$-terminology:

$$T(A) = \sqcap \; \forall f_j \colon A \sqcap \; \sqcap \; v_i \downarrow w_i.$$

---

[18] I use the term *features* because single-valued roles are essentially the same as features in *feature logic* (see, e.g., [Nebel and Smolka, 1990]).

[19] Note that coreference constraints lead to undecidability of subsumption in acyclic terminologies if the role chains in the constraint are not features but ordinary roles [Schmidt-Schauß, 1989]. If the role chains are built out of features, however, one can use the technique described in [Aït-Kaci, 1984] to obtain a polynomial subsumption algorithm.

Then

$$* \overset{S}{\Leftrightarrow} w \textit{ iff } [\![A]\!]^I \subseteq [\![v \downarrow w]\!]^I \textit{ for all models } I \textit{ of } T.$$

Proof: Let I be a model of T and assume $v \overset{S}{\leftrightarrow} w$, where $v = xv_iy$ and $w = xw_iy$. Now we know for all $d \in [\![A]\!]^I$: $[\![x]\!]^I(d) \subseteq [\![A]\!]^I$ (because of $\sqcap\ \forall f_j\colon A$). From that it follows that $[\![xv_i]\!]^I(d) = [\![xw_i]\!]^I(d)$, hence $[\![v]\!]^I(d) = [\![w]\!]^I(d)$ for all $d \in [\![A]\!]^I$. By induction, we can conclude that $[\![A]\!]^I \subseteq [\![v \downarrow w]\!]^I$ if $v \overset{S}{\Leftrightarrow} w$.

For the other direction assume that $[\![A]\!]^I \subseteq [\![v \downarrow w]\!]^I$ for all models I of T. Let $[x]_S$ denote the equivalence class of x w.r.t. $\overset{S}{\Leftrightarrow}$. Now we construct a particular model of T as follows:

$$\mathcal{D} = \{[x]_S \mid x \in \mathbf{F}^*\}$$
$$[\![f_j]\!]^I = \{[x]_S \mapsto \{[xf_j]_S\}\}$$
$$[\![A]\!]^I = \mathcal{D}.$$

Obviously, I is a model of T since

1. for all $d \in [\![A]\!]^I$ it holds that $[\![f_j]\!]^I(d) \in [\![A]\!]^I$ for all $f_j \in \mathbf{F}$, and
2. $[\![v_i]\!]^I(d) = [\![w_i]\!]^I(d)$ for all pairs $\{v_i, w_i\}$ of the Thue system $\mathcal{S}$ because $[\![v_i]\!]^I([x]_S) = \{[xv_i]_S\} = \{[xw_i]_S\} = [\![w_i]\!]^I([x]_S)$.

Because of our assumption, we know that $[\![v]\!]^I(d) = [\![w]\!]^I(d)$ for all elements $d \in [\![A]\!]^I = \mathcal{D}$. Thus, in particular, we have $[\![v]\!]^I([\varepsilon]_S) = [\![w]\!]^I([\varepsilon]_S)$, hence $[\varepsilon v]_S = [\varepsilon w]_S$, hence $[v]_S = [w]_S$, which means $v \overset{S}{\Leftrightarrow} w$.

From that the undecidability of subsumption w.r.t. descriptive semantics follows immediately.

Theorem 3 Subsumption w.r.t. descriptive semantics in general $\mathcal{TLC}$-terminologies is undecidable.

Proof: Since the word problem in Thue systems is undecidable, and it can be reduced to subsumption w.r.t. to descriptive semantics, subsumption w.r.t. descriptive semantics is undecidable.

As should be obvious, adding coreference constraints to our language does not change the monotonicity of Γ, i.e., it makes sense to ask about the behavior of subsumption under *lfp*- and *gfp*-semantics. It is easy to see that the above result applies to *gfp*-semantics, as well.

Corollary 8 Subsumption w.r.t. *gfp*-semantics in general $\mathcal{TLC}$-terminologies is undecidable.

Proof: Since the first part of lemma 2 applies to all models, it applies to *gfp*-models, as well. The model constructed in the second part of the proof is a *gfp*-model, as can be easily verified.

Unfortunately, the proof technique used above does not seem to be usable for showing *lfp*-subsumption to be undecidable. However, since we ruled out this semantics in Section 11.4.5 because of other reasons, we will not dig deeper at this point.

In general, these undecidability results mean that terminological cycles are not always tolerable. In particular, when coreference constraints are part of the language, the unrestricted use of terminological cycles should be prohibited.

11.6 CONCLUSIONS

Terminological cycles present conceptual and algorithmic problems for terminological representation systems. As shown in Section 11.4, it is possible to extend the standard semantics of terminological representation formalisms to cover cyclic terminologies. However, it is not completely obvious which style of semantics is the best one. Greatest fixpoint semantics has the advantage that it leads to a conceptually simple subsumption relation, which is identical to language inclusion of the nondeterministic automata corresponding to the terminology. However this style of semantics cannot be extended to cover more powerful formalisms. Descriptive semantics, on the other hand, is the most straightforward extension of the standard semantics, covers all conceivable terminological formalisms, and permits interesting inferences in hybrid representation systems, but leads to subsumption relationships which are not fully obvious—except if one considers the structure of the deterministic automata corresponding to a terminology. Finally, it was shown that the unrestricted use of terminological cycles can lead to undecidability. In particular, it was shown that adding terminological cycles to an essential subset of the terminological formalism used in the CLASSIC systems results in undecidability.

ACKNOWLEDGMENTS

This paper greatly profited from discussions with Franz Baader, Kai von Luck, Bob Mac Gregor, Bernd Mahr, Peter Patel-Schneider, Christof Peltason, Albrecht Schmiedel, Jim Schmolze, Gert Smolka, and Marc Vilain. In particular Franz helped me to get a deeper understanding of some of the subtle points in subsumption determination in cyclic terminologies. Also, Alfred Kobsa and Peter Patel-Schneider provided valuable comments on this paper.

References

Aït-Kaci, H. 1984. *A Lattice-Theoretic Approach to Computations Based on a Calculus of Partially Ordered Type Structures.* PhD thesis, University of Pennsylvania, PA.

Baader, F. 1990. Terminological cycles in KL-ONE-based knowledge representation languages. In *Proceedings of the Eighth National Conference of the American Association for Artificial Intelligence.* AAAI, Menlo Park, CA.

Borgida, A., Brachman, R.J., McGuinness, D.L. and Resnick, L.A. 1989 CLASSIC: A structural data model for objects. In *Proceedings of the 1989 ACM SIGMOD International Conference on Management of Data*, pp. 59–67.

Brachman, R.J. 1979. On the epistemological status of semantic networks. In *Associative Networks: Representation and Use of Knowledge by Computers*, Findler, N.V. (ed.), pp. 3–50. Academic Press, New York.

Brachman, R.J. and Levesque, H.J. 1982. Competence in knowledge representation. In *Proceedings of the Second National Conference of the American Association for Artificial Intelligence*, pp. 189–192. AAAI, Menlo Park, CA

———. 1984. The tractability of subsumption in frame-based description languages. In *Proceedings of the Fourth National Conference of the American Association for Artificial Intelligence*, pp. 34–37. AAAI, Menlo Park, CA.

Brachman, R.J. and Schmolze, J.G. 1985. An overview of the KL-ONE knowledge representation system. *Cognitive Science*, 9(2):171–216.

Brachman, R.J., Gilbert, V.P., and Levesque, H.J. 1985. An essential hybrid reasoning system: Knowledge and symbol level accounts in KRYPTON. In *Proceedings of the Ninth International Joint Conference on Artificial Intelligence*, pp. 532–539. IJCAI proceedings are available from Morgan Kaufmann Publishers, San Mateo, CA.

Brachman, R.J., Borgida, A., McGuinness, D.L., Patel-Schneider, P., and Resnick, L.A. 1991. Living with CLASSIC: When and how to use a KL-ONE-like language. This volume.

Edelmann, J.E. and Owsnicki, B. 1986. Data models in knowledge representation systems: A case study. In *GWAI-86 und 2. Österreichische Artificial-Intelligence-Tagung*, Rollinger, C.-R. and Horn, W. (ed.s), pp. 69–74. Springer-Verlag, Berlin.

Garey, M.R. and Johnson, D.S. 1979. *Computers and Intractability—A Guide to the Theory of NP-Completeness.* Freeman, San Francisco, CA.

Hollunder, B., Nutt, W., and Schmidt-Schauß, M. 1990. Subsumption algorithms for concept description languages. In *Proceedings of the Ninth European Conference on Artificial Intelligence*, pp. 348–353.

Kaczmarek, T.S., Bates, R., and Robins, G. Recent developments in NIKL. In *Proceedings of the Fifth National Conference of the American Association for Artificial Intelligence*, pp. 978–987. AAAI, Menlo Park, CA.

Kobsa, A. 1991. Utilizing knowledge: The components of the SB-ONE knowledge representation workbench. This volume, Chapter 15.

Levesque, H.J. and Brachman, R.J. 1987. Expressiveness and tractability in knowledge representation and reasoning. *Computational Intelligence*, 3:78–93.

Lewis, H.R. and Papadimitriou, C.H. 1981. *Elements of the Theory of Computation.* Prentice Hall, Englewood Cliffs, N.J.

Lipkis, T. 1982. A KL-ONE classifier. In *Proceedings of the 1981 KL-ONE Workshop*, Schmolze, J.G. and Brachman, R.J. (ed.s), pp. 128–145, Cambridge, MA. The proceedings have been published as BBN Report No. 4842 and Fairchild Technical Report No. 618.

Lloyd, J.W. *Foundations of Logic Programming*. Springer-Verlag, Berlin, West Germany.

Mac Gregor, R. 1988. A deductive pattern matcher. In *Proceedings of the Seventh National Conference of the American Association for Artificial Intelligence*, pp. 403–408. AAAI, Menlo Park, CA.

Nebel, B. 1988. Computational complexity of terminological reasoning in BACK. *Artificial Intelligence*, 34(3):371–383.

———. 1990a. *Reasoning and Revision in Hybrid Representation Systems*, volume 422 of *Lecture Notes in Computer Science*. Springer-Verlag, Berlin, West Germany.

———. 1990b. Terminological reasoning is inherently intractable. *Artificial Intelligence*, 43:235–249.

Nebel, B. and Luck, K. von. 1988. Hybrid reasoning in BACK. In *Methodologies for Intelligent Systems*, Ras, Z.W. and Saitta, L. (ed.s),volume 3, pp. 260–269. North-Holland, Amsterdam, Holland.

Nebel, B. and Smolka, G. 1990. Representation and reasoning with attributive descriptions. In *Sorts and Types in Artificial Intelligence*, Bläsius, K.-H., Hedtstück, U., and Rollinger, C.-R. (ed.s), pp. 112–139. Springer-Verlag, Berlin, West Germany.

Neches, R., Swartout, W.R. and Moore, J.D. 1985. Explainable (and maintainable) expert systems. In *Proceedings of the Ninth International Joint Conference on Artificial Intelligence*, pp. 382–389. IJCAI proceedings are available from Morgan Kaufmann Publishers, San Mateo, CA.

Owsnicki-Klewe, B. 1988. Configuration as a consistency maintenance task. In *GWAI-88. 12th German Workshop on Artificial Intelligence*, Hoeppner, W. (ed.), pp. 77–87. Springer-Verlag, Berlin.

Patel-Schneider, P.F., Brachman, R.J., and Levesque, H.J. 1984. ARGON: Knowledge representation meets information retrieval. In *Proceedings of the First Conference on Artificial Intelligence Applications*, pp. 280–286.

Patel-Schneider, P.F. 1984. Small can be beautiful in knowledge representation. In *Proceedings of the IEEE Workshop on Principles of Knowledge-Based Systems*, pp. 11–16. An extended version including a KANDOR system description is available as AI Technical Report No. 37, Palo Alto, Cal., Schlumberger Palo Alto Research, October 1984.

———. 1986. A four-valued semantics for frame-based description languages. In *Proceedings of the Fifth National Conference of the American Association for Artificial Intelligence*, pp. 344–348. AAAI, Menlo Park, CA.

———. 1989a. A four-valued semantics for terminological logics. *Artificial Intelligence*, 38(3):319–351.

———. 1989b. Undecidability of subsumption in NIKL. *Artificial Intelligence*, 39(2):263–272.

Schild, Klaus. 1988. Undecidability of $\mathcal{U}$. KIT Report 67, Department of Computer Science, Technische Universität Berlin, Berlin, West Germany, October 1988.

Schmidt-Schauß, M. and Smolka, G. 1991. Attributive concept descriptions with unions and complements. *Artificial Intelligence*, 47. To appear.

Schmidt-Schauß, M. 1989. Subsumption in KL-ONE is undecidable. In *Proceedings of the First International Conference on Principles of Knowledge Representation and Reasoning*, Brachman, R.J., Levesque, H.J., and Reiter, R. (ed.s), pp. 421–431.

Schmolze, J.G. and Brachman, R.J. (ed.s). *Proceedings of the 1981 KL-ONE Workshop*, Bolt, Beranek, and Newman Inc., Cambridge, MA, BBN Report No. 4842.

Schmolze, J.G., and Israel, D.J. 1983. KL-ONE: Semantics and classification. In *Research in Knowledge Representation and Natural Language Understanding, BBN Technical Report, No. 5421*, pp. 27–39. Bolt, Beranek, and Newman Inc., Cambridge, MA, 1983.

Schmolze, J.G. 1989. *The Language and Semantics of NIKL*. Technical Report 89–4, Department of Computer Science, Tufts University, Medford, MA.

Smolka, G. 1989. *Feature Constraint Logics for Unification Grammars*. IWBS Report 93, IBM Germany Scientific Center, IWBS, Stuttgart, West Germany, November 1989. To appear in *Proceedings of the Workshop on Unification Formalisms—Syntax, Semantics, and Implementation*. Titisee, April 1988, The MIT Press.

Sondheimer, N.K. and Nebel, B. 1986. A logical-form and knowledge-base design for natural language generation. In *Proceedings of the Fifth National Conference of the American Association for Artificial Intelligence*, pp. 612–618. AAAI, Menlo Park, CA.

Swartout, W.R. and Neches, R. 1986. The shifting terminological space: An impediment to evolvability. In *Proceedings of the Fifth National Conference of the American Association for Artificial Intelligence*, pp. 936–941.

Tarski, A. 1955. A lattice-theoretical fixpoint theorem and its applications. *Pacific Journal of Mathematics*, 5:285–309.

Vilain, M.B. 1985. The restricted language architecture of a hybrid representation system. In *Proceedings of the Ninth International Joint Conference on Artificial Intelligence*, pp. 547–551. IJCAI proceedings are available from Morgan Kaufmann Publishers, San Mateo, CA.

von Luck, K., Nebel, B., Peltason, C., and Schmiedel, A. 1987. *The Anatomy of the BACK System*. KIT Report 41, Department of Computer Science, Technische Universität Berlin, Berlin, West Germany.

Webber, B.L. and Bobrow, R.J. 1980. Knowledge representation for syntactic/semantic processing. In *Proceedings of the First National Conference of the American Association for Artificial Intelligence*, pp. 316–323. AAAI, Menlo Park, CA.

12

LOGICAL DIMENSIONS OF SOME GRAPH FORMALISMS

Wlodek Zadrozny
(IBM T. J. Watson Research Center, New York)

Abstract

One can imagine that in knowledge representation and reasoning systems graphs could appear not only for psychological but also for formal reasons. In a graph-based logic, syntax, proof theory and semantics (or model theory) would refer to graph-theoretic properties of terms that are manipulated. The main thesis of this chapter is that, to our best knowledge, there is yet no such graph-based logic. But we believe that a graph-based logic of concepts can be formulated. In this context, we discuss logical properties of three knowledge representation formalisms that directly refer to graph-theoretic properties: conceptual graphs (Sowa), higraphs (Harel), and the three-level semantics (Zadrozny). We describe the relationships among concepts that are made explicit in those formalisms (respectively): the structure of propositions, the structure of a model, and the plausibility of interpretations.

As a conclusion we formulate the thesis that the adequacy of a formalism should be judged by its capacity to offer new tools, which seems to be a more quantifiable criterion than fidelity to intuitions (see also [Israel, 1983]).

12.1 MOTIVATION

Harel [1988] has proposed *higraphs* (abbreviated HGs) as a visual formalism suited for many applications, including knowledge representation. His treatment of the subject is formal, so that higraphs can be "manipulated, maintained and analyzed by computers"; but these forms are also assumed "to be generated, comprehended, and communicated by humans." Earlier, Sowa [1976, 1984] introduced *conceptual graphs* (CGs, for short) as a knowledge representation language, his aims being quite similar to those of Harel's, although he emphasized natural language as the main domain of application. Both formalisms seem to be quite expressive; and the natural question arises about their strengths and their relationship to logic. The third formalism we are to discuss—the *three-level semantics* (see also [Zadrozny and Jensen, 1991])—does not use graphs to represent concepts or propositions, but in developing its notion of a (default) proof and an interpretation it uses graph-theoretic terms, like *dominance*, *link*, or *distance*.

The main question we want to explore is whether graphs appear in these formalisms just for psychological reasons (people like them) or perhaps they also have some formal function.

We discuss these formalisms from the perspective of natural language understanding (NLU). In many NLU programs, trees are used to represent the structure of sentences; graphs are used for the same purpose, as well as to represent the attribute-value structure of the parse trees; connections and distances are incorporated into marker passing or activation-spreading algorithms. Sowa's CGs have already been applied in NLU, HGs have such a potential, and the three-level semantics is currently being implemented as a part of an NLU system.

Usually, relations that are explicitly represented are easier to compute. An ideal representation should also be expressive and easy to use, and it should have a formal semantics. We believe that the transfer of techniques and insights among various formalisms will give more adequate representations for NLU.

From a logical point of view, knowledge representation systems are usually discussed along the following dimensions:

- *Syntactic*: What are the classes of well-formed expressions in these formalisms? Is one class bigger than the other?
- *Semantic*: What are their models? How can they be constructed? In other words, what are the entities the formalisms deal with, and what kind of relations can be expected to hold among them?
- *Proof theoretic*: What kind of inferences do these formalisms support? What kind of syntactic structures can be built by applying the rules and can any graph be derived?
- *Decidability and computational complexity*: How difficult is it to formally manipulate these objects? How difficult is it to prove something about (or with) them?

Since we want to deal with graph-based formalisms, we should add a new aspect: whether these formalisms use graphs in semantically, or just psychologically, significant ways?

We want to study the three systems (CGs, HGs, and the three-level semantics), because they stress different aspects of knowledge representation, and they offer different tools. These tools, we believe, can be combined but analyzing them is a prerequisite of engineering.

12.2 CONCEPTUAL GRAPHS

Sowa [1984] introduced CGs, gave semantics of "first-order" CGs (FOCGs), proved the soundness and completeness of this system by mapping it into first-order logic, and applied the graphs to a variety of problems. Work on extending the language and broadening the areas of application was later continued by Sowa, Fargues et al. [1986], and others. It seems to us that the underlying semantic assumption of these extensions was that, if necessary, a mapping from them into an extension of classical logic (e.g., a modal logic, in the case of CGs with modalities) can be found. This assumption is almost certainly correct for large subsystems of these extended CGs. This work however has not been done. In particular we do not know the exact expressive power of the following:

- CGs allowing set quantifiers (or other quantifiers):

  Example. Sowa (There is more ...) uses *Dist* {*} (which stands for the distributive reading of the set quantifier) and *Col* {*} (collective) as set quantifiers with the intended meaning described by the correspondence of the conceptual graph

  [BLOCK: Dist{*}] ← (PTNT) ← [SUPPORT] → (INST) →

  → [PYRAMID: Col{*}@3]

  with the sentence *Some blocks are each supported by three pyramids.*

  Here and in the next example, INST, PTNT, OBJ, AGT stand for "instrument," "patient," "object," and "agent."

How much set theory do we need to deal with sentences containing Col and Dist? No precise answer has been given, although some work in that direction has been done by Gardiner et al. [1989]. In general, the problems with sets in computational contexts are nontrivial as the papers of Beeri et al. [1987] or Shmueli and Naqvi [1987] prove.

- CGs with "propositions": They are needed, for instance, to model propositional attitudes.

  Example.

  [PERSON: 'John'] ← (AGT) ← [BELIEVE] → (OBJ) →

  [PROPOSITION:

  [BLOCK: Dist{*}] ← (PTNT) ← [SUPPORT] → (INST) →

  → [PYRAMID: Col{*}@3]]

  John believes that some blocks are each supported by three pyramids.

How weak would the corresponding higher order logic be?

It is not clear whether the sum of all these extensions is consistent. This is an important question if we want to have one supertheory of representation. On the other hand, we can view all these extensions as separate theories, and then we face a problem of assigning semantic roles to these extensions, which means finding appropriate logics for different fragments of natural language and ways of combining them.

The presence of graph-theoretic concepts in the logic of conceptual graphs can be summarized as follows:

- CGs represent formulas/propositions. A collection of CGs represents a theory (Sowa [1984, p. 152] talks about its consistency).
- Since a model can be viewed as a collection of grounded formulas, one can represent a model as a collection of CGs, i.e., a theory.
- The inference rules can be expressed in graph-theoretic terms, like *projection*, *restriction*, and *matching* (compare Fargues et al. [1986]).
- But, since the theory of FOCGs corresponds to first-order logic, its semantics is standard and graphs can be eliminated without any loss in the expressive power.
- Because of the above correspondence and the undecidability of satisfaction, there is no algorithm for deriving a model for a collection of CGs.
- Models of a collection of CGs can be infinite.
- Graph properties of background knowledge, like proximity or connectedness, play almost no semantic role (except for the lattice of types).

Notice the conflict between the need for expressive power in order to handle natural language expressions and the difficulty in inferencing and constructing a model. Sowa's work addresses only the first problem. One the other hand, graphs and higraphs offer some help in dealing with the complexity issue, see Sections 12.3 and 12.4. The trade-offs between the expressive power and computability are discussed by Levesque and Brachman [1985], and their insights apply to graph-based formalisms, too. And although for some purposes the low complexity of higraphs can be an advantage, CGs have a lot to offer: Slagle and Vayghan [1988] list more than two dozen requirements for a knowledge representation system and argue that CGs satisfy most of them. They may be right, but we believe that certain types of information can be represented better by higraphs and their derivative—state charts; namely, information about structure, flow of control, and time. For how this can be done, the reader should consult Harel [1988]; we, in the next section, will deal only with logical properties of higraphs.

Representation systems based on CGs are intuitively appealing, and practically useful, even if not completely understood and formalized. The issues we have raised might provide some guidance into how one could enhance the formalism.

Future research on at least some of them might bring insights about knowledge representation, new algorithms, and perhaps interesting connections set theory, graph theory, higher order and "exotic" logics, and other areas. Some of these possible connections will be discussed in Section 12.5.

12.3 HIGRAPHS

We now present Harel's formalism of higraphs [Harel, 1988]. This section will be longer than the one on CGs because this formalism is less popular. Also, we find it necessary to actually prove something about higraphs, while in the case of CGs this basic work has been already done (although incompletely!).

As an element of our analysis of available tools, we establish a correspondence between higraphs and *datalog* programs, i.e., PROLOG programs without negation, function symbols, recursion, and without sharing of variables in the body of a rule. A few examples are intended to develop some intuitions about higraphs, whose formal role in knowledge representation will be discussed at the end of the section.

Definition. A *higraph* is a quadruple $H = (B, \sigma, \pi, E)$ where B is a finite set of ***blobs*** and E is a set of ***edges*** (a binary relation on blobs). The ***subblob*** function

$$\sigma : B \rightarrow 2^B$$

assigns to each blob $x \in B$ the set $\sigma(x)$ of its subblobs; it is assumed that the function is cycle free. The function

$$\pi : B \rightarrow 2^{B \times B}$$

introduces an equivalence relation on the blobs; these classes of equivalence for a given blob x will be denoted as $\pi_i(x)$. The ***atomic blobs***, denoted by $\boldsymbol{A}$, are those that do not have any subblobs, see Figure 12.1.

In this formalism no assumptions are made about what kind of relations can be denoted by edges of a higraph. Therefore in all the cases we consider, by *semantics* we will mean a *semantics of blobs*. The complications introduced by edges will be discussed separately.

12.3.1 The Inclusion Semantics

According to Harel, a ***model*** for a higraph H is a pair (D, μ), μ is a function on blobs:

$$\mu : \boldsymbol{A} \rightarrow 2^D$$

and the denotations of different atomic blobs have empty intersections. If a blob does not contain a Cartesian product we set

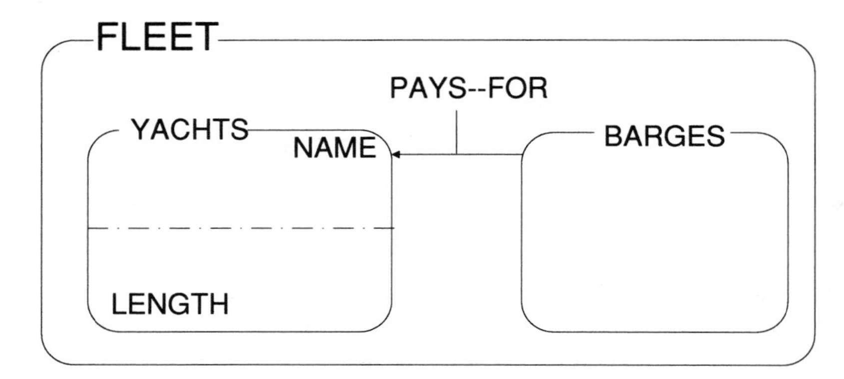

Figure 12.1: A higraph representing a FLEET of YACHTS and BARGES. The YACHT blob is a Cartesian product of NAME and LENGTH. The profit from the barges PAYS-FOR the upkeep of yachts. The semantics of this operation is not specified by the higraph, so the payments can be done collectively or individually.

$$\mu(x) = \bigcup\{\ \mu(y) : y \in \sigma(x)\ \}$$

and in the general case

$$\mu(x) = \prod_{i=1}^{k_x} (\bigcup\{\mu(y) : y \in \pi_i(x)\})$$

(Harel uses unordered Cartesian product).

The semantic relation E_M on $\mu(x)$'s is defined as $(\mu(x),\ \mu(y)) \in E_M$ *iff* $(x,y) \in E$, i.e., E_M is a collection of relations on the domain D.

Example: Two higraphs shown in Figure 12.2 are described by the classes of abstraction π_i (instead of the equivalence relation π) and by the subblob relation σ.

The formulas below describe the graphs and their models

(a) $\sigma(A) = \{B, E\}$, $\pi_1(A) = \{B, E\}$, $\sigma(E) = \{C, D\}$, $\pi_1(E) = \{C\}$, $\pi_2(E) = \{D\}$ (hence $E = C \times D$).

$$\mu(A) = \bigcup\{\mu(y) : y \in \pi_1(A)\}\ (= B \cup (C \times D))$$

(b) $\sigma(A) = \{B, E\}$, $\pi_1(A) = \{B\}$, $\pi_2(A) = \{E\}$, $\sigma(E) = \{C, D\}$, $\pi_1(E) = \{C, D\}$, (hence $E = C \cup D$).

$$\mu(A) = \prod_{i=1}^{2} (\bigcup\{\mu(y) : y \in \pi_i(A)\})(= B \times E = B \times (C \cup D))$$

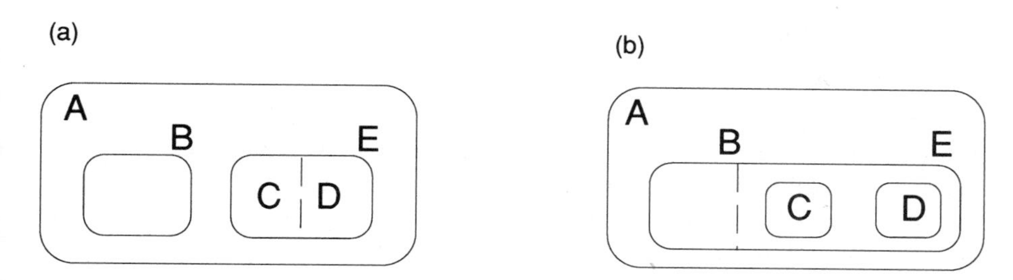

Figure 12.2: Two collections of blobs. The difference in the equivalence classes π_1 makes the higraph (a) a union of blobs, and (b) a Cartesian product.

Notice that a diagram of a higraph is its model. This relation is not 1–1, because if a contour C is included in a contour B, which is included in a contour A, such a diagram is a model of two higraphs: in the first one $\sigma(A) = \{B\}$, $\sigma(B) = \{C\}$; for the other one we have $\sigma(A) = \{B, C\}$, $\sigma(B) = \{C\}$.

Harel has shown that this inclusion semantics (a blob is a union of its sub-blobs) is suitable for visualizing information and for representing (among other things) ISA hierarchies.

12.3.2 Higraphs and Horn Logic

We know that the FOCGs correspond to formulas of first-order logic; it is then reasonable to ask: What is the class of formulas HGs correspond to? It turns out that under the type of semantics we described above, higraphs correspond to a subclass of datalog programs.

Theorem 3.1. There is a 1–1 embedding of higraphs into *datalog*$^{-}$—datalog programs without recursion, and without sharing of variables in the body of rules.

Proof. We define the mapping as follows:

1. Each atomic blob $a \in \boldsymbol{A}$ gets assigned (in a 1–1 way) a name of a unary relation $a(x)$;
2. Each $\pi_i(A) = \{A_1, ..., A_{n_i}\}$ is mapped into the disjunction

   $P_i\ (X) \leftarrow A_1(X)$
   $P_i\ (X) \leftarrow A_2(Y)$
   ...
   $P_i\ (Y) \leftarrow A_{n_i}(Y)$

   (X, Y denote the tuples of variables—some of A_i's can be the products of their subblobs)

3. After all $\pi_i(A)$, for $i \leq k$, have been mapped into P_i (X)'s, we define

   $A(X_1, \ldots, X_k) \leftarrow P_1(X_1)$ & ... & $P_k(X_k)$.

   Note. Since $P_i(X)$ can have more than one definition with Xs of different arity, the last step produces a scheme from which a program is generated by substituting all allowable tuples of variables for each X_i. By adding to datalog the tuple constructor and the equality, we can easily find another translation of blobs, in which the last step actually gives a program.
4. Finally, the presence of the semantic relation E between two blobs A_1 and A_2 can be encoded by: $e(X_1, X_2) \leftarrow A_1(X_1)$ & $A_2(X_2)$.

Notice that all these steps are 1–1, and that we get recursion free program because the subblob function σ contains no cycles.

We can, by reversing the mapping, prove the converse. As a result we get:

Theorem 3.2. There is an isomorphism between *datalog* programs and higraphs.

In most situations, the encoding of blobs belonging to the domain of E (step (4), above) would give us a representation that would be too weak to express an intended meaning of the relation E. (Remember that the semantics of E is not part of the semantics of higraphs). For instance, if the edge "married-to" links two blobs "men" and "women," the above interpretation would give

$\forall x, y\ [married(x,y) \leftarrow woman(x)\ \&\ man(y)]$

while clearly the intended interpretation may be

$\forall x, \exists y\ [married(x,y)\ \&\ man(y) \leftarrow woman(x)]$ and
$\forall x, \exists y\ [married(x,y)\ \&\ woman(y) \leftarrow man(x)]$

(every woman is married to some man, and *vice versa*) or

$\exists\ x, y\ [married(x,y)\ \&\ woman(y)\ \&\ man(x)]$

(some women are married to some men). Since neither of these is equivalent to a universal formula, they cannot be expressed in datalog. But we can interpret the datalog formulas as constraints on types of objects that can enter the relation E; for instance, *married*(x,y) is a relation between men and women, not yachts.

The upshot is that, depending on the semantics of links, the expressive power of higraphs is at least equal to recursion-free datalog programs. The upper limit is more difficult to assess; if edges can link only two blobs, then under the semantics we just have sketched, the expressive power would be less or equal to the union of $\exists\forall$and $\forall\exists$ formulas.

12.3.3 Another Semantics for Higraphs: Mapping into Sets

Under this semantics, blobs are mapped into finite sets; Harel [1988] mentions this possibility. We would like to say a few words about it, to show that more than one semantics for higraphs is possible. Moreover, in a three-dimensional representation envisioned by Harel, the inclusion semantics and the set membership semantics can easily be combined.

To save space we will not talk about the Cartesian product now. A model for a higraph H is as before a pair (D, μ), and as before μ is a function on blobs, but now $\mu: A \rightarrow D$ and $\mu(x) = \{ \mu(y) : y \in \sigma(x) \}$, which means that a (nonatomic) blob is treated as the *set of its subblobs*. As before, we can define a relation E_M *on* $\mu(x)$'s. This semantics makes it easy to represent other types of information, e.g., encode the structure of objects we encounter in situation semantics [Barwise and Perry, 1983]. But the postulate that blobs/sets are well founded—i.e. there are always atomic blobs "at the bottom"—should be abandoned, if we care about representing self-reference. The required modification would make the subblob function σ correspond to the tagged graph of a not-necessarily-well-founded set (compare [Barwise and Etchemendy, 1987]). Such a modification allows us to represent the phrase

The man who mistook his wife for a hat

as a higraph, with the referent of "his" being the whole phrase, containing itself as a subgraph. (But notice the difficulty of representing cycles with rectangles).

12.3.4 Comments on Some Formal Aspects of Higraphs

- Intuitively, the diagrams of higraphs—and we think of higraphs in terms of their diagrams—are like models, not formulas. So the diagrams of HGs and CGs (a CG is a formula/proposition) have different logical functions. Notice for instance that $A \rightarrow B$ and $A \rightarrow C$ will presented as

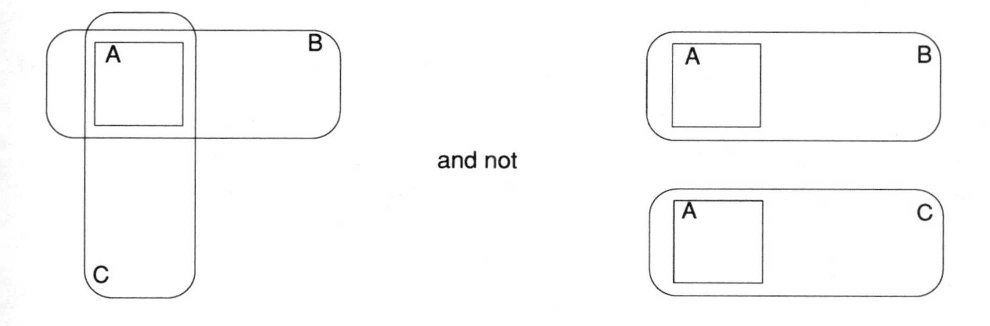

Moreover such a theory gives only a partial specification of blobs: $A \in \sigma(B)$, $A \in \sigma(C)$, but in a higraph either B is a subset of C or not. Finally, as with Horn clauses, there is no disjunction in the conclusion of a rule.

- Higraphs seem to represent well the structural properties of objects; there is no disjunction, which can be understood as the dictum "if you know the object, you must know its parts." State charts (also in [Harel, 1988]) can represent the dynamics of actions.
- Although Harel's paper does not mention the possibility of using the higraphs for inference, the potential for such a use is obvious—especially after we have established the correspondence of higraphs with recursion-free datalog programs.
- Reading off information from a higraph can be formalized.

HGs use containment of blobs to represent inclusion or membership. From the point of view of NLU, they provide a convenient representation of the structure of records, as well as of information about coreference and about the structure of discourse entities. The expressive power of HGs can probably be increased by combining them with CGs. Formal specifications for an extension of FOCGs by addition of the Cartesian product and inclusion do not seem to be too difficult to write. State charts may offer a neat way of representing temporal constraints among events.

12.4 GRAPHS GUIDE INFERENCE IN THE THREE-LEVEL SEMANTICS

In this section we present an example of how inference can depend on graph properties of a knowledge base. Some inheritance nets have this feature—conclusions drawn from a net can actually depend on the distance between predicates (compare for example [Touretzky, 1984]); path-based inference appears also in Shapiro's SNePS [Chapter 3, this volume]. (The semantics of SNePS and of inheritance nets is discussed by Israel [1983].) We now want to present a system with a lot of expressive power where inferencing depends additionally on a position of a theory in a partial ordering of theories and on coherence links between them.

We do not have enough space here to present a formal and thorough exposition of the three-level semantics, but its main ideas are as follows:

1. Reasoning takes place in a three-level structure consisting of a *referential level* **R** (a partial order of theories representing background knowledge), an *object level* (describing current situation), and a *metalevel* (constraining types of models).
2. The referential level is a collection of graphs whose nodes correspond to theories describing background knowledge, and whose links represent the partial orderings on these theories (see Section 12.4.1).

3. An object-level theory T is augmented by theories from the referential level by extending paths from subformulas of T to corresponding theories of **R**. The resulting new, *consistent*, theories $PT(T)$ can be then further extended to $PT(PT(T))$, and so on.
4. Models of such extensions are then built, subject to metalevel constraints.

We will illustrate the first three points using an example; more information about the system can be found in Zadrozny and Jensen [1991]. The reader is asked to notice that extending paths corresponds to reasoning by default, and thus we do not obtain logical truths but only most-plausible interpretations.

12.4.1 The Referential Level

The next few paragraphs will be devoted to an analysis of interaction of background knowledge with a logical representation of a text. We will describe two modes of such an interaction; both seem to be present in our understanding of language. One exploits differences in plausibility of meanings of words and phrases in absence of context; e.g., the difference between central and peripheral senses, or between frequent and rare meanings. The other takes advantage of connections between those meanings. We will illustrate the theory by the example based on Zadrozny and Jensen [1991].

Example: Assume that the sentence

Entering the port, a ship brought a disease.

has been translated into the logical formula (ignoring the past tense of "bring" and the progressive of "enter"):

$$S : enter(s, p) \;\&\; ship(s) \;\&\; port(p) \;\&\; bring(s, d) \;\&\; disease(d)$$

(s, p, d are all constants).

Our assumptions about the structure of background knowledge are listed in Section 12.4.1:

- A *referential level* **R** is a structure

  $\mathbf{R} = \{ (\psi, <_\psi) : \psi \in \mathit{Formulae} \}$

  where—for each ψ—$<_\psi$ is a partially ordered (by a relation of plausibility) collection of implications $\psi \rightarrow T_\psi$.

  The term $\psi \rightarrow T$ stands for the theory $\{ \psi \rightarrow \tau : \tau \in T \}$.
- It is convenient to assume also that all formulas, except "laws"—which are supposed to be always true—have the least preferred *empty interpretation* ϕ.

- We suppose also that interpretations are additionally ranked according to the canonical partial ordering on subformulas. The ranking provides a natural method of dealing with exceptions, like in the case of finding an interpretation of α & ρ & β with **R** containing ($\alpha \rightarrow \gamma$) ($\alpha$ & $\beta \rightarrow \neg \gamma$), where $\neg \gamma$ would be preferred to γ—if both are consistent, and both defaults are equally preferred. This means that preference is given to more specific information. For instance, the sentence *The officer went out and struck the flag* will get the reading "lowered the flag," if the appropriate theory of *strike*(*x*,*y*) & *flag*(*y*) is part of background knowledge; if not, it will be understood as "hit the flag," assuming that *strike*(*x*,*y*) $\rightarrow$ *hit* (*x*, *y*) is in **R**.

The referential level **R** may contain the theories listed below. Since we view a dictionary as an (imperfect) embodiment of a referential level, we have derived the formulas in every theory T_ψ from a dictionary definition of the term ψ. We believe that even such a crude model can be useful in practice, but a refinement of this model will be needed to have a sophisticated natural language understanding system. (All free variables in the formulas below are implicitly universally quantified).

$\psi \rightarrow T_\psi$
enter(*x*,*y*) $\rightarrow${ *come_in*(*x*,*y*); *place*(*y*) , ... } (e1)
enter(*x*,*y*) $\rightarrow${ *join*(*x*,*y*) & group(*y*); **typically**: *professionals*(*y*) } (e2)
ship(*x*)$\rightarrow${ *large_boat*(*x*) ; $\exists$ *y carry*(*x*,*y*) & (*people*(*y*) $\ddagger$ *goods*(*y*)) , ... } (s1)
ship(*x*)$\rightarrow${ (*large_aircraft*(*x*) $\vee$ *space_vehicle*(*x*)) ; ... } (s2)
bring(*x*,*y*) $\rightarrow${ *carry*(*x*,*y*) ; ... } (b1)
bring(*x*,*y*) $\rightarrow${ *cause*(*x*,*y*) ; ... } (b2)
disease(*y*)$\rightarrow${ *illness*(*y*) ; ... } (de1)
disaster(*y*) $\rightarrow${ ... ; $\exists$*x cause*(*y*,*x*) & *harm*(*x*) ... } (drl)
port(*x*) $\rightarrow$ { *harbor*(*x*) ; ... } (pl)
(...)

The theories, which we describe here only partially, restricting ourselves to their relevant parts, represent the meanings of concepts. We assume that (e1) ("to come in") is a more plausible meaning (*a* theory of) of "to enter" than (e2) ("to join a group, usually of professionals"), i.e., e1 > e2. Similarly, (s1) is assumed to be more plausible than (s2), and so on. This particular ordering of theories is based on the ordering of meanings of the corresponding words in dictionaries (derived and less frequent meanings have lower priority). But one can imagine deriving such orderings by other means, such as statistics.

The partial order $<_{enter}$ has the theories $\{e1, e2, \phi\}$ as its domain; ϕ is the least preferred empty interpretation corresponding to our lack of knowledge about the predicate, it is used when both e1 and e2 are inconsistent with a current object theory. The domain is ordered by the relation of preference $e1 > e2 > \phi$.

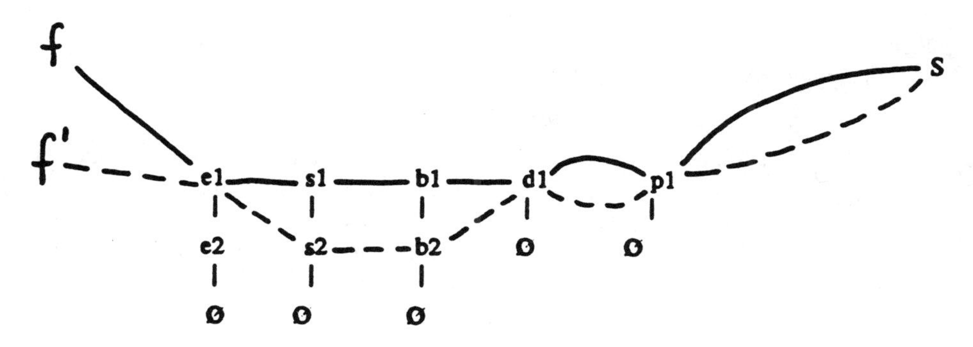

Figure 12.3: The partial ordering of theories of the referential level **R** and the ordering of the interpretations. Since s1 and b1 dominate (respectively) s2 and b2, the path *f* represents a more plausible interpretation than *f'*.

12.4.2 Using Dominance

In Figure 12.3, the theories of "enter," "ship," etc. and the partial orders are represented graphically; more plausible theories are positioned higher. A path through this graph chooses an interpretation of the sentence *S*. For instance, the path $f = \{ e1, s1, p1, b1, d1 \}$ and S say together that

A large boat (ship) that carries people or goods came into the harbor and carried a disease (illness).

Since it is the "highest" path, *f* is the most plausible (relative to **R**) interpretation of the words that appear in the sentence. Because it is also consistent, so it will be chosen as a best interpretation of *S*, (compare [Zadrozny, 1987a, 1987b]). Another theory, consisting of $f' = \{ e1, s2, p1, b2 , d1 \}$ and S, saying that

A space vehicle came into the harbor and caused a disease/illness

is less plausible according to that ordering. As it turns out, *f'* is never constructed in the process of building an interpretation of a paragraph containing the sentence *S*, unless assuming *f* would lead to a contradiction, for instance with a higher level context of a science fiction story.

The collection of these most plausible consistent interpretations of a given theory *T* is denoted by $PT_<(T)$. Then *f* belongs to $PT_<(\{S\})$, or more exactly to $PT_<(Theory(\{S\}))$, but this is not true for *f'*.

12.4.3 Adding Coherence

The reasoning that led to the interpretation *f* was based on the partial ordering of the theories of **R**. We want to exploit now another graph-related property of the theories of **R**—their coherence. Finding interpretation of a natural language text or sentence typically involves an appeal to coherence. Consider

S2: Entering the port, a ship brought a disaster.

Using the coherence link between (b2) and (dr1)—the presence of *cause*(*,*) in the theories of "bring" and "disaster"—we can find a partial coherent interpretation $PT_C(\{S2\})$ of $S2$. In this interpretation, theories explaining the meanings of terms are chosen on the basis of coherence, which for the purpose of this chapter can be simply understood as sharing of predicates among theories of **R**. Thus, when building an interpretation of $S2$, we disregard the ordering (see Figure 12.3); instead, we try to form a chain of theories such that any two consecutive theories share at least one predicate. This makes (b2), "to bring" means "to cause," plausible, and therefore (b2) would be included in $PT_C(\{S2\})$.

A finer interpretation of an object level theory T—its *partial theory*—is obtained by the iteration:

$$PT(T) = PT_<(PT_C(Th(T)))$$

PT is well defined after we specify that PT of a set of theories is the set of the PTs, for both $<$ and C.

Notice that coherence does not decide between (e1) and (e2) given the above **R**, but the iteration produces two theories of $S2$, both of which assert that the meaning of "ship entered" is "ship came."

A ship/boat came into the harbor/port and caused / brought a disaster.

A ship/boat came into the harbor/port and carried / brought a disaster.

$PT(\{S1\})$ contains only one interpretation—*A ship/boat came into the harbor/port and carried/brought a disease*, which is the one that was given by *f*.

Iterating the function PT allows us to obtain step by step refinements $PT($ ... $PT(\{S2\})$ ... $)$ of the first approximation $PT(\{S2\})$; typically only a few steps of such iteration are needed to find answers to *wh*-questions. The closure under PT behaves very much like the standard deductive closure, except it is nonmonotonic (more about the logic of PT can be found in Zadrozny [1987b, forthcoming]).

We have shown that finding an interpretation of a sentence depends on two graph-theoretic properties—coherence and dominance. Coherence is a purely "associative" property; we are interested only in the existence of links between represented concepts/theories. Dominance uses the directionality of the partial orders. Both guide inference. The paths through the graph of background knowledge depend on the proximity relation in two ways: topmost members of the partial orders are assumed to be closer to object theories than lower ones; moreover, because the paths are allowed to produce only consistent theories, the order in which theories are formed, which is a function of distance, matters.

Notice that by using coherence and dominance we are actually putting constraints on how inferences should be made; thus (the monotonic part of) the logic we obtain is stronger than first-order logic, the information contained in **R** distorts the relation of entailment. Although this logic is not necessarily the best tool to reason about cardinal numbers in set theory, these and other constraints make it more suitable to represent inference processes of natural language. This formalism is obviously compatible with conceptual graphs or higraphs; we can partially order collections of CGs and HGs, and we can define appropriate coherence relations.

12.5 A GRAPH-BASED REPRESENTATION FORMALISM?

"Graphs" offer some advantages over the standard first-order logic. First, they can be used to guide inference, by restricting the amount of relevant information; second, as we argue in Zadrozny and Jensen [1991], they allow shallow inference based on semantic criteria; third, in contrast with standard logic, if inconsistencies appear they can be localized. This last property also has computational advantages—detecting inconsistency and proving it are, in general, computationally intractable.

In our discussion of graph-related representations we have observed that:

- Topological or metric properties of some spaces of abstract objects can guide inference. We can assume that proximity in such spaces is *semantically* significant. This fact has been exploited in semantic networks and ISA hierarchies.
- In particular, it is possible to constrain reasoning and make it resource-bounded using graph properties like dominance and coherence (Section 12.4).
- First-order logic, especially in the form of conceptual graphs, makes certain types of knowledge readable. Until we are able to communicate with computers using natural language, first-order logic is perhaps the easiest formal language to carry conversations with them (Section 12.2).
- *Datalog*$^{-}$ programs (i.e., computationally easy fragments of first order logic) can be very conveniently modeled as blobs of higraphs (Section 12.3).
- We have noticed some gaps in the theory of conceptual graphs:

  1. How to handle extensions of FOCGs?

     Sowa [1989] is aware of the problem and suggests abduction as a method for "extracting relevant chunks from the knowledge soup to construct a theory which makes deduction possible." This very much agrees with the approach we presented in Section 12.4, where we used coherence and dominance as two methods of abduction.

  2. Lack of graph-based model theory.

> The problem is how to use conceptual graphs to represent models of a theory given as a set of CGs. Conceptual graphs would now have to be restricted in order to represent only grounded relations, functions, and terms.

Imagine a system that uses higraphs to represent the structure of terms, and conceptual graphs for propositions; inference could be guided by topological properties of graphs representing knowledge, as it is in inheritance networks with exceptions and the three-level semantics; models would be graphs, too; state charts and modal extensions of conceptual graphs would show changes in time. In addition, we would have in such a system all kinds of hierarchies and inheritance, we could construct complex concepts from simple ones and talk about the structure of concepts. No doubt, the expressive power of such a formalism would be great; in particular it would satisfy almost all of the more than two dozen requirements set forth by Slagle and Vayghan [1988]. It seems to us that a such a scheme could be put together; it could for instance be programmed in a system like the Cambridge higher order logical language (HOL).

But would an NLU system with such a powerful engine and tons of useful information presented in a graph format be able to find correct interpretations of nontrivial texts? Probably not—even if transparency of such a system were maintained by adding an abstraction mechanism of the sort discussed by Harel [1988], and if the problems of managing the extensions of the CGs theory were solved.

We believe that without constraints on the structure of terms and propositions (conceptual graphs), and on inference and semantics, such a system could represent anything, not only concepts. It would not differ for instance from set theory, where "everything," i.e., all mathematically possible structures, can be represented. In addition, its logic would be too general to guarantee flawlessness of conclusions. The system could help a human in navigating through a knowledge base, but it would not operate correctly on an "automatic pilot."

Some elementary examples of the possible constraints can be found in this list: not too many elements in a set (on terms); no relations of arity greater than three, and no concepts like "grue"—green before 1969 and blue after (on conceptual graphs/propositions); long proofs and explanations are suspect (on inference), no infinite models (on semantics).

Current topo-visual representations may help in finding and formulating such constraints. After we have discovered enough of them, we may hope for a graph-based logic—an ideal representation that would be expressive, explicit, and easy to use.

From a formal point of view, building such a system will be worth the effort only if it leads to new reasoning patterns, a new notion of the logical consequence or/and a new concept of semantics. Such a new system can be interpretable in a standard logic, but it can't be isomorphic to it, and it must be worth studying on its own. Our position differs here from that of Israel [1983]: "A crucial condition of adequacy to be satisfied is fidelity to some of the intuitions of the creators of the formalism." We believe that a system is worth studying if it offers new tools. Kepler's ellipses were quite counterintuitive, but they certainly have made the casting of horoscopes easier.

ACKNOWLEDGMENTS

I'd like to thank John Sowa and David Harel for answering my questions about conceptual graphs and higraphs. I have profited from the comments of Ben Kuipers, Doug Skuce, and other participants of the Workshop on Formal Aspects of Semantic Networks; I thank them too.

References

Barwise, J. and Perry, J. 1983. *Situations and Attitudes.* MIT Press, Cambridge, MA.

Barwise, J. and Etchemendy, J. 1987. *The Liar.* Oxford University Press.

Beeri, C., Naqvi, S., Ramakrishnan, R., Shmueli, O., and Tsur, S. 1987. Sets and negation in a logic database language (LDL-1). In *Proceedings of the Sixth ACM Conference on PODS*, San Diego.

Fargues, J., Landau, M-C., Dugourd, A. and Catach L. 1986. Conceptual graphs for semantic and knowledge processing. *IBM J. of Res. and Dev.*, 30(1):70–79.

Gardiner, D.A., Tjan, B.S. and Slagle, J.R. 1989. *Extended Conceptual Structure Notation.* University of Minnesota Computer Science Technical Report TR 89–88. Minneapolis, MN. Also in *Proceedings of the Fourth Annual Workshop on Conceptual Graphs*, Detroit, MI, August 1989.

Harel, D. 1988. On visual formalisms. *Communications of ACM*, pp.514–530.

Israel, D.J. 1983. Interpreting network formalisms. *Computer and Mathematics with Applications*, 9(1):1–13.

Levesque, H.J. and Brachman R.J. 1985. A fundamental tradeoff in knowedge representation and reasoning (revised version). In *Readings in Knowledge Representation*, Brachman R.J. and Levesque, H.J. (ed.s.). Morgan Kaufmann Publishers, San Mateo, CA.

Shapiro, S. 1991. Cables, paths and subconscious reasoning in propositional semantic networks. Chapter 4, this volume.

Shmueli, O. and Naqvi, S. 1987. Set grouping and layering in Horn clause programs. *Proceedings of the International Conference on Logic Programming*, Melbourne.

Slagle, J.R. and Vayghan, J.A. 1988. Knowledge representation and conceptual structures. *Proceedings of the Third Annual Workshop on Conceptual Graphs*, St Paul, Minnesota.

Sowa, J.F. 1989. *Crystallizing Theories out of Knowledge Soup.* Unpublished manuscript.

———. 1984. *Conceptual Structures*. Addison-Wesley, Reading, MA.

———. 1976. Conceptual graphs for a data base interface. *IBM J. of Research and Development*, 20:336–357.

Touretzky, D.S. 1984. Implicit ordering of defaults in inheritance systems. *Proceedings of AAAI-84*, pp. 322–325.

Zadrozny, W. 1987a. Intended models, circumscription and commonsense reasoning. *Proceedings of IJCAI-87*. IJCAI Proceedings are available from Morgan Kaufmann Publishers, San Mateo, CA.

———. 1987b. A theory of default reasoning. *Proceedings of AAAI-87*.

———. Forthcoming. A three-level theory of reasoning with applications.

Zadrozny, W. and Jensen, K. 1991. Semantics of paragraphs. *Computational Linguistics*.

PART III

SYSTEMS FOR KNOWLEDGE REPRESENTATION

The chapters in Part III present complete systems that implement semantic networks and use them for knowledge representation and reasoning. Although these chapters emphasize implementations and applications, they also address important theoretical issues of knowledge representation. Some of the most difficult and subtle issues, in fact, only become apparent when the systems are tested on real applications. As Rich Thomason said in the panel discussion, "We ought to strive for a kind of tight feedback loop where the theoretical work pays close attention to the problems of practitioners, and practitioners look to theories for models that help them to deal with their concerns." These chapters close the cycle that was begun in Part I and lead the way to the next cycle of theory.

SURVEY OF CHAPTERS

The first three chapters in Part III discuss systems that have evolved from KL-ONE and its research tradition. The original KL-ONE system was built by Ron Brachman as part of his PhD research at Harvard University. Since Brachman's thesis adviser was William Woods, KL-ONE was designed in response to the issues that Woods raised in "What's in a Link" and now discusses further in Chapter 1 of this book. Further development of KL-ONE was continued at Bolt, Beranek and Newman, by Brachman, Woods, and their colleagues. KL-ONE itself was distributed to other researchers around the world, who developed similar systems and made *KL-ONE-like* a generic term for a family of knowledge representation systems. In Chapter 13, Robert MacGregor surveys the evolution of the KL-ONE family and analyzes their unifying architectural features. He discusses the tradeoffs between expressive power and computational complexity and the ways in which the system designers have responded to the users' requirements. In Chapter 14, Ron Brachman and his colleagues present a new KL-ONE-like system called CLASSIC. After introducing the main features of CLASSIC, they present examples that illustrate typical applications. Since the examples are characteristic of many practical applications, they should also be of interest to people who are using other semantic networks and related knowledge representations. In Chapter 15, Alfred Kobsa describes the SB-ONE knowledge representation workbench. Besides a KL-ONE-like representation and reasoning system, SB-ONE supports tools for the development of conceptual knowledge bases for natural language systems. Among the tools are a sophisticated graphics interface, a consistency maintenance system, a mechanism for partitioning a knowledge base, and interfaces to other languages, including Prolog and the Babylon frame system.

The next two chapters describe systems for model-based reasoning with graphs as the structural units. In Chapter 16, Roger Hartley and Michael Coombs describe their method of *model generative reasoning*, which solves problems by joining conceptual graphs to build models. Their two basic operators are *specialize* and *fragment*. The specialize operator supports abductive reasoning by generating hypotheses, and the fragment operator removes potential incoherences while preserving coherence with observation. In Chapter 17, Rattikorn Hewett and Barbara Hayes-Roth show how models for specific domains can be developed as specializations of *prime models*, which are general enough to apply to many different domains. The human respiratory system, for example, can be modeled as a specialization of fluid flow. They use networks both for the structural elements of their models and for the *belief networks* that show logical and probabilistic dependencies.

The last two chapters of this book present systems that bring together many features that were discussed separately in earlier chapters. In Chapter 18, Paul Jacobs shows how a natural language processor can call upon a knowledge representation system in both analysis and generation. In analysis, it uses background knowledge for disambiguating sentences and for constructing a semantic representation. In generation, it uses the knowledge for guiding lexical choice and for selecting linguistic structures. He uses the ACE network representation for both the lexical definitions and the meaning of sentences. In Chapter 19, Doug Skuce presents a method of *conceptually oriented description*, which integrates AI techniques of knowledge representation with the research on abstract data types in programming languages. He argues that ideas taken from algebraic specification languages can help to unify such diverse notions as frames, objects, functions, logical constraints, and temporal phenomena. Using those ideas, he has developed a system for supporting the tasks of knowledge acquisition, representation, and management.

13

THE EVOLVING TECHNOLOGY OF CLASSIFICATION-BASED KNOWLEDGE REPRESENTATION SYSTEMS

Robert Mac Gregor
(USC/Information Sciences Institute, Marina del Rey)

Abstract

This chapter attempts to characterize the technology that has evolved within the KL-ONE family of knowledge representation systems. Key features of these systems are that they are logic based, they support a specialized term-forming language, and they implement a specialized reasoner called a *term classifier*. We begin by introducing some of the concepts commonly used in the KL-ONE literature, and we provide a brief sketch of the history of this family of systems. Next, we summarize the current state of this technology, and identify some of its major contributions. We close with a look at some issues that are still regarded as controversial within the research community.

13.1 INTRODUCTION

The field of knowledge representation has not yet achieved the development of a general-purpose knowledge representation system (KRS). In most cases, the authors of a particular KRS and the application programmers using that KRS are the same group of people. There exist no generally agreed on principles that indicate, among other things, what the capabilities of a KRS should be, or how to characterize the quality or level of interaction between a KRS and a user or application program.

The systems belonging to the KL-ONE [Brachman and Schmolze, 1985] family of KRSs constitute a partial exception to the previously mentioned state of affairs. This chapter outlines major principles that have been adopted by these systems, describes key features of several individual systems, and tries to identify unifying architectural themes among the various implementations that could evolve into a general purpose knowledge representation technology.

KL-ONE and its descendants share a commitment to the following architectural features:

- They are logic-based (i.e., they appeal to first-order logic for their semantics).
- They draw a distinction between *terminological* and *assertional* knowledge,[1] and each system implements its own specialized term-forming language.
- They include a *classifier* that organizes terms (concepts) into a taxonomy, based on subsumption relationships between terms.

We shall refer to knowledge representation systems that exhibit these features as *classification-based*, or *term classification* (TC) systems. The technology developed for TC systems has probably seen more extensive application than that of any other family of KRSs, and hence represents an important contribution of the field of knowledge representation.

The principle objective of this chapter is to introduce important technical ideas that have emerged during the development of various TC systems. We also attempt to provide a historical perspective on this family of systems—when appropriate, we associate particular systems with certain of these ideas. A few of the ideas that have emerged have not withstood the test of time, while others are currently considered to be controversial. Our hope is that this chapter will help readers to better understand the current state of this technology.

Section 13.2 gives a brief outline of the origins of the KL-ONE family of systems; Section 13.3 describes the architectural parameters that distinguish TC systems from other KRSs; Section 13.4 summarizes the architectural features and individual technological contributions of several TC systems; Section 13.5 discusses the overall merit of classification-based technology as it could be employed within a general purpose KRS; Section 13.6 discusses an issue that is still controversial within the TC community, which is, "How expressive should a terminological language be?"

---

[1] These terms are defined in Section 13.3.

13.2 BACKGROUND

The KL-ONE language was originally formulated within Ron Brachman's Ph.D. dissertation [Brachman, 1978]. KL-ONE generated a relatively large amount of interest in the early 1980s, as evidenced by the organizing of two KL-ONE workshops [Schmolze and Brachman, 1982]. During this time, researchers at Bolt Beranek and Newman and at USC's Information Sciences Institute were formalizing the semantics for KL-ONE, and they built the first KL-ONE classifier [Schmolze and Lipkis, 1983].

KL-ONE's implementers discovered that serious computational complexity problems inherent in the semantics of the KL-ONE language prevented construction of an efficient reasoner for the KL-ONE language. Subsequent to the original KL-ONE system, numerous other systems have been developed that adhere to the basic principles established for KL-ONE, but which have refined or eliminated various aspects of the KL-ONE language in order to achieve a more efficient and complete reasoning capability. These systems include NIKL, KRYPTON, KL-TWO, KANDOR, BACK, LOOM, and CLASSIC.

A hybrid technology is emerging from the experiments represented by these systems that is making possible the construction of efficient, general-purpose KRSs.

13.3 CLASSIFICATION-BASED TECHNOLOGY

A classification-based KRS includes two languages: a *terminological* language and an *assertion* language. A terminological language [Brachman and Levesque, 1982; Brachman et al., 1983] is designed to facilitate the construction of expressions that describe classes of individuals. For example, the phrase "a brown, three-legged dog" describes any dog that is brown and has three legs, while the phrase "a father all of whose children are college graduates" describes a subset of the class of all fathers. The formal constructs in a terminological language that correspond to these phrases are called terms or *concepts*.

The purpose of an assertion language is to state constraints or facts that apply to a particular domain or world. For example, we can assert that "Rover is a brown, three-legged dog."

Frequently referenced concepts are usually given names. These names function as unary predicates within the assertion language. In the LOOM system, the declaration

```
(defconcept B3LD
   :is (:and Dog Brown-Thing
             (:exactly 3 has-leg)))
```

assigns the name B3LD to the concept representing "a brown, three-legged dog." The assertion B3LD(Rover) states that Rover is a dog, is a brown thing, and has exactly three legs.

A concept definition states a necessary and sufficient condition for membership in the extension of that concept. In other words, each thing that satisfies the definition of a concept C must be an instance of C, and conversely, every instance of C necessarily satisfies C's definition. For example, the LOOM declaration

```
(defconcept Successful-Father
   :is (:and Father
             (:all has-child College-Graduate))) }
```

adds to a knowledge base the axiom

```
(all x)(Successful-Father(x) iff (Father(x) and
                                  (all y) (has-daughter(x,y) implies
                                          College-Graduate(y)))) }
```

Concepts in a classification-based KRS are organized into a "taxonomy" based on a "subsumption" relationship that relates each pair of concepts: A concept *C subsumes* a concept *D* if any individual satisfying the definition for *D* necessarily satisfies the definition of *C*. Thus, if *C* subsumes *D* then the extension of *C* is a superset of the extension of *D*.

A concept *classifier* computes subsumption relationships between concepts. For example, a classifier will determine that the concept Brown-Dog, defined as

```
(defconcept Brown-Dog
   :is (:and Dog Brown-Thing)),
```

subsumes the concept B3LD, while the concepts Dog and Brown-Thing each subsume the concept Brown-Dog.

The subsumption relation induces a partial ordering among the concepts in a knowledge base. The process of inserting a new concept into a taxonomy of concepts so that more general concepts are positioned above it, while less general ones are positioned below it is called *classification.*

Given any language with the expressive power of the first-order predicate calculus (FOPC), the general problem of computing a subsumption relation between two arbitrary concepts is as hard computationally as the problem of determining if two arbitrary first-order logical expressions are equivalent. Hence, in the general case the problem of computing subsumption relationships is recursively undecidable. Furthermore, various theoretical results [Brachman and Levesque, 1984; Nebel, 1988] have shown that for all but very restricted languages the subsumption problem is intractable (NP- or co-NP-hard). Because classification of concepts is so difficult, all of the terminological languages developed for TC systems represent proper subsets of FOPC. In Section 13.4, we will discuss how the trade-off between terminological expressiveness and completeness (of classification) has been resolved for several of the TC systems.

While there is reasonable agreement within the TC community on what terminological capabilities a KRS should provide [Patel-Schneider et al., 1985], there is as yet no comparable consensus on what the assertional component of a KRS should look like. However, we can identify two features, each of which appears in the assertional component of several of the more recent TC systems, that may eventually become established characteristics of classification-based technology. The first feature is a general capability for specifying the attachment of constraints to concepts, and the second is an object-centered approach to the assertional reasoning component.

Three systems, LOOM, MESON, and CLASSIC, permit the specification of *implication* relationships between pairs of concepts, e.g., one can assert for any concepts *C1* and *C2* that membership in *C1* implies membership in *C2*. Unlike a subsumption relation, which is an analytic relationship and hence must be true for all possible models, an implication relationship defines a constraint that must be true for some particular model or models, but is not necessarily true in all models. For example, we might state

```
(implies Successful-Father Relieved)
```

to indicate that for a particular world, if a father has gotten all of his children through college, he is relieved (at least until he sires another child). The `implies` operator permits one to state conditions for a concept that are necessary but not sufficient (or *vice versa*), and hence represents a valuable extension to a system's representational capabilities.

The BACK, LOOM, and CLASSIC systems each implement an assertional component wherein all asserted facts must take the form either of unary predications (e.g., `B3LD(Rover)`; `Successful-Father(Fred)`) or binary predications (e.g., `has-child(Fred,Sally)`; `has-leg(Rover,L2)`). In these systems one *cannot* assert, for example "Either Fred is a father or Joe is a father." By excluding more complex assertions, these systems are able to manage the factual portion of a knowledge base more efficiently than would be possible if they attempted to represent arbitrary propositions.

The set of concepts that an individual in a knowledge base belongs to is called the *type* of that individual. An individual's type represents a summary of the system's current knowledge about an individual. Each of the above three systems implements an assertional reasoner called a *recognizer* whose function is to maintain current values for the types of all individuals in a knowledge base [Mac Gregor, 1988]. Thus, we see that the focus of the recognizer is on the facts as they pertain to individuals, i.e., the recognizer is object centered.

13.4 A KL-ONE FAMILY HISTORY

Here we select a number of important classifier technology issues, and trace the evolution of each of them by citing contributions made by individual TC systems. The issues are: terminological languages and term classifiers, assertion languages, rule/constraint languages, truth maintenance, and system performance. At the end of this section we summarize what we perceive to be the current state of classification-based technology: We list a number of areas where the TC research community seems to have arrived at a consensus, and also point out a few areas where there exists a diversity of opinions.

13.4.1 Terminological Languages and Term Classifiers

KL-ONE has a relatively rich terminological language, designed to facilitate the expression of definitions that commonly arise in the processing of natural language [Brachman and Schmolze, 1985]. The developers of the first KL-ONE classifier made an empirically based discovery that some subsumption-related inferences are easier to compute than others. As a consequence, the KL-ONE classifier treats the KL-ONE language very unevenly—some constructs are fairly well understood by the classifier, while others get shortchanged or are completely ignored. NIKL (New Implementation of KL-ONE, see [Robins, 1986]) was conceived as a slim, trim version of KL-ONE. The algorithm designed for the NIKL classifier was quite efficient (30 times faster than the KL-ONE classifier), but it too was inferentially incomplete.

The desire to build a system that could be relied on to find all valid subsumption relations spawned a search for (smaller but still useful) term languages for which an efficient and inferentially complete subsumption algorithm could be demonstrated. KRYPTON's designers started with a term language that was still too expressive (described in [Brachman et al., 1983]), and they subsequently had to trim it down to achieve a tractable subsumption algorithm. The classification algorithms developed for the KANDOR [Patel-Schneider, 1984] and BACK [von Luck et al., 1987] systems were subsequently shown to be incomplete [Nebel, 1988]. The term language chosen for the CLASSIC system [Borgida et al., 1989] represents the first system that is, roughly speaking, "as expressive as possible" while preserving computational tractability and completeness of inference.

Given that several inferentially incomplete systems have been developed and used successfully in applications, one might ask "How necessary is it that a system provide an inferentially complete classification algorithm?" Section 13.6 below discusses this question in more detail.

13.4.2 Assertion Languages

KL-ONE's assertion language was never fully developed, while the NIKL project ended before its developers could design an assertion language for NIKL. Thus, KRYPTON was the first TC system to have a genuine assertion language. KRYPTON was the first system to formally distinguish two separate reasoning components: the terminological reasoner (TBox) and the assertional reasoner (ABox). KRYPTON's ABox embraced the entire first-order predicate calculus, and hence required a (resolution-based) theorem prover to perform its inferences. KRYPTON was far too slow and fragile to be a knowledge server in an on-line application.

In order to achieve satisfactory performance, subsequent TC systems have opted for much less expressive ABoxes. KANDOR's ABox established a baseline by supporting only fully grounded unary and binary predications (atomic formulas). KL-TWO's ABox supported a quantifier-free predicate calculus with equality [Vilain, 1985]. However, its performance was barely adequate, and recent systems have retreated back to KANDOR-like ABoxes. The BACK system, which added limited quantification into its ABox to "balance the expressiveness" between TBox and ABox, first achieved the current conception of what an ABox should contain [Nebel and von Luck, 1987].

13.4.3 Rules/Constraints

LOOM's designers discovered that a hybrid TBox/ABox architecture extends very naturally to accomodate rules of the form

```
(all x) (A(x) implies B(x))
```

where A and B are arbitrary term expressions (defining one-place predicates). These rules are used most commonly to specify additional necessary conditions that augment a concept definition, i.e., the rules place additional *constraints* on the concept. A report on the MESON system [Owsnicki and Klewe, 1988] describes what is probably the first use of rules in a classification-based application.

Remark: From an epistemological viewpoint, these rules must be considered a part of the ABox. Countering this formal viewpoint is the observation that programmers of TC-derived applications naturally group rules together with term definitions. Additionally, a modified term-classifier provides most of the inferential mechanism needed to reason with rules. Hence, it is usually most convenient to regard rules as a form of knowledge that belongs to neither the TBox nor the ABox.

13.4.4 Truth Maintenance

Term classifiers are inherently forward-chaining reasoners—newly introduced concepts are automatically classified against all other concepts in a concept taxonomy. The more recent TC systems (e.g., KL-TWO, BACK, LOOM, CLASSIC) have chosen to use forward-chaining recognizers (instance matchers) as well: Each time an ABox instance is introduced or modified, these systems automatically revise any changes in the previously computed *instance-of* links that relate instances to concepts.

If a system permits *retractions* as well as assertions of ABox facts, *and* if it caches the results of instance matching (e.g., if it forward-chains), then to preserve correctness of the *instance-of* computations the system must include some form of truth-maintenance (TMS) facility. The function of a TMS is to insure that any point in time, (1) all facts inferrable by the matcher have been inferred, and (2) logical support (a proof) exists for each inferred fact. As facts are asserted or retracted, the TMS will continuously revise the set of inferred facts.

KL-TWO, the first TC system to put all of the major components (TBox, ABox, TMS) into a single system, uses the TMS capability built into the RUP system [McAllester, 1982]. LOOM and CLASSIC have each implemented their own TMSs. We are predicting that the incorporation of TMS facilities into TC systems will become more prevalent as classification-based technology continues to mature. Unless they abandon their commitment to a forward-chaining architecture, TC systems without TMSs are limited to supporting only applications whose knowledge bases change monotonically.

13.4.5 System Performance

A challenge to implementers of TC systems is to build a system that can respond fast enough so that the system can function as the knowledge server in an on-line application. To function as an on-line knowledge server, a system must get adequate response time from each of its TBox, ABox, and truth maintenance components.

The concept classifier designed for NIKL set a very high standard for TBox performance, and modern concept classifiers include only a few architectural improvements. Whether or not this classifier is considered fast enough turns out to depend on how it is used: In the KL-TWO and BACK implementations, the concept classifier is used both for classifying concepts and for matching instances—their strategy is to match an instance by creating a concept describing it and classifying that new concept. This strategy turns out to be elegant but suboptimal—much better performance can be achieved by substituting a specialized instance matching test in place of the subsumption test for concepts (see [Mac Gregor, 1988]).

While KL-TWO demonstrated the feasibility of combining TBox, ABox, and truth maintenance reasoners into a single system, its on-line performance is barely adequate. Consequently, when designing LOOM's TMS, we had to wonder whether or not satisfactory performance was possible when a TMS is included in the TBox/ABox architecture. To maximize our chances for success, we chose to develop a highly specific truth maintenance algorithm tuned to the data structures maintained by the classifier. This experiment has been a success—LOOM applications routinely run with the truth maintenance component monitoring all ABox activity.

13.4.6 Summary of Current KL-ONE Technology

The defining characteristics of a TC system are (1) its *term-definition language*, and (2) its use of a *concept classifier*. There are a number of other characteristics that we believe will become standard within the field: (3) a *database-like* (object-centered) *assertion language*; (4) a *forward-chaining recognizer*; (5) a *rule language* similar to that described in Section 13.4.3; (6) automatic *detection of inconsistent knowledge* (this is an almost free by-product of classification technology).

There are a couple of features for which no consensus exists, but which we predict will eventually become established components in the technology: (7) *retraction* of (ABox) facts—among LOOM users at USC's Information Sciences Institute, only the natural language researchers aren't routinely using LOOM's retraction facility, and they have indicated a need for default reasoning, which implicitly relies on a retraction capability. And, going slightly out on a limb, (8) *default reasoning*—every one of LOOM's users has requested that it provide some sort of nonmonotonic reasoning capability.[2]

No consensus has been achieved on the question of how expressive the term language should be. LOOM and CLASSIC, the two most recently built systems, stand at opposite sides of this question. Section 13.6 examines this question in more detail.

13.5 CONTRIBUTIONS OF KL-ONE TECHNOLOGY

This section surveys some key ideas that the experience offered by the succession of TC systems contributes to the field of knowledge representation. The classically cited contribution of these systems is that they sharply categorize

---

[2] The LOOM language includes a default logic. The fact that the classification technology is relatively efficient at detecting inconsistency and computing subsumption relations makes it particularly well-suited for supporting specificity-based defaults.

knowledge as being either terminological or assertional. The benefits of this approach are argued for in [Brachman and Levesque, 1982; Brachman et al., 1983; Swartout and Neches, 1986]. However, the *formal* distinction between terminological and assertional knowledge (hinted at in our comparison of the "subsumes" and "implies" relations) is somewhat esoteric. Our experience with NIKL and LOOM suggests that drawing such a distinction confuses (all but the most sophisticated) users as often as it helps them.

We consider a major contribution to be the new perspectives the various TC systems offer on how to choose a subset of FOPC. Logic programming advocates often take the view that the syntax and semantics of Horn clause logic is inscribed on clay tablets. TC systems, which base their choice of representation primarily on utility, and only secondarily on computational elegance, have developed a collection of logics that uniformly reject the traditional Horn clause approach. For example, each terminological dialect includes some form of existential quantifier, and all of the assertion languages support open-world semantics. Support for bidirectional implications (between concepts) is a mandatory feature of a TC system.[3]

We suggest that the ability to represent biconditionals (if-and-only-if statements) should be a requirement of any KRS. This requirement allows us to conclude, for example, that PROLOG, which has no definitional capabilities, cannot serve the function of a KRS. Because PROLOG users frequently suffer the delusion that one *can* define terms in PROLOG, we offer a small counterexample. Suppose we assert the following in PROLOG:

```
grandparent(X,Y) :- parent(X,Z), parent(Z,Y).
grandparent(fred,joe).
```

If the above PROLOG rule actually constituted a definition for `grandparent`, then from these two statements we should be able to infer, among other things `(exists Z) parent(fred,Z)`. This would contradict the closed-world semantics of PROLOG, which in the above case implies `not((exists Z) parent(fred,Z))`. PROLOG is designed to permit only the specification of sufficient conditions for membership in a concept or relation, and has no facilities for specifying necessary conditions.

KL-ONE concepts have been characterized as "frames implemented in logic." As such, they combine the principled semantics of logic with the efficiency and naturalness of representation provided by frame systems. A typical frame system derives most of its power and efficiency from its reliance on an *inheritance* mechanism that propagates features from one frame to another. Within a TC system, all

---

[3]The LOOM language includes (backward-chaining) Horn rules. A discussion of how an extended terminological logic like that in LOOM differs from a conventional Horn logic that has been extended to include terminological operators (e.g., LOGIN [Anti-Kaci and Nasr, 1986]) lies outside the scope of this chapter.

logical constraints that apply to a particular concept are propagated (inherited) to all of its subconcepts as a by-product of the classification process.

The automatic inheritance of constraints down a subsumption hierarchy provides several benefits. Among them

- users can inspect individual concepts to see if the constraints that logically apply match the user's own expectations;
- the system automatically detects concepts that inherit conflicting constraints;
- inherited constraints and subsumption links represent cached deductions that can be referenced by other reasoners, yielding significant performance increases for certain classes of deductive queries.

The concept-centered terminological reasoning cited in the previous subsection represents a special case of a more general phenomenon exhibited by many TC systems, which is that they favor forward-chaining inference mechanisms. The constraint propagation mechanisms (recognizers) employed within the assertional components are also forward-chaining reasoners.

The combination of a concept-centered terminological reasoner and an object-centered assertional reasoner yields a relatively efficient hybrid reasoner that can perform computations that are beyond the abilities (from a practical standpoint) of a backward-chaining reasoner. For example, the object-centered, forward-chaining architecture makes it feasible for a system to automatically detect constraint violations as facts are introduced into a knowledge base. This capability enables

- automatic data validation;
- early detection of infeasible states during search;
- determination of whether the application of a default rule would lead to a contradiction.

The benefits that accompany the use of a forward-chaining assertional component come at a price—each revision of the fact base can trigger a number of inferences. Each of these inferences may or may not represent a useful deduction. Because the cost of forward-chaining is sometimes unreasonably high, LOOM implements a mixed strategy wherein concepts can be marked as either forward or backward chaining. The instantiation relationships of concepts marked as forward chaining are continuously truth-maintained, while instantiation relationships of backward-chaining concepts are computed only on demand (and then discarded).

13.6 AN ARGUMENT FOR TERMINOLOGICAL PROMISCUITY

Many or most TC systems were originally developed with the intention of constructing a sound and complete classifier for their terminological language. In consequence, the terminological languages of these systems are strictly limited in their expressivity. Proponents of this "small is beautiful" line of thinking argue that an incomplete system cannot be trusted—that the system may fail to find a valid inference at a critical moment in a running application.

There is a variety of evidence suggesting that a KRS with an expressive terminological language (and an incomplete classifier) is a more useful tool than a KRS with a small terminological language (and a complete classifier). In this section we present arguments in favor of implementing an expressive ("promiscuous") terminological language, and also propose an architecture that may turn out to allow us the best of both worlds.

Users Want More Expressivity. The problem of computing subsumption relationships between NIKL concepts was shown in [Schmidt-Schauss, 1989] to be recursively undecidable. Hence, the NIKL language is considered by the TC purists to be too expressive. Nevertheless, participants at a NIKL workshop [Moore, 1986] compiled a substantial list of capabilities they wanted to see added to NIKL, including numerous extensions to its terminological language. Although LOOM incorporates nearly all of the proposed extensions to NIKL, LOOM users are requesting still more language extensions. Hence, we perceive a large gap between what users say they want, and what many purveyors of TC systems are willing to give them.

Wherein Resides the Scruffiness? A small, elegant KRS embedded in a larger, incomplete (i.e., scruffy) application program yields a scruffy application. When the focus is on the end product, rather than the tool, we observe that the argument for completeness becomes untenable in the general case. Our experience with NIKL and LOOM suggests that when application programmers need to represent something, and the KRS can't help them, they invent their own representation, and the result is nearly always inferior to what a skilled knowledge representation developer could produce. We prefer that the bulk of an application's knowledge structuring constructs occur within a KRS rather than outside of it.

The Complexity of Subsumption is Irrelevant. Suppose a student of formal grammars tells a language implementor that the equivalence problem for deterministic context-free languages is undecidable. The implementor's response is "Who cares! All I care about is parsing, and we can do that in polynomial time." Similarly, in using hybrid TC reasoners, all of the focus at runtime is on the recognition process (computing the types of individuals), not on classification. Bernhard Nebel has shown that although the BACK classifier is incomplete, under certain well-defined circumstances[4] the BACK recognizer *is* complete [Nebel, 1989]. We anticipate that these results can be pushed much farther, so that completeness of recognition will be demonstrated for terminological languages more expressive than BACK's.

There is no RIGHT Terminological Language. Gert Smolka [Smolka, 1988] has formalized a terminological language he calls a "feature logic" that (1) is tailored to match the requirements of a unification-based natural language parser (i.e., the application is significant); (2) has a complete classification algorithm; and (3) looks very different from traditional terminological languages. For example, his feature logic includes operators for representing disjunction and negation of concepts. These operators have been considered taboo by most purveyors of TC systems.

It is feasible to design a terminological language expressive enough to include, for example, both Smolka's feature logic and CLASSIC's terminological language as (proper) subsets, and to build an incomplete classifier for the language that makes complete inferences over these (and other) language subsets. Such a terminological language might be called *promiscuous*, since it aims to satisfy several different classes of users.

We envision that a KRS implementing a promiscuous terminological language would permit individual application programs to indicate which subset of the language they intended to use. The KRS would then flag occurrences of references to concepts that lay outside of the indicated subset. Let us call a concept "first-class" if (1) it is expressed in the indicated language subset, and (2) all concepts referenced within its definition are also first-class concepts. Concepts that are not first-class concepts will be called "second-class" concepts. As long as all factual assertions to our knowledge base reference only first-class concepts, then our recognizer is capable of performing complete inferences with respect to the stated assertions and all first-class concepts.

Second-class concepts can be "safely" employed within queries or patterns. Also, the specification of constraints involving second-class concepts may improve the efficiency or integrity of an application in certain situations, and ought to be permitted as long as the correctness of the application doesn't depend on this "second-class knowledge."

Thus, for those users who insist on completeness, we propose a two-tiered approach to using concepts, wherein no restrictions are placed on how first-class concepts may be used, while second-class concepts may be used only when certain conventions are obeyed. This two-level approach to concept usage is analogous to the situation in the field of relational database systems, where relations are classed

[4] Roughly speaking, the asserted knowledge must be *vivid* in the sense of [Levesque, 1986].

as either "base" relations or "view" relations, and strong restrictions apply to the usage of the view relations.

We have argued that a large gap exists between what users want from a KRS and what many purveyors of TC systems are prepared to give them. Further, we have argued that the negative complexity results for subsumption are irrelevant, since a properly designed hybrid recognizer uses a classifier only to improve the efficiency of the recognition process, not for making it complete.

Instead, we propose implementing a promiscuous terminological language. Such a language would be well positioned to take advantage of any additional positive complexity results obtained for the recognition problem. Furthermore, the availability of a promiscuous terminological language will encourage experiments to determine empirically what terminological subsets are used in real application programs. The implementors of the LOOM language are pursuing this promiscuous approach to terminological reasoning.

13.7 CONCLUSIONS

Several architectural trends have emerged as the TC systems have evolved. All of the TC systems restrict the expressivity of the terminological language, while most of them also restrict the expressivity of the assertion language. Hence, most of them (all but KRYPTON) implicitly favor sacrificing expressiveness in order to obtain more efficient and/or more complete reasoning within the subset of logic that they have chosen to support.

Although no dominant architecture exists for this family of systems, the strongest contender is a hybrid architecture that contains both a classifier, to perform terminological reasoning, and a recognizer, to perform assertional reasoning. The core reasoners in most of these systems adopt an object-centered, forward-chaining style of deduction that represents a generalization of the kind of inference performed by the inheritance mechanisms of frame-based systems.

There is still a way to go before the technology common to a majority of TC systems has reached the point where it would translate into a general-purpose KRS. Beyond the consensus that a KRS should provide explicit support for a terminological language, there is no agreement as to what constructs the terminological language ought to include, or to what degree its expressivity should be limited. The focus of most of these systems has been entirely on reasoning within the bounds of first-order logic, and hence the experience gained from the current family of TC systems gives no guidance regarding what kinds of support a KRS should provide for extra-logical reasoning.

What the classification-based technology *does* offer is a good base on which to grow a well-rounded KRS. After a period of dormancy, we are experiencing a resurgence of activity by developers of TC systems, so the opportunity exists for these systems to grow well beyond the bounds established by the current technology.

ACKNOWLEDGMENTS

This research was sponsored by the Defense Advanced Research Projects Agency under Contract MDA903-87-C-0641.)

References

Ait-Kaci, H. and Nasr, R. 1986. LOGIN: A logic programming language with built-in inheritance. *The Journal of Logic Programming*, 89:185–215.

Borgida, A., Brachman, R.J., McGuinness, D.L., and Resnick, L.A. 1989. CLASSIC: A structural data model for objects. In *Proceedings of ACM-SIGMOD-89*, Portland, Oregon.

Brachman, R. 1978. A structural paradigm for representing knowledge. Bolt Beranek and Newman, Inc.

Brachman, R.J. and Levesque, H.J. 1982. Competence in knowledge representation. In *AAAI-82, Proceedings of the National Conference on Artificial Intelligence*. AAAI, Menlo Park, CA.

———. 1984. The tractability of subsumption in frame-based description languages. In *AAAI-84, Proceedings of the National Conference on Artificial Intelligence*. AAAI, Menlo Park, CA.

Brachman, R.J. and Schmolze, J.G. 1985. An overview of the KL-ONE knowledge representation system, *Cognitive Science*, August, pp. 171–216.

Brachman, R., Fikes, R. and Levesque, H. 1983. KRYPTON: A functional approach to knowledge representation. *IEEE Computer*, September.

Forgy, C.L. 1982. Rete: A fast algorithm for the many pattern/Many object pattern match problem. *Artificial Intelligence*, 19:17–38.

Levesque, H.J. Making believers out of computers. *Artificial Intelligence*, 30(1).

von Luck, K., Nebel, B., Peltason, C., and Schmiedel, A. 1987. *The Anatomy of the BACK System*. Technische Universitat Berlin, KIT Report 41.

Mac Gregor, R. 1988. A deductive pattern matcher. In *AAAI-88, Proceedings of the National Conference on Artificial Intelligence*. AAAI, Menlo Park, CA.

McAllester, D.A. 1982. *Reasoning Utility Package User's Manual*. AI Memo 667, Massachusetts Institute of Technology, Artificial Intelligence Laboratory.

Moore, J. 1986. *NIKL Workshop Summary*. USC/Information Sciences Institute.

Nebel, B. 1988. Computational complexity of terminological reasoning in BACK. *Artificial Intelligence*, 34(3).

———. Forthcoming. Reasoning and revision in hybrid knowledge representation systems.

Nebel, B. and von Luck, K. 1987. Issues of integration and balancing in hybrid knowledge representation systems. German Workshop on Artificial Intelligence, *GWAI-87*, K. Morik, Springer, Berlin (Germany), pp. 114–123.

Owsnicki-Klewe, B. 1988. Configuration as a consistency maintenance task. German Workshop on Artificial Intelligence, *GWAI-88*, W. Hoeppner, Springer, Berlin (Germany), pp. 77–87.

Patel-Schneider, P. 1984. Small can be beautiful in knowledge representation. In *Proceedings of the IEEE Workshop on Principles of Knowledge-Based Systems*, Denver, Colorado, pp. 11–16.

Patel-Schneider, P.F., Gilbert, V.P., and Brachman, R.J. 1985. *Hybrid Knowledge Representation Systems*. Schlumberger Palo Alto Research, Palo Alto, CA.

Robins, G. 1986. *The NIKL Manual*. USC/Information Sciences Institute.

Schmidt-Schauss, M. 1989 Subsumption in KL-ONE is Undecidable. In *Proceedings of the First International Conference on Principles of Knowledge Representation and Reasoning (KR-89)*, Toronto, Canada, pp. 421–431)

Schmolze, J. and Brachman, R. (ed.s). 1982. *Proceedings of the 1981 KL-ONE Workshop*. Fairchild, No. 618.

Schmolze, J. and Lipkis, T. 1983. Classification in the KL-ONE knowledge representation system. In *Proceedings of the Eighth International Joint Conference on Artificial Intelligence*. IJCAI proceedings are available from Morgan Kaufmann Publishers, San Mateo, CA.

Smolka, G. 1988. *A Feature Logic with Subsorts*. IBM Deutschland, Stuttgart, West Germany, LILOG Report 33.

Swartout, W. and Neches, R. 1986. The shifting terminological space: an impediment to evolvability. In *AAAI-86, Proceedings of the National Conference on Artificial Intelligence*. AAAI, Menlo Park, CA.

Vilain, M. 1985. The restricted language architecture of a hybrid representation system. In *Proceedings of the Ninth International Joint Conference on Artificial Intelligence*, pp. 547–551. IJCAI proceedings are available from Morgan Kaufmann Publishers.

Vilain, M. and Bolt Beranek and Newman. 1984. *KL-TWO, A Hybrid Knowledge Representation System*.

14

LIVING WITH CLASSIC:

When and How to Use a KL-ONE-Like Language

Ronald J. Brachman
Deborah L. McGuinness
Peter F. Patel-Schneider
Lori Alperin Resnick
(AT&T Bell Laboratories, Murray Hill)

Alexander Borgida
(Rutgers University, New Brunswick)

Abstract

CLASSIC is a recently developed knowledge representation system that follows the paradigm originally set out in the KL-ONE system: It concentrates on the definition of structured concepts, their organization into taxonomies, the creation and manipulation of individual instances of such concepts, and the key inferences of subsumption and classification. Rather than simply presenting a description of CLASSIC, we complement a brief system overview with a discussion of how to live within the confines of a limited object-oriented deductive system. By analyzing the representational strengths and weaknesses of CLASSIC, we consider the circumstances under which it is most appropriate to use (or not use) it. We elaborate a knowledge engineering methodology for building KL-ONE-style knowledge bases, with emphasis on the modeling choices that arise in the process of describing a domain. We also address some of the key difficult issues encountered by new users, including primitive vs. defined concepts, and differences between roles and concepts, as well as representational "tricks-of-the-trade," which we believe to be generally useful. Much of the discussion should be relevant to many of the current systems based on KL-ONE.

14.1 INTRODUCTION

Work on the KL-ONE knowledge representation system [Brachman and Schmolze, 1985] in the late 1970s inspired the development of a number of frame-based representation systems. These systems have all embraced the ideas of frames as structured descriptions, differentiation between terminological and assertional aspects of knowledge representation, and the central nature of subsumption and classification inferences. At this point there are at least a dozen systems with this shared philosophy and heritage, with widespread international distribution and much ongoing development. All told, there is a large and growing population of users of KL-ONE-like systems.

While the KL-ONE family has garnered its share of technical publications, virtually all of its literature has described technical details of language design, inference complexity, and semantics. One key issue, of concern to the growing community of users, has remained relatively ignored:[1] How does one go about developing a knowledge base with one of these languages? It is one thing to understand the syntax and semantics of a formal knowledge representation language, but quite another to comprehend how to take a complex domain and represent it appropriately with the constructs afforded by the language.

In this chapter, we attempt to capture some of the lore of building knowledge bases in KL-ONE-like systems. We do this in the context of CLASSIC, a new frame-based description system inspired by KL-ONE and most immediately descended from KANDOR [Patel-Schneider, 1984] (and, as it turns out, closely related to BACK [Peltason et al., 1987]). CLASSIC adopts the point of view that a knowledge base can be treated as a deductive database, in this case one with an object-centered flavor. Because of its intended role as a database-style repository, CLASSIC intentionally limits what the user can say. As a benefit, all inferences can be done in a timely manner. All KL-ONE-like languages are limited in some way, and learning to live with such limitations is one of the keys to making good use of these systems in knowledge-based applications.

CLASSIC has a number of novel features that distinguish it from other KL-ONE-like systems, but here we concentrate less on interesting new developments

---

[1] An exception is a recent paper on how to build medical knowledge bases in the NIKL language [Senyk et al., 1989]. Discussion regarding "ontological engineering" in CYC [Lenat and Guha, 1990] is also somewhat relevant here.

in the language and focus instead on how to make good use of it.[2] To that end, we first give a brief introduction to the formalities of CLASSIC. We then address the key issue of when a system like CLASSIC is appropriate for an application and when it is not. While we cannot give a comprehensive formula for when to use the system, we have tried to give some insight into its strengths and weaknesses, and thus which applications may be best suited to its abilities.

Since CLASSIC and some other KL-ONE-like systems emphasize certain issues relating to terminology and classification that are not common in other KR systems, there tend to be a number of subtle ideas that a user must grasp before he or she can make best use of such systems. Therefore, we address ourselves to several important ideas that may be difficult for the novice user of CLASSIC. These involve, among other things, the differences between primitive and defined concepts and some differences in working with concepts and individuals. We also address the perennial issue of when to make something a concept or a role. Subsequently, we present some guidelines for developing CLASSIC knowledge bases, including a sketch of a knowledge engineering methodology that has worked for us in recent applications. Finally, we offer some "tricks of the trade" for CLASSIC users—some tips on ways to represent certain information that are not obvious from the syntax of the language. For example, judicious use of "test" concepts and CLASSIC rules can provide a facility for integrity checking. All in all, we try to give the potential user an idea not so much of what CLASSIC is, but rather how best to live with it and make it work well in an application.

14.2 THE CLASSIC KNOWLEDGE REPRESENTATION SYSTEM

CLASSIC[3] is a frame-based knowledge representation system; i.e., its primary means of representation is in describing objects as opposed to asserting arbitrary logical sentences. It allows the user to make assertions about objects (e.g., "Kalin-Cellars-Semillon is a wine," and "Mary drinks Marietta-Old-Vines-Red") and to describe classes of objects (e.g., "a wine made from Cabernet-Sauvignon and Merlot grapes"). The frames in CLASSIC—which we call "concepts"—are interpreted as descriptions rather than assertions. Thus, if we define a wine as a

---

[2] The interested reader is referred to [Borgida et al., 1989] and [Brachman et al., 1990] for details on CLASSIC and its novel contributions.

[3] CLASSIC stands for "**CLASS**ification of **I**ndividuals and **C**oncepts." It has a complete implementation in Common LISP.

drink with a number of other properties, then being a drink is a necessary part of being a wine, and no wine can violate this requirement.

There are three kinds of formal objects in CLASSIC:

- *Concepts*, which are descriptions with potentially complex structure, formed by composing a limited set of description-forming operators (e.g., WHITE-FULL-BODIED-WINE[4] might represent the concept of a WINE whose color property is restricted to being White and whose body is Full). Concepts correspond to one-place predicates, and thus are applied to one individual at a time;
- *Roles*, which are simple formal terms for properties (e.g., grape might represent the grape(s) a wine is made from). Roles correspond to two-place predicates, and are used to relate two individuals at a time. Roles that must be filled by exactly one individual are called *attributes* (e.g., color might be an attribute representing the color of a wine);
- *Individuals*, which are simple formal constructs intended to directly represent objects in the domain of interest. Individuals are given properties by asserting that they satisfy concepts (e.g., "Chardonnay is a GRAPE") and that their roles are filled by other individuals (e.g., "Kalin-Cellars-Semillon's color is White").

Concepts and individuals in CLASSIC are divided into two realms: *CLASSIC* and *HOST*. *CLASSIC* concepts are used to represent classes of real-world individuals of a domain, while *HOST* concepts are used to describe individuals in the implementation language (currently Common LISP), such as numbers and strings. We treat *HOST* concepts and individuals differently from their *CLASSIC* counterparts by not allowing them to have roles (e.g., we cannot attach any properties to the integer 3).

Concepts and individuals are put into a taxonomy, or hierarchy. A more general concept will be above a more specific concept in the taxonomy. For example, if there were a concept for "a wine made from Cabernet-Sauvignon and Merlot grapes," then this would be a more specific concept than "a wine made from at least one grape," because the first concept describes wines made from at least two grapes. In the taxonomy, individuals are found underneath all the concepts that they satisfy. For example, the individual Kalin-Cellars-Semillon, which happens to be a wine whose color is white, would be under the concept WHITE-WINE in the taxonomy. To maintain this taxonomy CLASSIC also determines the derivable

---

[4] Throughout this chapter, we use the following orthographic conventions: CONCEPT-NAME: typewriter font, uppercase; Individual-Name: typewriter font, capitalized; role-name: typewriter font, lowercase; *REALM*: slanted, uppercase; **function-name**: boldface roman, lowercase; **CLASSIC-OPERATOR**: boldface roman, uppercase.

properties of all individuals and concepts—inheriting properties from more general descriptions as well as combining properties as appropriate.

There are numerous deductive inferences that CLASSIC provides:

- *Completion*: Logical consequences of assertions about individuals and descriptions of concepts are computed; there are a number of "completion" inferences CLASSIC can make:
  - *Inheritance*: Restrictions that apply to instances of a concept must also apply to instances of specializations of that concept. In a sense, then, properties are "inherited" by more specific concepts from those that they specialize.
  - *Combination*: Restrictions on concepts and individuals can be logically combined to make narrower restrictions.
  - *Propagation*: When an assertion is made about an individual, it may hold logical consequences for some other, related individuals. CLASSIC "propagates" this information forward when an assertion is made.
  - *Contradiction detection*: It is possible to accidentally assert two facts about an individual that are logically impossible to conjoin. CLASSIC detects this kind of contradiction.
  - *Incoherent concept detection*: It is possible to accidentally give a concept some restrictions that conbine to make a logical impossibility, thereby not allowing any instances of the concept to be possible. CLASSIC detects this kind of inconsistent description.
- *Classification and subsumption*:
  - *Concept classification*: All concepts more general than a concept and all concepts more specific than a concept are found.[5]
  - *Individual classification*: All concepts that an individual satisfies are determined.
  - *Subsumption*: Questions about whether or not one concept is more general than another concept are answered (this is important during concept classification).
- *Rule application*: Simple forward-chaining rules have concepts as antecedents and consequents. When an individual is determined to satisfy the antecedent of a rule, it is asserted to satisfy the consequent as well.

CLASSIC has a uniform, compositional language, with term-forming operators for creating descriptions of concepts and individuals. The grammar for this language can be found in Figure 14.1 (we discuss the operators below). Note that

[5] Note that object-oriented programming languages usually have inheritance, but not classification.

```
<concept-expr> ::=        THING | CLASSIC-THING | HOST-THING |
                          <concept-name> |
                          (AND <concept-expr>+) |
                          (ALL <role-expr><concept-expr>) |
                          (AT-LEAST <positive-integer><role-expr>) |
                          (AT-MOST <non-negative-integer><role-expr>) |
                          (FILLS <role-expr> <individual-name>+) |
                          (SAME-AS <attribute-path><attribute-path>) |
                          (TEST-C <fn><arg>*) |
                          (TEST-H <fn><arg>*) |
                          (ONE-OF <individual-name>+) |
                          (PRIMITIVE <concept-expr> <index>) |
                          (DISJOINT-PRIMITIVE <concept-expr> <group-index> <index>)
<individual-expr> ::=     <concept-expr>
<concept-name> ::=        <symbol>
<individual-name> ::=     <symbol> | <cl-host-expr>
<role-expr> ::=           <mrole-expr> | <attribute-expr>
<mrole-expr> ::=          <symbol>
<attribute-path> ::=      (<attribute-expr>+)
<attribute-expr> ::=      <symbol>
<cl-host-expr> ::=        <string> | <number> |
                          '<COMMONLISP-expr> | (quote <COMMONLISP-expr>)
<fn> ::= a function in the host language (COMMON LISP) with three-valued logical return type
<arg> ::= an expression passed to a test function
<index> ::=               <number> | <symbol>
<group-index> ::=         <number> | <symbol>
```

Figure 14.1: The CLASSIC grammar

individuals can be described with the same expressiveness as concepts. Information can be added to existing individuals, and information can also be retracted from them, with the appropriate consequences.

We should add that we have taken the approach in CLASSIC that a knowledge representation system should be small and simple (i.e., limited in expressive power), so that its response time is quick, and thorough inference can be peformed. Thus, a user cannot expect to program arbitrary computations in CLASSIC. One should envision CLASSIC as being one component within a larger application system, where it would be used to represent the domain knowledge of the system and calculate a limited set of domain-independent inferences from that knowledge. Other modules in the system would be responsible for the more complicated inferences relating to the particular domain and task.

14.2.1 Knowledge Base Components

The CLASSIC operators are used to form conjunctions, role restrictions, test restrictions, enumerated concepts, and primitive and disjoint primitive concepts. The typical way of describing a new concept or individual in CLASSIC is to give a list of more general concepts (or in the case of an individual, a list of concepts that are satisfied by the individual), and then a list of restrictions that specify the ways in which this new concept or individual differs from these more general concepts. At the end of this subsection, we also discuss the rule component of CLASSIC.

14.2.1.1 Named Concepts and Conjunction

The simplest type of concept expression is a single symbol designating a concept. CLASSIC starts off with a number of built-in named concepts, including `THING`, `CLASSIC-THING`, `HOST-THING`, and concepts for each of the Common LISP types.[6] These names can be used in other concept expressions to build up complex definitions. While the user can create a new name and make it directly synonymous with an existing one, the simplest, useful means of building a compound concept expression is the **AND** operator, which creates a new concept that is the conjunction of the concepts given as arguments. For example, if `WHITE-WINE` and `FULL-BODIED-WINE` are two concepts that have been previously defined, we can define their conjunction as

```
(AND WHITE-WINE FULL-BODIED-WINE)
```

and call it `WHITE-FULL-BODIED-WINE`. This name can then be used in later concept definitions. Note that the **AND** operator can be applied to *any* concept expressions (as long as any names are defined before they are used), not just simple named ones (see Section 14.2.1.2 and following for examples).

14.2.1.2 Role Restrictions

The five operators **ALL**, **AT-LEAST**, **AT-MOST**, **FILLS**, and **SAME-AS** form expressions known as *role restrictions*, and can be used only in *CLASSIC* concepts and individuals, not in their *HOST* counterparts. As specified in the grammar, a role restriction is itself a well-formed concept.

A universal value restriction, or **ALL** restriction, specifies that all the fillers of a particular role must be individuals described by a particular concept expression. For example, a `CALIFORNIA-WINE` might be defined as a wine whose region is a California region, where the California regions are Napa Valley, Sonoma Valley, etc. The `region` role restriction would be written

```
(ALL region CALIFORNIA-REGION).
```

---

[6] Technically, `THING`, `CLASSIC-THING`, and `HOST-THING` are primitive concepts, with the latter two being disjoint (see Section 14.2.1.3). The concepts for the Common LISP types are formed using the **TEST-H** construct (see also Section 14.2.1.3), so that all instances of them can be recognized automatically.

AT-LEAST and **AT-MOST** restrictions restrict the minimum and maximum number of fillers allowed for a given role on a concept or individual. For example, part of the definition of a wine might be that it is made from at least one kind of grape, which would be written

```
(AT-LEAST 1 grape),
```

where `grape` is a role.

The **FILLS** operator specifies that a role is filled by some specified individuals (although the role may have additional fillers). For example, we might define the concept `CHARDONNAY-WINE` as a wine whose grapes include chardonnay; the restriction would be written as

```
(FILLS grape Chardonnay).
```

A **SAME-AS** restriction requires that the individual found by following one attribute-path is the same individual as that found by following a second attribute-path. For example, suppose that there is a food and a drink associated with each course at a meal. Then the concept `REGIONAL-COURSE` might be defined as a course where the food's region is the same as the drink's region. This would be written as

```
(AND MEAL-COURSE (SAME-AS (food region) (drink region))).
```

14.2.1.3 Other Restrictions

Tests: There are two operators that allow procedures to be used in specifying concepts: one is used in *CLASSIC* concepts (**TEST-C**), and one is used in *HOST* concepts (**TEST-H**).[7] A test restriction requires that an individual must pass the test to satisfy the restriction. For example, the concept `EVEN-INTEGER` might be defined as the conjunction of the built-in concept `INTEGER` and a test to see if the integer is an even number:

```
(AND INTEGER (TEST-H evenp))
```

(assuming **evenp** is a function in the host language). The individual currently being tested is assumed to be the first argument to the function, and other arguments can be specified as well. Since *CLASSIC* individuals may change, the test functions return one of three values when applied to a *CLASSIC* individual:

[7] There are two different operators for tests in order to allow CLASSIC to recognize the realm of any concept directly from its expression. While it can do this with all other constructs, since tests are opaque, CLASSIC cannot tell just by looking whether an unmarked test concept is a *CLASSIC* concept or a *HOST* concept. Thus we have two operators, which directly indicate the realm.

- NIL: the individual is inconsistent with this restriction.
- ?: unknown, i.e., the individual is currently consistent with the restriction, but if information is added to the individual, the individual may become either inconsistent with or provably described by the restriction. In other words, the individual neither provably satisfies the restriction nor provably falsifies it.
- T: the individual definitely passes the test; i.e., it provably satisfies it.

Test functions must be monotonic; that is, it should not be possible for the same test function to return T (or NIL) for an individual at one time and NIL (T) at a later time, unless an explicit retraction (see Section 14.2.3) has been done in between.

Enumerated Concepts: A **ONE-OF** concept (or enumerated concept) enumerates a set of individuals, which are the only instances of the concept. For example, a wine whose body could be either full or medium would have the restriction

(**ALL** body (**ONE-OF** Full Medium)).

Primitive Concepts: Normally, when one gives a CLASSIC definition for a concept, it is both necessary and sufficient. For example, if we define a FULL-BODIED-WHITE-WINE as a FULL-BODIED-WINE and a WHITE-WINE, we expect the relationship to be an "if and only if" relationship. The **PRIMITIVE** and **DISJOINT-PRIMITIVE** operators allow a user to form concepts that cannot be fully specified by necessary and sufficient conditions. These operators can only define concepts in the *CLASSIC* realm. If we want to define a wine as a drink with special properties we do not want to or cannot fully specify, we would define the concept WINE as (**PRIMITIVE** POTABLE-LIQUID *wine*), with *wine* being an arbitrary symbol (the *index*) used simply to distinguish this concept from others.[8] WINE is then known to be different from any other **PRIMITIVE** concepts defined under POTABLE-LIQUID (i.e., those with different indices—see the discussion on indices in Section 14.4.1). A **DISJOINT-PRIMITIVE** concept is just like a **PRIMITIVE** concept, except that any concepts within the same "disjoint grouping" are known to be disjoint from each other, and thus, no individual can be described by two **DISJOINT-PRIMITIVE**s in the same disjoint grouping. For example, if we know that fish and shellfish are both types of seafood, and nothing can be both a fish and a shellfish, then we could define fish and shellfish as disjoint primitives under seafood within the same disjoint grouping. That is, we would define the concept FISH as (**DISJOINT-PRIMITIVE** SEAFOOD *type* *fish*), and we would define the

---

[8] Any symbol at all can be used as an index. We use symbols that mirror the names of the concepts just to make it easier to keep them straight. There is absolutely nothing special about the symbol "*wine*."

concept SHELLFISH as (**DISJOINT-PRIMITIVE** SEAFOOD *type* *shell-fish*), where *type* is an arbitrary symbol designating the grouping.

14.2.1.4 Rules

Aside from the language constructs used in forming concept and individual expressions, CLASSIC allows for forward-chaining rules. A CLASSIC *rule* consists of an antecedent and a consequent, both of which are concepts, where the antecedent must be named. As soon as an individual is known to satisfy the antecedent concept, the rule is "triggered," and the individual is also known to satisfy the consequent concept. For example, if there is a rule that says that the best wine for a dessert course is a full-bodied, sweet wine, then if Mary is eating a dessert course, the rule is fired and CLASSIC will deduce that her course is one whose wine is full-bodied and sweet. Consequents of rules are treated as derived information—if the antecedent of a rule is retracted from an individual, then the consequent is also retracted (see Section 14.2.3). (This differs from the treatment of rules in typical rule-based systems, such as OPS, where the consequents of retracted antecedents remain in the knowledge base.)

14.2.2 Knowledge Base Inferences

CLASSIC provides a number of different deductive inferences. The three main types are completion, classification/subsumption, and rule application. *Completion* involves computing the implicit logical consequences of assertions about individuals and descriptions of concepts. For example, when a new concept is defined in terms of existing concepts, *inheritance* is used to determine all of the properties of the new concept—the new concept "inherits" all of the properties from the existing concepts. Thus, if WINE is defined to have exactly one body, flavor, and color, and WHITE-WINE is defined as a WINE whose color is white, then WHITE-WINE will inherit the properties that it has exactly one body, flavor, and color, in addition to having the color white. When a new individual is described in terms of existing concepts, it inherits the properties of those concepts. For example, if Chateau-d-Yquem-Sauterne is an individual that is, among other things, a WHITE-WINE, then it inherits from WHITE-WINE the property that its color is white. It also inherits from WINE the properties that it has exactly one body, flavor, and color.

When a new concept or individual is created, all of its properties are *combined*, which can lead to a number of conclusions. Suppose that the concept FULL-OR-MEDIUM-BODIED-WINE is defined as a wine whose body is either full or medium:

```
(AND WINE (ALL body (ONE-OF Full Medium))),
```

and the concept MEDIUM-OR-LIGHT-BODIED-WINE is defined as a wine whose body is either medium or light:

```
(AND WINE (ALL body (ONE-OF Medium Light))).
```

Suppose that we define the concept SPECIAL-BODIED-WINE as both a FULL-OR-MEDIUM-BODIED-WINE and a MEDIUM-OR-LIGHT-BODIED-WINE:

```
(AND FULL-OR-MEDIUM-BODIED-WINE
     MEDIUM-OR-LIGHT-BODIED-WINE).
```

CLASSIC combines the properties inherited on the body role by intersecting the two **ONE-OF** restrictions, and discovers that the body for SPECIAL-BODIED-WINE must be Medium.

As another example, suppose that Mary wants to serve a regional course (the food and drink are from the same region). She is not very knowledgeable about regions of wines, but she would like to serve a Chianti wine. She knows it is from either France or Italy, so she decides to serve either boeuf bourguignonne or lasagna—whichever one is consistent. She attempts to create an individual course with the following definition (note: CHIANTI is considered a general class here, Boeuf-Bourguignonne an individual food):

```
(AND REGIONAL-COURSE
     (ALL drink CHIANTI)
     (FILLS food Boeuf-Bourguignonne)).
```

CLASSIC will not accept this course description, because the food and drink are from different regions. If Mary were instead to create the course description with the food being Lasagna, the assertion would be successful.

When combining properties of an individual, CLASSIC may discover that a role is *closed*, i.e., it can have no more fillers. For example, suppose a wine is defined to have exactly one maker, which is a winery. If the individual Kalin-Cellars-Semillon is known to be a wine with maker Kalin-Cellars, perhaps represented as

```
(AND WINE (FILLS maker Kalin-Cellars)),
```

then the maker role is implicitly closed by CLASSIC on Kalin-Cellars-Semillon, since it can have no more fillers. Thus, if the user tries to add a filler to the maker role, this will cause an error. The user may also explicitly close a role (see Section 14.2.3).

When a new individual is created, inheritance and combination of properties may also cause certain information to be *propagated* to another individual. For example, suppose we know that Sue drinks Chateau d'Yquem Sauterne, and we tell CLASSIC that Sue drinks only dry wines. The information is then propagated that the individual Chateau-d-Yquem-Sauterne must be a dry wine. *Contradiction detection* will take place during propagation of properties. In this example, if Chateau d'Yquem Sauterne were already known to be a sweet wine, a contradiction would be detected. When a contradiction is found on an individual, the assertion that caused the contradiction is retracted (i.e., that Sue drinks only dry wines), and all the inferences done up to the point of discovering the contradiction are undone (`Chateau-d-Yquem-Sauterne` is reverted to being a sweet wine).

When a new concept is defined, and all of its properties are inherited and combined, CLASSIC determines whether the concept is *incoherent* (i.e., if the concept can have no instances because it contains inconsistent information). For example, if the concept `FULL-BODIED-WINE` is a wine whose body must be full, `MEDIUM-BODIED-WINE` is a wine whose body must be medium, and a wine must have exactly one body, then

```
(AND FULL-BODIED-WINE MEDIUM-BODIED-WINE)
```

will be detected to be an incoherent concept, since a wine cannot have a body of both full and medium at the same time—it cannot have more than one body.

When a new concept is defined, *classification* is used to find all concepts more general than the new concept and all concepts more specific than it. For example, suppose that the concept `FULL-BODIED-WHITE-WINE` is defined as a `WINE` whose `body` is `Full` and whose `color` is `White`. When it is classified, the concepts `FULL-BODIED-WINE` and `WHITE-WINE` would be found as parent (more general) concepts (assuming these concepts have been previously defined), while the concept `FULL-BODIED-STRONG-WHITE-WINE` would be found as a child (more specific) concept (assuming it has been previously defined). During classification, *subsumption* is used to determine whether one concept is more general than another concept. In this example, `FULL-BODIED-WINE` would be found to *subsume* `FULL-BODIED-WHITE-WINE`, since it is impossible to have an instance of the latter that is not an instance of the former. Rules are ignored when determining whether one concept subsumes another.

When a new individual is created, classification is also invoked, to find all concepts that are satisfied by the individual. For example, suppose that the individual `Forman-Chardonnay` is known to be a `WINE` whose `body` is `Full`, whose `color` is `White`, and whose `flavor` is `Moderate`. When it is classified, it would satisfy the concept `FULL-BODIED-WHITE-WINE`, but not the concept `FULL-BODIED-STRONG-WHITE-WINE`. When a new concept with a test restriction is defined, and a subsumption test is done between that concept and another existing concept, also containing a test restriction, the Common LISP functions are not analyzed to see if one is more general than another. However, when a new individual is created, and a check is done to see if that individual satisfies an existing concept containing a test restriction, the test function is run on the individual to see if the individual satisfies the restriction.

As discussed in Section 14.2.1.4, a CLASSIC rule consists of an antecedent and a consequent, both of which are concepts. When an individual is known to satisfy the antecedent concept of a rule, the *rule is applied*, or "triggered," and the individual is also known to satisfy the consequent concept. In the example from Section 14.2.1.4, when Mary is known to be eating a dessert course, the rule is fired that asserts that the wine she drinks with the course is a full-bodied, sweet wine. If she is known to be drinking a dry wine, then a contradiction is signaled, because the information implied about the wine she is drinking is inconsistent.

14.2.3 Knowledge Base Operations

There are a number of operations a user can perform on a knowledge base in CLASSIC. The user can *query* the knowledge base for information, by asking questions like the following:

- "What are all the instances of this concept?" ("Which individuals satisfy this description?")
- "Which concepts does this individual satisfy?"
- "Which individuals fill role `r` on individual `I`?"
- "How is role `r` restricted on concept `C` (or on individual `I`)?"

A user can *define* a new concept, role, or individual. This may cause any of a number of inferences to be performed (see Section 14.2.2). A user can also *add* information to a known individual. For example, if the user originally asserts that `Mary` has exactly one `child`, she might later assert that `Mary`'s child is `Sue`. Concept definitions cannot be modified, although a user can add new rules with any concept as an antecedent at any time.

A user can assert about an individual that a specific role is *closed*; i.e., its current fillers are the only fillers (unless a role is closed, explicitly with a function call, or implicitly when the number of fillers reaches the **AT-MOST** restriction, it may have more fillers, since there is no closed-world assumption in CLASSIC—see Section 14.4.7). There is no **CLOSE** operator in the expression language. Instead, there is a separate function used to close a role on an individual.[9]

Information that has previously been asserted about an individual can be *retracted* in CLASSIC. For example, suppose `Mary` was originally defined to be a `PERSON`, and then she is asserted to be a `NON-WINE-DRINKER` (a person who drinks no wines). If someone then sees `Mary` drinking wine, he or she could retract the information that `Mary` is a `NON-WINE-DRINKER`. In that case, `Mary` would revert back to being simply a `PERSON`, and any inferences that may have been

[9] This is because a **CLOSE** operator would provide a different kind of knowledge (autoepistemic) from all other operators.

made due to her being a NON-WINE-DRINKER are undone. The user can also retract rules that have been added to the knowledge base. No other information about concepts can be changed.

14.3 WHEN IS CLASSIC APPROPRIATE?

As we have seen, CLASSIC includes both a language for representing certain kinds of knowledge, and a system that supports the manipulation of descriptions in this language. As such, it is part of a large family of computer systems variously known as knowledge base or database management systems. As with all such systems, CLASSIC has certain characteristics that make it appropriate for some applications and inappropriate for others. These key characteristics include the following:

- *Object-centered*: All individuals have a unique, intrinsic, and immutable identity obtained at time of creation. The user cannot form arbitrary logical sentences.
- *Terminological*: The system supports the definition of complex "noun phrases" in the form of concepts (and the discovery of their interrelationships). These concepts can then be used to make assertions about objects. CLASSIC is therefore good at describing complex objects, but not particularly suitable for making complex assertions, such as ones involving multiple quantifiers or disjunction.
- *Deductive*: CLASSIC is not just a passive repository for unconnected assertions, like a relational database; the system actively searches to find an entire class of propositions entailed by the facts it has been explicitly told.
- *Incremental*: Partial, incomplete descriptions of individuals are acceptable.
- *Supports knowledge retraction*: The system tracks dependencies between facts and allows certain facts to be retracted.
- *Supports simple rules*: These are applied in a simple forward chaining manner, whenever appropriate individuals are found.
- *Supports procedural tests*: Complex concepts, not otherwise expressible in CLASSIC, can be described procedurally in the host language, so that individuals satisfying them can be recognized.
- *Well-integrated with the host language*: CLASSIC allows values from the host programming language to be managed as instances of their own classes without requiring them to be "encoded" as CLASSIC individuals.

These characteristics allow CLASSIC to provide a great deal of power for certain types of applications but also limit its utility in some situations.

14.3.1 When to Use CLASSIC

The most notable feature of CLASSIC's family of languages is the "self-organization" of the concepts defined: Because concepts have clear definitions, it is possible to have the *system* organize them into the subsumption hierarchy, rather than have the user specify their exact place. This is important because standard logic and production systems, for example, do not address the knowledge engineering issue of organizing large collections of knowledge. Thus, CLASSIC, and more generally, its "sibling" languages can be exploited in any domain where it is useful to organize a large set of objects that can naturally be represented in terms of "features" or "roles." For example, it has been argued that this kind of automatic classification is a useful way of organizing a large set of rules in an expert system [Yen et al., 1989]: by classifying the left-hand sides, the system automatically calculates a well-founded specificity ordering over the rules (the generalization hierarchy); this can be used directly in conflict resolution.

Another example of such a family of applications would be information retrieval, where every object[10] has a complex description, and a query may be phrased as a description of objects having a certain structure (e.g., "find all meals with at least two courses, each of which has a sweet wine as its drink"). In such cases, the descriptions can be classified with respect to each other so that similar objects are grouped together. This can provide a much more sophisticated indexing scheme than simple keyword schemes, without increasing retrieval time significantly since everything is preclassified. (The cost for this type of system is at concept classification time, but presumably that would not be a problem in a library scenario.) The LASSIE system [Devanbu et al., 1989, 1990] is one example of such an application: It maintains information about a large software system and its components, viewed from multiple perspectives, and it can be queried as part of the effort of understanding the software system. LASSIE accepts queries in the form of structured object descriptions (e.g., "an action that drops a user from a call and is caused by a button-push by an attendant"), and uses classification to find all matching instances of the query. LASSIE was first implemented in the KANDOR language, and has now been converted to CLASSIC.

Because the hierarchy of concepts can change dynamically, CLASSIC and its close relatives are also more appropriate for database-like applications that have an *evolving schema*—the normal state of affairs in design and specification efforts, for example. In contrast, standard database management systems are relatively poor at supporting schema changes, in comparison to straight updates to data.

Another important class of applications consists of those involving incrementally evolving descriptions. In contrast to standard repositories of data, such as

---

[10] An object might be a text document, some software component, a chemical compound, a meal, etc.

traditional databases, a CLASSIC knowledge base allows the user to maintain a partial, incomplete view of the domain of discourse, a view in which information is incrementally acquired. The following are some of the features of CLASSIC that support this:

- Role fillers of individuals can be described in ways other than by simple enumeration; for example, it is possible to
  - assert how many objects an individual is related to via some role, without knowing the actual objects; e.g., "every wine has at least one object related to it via the `grape` role."
  - describe the fillers of a role, without knowing them; for example, "all the fillers of the `drink` role for this course are from France."
- Incomplete information may be gradually refined as new knowledge is acquired; thus
  - a particular meal can be said to have at least three courses, and then later discovered to have at least four;
  - a particular individual may first be known to be an instance of `FRUIT` (some primitive class), and then later be discovered to be an instance of `GRAPE` (a more specialized primitive class), without knowing the exact variety of grape (each of which is a primitive subclass of `GRAPE`).
- The "closed-world assumption," normally invoked in data and knowledge bases, views the state of knowledge to be complete at any time; therefore when additional information (not contradicting past data) is added, one is often faced with the problem of having to retract certain conclusions that were reached "too hastily." The absence of the closed-world assumption in CLASSIC avoids these problems by not drawing conclusions until all information is known, and hence CLASSIC supports incremental filling-in of a partially known situation.

This ability to handle partial knowledge can be usefully exploited in such tasks as the design or configuration of artifacts (where something is being created, without having an exact idea of all its parts until it is completed), or the "detective" process involved in recognizing objects from clues discovered over time (e.g., identifying criminals). Languages in the KL-ONE family have been used for such purposes in configuration tasks [Owsnicki and Klewe, 1988], among others.

CLASSIC is also suitable for applications that want to enforce constraints on collections of facts because inheritance is strict and "trigger"-like rules are available. We have one application (a configurator) that uses CLASSIC mostly as an integrity checker. This application makes use of inheritance by putting constraints on high-level concepts and then lets CLASSIC enforce the constraints on all sub-concepts, avoiding the redundancy that would be necessary in many database implementations of the same facts.

CLASSIC, unlike other languages of its kind, has been designed to allow the relatively easy integration of individuals from the host programming language in a manner consistent with *CLASSIC* individuals. This makes CLASSIC easier to use in situations where values such as integers, etc., need to be stored in the knowledge base, and in the case of languages like Common LISP, it allows arbitrary data structures and programs to be kept in a CLASSIC knowledge base—an important feature for AI applications to software engineering, for example.

Because of the object-centered nature of CLASSIC, individuals can be created without knowing some or all of their final descriptors. This allows a user to take the following set of steps: (1) create some new "dummy" individual; (2) relate it to some existing individual (e.g., as a role filler); and (3) inspect the KB to see what additional descriptors have been attached to the dummy individual as a result of rule firings and other deductions. The result is a technique for obtaining so-called "intensional" answers to queries—descriptions of conditions that must hold of *any* individual, currently existing or not, which satisfies certain relationships (see [Borgida et al., 1989] and Section 14.6.7 for more details). Such querying is not supported by traditional databases.

14.3.2 When Not to Use CLASSIC

Previous sections have mentioned the goals and philosophy behind the design of CLASSIC. In keeping with our principles of providing effective reasoning services, certain expressive features have been deliberately left out of the language. These features obviously influence the situations where CLASSIC is appropriate as a representation tool.

Because of its object-centered nature, CLASSIC is likely to be cumbersome to use in cases where mathematical entities such as tuples, sequences, geometric entities, etc. are the center of attention. This is because such entities usually have a notion of "equality" based on (recursive) component identity. For example, calendar dates are structured objects, and it seems natural to model them as CLASSIC individuals with three attributes: `day`, `month`, and `year`. However, object identity may provide surprising results: If we are tracking the date on which wines are bottled through an attribute `bottled-on`, and we are interested in finding out whether two bottles `Wine-bottle-53` and `Wine-bottle-661` were bottled the ame day, then simply checking that `Wine-bottle-53`'s `bottled-on` is the same as `Wine-bottle-661`'s `bottled-on` may result in the answer "false" even if the two dates have the same `day`, `month`, and `year`. In order to avoid such problems, the user would have to search the knowledge base before entering any date, to make sure that a date with the same attribute values did not already exist.[11]

With CLASSIC, an application requiring simple retrieval of told facts, with no interest in derived consequences or a complex query language, will pay an unnecessary performance penalty (both in time and in space) during the processing of input data, and especially in the revision of told facts, since updates would normally be quite simple in that case. Furthermore, at least at the moment, CLASSIC does not have efficient data access facilities built-in in order to handle very large numbers of individuals, such as desired in data processing applications.

Since CLASSIC does strict inheritance, defaults and exceptions are not easily encoded in the language. If an application is inherently oriented toward defaults, CLASSIC should not be the language of choice. If, however, there are only a small number of certain kinds of defaults, CLASSIC may be adequate (see Section 14.6.3).

CLASSIC provides only a limited form of rules, where both the antecedent and the consequent refer to the membership of a *single* individual in some concept (which of course might be structured). Applications requiring complex conditions in the antecedent are much more difficult to handle properly. First, CLASSIC supports neither full negation nor full disjunction, so these constructs are not usually available for expressing complex trigger conditions (but see Sections 14.6.1 and 14.6.2). Nor is it possible to write rules that are triggered by the existence of two or more individuals that are not directly related by some chain of roles (e.g., "if there exist wines x and y such that one is twice as old as the other, then…"). One could consider using something like OPS5 as a front-end rule-processing system and use CLASSIC as a back-end structured working memory. An alternative explored in [Yen et al., 1989] has been to expand the role of the knowledge base to manage both the space of rules and the policy of rule firing.

CLASSIC does not have full negation. If an application will constantly need to refer to a concept that includes everything that is not an instance of some other concept, then the application is not well suited for CLASSIC. Limited uses of negation are discussed in Section 14.6.1.

Classification systems such as CLASSIC are usually implemented as forward-chaining inference systems. (By way of contrast, queries in PROLOG and databases augmented with recursive rules are usually processed by working backward from the query to the database of explicitly asserted facts.) This means that

[11] In CLASSIC, this problem could sometimes be resolved through the use of complex objects in the host language domain, as long as the host language performs equality checking in a component-wise fashion on certain data structures, such as is the case with Common LISP's **equal** predicate. However, in that case, the internal structure of the objects of interest (e.g., dates) would not be accessible to CLASSIC for reasoning.

the addition of new concepts or individuals is time-consuming, though retrieval is more efficient. Therefore if updates are frequent and time-critical, current implementations would make such systems less than ideal when the number of objects becomes large.

Because CLASSIC distinguishes individuals from (generic) concepts and does not support "metaconcepts," CLASSIC itself is not suitable in situations where some individual may in certain cases be viewed as a class with instances. For example, there is no direct way to associate with the concept `WINE` a specific value through a role such as `average-age` or `maximum-sugar-content`—roles that do not make sense when applied to individual bottles of wine. Note however that this is not an intrinsic lack of KL-ONE-style languages—it could easily be remedied in future generations.

Similar problems arise in situations where the "ontology" of the domain is not self-evident: In a knowledge base about wines, does an instance `Kalin-Cellars-Chardonnay` of the concept `CHARDONNAY-WINE` correspond to a specific kind of wine, to a particular vintage ("the 1985 one"), or even more specifically, to a particular bottle? In the case of the vintage, is it after bottling, or later on, or both? Such shifts of perspective are not easily supported by knowledge representation languages that maintain a strict distinction between individuals and concepts (see Section 14.5.1.1).

Finally, CLASSIC and its relatives have general (weak) reasoning procedures, and do not support the direct and efficient addition of specialized kinds of inferences. This means that applications needing to make intensive use of temporal reasoning or spatial reasoning, for example, would find it difficult to have CLASSIC deduce the desired relationships (but see [Litman and Devanbu, 1990] for an extension to CLASSIC that makes it more useful in planning applications).

While some of the above limitations are inherent to the object-centered view of CLASSIC, extensions to the system may eventually relax some of the other restrictions. Under active consideration now are the addition of defaults, a more elaborate rule framework, and large-scale data storage facilities with a powerful query language.

14.4 DIFFICULT IDEAS

Once you have decided to use CLASSIC to build a knowledge base it is important to understand several subtle issues. We will address these in relation to CLASSIC; however, many are equally applicable to the other languages in the KL-ONE family. The issues concern the philosophy of the language and knowledge base design, and can affect decisions concerning the gross structure of the KB. The issues include the amount and kind of information that should go into a concept definition, individuals versus concepts, CLASSIC's detection of incoherencies in role fillers, when rule application occurs, how CLASSIC handles unknown individuals, how updates are done, and the impact of eschewing a closed-world assumption. Two other key (and somewhat difficult) ontological considerations are covered in Section 14.5.1.

14.4.1 Primitive and Defined Concepts

It has been traditional in the KL-ONE family of languages to provide for two kinds of concepts—defined and primitive. A defined concept is like a necessary "if and only if" statement in logic. For example, if a white wine is defined to be exactly a wine whose color is white, then deductions can be done in two directions:

- if we know something is a white wine, then we know that it is a wine and it is white;
- if we know something is a wine and has color white, then we know it is a white wine.

In other words, this kind of definition includes necessary and sufficient conditions for membership in the class. So, if `WHITE-WINE` is defined in the obvious way, any object that is asserted to be one will be both a wine and something whose color is white; also, anything that is known to be a wine and have white color will be classified as a `WHITE-WINE`.

A primitive concept includes only necessary (but not sufficient) conditions for membership. In contrast to defined concepts, primitive concepts support deductions in only one direction (like an "if" statement instead of an "if and only if" statement). For example, it is hard to define "wine" completely. So one might say that, *among other things*, a wine is something that has a `color` that is either `Red`, `White`, or `Rose`. In this case, when CLASSIC is told that something is a wine, it will infer that it has a value restriction on the `color` role, but just because something has a `color` role filled with value `Red`, CLASSIC does *not* infer it to be a wine.

Determining whether a concept should be primitive or defined is a key aspect of building a CLASSIC KB. The basic idea is that a primitive concept is appropriate when no complete definition exists or when only part of a completely known definition is relevant. In the former case, we have no choice but to use a primitive concept—if we use a defined concept, accidental and inappropriate "only if" deductions will be sanctioned. In the latter case, there may be no need to bother with a complete definition if the application never demands that the system automatically recognize an instance of the concept. If the user can be guaranteed to assert class membership directly, then a full definition of a concept like `WINE` is not necessary, even if one is possible. Defined concepts are appropriate when the complete definition is known and relevant, or when one wants the *system* to determine membership in a class. Primitive concepts are usually found near the top of a generalization hierarchy and defined concepts typically appear as we move further down by specializing general concepts with various restrictions.

In CLASSIC, primitive concepts are distinguished by indices. Thus concepts FOOD and WINE could be defined as CLASSIC terms (**PRIMITIVE** CLASSIC-THING *food*) and (**PRIMITIVE** CLASSIC-THING *wine*) respectively; the indices *food* and *wine* allow these two concepts to be different, and at the same time permit synonyms to be defined: FAVORITE-BEVERAGE might also be defined as (**PRIMITIVE** CLASSIC-THING *wine*). The use of indices reinforces that the meaning of a primitive concept definition is contained in its expression—as is the case with all other CLASSIC descriptor types—while the name is simply a label that helps the user. Defined concepts do not need an index as they are distinguished from other concepts by their very definitions. Synonyms can also be created by defining two concepts with equivalent descriptions. Both the concept names may be used later, but in the concept hierarchy they refer to the same entity.

In general, there are three reasons to consider creating a defined concept in systems like CLASSIC:

1. The most important reason is simply that the meaning of an important domain term can be fully defined within the language. In many cases, there will be a natural name in the domain for the concept and an obvious set of necessary and sufficient conditions. For example, OENOLOGIST might be defined as a PERSON who studies wines. There will be many of these concepts in an artificial domain, and few if the domain covers mainly naturally occurring objects.
2. In some ontologies, it can be useful to organize the antecedents of rules into a taxonomy. Rules can be organized so that each consequent is associated with an antecedent at the right level of generality, and rules that apply to more general situations can be inherited and applied in specific situations. This allows classification—and not just direct assertion—to determine when a rule is invoked. For example, as in our sample knowledge base (see Section 14.5.3), we might have partial knowledge about an appropriate wine associated with the general property that a course's food is seafood (i.e., the wine's color must be white), and another fact associated with a more specific property, for example, that the course's food is shellfish (i.e., the wine must be full-bodied). Organization of the antecedents into a hierarchy makes the ontology clearer and makes knowledge base maintenance substantially easier. Here a defined concept is simply used to express the antecedent of a rule, and need not correspond to any natural class in the domain; such concepts will most likely not have any naturally occurring names in the domain. In our sample KB, we have used constructed names like "SHELLFISH-COURSE" for these concepts, although such names hold no significance other than as placeholders (the antecedents of rules in CLASSIC must be named).

3. For some primitive concepts, there may be a number of ways that class members can be recognized, even if there is not a single necessary and sufficient definition. A final use for defined concepts is to express sufficiency conditions for recognition of members of an otherwise primitive class. For example, while PERSON would most likely be primitive in most ontologies, conditions like "featherless biped" and "child of a person" might be considered sufficient conditions for determining personhood. In CLASSIC, one can use a defined concept to represent each set of sufficient conditions (e.g., FEATHERLESS-BIPED would be a defined concept). Each such concept would be the antecedent of a rule whose consequent was the primitive concept whose members were to be recognized (PERSON, in this case).

14.4.2 Definitional and Incidental Properties

It is important in CLASSIC to distinguish between a concept's true definition and any incidental properties that its instances all share. For example, consider red Bordeaux wines, which are always dry. The color and the region would clearly be part of the definition of the concept RED-BORDEAUX-WINE, since this constitutes part of the very meaning of the term. But the property of being dry is certainly not part of the meaning of "red Bordeaux wine," even if it is a (contingent) universal property of red Bordeaux. Thus, in a CLASSIC-style representation the first two properties, (**FILLS** color Red) and (**FILLS** region Bordeaux), would be part of the concept RED-BORDEAUX-WINE, whereas the third would be expressed as a rule, whose consequent would be (**FILLS** sugar Dry) and whose antecedent would be RED-BORDEAUX-WINE.

The distinction between definitions and incidental properties is not important in KR systems that do not perform classification, as it has no effect on how these systems work. However, in CLASSIC, since they represent only necessary, and not sufficient conditions, rules do not participate in either recognition or classification. So, for example, putting the "dryness" property into the definition of RED-BORDEAUX-WINE would mean that a wine would have to be dry to be recognized as a RED-BORDEAUX-WINE (as opposed to having "dryness" automatically asserted about wines that have already been recognized as RED-BORDEAUX-WINES); it would also mean that RED-BORDEAUX-WINE would be inappropriately classified under the concept DRY-WINE. (See also Section 14.5.3, especially footnote 19.)

This type of inappropriate classification also affects primitive concepts. Consider the earlier primitive definition of WINE as something that has, among other things, a color that is either Red, White, or Rose:

```
(PRIMITIVE (AND (ALL color (ONE-OF Red White Rose))
                (AT-LEAST 1 color))
           *wine*).
```

Another way to view this might be to make `WINE` an atomic primitive concept (i.e., directly below `CLASSIC-THING`), and use a rule to express the color restriction. In both cases, since `WINE` is primitive, the color restriction would not be used to answer subsumption questions. Also, if an individual were stated to be a wine, in both cases, the individual's `color` role would be checked for consistency with the restriction. However, there is an important difference. If we added a defined concept, `COLORED-THING` (something that has at least one color), then if `WINE` were only a primitive thing that had a color restriction in a rule, it would not be classified under `COLORED-THING`. The `WINE` concept that included the restriction as part of its meaning would, on the other hand, get classified under `COLORED-THING`.

The distinction between definitional and incidental properties must be carefully made for *all* concepts in CLASSIC, not just defined concepts. In general, the user must decide on ontological grounds whether a restriction should be taken as part of the *meaning* of a concept (and thus participate in classification and recognition) or simply as a derived property to be inferred once class membership is ascertained. The difference between primitive and defined concepts is that in the former case class membership must be asserted directly (by the user or a rule), and in the latter the system can determine it.

14.4.3 Concepts and Individuals

Although in some ways concepts look very similar to individuals (e.g., CLASSIC's syntax allows the same types of expressions for each), there are some subtle (and some not so subtle) differences between them. It is useful to understand some of the important distinctions when trying to understand CLASSIC's classification and deductive processes. First, individuals have unique identities and are countable. An individual can be described by concept expressions that apply to it, but there is a uniqueness assumption that guarantees that two individuals with different names—even with the same description—will be different individuals. Concepts are descriptions and because of the compositional nature of descriptions, the concept space is infinite. The concept hierarchy could include things like full-bodied-wines, full-bodied-white-wines, full-bodied-white-medium-flavored-wines, etc. When considering the knowledge base, it makes sense to count the individual wines but it is not clear how or why one would want to count all the descriptions of those wines.

Next, facts in the world can change, and thus individuals can change, too. One might want to add information to a particular individual or perhaps change something about it, for example, the price of a wine. In contrast, concept definitions and their relationships to each other do not change. Once someone defines a white wine, say as a wine whose color is white, CLASSIC will continue to classify all individuals and concepts with respect to this definition until someone reloads the entire knowledge base. A more subtle issue is that retraction and addition of facts about individuals do not change the concept classification hierarchy. Individuals, and their classification, can change through assertion and retraction of facts; but the semantics of CLASSIC was designed to make the concept hierarchy be immune to changes in individuals. (The concept hierarchy would change monotonically if a new concept definition were added.)

For example, given a concept PICNIC-BASKET defined as

```
(AND BASKET
     (AT-LEAST 2 drink) (AT-MOST 2 drink) (ALL drink WINE)
     (AT-LEAST 3 food) (ALL food EDIBLE-THING)),
```

a CALIFORNIA-PICNIC-BASKET defined as

```
(AND PICNIC-BASKET (ALL drink CALIFORNIA-MADE)),
```

and a KALIN-CELLARS-BASKET defined as

```
(AND PICNIC-BASKET
     (FILLS drink Kalin-Cellars-Chardonnay Kalin-Cellars-Cabernet)),
```

then even though both the wines in the definition of KALIN-CELLARS-BASKET happen to be made in California, KALIN-CELLARS-BASKET will be classified under PICNIC-BASKET but *not* under CALIFORNIA-BASKET. The motivation is that the concept hierarchy should not have to change if the incidental facts about one individual changed. If Kalin Cellars moved its winery to Oregon, we would not want to have to reclassify the concept KALIN-CELLARS-BASKET. Note, however, that if there were an individual Kalin-Cellars-Basket-1 that was a KALIN-CELLARS-BASKET, this would in fact be classified under CALIFORNIA-BASKET. The difference is that this is an *individual*, and as such it is classified based on the known properties of all individuals, including its role fillers. Concepts are not classified based on properties of individuals; they are only classified based on information that is *necessarily* true. The individual Kalin-Cellars-Basket-1 could later be reclassified if the properties of either Kalin-Cellars-Chardonnay or Kalin-Cellars-Cabernet were changed or modified.

As mentioned previously, in CLASSIC, rules function differently with respect to concepts and individuals. Rules are associated with concepts but they are not "fired" until an individual is found to be an instance of the concept. Thus, although there may be a rule that says that wines for seafood courses must be white, this rule would not be enforced until there was a known individual seafood course.

14.4.4 Rule Application

A rule (see also Sections 14.2.1.4 and 14.6.4) is not actually "fired" until an individual is found to be an instance of the antecedent concept. Thus, if one creates a rule that says that white wines must be drunk with seafood courses, this information does not get propagated until a seafood course exists. One ramification of this is that in order to test all the rules in a knowledge base—e.g., for global consistency—one needs to create individual instances of all the concepts that are the antecedents of rules. For example, consider the SEAFOOD-COURSE concept above and a concept SHELLFISH-COURSE that is a kind of SEAFOOD-COURSE with a rule stating that the wine drunk with a SHELLFISH-COURSE must be a full- or medium-bodied wine. In order to check consistency of the rules and to observe restrictions appearing on the wines of courses, individual seafood and shellfish courses would need to be created. Once we created a shellfish course with an associated wine, we would find that the wine would be restricted to being a white, full- or medium-bodied wine.

Because the right-hand sides of rules are concepts and not commands, it is not possible for a retraction to result from the application of a rule. Thus, the only thing that a rule may do is state that if an individual is found to be an instance of the antecedent concept, then it is an instance of the consequent concept. If this is not consistent with the other facts in the knowledge base, then the statement about the individual that triggered the firing of the rule would not be allowed as input to the knowledge base.

It should be noted that rules work in one (and only one) direction. In the previous example, because a course is a seafood course, then we know that the wine for the course must be a white wine. The system would not make the backward inference that because a wine for a course is not a white wine, then the course must not be a seafood course.

14.4.5 Unknown Individuals in CLASSIC

One of the advantages of CLASSIC, as pointed out earlier, is that it allows the description of partially known objects. For example, one way to give information about "null values"—values that exist but are not currently known to the KB—is through identities between attribute paths. We can say, for example, that the Thanksgiving Day menu will have the same drink for lunch as for dinner (by adding (**SAME-AS** (lunch drink) (dinner drink)) to the description of Thanksgiving-Day-Menu), without knowing the identity of the lunch, dinner, or drink objects.

More usually, it is possible to give filler information about roles of unknown objects; for example, one can take an individual course, Course-1, and add to its description the restriction

```
(ALL drink (FILLS grape Riesling))
```

to state that the wine served with it is made from Riesling grapes, without knowing the actual wine to be served.

These examples might make one believe that the system actually creates and maintains CLASSIC individuals for all entities in the domain implied by the current knowledge base (these are sometimes called "Skolem individuals"). This, however, is not the case. We cannot say that some restaurant's wine list includes the drink of `Course-1`, and then, later on, when we find out what is the specific drink of `Course-1`, expect it to show up on the wine list.

In the current implementation of CLASSIC the processing of individuals is complete only in the case when the fillers of roles are all known. The following two examples illustrate incompleteness that occurs when some role fillers are not known.

First, in order to determine that some individual `Ind` is an instance of a concept of the form `(`**`ALL`**` p (`**`ALL`**` q C))`, it is sufficient to know the complete set of the `q`'s of the `p`'s of `Ind` without necessarily knowing the `p`'s of `Ind`. `Course-1` above illustrates this possibility: we know that the `grape`s of the `drink`s of `Course-1` include `Riesling`, but we don't know the `drink`s; if `Riesling` were known to be a fruit and the `grape` role could have at most one filler, a more complete reasoner would recognize `Course-1` as an instance of the concept

```
(ALL drink (ALL grape FRUIT)).
```

For the current implementation, we believe that situations in which such conclusions can be reached are sufficiently rare that we have chosen to avoid the ever present overhead of looking for them.

Second, the implementation does not perform case analysis over the set of possible fillers for some role or role-path. This means that even if `Course-2` has one drink, which is either `Mouton-Cadet` or `Chateau-Lafite`, and both are made in France, the system will fail to recognize that no matter which object is the actual filler of `drink`, `Course-2` should be an instance of the concept

```
(ALL drink (FILLS made-in France)).
```

We emphasize that the above incompleteness arises only in the presence of the constructions `(`**`ALL`**` p (`**`FILLS`**` q ...))` and `(`**`ALL`**` p (`**`ONE-OF`**` ...))`, used because the actual fillers of the `p` role are not yet known. In the current implementation, when information about individuals is incomplete in this way, the subsumption mechanism normally used for concepts is used (since that deals with descriptions intended to be incomplete). However, with that mechanism, the properties of individuals are not considered (e.g., the regions of the wines in the above example; for the reasons for this, see Section 14.4.3), even though they ought to be when processing individuals.

14.4.6 Updates

As mentioned in Section 14.2.3, CLASSIC allows information that has been explicitly asserted by the user about individuals to be retracted. However, CLASSIC does not allow retraction of information that has been *derived* from other information. This is best explained with an example.

Let us begin with an individual that has a restriction on all of the fillers of a role and a known filler for that role, and then try to retract the restriction on the filler. If CLASSIC were told that Lori drinks only kosher wines and that one of the wines that she drinks is `Shalom-Cream-White-Concord`, then `Shalom-Cream-White-Concord` would be inferred to be kosher (by a propagation inference). If at some point, we actually were to discover that `Shalom-Cream-White-Concord` was not kosher, we might want to retract that fact from our knowledge base. CLASSIC would not allow this retraction since its knowledge about this fact is considered to be *derived* information. CLASSIC would force the retraction of some piece of *user-stated* information that led to the conclusion that `Shalom-Cream-White-Concord` was kosher. For example, the user could retract either the fact that Lori drinks `Shalom-Cream-White-Concord` or the fact that Lori drinks only kosher wines.

The reason for disallowing retraction of derived information is to maintain consistency of the knowledge base. If CLASSIC allowed direct retraction of the fact that `Shalom-Cream-White-Concord` was kosher, then if someone asked if it was, it would be unclear how to answer: if the **ALL** restriction on `Lori`'s `drinks` role were enforced, the answer would be "yes"; if the directly stated facts on `Shalom-Cream-White-Concord` were examined, the answer would be "no." Also, if CLASSIC allowed retraction of derived information, some updates would appear never to have occurred. CLASSIC's approach to updates is to retract the stated information and automatically retract all derived information that was based on that information. Then the system rederives all facts that hold in the new situation. If CLASSIC allowed the retraction of the fact that `Shalom-Cream-White-Concord` was kosher, then following this algorithm, it would have to reclassify `Shalom-Cream-White-Concord`. It would once again find that `Shalom-Cream-White-Concord` was a wine that Lori drank and then it would propagate the restriction that the wine must be kosher. Thus the knowledge base would simply revert back to the previous state wherein `Shalom-Cream-White-Concord` was kosher; the update would appear never to have occurred. The only other way to maintain consistency would be for CLASSIC to retract a piece of information that led to the derived information. In this case, it is not clear which piece of information that should be, thus it seems appropriate to force the user to make the choice.

14.4.7 No Closed-World Assumption

CLASSIC does not work under the closed-world assumption (CWA) for individuals, that is, it does *not* assume that anything that it does not know is false. Thus, if some basket were known to have two specific wines in it, CLASSIC would not assume that it had *only* two wines in it—it would deduce only that the basket had *at least* two wines in it. So if this same basket had three things to eat in it and we knew that PICNIC-BASKETs by definition had at least three things to eat and at most two wines in them, this basket could not be classified as a PICNIC-BASKET. It would only be classified as such when the drink role became "closed"—i.e., when CLASSIC was told or it derived that there could be no other fillers for the drink role. This example shows that in general an individual cannot be classified under a concept with an **AT-MOST** restriction until the corresponding role is closed. The same is true for concepts with **ALL** restrictions.[12]

A role can be closed in two ways. The user may explicitly tell CLASSIC that a particular role on an individual will have no more fillers. Alternatively, the system may derive that a role must be closed. If the system is told that an individual is an instance of a PICNIC-BASKET, and it also knows that PICNIC-BASKET contains the wines Kalin-Cellars-Chardonnay and Marietta-Zinfandel, then CLASSIC can deduce that the role is closed since the definition of PICNIC-BASKET states that there may be at most two wines.

14.5 BUILDING CLASSIC KNOWLEDGE BASES

Once it has been determined that CLASSIC is an appropriate language to use in describing a domain, and some of the more subtle language issues are well in hand, there is still the significant problem of designing the knowledge base given the domain structure. While not identical to the traditional expert systems process, the process of developing a CLASSIC KB is a form of knowledge engineering, where the key is finding the right way to break the domain into objects and their relationships. While there is no single method for producing such an ontology, we discuss some general issues to consider and offer one possible process for creating a knowledge base. We also present parts of a CLASSIC knowledge base, to illustrate the style of description of a typical domain representation.

---

[12] There is one way to classify an individual with respect to concepts with **AT-MOST** or **ALL** restrictions. If the individual in question has a restriction (either directly or by inheritance), then CLASSIC can make deductions based on this restriction, including determining that it implies the target **AT-MOST** or **ALL** restriction. If, for example, CLASSIC is trying to classify something as a CALIFORNIA-BASKET and its drink role is not closed, but it does have a restriction that all its drinks are made in the Napa Valley, and we know that everything that is made in Napa Valley is made in California, then even without knowing all the fillers of the drink role, CLASSIC can make the deduction that it satisfies the **ALL** restriction on drink of CALIFORNIA-BASKET.

14.5.1 Basic Ontological Decisions—Individuals and Roles

Since frame systems like CLASSIC are object-centered, the key idea is to determine what the "objects" in the domain are. This involves the specification of the individual items about which information can be gathered and asserted (the *individuals* of the domain), as well as the specification of classes of those items that share common properties (the *concepts*). The properties of the individuals and the relationships between them are then represented as *roles*. This is all complicated by two key facts: What constitutes an "individual" is not always clear (different levels of abstraction are possible), and some terms seem equally well expressible as concepts and as roles. In all of these cases, the knowledge engineer needs to make a determination fairly early in the KB design process.

Let us consider these two issues in turn, and then we will discuss a general procedure for getting a domain characterized in CLASSIC.

14.5.1.1 Individuals versus Concepts

Imagine that we are developing a knowledge base of foods and wines. Intuitively, it would seem clear that items like `WINE` and `WHITE-WINE` (a wine whose color is white) should be concepts. It is likewise reasonably clear that `CHARDONNAY-WINE` (a wine made from the chardonnay grape) should also be a concept. However, things are not so simple when we attempt to represent a single "wine."

In some knowledge bases, for example in an application that will recommend a wine to a patron for a general class of entrees (e.g., shellfish), an individual winery's varietal (e.g., Forman Chardonnay) will be an appropriate individual. In our sample knowledge base (Section 14.5.3), we use this as the level of our individuals. However, for some problems, this level might not be fine-grained enough. For the discriminating wine-drinker, the vintage of a particular wine may be critical, and thus `FORMAN-CHARDONNAY` would have to be a concept, in order that `1981-Forman-Chardonnay` could be an individual. Or, it might be necessary in some applications to make individual bottles of wine be individuals in CLASSIC.

While different kinds of objects can be considered individuals from different points of view, in a system like CLASSIC we are forced to make a commitment at the outset. In that case, the key question to ask is, which objects would be appropriate to *count* in an application? Or, alternatively, in a retrieval application, which objects would be best to retrieve given a query? For a wine-advisory application, the answer given by a wine steward to the question, "How many wines do you stock?" would indicate which items to count as individuals (e.g., `Forman-Chardonnay`). Alternatively, one could count as individuals the items appearing on a menu (e.g., winery, varietal, and vintage).

Whatever level we fix for our individuals, any other descriptions in the domain that could be considered individuals from some other point of view can be handled in one of two less-than-ideal ways. First, they could simply be represented as concepts. Thus, if `1981-Forman-Chardonnay` were an individual, `FORMAN-CHARDONNAY` would be a concept, and the former would probably be described by the latter. An alternative would be to allow both objects to be individuals. But since CLASSIC does not currently support a "metadescription" facility, this representation would be incomplete in an important way, in that CLASSIC would maintain no relationship at all between the two individuals. One could go so far as to place a `generic-varietal` role on `1981-Forman-Chardonnay` and fill that role with `Forman-Chardonnay`, but CLASSIC would treat that role just as any other, and no properties of the more generic varietal individual would be inherited by the more specific vintage one.

14.5.1.2 Concepts versus Roles

As mentioned, another key distinction that the user of a language like CLASSIC is forced to make is that between concepts and roles. A number of people working with KL-ONE-like languages have reported having difficulty deciding whether something should be a concept or a role. Terms like "father," "landlord," etc., can be used equally well in either sense. For example, "Ron is a new father" uses *father* as a concept. "Ron is the father of Rebecca" uses it as a role. Even a more straightforward term like "grape"—an obvious candidate for concepthood—can present a problem. We can easily imagine the properties of grapes (`color`, `where-grown`, `age-of-vines`, etc.), and can visualize `GRAPE`'s place in a taxonomy of types of foods. However, it is equally plausible to imagine a `grape` role for the concept of `WINE`, indicating the kind of grape a wine is made from. Should *grape* be a concept, a role, or both?

While the treatment of any particular domain term will really depend on the application, there are some general guidelines to use when trying to design concepts and roles. Since part of the problem is the use of nouns in natural languages to correspond to both concepts and roles, we need to look beyond the surface properties of words. In languages like English, certain nouns seem to reflect items that have existence independent of any others (e.g., "person," "apartment," "wine," "grape"), and others reflect items that depend on others for their existence (e.g., "father," "landlord," "vintage," "skin"). The former most obviously correspond to one-place predicates in first-order logic. We would have no trouble describing an individual by one of these terms without reference to any other individuals on whose existence they depend. Thus, we could independently characterize an object as a grape without needing to make reference to any wines made of out of such grapes, nor would there ever have to be any. The description of an item as a grape would stand on its own, without implying the existence of any unmentioned individuals.[13]

On the other hand, while we might naturally use some terms from the latter set as if they were also one-place predicates (e.g., "Deb is a landlord"), *they in actuality imply the existence of a second argument* (e.g., whom Deb is the landlord *of*). In this case, the primary representation in CLASSIC should be as a role. Any interpretation of the term as a concept would be *derivative* from its interpretation as a role, since there is always an *implied* second argument.

The clear guideline for discrimination between concepts and roles is thus the determination as to whether a description can stand on its own without implying an unmentioned object related to the object in question. In an intuitive ontology, `SHELLFISH` would clearly be a concept, and `vintage` would clearly be a role. There are some cases—including those just mentioned—where it will be quite easy to determine which is which. In the case of an unquestionable concept like `SHELLFISH`, it is almost impossible to imagine using the term in a phrase like, "the shellfish of ⟨something else⟩." That is, it would be very hard to imagine a property of something called its "shellfish." In the case of an unquestionable role like `vintage`, it is almost impossible to consider using the term *without* the "of" phrase. For example, it is unusual to use "vintage" in any other way than as the vintage *of* a particular wine.

Unfortunately, most terms will not be so pure in their natural use. However, the basic guideline still applies. Even though we can refer to a "wine's grape" (i.e., its composition), the concept of a grape stands on its own and does not need to lean on the existence of any wines. Even though someone is referred to as a "father," that description is not truly meaningful without taking into account the implied child. One interesting difference between these two cases (in which a term can be used either as a concept or as a role) is that in the latter case, the value restriction used for the `father` role would have a different name (`MAN`) from the role, whereas it seems most natural in the former case to name the role with the same name as the value restriction (the `grape` role of a `WINE` would be filled by a `GRAPE`). It would seem somewhat silly and uninformative to have the value restriction of the `father` role be `FATHER`. This is because the *only* difference between the concept `MAN` and any proposed concept like `FATHER` is the man's *playing the role* of father. One could find all of the fathers in a knowledge base simply by finding the set of men and then discarding those not known to fill the father role for some individual. The concept of a father clearly has its meaning compositionally dependent on the meaning of the `father` role.

---

[13] This discussion is intended to be intuitive, and relies only on a naive understanding of the ontology of the world. It is not intended to envoke deep discussion about existence, objecthood, or any other metaphysical issues.

In the history of KL-ONE-style languages, proposals have been made for a type of object called a *qua-concept* [Freeman, 1982], which would be a concept whose meaning is dependent on some role. FATHER as a qua-concept would have a slightly different structure than, say, MAN, reflecting the dependence of someone's being a father on the existence of another individual (some interesting property inheritance can be done in this case as well). CLASSIC, however, has no facility for this, so the best one can do is adhere to some reasonable conventions. If a separate concept for the role father is truly necessary (e.g., to act as a value restriction for some other role), consider naming it MAN-qua-father, to indicate the functional dependence. This concept would be a subconcept of MAN, and it could be made to work as if it were a qua-concept through the use of a procedural test, so that at least classification of all fathers could be achieved automatically.[14]

In the case of a WINE's grape, one could use the same name for the role and the concept without resorting to any other mechanism. CLASSIC will not get confused; however, users might. Thus, for clarity, it might be safer either to preface the role name with "has" to clearly distinguish the two senses (i.e., has-grape would be a role of WINE), or to create a compound concept name so that the role name will be simple. In our sample knowledge base in Section 14.5.3, we do the latter, creating the category of a WINE-GRAPE, and using grape as a role for WINE. In many cases, there is a natural role name to use so that this problem will not even arise. Such is the case with a term like "vintage," where the value restriction of the vintage role for WINE would be YEAR. It is also not required in any way that the names of roles should be nouns. made-from would be a perfectly reasonable name for the role we have been calling grape.

Finally, one should in general consider using roles to represent *parts* of objects, *intrinsic properties* (e.g., the color of a wine), and *extrinsic properties* (e.g., the price of a wine, which is not an intrinsic feature, but rather set in some external way), as well as for functionally defined terms like "vintage."

14.5.2 A Simple Knowledge Engineering Methodology for CLASSIC

When attempting to analyze a domain and build a CLASSIC-style representation, it is often difficult to know how to begin. Over the years, we have developed some guidelines for building knowledge bases that break the process down into a series of steps, starting with a rough cut at the domain ontology and then refining the representation in several passes. While this method may oversimplify the knowledge representation process, it may be useful in many application areas,

[14] What will be missing in this case is the automatic recognition that an OLD-FATHER is a FATHER, since no subsumption is computed on test functions (assuming FATHER and OLD-FATHER each had a single test function to compute their membership).

especially for those who are just getting started in using CLASSIC or other languages like it. We continue using our wine and meal examples. We have included below sketches of portions of the evolving KB to exemplify most of the steps.

1. *Enumerate Object Types*. First, without making any fine-grained distinctions, it is useful to try to write down a list of all types of objects you would ever care to make statements about or explain to a user. For example, important wine-related object types will include *wine*; *grape*; *winery*; *location*; a wine's *color*, *body*, *flavor*, and *sugar-content*; different types of *food*, like *shellfish* and *red-meat*; subtypes of wine such as *white wine*; etc. The key thing initially is to get a comprehensive list of names without worrying about overlap between concepts or any properties that the items might have.

1. Object types

body sugar white-wine
color wine fish food
grape location dry-wine
winery red-meat
seafood

2. *Distinguish Concepts from Roles*. Looking at the list, make a major cut by distinguishing between objects that have independent existence and those that depend on other objects for their existence (see Section 14.5.1.2). The former will be concepts, the latter must be roles. For example, wines will exist as independent objects, as will wineries, but the body of a wine and its sugar content are more appropriately thought of as roles. In developing a CLASSIC KB, it is also necessary to distinguish which roles are *attributes*, i.e., which ones have exactly one filler. Thus, `color` might be an attribute, since a given wine can have only one color, and `grape` would be a regular, multiply fillable role, since a wine can be made from more than one type of grape.

2. Concepts vs. Roles

WINE	sugar (a)
WINERY	body (a)
WHITE-WINE	flavor (a)
DRY-WINE	color (a)
FOOD	grape
FISH	region (a)
RED-MEAT	
SEAFOOD	
GRAPE	

3. *Develop Concept Taxonomy*. Group the concept objects into a hierarchical taxonomy by asking if by being an instance of a type, an object will necessarily (i.e., by definition) be an instance of some other type. The latter will then

be above the former in the hierarchy. For example, if something is a WHITE-WINE, it will necessarily be a WINE. Thus WHITE-WINE will be a descendant of WINE in the taxonomy. Remember that it is possible for a type to be an immediate descendant of more than one other type. For example, a DRY-WHITE-WINE must be both a DRY-WINE and a WHITE-WINE.[15]

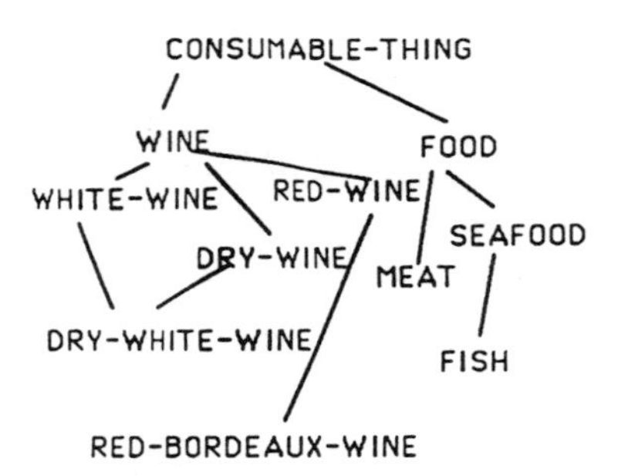

4. *Individuals.* Isolate the set of key individuals that will be important in all uses of the application. For example, wine colors like red, white, and rose, and wine sugar levels like dry and sweet will be critical in the definition of concepts like WHITE-WINE and DRY-WINE. For each individual, try to determine all of the concepts that aptly describe it.

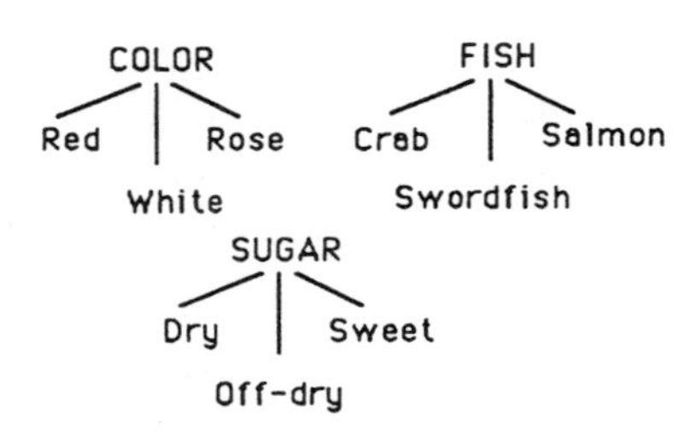

5. *Determine Properties and Parts.* Once the basic ontology is laid out, with the taxonomic relationships between concepts being fairly clear, it is time to turn

---

[15] Note that once the final representation of a concept like DRY-WHITE-WINE is completed, CLASSIC will be able to determine automatically that it is a subconcept of the other two concepts. However, when developing the domain ontology, it is not a bad idea to sketch out these relationships by hand; once the formal representation is constructed and everything is classified, the user can check the resulting taxonomy against his/her original conception of the domain, to see if the formal representation is correct.

attention to the internal structure of the concepts. For each concept enumerated so far, write down a list of its properties. These should include

- *"intrinsic" properties* like the color and body of a wine;
- *"extrinsic" properties* like a wine's name and its price;
- *parts*, if the type of object is structured; these can be both physical and abstract "parts" (e.g., the courses of a meal, the grape of a wine, the casks of a winery).

Record also any key relationships between individual members of the class and other items (e.g., relationships like employee that might not be considered properties or parts of a winery). Each of the above relationships should be assigned to a role (while it is useful to distinguish between parts and other properties, CLASSIC and related languages do not have any formal mechanism for distinguishing among different types of roles). It is reasonable to expect that many of the roles will be used in many concepts. Each of the items determined to be a role in Step 2 should be accounted for.

Note: Some of the roles determined to be relevant to a concept in this step will ultimately end up playing a part in the *definition* of the concept, and some will be used to express *derived* properties. In other words, some of the role restrictions generated in steps 6–9 must be satisfied for an individual to be considered to satisfy a concept; the other restrictions will be appropriate to infer about the individual once it is determined to satisfy the concept definition. For example, a value restriction like (**FILLS** color White), derived in step 7, will be part of the meaning of WHITE-WINE; this means that an individual will need to have its color be provably white before it will be placed in that category. The same restriction could, however, be a derived property of CHARDONNAY-WINE, since it is not necessary to determine that a wine is white before deciding that it is a chardonnay (it need only be known that it is made with a chardonnay grape). Keep this in mind for step 10. Also, see Section 14.4.2 for more on this distinction.

5. Properties

WINE	
CONSUMABLE-THING	
intrinsic:	color
	body
	grape
	sugar ...
extrinsic:	name
	price
	region ...

6. *Determine Number Restrictions.* For each concept and each role that is relevant to its meaning, determine the cardinality of the set of role fillers (e.g.,

that a wine can have only one region but several grapes). These will be expressed in CLASSIC as **AT-LEAST** and **AT-MOST** restrictions.

6. Cardinality

WINE	
CONSUMABLE-THING	
color	1
body	1
grape	>=1
sugar	1
name.	>=1
price	>=1
region	1

7. *Determine Value Restrictions.* For each concept and each of its relevant roles, determine the class of values that can appropriately fill the role. These "value restrictions" (e.g., that the `region` of a `WINE` must be a geographic region) will be expressed in **ALL** restrictions. In the event that a role must be filled by a single individual (e.g., a `CHARDONNAY-WINE` must have its `grape` role filled by exactly `Chardonnay`), or a fixed set of individuals, use the **FILLS** construct in conjunction with an **AT-MOST** restriction. If there is more than one potential filler (not all of which must necessarily fill the role), but the set of candidates is a fixed set of individuals, use the **ONE-OF** construct (e.g., a `NON-SWEET-WINE` has as the fillers of its `sugar` role the set `(`**`ONE-OF`**` Dry Off-Dry)`).

7. Value Restricitions

WINE		
CONSUMABLE-THING		
color	1	COLOR
body	1	BODY
grape	>=1	GRAPE
sugar	1	SUGAR
name	>=1	STRING
price	>=1	DOLLAR-AMOUNT
region	1	REGION

7. More Value Restrictions

RED-BORDEAUX-WINE	
WINE	
color	Red
region	Bordeaux

8. *Detail Unrepresented Value Restrictions.* For each value restriction thus needed, make sure that the appropriate concept exists in the previously generated general taxonomy. If it had previously been proposed, add it to the general taxonomy (for example, it is probable that we had not thought to create the concept of a geographic region prior to thinking about the structure of `WINE`). If the concept will be important in the domain model, go through all of the above steps for that new concept and any related ones you neglected to create before. For example, if you determine that the `grape` of a `WINE` must

be a WINE-GRAPE, and the concept of such a grape is important, consider creating specialized subconcepts that might be useful (e.g., CHARDONNAY). For each of the new concepts, consider its properties and relations to other concepts and individuals.

9. *Determine Interrole Relationships.* For each concept, enumerate any relationships among its roles that might be important to your domain knowledge (for example, it might be important to restrict the suggested-retail-price of a WINE such that it is the WINE's maker's marketing-rep that sets it). CLASSIC and languages like it have only limited means of expressing these interrole restrictions, but they are useful to enumerate. For a CLASSIC representation, any constraint that can be expressed as an equality between two chains of attributes on the same object can be expressed with the **SAME-AS** construct. Any other constraints must be expressed in opaque form with the **TEST-C** or **TEST-H** construct.

9. Constraints

```
WINE
CONSUMABLE-THING
  color   1     COLOR
  body    1     BODY
  grape  >=1    GRAPE
  sugar   1     SUGAR
  name   >=1    STRING
  price  >=1    DOLLAR-AMOUNT
                (maker market-rep price)
  region  1     REGION
```

10. *Distinguish Essential and Incidental Properties.* At this point, for each concept, we will have determined a set of parent concepts (expressed in the taxonomy) and a set of restrictions, namely number, value, interrole equality (**SAME-AS**), and opaque test restrictions. For each concept, look over this set, think about what it would mean to be a member of the class specified by the concept, and isolate the set of concepts and restrictions that would appropriately constitute a set of essential properties. These properties would be sufficient for determining membership in the concept in question. For example, with a RED-BORDEAUX-WINE, the fact that it is a WINE whose color is Red and whose region is Bordeaux would be essential to its definition. Its sugar content would be an incidental property and would not be necessary to know before determining that something was a red Bordeaux. The essential properties would constitute the definition of the concept while the other properties would then be expressed as the consequents of *rules* associated with the concept (e.g., RED-BORDEAUX-WINE would have a rule asserting that the wine is a DRY-WINE; thus the sugar content need not be known in order to determine that something is a red Bordeaux, but it would be universally true of all red Bordeaux wines).

10. Rules

```
RED-BORDEAUX-WINE
-----------------------
WINE
 color      Red
 region     Bordeaux
-----------------------
rules:  DRY-WINE
```

11. *Distinguish Primitive and Defined Concepts.* Determine if each proposed concept definition is complete. That is, do the conditions determined by the above steps constitute a complete set of necessary and sufficient conditions for the concept? In the case of a `RED-BORDEAUX-WINE`, the conditions that it is a `WINE`, that its `color` must be exactly `Red`, and that its `region` must be `Bordeaux` would indeed be both necessary and sufficient. For those items whose definitional complement is not fully sufficient, make the concepts primitive. For example, we may not consider `WINE` to be fully defined as a `POTABLE-LIQUID` with at least one `grape`; we would not want every liquid made from grapes to be considered a wine. Thus `WINE` would have to be primitive.
12. *Determine* **DISJOINT-PRIMITIVE** *Concepts.* For those concepts determined to be primitive, determine if any are mutually exclusive. Group those so determined into clusters under a common superconcept.[16] Typically, the highest concepts in the hierarchy will be primitive and disjoint. For example, `SHELLFISH` and `FISH` would be good candidates for disjoint primitive concepts with a mutual parent of `SEAFOOD`. They are disjoint because no individual can be described by more than one of them at a time, and they are primitive because in this domain we are not interested in any internal structure or further description of individuals that satisfy these descriptions (we will typically declare by fiat that `Crab` is a `SHELLFISH`, without expecting CLASSIC to be able to determine it by itself). Use the **DISJOINT-PRIMITIVE** construct to specify these concepts.

The result of translating the informal representation created above into CLASSIC will be a knowledge base of concepts, roles, individuals, and rules (note that a concept must be defined prior to its first use, since there are no circular definitions allowed; however, a concept can be used in the consequent of a rule that is associated with it). The concepts will have a set of necessary, and sometimes, necessary and sufficient conditions expressed as sets of more general concepts and

[16] In CLASSIC, there can be several disjoint groupings under the same concept, with the assumption that there is a common dimension along which all the items in a grouping differ (imagine, for example, grouping subconcepts of `PERSON` by gender or by age). Thus the **DISJOINT-PRIMITIVE** construct requires the user not only to specify the parent concept, but to name a grouping into which to put the primitive being specified.

restrictions (those concepts with no sufficient conditions would be constructed using the **PRIMITIVE** or **DISJOINT-PRIMITIVE** operators). The parents and restrictions on a concept would be conjoined with the **AND** operator, and each restriction would be expressed with an **ALL**, **AT-LEAST**, **AT-MOST**, **FILLS**, **SAME-AS** or **ONE-OF** operator (or a **TEST-C** or **TEST-H**, if appropriate). Named concepts would also be the antecedents of rules expressing necessary conditions—descriptions that would follow once something was determined to be a member of the class. Figure 14.2 shows both the schematic form and the CLASSIC form of the two examples we have been following.

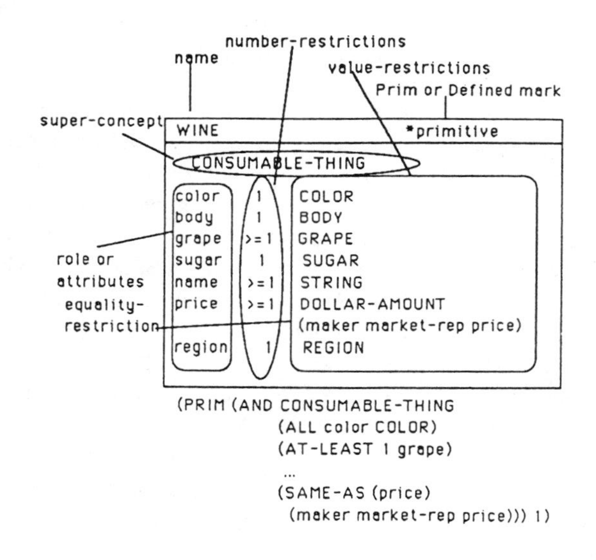

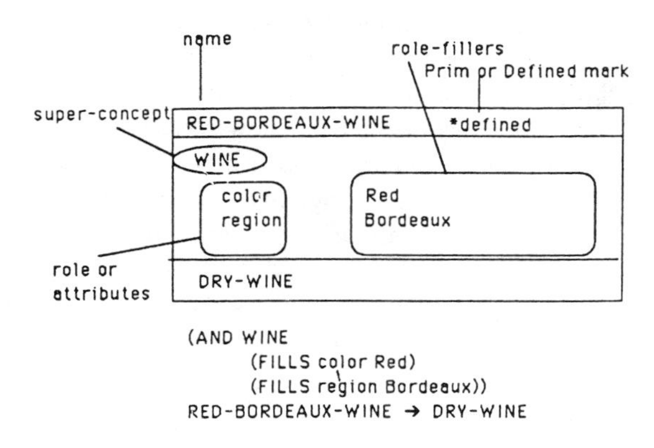

Figure 14.2

14.5.3 A Sample Knowledge Base

In order to illustrate the general ways a user will use CLASSIC to build a knowledge base, we will now consider some sample definitions from the world of wines and meals. The basic goal here is to allow a user to describe the food eaten at a particular course of a meal (in a very simple way), and have the KB recommend an appropriate set of wines. The knowledge is organized so that a new wine can be described in a number of different ways (e.g., it might be asserted to be a late-harvest Semillon, or a white wine from the Loire region); it is then classified with respect to a general set of useful wine types (e.g., CHARDONNAY-WINE). Once the wine is classified, properties not directly asserted by the user are derived using rules whose antecedents are the general wine types (e.g., if all chardonnays are either full- or medium-bodied, this information will be represented as a rule whose antecedent is the concept of a chardonnay wine). Thus wines can be entered in a variety of ways—by region, by varietal, by color, etc.—and ultimately as much as possible about their color, body, sweetness, etc., will be ascertained automatically.

In parallel to the hierarchy of useful wine types, we have a simple hierarchy of food types. The food types are used to describe a course the user is considering having (e.g., "a MEAL-COURSE[17] whose food is a SHELLFISH"). The connection between wines and food is to be made via a hierarchy of course-types (e.g., SHELLFISH-COURSE). Each useful course-type (not every possible course-type forces a choice of wines) has an associated rule that states what characteristics are required of its wine (e.g., seafood courses demand white wines, oyster courses need sweet wines). The system makes a "recommendation" in a simple forward-chaining way: The user's course-type is classified, rules applying to it are inherited from all descriptions that apply to the course, the rules are fired, and the consequents assert various constraints on the drink of the course. The user can then examine the drink role of the course to see what characteristics are necessary for the wine, as well as which wines are compatible with those characteristics. This is an example of a simple forward-chaining constraint propagation application. The value of organizing the knowledge in this fashion is that the wine descriptions are decoupled from the requirements for each course type. A new wine can be added, a given wine can easily have its characteristics changed, or a given food can be associated with different wine characteristics, all by making only local changes.

Figure 14.3 shows the top few levels of the concept hierarchy for our wine and food KB.

In the subsequent figures illustrating our concepts, we do not present the information in the exact form in which we would type it to CLASSIC—that would

[17] In the sample KB, we use course for the role of a course at a meal, and MEAL-COURSE for the concept of a course.

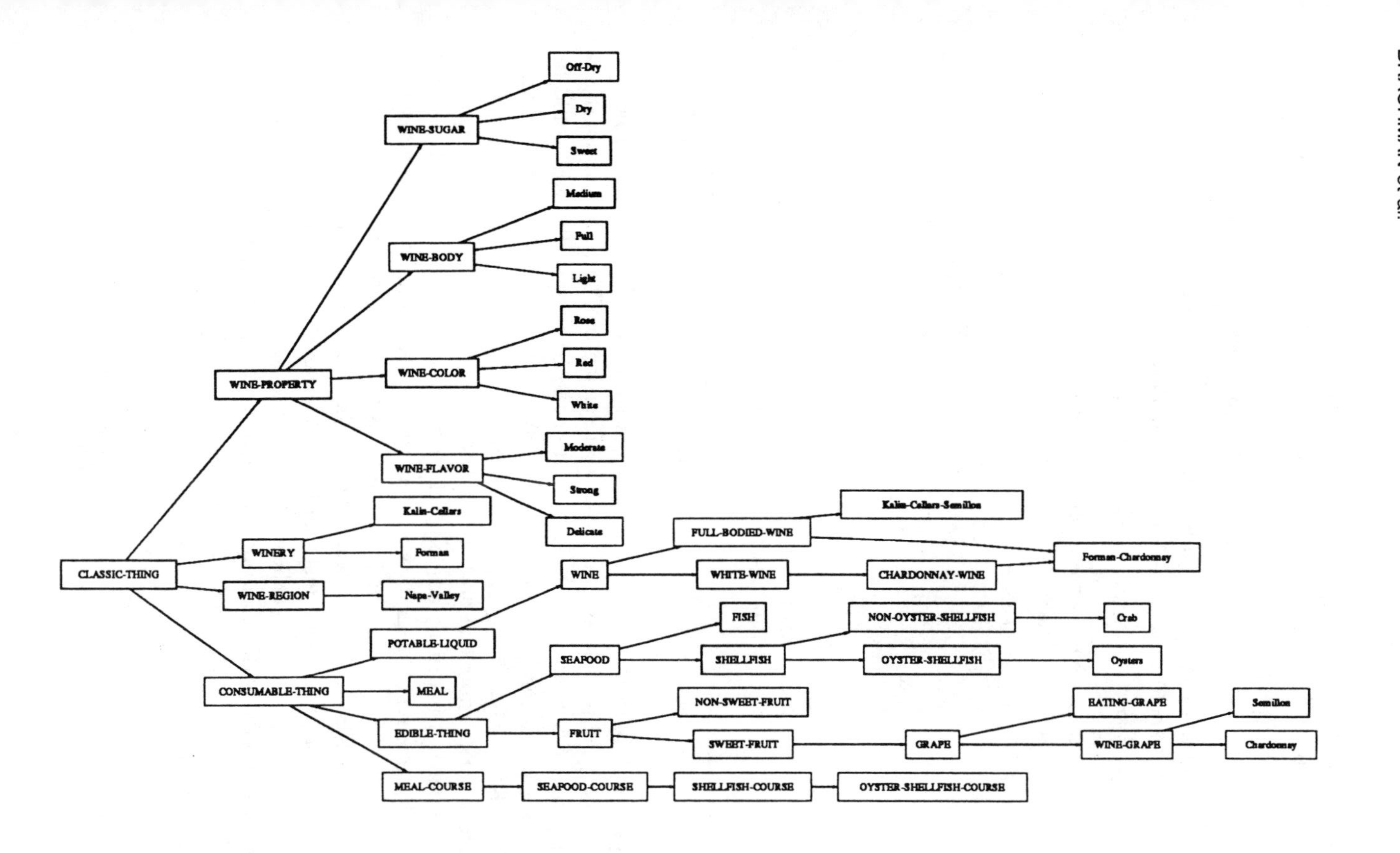

Figure 14.3: Hierarchy of the sample knowledge base

involve for each item a call to a Common LISP function. Instead, we have used the notation in Figure 14.4 to signify the type of description being defined or applied.

Thus, for example,

```
WINE-COLOR ⇔ (AND WINE-PROPERTY (ONE-OF White Rose Red))
```

would mean that WINE-COLOR is fully defined as a WINE-PROPERTY whose only possible instances are White, Rose, and Red. Similarly,

```
SEAFOOD-COURSE ⊃ (ALL drink WHITE-WINE)
```

would mean that if an object were determined to be a SEAFOOD-COURSE, it automatically follows that all of its drinks are WHITE-WINEs. The two definitions,

```
MEAL-COURSE ⊗1+⇒ CONSUMABLE-THING,
                 (AND  (AT-LEAST 1 food)
                       (ALL food EDIBLE-THING)
                       (AT-LEAST 1 drink)
                       (ALL drink POTABLE-LIQUID))
```

and

```
MEAL ⊗1+⇒ CONSUMABLE-THING,
          (AND (AT-LEAST 1 course)
               (ALL course MEAL-COURSE))
```

would mean that MEAL-COURSE and MEAL were both specializations of CONSUMABLE-THING, they were mutually disjoint, and they each had the additional properties specified.

Figure 14.5 illustrates the beginning of our wine and food KB. Since roles are used in concept definitions, and, in the current version of CLASSIC, do not themselves depend on any other constructs, the roles to be used in the KB would be defined first. In this case, we assume the following roles are defined at the beginning of the KB: color, body, flavor, sugar, region, grape, maker, drink, food, and course (note that all but grape and course are attributes). After the roles are defined, it is usually a good idea to define the classes of objects that are used only in value restrictions of other concepts. In the figure, we define a simple primitive, WINE-PROPERTY, which will serve as the parent for all wine-properties later used in the KB.[18] Since we want wines to have colors, and we can specify in advance all of the individuals that can be wine colors, we create a defined subconcept of WINE-PROPERTY called WINE-COLOR, specifying all of its possible instances with a **ONE-OF** description. Similarly, we create the wine-properties of WINE-BODY, WINE-FLAVOR, and WINE-SUGAR.

---

[18] As illustrated, WINE-PROPERTY is a member of disjoint grouping number 1 of CLASSIC-THING. In Figure 14.6, we illustrate the other concepts that are disjoint from this one.

expression	*meaning*
c $\Leftrightarrow$ e	c is fully defined by the expression e
c $\Rightarrow$ e	c is a primitive subconcept of the concept represented by e
c $\otimes_i\Rightarrow$ e	c is a disjoint primitive subconcept of the concept represented by e, in the disjoint grouping labeled "i"
c $\otimes_i^+\Rightarrow$ e, E	c is the combination of the expression E and a (unnamed) disjoint primitive subconcept of the concept represented by e (which is in the disjoint grouping labeled "i")
c $\supset$ e	c is the antecedent of a rule whose consequent is e
i $\rightarrow$ e	i is an individual and is asserted to have the properties described by e
r $\mapsto$	r is a role
r $\overset{!}{\mapsto}$	r is an attribute

Figure 14.4: Symbols used to describe the sample knowledge base

Wine and Meal Knowledge Base.

After defining the roles, define value restriction concepts and individuals to be used in further definitions.

color $\overset{!}{\mapsto}$
body $\overset{!}{\mapsto}$
flavor $\overset{!}{\mapsto}$
sugar $\overset{!}{\mapsto}$
region $\overset{!}{\mapsto}$
grape $\mapsto$
maker $\overset{!}{\mapsto}$
drink $\overset{!}{\mapsto}$
food $\overset{!}{\mapsto}$
course $\mapsto$

WINE-PROPERTY $\otimes_1\Rightarrow$ CLASSIC-THING

WINE-COLOR $\Leftrightarrow$ (AND WINE-PROPERTY (ONE-OF White Rose Red))

WINE-BODY $\Leftrightarrow$ (AND WINE-PROPERTY (ONE-OF Light Medium Full))

WINE-FLAVOR $\Leftrightarrow$ (AND WINE-PROPERTY (ONE-OF Delicate Moderate Strong))

WINE-SUGAR $\Leftrightarrow$ (AND WINE-PROPERTY (ONE-OF Sweet Off-Dry Dry))

Figure 14.5: Sample knowledge base—roles and some basic value restrictions

Define the other topmost concepts.

WINERY $\otimes_1\Rightarrow$ **CLASSIC-THING**
WINE-REGION $\otimes_1\Rightarrow$ **CLASSIC-THING**
CONSUMABLE-THING $\otimes_1\Rightarrow$ **CLASSIC-THING**

EDIBLE-THING $\otimes_1\Rightarrow$ **CONSUMABLE-THING**
POTABLE-LIQUID $\otimes_1\Rightarrow$ **CONSUMABLE-THING**

SEAFOOD $\otimes_1\Rightarrow$ **EDIBLE-THING**
FRUIT $\otimes_1\Rightarrow$ **EDIBLE-THING**

SHELLFISH $\otimes_1\Rightarrow$ **SEAFOOD**
FISH $\otimes_1\Rightarrow$ **SEAFOOD**

Define some instances of **WINERY** and **WINE-REGION**.

Forman $\rightarrow$ **WINERY**
Kalin-Cellars $\rightarrow$ **WINERY**
Napa-Valley $\rightarrow$ **WINE-REGION**

Define **WINE-GRAPE** and some instances of it.

SWEET-FRUIT $\otimes_1\Rightarrow$ **FRUIT**
GRAPE $\otimes_1\Rightarrow$ **SWEET-FRUIT**
EATING-GRAPE $\Rightarrow$ **GRAPE**
WINE-GRAPE $\Rightarrow$ **GRAPE**
Chardonnay $\rightarrow$ **WINE-GRAPE**
Semillon $\rightarrow$ **WINE-GRAPE**

Figure 14.6: Sample knowledge base—more general concepts

Next we create the top part of the main hierarchy. Because concepts and roles must be defined before they are used, a CLASSIC KB file will generally proceed from most general concepts to most specific ones. In Figure 14.6, we define a few high-level primitive concepts. The simple world we are describing is broken into four disjoint parts: WINE-PROPERTYs, WINERYs, WINE-REGIONs, and CONSUMABLE-THINGs (this will be used for foods and wines, as well as meals and courses—special categories needed to trigger the inferences about wine types for different foods—see Figure 14.10). In Figure 14.6 we also define several types of CONSUMABLE-THING, and then some representative instances of WINERY and

Define the concept of a wine.

```
WINE  =>  (AND POTABLE-LIQUID
               (AT-LEAST 1 color)
               (ALL color WINE-COLOR)
               (AT-LEAST 1 body)
               (ALL body WINE-BODY)
               (AT-LEAST 1 flavor)
               (ALL flavor WINE-FLAVOR)
               (AT-LEAST 1 sugar)
               (ALL sugar WINE-SUGAR)
               (AT-LEAST 1 region)
               (ALL region WINE-REGION)
               (AT-LEAST 1 grape)
               (ALL grape WINE-GRAPE)
               (AT-LEAST 1 maker)
               (ALL maker WINERY))
```

Figure 14.7: Sample knowledge base—`wine`

`WINE-REGION`. We then include some information about grapes that will be needed later. Note that there may be some grapes used for eating that are also used for making wine, so `EATING-GRAPE` and `WINE-GRAPE` have been defined as primitive but not disjoint concepts under `GRAPE`.

So far, we have created only simple primitive concepts. CLASSIC allows the construction of much more complex, but still primitive concepts. For example, we might want to give `WINE` some complex necessary conditions as part of its meaning, but tell CLASSIC that the conditions we give it are not sufficient for recognizing wines. We would accomplish this by defining `WINE` as a primitive with a complex expression, as illustrated in Figure 14.7.

We can read this definition of `WINE` as something like, "a wine is, among other things, a potable liquid with exactly one color [because `color` is an attribute], which must be a wine-color, exactly one body, ..."

Once we have the key basic concept of a `WINE` defined, we can describe the more specialized types of wines we would like to be able to recognize automatically. Figure 14.8 illustrates three fully defined wine subconcepts. For example, a `WHITE-WINE` is fully defined as a wine whose color is white. The condition that the color of a `WHITE-WINE` must be exactly `White` is sufficiently stated as `(`**`FILLS`** `color White)`, since `color` has been defined as an attribute, and an attribute has exactly one filler. In the case of `CHARDONNAY-WINE`, whose `grape` role must be filled by exactly the individual `Chardonnay`, the definition of `WINE` says that a `CHARDONNAY-WINE` (or any wine) must have at least 1 grape, and the restriction on

CHARDONNAY-WINE, (**ALL** grape (**ONE-OF** Chardonnay)), specifies what that grape is, and that there can be no additional fillers for the grape role. Returning to WHITE-WINE, note that White is consonant with the general value restriction previously stated for the color role of WINE (i.e., White is a WINE-COLOR). In any case, CLASSIC will recognize any wine whose color is determined to be white *by any means* (user assertion, rule firing, propagation from some other assertion, etc.) as an instance of WHITE-WINE.

Figure 14.7 also illustrates some rules based on CHARDONNAY-WINE. Since we have stated nothing specific about the Chardonnay grape (i.e., it is never stated that wines made from this grape are white), we have a rule stating that chardonnays have color white. Thus, any wine whose grape is recognized to be exactly Chardonnay will end up being a WHITE-WINE as well, since the rule will assert that its color is white, and classification will use the fact that it is a wine and also white to determine that it is a WHITE-WINE.[19] We also include rules about the body and flavor of Chardonnays.

Once we have the wine hierarchy defined, it is reasonable to create and describe individuals for various particular wines. Figure 14.9 illustrates two typical descriptions of such individuals. Note that by inheritance Forman-Chardonnay will end up with all known properties of CHARDONNAY-WINEs (as well as of WINEs in general), as well as the individual properties stated in the figure. As we mentioned above, once this individual is created, it will be classified under all appropriate defined concepts, such as FULL-BODIED-WINE. In addition, in this case, the rule that says that chardonnays are always white will fire, and Forman-Chardonnay will end up being classified as a WHITE-WINE as well. Also note that Kalin-Cellars-Semillon is only partially described, in that we have stated that one of its grapes is Semillon, but have not closed the grape role.

In Figure 14.10 we illustrate some simple primitive concepts that will appear below SHELLFISH in the hierarchy. We then represent the concepts MEAL-COURSE and MEAL as disjoint primitive concepts under CONSUMABLE-THING (disjoint also from POTABLE-LIQUID and EDIBLE-THING—see Figure 14.6), but having complex structure. A MEAL-COURSE is defined as having exactly one food and exactly one drink (recall that food and drink are attributes), while a MEAL is defined as having at least one course. In this simple application, the type of food served at a course will be stated directly; the categorization of the course on the basis of this food will then be used to trigger rules constraining the properties of any wine

[19] Note that if we had included the white color restriction as part of the definition of CHARDONNAY-WINE, it would have made that restriction one of the conditions necessary for a wine to have before it could be determined to be a chardonnay wine. Since the essential property of being a chardonnay wine is having the right grape, then the white color is a derivative property that should not be included in the basic concept definition. Thus we use a rule to assert that chardonnays are white.

Define some subcategories of wines.

A white wine is a wine whose color is white.

```
WHITE-WINE  ⇔  (AND WINE (FILLS color White))
```

A full-bodied wine is a wine whose body is full.

```
FULL-BODIED-WINE  ⇔  (AND WINE (FILLS body Full))
```

A `CHARDONNAY-WINE` is a wine with exactly one grape, which is `Chardonnay`.

```
CHARDONNAY-WINE  ⇔  (AND WINE (ALL grape (ONE-OF Chardonnay)))
```

Now assert some rules about Chardonnay wines.

Chardonnays are always white.

```
CHARDONNAY-WINE  ⊃  (FILLS color White)
```

Chardonnays are always either full- or medium-bodied wines.

```
CHARDONNAY-WINE  ⊃  (ALL body (ONE-OF Full Medium))
```

Chardonnays are not delicate.

```
CHARDONNAY-WINE  ⊃  (ALL flavor (ONE-OF Strong Moderate))
```

Figure 14.8: Sample knowledge base—defined wine subconcepts

Create and describe some individual wines.

```
Forman-Chardonnay  →  (AND CHARDONNAY-WINE
                           (FILLS body Full)
                           (FILLS flavor Moderate)
                           (FILLS sugar Dry)
                           (FILLS maker Forman))

Kalin-Cellars-Semillon  →  (AND WINE
                                (FILLS grape Semillon)
                                (FILLS body Full)
                                (FILLS flavor Strong)
                                (FILLS sugar Dry)
                                (FILLS maker Kalin-Cellars))
```

Figure 14.9: Sample knowledge base—individual wines

Define some primitive food-types.

```
OYSTER-SHELLFISH  ⊗1⇒  SHELLFISH
NON-OYSTER-SHELLFISH  ⊗1⇒  SHELLFISH
```

Create some instances of foods.

```
Oysters  →  OYSTER-SHELLFISH
Crab  →  NON-OYSTER-SHELLFISH
```

Define the concepts for a course and a meal

```
MEAL-COURSE  ⊗1+⇒  CONSUMABLE-THING,
                   (AND (AT-LEAST 1 food)
                        (ALL food EDIBLE-THING)
                        (AT-LEAST 1 drink)
                        (ALL drink POTABLE-LIQUID))

MEAL  ⊗1+⇒  CONSUMABLE-THING,
            (AND (AT-LEAST 1 course)
                 (ALL course MEAL-COURSE))
```

Figure 14.10: Sample knowledge base—foods, meals, and courses

served. Thus, the food concepts and individuals need no internal structure. A course individual will be classified under a specific type of course (e.g., SEAFOOD-COURSE in Figure 14.11) as soon as its food is known, and the drink role will be used to accumulate properties of the wine for the given course.

Finally, to allow our knowledge base to perform the appropriate inferences when we describe an individual course, we will need a set of rules that constrain the type of wine to be drunk with each appropriate food type. In some cases, we can have very general rules, such as seafood requiring white wines, and in others we can have very narrowly applicable ones, such as oysters requiring sweet wines. Each rule is associated with the appropriate concept in the KB, as illustrated in Figure 14.10. When a given course is described (such as Course-256 in the figure), all rules that apply will be inherited and triggered. In the case of Course-256, since the food of the course is oysters, the course will be classified as an OYSTER-SHELLFISH-COURSE: Because food is an attribute, the food role of Course-256 is closed as soon as it is asserted that it is filled with Oysters; with Oysters as the only filler of that role, the **ALL** restriction on OYSTER-SHELLFISH-COURSE is satisfied. The classification of Course-256 as an OYSTER-SHELLFISH-COURSE makes applicable all rules from OYSTER-SHELLFISH-

Define some concepts that allow recognition of course-types, which will be antecedents of rules constraining wines.

```
SEAFOOD-COURSE  ⇔  (AND MEAL-COURSE (ALL food SEAFOOD))
```

Note that SHELLFISH-COURSE will be classified under SEAFOOD-COURSE and OYSTER-SHELLFISH-COURSE will be classified under SHELLFISH-COURSE:

```
SHELLFISH-COURSE  ⇔  (AND MEAL-COURSE (ALL food SHELLFISH))

OYSTER-SHELLFISH-COURSE  ⇔  (AND MEAL-COURSE (ALL food OYSTER-SHELLFISH))
```

Now assert rules pertaining to course-types:

```
SEAFOOD-COURSE  ⊃  (ALL drink WHITE-WINE)

SHELLFISH-COURSE  ⊃  (ALL drink
                          (AND (FILLS body Full)
                               (ALL flavor (ONE-OF Moderate Strong))))

OYSTER-SHELLFISH-COURSE  ⊃  (ALL drink (FILLS sugar Sweet))
```

Create a specific course with oysters as food.

```
Course-256  →  (AND MEAL-COURSE (FILLS food Oysters))
```

Figure 14.11: Sample knowledge base—course-types with rules

COURSE, SHELLFISH-COURSE, and SEAFOOD-COURSE. The drink of Course-256 will thus be constrained to be a sweet (from OYSTER-SHELLFISH-COURSE), full-bodied (from SHELLFISH-COURSE) white wine (from SEAFOOD-COURSE), of either moderate or strong flavor (from SHELLFISH-COURSE).

14.6 TRICKS OF THE TRADE

The expressive limitations of CLASSIC mean that there are many things that it cannot directly represent. After building a number of knowledge bases using the system, we have found some ways of getting around some of these expressive limitations.

The reason these techniques are presented in a separate section is that the meanings that CLASSIC places on the resultant concepts are different from their intuitive meanings. Under some circumstances CLASSIC will act in a way inconsistent with the intuitive meanings. Often this divergence only shows up when certain types of extra information are added to the knowledge base—if this extra information is never added, then CLASSIC will adhere to the intuitive behavior.

(For example, see the first way of representing a limited form of negation in Section 14.6.1.) Therefore, the knowledge base designer must be extremely careful when using these techniques.

These techniques are most useful when used sparingly. If a designer finds it necessary to use a large number of these "tricks," then perhaps CLASSIC should not be used for the application.

14.6.1 Negation and Complements

As noted before, there is no full negation in CLASSIC, but there are a few ways to represent limited forms of negation or complements.

One method can be used to define the concept of nonsweet wines. Given that wines have exactly one filler for their `sugar` role, and that the only possible fillers for the `sugar` role of wines are `Dry`, `Off-Dry`, and `Sweet`, a nonsweet wine can be defined as

```
(AND WINE (ALL sugar (ONE-OF Dry Off-Dry))).
```

Since `WINE-SUGAR` has exactly three instances, this concept is the complement of sweet wines (`WINE`s with filler `Sweet` for their `sugar` role) in the universe of wines.

However, this trick does not work as well when a restriction is based on a primitive concept (i.e., `WINE-GRAPE`) and not on a **ONE-OF** concept (i.e., `WINE-SUGAR`). A non-chardonnay wine can be defined as

```
(AND WINE (ALL grape (ONE-OF Semillon))),
```

since `Chardonnay` and `Semillon` are the only grapes in the KB. However, if a new grape is added to the KB (i.e., `Riesling`), then this definition would no longer represent the wines made from all grapes except chardonnay.

Another form of negation can be represented with disjoint primitives. If the concepts `FISH` and `SHELLFISH` are disjoint primitives under the concept `SEAFOOD`, then there can be no individuals belonging to both `FISH` and `SHELLFISH`. However, in this situation, it is possible for something to be a seafood and neither a fish nor a shellfish, and thus `FISH` is not exactly the relative complement of `SHELLFISH` with respect to `SEAFOOD`.

Finally, test concepts can also be used to capture part of the meaning of complements. A test function that returns false if an individual satisfies some concept, true if the individual cannot possibly satisfy it, and unknown otherwise, can be used to create a complement concept. However, there is a small problem with this method of complementation. The complement concept will not be recognized as disjoint from the other concept, so, for instance, the conjunction of the two concepts will not be considered incoherent, although it cannot, in reality, have any instances.

14.6.2 Disjunction

Although there is no "**OR**" operator in the CLASSIC language, disjunction can be captured in some special cases.

The first of these is simply a **ONE-OF** concept, which provides an extremely simple and uninteresting case of disjunction (of the individuals in the set). The second case builds on the first by using the **ONE-OF** concept in a value restriction. For example, the concept

```
(AND WINE (ALL grape (ONE-OF Semillon Sauvignon)))
```

represents the disjunction of wines made from semillon grapes and wines made from sauvignon grapes. Once a disjunctive concept like this is formed with a **ONE-OF** embedded in an **ALL**, such a concept can in turn be used in another **ALL** restriction, thus allowing arbitrarily deep nesting.

The above types of disjunction are not really tricks at all. They represent true disjunction—however, only certain, very limited, types of disjunction can be represented this way.

General disjunction can be crudely approximated, however, by using a simple trick. When one concept subsumes others, then it subsumes their disjunction, and can, under some circumstances, act like their disjunction. For example, in Figure 14.6, `SEAFOOD` subsumes the disjunction of `SHELLFISH` and `FISH`. If no individuals become instances of `SEAFOOD` without becoming instances of either `SHELLFISH` or `FISH` then `SEAFOOD` can be considered to be the disjunction of `SHELLFISH` and `FISH`. Because there may be instances of `SEAFOOD` that are neither `SHELLFISH` nor `FISH`, this is not true disjunction. (Learning that an individual is not an instance of `FISH` does not make it an instance of `SHELLFISH`.)

14.6.3 Defaults

CLASSIC enforces a strict inheritance hierarchy and does not provide a default operator. However, a limited form of defaults can be represented with the aid of rules and test functions.

For example, to make wines have default color red, use a test function (perhaps called **no-known-color**) that returns true if the number of currently known fillers of the `color` role is zero, and false otherwise[20] and use it in the concept `WINE-CAUSE-DEFAULT-RED`, defined as

```
WINE-CAUSE-DEFAULT-RED ⇔ (AND WINE (TEST-C no-known-color))
WINE-CAUSE-DEFAULT-RED ⊃ (FILLS color Red).
```

---

[20] This is different from knowing that there are no *possible* fillers for the `color` role, as CLASSIC can represent individuals, such as instances of `WINE`, for which there must be a filler for a role without knowing the actual filler.

This will cause wines that are not given a color to become red wines because they will pass the test function, become instances of WINE-CAUSE-DEFAULT-RED, and be given color Red as a result of the firing of the rule above.

WARNING: Small changes to the implementation of CLASSIC could cause this trick to fail—it uses a test function that violates the conditions placed on test functions. (Test functions in CLASSIC should be monotonic, i.e., adding information cannot cause the result of a test function to change from true to false, or *vice versa.*) *Use this trick with extreme caution.*

14.6.4 More Powerful Rules

Rules are an important part of CLASSIC, but are limited in that the antecedent of a rule can only be a named CLASSIC concept. However, using test restrictions in the antecedent of rules allows arbitrary pattern matching to determine rule applicability. For example, we might want to extend the wine example to consider vintages and then conclude that if some wine is from a good vintage year then it is expensive. The definition of "good vintage" might be quite complicated and not expressible in CLASSIC without using a test restriction.

This method does not cause any particular problems, aside from the general problem inherent in the use of (opaque) test functions, as long as the test conforms to the conditions placed on test functions. However, excessive use of test functions can cause performance degradation if the test concepts end up near the top of the concept hierarchy, where their tests will be run frequently.

14.6.5 Integrity Checking

Rules can also be used to provide a sort of integrity checking, by using test concepts as their conclusions. In this case, once an individual is found to satisfy the antecedent of the rule, it is made an instance of the test concept. Part of this process is to run the test function on the individual; if the individual is inconsistent with the test function then the individual is also removed from the antecedent concept. In this way complicated integrity constraints can be created for otherwise test-free concepts.

For example, we might want to check that late-harvest grapes have a sugar content of at least 30 brix. This can be done by creating a rule

LATE-HARVEST-GRAPE ⊃ (**TEST-C sugar-at-least-30**)

where **sugar-at-least-30** returns unknown if there is no currently known filler of the sugar-content role of a grape, true if the filler is known and is at least 30, and false otherwise.

This is different from including the test condition as part of LATE-HARVEST-GRAPE in two ways. First, the test does not become part of the definition of the concept so it will not be subsumed by another concept that happens to incorporate the same test. Second, if LATE-HARVEST-GRAPE is a defined concept then individuals can be recognized as its instances without passing the test; they are forced to be (and remain) consistent with the test.

14.6.6 Restrictions on Roles

The CLASSIC language supports restrictions of the form "all of the drinks in a picnic basket are wines," and "a picnic basket has at least one drink," but there is no operator for saying precisely "at least two of the drinks in a picnic basket are white wines."[21]

When this sort of restriction is needed, a test can be used. For example, a test function to determine if at least two of the drinks in a picnic basket are white wines can be written as follows:

- If there are two known fillers of the `drink` role of the picnic basket that are instances of WHITE-WINE then return true;
- otherwise, if there can be at most one filler of the `drink role` of the picnic basket, then return false;
- otherwise, if all the fillers of the `drink` role of the picnic basket must be white wines because the type of its drinks is subsumed by WHITE-WINE, and there must be at least two drinks for the picnic basket, then return true;
- otherwise, if all the picnic basket's drinks are known, then if there is at most one of them that is an instance of WHITE-WINE then return false;
- otherwise return unknown.

As with all tests, CLASSIC treats the function as a black box and will not discover any subsumption relationships between different test functions. This can pose a problem here because there are a large number of possible subsumption relationships between these sorts of restrictions. For example, "at least two of the drinks in a picnic basket are white wines" subsumes "at least three of the drinks in a picnic basket are full-bodied white wines," but CLASSIC cannot discover these relationships, which depend on the behavior of test functions.

Further, this test function contains a potentially dangerous "closed-world assumption" in that it assumes that a drink that is not known to be an instance of WHITE-WINE will never be an instance of WHITE-WINE. Since CLASSIC allows the acquisition of extra information about individuals, it is possible that a drink could later become an instance of WHITE-WINE, thus invalidating the conclusion drawn by this test function.

---

[21] This is a deliberate omission, as the inclusion of such operators makes determining subsumption computationally intractable [Nebel, 1988].

14.6.7 Dummy Individuals

As mentioned in Section 14.3.1, CLASSIC can answer queries about mandated properties of fillers of roles without knowing the identity of the fillers. Some of these queries can be answered by getting the value restriction for the role. For example, `Course-256` from Figure 14.11 must have the `body` of all its `drinks` be `Full`, since it has the property

```
(ALL drink (FILLS body Full)),
```

by virtue of its being a `SHELLFISH-COURSE`. This can be determined by CLASSIC without knowing the actual `drink` of the course.

However, this method does not pick up the rules that might be applied to the role filler. For example, under the definitions,

```
KOSHER-WEDDING ⇔ (AND WEDDING (ALL meal KOSHER-MEAL))
   KOSHER-MEAL ⊃ (ALL course (ALL drink KOSHER-WINE))
Lori's-Wedding → KOSHER-WEDDING,
```

the value restriction for the `drink` of any `course` of the meal at `Lori's-Wedding` would not be known to be a `KOSHER-WINE`, even though the `meal` at `Lori's-Wedding` must be a `KOSHER-MEAL` and there is a rule on `KOSHER-MEAL` asserting that all the `drinks` of each `course` must be `KOSHER-WINEs`. To pick up this restriction it is necessary to create a "dummy" meal for `Lori's-Wedding`. Then the rule will fire, and assert the restriction that the `drink` for each course of this dummy meal must be a `KOSHER-WINE`.

The creation of dummy individuals must be performed with care, as CLASSIC assumes that they are distinct from all other individuals. Thus when the real meal is found, it cannot just be added, but, instead, either the dummy individual must be removed as a filler, or the two individuals must be merged in an application-dependent manner. It is best to use a dummy individual to answer the query, and then immediately remove it.

14.7 CONCLUSION

By now it is clear that learning a programming language involves more than just learning its syntax and semantics: There are usually an associated methodology or paradigm of use that needs to be absorbed, a collection of techniques for handling various special situations, warnings about frequent pitfalls, and the recognition that some other language might be more appropriate for a specific programming task. For example, in order to use PROLOG expertly one should, among other things, understand the paradigm of logic programming, the trick of building data structures with unbound variables (which are assigned a value later in the computation), the problems of negation by failure, and the cost of nondeterministic search/backtracking.

Knowledge representation languages are no different in this respect. For this reason, we have chosen to provide in this chapter more than just the description of an existing, implemented classification-based frame language. We have attempted to present the paradigm of using such languages by working through examples and by listing situations in which CLASSIC is likely to be useful. Additionally, we have indicated under what circumstances languages like CLASSIC may prove to be less than ideal. We have also assembled from our experiences of using the language and teaching it to others a collection of potentially confusing distinctions, together with "tricks of the trade" for representing special situations. Most importantly, we have presented a methodology for working through a domain and producing a knowledge base that reflects the domain structure in CLASSIC terms.

References

Borgida, A., Brachman, R.J., McGuinness, D.L., and Resnick, L.A.. 1989. CLASSIC: A structural data model for objects. In *Proceedings of the 1989 ACM SIGMOD International Conference on Management of Data*, pp. 59–67.

Brachman, R.J. and Schmolze, J.G. 1985. An overview of the KL-ONE knowledge representation system. *Cognitive Science*, 9(2):171–216.

Brachman, R.J., Borgida, A., McGuinness, D.L., Patel-Schneider, P.F., and Resnick, L.A. In preparation. The CLASSIC knowledge representation system.

Devanbu, P., Brachman, R.J., and Selfridge, P.G. 1990. LaSSIE-a classification-based software information system. In *Proceedings of the International Conference on Software Engineering*. IEEE Computer Society.

Devanbu, P., Selfridge, P.G., Ballard, B.W., and Brachman, RJ. 1989. A knowledge-based software information system. In *Proceedings of the Eleventh International Joint Conference on Artificial Intelligence,* pp. 110–115. IJCAI proceedings are available from Morgan Kaufmann Publishers, San Mateo, CA.

Freeman, M.W. 1982. The qua link. In *Proceedings of the 1981 KL-One Workshop,* Schmolze, J.G. and Brachman, R.J. (ed.s), pp. 54–64. Bolt Beranek and Newman Inc., Jackson, NH.

Lenat, D.B. and Guha, R.V. 1990. *Building Large Knowledge-Based Systems*. Addison-Wesley, Reading, MA.

Litman, D. and Devanbu, P. 1990. *Clasp: A Plan and Scenario Classification System.* AT&T Bell Laboratories.

Nebel, B. 1988. Computational complexity of terminological reasoning in BACK. *Artificial Intelligence*, 34(3):371–383.

Owsnicki-Klewe, B. 1988. Configuration as a consistency maintenance task. In *Proceedings of GWAI-88—The 12th German Workshop on Artificial Intelligence,* Hoeppner, W. (ed), pp. 77–87. Springer-Verlag.

Patel-Schneider, P.F. 1984. Small can be beautiful in knowledge representation. In *Proceedings of the IEEE Workshop on Principles of Knowledge-Based Systems,* pp. 11–16. IEEE Computer Society. A revised and extended version is available as AI Technical Report Number 37, Schlumberger Palo Alto Research, October 1984.

Peltason, C., von Luck, K., Nebel, B., and Schmiedel, A. 1987. *The User's Guide to the Back System.* KIT-Report 42, Fachbereich Informatik, Technische Universität Berlin.

Senyk, O., Patil, R.S., and Sonnenberg, F.A. 1989. Systematic knowledge base design for medical diagnosis. *Applied Artificial Intelligence*, 3(2–3):249–274.

Yen, J., Neches, R., and Mac Gregor, R. October 1989. Using terminological models to enhance the rule-based paradigm. In *Proceedings of the Second International Symposium on Artificial Intelligence.*

15

UTILIZING KNOWLEDGE:

The Components of the SB-ONE Knowledge Representation Workbench

Alfred Kobsa
(University of Saarbrücken, Germany)

Abstract

SB-ONE is a knowledge representation workbench specifically designed for the construction and exploitation of conceptual knowledge bases in natural language systems. At the heart of the system lies the SB-ONE language, which allows for the representation of conceptual knowledge and simple existential assertions. The kernel language has been extended by "metastructures," which permit the description of objects in a represented domain both as individuals and as pairs of a relation. Knowledge can be assigned to partitions, which may themselves be ordered in inheritance hierarchies. The construction of SB-ONE knowledge bases is facilitated by functional, textual, and graphics-based interfaces; a consistency maintenance system for the syntactic well-formedness of SB-ONE knowledge bases; a classifier; and a realizer. Additional utilities operating on SB-ONE that are briefly described include a pattern matcher, a spreading-activation mechanism, an interpreter and classifier for SB-ONE to SB-ONE translation rules, an integration mechanism for an external frame-based representation, and a connection between SB-ONE and an extended PROLOG.

15.1 INTRODUCTION

Relatively early in the history of research on natural language (NL) systems it was acknowledged that a knowledge representation (KR) component forms a central core of such systems. Consequently, a large number of representational schemata have been developed in the 1970s, of which only a few have survived: the

KL-ONE language family [Brachman and Schmolze, 1984], SNePS [Shapiro and Rapaport, 1987; Kumar, 1990], KODIAK [Wilensky, 1986; Wilensky et al., 1988] and conceptual graphs [Sowa, 1984], to name just the most frequently used.[1] Most of this research was strongly focused on the development of knowledge representation *languages* rather than on the development of integrated and easily usable knowledge representation *systems*. Only limited support is available to the knowledge engineer who develops a knowledge base, and only a few utilities exist that make it easier to utilize a developed knowledge base. Often, new knowledge must be entered in a LISP-like form, or even the implementation structures must be accessed. Assistance to the knowledge engineer is restricted to the rejection of syntactically incorrect definitions, and to the classification (i.e., correct positioning in a hierarchy) of new structures in the knowledge base. Thus the construction of only middle-sized knowledge bases becomes already quite cumbersome, and without an extra drawing on a sheet of paper knowledge engineers can quickly loose perspective.

In this chapter, an integrated knowledge representation workbench for conceptual knowledge will be presented. This workbench is based on a representation language that fits loosely into the KL-ONE paradigm. In the design of the system, special emphasis was put on supporting the knowledge engineer in building, browsing, and correcting knowledge bases for natural language dialog systems. These operations on the knowledge base should be performable in an easy and natural way, which is made possible mainly through the following three system components:

- A *graphics-based user interface*, which exploits the high screen resolution and the window, menu, and mouse interaction facilities of modern AI workstations. This interface provides the knowledge engineer with a pictorial representation of the current knowledge base. Most representational units are mouse-sensitive. The knowledge engineer can augment and change the knowledge base using direct-manipulative operations performed on this pictorial representation (if the size of the graphical representation exceeds that of the screen, the display can be scrolled in all directions). Moreover, trace, checkpoint, and undo mechanisms as well as a connection to a laser printer are available.
- A *maintenance system for the syntactic well-formedness of the knowledge base*. This system recognizes and rejects entries that violate the conditions for syntactic well-formedness. Inconsistent entries are rejected, while *incomplete* definitions are tolerated and recorded in an "agenda" that keeps track of what

---

[1] In the last few years, PROLOG also received strong interest as a KR language in research on natural language systems [Pereira and Shieber, 1987].

completions have still to be made. On request (e.g., at the end of a terminal session), the system will ask the knowledge engineer for the missing structures. The agenda can instead also be stored until the next session.

- A *classifier*, which supports the correct positioning of new knowledge definitions in the current knowledge base. The classifier can be used for testing the knowledge base as a whole, or just for testing individual definitions. On the basis of the current knowledge base, an interactive enhancement system to the classifier can ask the knowledge engineer for additional information on the knowledge item just entered and thus assist him/her in determining its correct position.

While these SB-ONE components facilitate the *construction* of knowledge bases, a large number of additional utilities of the SB-ONE workbench help in the *exploitation* of developed knowledge bases. These include a pattern matcher, a spreading-activation mechanism, an interpreter and classifier for SB-ONE to SB-ONE translation rules, an integration mechanism for a frame-based knowledge representation, and a connection between SB-ONE and an extended PROLOG. Moreover, the kernel language has been enhanced by partitions that can be ordered in an inheritance hierarchy, and by "metastructures" that allow for the description of objects in a represented domain both as individuals and as pairs of a relation.

Not surprisingly, these complex processes rely heavily on a precisely defined syntax and interpretation of the representation language. Great care has therefore been taken to clearly define SB-ONE on an epistemological, notational, and interpretational level. Moreover, the SB-ONE workbench has been crafted specifically to meet the needs of knowledge engineers who aim at building knowledge bases for natural language dialog systems. Many of the representation elements contained in SB-ONE have already proven valuable in NL-oriented knowledge representation, particularly in the KL-ONE environment [Brachman, 1978; Brachman et al., 1979; Brachman and Schmolze, 1984; Nebel and Sondheimer, 1986]. A preliminary version of SB-ONE has been used in a major natural language dialog system (XTRA, [Allgayer et al., 1989a, 1989b]) since 1986. Experiences from this application have influenced the design of the language, in particular the introduction of additional representational elements. The orientation toward natural language research also becomes manifest in a number of decisions on what to display and make graphically accessible on the terminal screen. Currently, SB-ONE is also being employed in natural language generation systems for the description of events in visual scenes [André et al., 1988] and for multimodal technical descriptions [Wahlster et al., 1991], as well as in an interest-based natural language dialog system [Allgayer et al., 1990].

In the remainder of this chapter, the components of the SB-ONE workbench will be described. First, the SB-ONE *language* will be surveyed, which allows for the representation of conceptual knowledge and simple existential assertions.

Extensions to the language (namely metastructures and partitions) are discussed in Sections 15.3 and 15.4, respectively. The subsequent sections describe the three different interfaces of the SB-ONE workbench, the maintenance system for the syntactic well-formedness of SB-ONE knowledge bases, the classifier and the realizer, and several other system components. In Section 15.9, finally, the implementation of SB-ONE is briefly described.

15.2 THE SB-ONE KNOWLEDGE REPRESENTATION LANGUAGE

15.2.1 Overview

The SB-ONE language [Profitlich, 1989, 1990; Kobsa, 1990b] is a representation language for conceptual knowledge and simple existential assertions, which fits loosely into the KL-ONE paradigm [Brachman, 1978; Brachman and Schmolze, 1984]. When describing the SB-ONE knowledge representation language, three perspectives can be distinguished:

- On the *epistemological level* (the term is due to [Brachman, 1978]), the *knowledge representation elements* which a KR language provides for representing knowledge are specified (as are, e.g., individual constants, predicates, functions, etc. in the case of predicate logic). On this level, moreover, rules exist that lay down how well-formed *KR expressions* can be formed from KR elements (these rules are formulated in first-order predicate logic).
- On the *interpretational level*, a so-called *interpretative domain* $\mathcal{D}$ exists, which is an abstraction of real-world states of affairs. The domain consists of so-called *individuals*, and binary relations between individuals. An *interpretation* expresses the meaning of KR elements and expressions by relating them to this interpretative domain.
- On the notational level, KR *symbols* are assigned to each KR element, and rules exist on how to form complex KR *structures* out of these individual symbols (these rules parallel the well-formedness conditions for KR expressions). For SB-ONE, there exist two kinds of notation: A graphical notation, which is practically identical with the display of the graphical user interface; and an additional "linear" notation (similar to the notations of formal logic), which, when used, makes proofs and definitions easier and shorter.

In the remainder of this section, the epistemological and interpretational levels will be briefly described. The two different notations for SB-ONE will be illustrated by examples only.

15.2.2 Epistemological Level

15.2.2.1 Representational Elements

The representational elements of SB-ONE can be divided into those pertaining to the *general level* and those pertaining to the *individualized level.* On the former level, concepts and relationships between concepts are defined, and on the latter, defined concepts are utilized for making simple existential assertions. The most important representational element of SB-ONE is the *general concept.* Formally, a general concept *gc* is a structured object consisting of:

- a unique one-placed *concept predicate* over individuals of $\mathcal{D}$,
- a *concept name* (optional),
- a set of *attribute descriptions* $gad_{i_1}(gc),\ldots, gad_{i_n}(gc)$ pertaining to *gc*, and
- a legal combination of so-called *concept types.*

A general concept characterizes the set of individuals in $\mathcal{D}$ which is denoted by its predicate. This characterization is given by its attribute descriptions $gad_{i_1}(gc),\ldots, gad_{i_n}(gc)$, which describe properties of the individuals in the denotation of *gc*. A property, in turn, is a binary relation of an individual with another individual in $\mathcal{D}$.

An attribute description $gad_i(gc)$ of a concept *gc* also forms a structure, whose constituents describe a property in more detail:

- the *role predicate* of the attribute description denotes a relation in $\mathcal{D}$;
- the *role name* (optional) can be used for giving the attribute description a name;
- the *value restriction concept* restricts the individuals in the second argument of the relation to elements of its denotation;
- the *default value restriction* specifies the *usual* restrictions on the second argument of the relation;
- the *number restriction* indicates how many of the individuals in the denotation of *gc* possess the attribute in the minimal, maximal, and default cases;
- the *modality* indicates whether *all* or *some* of the individuals in the denotation of *gc* possess the respective attribute (in the former case, the attribute description is called 'necessary', in the latter case 'optional').

Several concept types exist in SB-ONE, including the following:

Defined concepts: their attribute descriptions specify necessary and sufficient conditions as to whether or not the concept (i.e., its predicate) can be applied to an individual;

Primitive concepts: their attribute descriptions specify necessary but not sufficient conditions;

Singleton concepts: the cardinality of their denotation is at most one.

Figure 15.1 contains several different kinds of concepts and attribute descriptions (concepts are depicted by ovals, and attribute descriptions by small circles). The concepts *CAR*, *BUS*, *TRAIN*, etc. do not possess any attribute descriptions. They have therefore been declared as primitive (which is marked by the asterisks). The concept 'PHYSICAL TRANSFER' possesses five attribute descriptions with the role names 'agent', 'object', 'origin', 'destination' and 'means-of-transport'. Value restriction concepts for these attribute descriptions are 'PERSON', 'PHYSICAL OBJECT', twice 'LOCATION', and 'VEHICLE', respectively. The number restriction of all these attribute descriptions is (1,1,1), except (1,INF,1) for 'object' (i.e., in a physical transfer, one to arbitrarily many objects are moved; the default is one). By default, all modalities are 'necessary'. The concept type of PHYSICAL TRANSFER is 'defined', i.e., the five attribute descriptions constitute both necessary and sufficient conditions for the applicability of the concept to individuals of $\mathcal{D}$.

Other representational elements in SB-ONE are the *SB-ONE relations* between concepts and attribute descriptions (these should not be confused with the relations in the domain $\mathcal{D}$). Here are the SB-ONE relations of the general level:

- The *restriction relation* between two attribute descriptions $gad_j(gc_2)$ and $gad_i(gc_1)$ specifies that $gad_j(gc_2)$ is stricter than $gad_i(gc_1)$, in that the value restriction of $gad_j(gc_2)$ is in a specialization relation (see below) with the value restriction of $gad_i(gc_1)$, and/or that the number restriction of $gad_j(gc_2)$ is a subinterval of that of $gad_i(gc_1)$. In Figure 15.1, the attribute descriptions 'agent', 'object', 'origin', 'destination' and 'means-of-transport' of TAX DEDUCTIBLE COMMUTING are all in a restriction relation with the corresponding attribute descriptions of PHYSICAL TRANSFER, since in all cases the value restriction of the subordinate attribute description is more specific than that of the superordinate attribute description. In Figure 15.1, restriction relations are depicted by dotted arrows with the label 'RES'.
- The *specialization relation* between two concepts (abbreviated ($spec(gc_2,gc_1)$)) indicates that gc_2 is a more special concept description than gc_1. The concept gc_2 is called a *subconcept* of gc_1 in this case. A necessary condition for gc_2 being a subconcept of gc_1 is that gc_2 must possess more attribute descriptions than gc_1, or at least one that is in a specialization relation with one of the attribute descriptions of gc_1. The *spec* relation is transitive.
- The *isa* relation, which forms the basis of the *spec* relation. Only the *isa* relation, but not *spec*, is available to the knowledge engineer. In Figure 15.1, *isa* relations are depicted by double-lined arrows.

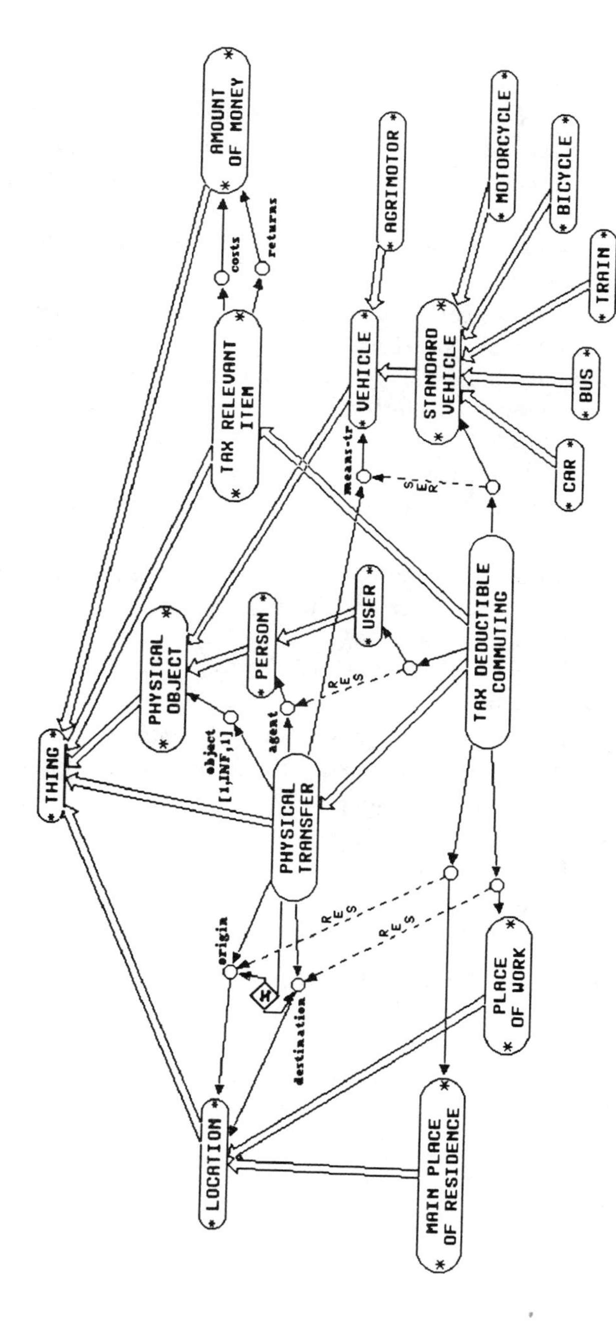

Figure 15.1: Example of an SB-ONE knowledge base

- The *inheritance relation* expresses that two attribute descriptions of two different concepts in a *spec* relation describe the same facts in the domain. In Figure 15.1, not only TAX RELEVANT ITEM, but also TAX DEDUCTIBLE COMMUTING possesses the attribute descriptions 'costs' and 'returns' (this is not depicted graphically). The latter are in an inheritance relation with the former.
- The *inversion relation* expresses some sort of inverse relationship between two attribute descriptions of different concepts.
- The *role value map* expresses certain set-theoretical relationships (namely set equality, disjointness, or inclusion) between the denotations of "chains" of attribute descriptions. In Figure 15.1, a role value map expresses that for physical transfers the destination must not be the same as the origin (both attribute description chains have a length of one in this example).
- The *differentiation relation* specifies that the denotation of an attribute description $gad_i(gc)$ is partitioned by the denotations of attribute descriptions $gad_{i_1}(gc),..., gad_{i_n}(gc)$.
- The *disjointness relation* between concepts $gc_1,..., gc_n$ specifies that the denotations of two or more concepts are disjoint (which implies, among other things, that a common subconcept of *all* $gc_1,..., gc_n$ cannot exist. In Figure 15.1, *CAR*, *BUS*, *TRAIN*, *BICYCLE* and *MOTORCYCLE* should be declared as disjoint.
- The *nondisjointness relation* is the "negation" of the disjointness relation.
- The *exhaustiveness relation* expresses that the denotations of subordinate concepts exhaustively cover the denotation of a superordinate concept. In Figure 15.1, an exhaustiveness relation could be stated between the above-mentioned concepts and *STANDARD VEHICLE*.
- The *nonexhaustiveness relation* is the "negation" of the exhaustiveness relation.

Only universally quantified assertions about the domain $\mathcal{D}$ can be constructed with the knowledge representation elements discussed so far. More specifically, assertions can be made about all individuals in the denotation of a concept predicate, and about all pairs of individuals in the denotation of a role predicate in a general attribute description. So-called "individualized" elements in the SB-ONE knowledge representation language allow assertions to be made about single individuals in the domain.[2] Not all kinds of assertions are permitted, however: Only elements for constructing *existential* assertions exist in SB-ONE. The individual-

---

[2] SB-ONE$^+$, an enhancement of SB-ONE [Allgayer, 1990], additionally allows assertions about sets to be made.

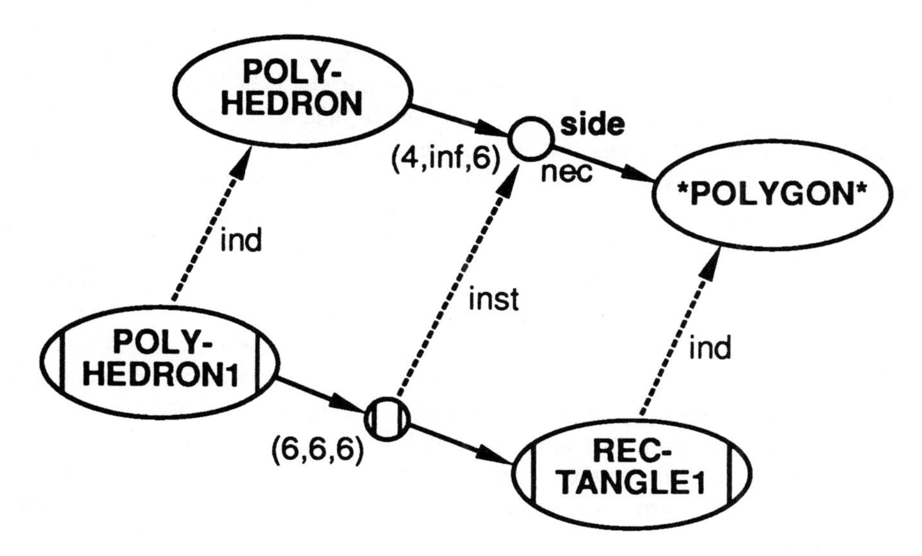

Figure 15.2: Example of the individualized level

ized level is based on four knowledge representation elements: *individualized concepts* and *individualized attribute descriptions*, and the *individualization* and *instantiation relations*. The latter are employed for linking individualized concepts and attribute descriptions to their general counterparts. The existence of individuals and pairs of individuals in the denotations of the respective concept and role predicates is thereby asserted.

An example of the individualized level is given in Figure 15.2. In the upper part, the concept 'POLYHEDRON' is defined as having 4 to arbitrarily many sides (6 by default), all of which are *POLYGONs*. The lower part asserts the existence of one individual in $\mathcal{D}$ to which the predicate of POLYHEDRON can be applied, and of six individuals to which the predicate of *POLYGON* can be applied (the number restriction (6,6,6) on the individualized level should be regarded as an abbreviation for six identical individualized structures).

15.2.2.2 Well-Formed SB-ONE Expressions

In the preceding section, all *elements* of the SB-ONE knowledge representation language have been presented. However, these are not independent of each other. Instead, nearly all SB-ONE relations between concepts or attribute descriptions imply the existence or absence of other SB-ONE relations. For instance, if $isa(gc_2,gc_1)$ holds true then neither $isa(gc_1,gc_2)$, nor $isa(gc_2,gc_3)$ and $isa(gc_3,gc_1)$ with $gc_2 \neq gc_3$ and $gc_3 \neq gc_1$ may hold true.

A large number of such *syntactic constraints* exist for most representational elements of SB-ONE (see [Kobsa, 1990b]). Their purpose is both to rule out logical inconsistencies (as in the above case of *isa*), and to induce the knowledge engineer to define "good" knowledge bases. For instance, if two attribute descriptions $gad_{i_2}(gc_2)$ and $gad_{i_3}(gc_3)$ are supposed to have the same denotation, this can only be expressed through the introduction of a $gad_{i_1}(gc_1)$ *with* $spec(gc_2,gc_1)$, $spec(gc_3,gc_1)$, $inh(gad_{i_2}(gc_2),gad_{i_1}(gc_1))$ *and* $inh(gad_{i_3}(gc_3), gad_{i_1}(gc_1))$, *but not via identical names. This requirement was added to induce the knowledge engineer to introduce missing superordinate concepts and to thus improve the quality of the knowledge base.*

The SB-ONE elements, moreover, do not exist autonomously, but form only the building blocks for the SB-ONE *expressions*. Starting with a "root concept" gc_0 (which is usually named 'THING'), the well-formedness of SB-ONE expressions can be recursively defined by referring to the set of all syntactic constraints of all SB-ONE elements. This set thus forms a *theory* $\mathcal{T}$ of well-formed SB-ONE expressions (which is first order since the syntactic constraints are formulated in first-order predicate calculus).

15.2.3 The Interpretation of SB-ONE

Until now, the meaning of the representational elements of SB-ONE has been explained only in an informal and more or less intuitive way. It is necessary, however, that the meaning of representational expressions and structures be made as clear as possible, both for reasons of communication (everybody should interpret the same KR structure in the same way), and for a theoretical and practical evaluation of the behavior of processes operating on the KR structure (e.g., for verifying whether processes operating on a KR structure really yield the desired result). Moreover, a precise interpretation makes it possible to clarify the capabilities and limits of a KR system, i.e., helps to determine what can and what cannot be represented when it is used.

In the field of formal logic, the favorite way for specifying the meaning of symbol structures is to map them into a mathematical structure that is so simple that it can be claimed to be "intuitively comprehensible," or into one that can itself be mapped into an intuitively comprehensible structure in a well-defined way. "Intuitive comprehensibility" of such a structure (which we will call *interpretative domain*) can be construed as implying that, for each element type of this structure, it is possible to identify those things in the world which belong to that type and those which do not.

In SB-ONE, the interpretative domain $\mathcal{D}$ consists of a set of *individuals* I and binary relations between these individuals. A *denotation function* Δ maps the predicates of general concepts into subsets of I, and the predicates of attribute descriptions into relations, i.e., subsets of $I \times I$. For the SB-ONE relations, an *interpreta-*

tion function $\Im$ determines an interpretation value from $\{0,1\}$, depending on whether or not certain conditions hold in $\mathcal{D}$. For instance, $\Im(spec(gc_2,gc_1)) = 1$ if and only if $\Delta(gc_2)$ is a subset of $\Delta(gc_1)$. For further details, see [Kobsa, 1990b].

15.3 META-SB-ONE

SB-ONE is neutral with respect to what kinds of things in the domain to be modeled should be regarded as individuals (and hence be represented by concepts), and what should be regarded as relations (and thus be represented by attribute descriptions). The decision as to how to represent certain conceptual knowledge is entirely left to the knowledge engineer who models a domain using SB-ONE. [Brachman et al., 1990] present a guideline for the discrimination between concepts and attribute descriptions, namely to determine "as to whether a description can stand on its own without implying an unmentioned object related to the object in question." If so, the description at hand would constitute a concept, otherwise an attribute description of the unmentioned object. Independently, a number of conventions as to what should be regarded as concepts and what as attribute descriptions have emerged in the field of natural language processing, since certain forms of representation have turned out to be more advantageous for natural language applications than others. For instance, if actions are regarded as individuals rather than relations, it is easier to specify the relationship between the semantic cases [Fillmore, 1968] of the natural language verbs that describe these actions and the attributes of these actions (such as the agent, object, etc.). But even in the field of natural language processing, these conventions are often broken for various reasons.[3] In fields such as expert systems or conceptual modeling for databases, no such convention seems to exist anyway as yet.

This arbitrariness in the representation of knowledge via concepts or attribute descriptions does not seem harmful as long as knowledge bases are used in isolation only. As soon as one wants to combine the conceptual knowledge of two or more knowledge bases, representational variants for the same knowledge pose serious problems. One solution would be to decide on one variant, and suppress the other in the combined knowledge base. This, however, means that processes that expect the suppressed version can no longer operate on the combined knowledge base.

The solution pursued in the development of SB-ONE was to enhance the language in such a way that objects in the world can be regarded both as individuals and as pairs of a relation, so that the same knowledge can be represented both

---

[3] Also, the example of action representation seems to contradict the above guideline of [Brachman et al., 1990], since an action like 'give' is related to unmentioned objects (e.g., the object being given, as well as the agent of this action), but is nevertheless represented by a concept.

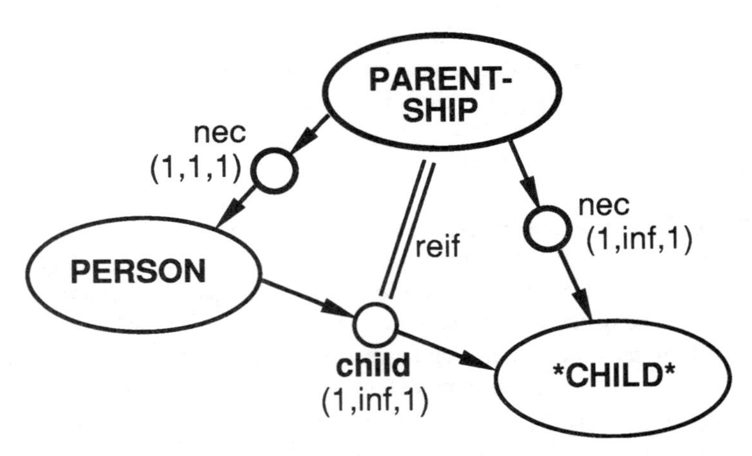

Figure 15.3: Example of a metaconcept and the reification relation

through concepts and through attribute descriptions. For achieving this, both the interpretative domain and the representational elements of SB-ONE must be augmented (the resulting language was called 'Meta-SB-ONE'). Different linearly ordered *ontological levels* are introduced into the interpretative domain $\mathcal{D}$, and each individual in $\mathcal{D}$ is assigned to one of these levels. The *reifies relation* is introduced between higher level individuals and pairs whose elements belong to a lower level (which expresses that a higher level individual "stands for" a lower level pair). Two new representational elements are introduced on the general level, namely so-called *metaconcepts* (they possess two special attribute descriptions), and the reification relation (*reif*) between metaconcepts and attribute descriptions. If an attribute description is *reified*, the assertions expressed by this attribute description become additionally represented by the metaconcept and its special attribute descriptions. An example is given in Figure 15.3, which also illustrates the graphical notation of metaconcepts and the reification relation. In this example, the attribute description 'has-child' of PERSON with value restriction *CHILD* has been reified into the metaconcept 'PARENTSHIP' with two special attribute descriptions whose value restrictions are PERSON and *CHILD*, respectively.

Metaconcepts and the reification relation are governed by a number of syntactic constraints, the most important being that one special attribute description of the metaconcept of an attribute description $gad_i(gc)$ must have gc as its value restriction, and the other the value restriction of $gad_i(gc)$. Other constraints refer to several of the SB-ONE relationships described in Section 15.2.2.1. The denotation function Δ must be slightly redefined in that all individuals of $\mathcal{D}$ that are in the denotation of a concept must pertain to the same ontological level. Thus each concept maps into a subset of the individuals of a single ontological level of $\mathcal{D}$. In a well-formed Meta-SB-ONE knowledge base, a separate root concept gc_{0_i} is introduced for each ontological level *i*. All these root concepts are disjoint from each other. An additional requirement for attribute descriptions of a concept of a certain level is that only concepts of the same or a lower level may be employed as value restrictions. This constraint, together with the different root concepts for each ontological level, guarantee that the ontological distinctions of the interpretative domain are also syntactically observed (e.g., by the classifier, see Section 15.7). Reification may occur arbitrarily often, i.e., attribute descriptions of metaconcepts may again be reified, etc. A set of individuals of the next higher ontological level in the interpretative domain is thereby described each time. It is doubtful, however, whether a double or even multiple reification makes sense. In practical applications, single reification will most probably be sufficient.

15.4 PARTITIONS AND PARTITION INHERITANCE

15.4.1 SB-PART

Knowledge that is represented using the SB-ONE knowledge representation workbench need not be stored in a single large knowledge base. With the enhancement system SB-PART [Scherer, 1990a, 1990b], an arbitrary number of so-called *partitions* can be maintained, each of which contains knowledge expressed in SB-ONE. These partitions may be completely independent of each other, or they may be ordered in an arbitrary *inheritance hierarchy*.[4] In the latter case, a subordinate partition inherits the contents of all superordinate partitions. It thereby becomes possible, for instance, to store the common contents of two or more partitions in a common superordinate partition, from which these contents can be inherited. This minimizes redundancy in the knowledge representation and allows for the clear separation of shared knowledge.

Figure 15.4 gives an example of a possible partition hierarchy in SB-PART. The aim of this example is merely to demonstrate the expressive power of the formalism; examples of meaningful applications will be given below. The hierarchy consists of one root partition (P1), one intermediate partition (P2), and three leaf partitions (P3, P4, and P5). The concepts gc_1, gc_2 and gc_3, and the attribute description gr_1[5] are inherited from P1 and are thus also accessible in P2, P3, P4, and P5. In P3, gc_2 is regarded as a subconcept of gc_1; whereas in P4, it is gc_1, which is a subconcept of gc_2 (gc_1, and indirectly gc_6, therefore inherit gr_1 from gc_2 in P4). In

---

[4] Partition hierarchies may be arbitrary directed acyclic graphs. SB-PART also allows for the construction of more than one independent parallel hierarchy. A knowledge item can then be assigned to different partitions in different hierarchies without any need for a duplication of this item.

[5] Assume that gr_i denotes an attribute description with empty number and value restrictions.

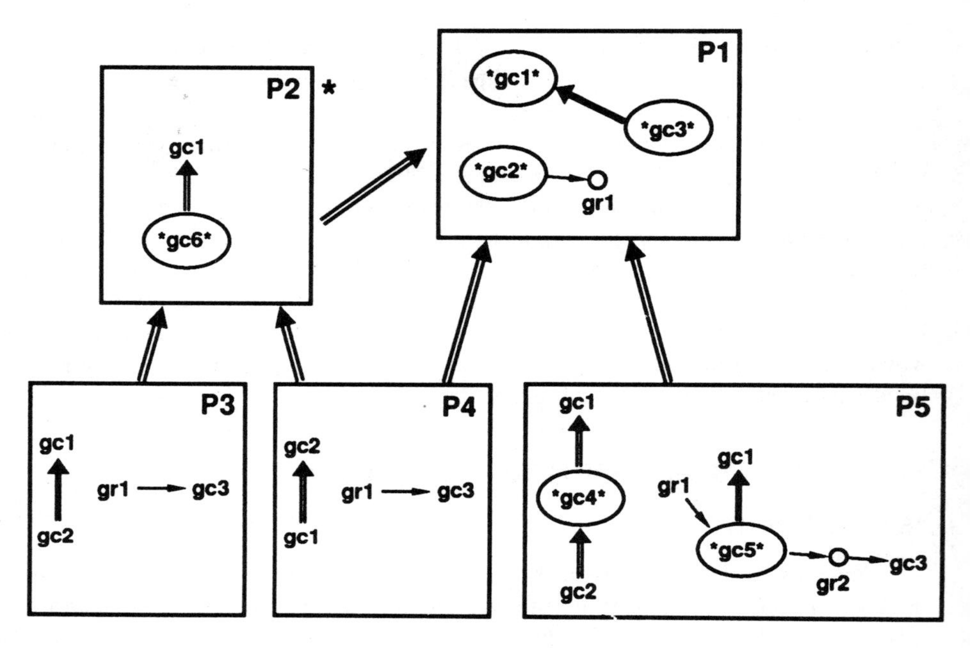

Figure 15.4: Example of a partition hierarchy

P5, finally, a new concept has been introduced between gc_1 and gc_2. The attribute description gr_1 which gc_2 possesses in P1 has no value restriction in this partition. In P3 and P4, this function is filled by the concept gc_3, which is inherited from P1. In P5, a new concept gc_5 (which is local to P5) has been made the value restriction of gr_1. This concept possesses an attribute description of its own (namely gr_2) with the inherited gc_3 as value restriction.

The attribute description gr_1 which gc_2 possesses in P1 has no value restriction in this partition. In P3 and P4, this function is filled by the concept gc_3, which is inherited from P1. In P5, a new concept gc_5 (which is local to P5) has been made the value restriction of gr_1. This concept possesses an attribute description of its own (namely gr_2) with the inherited gc_3 as value restriction.

As can be seen from Figure 15.4, a consequence of this distribution of knowledge structures over a partition hierarchy is that the contents of partitions need not necessarily be syntactically complete (e.g., as in the case of gr_1 in P1, an attribute description need not possess a value restriction concept within the same partition). Syntactic well-formedness as specified in Section 15.2.2.2 can no longer be guaranteed within a single partition; it can only be required for the contents of a whole *view*, i.e., for the union of all knowledge structures in all partitions on all paths leading from a leaf partition to all root partitions of the hierarchy.

SB-PART supports the addition and deletion of partitions in a partition hierarchy via a graphics-based and a functional interface. Within each view, SB-ONE structures may be added, removed, or revised using any of the SB-ONE interfaces described in Section 15.5. Knowledge can also be transferred from one partition to another. The results of all these operations are analyzed, however, with respect to whether the constraints of well-formed SB-ONE are observed in all views affected by these operations. If this is not the case, the operation is retracted. If an entry is present in more than one partition/view, it will automatically be transferred to their common superordinate partition, if such a partition exists for exactly these partitions/views. This propagation is not desirable, however, if all subordinates of this common superordinate partition have not yet been created. Partitions can therefore be marked as *primitive* to prevent an automatic "upward propagation" from their subpartitions. In Figure 15.4, this is the case for partition P2 (its primitiveness is marked by an asterisk). Therefore, the information that gc_3 is the value restriction of gr_1 was not transferred to P2, although it is contained in all (current!) subpartitions of P2. An application of primitive partitions in the field of user modeling is described in [Kobsa, 1990a].

Note also that classification and realization (see Section 15.7) must now be performed on *each* view. The results may differ depending on how concepts were defined in the respective views. Thus it is possible that the concept 'WHALE' becomes classified as a subconcept of 'MAMMAL' in one view, and—due to different attribute descriptions—as a subconcept of 'FISH' in another view.

15.4.2 Applications of the Partition Mechanism

The partition hierarchy of SB-ONE can be used for a wide variety of applications in which it is important to store shared knowledge together with conflicting knowledge in a redundancy-free manner. This includes the following:

Tentative maintenance of alternatives: During the development of SB-ONE knowledge bases, alternatives may be explored by creating parallel subpartitions of a common root partition. The alternative branches can be expunged or merged with the common superordinate partition later. Possible applications are the concurrent development of knowledge bases by multiple knowledge engineers [Mays et al., 1990; Lenat and Guha, 1990], or the exploration of alternative strategies by expert systems.[6]

---

[6] Expert system shells therefore frequently possess so-called 'contexts' or 'worlds' [Carnegie Group, 1985; Clayton, 1985; Intellicorp, 1987], and also a few early AI programming languages included similar mechanisms [Sussman and McDermott, 1972]. The SB-PART partitions are far more complex, though (see [Scherer, 1990a] for a comparison).

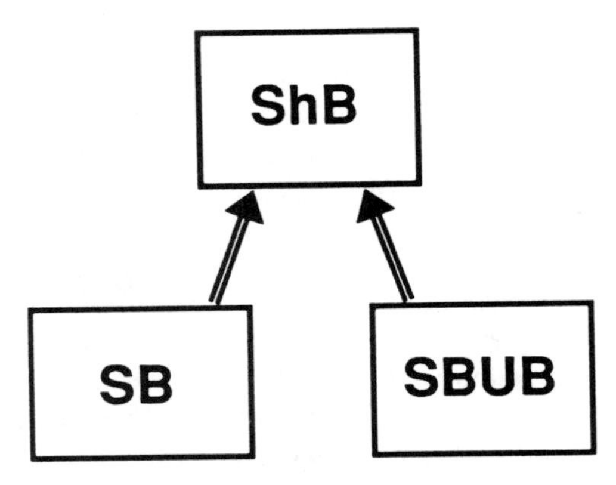

Figure 15.5: Example of a simple user model based on a partition hierarchy

Integration of conceptual knowledge bases: Mechanisms are being developed which allow for the integration of multiple external conceptual knowledge bases into SB-ONE knowledge bases (see Section 15.8). The external knowledge bases are thereby not duplicated or translated, but regarded as external superordinate partitions from which knowledge is inherited by a common subordinate SB-ONE partition.

User modeling: Figure 15.5 shows a very simplified example of how a partition hierarchy can be employed for a redundancy-free representation of the conceptual knowledge of a user, as well as of his or her misconceptions. The view with leaf partition 'SB' contains the system's knowledge, and the view with leaf partition 'SBUB' the user's knowledge.[7] The conceptual knowledge that is shared by the user and the system is stored in partition 'ShB' and is thus inherited both by 'SB' and 'UB'. Only beliefs that are not shared (namely the expert knowledge of the system and the misconceptions of the user) must be stored in 'SB' and 'UB', respectively. As can be seen from Figure 15.4, different opinions may exist about practically all properties of concepts which can be expressed using SB-ONE, including their superconcepts and subconcepts, attribute descriptions, disjointness, exhaustiveness, and consequently also their position in the concept hierarchy.

SB-PART can represent not only assumptions about individual users, but also stereotypical assumptions about the conceptual knowledge of certain user subgroups. Commonalities between user subgroups can thereby be collected in superordinate partitions. A variety of possible set-theoretical relationships between

---

[7] 'SB' stands for '**s**ystem **b**elieves', 'UB' for '**u**ser **b**elieves', and 'ShB' for '**sh**ared **b**eliefs'.

stereotypes have been proposed (and partly empirically investigated) in the field of user modeling (see, e.g., [Rich, 1979; Sutcliffe and Old, 1987; Fischer et al., 1988; Chin, 1989]). In [Kobsa, 1990a], the user modeling shell system BGP-MS is described; BGP-MS allows for the development of user modeling components in dialog systems. The representation of user models and of stereotype hierarchies in BGP-MS is based on SB-ONE and its partition mechanism. With BGP-MS, much more complex user models than that depicted in Figure 15.5 can be represented: for instance, the model of user beliefs and goals developed for XTRA consists of a hierarchy of 37 different partitions [Kobsa, 1988; Scherer, 1990b].

15.5 INTERFACES TO THE SB-ONE WORKBENCH

Good user interfaces are extremely important for usable software systems. For instance, [Bobrow et al., 1986] estimate that 30–50% of the program code in expert systems is devoted to the user interface. The same holds true for the SB-ONE workbench, which offers three types of interfaces for retrieval and update operations on SB-ONE knowledge bases: a functional interface, a TELL/ASK interface, and a graphics-based interface. The knowledge engineer can employ any of these interfaces, whereas application systems that use SB-ONE as a knowledge representation subcomponent can employ only the functional and the TELL/ASK interfaces. Before update operations specified via these interfaces are executed, they are examined by the maintenance system for syntactic well-formedness (see Section 15.6) as to whether their results will again yield well-formed SB-ONE structures.

15.5.1 The Functional Interface

SB-ONE's functional interface [Profitlich 1989, 1990] offers a set of about 150 LISP functions with which SB-ONE knowledge bases can be accessed and updated. Here are four examples:

define-general-concept

&key (*type* *default-concept-type*) *name* (*supers* '(GC0)) *subs others*

defines a new general concept of type *type* (which may take on 'defined', 'primitive' and 'singleton'; the default value is the value of *default-concept-type*), concept name *name*, superconcepts *supers* (the default is gc_0), subconcepts *subs*, and the non-SB-ONE properties *others*.

define-general-role

domain range &key *name* (*card* *default-cardinality*) (*nec* *default-necessity*) *dvr others*

defines a new general attribute description of concept *domain* with value restriction *range*, name *name*, number restriction *card* (the default value is the value of *default-cardinality*), modality *nec* (the default value is the value of *default-necessity*) default value restriction *dvr*, and the non-SB-ONE properties *others*.

get-direct-superconcepts *concept*
yields all direct superconcepts of concept *concept*.

test-direct-superconcepts *concept1 concept2*
tests whether *concept1* is a direct superconcept of *concept2*.

15.5.2 The TELL/ASK Interface

The TELL/ASK interface consists of the TELL/ASK language $\mathcal{L}_{SB\text{-}ONE}$+ and an interpreter which accesses SB-ONE[8] via its functional interface [Allgayer, 1989]. The TELL language often allows knowledge definitions to be made in a more compact form than is possible with the functional interface, particularly as far as concept definitions are concerned.[9] For instance, a concept CName with an attribute description RName can be defined as follows:

```
primelemrole
    (RName
     domain-range (defconcept (CName
                               supers (ConceptList)
                               nr (RName NRTriple)
                               necres(RName NecSpec))))
```

The retrieval language ASK has a PROLOG-like syntax and is combined with a continuation-based solution generator to simulate a PROLOG-like query processing. For instance, when the predicate (**supers** *subc superc*) is evaluated, *T* will be returned if both *subc* and *superc* are SB-ONE concepts which are in a *spec* relation. If one or both are variables, an instantiation of these variables with SB-ONE concepts will be sought so that the predicate is fulfilled. On request, the next solution will be supplied, etc. Thus, only a single predicate is needed in ASK where at least three different functions of SB-ONE's functional interface must be employed.

15.5.3 The Graphics-based Interface

Figure 15.6 gives an example of how knowledge bases can be edited with the graphics-based user interface SB-GRAPH [Kalmes, 1988, 1990]. The dark headpiece of the terminal screen contains the graphical icons for individualized con-

---

[8] Or more precisely SB-ONE^{+}, i.e., an extension of SB-ONE that allows for the representation of sets [Allgayer, 1990].

[9] The functional interface, on the other hand, can be employed by the graphics-based interface described below; it also allows for revision and deletion operations.

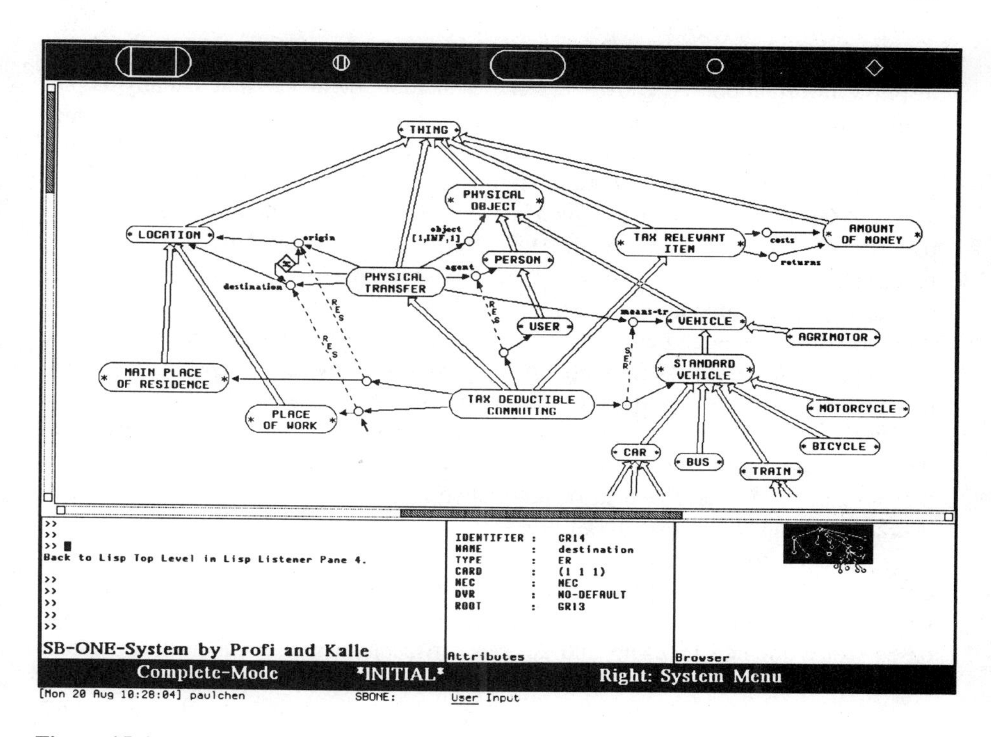

Figure 15.6: The graphical interface of the SB-ONE workbench

cepts and attribute descriptions, general concepts and attribute descriptions, and role value maps. New entries into the knowledge base are defined by clicking on one of these icons using the mouse, dragging them into the central window, and positioning them at an appropriate location with another mouse click. Additional information such as the names of concepts or attribute descriptions, the number restrictions of attribute descriptions, or the view or partition (see Section 15.4.1) into which the new entry should be placed is supplied by filling in pop-up menus associated with these icons (for most entries, the knowledge engineer may specify default values). Both the displayed nodes (and their attached links) as well as their labels can be easily moved around on the terminal screen. The knowledge engineer can scroll the screen in all directions, save and retrieve knowledge bases, and correct entries with an unlimited undo facility.

In the lower right part of the terminal screen, the complete knowledge base is displayed in reduced size. The black rectangle marks that portion of the total knowledge base that is currently displayed. A scrolling of the central display causes the rectangle to move correspondingly, and a locational displacement of this rectangle will change the central display. The middle area in the lower part of the screen displays information on knowledge representation elements that usually is not graphically displayed. For obtaining this information, the mouse icon must merely touch the respective representational element. The lower left window, finally, contains a LISP interface. Under normal circumstances, it will not be needed.

SB-GRAPH has been designed in accordance with important design principles for user interfaces [Card et al., 1983, Norman and Draper, 1986], including the requirement of operation consistency, conformity of the system behavior with user expectations, customizability and direct feedback. Features particularly required in interfaces to knowledge bases [Hammwoehner and Thiel, 1986; Kalmes, 1990] are also present in SB-GRAPH, including navigation, browsing, snapshot, and undo mechanisms. Special attention has been given to consistent direct-manipulative interaction [Shneiderman, 1983; Hutchins et al., 1986] with the graphical display of the knowledge base: Knowledge bases can be edited using mostly only operations that pertain to the visual world of the display, namely pointing actions and move operations using the mouse.

SB-GRAPH has hitherto been used for small or medium-sized knowledge bases only (one with 800 concepts and 2,000 attribute descriptions is by far the largest). Enhancements necessary for an adequate operation on larger knowledge bases would include focusing and abstraction mechanisms. Focusing mechanisms would allow the knowledge engineer to operate on subsets of the knowledge base. The contents of these subsets would in part have to be specified by the knowledge engineer. This kernel could then be automatically complemented by the interface, by using heuristics based on the structure of the current knowledge base and possibly also a user model. Abstraction mechanisms would allow subsets of the knowledge base to be regarded as unstructured higher level items, and to *reference* these items in knowledge definitions (e.g., in a *spec* relation). The maintenance system for syntactic well-formedness could regard such references as an additional constraint in its *incomplete mode* (see Section 15.6), in the sense that the final referent must not only fulfill all SB-ONE constraints but must also be contained in the subset denoted by the referenced higher level item.

15.6 A MAINTENANCE SYSTEM FOR THE SYNTACTIC WELL-FORMEDNESS OF SB-ONE KNOWLEDGE BASES

Update operations on well-formed SB-ONE knowledge bases (see Section 15.2.2.2) which are specified via any of the three above-mentioned interfaces are examined as to whether their results will again yield well-formed SB-ONE. Basically, each of these operations adds or removes one or more instantiated knowledge representation elements described in Section 15.2.2.1. An operation yields a syntactically *inconsistent* SB-ONE knowledge base if the union of newly entered SB-

ONE elements and the current SB-ONE knowledge base is inconsistent under $\mathcal{T}$, the first-order theory about well-formed SB-ONE expressions. An operation yields a syntactically *incomplete* SB-ONE knowledge base if the union of the new entries, the current knowledge base and $\mathcal{T}$ is not fully instantiated, i.e., contains existentially bound or free variables (which means that a number of SB-ONE elements have still to be defined, yet certain characteristics of them could already be inferred from the syntactic constraints of SB-ONE).

The maintenance system for the syntactic well-formedness of SB-ONE knowledge bases ("well-formedness maintenance system" for short) operates in two modes: in its *complete* mode, it rejects operations that result in incomplete or inconsistent SB-ONE (the knowledge engineer will possibly be asked for missing SB-ONE elements), whereas in its *incomplete* mode it rejects only operations that yield inconsistent SB-ONE. An operation that has not been rejected is immediately executed in the SB-ONE knowledge base.

The purpose of the incomplete mode is to allow the knowledge engineer to concentrate on the definition of the essentials of a knowledge base, and to leave the rest for later. For instance, the knowledge engineer can enter an attribute description without having to account for its value restriction, or for the concept to which the attribute description pertains. Additional information imposes constraints on the missing elements; e.g., if a superordinate attribute description, but not a value restriction was given for the currently entered attribute description, then the value restriction of the superordinate attribute description must be a superconcept of or equal to the missing value restriction (see Section 15.2.2.1). The well-formedness maintenance system introduces variables for missing concepts, records in an *agenda* what information must still be supplied in order that the knowledge base becomes syntactically complete, and stores the constraints that apply to the missing elements. The agenda and the constraints can be inspected by the knowledge engineer when she or he wants to complement the knowledge base. Since both structures can be saved together with the incomplete knowledge base, the knowledge engineer can freely decide on when to supply the missing information. Classification (see Section 15.7) is only possible in a syntactically complete knowledge base, however, since subsumption can mostly not be determined in incomplete knowledge bases.

The complete mode of the well-formedness maintenance system has been implemented procedurally, and the incomplete mode as a simple forward-chaining mechanism. Although this guarantees efficient tests for well-formedness when an SB-ONE knowledge base is augmented, serious problems arise if knowledge representation elements are retracted from a knowledge base since it is difficult to determine which previously drawn implications are then no longer justified. Some sort of reason maintenance system [McAllester, 1990] would be necessary to record these dependencies. Instead, deletion operations have been constrained in the SB-

ONE workbench in such a way that they cannot be performed in an arbitrary order, but only in one whose effects can still be controlled by the well-formedness maintenance system.

15.7 THE CLASSIFIER AND THE REALIZER

Classification (see [Schmolze and Israel, 1982; Schmolze and Lipkis, 1983]) is a special kind of deduction, which infers new *isa* relations between defined concepts in SB-ONE knowledge bases. The denotation of the predicates of these concepts can be computed on the basis of their attribute descriptions. The so-called *classifier* determines for a given concept *gc* the most specific superordinate concepts based on the attribute descriptions of *gc* and the current knowledge base.

Although only the *isa* relation is available to the user of the SB-ONE workbench, all *isa* relations of a specific concept in a knowledge base may be declared as "tentative," and their verification requested. In this case, the SB-ONE classifier will regard these relations as *spec* relations and compute the most specific subset relationships for the concept in question. If the "incomplete mode" of the maintenance system for syntactic well-formedness (see Section 15.6) was selected, the agenda must be empty before classification can take place. The knowledge engineer may also declare *all* the *isa* relations of the knowledge base as being tentative. In this case, the SB-ONE classifier will iteratively classify all concepts.

A closely related type of deduction is the so-called "realization" [Mark, 1982] of individualized concepts and attribute descriptions in a given SB-ONE knowledge base. For an individualization *ic* of a general concept gc_1, the realizer determines the most specific concept gc_2 with *spec* (gc_2, gc_1) such that the individual whose existence is postulated by *ic* is not only an element of $\Delta(\mathbf{gc}_1)$, but also of $\Delta(\mathbf{gc}_2)$. Additional *inst* relations between the attribute descriptions of *ic* and those of gc_2 are also deduced. An example is given in Figure 15.7, which enhances Figure 15.2 by additional general concepts. In this example, the classifier would recognize that POLYHEDRON1 is not only an individualization of POLYHEDRON, but also of BLOCK since its attribute descriptions also fulfill the requirements expressed by the attribute description 'face' of 'BLOCK'. Realization is strongly based on classification: For the determination of the most specific gc_2, a general dummy concept is created that possesses the same attribute descriptions as *ic* (to illustrate this, the reader should regard all individualized structures of Figure 15.7 as general structures, and the *ind* and *inst* relations as *spec* and *restr* relations, respectively). After this concept has been classified, the sought gc_2 is the immediate superconcept of it, or identical to it. If an individualized concept is the individualization of more than one general concept (which is not permitted in the current version of SB-ONE), the realizer would determine *all* most specific concepts of which *ic* is also an individualization.

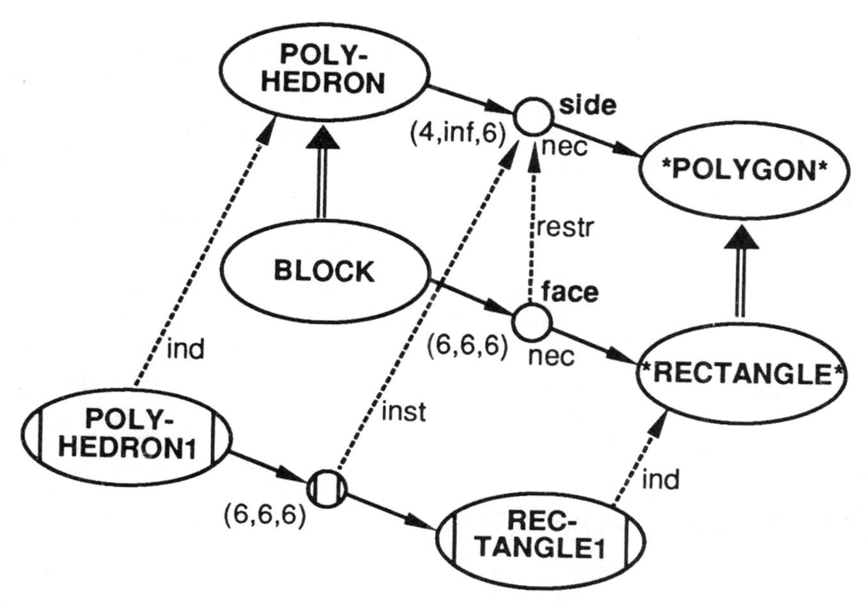

Figure 15.7: Example of realization in SB-ONE

Both classification and realization are crucial in NL systems for the following reasons:

- The access to a knowledge base becomes more efficient if all concepts are guaranteed to be in their "correct" positions in the concept hierarchy.
- The representation of the user's natural language input (which is an individualization of general SB-ONE structures onto which the input was mapped) can be better analyzed. For an example, see Figure 15.6, which shows an excerpt of one of XTRA's [Allgayer et al., 1989b] knowledge bases: XTRA would realize the user's input sentence "I go daily from Saarbrücken to Völklingen" as being an individualization of TAX DEDUCTIBLE COMMUTING, and not only of PHYSICAL TRANSFER if it has the information that Saarbrücken is the user's MAIN PLACE OF RESIDENCE, that Völklingen is his or her PLACE OF WORK, and that this action has costs and returns.
- Patterns can normally be matched more efficiently in a knowledge base if they are realized or classified before the matching takes place. Of particular interest is the classification of the patterns (i.e., the left-hand sides) of *rules* [Yen et al., 1988; Reinert, 1990, 1991]. If this has been performed, the spe-

cialization relationship between patterns can be exploited in the search for applicable rules as well as the selection among conflicting applicable rules.

The current SB-ONE classifier is described in more detail in [Profitlich, 1989, 1990]. Several parameters (which have default settings) determine whether a single concept or the whole knowledge base should be classified, and specify the start concept and the behavior of the classifier in the case of identical definitions of two concepts or cyclic definitions. No analysis has as yet been made as to the complexity and completeness of this algorithm. Recently, this classifier has been enhanced by an *interactive* classification component [Jansen-Winkeln et al., 1990, 1991], which was first proposed by [Finin and Silverman, 1984]. This component uses the structure of the current knowledge base to ask the knowledge engineer for possible additional properties of a concept that is currently being entered. A comparison of the SB-ONE classifier with weaker connectionist methods of classification has been made in [Kobsa, 1989].

15.8 ADDITIONAL COMPONENTS OF THE SB-ONE WORKBENCH

The SB-ONE workbench comprises additional utilities and tool systems that operate on SB-ONE knowledge bases. At the moment, the following systems are available:

SB-ONE Matcher a powerful network matcher for SB-ONE structures which allows for the introduction of variables for concepts and attribute descriptions that are to be matched [Aue et al., 1989]. This mechanism is currently being expanded so that conjunctions and disjunctions of patterns can also be matched.

SPREADIAC a spreading-activation mechanism that supports the definition of activation path patterns and activation damping factors [Schäfer, 1990]. It can be used for detecting the shortest path of SB-ONE elements that connects certain concepts or attribute descriptions. This mechanism can be employed, e.g., for finding referents of noun phrases that have only been mentioned implicity in the previous dialog, for simple information retrieval, and for ranking of nonunique results of the SB-ONE matcher.

SB-TRANS an interpreter for translation rules from SB-ONE to SB-ONE [Reinert, 1990, 1991]. These rules may be attached to SB-ONE concepts in a source knowledge base, which are to be translated into a target knowledge base. In XTRA, this mechanism is exploited for a bidirectional translation between a language-related SB-ONE knowledge base (into which natural language input of the user is mapped, and from which natural language output of the system is generated) and another

SB-ONE knowledge base which contains a "deeper" representation of the domain of discourse [Allgayer et al., 1989a, 1989b]. The interpreter makes twofold use of the concept hierarchy in the source knowledge base. First, not only the rules that are directly attached to the concept to be translated, but also those attached to its superconcepts are tested for applicability. Second, applicability is tested and the most specific applicable rule determined by classifying the left-hand sides of these rules, and also the concept to be translated. The right-hand side of the most specific applicable rule is then merged with the right-hand sides of its superordinate rules (more specific actions thereby override less specific ones), and the resulting action is executed in the target knowledge base.

BABY-BONE a tool system that allows for the integration of a BABYLON frame knowledge base [di Primio and Brewka, 1985; Christaller et al., 1988] into an SB-ONE knowledge base [Bolz and Weber, 1990]. The contents of the frame knowledge base form virtual SB-ONE concepts and attribute descriptions and are inherited into the combined knowledge base using an extension of the partition mechanism described in Section 15.4. The frame knowledge base can thereby be fully integrated into SB-ONE. For instance, frames can become the superconcepts or subconcepts of SB-ONE concepts, or the value restrictions of SB-ONE attribute descriptions, etc. The integration guarantees that processes that operate exclusively on BABYLON do not "recognize" this connection with SB-ONE, and processes that operate on SB-ONE do not "recognize" that some of the SB-ONE concepts and attribute descriptions are only virtual objects. The system is currently being enhanced in such a way that also other external knowledge bases (e.g., Loom [Mac Gregor, 1988, 1991]) can be integrated into SB-ONE, and that information from different sources can be merged.

MOTHOLOG an extended PROLOG interpreter which accepts negation and disjunction both in the antecedent and in the consequent parts of the PROLOG rules [Bartsch *et al.*, 1990]. Moreover, MOTHOLOG predicates can be equated with SB-ONE concepts; these predicates are then evaluated by a search in an SB-ONE knowledge-base, using the continuation-based solution generator $\mathcal{L}_{\text{SB-ONE}}+$ described in Section 15.5.2, in order to simulate a PROLOG-like query processing.

SB-TWO which actually cannot be regarded as an enhancement of SB-ONE, but is rather an independent system of its own that makes use of SB-ONE, $\mathcal{L}_{\text{SB-ONE}}+$ and of MOTHOLOG. SB-TWO is aimed at forming a semantic representation language for the representation of the meaning of natural language sentences. Special emphasis is on the adequate representation of the scope and several other characteristics of noun phrases. For a more detailed discussion of these issues see [Allgayer and Reddig, 1990].

15.9 IMPLEMENTATION

The SB-ONE Workbench is written in Common LISP and has been run on Symbolics 36xx (full graphics-based interface available as described in Section 15.5.3), HP 9000 (reduced graphics facilities) and VAX 8700 (no graphics-based interface). SB-ONE knowledge bases are implemented in ASCON [Bosch, 1988], a network storage system with a powerful pattern-matching language, which is fairly efficient due to extensive hashing. Retrieval time efficiency has been given priority over definition and update time efficiency. Most inherited information about concepts has therefore been cached in the network implementation, and other information has been precomputed. The retrieval processes in SB-ONE knowledge bases could thereby be speeded up considerably (see [Schmolze, 1989] for similar experiences in NIKL).

SB-ONE has been used in the XTRA natural language dialog system [Allgayer et al., 1989a, 1989b] since 1986. More recently, SB-ONE has been employed for the representation of conceptual hierarchies in a natural language generation system for the description of visual scenes in a soccer domain (VITRA, see [André et al., 1988; Hays, 1989]) and for the representation of document structures and graphical knowledge in a generation system for multimodal technical descriptions (WIP, [Wahlster et al., 1991]). Envisaged applications include the dialog system (PRACMA, see [Allgayer et al., 1990]) and the representation of nonlinguistic knowledge in the multiparty dialog system DISCO.

ACKNOWLEDGMENTS

The research reported here has been supported by the German Science Foundation in its Special Collaborative Research Programme No. 314 on AI and Knowledge-Based Systems. I would like to thank Jürgen Allgayer, Markus Bolz, Roman Jansen-Winkeln, Joachim Kalmes, Bob Mac Gregor, Harold Paredes-Frigolett, Carola Reddig-Siekmann, Douglas Skuce, and most of all Bernhard Nebel, Hans-Jürgen Profitlich and Thomas Weber for their comments on earlier versions of this paper.

References

Allgayer. J. 1989. $\mathcal{L}_{SB\text{-}ONE}+$: *Die Zugangssprache zu SB-ONE*$^{+}$. Unpublished manuscript, SFB 314: AI—Knowledge-Based Systems, Department of Computer Science, Univ. of Saarbrücken, Saarbrücken, Germany.

Allgayer, J. and Reddig, C. 1990. What's in a 'DET': Steps towards determiner-dependent inferencing. In *Artificial Intelligence IV: Methodology, Systems, Applications*, Jorrand, R. and Sendov, B. (ed.s). North-Holland, Amsterdam, Netherlands.

Allgayer, J., Harbusch, K., Kobsa, A., Reddig, C., Reithinger, N., and Schmauks, D. 1989a. XTRA: A Natural-language access system to expert systems. *International Journal of Man–Machine Studies*, 31:161–195.

Allgayer, J., Jansen-Winkeln, R., Reddig, C., and Reithinger, N. 1989b. Bidirectional use of knowledge in the multimodal NL access system XTRA. In *Proceedings of the 11th IJCAI*, pp. 1492–1497, Detroit, MI.

Allgayer, J., Kobsa, A., Reddig, C., and Reithinger, N. 1990. PRACMA: PRocessing Arguments between Controversially-Minded Agents. In *Proceedings of the Fifth Rocky Mountain Conference on Artificial Intelligence: Pradmatics in Artificial Intelligence*, pp. 63–68, Las Cruces, NM.

———. 1990. SB-ONE^{+}: Representing sets efficiently. In *Proceedings of the Ninth European Conference on Artificial Intelligence*, pp. 13–18, Stockholm, Sweden.

André, E., Herzog, G., and Rist, T. 1988. On the simultaneous interpretation of real world image sequences and their natural language description: The system soccer. In *Proceedings of the 8th ECAI*, pp. 449–454, Munich.

Aue, D., Heib, S., and Ndiaye, A. 1989. *SB-ONE Matcher: Systembeschreibung und Benutzeranleitung*. Memo 32, Projekt XTRA, Fachbereich Informatik, Universität Saarbrücken, Deutschland.

Bartsch, W., Kader, A.D., Raasch, I., and Schmitt, R. 1990. *MOTHOLOG: Ein Prolog Interpreter zum erklärbaren Beweisen disjunktiver und negativer Ziele*. Memo, SFB 314: KI—Wissensbasierte Systeme, Fachbereich Informatik, Univ. Saarbrücken, Saarbrücken, Deutschland.

Bobrow, D.G., Mittal, S., and Stefik, M.J. 1986. Expert systems: Perils promise. *Communications of the ACM*, 29(9):880–894.

Bolz, M. and Weber, T. 1990. *BABY-BONE: Ein System zur Integration von Babylon-Frames und SB-ONE*. Arbeitsbericht 4, SFB 314: AI—Knowledge-Based Systems, Department of Computer Science, Univ. of Saarbrücken, Saarbrücken, Germany.

Bosch, G. 1988. *ASCON*. Unpublished Manuscript, SFB 314: AI—Knowledge-based Systems, Department of Computer Science, Univ. of Saarbrücken, Saarbrücken, Germany.

Brachman. R.J. 1978. *A Structural Paradigm for Representing Knowledge*. Technical Report 3605, Bolt Beranek and Newman, Cambridge, MA.

Brachman, R.J. and Schmolze, J.G. 1984. *An Overview of the KL-ONE Knowledge Representation System*. Technical Report 655, Fairchild Laboratory for Artificial Intelligence Research, Palo Alto, CA.

Brachman, R.J., Bobrow, R.J., Cohen, P.R., Klovstad, J.W., Weber, B.L., and Woods, W.A. 1979. *Research in Natural Language Understanding*. Technical Report 4274, Bolt Beranek and Newman, Cambridge, MA.

Brachman, R.J., McGuinness, D.L., Patel-Schneider, P.F., Alperin Resnick, L., and Borgida, A. 1991. Living with CLASSIC: When and How to Use a KL-ONE-Like Language. This volume, Chapter 14.

Card, S.K., Moran, T.P., and Newell, A. 1983. *The Psychology of Human–Computer Interaction.* Lawrence Erlbaum Associates, Hillsdale, NJ.

Chin, D.N. 1989. KNOME: Modeling what the user knows in UC. In *User Models in Dialog Systems*, Kobsa, A. and Wahlster, W. (ed.s), pp. 74–107. Springer, Berlin, Heidelberg.

Christaller, T., di Primio, F., and Voss, A. 1988. *Die KI-Werkbank BABYLON.* Addison-Wesley, Bonn, Germany.

Clayton, B.D. 1985. *ART Programming Tutorial, Version 1.0.* Inference Corporation, Los Angeles, CA.

Carnegie Group Inc. 1985. *CRL Reference Manual*, Pittsburgh, PA.

Fillmore, C.J. 1968. The case for the case. In *Universals in Linguistic Theory*, E. Bach and R. Harms, (ed.s), pp. 1–88. Holt, Rinehart and Winston, New York.

Finin, T. and Silverman, D. 1984. *Interactive Classification: A Technique for the Acquisition and Maintenance of Knowledge Bases.* Technical Report MS-CIS-84–17, Department of Computer and Information Science, Univ. of Pennsylvania, Philadelphia, PA.

Fischer, G., Lemke, A., and Nieper-Lemke, H. 1988. *Enhancing Incremental Learning Processes with Knowledge-Based Systems.* Technical Report CU-CS-392–88, Department of Computer Science, Univ. of Colorado, Boulder, CO.

Hammwoehner, R. and Thiel, U. 1986. Graphische Kommunikations—und Präsentationsformen für komplexe Wissens—und Textstrukturen: Zur Konzeption eines graphischen Interface für ein wissensbasiertes Textkondensierungssystem. In *Kognitive Aspekte der Mensch-Computer-Interaktion*, Dirlich, G., Freksa, C., Schwatlo, U., and Wimmer, K. (ed.s), pp. 165–177. Springer, Berlin, Heidelberg.

Hays, E.M. 1989. Two views of motion: On representing move events in a lagnuage-vision system. In GWAI-89. P*roceedings of the 13th German Workshop on Artificial Intelligence*, Metzing, D. (ed.). Eringerfeld, Deutschland, pp. 312–317. Springer, Berlin, Heidelberg.

Hutchins, E.L., Hollan, J.D., and Norman, D.A. 1986. Direct manipulation interfaces. In *User-Centered System Design*, Norman, D.A. and Draper, S.W. (ed.s). Lawrence Erlbaum Ass., Hillsdale, NJ.

Jansen-Winkeln, R.M., Ndiaye, A., and Reithinger, N. 1990. FSS-WASTL: Interactive knowledge acquisition for a semantical lexicon. Paper to be submitted, 1991.

Kalmes, J. 1988. *SB-Graph User Manual (Release 0.1).* Memo 30, Project XTRA, Department of Computer Science, University Saarbrücken, Germany. (In German.)

———. 1990. *SB-Graph: Eine graphische Benutzerschnittstelle für die Wissensrepräsentationswerkbank SB-ONE.* Memo 44, Projekt XTRA, Fachbereich Informatik, Universität Saarbrücken, Deutschland, 1990.

Intellicorp. 1987. *KEEworlds Reference Manual, KEE Version 3.1.*

Kobsa, A. 1988. User models and discourse models: United they stand... *Computational Linguistics*, 14:91–94.

———. 1989. *Conceptual Hierarchies in Classical and Connectionist Architecture.* Technical Report 89–010, International Computer Science Institute, Berkeley, CA.

———. 1990a. Modeling the user's conceptual knowledge in BGP-MS, a user modeling shell system. *Computational Intelligence*, 5(4).

———. 1990b. *The SB-ONE Knowledge Representation Workbench.* Memo 50, SFB 314: AI—Knowledge-Based Systems, Department of Computer Sciene, Univ. of Saarbrücken, Saarbrücken, Germany.

Kumar, D. (ed). 1990. *Current Trends in SNePS—Semantic Network Processing System.* Springer-Verlag, Berlin.

Lenat, D.B. and Guha, R.V. 1990. *Building Large Knowledge Bases.* Addison-Wesley, Reading, MA.

Mac Gregor, R.M. 1988. A deductive pattern matcher. In *AAAI-88: Proceedings of the National Association for Artificial Intelligence*, pp. 403–408, St. Paul, MN.

MacGregor, R 1991. Using a description classifier to enhance deductive inference. In *Proceedings of the Seventh IEEE Conference on AI Applications*, Miami, FL, to appear.

Mark, W. 1982. Realization. In *Report No. 4842: Proceedings of the 1981 KL-One Workshop*, Schmolze, J.G. and Brachman, R.J. (ed.s), pp. 78–89. Bolt Beranek and Newman, Boston, MA.

Mays, E., Lanka, S., Dionne, B., and Weida, R. 1990. A persistent store for large shared knowledge bases. In *Proceedings of the Sixth IEEE Conference on Artificial Intelligence Applications*, pp. 169–175, Santa Barbara, CA.

McAllester, D. 1990. Truth maintenance. In *Proceedings of the AAAI-90*, pp. 1109–1116, Boston, MA.

Nebel, B. and Sondheimer, N.K. 1986. NIGEL gets to know logic. An experiment in natural language generation taking a logical, knowledge-based view. In *GWAI-86 und 2. Österreichische Artificial-Intelligence-Tagung,* Rollinger, C.-R. and Horn, W. (ed.s), Ottenstein, Austria, pp. 75–86. Springer, Berlin, Heidelberg.

Norman, D. A. and Draper, S.W. (ed.s). 1986. *User-Centered System Design.* Lawrence Erlbaum, Hillsdale, NJ.

Pereira, F.C.N. and Shieber, S.M. 1987. *Prolog and Natural-Language Analysis.* CSLI, Stanford, CA.

di Primio, F. and Brewka, G. 1985. BABYLON: Kernel system of an integrated environment for expert systems development and operation. In *Proceedings of the Fifth International Workshop on Expert Systems and their Applications*, pp. 573–583, Avignon, France.

Profitlich, H.-J. 1989. *Das SB-ONE Handbuch.* Version 1.0. Memo 33, SFB 314: AI—Knowledge-Based Systems, Department of Computer Science, Univ. of Saarbrücken, Saarbrücken, Germany.

———. 1990. *SB-ONE: Ein Wissensrepräsentationssystem basierend auf KL-ONE.* Memo 43, SFB 314: AI—Knowledge-Based Systems, Department of Computer Science, Univ. of Saarbrücken, Saarbrücken, Germany.

Reinert, J. 1990. *SB-TRANS: Conflict Free Net-to-Net Transformation Based on Incrementally Classified Rules.* Unpublished Manuscript, SFB 314: AI—Knowledge-Based Systems, Department of Computer Science, Univ. of Saarbrücken, Saarbrücken, Germany.

Rich, E. 1979. *Building and Exploiting User Models.* Ph.D. Thesis, Department of Computer Science, Carnegie-Mellon University, Pittsburgh, PA.

Schäfer, R. 1990. SPREADIAC: Intelligente Pfadsuche und -bewertung auf Vererbungsnetzen zur Verarbeitung impliziter Referenzen. In *GWAI-90: 14th German Workshop on Artificial Intelligence* Marburger, H. (ed)., pp. 231–235, Springer-Verlag, Berlin, Germany.

Scherer, J. 1990a. *SB-PART: Ein Partitionsmechanismus für die Wissensrepräsentationssprache SB-ONE*. Master's thesis, Department of Computer Science, Univ. of Saarbrücken, Saarbrücken, Germany.

———. 1990b. *SB-PART Handbuch: Version 1.0*. Memo 47, SFB 314: AI—Knowledge-Based Systems, Department of Computer Science, Univ. of Saarbrücken, Saarbrücken, Germany.

Schmolze, J. and Israel, D. 1982. *KL-ONE: Semantics and Classification. Research in Knowledge Representation and Natural Language Understanding*. Report No. 5421, pp. 27–39. Bolt Beranek and Newman, Boston, MA.

Schmolze, J.G. and Lipkis, T.A. 1983. Classification in the KL-ONE knowledge representation systems. In *Proceedings of the Eighth IJCAI*, pp. 330–332, Karlsruhe, FRG.

Schmolze, J.G. 1989. *The Language and Semantics of NIKL*. Technical Report 89–4, Department of Computer Science, Tufts University, Medford, MA.

Shapiro, S.C. and Rapaport, W.J. 1987. SNePS considered as a fully intensional propositional semantic network. In *The Knowledge Frontier*, Cercone, N. and McCalla, G. (ed.s), pp. 262–315. Springer, New York.

Shneiderman, B. 1983. Direct manipulation: A step beyond programming languages. *IEEE Computer*, 16(8):57–69.

Sowa, J.F. 1984. *Conceptual Structures: Information Processing in Mind and Machine*. Addison-Wesley, Reading, MA.

Sussman, G.J. and McDermott, D.V. 1972. From PLANNER to CONNIVER: A genetic approach. In *Proceedings of the AFIPS Fall Computer Conference*, pp. 1171–1179.

Sutcliffe, A.G. and Old, A.C. 1987. Do Users Know They Have User Models? Some Experiences in the Practice of User Modelling. In *Human–Computer Interaction: INTERACT-87*, Bullinger, H.-J. and Shakel, B. (ed.s), pp. 35–41. North-Holland, Amsterdam, 1987.

Wahlster, W., André, E., Bandyopadhyay, S., Graf, W., and Rist, T. 1991. WIP: The coordinated generation of multimodal presentations from a common representation. In *Computational Theories of Communication and their Applications: Problems and Prospects*, Ortony, A. Slack, J., and Stock, O. (ed.s). Springer-Verlag, Berlin, Germany.

Wilensky, R., Chin, D.N., Luria, M., Martin, J., Mayfield, J., and Wu, D. 1988. The Berkeley UNIX consultant project. *Computational Linguistics*, 14:35–84.

Wilensky, R. 1986. *Some Problems and Proposals for Knowledge Representation*. Report UCB/CSD86/294, Computer Science Division (EECS), University of California, Berkeley, CA.

Yen, J., Neches, R., and Mac Gregor, R. 1988. *Classification-Based Programming: A Deep Integration of Frames and Rules*. Technical Report ISI/RR-88–213, Information Science Institute, Marina del Rey, CA.

16

REASONING WITH GRAPH OPERATIONS

Roger T. Hartley and Michael J. Coombs
(New Mexico State University, Las Cruces)

Abstract

Problem solving is an analog to scientific method, wherein abduction and deduction operate in a cyclic fashion to generate and refine a series of hypotheses that purport to explain the observed data. *Model generative reasoning* implements this cycle through a family of operations on representations based on conceptual graphs. *Specialize*, the operator that implements abduction, generates alternative hypotheses. *Fragment* removes potential incoherences from hypotheses, while preserving coherence with the observations. This is seen as a form of deduction with the aim of allowing more hypotheses to be generated in the next cycle.

16.1 PROBLEM SOLVING AND NOISY DATA

In essence, problem solving is a two-part process. There is a data-driven side, where making observations, filtering them, and generating hypotheses from them is important. There is also another side, that is more goal driven: Evaluation of hypotheses against new data can, and does, lead to reformulation or even rejection of these hypotheses. Typically problem-solving machines are good at the first but less so at the second part. Heuristic search enables this sort of efficient generation, leading to excellent systems for planning, where the prime aim is to reach some desired goal without interference from the environment [Chapman, 1987]. When, however, data are incomplete, incoherent (i.e., unexpected), or just irrelevant, such techniques will fail.

In these difficult cases, what is needed is a principled way of handling noisy data. The gaps in incomplete data should be filled, the incoherencies removed, and the irrelevancies ignored. We will present, in this chapter, mechanisms for doing all of these, and place these mechanisms in a problem-solving framework. To do this we will contrast our approach with that based on theorem proving. In particular the nonmonotonic approach to noisy data through the ATMS [Reiter and de Kleer, 1987] can be seen as only solving one of the problems associated with noisy data: incoherence that presents itself through logical inconsistency.

16.1.1 Hypotheses, Explanation, and Abduction

All problem solvers generate hypotheses, and in general we can classify all such mechanisms as *abductive*. However, the use to which these subsequent hypotheses are put separates what we might call *logical abduction* from the more pragmatic use of the term in scientific reasoning [Peirce, 1957].

Many authors have pointed out that abduction is an unsound logical inference from consequent to antecedent, as in:

$$\frac{A \rightarrow B \quad B}{A}$$

Another way to look at such an inference is that if B is true, and $A \rightarrow B$, then A explains B. This is the basis of the methods described by Levesque [1989] and Poole [1989]. Explanations are hypothetical structures generated to fit some set of observations (not just one as the above simplification implies) and have only the status of "possible" in the system. However, if they were true, then the consequent would follow naturally by deduction. Finding an explanation in a logical system then amounts to finding an expression, that, if it were true, would imply the input (the axioms). In order to find out how this works, we need to analyze the use of rules (logical implications) in such systems.

There are four main uses of a rule:

1. As a selectional constraint on types, e.g., all Us are Vs:
   $\forall x\, U(x) \rightarrow V(x)$
2. as an Aristotelian definition, e.g., if something has properties A, B, C, etc., then it is a V
   $\forall x\, A(x) \wedge B(x) \wedge C(x) \ldots. \rightarrow V(x)$
3. as a contingent, or schematic definition, e.g., if something is a V, then it has properties A, B, C, etc.
   $\forall x\, V(x) \rightarrow A(x) \wedge B(x) \wedge C(x) \ldots.$

4. to express causality, e.g., if P, Q, R all happen, then X, Y, Z will happen as a direct consequence
   $P \wedge Q \wedge R \ldots\ldots \rightarrow X \wedge Y \wedge Z \cdots$

To illustrate these types of rule, consider the following abductive inferences:

1. $$\begin{array}{l} car(a) \\ \forall x\, ford(X) \rightarrow car(x) \\ \hline possible(ford(a)) \end{array}$$

In other words, if a car a is observed, then it is possibly a Ford. Of course, this is not an explanation of *why* a is a car, but it does shed a little more light on the subject. There may well be other types of car (Chevrolet, Subaru etc.) and these would be equally likely inferences. The question of the goodness of an explanation is one for the pragmatics of abduction. Poole has pointed out, however, [Poole, 1989] that there are several possible accounts of what constitutes the best explanation.

2. $$\begin{array}{l} car(a) \\ \forall\ x\ has\text{-}wheels(x) \wedge has\text{-}engine(x) \wedge has\text{-}drivers\text{-}seat(x) \rightarrow car(x) \\ \hline possible(wheels(a) \wedge has\text{-}engine(a) \wedge has\text{-}drivers\text{-}seat(a)) \end{array}$$

This abductive inference stands a little better as an explanation; it at least shows why a is a car, based on the limited knowledge on hand about cars. Note that if both of the above rules were available, and a criterion of goodness was expressed as the simplest explanation is the best, then the first would be preferred over the second.

3. $$\begin{array}{l} at(a,b) \\ \forall\ xyz\ person(x) \wedge car(y) \wedge drive(x,y) \wedge location(z) \rightarrow at(x,z) \wedge at(y,z) \\ \hline possible(\exists\ y\ person(a) \wedge car(y) \wedge drive(a,y) \wedge location(b)) \end{array}$$

Here we infer an existential result (as pointed out by Poole) because we have no evidence about the car if we assume a is a person. The other possible inference is:

$$possible(\exists\ y\ person(y) \wedge car(a) \wedge drive(y,a) \wedge location(b))$$

It is also possible that the observations are existentially quantified; e.g., with the fact:

4. $\exists xy\ at(a,x) \wedge drive(y,b)$

This, with the same rule as in (3), gives the inference:

$$possible(\exists x\ person(a) \wedge car(b) \wedge drive(a,b) \wedge location(x))$$

Finally an example that gets closer, we believe to the reason abduction is important. If we have the facts:

5. $at(a,b)$ *and*
   $has\text{-}engine(c)$

which seem to be unconnected, the job of abduction is to *glue* them together in a single hypothesis. The inference we might look for, and one that is clearly an explanation of why these two pieces of data are observed together is:

$$person(a) \wedge car(c) \wedge drive(a,c) \wedge location(b) \wedge at(c,b)$$

This hypothesis glues the facts together, through the definition of a car and the driving rule.

16.2 AN OPERATOR FOR ABDUCTION: SPECIALIZE

We will describe an single operator, *specialize*, which mechanizes the process of abduction illustrated in the above examples. It is composed of two more primitive operators, *cover* and *join*, that operate on conceptual graphs [Sowa, 1984]. This leads to the slogan:

Abduction = cover + join

Conceptual graphs are connected, directed, bipartite graphs where the nodes are labeled with either a concept type or a relation name. There are restrictions on the edges, however, that are used to preserve semantic coherence (Sowa calls this *canonicality*). A relation node may have only one ingoing edge, but any number of outgoing edges. A concept node may have any number of edges, in or out. For the purposes of this chapter, however, this family of graphs will be reduced to a *concept graph* by eliminating all relation nodes (thus reducing the number of colors to one) and the directionality of the edges. This can clearly be done for any conceptual graph (there is a small problem with relations of degree greater than two, but this need not concern us here). Figure 16.1 shows a conceptual graph and its reduction to the corresponding concept graph. The reason we can work with the simplified graph is that specialize and its dual, *fragment*, only work on the concept nodes of the conceptual graph, through the operation *join*. The relational nodes, since they do not take part in join, can effectively be omitted. This is in contrast to the logic-based methods, which almost always match predicates (relations) first, and leave object matching to some form of unification.

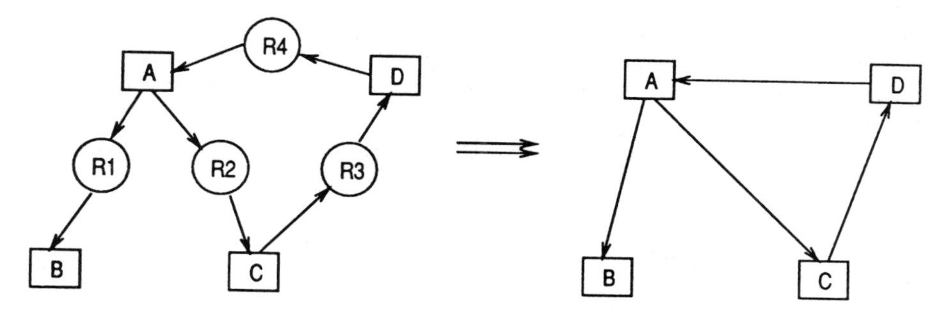

Figure.16.1: A conceptual graph and its concept graph reduction

The functionality of *specialize* is:

$$specialize: 2^{\mathcal{F}} \times 2^{\mathcal{D}} \rightarrow 2^{\mathcal{H}}$$

where $\mathcal{F}$ is a set of input graphs, $\mathcal{D}$ is a set of *definitions* (conforming to the rule types 2, 3 and 4 above, i.e., Aristotelian, schematic, or causal) and $\mathcal{H}$ is the resultant set of hypotheses produced by *cover* and *join*. It is the composition of the two operations *join* and *cover*:

$$specialize = join \circ cover$$

16.2.1 The Operator Cover

It is the job of *cover* to choose an appropriate subset of a set of stored graphs $\mathcal{D}$, that cover all of the concepts in a given subset of graphs taken from a set $\mathcal{F}$. If the conceptual content of a graph g is given by $C(g)$ and the maximal common subtype of two concepts c_1 and c_2 is given by $M_b(c_1,c_2)$ then the functionality of cover is given by:

$$cover: \mathcal{F} \times 2^{\mathcal{D}} \rightarrow 2^{\mathcal{D}}$$
where for $f \in \mathcal{F}$, $\forall c \in C(f)\ \exists\ c_d, d \mid c_d \in C(d)$ for some $d \in \mathcal{D}$
and $M_b(c,c_d)$ exists

In other words, every concept in f must have at least one concept in the set of graphs $\mathcal{D}_C$, where their maximum common subtype exists; i.e., is not bottom. There are problems with graphs containing duplicate labels, but these can be solved by ensuring that there are sufficient quantities of covering concepts from graphs in $\mathcal{D}$ for the concepts in f.

The choice of an appropriate subset, since there can be many that satisfy the above condition, is a matter for the pragmatics of the problem. The Maryland group [Nau and Reggia, 1986] have used this idea of set covering (as have many others) in their diagnostic work, but deal with expressions at the propositional level rather than at the object level as we do here. They point out that although a parsimonious *cover* may be appropriate when simplicity is called for (compare Occam's razor) there may be cases when less than parsimonious *cover* is safer, or simply better as an explanation.

Parsimonious *cover* may be produced my minimizing the Boolean expression:

$\wedge_c \vee_i d_i$, where $c \in C(f), C(d_i)$

As a simple example:

let $C(f) = \{a, b, c\}$
$C(d) = \{a, b\}$
$C(d_1) = \{c, d, e\}$
$C(d_2) = \{a, c, d\}$

Parsimonious *cover* is then the minimization of:

$(d_1 + d_3).(d_1).(d_2 + d_3)$
or, $d_1 d_2 + d_1 d_3$, eliminating $d_1 d_2 d_3$

16.2.2 The Operator *Join*

Cover just produces an appropriate subset of $\mathcal{D}$. The job of producing an explanatory hypothesis is left to the binary operation *join* (actually *maximal join*). As an operation on single concept nodes, *join* merges two graphs at a single point where both graphs contain the same concept label. *Maximal join* (we will usually refer to this as just *join*) will not only allow restrictions in that a concept label can be replaced by a label of any subtype but also will merge the two graphs on the maximum number of nodes (see [Sowa, 1984]). An example is given in Figure 16.2. The functionality of join is:

maximal join: $\mathcal{G} \times \mathcal{G} \rightarrow 2^{\mathcal{G}}$

There can be more than one maximal *join*, hence the powerset notation on the set of all graphs *G*. *Join* is a binary operation, but multiple graphs can be joined by composing it with itself. Unfortunately, there is good reason to believe that *join* is not commutative when semantic considerations come into play [Pfeiffer and Hartley, 1989]; but for now we will assume there is no problem.

Since restrictions are allowed, it is clear that two nodes are joinable as part of a maximal join operation if they contain types that have a maximal common subtype. So PET can be restricted to DOG, and so can MAMMAL. Thus nodes containing PET and MAMMAL join to produce DOG. If two concepts have only $\perp$ (bottom) as their common subtype, then the maximal common subtype is not considered to exist. The reason the same constraint was placed on the operator cover was to ensure that the covers returned are maximally joinable; i.e., that the fact

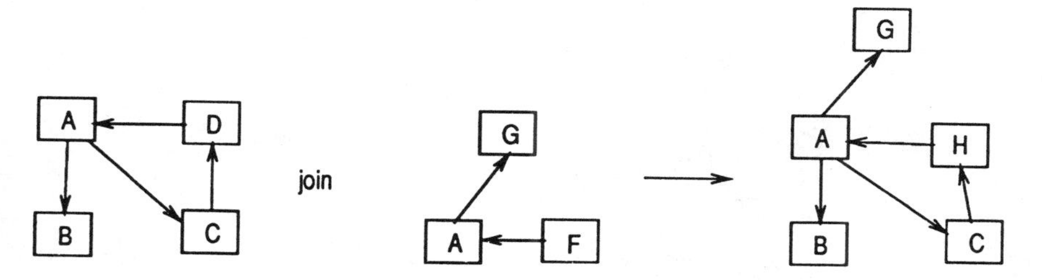

Figure 16.2: An example of *maximal join* ($Mb(D,F) = H$)

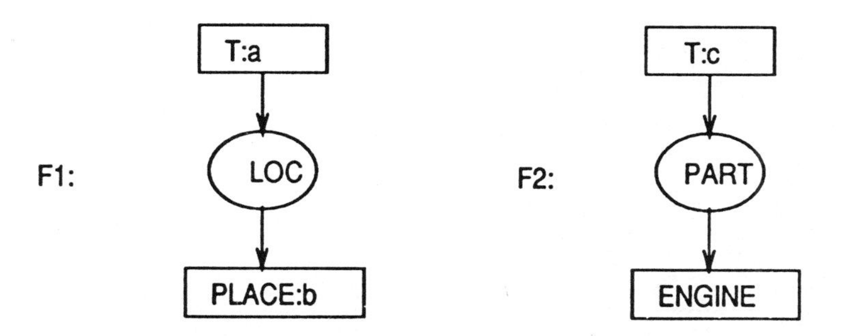

Figure 16.3: The "driving" facts

graph *f* is joinable to the graphs that cover it. That this is an abductive inference in the logical sense may be seen from the following equivalent presentation:

$$\frac{\begin{array}{l} PET(a) \\ MAMMAL(a) \\ \forall x\, DOG(x) \rightarrow PET(x) \\ \forall x\, DOG(x) \rightarrow MAMMAL(x) \end{array}}{DOG(a)}$$

If we now look at example (5) above, the facts might be represented as in Figure 16.3, and the covering graphs as in Figure 16.4. These graphs add information that the logical representation leaves out, however these are mandated by the need to form canonical graphs. The equivalent in logic would be a full intensional logic with type restrictions on the placeholders, but the graphs have not prejudiced the argument that the appropriate hypothesis is obtained by joining all four graphs together, as shown in Figure 16.5.

The major addition to the driving graph is the actor node in the diamond-ended box (Figure 16.4 and 16.5). In an extension to conceptual graphs [Hartley, forthcoming], these nodes can express the temporal relationships between states

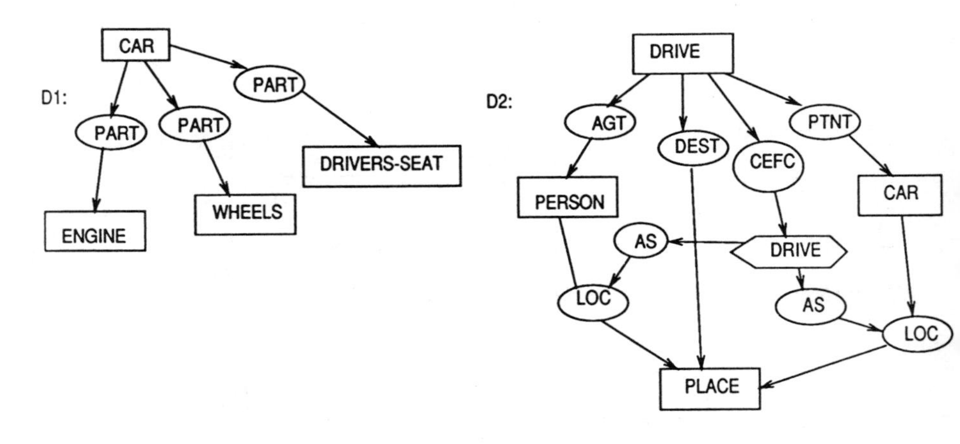

Figure 16.4: The covering graphs for Figure 16.3

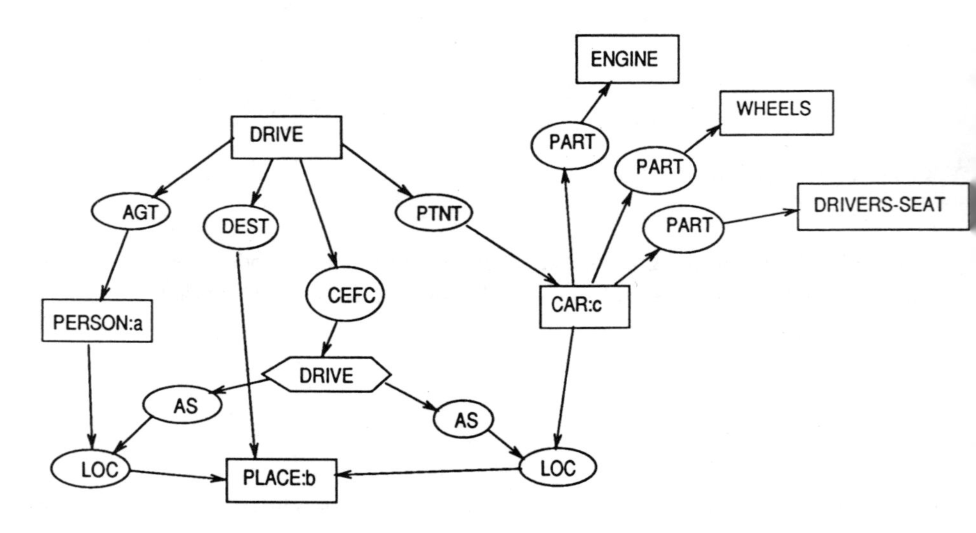

Figure 16.5: The maximal join of Figures 16.3 and 16.4

and events in order to represent procedures qualitatively. In the example, the causal relationship between the two states CAR→LOC→PLACE and PERSON→LOC→ PLACE is made through the actor, with the DRIVE event as mediator. The temporal relations between the state relations (the LOC nodes) and the event concept (DRIVE) designate a particular relation between the interval over which the event takes place, and the interval over which the state holds. CEFC (Continuous Enabling Finish Condition) and AS (Assert State) together mean that the end point of the event interval coincides with the start of the state interval, which is open-ended. In other words, the state comes into existence when the event stops. However, these extra nodes play no part in *cover* or *join*, and will not be discussed further.[1] The join will only occur if the following type relationships hold:

$M_b(CAR, PHYS\text{-}OBJ) = CAR$
$M_b(CAR, TRANSPORT) = CAR$

It should be noted that a person, an engine, and a drivers seat are all physical objects, as is the car. These relationships potentially give alternative joins. Thus instead of placing the person *a* at the place *b*, the join could place any of the other objects, for instance the engine, at *b*. This sort of thing may produce a violation of canonicality (e.g., giving a pipe three ends instead of two ends and a middle) but may also be prevented by knowledge of the *conformity* of individuals to types. Again, the FOPC form does not contain this information, but *a* may conform to PERSON but not to ENGINE.

In essence, therefore, the resultant graphs produced by join can be seen as abductive inferences from the facts and those definitions, causal or Aristotelian, that cover them. The result is hypothetical in nature because the maximal common subtype restriction of two types leads to the same unsound inference rule that an logical abductive rule makes. Additionally, however, constraints stemming from canonicality and conformity increase the likelihood of the inference. Figure 16.6 contains a more intuitive Venn-like diagram of *specialize* where each enclosed region contains at least one concept node. *F1* and *F2* are two fact graphs, and *D1* and *D2* are two covering definitions. *D1* covers all of *F1* and one node of *F2*, *D2* covers all of *F2* and two nodes of *F1*. *D1* and *D2* together cover all of the nodes in both facts.

16.3 AN OPERATOR FOR DEDUCTION: *FRAGMENT*

In Section 16.4 we will show how problem solving can be seen as a cycle of abduction and deduction. Any operator used for deduction had better be logically sound (although human problem solvers use a variety of unsound inferences, typically based on analogy). The inverse of the operation *join* is *project*, based on the same idea of merging two graphs, but this time taking the minimal common supertype of the concepts (M_p). Just as *join* is maximal, so *project* is as well. However,

---

[1] The model generative reasoning system includes an extension to conceptual graphs to represent causal/temporal relationships and to allow these to be combined from different sources and used for prediction [Hartley, op cit]. Effectively this is forward use of rules.

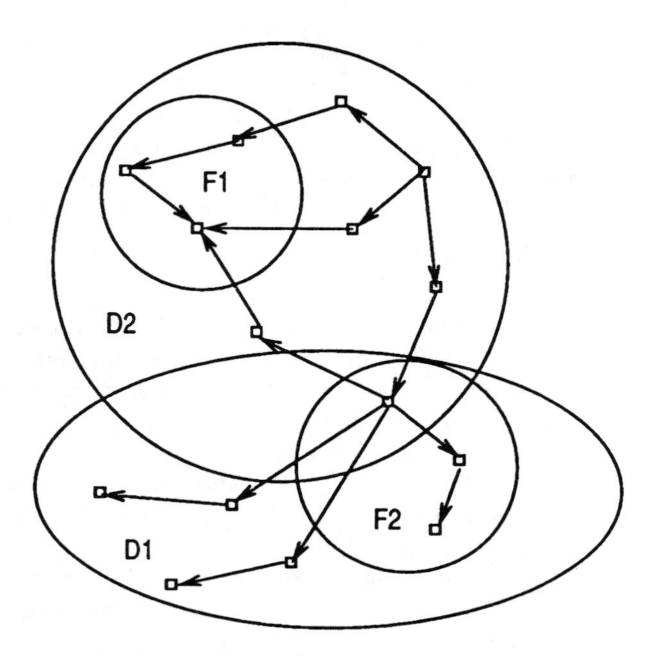

Figure 16.6: *Specialize* in a set diagram form

when we say *project*, we will always mean *maximal projection* unless explicitly stated. The other difference is that all nodes that do not have a common supertype are dropped for the resultant graph. Again just as bottom was not allowed with *join*, so top is not allowed with *project*. If *join* is likened to set union, in that all nodes not joinable are just left alone and come along for the ride, then *project* is like set intersection. All nodes that are not projectable are simply dropped from the resultant graph, along with their associated relation nodes.

All the abductive inferences in Section 16.1 can be reversed into deductive inferences if the appropriate axioms are available. The conclusions are, of course, truth preserving. *Project*, however, is not a substitute for forward chaining through a rule. For instance, given the theory

$\forall x\ mammal(x) \rightarrow warm\text{-}blooded(x)$
$\forall x\ cat(x) \rightarrow mammal(x)$
$cat(a) \wedge has\text{-}tail(a)$

we could conclude *warm-blooded*(*a*). However, if the schema definition for warm-blooded mammals is projected with the fact about *a*, the result is the single node graph *mammal*(*a*), as Figure 16.7 shows; the other nodes are dropped out.

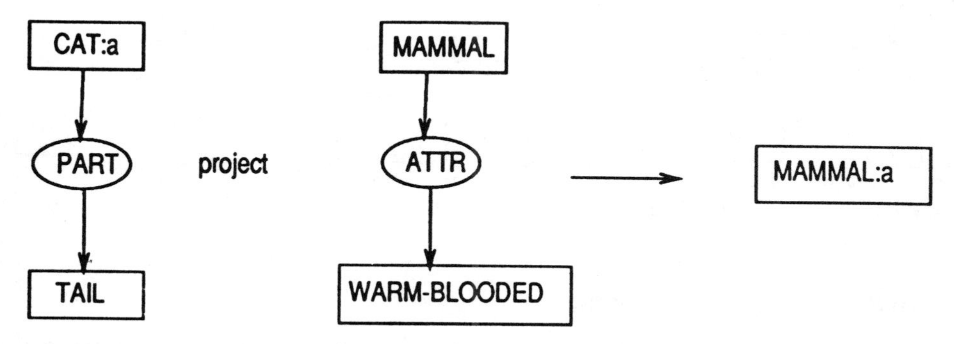

Figure 16.7: An example of projection

This is a valid conclusion, but it merely follows the subtype rule about all cats being mammals; it does not follow the schematic rule that all mammals are warm-blooded.

However, with the addition of an inverse operation to *cover*, in *specialize*, *project* can be turned into a useful operation. The inverse, which we call *uncover*, has the job of preserving factual information at the expense of definitional information. It breaks apart a hypothesis graph into unconnected pieces, or fragments which are by definition unjoinable. Hence the name for the operation: *fragment*. If *specialize* glues facts together with the minimum number of definitions, then *fragment* removes the minimum amount of glue to separate them again. It is important to note that *fragment* is not the true inverse of *specialize*. As we shall see in Section 16.4, a problem solver searches a space of potential solutions. An operator that merely retraces the steps of another is useless. The functionality is:

fragment: $2^{\mathcal{F}} \times \mathcal{H} \rightarrow 2^{\mathcal{H}}$

Here a set of fact graphs taken from $\mathcal{F}$ are projected into a single hypothesis $h \in \mathcal{H}$ to produce a set of fragments $\mathcal{H}$. It is not necessary for the subset $\mathcal{F}$ to be the set of facts that were originally covered to produce h.

16.3.1 The Operator Project

Project's functionality is the same as join:

maximal project: $\mathcal{G} \times \mathcal{G} \rightarrow 2^{\mathcal{G}}$

The example in Figure 16.8 shows projection with the reduced form of graphs. These operand graphs are the same as in Figure 16.2.

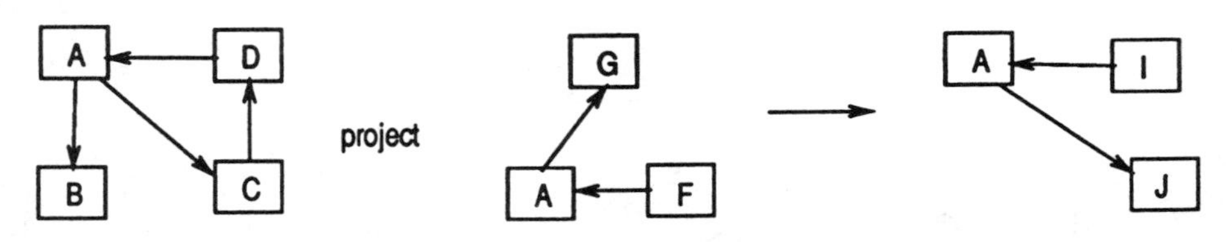

Figure 16.8: An example of projection ($Mp(D,F)$ = I and $Mp(G,C) = J$)

16.3.2 The Operator Uncover

The job of uncover is to undo some of the work that cover has done, but not all of it. It is best seen first in the set diagram form. In Figure 16.9 the regions labeled *F1* and *F2* are the regions of the graph that contain concept nodes to be projected onto by a given set of fact graphs. *D1*, *D2*, and *D3* are the definition graphs that originally made up the hypothesis graph. In fact these may already be fragments of definitions from previous fragmentations, but for the purpose of illustration, we will assume that the definitions are, as yet, intact within the hypothesis. Removing the links shown with a bar through them, and the node *n*1, splits the graph into two fragments. Which nodes to remove is a matter of searching out from the fact projections *F1* and *F2* (each fragment is thus guaranteed to contain at least one whole fact projection), adding nodes to each projection where they do not lie on a path to another projection (i.e., that connect within definitions), and removing one node that lies in the middle of each path to another projection. It can be seen from this example that *uncover* cuts links and removes information from definition graphs. Another way to say this is that facts are trusted, but definitions may have parts that are suspect. *Fragment*, through *uncover*, removes those untrustworthy parts. The fragments are then facts with good intensional information added (they could be called *assumptions*) and are available for further refinement through specialize. Moreover, the set of *fragments* produced by the operator are guaranteed not to join. They therefore correspond to separate hypotheses, and potentially to separate lines of thinking.

The functionality of uncover is:

uncover: $\mathcal{H} \times 2^{\mathcal{F}} \rightarrow 2^{\mathcal{H}}$

where $\forall\ \hbar \in H_{out}$, $\hbar$ is connected, and no concept in any $\hbar$ connects with any concept in another $\hbar$, and every $\hbar$ is of maximal size (i.e., $|C(\hbar)|$ is maximal)

16.3.3 An Example of Fragment Producing New Definitions

The example shown above is a good case where the fragments produced are of different sorts. The upper fragment only contains nodes from one definition and one fact. However, the lower one contains nodes from two definitions and one fact.

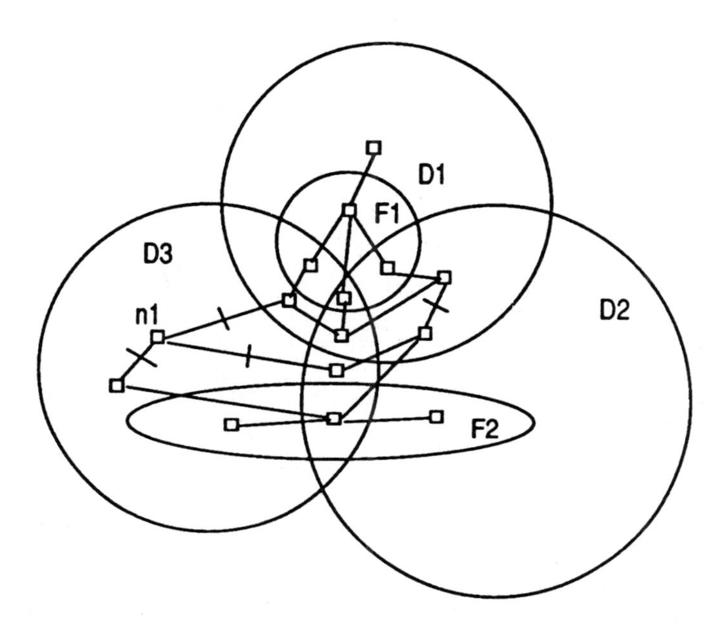

Figure 16.9: A set diagram showing uncover

If these fragments were to be available as definitions for use in specialize, then the lower fact could be covered by one definitions, instead of two as before. Furthermore, the number of nodes has been reduced, specifically the glue removed by *fragment*. *Fragment* can thus be seen as a way of reorganizing knowledge deductively such that future abductions can be made more efficiently. This seems to a different sort of learning from explanation-based methods, which typically are generalizations of successful solutions [DeJong and Mooney, 1986].

Figure 16.10 shows, in concept reduction form, an instantiation of the parts in the example in Figure 16.9. The seemingly unconnected facts can be glued together by the three murder schema definitions. DRIVE is covered by D1; PLACE and CAR are covered by D1, D2, or D3; and MURDER, VIOLENT, and 1ST-DEGREE by D2 *and* D3. All three definitions are thus needed to cover both facts. The five graphs join (there are no restrictions to subtypes to do) to produce Figure 16.11, which is the hypothesis that matches the form of Figure 16.9. *Fragment* removes the node PERSON (connected to PLACE), when used with the original facts, leaving the fragments shown in Figure 16.12. Here we used the original facts for *fragment*, to show that it is not the true inverse of specialize, although any facts that *project* into the hypothesis graph could have been used.

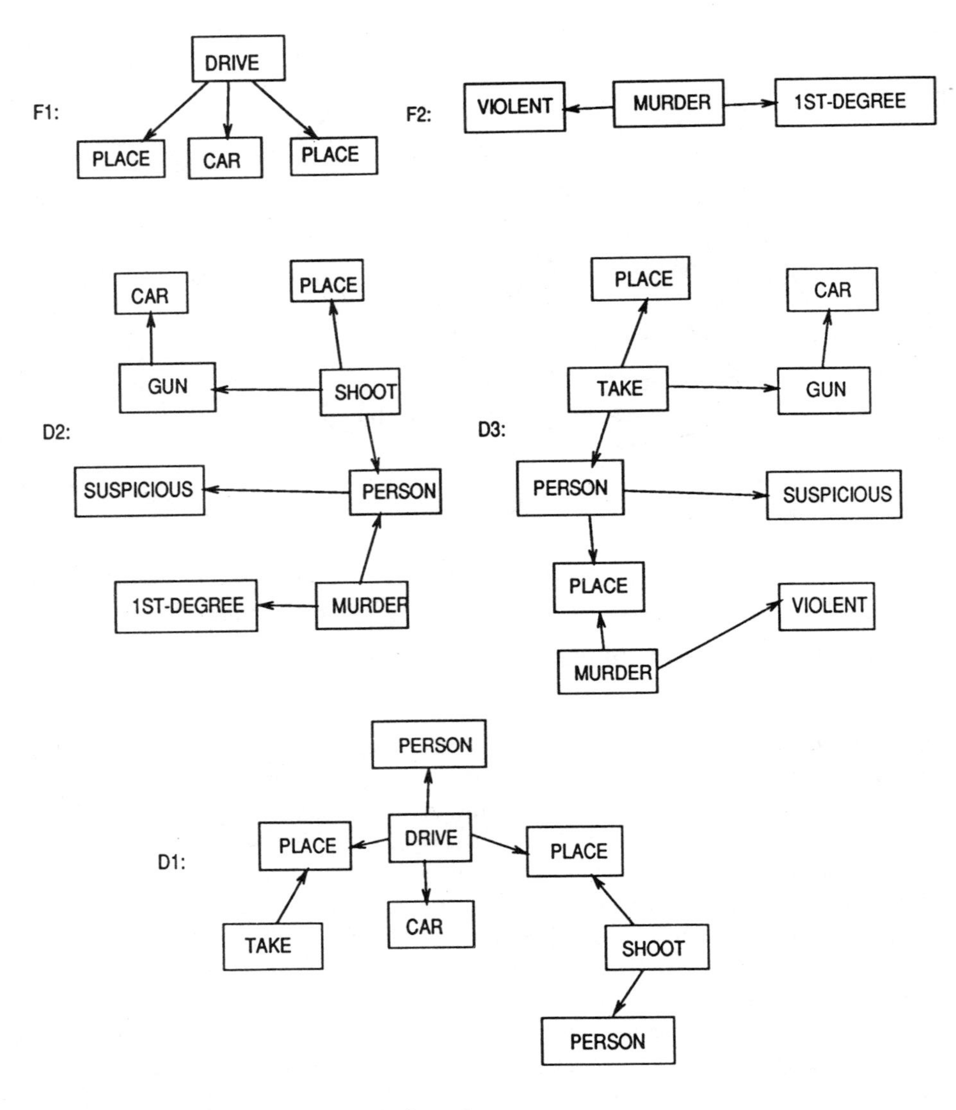

Figure 16.10: The "violent murder" graphs

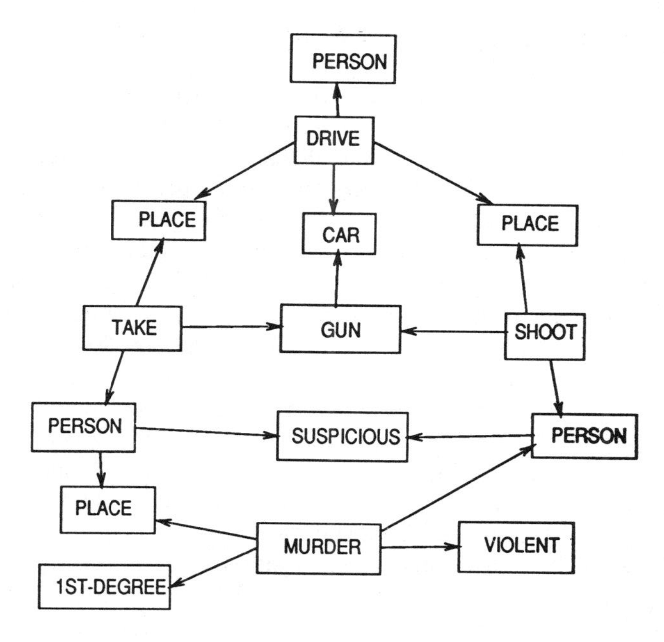

Figure 16.11: The "violent murder" hypothesis

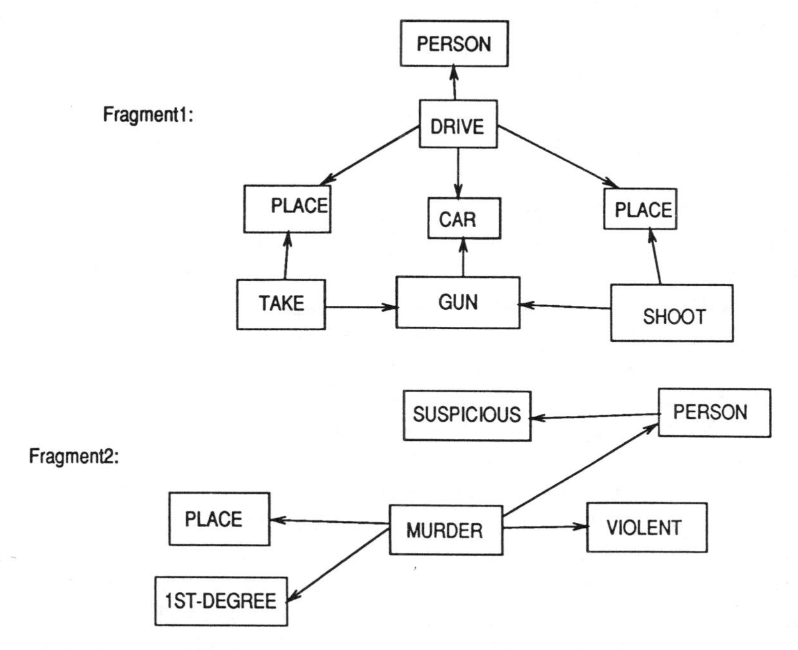

Figure 16.12: The "violent murder" fragments

16.4 THE PROBLEM-SOLVING CYCLE

The operators *specialize* and *fragment* can be seen as allowing search in a space of hypotheses. Since *specialize* is based on *join* and *fragment* on *project*, it is possible to consider the space as a generalization lattice, as in Figure 16.13. The relationships between the graphs in the lattice are specialize and generalize. A graph is more specialized than another if it restricts a node to a subtype, or adds a node. A graph is more generalized if it replaces a node with a supertype, or removes nodes. Even though the graph that is just a single node with label top can never be produced, it anchors the lattice at the top end. Similarly there is one single-node graph at the bottom of lattice, which is the (impossible) maximal join of all known graphs. If there exists at least one graph in the lattice that is a "correct" hypothesis, then the problem solver must drive the system into that area of the lattice. The subject of control is too lengthy for this paper, but abstractly the two operators act in a refinement cycle, together with a decision operator *evaluate* that stops the cycle when a satisfactory hypothesis is generated. Figure 16.14 shows a data-flow diagram where control is embodied in an operator *choose* that filters the three databases of facts, definitions, and hypotheses for *specialize* and *fragment*. The data type *graph* flows along all the arcs in the diagram.

Specialize produces alternative hypotheses for evaluation. When allowed, *fragment* breaks these unsatisfactory hypotheses apart, preserving factual connections, and allowing a new line of reasoning to emerge. The fragmented hypotheses become new input "facts" for specialize. They contain a fact as a subgraph, but also contain pieces of definitional, and therefore intensional, information. Another way to view this is to call them *assumptions*, grounded in fact, but deduced by *fragment* from a hypothesis. There are degenerate cases where *fragment* merely inverts the effect of *specialize*. In this case the system will loop. However, if the stored definitional knowledge is rich enough, this will not happen. *Cover*, being associational in nature, will explore the interconnections in the knowledge base in a classical semantic network fashion. A useful conjecture is that *specialize* and *fragment*, in tandem, can generate any canonical graph, and to discover the conditions under which this might be true, but this has yet to be proved. (We have proved it for specialize and another, simpler operator *generalize* [Fields et al., 1988b]), but not for *fragment*).

The cycle can also be seen as a weak problem-solving method, akin to the general techniques in SOAR [Laird et al., 1987]. Strength comes from good evaluation of hypotheses, particularly their rejection. We are also investigating the possibilities of controlling the search with some dynamic or even stochastic method, as in the genetic algorithm [Goldberg, 1988]. This is a view of problem solving that differs from the classical method based on a single line of reasoning, or even from the newer approach using multiple lines of reasoning such as found in the ATMS, wherein the system provides the problem solver with consistent alternative hypoth-

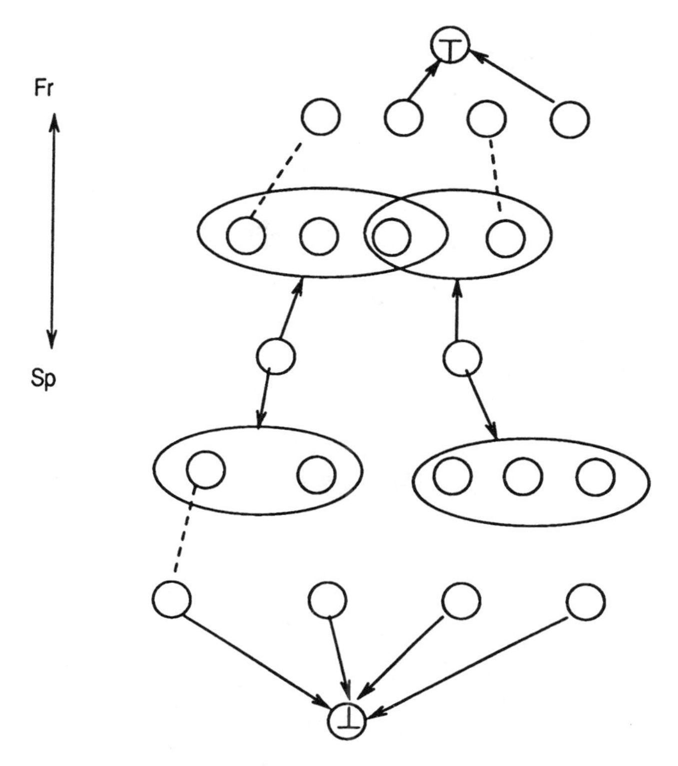

Figure 16.13: The *specialize/fragment* lattice

eses but makes no attempt to evaluate their worth. Now we might view problem solving as refinement of a population of hypotheses where the evaluation has two components. One is a static measure of worth; the other is a dynamic measure of the population as a whole. These measures can be heuristically combined and fed back to the problem solver in order to guide the choice of an operator and on what it should operate. See [Fields et al., 1988a] for more detail.

16.5 CONCLUSION

We have presented two operators, *specialize* and *fragment* that when taken together mimic the abduction/deduction cycle of scientific method. The addition of an evaluation operator allows the cycle to be used a weak method for problem solving. Parsimony in the suboperators *cover* and *uncover* ensure that potential solutions are as small as possible, and where a hypothesis is shown by evaluation to be inadequate, are modified as little as possible. Factual information is trusted

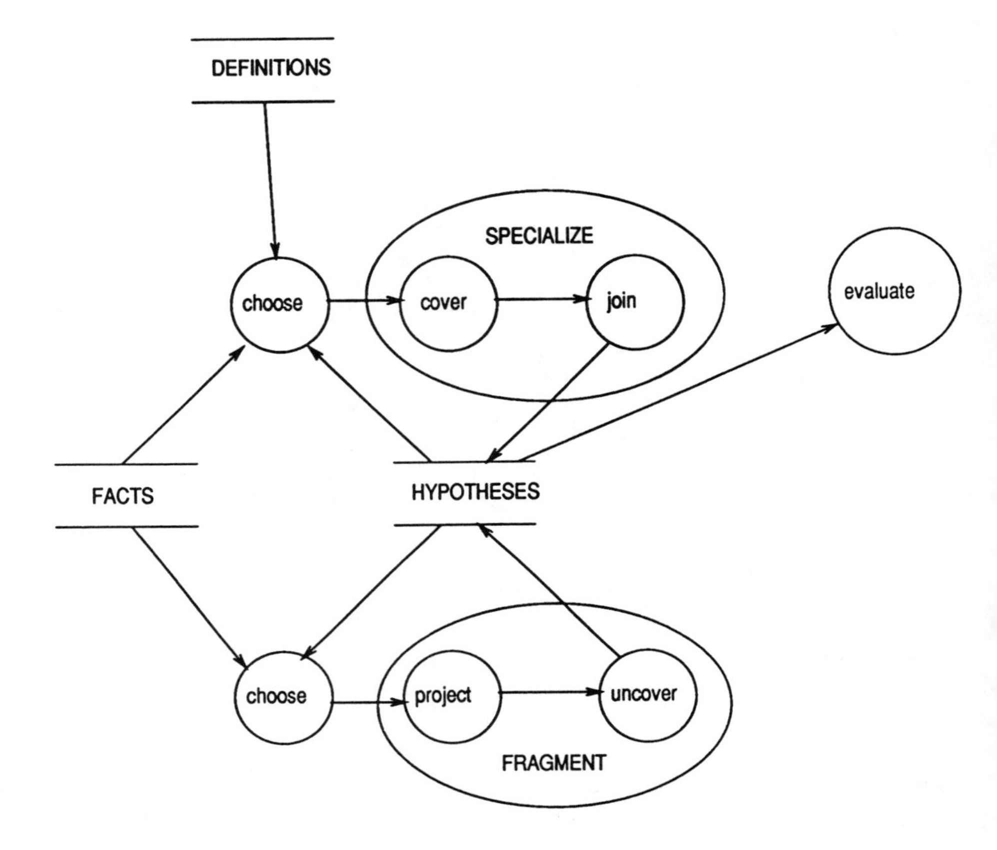

Figure 16.14: A data-flow diagram showing the relation of *specialize* and *fragment*

over stored knowledge, allowing the breaking of associations in definitional knowledge to effectively form new, better definitions. The operator specialize has been shown to perform abduction, or hypothesis generation, and fragment to perform a limited form of deduction; i.e., that necessary for hypothesis refinement.

References

Chapman, D. 1987. Planning for conjunctive goals. Artificial Intelligence 32:333–337.

DeJong, G., and R. Mooney. 1986. Explanation-based learning: An alternative view. *Machine Learning* 1:145–176.

Fields, C.A., Coombs, M.J., Dietrich, E.S., and Hartley, R.T. 1988b. Incorporating dynamic control into the Model Generative Reasoning system. *Proceedings of ECAI-88*, pp. 439–441.

Fields, C.A., Coombs, M.J., and Hartley, R.T. 1988. *The MGR Architecture is Turing Equivalent.* KSG working paper, Computing Research Laboratory, Las Cruces, NM.

Goldberg, D. 1988. *Genetic Algorithms in Search, Optimization, and Machine Learning.* Addison-Wesley, Reading, MA.

Hartley, R.T. and Coombs, M.J. 1988. Conceptual programming: Foundations of problem solving. In *Conceptual Graphs for Knowledge Systems*, Sowa, J., Foo, N., and Rao, P. (ed.s). Addison-Wesley, Reading, MA (in press).

Hartley, R.T. (1991, forthcoming). A uniform representation for time and space and their mutual constraints. *Computers and Mathematical Applications.*

Laird, J. E., Newell, A., and Rosenbloom, P.S. 1987. SOAR: An architecture for general intelligence. *Artificial Intelligence* 33:1–64.

Levesque, H. 1989. A knowledge-level account of abduction. *Proceedings of the Eleventh International Joint Conference on Artificial Intelligence*, Detroit, MI. pp. 1061–1073.

Nau, D. and Reggia, J. 1986. Relationships between deductive and abductive inference in knowledge-based diagnostic problem solving. In *Expert Data-base Systems: Proceedings of the First International Workshop*, Kerschberg, L. (ed.). Benjamin/Cummings, Redwood City, CA.

Peirce, C.S. 1957. *Essays in the Philosophy of Science.* Bobbs-Merrill, New York.

Pfeiffer, H.D. and Hartley, R.T. 1989. Semantic additions to conceptual programming. *Conceptual Graphs Workshop*, IJCAI-89.

Poole, D. 1989. Explanation and prediction: an architecture for default and abductive reasoning. *Computational Intelligence* 5:97–110.

Reiter, R. and de Kleer, J. 1987. Foundations of assumption-based truth maintenance systems: Preliminary report. *Proceedings of AAAI-87*, pp. 183–188. Morgan Kaufmann, San Mateo, CA.

Sowa, J.F. 1984. *Conceptual Structures.* Addison-Wesley, Reading, MA.

17

REPRESENTING AND REASONING ABOUT PHYSICAL SYSTEMS USING PRIME MODELS

Rattikorn Hewett and Barbara Hayes-Roth
(Stanford University)

Abstract

We propose an approach based on a network formalism for explicitly representing knowledge about physical systems at two levels of abstraction. Prime models explicitly represent the abstract structures and processes, both normal and abnormal, underlying classes of physical systems. Domain models explicitly represent the actual structures and processes that make up particular systems. Each domain model is viewed as an instance of a particular prime model. This approach has several advantages. It provides a basis for reasoning from first principles about individual domain models and yields building blocks for reasoning about more complex systems. It offers a compact representation of a potentially very large body of knowledge and makes the knowledge available for use in various reasoning tasks. In real-world applications we often have to deal with uncertain and incomplete information or domains where probabilistic reasoning is more appropriate. Thus, we explore a belief network, a well-known network used for representing and reasoning based on probabilistic thories. We discuss the trade-off between the proposed approach and the belief network and show how we can use prime models to represent and reason about physical systems under uncertainty.

17.1 INTRODUCTION

One aspect of the foundations of network representation involves analyzing the structures of knowledge representation schemes to determine how and what various network formalisms contribute to representational power, reasoning techniques and ease of use. In applying network formalisms, we deal with problems such as what type of representation is the most expressive and appropriate for our application and what kind of scheme allows us to use such a representation most effectively. This chapter is directed toward readers who would like to develop application systems that reason about physical systems using a conceptual semantic network as its knowledge representation. By physical systems we mean systems that can be either natural or man-made.

We propose a representation scheme based on a network formalism [Findler, 1979; Sowa, 1984] for explicitly representing knowledge about physical systems at two levels of abstraction. Prime models explicitly represent the abstract structures and processes, both normal and abnormal, underlying classes of physical systems. Domain models explicitly represent the actual structures and processes that make up particular systems. Each domain model is viewed as an instance of a particular prime model. For example, both the human respiratory system and urinary excretion system can be viewed as instances of a prime flow model, as can an ordinary water-delivery system. During reasoning about a domain model, any properties of the prime model may be instantiated. For example, an abstract causal relation, such as "blockage of a flow structure causes increased resistance in the structure, which causes decreased flow of the flow substance in the structure," may be instantiated for the respiratory system as, "blockage of the throat causes increased resistance in the throat, which causes decreased flow of air in the throat."

The proposed approach has several desirable properties. First, by representing multiple domain models as instances of a particular prime model, it provides a compact representation of a potentially very large body of knowledge. Second, by including within a prime model abstract representations of both the normal and abnormal mechanism, it provides a basis for reasoning from first principles [Davis, 1983, 1984; de Kleer, 1984; Genesereth, 1984; Hamscher, 1988; Kuipers, 1987] about individual domain models. Third, by representing both prime and domain models declaratively, it makes the knowledge available for use in various reasoning tasks. Finally, by modularizing knowledge of different prime and domain systems, it provides a capability for reasoning about more complex systems in a building block-like fashion, which is a desirable feature for incremental design and development.

In many real-world domains, many reasoning tasks require the ability to reason with uncertain information. A belief network [Pearl, 1986, 1988a, 1988b] is a well-known graphical probabilistic representation whose primary goal is to reason efficiently under uncertainty. Belief networks illustrate the role of networks as a representation scheme capable of producing efficient probabilistic inference. We compare the proposed approach to a belief network and discuss how the underlying principles of the two approaches affect their expressive power and reasoning power. Finally, we show how we can use the proposed approach to represent and reason about physical systems under uncertainty.

17.2 A REPRESENTATION SCHEME

This section describes our representation scheme, its general reasoning technique and illustrates the scheme with an example of a diagnostic reasoning task. Our representation is a semantic network [Findler, 1979; Sowa, 1984] whose objects represent concepts (in **bold**) and links represent relations among them (in *italic*). The two levels of abstraction we use to explicitly represent physical systems are prime models and domain models.

17.2.1 Domain Models

A physical system comprises a set of structures organized to support a set of related processes. Domain models explicitly represent the actual structures and processes that make up particular systems. Let D be a domain model. D is defined as a triple (S, P, R) where S is a set of system structures, P is a set of system processes and R represents relations among elements in S and P. D is modeled as a graph where a node can be any element of S or P and a link is an element of R. Note that a node alone can be a subgraph but not a subsystem of a domain model of a particular system. Figure 17.1 illustrates a part of a domain model for the human respiratory system, which can be mapped to the actual physical system. Here S and P are sets of nodes representing respiratory structures and respiratory processes respectively, and R is a set of links representing relations among these nodes. The model represents respiratory structures (e.g., **mouth**, **trachea**), respiratory processes (e.g., **inhale**, **exhale**) and their relationships including type and part-whole relations (e.g., *includes*), process relations (e.g., *occurs-in*), temporal relations (e.g., *precedes*) and spatial relations (e.g., *continues*). The description of the human respiratory model of Figure 17.1. is shown in Figure 17.2.

17.2.2 Prime Models

Many systems have analogous structures, common functions, behaviors and faults, and so are classified in the same class. Prime models explicitly represent the abstraction of both the normal and abnormal states of structures and processes underlying classes of physical systems.

Let S*, P*, and R* be abstractions of structures, processes and relations of a class of systems $\mathcal{D}$, respectively and $\leq$ denote a partial ordering relation, subtype, of a type hierarchy. Then D* = (S*, P*, R*) is an abstraction of the normal structures and processes of a system class $\mathcal{D}$ if $\forall$ D$\in$ $\mathcal{D}\exists$ a subgraph D′ of D and a projection

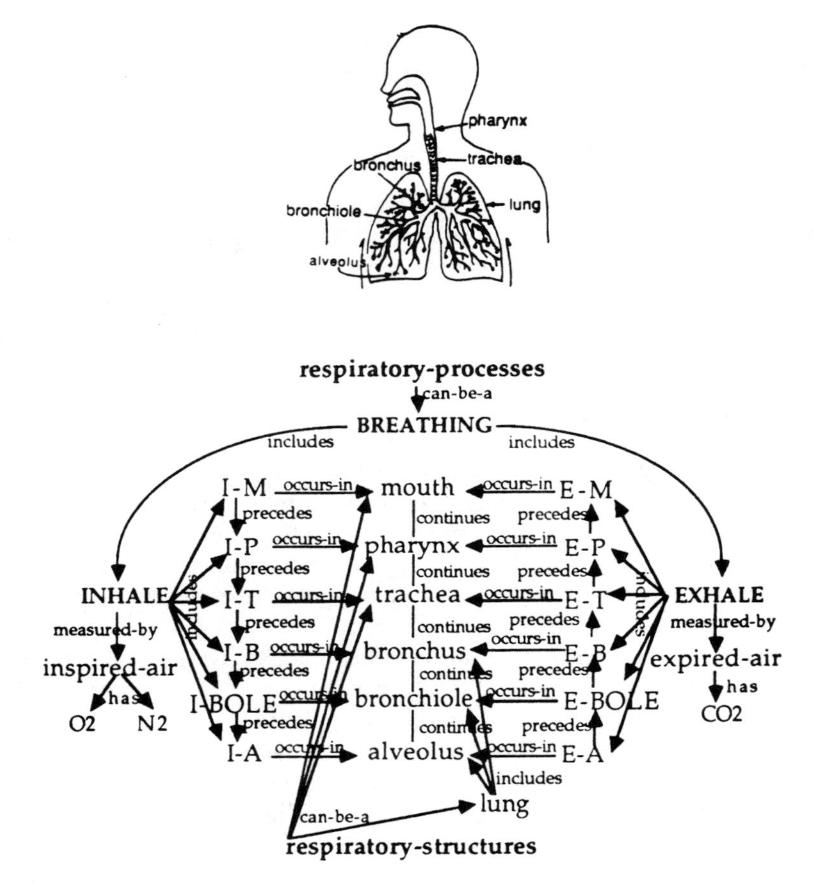

Figure 17.1: A domain model of human respiratory system

Respiratory processes can be a breathing process.
A breathing process includes inhale and exhale processes.
An inhale process is measured by inspired-air which has O_2 and N_2.
An inhale process includes

an inhale process occurring in the mouth, which precedes
an inhale process occurring in the pharynx, which precedes

•
•
•

The mouth abuts the pharynx which abuts the trachea, and so on.

Figure 17.2: Description of the human respiratory model

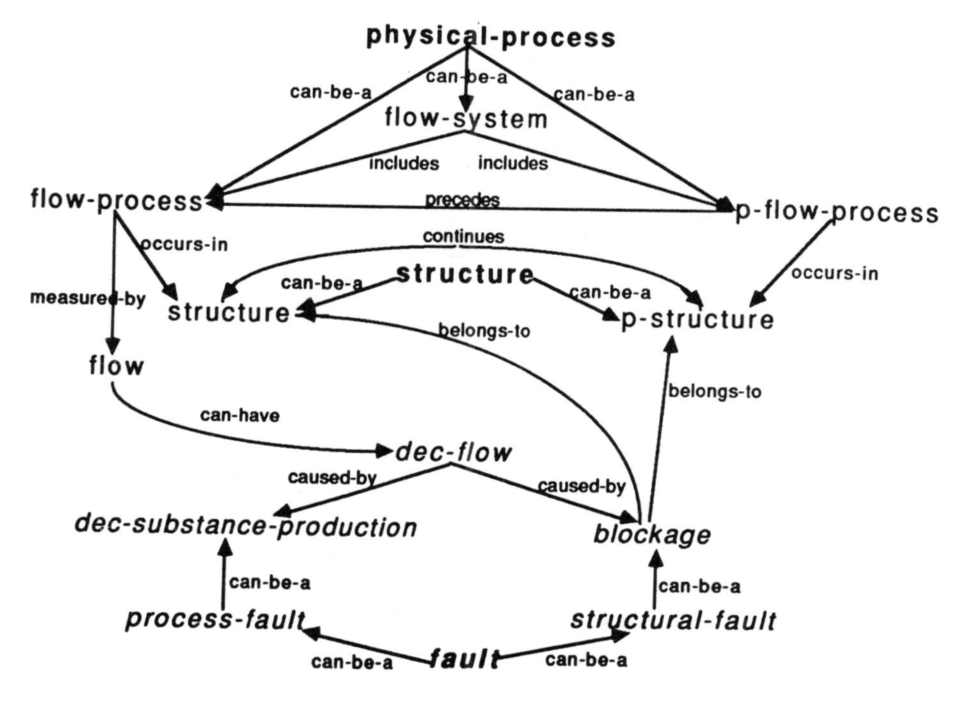

Figure 17.3: A prime flow model

π such that (1) $\pi D^* = D'$ and (2) $\forall$ concept c and relation r in D^*, πc and πr are a concept and a relation in D' respectively, where type(πc) $\leq$ type(c) and type(πr) $\leq$ type(r). A prime model $P_{\mathcal{D}}$ of a system class $\mathcal{D}$ is defined to be $D^* \cup$ abn(D^*), where abn(D^*) is a set of abstract faults and symptoms in this class.

For example, the human expiratory system involves a process in which a substance, CO_2-laden-air, is excreted by a structure, the lung, and then flows through a sequence of connected structures: the trachea, pharynx, and nose, out into the environment. Similarly, the human urine excretion system involves a process in which a substance, urine, is excreted by a structure, the kidney, and then flows through a sequence of connected structures: the ureter, bladder, and urethra, out into the environment. From these and other flow systems, we can abstract and represent a prime flow model, as shown in the top part of Figure 17.3, in which an abstract **flow-process** *occurs-in* an abstract **flow-structure**. The **flow-process** exhibits abstract process relations: *isa* type-of-process (e.g., **flow-process** *isa* **physical-process**), includes component-process (e.g., **flow-system** *includes* **flow-process**), precedes succeeding-process (e.g., **p-flow-process** *precedes* **flow-process**) and measured-by process-measurement (e.g., **flow-process** *measured-by* **flow**). The

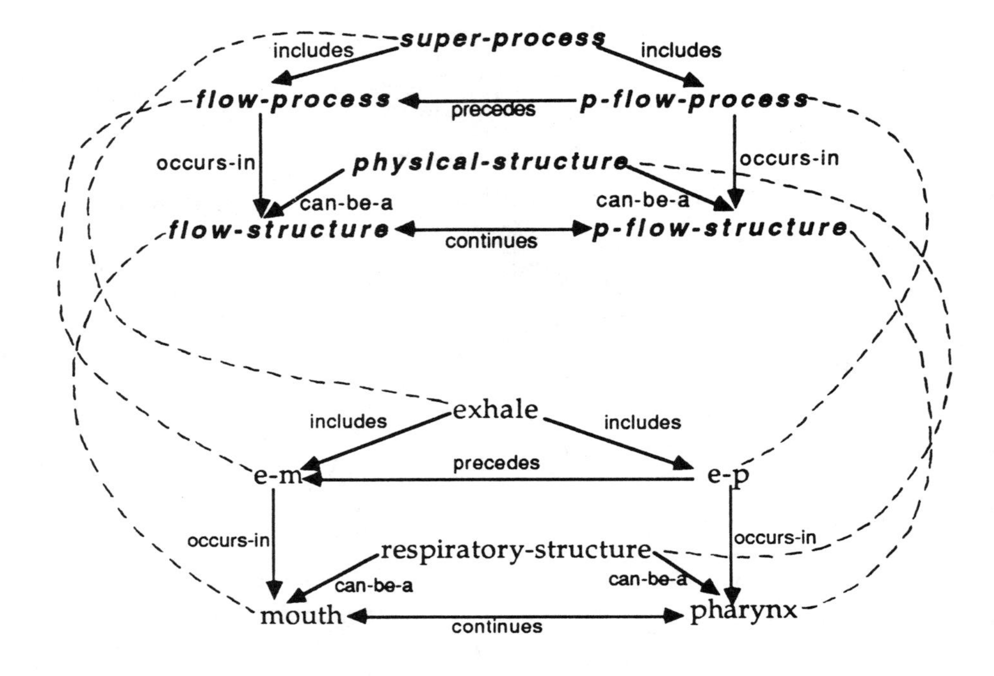

Figure 17.4: Respiration as an instance of the prime flow model

flow-structure exhibits generic structural relations: *isa* type-of-structure, *includes* component-structures, *continues* physically-connected-structures. Just as a particular flow system may be viewed as an instance of the prime flow model, each of its constituent structures and processes may be viewed as an instance of the corresponding element of the prime model. For example, the respiratory system, which is a flow system, includes the mouth, which is a flow structure. Figure 17.4 shows how a part of the human respiratory system is viewed as an instance of the prime flow model.

In addition to the abstraction of normal structure and behavior of the systems, prime models also abstract generic faults and the presenting symptoms of those faults. For example, for a prime flow model, given the generic symptom, decreased flow of a flow process, two potential underlying faults are: (1) blockage of a structure in which the faulty flow process occurs; and (2) blockage of a structure in which a predecessor of the faulty flow process occurs. The bottom part of Figure 17.3 represents abstract faults and symptoms of flow systems. For each type of symptom, abstract faults exhibit abstract relations: *isa* type-of-faults, *caused-by* type-of-fault, *can-be-had-by* process-measurement.

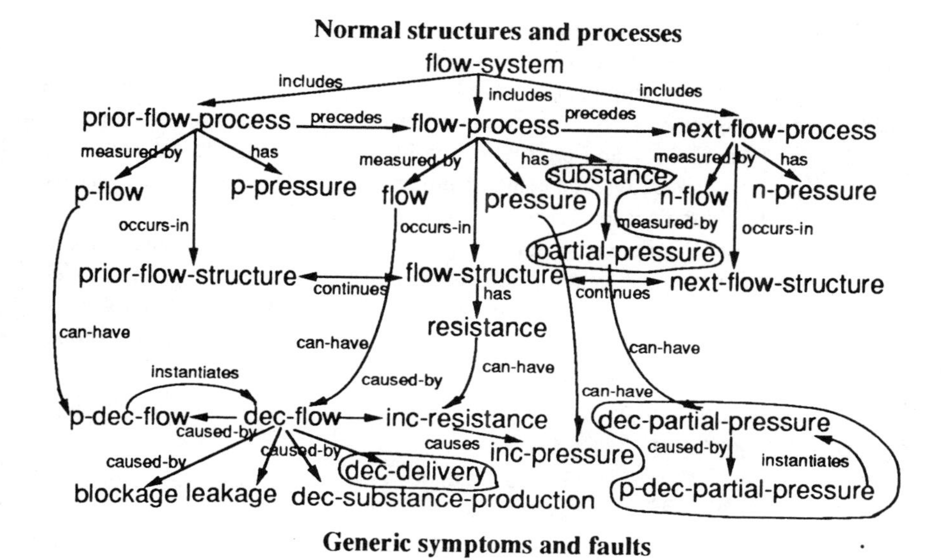

Figure 17.5: An evolution of a prime flow model

17.2.3 Construction and Evolution of Prime Models

The use of prime models presupposes substantial regularity within a class of systems. Although we have studied only a small number of domains so far, our experience suggests that these regularities exist. As we have extended the reasoning system with knowledge of new particular systems, or new scenarios involving those systems, we have needed to make only minor modifications to the original prime models. These modifications are primarily additions of more generic knowledge, which in most cases were valid and useful for the earlier systems considered as well.

To illustrate these findings, consider the evolution of our prime flow model. Beginning with the respiratory system, we developed a prime model of normal structure and function, and standard measurements, such as flow, pressure, and resistance. We also included generic structural faults that commonly occur in the respiratory systems, along with associated structural causes and effects. For example, "leakage of a flow structure decreases flow-substance in that structure." As discussed below, we used this model to diagnose and explain respiratory problems caused by several different types of structural faults occurring in any of the several different respiratory structures. At this stage the prime flow model has evolved from Figure 17.3 to Figure 17.5 (except circled areas).

We subsequently considered the circulatory system, extending our prime flow model to include generic process faults of the sorts that commonly occur in the circulatory system. For example, "decreased partial pressure of the flow-substance of the succeeding flow process." We used the extended prime model to diagnose and explain both respiratory and circulatory problems caused by the defined types of structural and process faults occurring in either system. These modifications are partially illustrated in the circled areas of Figure 17.5.

In general, considering a new domain system leads us to define generic faults that commonly occur in that system. At each point in the evolution of the model, we were able to use all of the faults previously defined so far to diagnose and explain instances of those faults as they occurred in any of the defined domain models.

17.3 USE OF MODELS

17.3.1 Reasoning Mechanisms

In general, reasoning about a particular domain may entail instantiation of relevant properties of the corresponding prime model. Given the network representation, this reasoning can exploit standard graph operations:

- *Graph Matching* finds a graph that matches or partially matches a given subgraph, in particular, a subgraph of a domain model that partially matches a graph of a prime model. Graph matching is similar to the operator graph projection mentioned in [Sowa, 1984]. It is being implemented with a generate and test technique [Rau, 1988].
- *Graph Instantiating,* which makes an instance of a given graph. In particular, those that are deduced during the reasoning.
- *Pattern Matching,* which compares two given graphs. The logical mechanism of this function is similar to that of the exact graph matching. Instead of generating and testing the tested graph if it completely matches the targeted graph, the tested graph is given. The function returns true if they match completely and false otherwise. This is useful in checking for terminal conditions during reasoning.
- *Causal Search,* which finds an object that follows a causal link from a given object in a prime model.
- *Context Search,* which finds an object in a domain model that has context corresponding to an abstract object in a corresponding prime model.

For example, Figure 17.6 illustrates the causal chains constructed during the diagnosis of the respiratory problem, decreased-CO_2-at-mouth. These causal chains are obtained by performing the following sequence of reasoning operations:

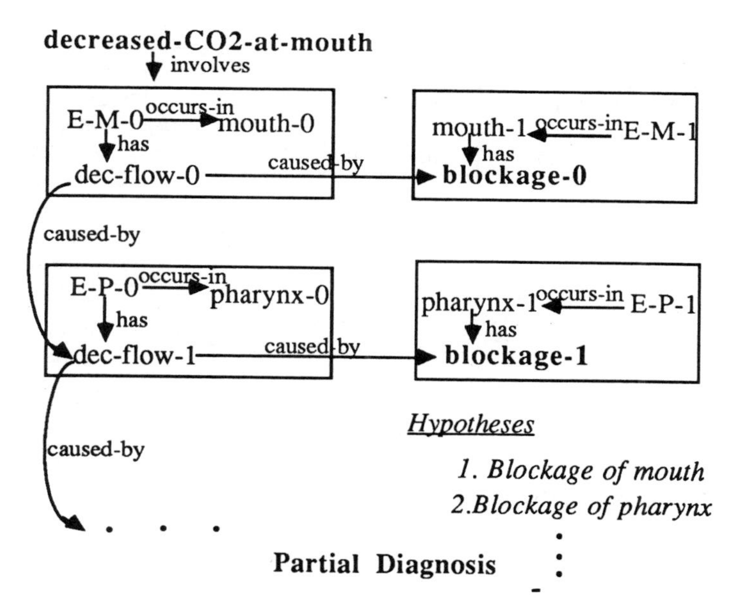

Figure 17.6: Identifying hypothetical faults

- Incorporate a representation of **decreased-CO_2**-at-mouth into the working model (by graph instantiation).
- Classify **decreased-CO_2**-at-mouth as an instance of **dec-flow** in the prime flow model (by graph matching).
- Identify a generic type of fault (e.g., **blockage** of the **flow-structure**) that can cause **dec-flow** (by causal search in the prime flow model).
- Identify a corresponding fault (e.g., blockage of the mouth) in the appropriate models (by context search).
- Instantiate the causal chain for the corresponding fault (e.g., **blockage of the mouth** causes **dec-flow** of CO_2 in the mouth) (by graph instantiation).

The reasoning process can continue until all hypotheses are generated. However, it is usually undesirable and infeasible to enumerate all possible chains of causes underlying an observed symptom. Therefore, the system must make judgements about which types of faults are more likely in the current context and use those judgements to make strategic decisions about which types of faults to hypothesize. For example, certain respiratory diseases might predispose a patient to structural faults, but not process faults. In this way, the system can narrow the search when contextual information strongly suggests a particular type of fault or broaden the search when such information is not available. Although we have shown a

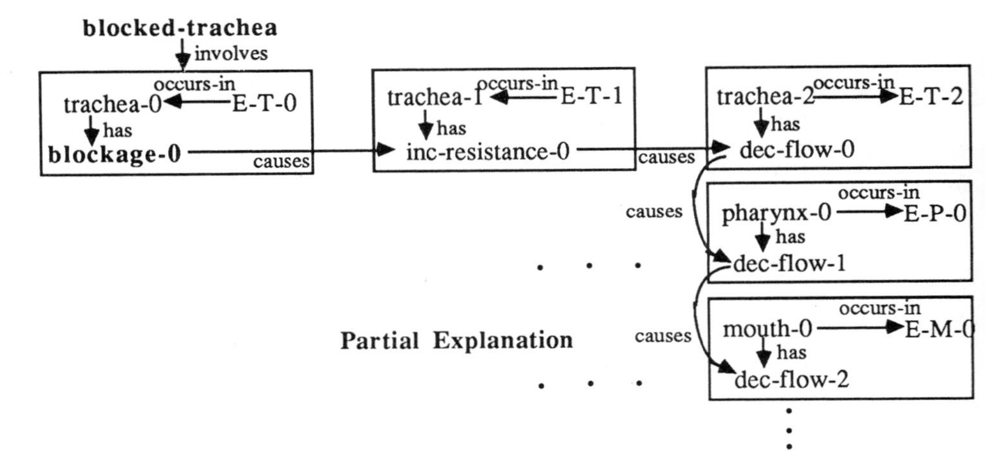

Figure 17.7: Explaining hypothesized fault

simple example here, these same basic reasoning operations can be used to identify more remote faults with longer and more complex causal chains to the presenting symptoms (see Section 17.3.3). Moreover, by reasoning in this fashion the diagnostic system can instantiate all known generic faults, some of them in several different domain contexts to produce a potentially very large differential diagnosis.

17.3.2 Flexible Use for Multiple Tasks and Multiple Domains

One advantage of this representation scheme is its flexible use of knowledge in the models. By representing both prime and domain models declaratively, the knowledge is available for use in multiple reasoning tasks. For example, the same prime and domain models can be used both to identify potential faults and explain the causal mechanisms underlying hypothesized faults. As illustrated in Figure 17.6, the prime flow model and the respiratory system model are used to generate hypotheses for a symptom **decreased-CO_2**-at-mouth. Figure 17.7 illustrates how the reasoning system uses the same prime and domain models to explain how a **blocked-trachea** can cause **decreased-CO_2**-at-mouth.

Another flexibility of our scheme is that each prime model can be applied in multiple domains. For example, the prime flow model is used to reason about several different biological system (e.g., respiration, circulation) and mechanical system (the ventilator). In collaboration with others, we are using our flow and diffusion prime models to reason about irrigation systems and semiconductor fabrication processes [Murdock and Hayes-Roth, 1990].

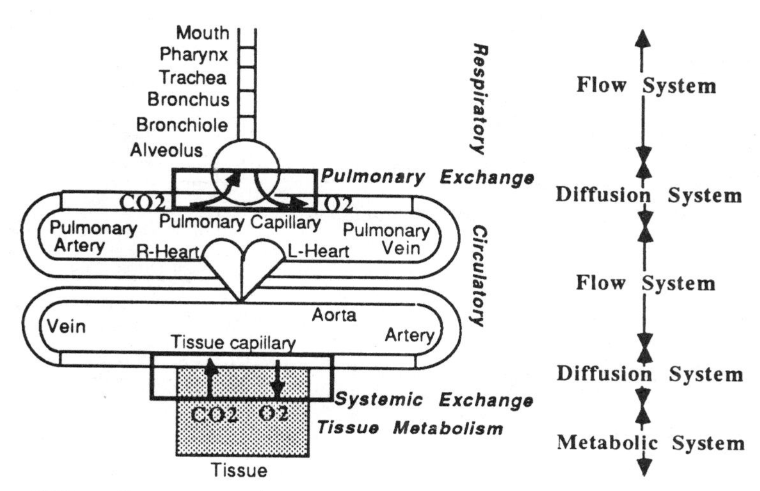

Figure 17.8: Gas transportation system

17.3.3 Building Blocks

Our scheme provides building blocks for reasoning about more complex systems, by modularizing knowledge of different prime and domain systems. For example, consider reasoning about the larger and more complex "gas transport system" for a patient using a mechanical ventilator. As shown in Figure 17.8, a conceptual view of gas (mainly O_2 and CO_2) transportation is a combination of six domain models: the mechanical ventilator (not shown), respiratory, pulmonary exchange, circulatory, tissue exchange, and tissue metabolic systems. The first two and the fourth are instances of a prime flow model, the last is of a prime metabolism model and the rest are of a prime diffusion model (indicated by the rightmost column of Figure 17.8). By integrating its knowledge of several domains and the corresponding prime models, these same mechanisms can be used to explain that a high respiration rate set at the ventilator and low temperature in the tissue metabolism system cause low arterial CO_2 in the circulatory system. The causal explanation is generated by stepping through relevant processes and structures of the domain models and instantiating causal effects from generic knowledge of the corresponding prime models in the corresponding domain context. Figure 17.9 shows partial reasoning steps to generate a causal explanation for low arterial CO_2.

17.4 ON REPRESENTING UNCERTAINTY

There are a number of reasoning systems that require an ability to deal with uncertain information. These systems usually deal with domains where there is not

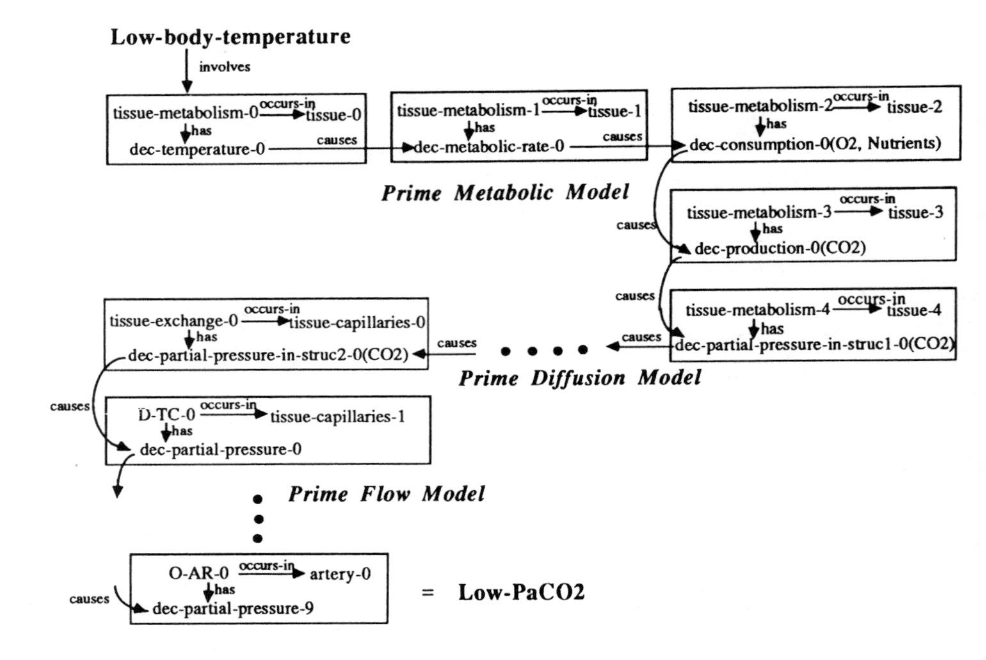

Figure 17.9: A partial explanation for low arterial CO_2

enough fundamental knowledge about systems behavior available and the degree of complexity is too high to obtain deterministic analysis, in which case probabilistic reasoning is more appropriate. This section attempts to develop a way to use our scheme for probabilistic reasoning by first considering an example of an existing probabilistic representation scheme. In particular, we consider another network representation called a *belief network*. We discuss how belief network representation differs from our scheme in terms of the results produced and their representational powers. Finally, we propose a way to handle uncertain information using our scheme.

17.4.1 Belief Networks

One formal approach to reasoning and representing uncertainty is a probabilistic representation called belief networks, also known as *Bayesian networks*, *causal networks*, or *influence networks* [Pearl, 1988a]. A belief network is an acyclic directed graph in which the nodes represent domain variables and the arcs represent direct dependencies between the linked variables. The strengths of dependencies among variables are quantified by conditional probabilities of the related variables. For example, Figure 17.10 illustrates a belief network that reflects

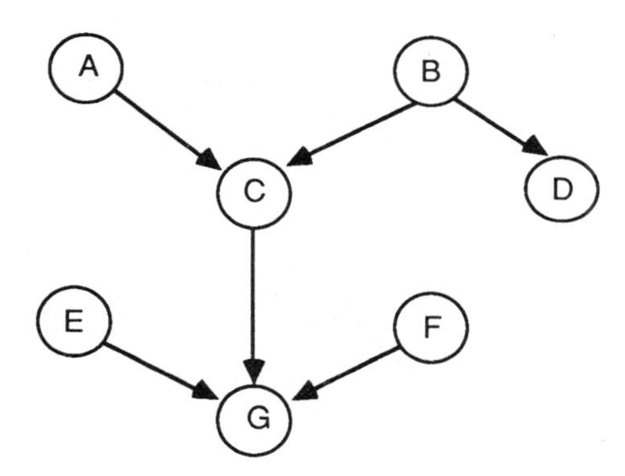

A: Blocked Lung
B: Leaking Lung
C: Decreased Expired CO2 in the Lung
D: Increased Peak Pressure
E: Blocked Throat
F: Leaking Throat
G: Decreased Expired CO2 in theThroat

Given
Prior Probabilities:
P(A), P(B), P(E) and P(F)
Conditional Probabilities:
P(C|A, B), P(C|A, ~B), P(C|~A, B), P(~A, ~B)
P(D|B), P(D|~B)
P(G|E, C, F), . . ., P(G|~E, ~C, ~F)

Figure 17.10: A belief network

causal knowledge of a human respiratory system. A decrease of the expired CO_2 in the lung (C) depends on whether the lung is blocked (A) and/or leaking (B). However, the blockage and leakage of the lung are independent. Similarly, a decrease of the expired CO_2 in the throat (G) is conditionally dependent on the blockage of the throat (E), a leak of the throat (F) and a decrease of expired CO_2 in the lung (C); and the leak in the lung can cause an increased peak pressure (D). The strengths of these dependencies are given by related conditional probabilities. For example, the link from B to D is quantified by P(D|B) (how likely is it that the peak pressure will increase, given that the lung leaks), and P(D|~B) (how likely is it that the peak pressure will increase, if there is no leakage in the lung). A completely specified belief network provides a basis to answer all probabilistic queries. For example, the joint distribution corresponding to the network of Figure 17.10 is given by:

$$P(A=a, B=b, C=c, D=d, E=e, F=f, G=g) = P(a)\,P(b)\,P(c|a, b)\,P(d|b)\,P(e)\,P(f)\,P(g|e, c, f)$$

where a, b,...., g are true or false values.

Probabilistic inference consists of belief propagation by a message-passing process through the network when new data are received. (See details in [Pearl, 1986, 1988a, 1988b]). As an example, Figure 17.11 illustrates five successive steps of belief propagation through the belief network shown in Figure 17.10. There are two types of messages: The black token represents the strength of causal support for the variable's descendants, and the white token represents the strength of evidential support for the variable's ancestors. In step (1), the network is in equilibrium and the state of belief depends on all prior probabilities as given in Figure 17.10. The new arrival data activates the two corresponding nodes, and white tokens are placed on their links, pointed toward their parents (step (2)). The parent nodes update the degree of belief and pass appropriate messages (tokens) to their

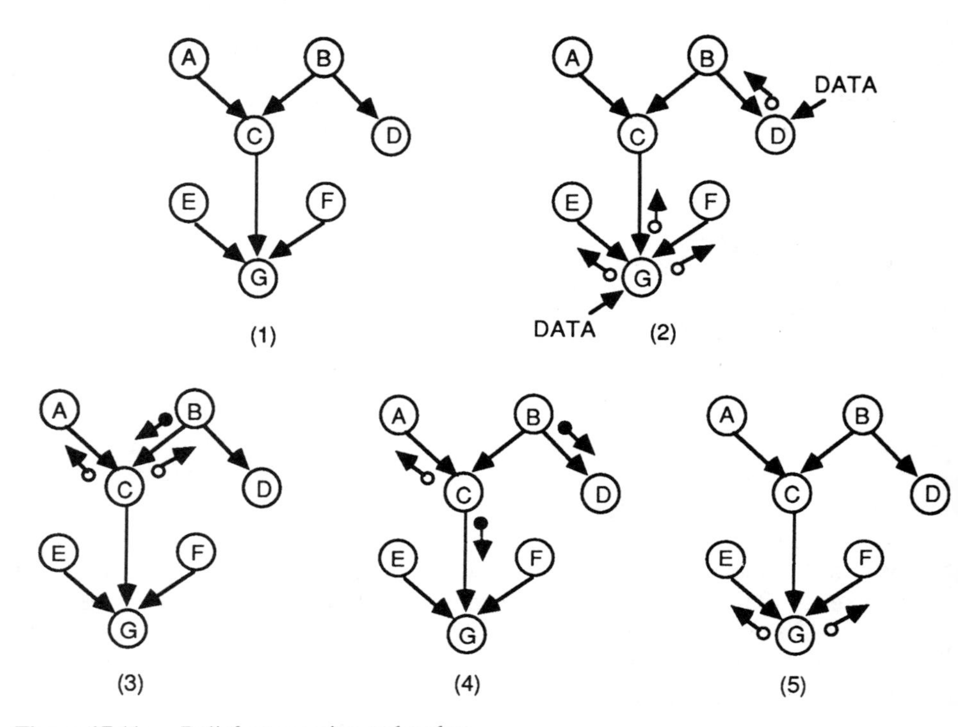

Figure 17.11: Belief propagation and update

neighbors i.e., white tokens to their parents and black for their children. The links through which the absorbed tokens have entered do not receive new tokens. C receives a white token, which triggers two white tokens to its parents; whereas B receives a white token, which triggers a black token delivered to C (step (3)). The process continues until all tokens are taken into consideration and thus the network reaches a new equilibrium with an updated belief from the new data.

There has been a lot of research on belief networks such as how to deal with networks with loops and some control issues. However, it is beyond the scope of this chapter to discuss them all. Interested readers should find more details of this subject in [Pearl, 1986, 1988a, 1988b].

17.4.2 Belief Networks versus Prime and Domain Models

Although both a belief network technique and the proposed scheme using prime models are based on a network formalism, their methodologies result in different representational and reasoning powers, as described below.

17.4.2.1 Expressive Power

In terms of knowledge content, belief networks provide an explicit representation of uncertainty (conditional probabilities), whereas prime models as described in Section 17.2 do not. Although, strictly speaking, the network formalism of the prime model approach can represent uncertainty the same way as belief networks, we choose not to do so. Because uncertainty is usually domain and context dependent, we exclude it from prime models in order to maintain their modularity and generality.

In terms of a full machinery of representation languages, aside from uncertainty, all knowledge that can be represented in belief networks can be represented in prime models. Since belief networks have one type of link whereas prime models have many, the set of knowledge that can be represented in prime models is a superset of the set of knowledge that can be represented in belief networks. For example, taking the diagnostic reasoning shown in Section 17.2.3, belief networks cannot represent the elementary knowledge that a certain flow process occurs in a certain flow structure or that a given structure is a flow structure.

Finally, belief network representation and reasoning techniques provide answer-producing procedures, whereas prime models provide a basis for reasoning from first principles that produces explanations as well as answers. For example, during diagnostic reasoning, a belief network representing the fact that **blockage-of-throat** *causes* **decreased-flow-of-air-at-throat** cannot explain what these variables are or how their causal connection occurs. By contrast, prime models explicitly represent the knowledge that (1) a flow process called exhalation that occurs in the throat has decreased air flow and (2) decreased flow of any flow process could be caused by blockage of the structure in which it occurs.

17.4.2.2 Storage Space

By representing multiple domain models as instances of particular prime models, our approach provides a compact representation of a potentially very large body of knowledge. On the other hand, the belief network probabilistic representation is domain or context dependent requiring storage of largely redundant information for each individual domain or context. Suppose the size of the network is the number of objects and links in the network. Let a be the size of the network representing the normality of the prime model and b be the size of the network representing the abnormality, in particular the dependency model, in the prime model, k be the number of domain models used during the reasoning and n be the maximum size of the domain models. Assuming that the representations are in the same granularity, for a given class of systems, the maximum storage cost for the prime models (CP) is equal to the storage cost for all domain models and the prime model i.e., $kn + a + b$. The maximum storage cost for the belief network representation (CB) is equal to the maximum storage cost for every system normal and abnormal behavior i.e., kn + kb. In fact when the number of domain models, k, is large enough, CP can reduce CB by 100 (kb – a – b)/(kn + kb) . In particular, k only has to be greater than 1 + a/b which is generally true in practice for systems with a very large body of knowledge.

17.4.2.3 Computational Time

With prime models, the computational time for reasoning is bounded by a graph matching operational time. (The computational times for other reasoning operations such as graph instantiating and causal search are either constant or linear in the size of the network.) For a simple complete graph matching (using a generate and test method [Rau, 1988]), the computational time bound is $O(g^{mn})$, where g is the number of graphs to be tested against, m is the size of the tested graph and n is the size of the given graph. On the average case, the computational time for this approach is much better because different link types allow the graph matching algorithm to discriminate unmatched graphs much faster. In a belief network without loops the computational time for propagation is linear in the size of the network [Pearl, 1986, 1988a]. However, computational time in the belief network is sensitive to the topological structure of the network. In fact, propagation through a network with loops is known to be NP-hard [Cooper, 1988]. Unfortunately, for a very large and complex body of knowledge, loops are likely to occur. Thus, for a less-complicated system, the belief network mechanism is more efficient, whereas for a more-complex system, prime models are more advantageous due to a reduction in the search space and the controls that can be used to guide the search in appropriate contexts. One technique for belief networks to cope with loops is by forming local groups of variables so that the resulting networks have no loops [Pearl, 1986]. This leads to the scheme for representing uncertainty using prime models, proposed in the following section.

17.4.3 A more appropriate representation

As discussed above, belief networks and prime models are almost complements of one another. We will now describe a representation scheme that is capable of handling uncertainty but at the same time is more feasible for a very large body of knowledge. The proposed scheme is to carefully integrate belief networks into local groups of domain models in the prime models scheme at an appropriate level of abstraction and context. For example, as illustrated in Figure 17.12, a diagnostic system that reasons about the human respiratory system might contain belief networks representing conditional probabilities of the cause of decreased flow in different contexts. For example, in a trauma case leakage has a higher probability than blockage, whereas in a postoperative case blockage has a higher probability than

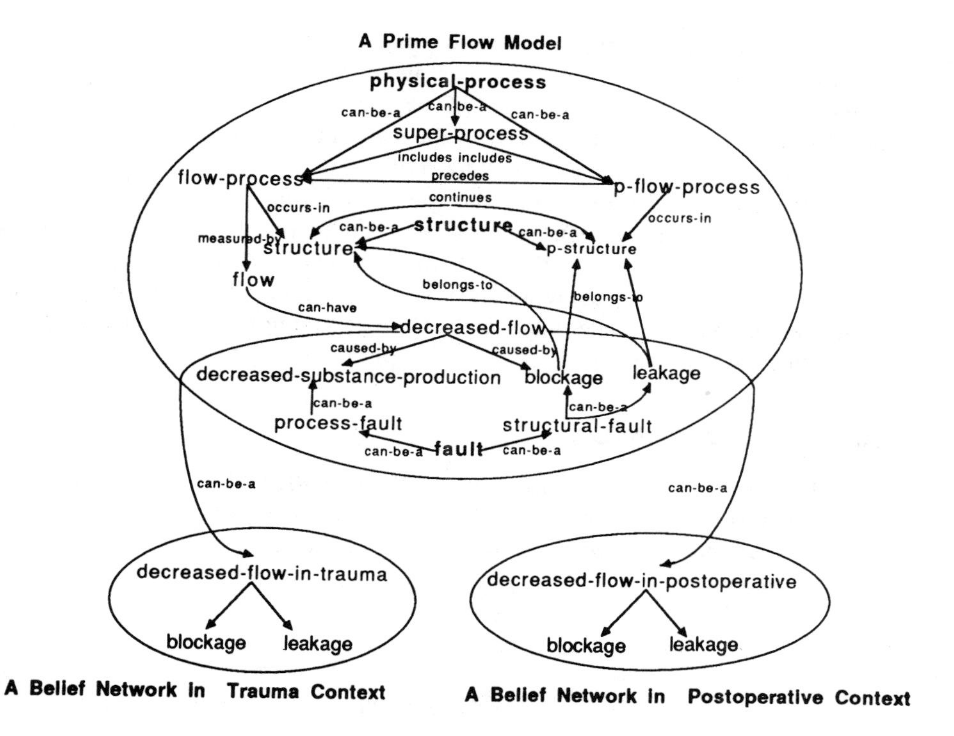

Figure 17.12: A proposed model for respiratory model with uncertain information

leakage. The system can make judgements about which probabilistic models to use based on its current context. By using prime models and integrated belief networks, the proposed scheme provides a compact representation that is capable of handling reasoning under uncertainty.

17.5 CONCLUSION

This chapter presents a representation scheme that explicitly represents knowledge about physical systems at two levels of abstraction: prime models and domain models. The proposed approach has several desirable properties. First, by representing multiple domain models as instances of a particular prime model, it provides a compact representation of a potentially very large body of knowledge. Second, by including within a prime model abstract representations of both normal and abnormal mechanism, it provides a basis for reasoning from first principles about individual domain models. Third, by representing both prime and domain models declaratively, it makes the knowledge available for use in various reasoning tasks. Finally, by modularizing knowledge of different prime and domain systems, it provides building blocks for reasoning about more complex systems. The proposed scheme described in Section 17.2 has been implemented in ICE, a blackboard-based diagnostic system as one of the reasoning components of the GUARDIAN system [Hayes-Roth et al., 1989] for monitoring intensive care patients.

We have started investigating the use of the proposed scheme to deal with uncertain information by comparing the proposed approach with a belief network. We conjecture that the integration of both approaches will yield a representation scheme that offers a compact representation and can explicitly represent and reason about physical systems under uncertainty. Our ongoing research explores aspects of integrating the two schemes.

ACKNOWLEDGMENTS

This research was supported by EPRI grant #RP2614-48. We thank John Sowa, Wlodek Zadrozny, and Roger Hartley for their comments on earlier versions of this paper and Ed Feigenbaum for sponsoring the work within the Knowledge Systems Laboratory.

References

Cooper, G. 1988. *Probabilistic Inference Using Belief Networks Is Np-hard*. Technical Report KSL-87-27, Stanford University, Stanford.

Davis, R. 1983. Reasoning from first principles in electronic trouble shooting. *International Journal of Man–Machine Studies*, 19:403–423.

———. 1984. Diagnostic reasoning based on structure and behavior. *Artificial Intelligence*, 24:347–410.

de Kleer, J. 1984. How circuits work. *Artificial Intelligence*, 24:205–280.

Findler, N.V. (ed.). 1979. *Associative Networks*. Academic Press, New York, NY.

Genesereth, M. 1984. The use of design description in automated diagnosis. *Artificial Intelligence*, 24:411–436.

Hamscher, W. 1988. *Model-based Troubleshooting of Digital Systems*. Ph.D. Thesis, A.I. Memo 1074, MIT Artificial Intelligence Laboratory.

Hayes-Roth, B., Washington, R., Hewett, R., Hewett, M. and Seiver, A. 1989. Intelligent monitoring and control. In *Proceedings of the Eleventh International Joint Conference on Artificial Intelligence*. IJCAI proceedings are available from Morgan Kaufmann Publishers, San Mateo, CA.

Kuipers, B. 1987. Qualitative simulation as causal explanation. *IEEE Transactions on Systems., Man, and Cybernettics*,17(3): 432–444.

Murdock, J. and Hayes-Roth, B. 1990. *Intelligent Monitoring and Control of Semiconductor Manufacturing*. Technical Report KSL-90-35, Stanford University, Stanford.

Pearl, J. 1986. Fusion, propagation and structuring in belief networks. *Artificial Intelligence*, 29:241–288.

———.1988a. *Probabilistic Reasoning in Intelligent Systems*. Morgan Kaufmann Publishers, San Mateo, CA.

———. 1988b. Evidential reasoning under uncertainty. In *Exploring Artificial Intelligence*, Shrobe, H. and AAAI (eds.). Morgan Kaufmann Publishers, San Mateo, CA.

Rau, L. 1988. Exploiting the semantics of conceptual graphs for efficient graph matching. *Proceedings of the Third Annual Workshop on Conceptual Graphs*, St. Paul, Minnesota.

Sowa, J. 1984. *Conceptual Structures: Information Processing in Mind and Machine*. Addison-Wesley, Reading, MA.

18

INTEGRATING LANGUAGE AND MEANING IN STRUCTURED INHERITANCE NETWORKS

Paul S. Jacobs
(GE Research and Development Center, Schenectady)

Abstract

Natural language systems must map between language and meaning. The mapping process is central to language analysis—producing an internal representation of an input text, and language generation—producing language to express an underlying knowledge representation. This language processing issue suggests using a representation that explicitly associates concepts with linguistic structures. Extending structured inheritance networks to include these associations helps in building efficient natural language processing systems that can perform both analysis and generation, and extend easily to new domains. The integration of language and meaning requires a representation that provides a general framework for mapping but adequately constrains the mapping process.

18.1 INTRODUCTION

Structured inheritance (SI) networks are semantic representations that specify a taxonomy of semantic categories along with their associated conceptual roles. These networks provide a sound basis for natural language processing, because both the semantic hierarchy and the semantic specification of the roles support semantic analysis and language generation. In language analysis, this structured knowledge aids in disambiguating word senses and roles. In generation, structured hierarchies can guide lexical choice and linguistic structure selection.

These semantic taxonomies, however, cover only part of the problem of knowledge representation for natural language processing. Language analysis requires mapping from words and surface structures into a conceptual representation, and language generation performs the inverse mapping. The vagueness and flexibility of language confound the problem of mapping between language and semantic structures. Treating this problem as part of knowledge base design suggests extending the framework of structured inheritance networks to cover linguistic structures and the complex relationships that associate them with meaning. Knowledge about linguistic expression, including the tangled connections between language and meaning, then becomes part of the taxonomy.

The knowledge representation task underlying natural language includes linguistic structures, word meanings, and constraints that combine linguistic and conceptual information. The knowledge representation must support, for example, representing words with similar meanings similarly, identifying paraphrases by shared representation, and distinguishing meaningful utterances or interpretations from anomalous ones. The following simple sentences illustrate these issues:

- (1a) Mary gave John a hug.
- (1b) Mary hugged John.
- (1c) John got a hug from Mary.
- (1d) ? John took a hug from Mary.

A language analyzer must determine, for example, that (1a), (1b),and (1c) have similar, if not identical, meanings: Not only is *hugging* the main event in these three sentences, but the roles of John and Mary in the event are the same. Sentence (1d), on the other hand, gets a question mark, indicating that is semantically "anomalous." At least, it is not the sort of sentence a language generator should produce.

What we know about linguistic expression from the above sentences is not contained at the level of the individual words. Substituting "kiss" for "hug," and "received" for "got," produces similar examples. Since it is difficult to represent constraints on this sort of expression in purely linguistic terms, it makes sense to use a uniform representation that can bring linguistic and conceptual knowledge together.

This uniformity of representation departs from the tradition, if not the theory, of most natural language programs. While several noteworthy efforts [Bobrow and Webber, 1980; Sondheimer et al., 1984; Hirst, 1987; Neal and Shapiro, 1987] have applied knowledge representation fundamentals to linguistic knowledge, all of these efforts handled mapping rules with a separate representation. James Allen's textbook [1987] presents a summary of this approach to semantic interpretation.

In practice, few natural language processing systems follow this model. Some use five or more different knowledge representations, including separate grammatical notations for analysis and generation, separate rule sets for mapping in each direction, and at least one conceptual representation. This eclectic design has some positive attributes: For example, it permits a group to compose a complete system by combining the best available modules, and it allows the evolution of each representation to suit a specific component of the system without impacting other modules. However, the separation of knowledge has some disastrous consequences: (1) it blocks transportability by posing five knowledge acquisition problems for each application, (2) it prevents integration where multiple knowledge sources combine in either analysis or generation, and (3) it increases program size and complexity.

The rest of this chapter will present a framework for extending semantic networks to associate linguistic and conceptual structures, addressing the problems of representing conceptual roles (Section 18.2), word senses (Section 18.3), and more complex lexical knowledge (Section 18.4). Section 18.5 will include some results of the application of this framework to large-scale natural language processing systems.

18.2 RELATING LINGUISTIC AND CONCEPTUAL ROLES

The problem of semantic interpretation, or producing a meaning representation of a linguistic input, comprises two main tasks: (1) determining concepts that correspond to words or other linguistic structures (sometimes described as *frame selection* or *word sense disambiguation*) and (2) determining how these concepts relate to one another (sometimes referred to as *case-slot disambiguation*). Language generation involves two corresponding functions: choosing a word that expresses a particular concept, and choosing a linguistic structure that expresses a conceptual relationship.

The first task above, representing word meaning, has an intuitive grounding, because we are conscious of ambiguity and nuances of meaning all the time. The second task, however, is less apparent. Here the problem, summarized well in [Allen, 1987], is to distinguish relations that are basically independent of the subtleties of linguistic structure but nevertheless underly the way language works. A "canonical," or classical, example of such a relationship appears in the following sentences:

- (2a) Mary gave John a book.
- (2b) Mary gave a book to John.

Among other things, a knowledge representation must capture the common meaning of these two sentences, as well as allow for easy inferences, such as that Mary had the book before and John has it after the *giving*. To accomplish this, most structured representations have a way of associating John with the *giving*, where John is explicitly identified as the *recipient* of the event in both (2a) and (2b).

The term *conceptual role* describes a relationship, like *recipient*, that groups linguistic expressions that have similar meanings, and allows for common inferences that are language independent. This corresponds loosely to many other terms, such as *slot*, *participant role*, *case role*, *thematic role*, and *theta-role*. Conceptual roles, like these other categories, include fixed relationships (such as *recipient*) that seem to go along with events, but also include many other less constrained relationships (such as *color* and *size*) Conceptual roles are more constrained, however, than slots, because they should not include arbitrary linguistic features or other relationships that do not capture linguistic generalizations or enable inferences.

The task of determining the conceptual roles of a linguistic input is rarely as simple as in (2a) and (2b), which seem to suggest that some simple mapping rules could collapse different linguistic structures into their common roles. Example (1a), for instance, shows how linguistic expressions often convey roles that are "deeper" than their literal interpretation. Having John as the *recipient* in (1a) would cause problems because, first, it wouldn't account for the similarity of meaning between (1a) and (1b), and second, because it might trigger false inferences, such as that Mary had the hug before the event, and John had it after.

Even sentences with a direct, literal interpretation can cause problems in deriving conceptual roles. For example, the following pair illustrates how the same surface relationship can express different conceptual roles:

- (3a) Mary loaded the wagon with hay.
- (3b) Mary loaded hay on (onto, in, into) the wagon.

In (3a) and (3b), either "wagon" or "hay" makes a reasonable direct object of the sentence, because both are reasonable conceptual *objects* (or *patients*). But each plays a more specific conceptual role as well. The wagon seems to combine or "fuse" the role of *object* with the wagon's role as a platform (hence "onto") and container (hence "into"). Similarly, the hay plays the role of the filler as well as *object*. Since (3a) and (3b) mean essentially the same thing, a good linguistic analyzer must determine these more specific roles.

The one-to-many relationship between linguistic roles and conceptual roles appears even in expressions like (1a). For example, the verb "kiss," like "load" can have two sorts of conceptual *objects* (the person being kissed and the body part being kissed), which can both also appear in the literal *recipient* role. Sentences (4) below illustrate these forms:

- (4a) Mary kissed John on the cheek.
- (4b) Mary kissed John's cheek.
- (4c) Mary gave John a kiss on the cheek.
- (4d) Mary gave John's cheek a kiss.

The examples presented so far show that different surface forms can often express the same conceptual roles, and the same surface forms can often express different conceptual roles. So the mapping between linguistic and conceptual relations is not one-to-one. Furthermore, while similar concepts often seem to be expressed similarly, the mapping relations depend heavily on the particular choice of words. For example, "load" in (3a) and (3b) is similar to "fill" and "store," yet each verb behaves slightly differently, as the following examples show:

- (5a) Mary filled the wagon with hay.
- (5b) * Mary filled hay on the wagon.
- (5c) Mary stored hay on the wagon.
- (5d) * Mary stored the wagon with hay.

Mapping from surface forms to conceptual roles is thus a difficult task. We will call the knowledge representation issue behind this difficulty the *Role Relationship Problem* [Jacobs, 1987a]. The problem is how to relate, in a reasonably general way, a surface construct to an underlying conceptual relationship. While the problem directly impacts disambiguation, there is a distinct problem of representing role relationships independent of the "direction" of mapping (i.e., analysis or generation).

Most systems, like Hirst's [1987], deal with role relationships within the lexicon, encoding explicitly for each word sense a set of syntactic slots (such as the direct object or the object of preposition "to") and their corresponding conceptual roles (such as *patient* or *destination*). This approach makes it easy to deal with subtle distinctions such as the difference between "load" and "store" but is unsatisfying because of the volume of information that must be repeated for words with similar meanings. On the other hand, the language defies general rules more often than it obeys them.

Having specific mapping rules causes a number of representation problems. First, the rules are generally directional, meaning a system has separate rules for language analysis and generation. Second, the inefficiency of repeating the rules for each word sense often limits semantic coverage by making it harder to add new word senses to the lexicon. Third, the specific rules hinder language acquisition, because new mapping relations cannot derive from general rules.

An attractive alternative approach to role relationships is to encode default relationships between linguistic and conceptual structures and to use specific information in the lexical or conceptual hierarchy to control and refine these generic relationships. The discussion that follows will further clarify the Role Relationship Problem with some examples, then describe the augmentations to structured representations that help to handle the problem.

18.2.1 The Conceptual Role of the Indirect Object

This section will take a simple example of the Role Relationship Problem and demonstrate how a particular knowledge representation framework helps to map between linguistic and conceptual roles.

The Role Relationship Problem manifests itself in determining the conceptual role of the indirect object in semantic interpretation, as in the following examples:

- (6a) Mary sold John a book.
- (6b) Mary did John a favor.
- (6c) Mary asked John a question.
- (6d) Mary charged John five dollars.

There is no necessary grammatical distinction among the sentences above, since the same dative verb phrase construct covers all four examples, and the same linguistic relation associates the verb with its indirect object ("John"). The problem is associating the indirect object with a conceptual role, such as *recipient.*

As the previous examples have shown, the relationship between indirect object and *recipient* is not a simple one-to-one mapping. John is the *recipient* in (6a), while in (6b) his role is *beneficiary*—distinct from recipient because one would paraphrase (6b) as "did a favor *for* John" rather than "...*to* John." In (6c) and (6d), John's role isn't as clear, but some of the usual inferences don't apply; for example, in (6c), John doesn't have the question after it's asked; in (6d), he doesn't get the five dollars.

Some simple extensions to network representations can capture some of the general mapping relationships while also helping with the many exceptions. The rest of this chapter will describe some of these extensions.

The ACE representation [Jacobs and Rau, 1985] augments the traditional features of structured inheritance networks with knowledge structures associating language and meaning, including lexical and syntactic hierarchies, explicit links between these hierarchies and semantic categories, and conceptual associations for representing and extending word senses. ACE evolved as an extension to a knowledge representation called KODIAK [Wilensky, 1986], which is similar to KL-ONE [Brachman and Schmolze, 1985], and uses an implementation of most of the features of KODIAK. Building the knowledge representation system before the natural language programs enforces uniformity and knowledge sharing between analysis and generation. Over a five-year period the KING generator [Jacobs, 1987b] and TRUMP analyzer [Jacobs, 1987a] have been developed, using the common framework of ACE.

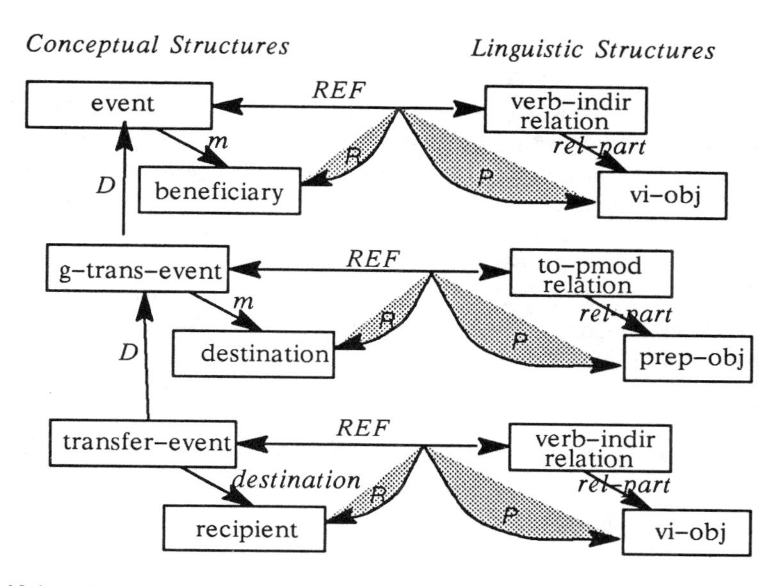

Figure 18.1: The REF structured association

18.2.2 REF Structures in ACE

The general knowledge structure that relates the indirect object to *recipient* in ACE is called REF (for "refer," although "express" would probably be a better term). REF associates a word with its meaning, and associates linguistic structures with conceptual roles. Figure 18.1 shows some REF associations. In the figure, "D" links (for DOMINATEs) join categories to their parents, "m" links (for MANIFEST) join categories to their roles, and the wavy links labeled "R" and "P" associate roles through "ROLE-PLAY." Diagonal lines with italicized labels represent a shorthand way of indicating ROLE-PLAY, marking a role with the name of a more general role.

Linguistic relations in Figure 18.1, such as *verb-indir* and *to-pmod*, are a way of representing linguistic structures independently from word order. The *verb-indir* relation includes a verb and its indirect object, and the to-pmod relation associates a verb with a prepositional phrase whose preposition is "to." Figure 18.1 shows these two linguistic relations and three REFs linking them to the conceptual roles *beneficiary*, *destination*, and *recipient* (The *destination* role, a generalization of *recipient*, includes destinations of physical transfers as well, as part of the generalized transfer event *g-trans-event*).

This REF link joins the indirect object to the *recipient* with a structured association similar to the relationship between conceptual roles in many representations, except that the role relationship applies only when an interpreter uses the REF association to produce a new structure, such as in analysis or generation. In both analysis and generation, REFs at specific levels generally override higher level REFs, so the indirect object will express the *recipient* rather than *beneficiary* when the event described has a *recipient*.

The REFs shown here link abstract linguistic entities to abstract concepts, thus providing a set of general role relationships along with a hierarchy in which role preferences can be expressed (such as the preference for *recipient* over *beneficiary* in transfer events). In order to use these links in interpreting examples such as those given earlier, the senses of words must be subcategories of the abstract concepts, and specific knowledge about words must control which role relationships apply in the case of exceptions or conflicts. The next sections deal with how REF associations relate to specific concepts, and with how linguistic knowledge can control these associations.

18.3 REPRESENTING CORE AND EXTENDED WORD SENSES

The introduction pointed out that the flexibility of language confounds the problem of relating linguistic and conceptual structures. Some of the most common words in the language are also the most vague or polysemous (having multiple senses), and some of the most common concepts are expressed in many different ways. Relating words to word senses seems to require expressing relationships among associated concepts and providing these relationships with a context.

Word senses and role relationships go together because the sense of a word usually determines what conceptual roles to expect, as well as what default inferences use those roles. Along with these inferences, we want to have similar representations of the roles of expressions with similar meanings, even when different words are used. The following illustrates a "canonical" example of different sentences that can express the same event:

- (6a) Mary sold John a book.
- (7a) John bought a book from Mary.

In these examples, the representation of the *buying* and *selling* events must reflect the fact that the two can express the same complex event, as well as that the underlying roles of John, Mary, and the book are the same (or, at least, compatible). A typical way of dealing with the similarity between *buying* and *selling* is to postulate a common complex event that underlies the verbs "buy" and "sell." We will call this event *commercial-transaction*.

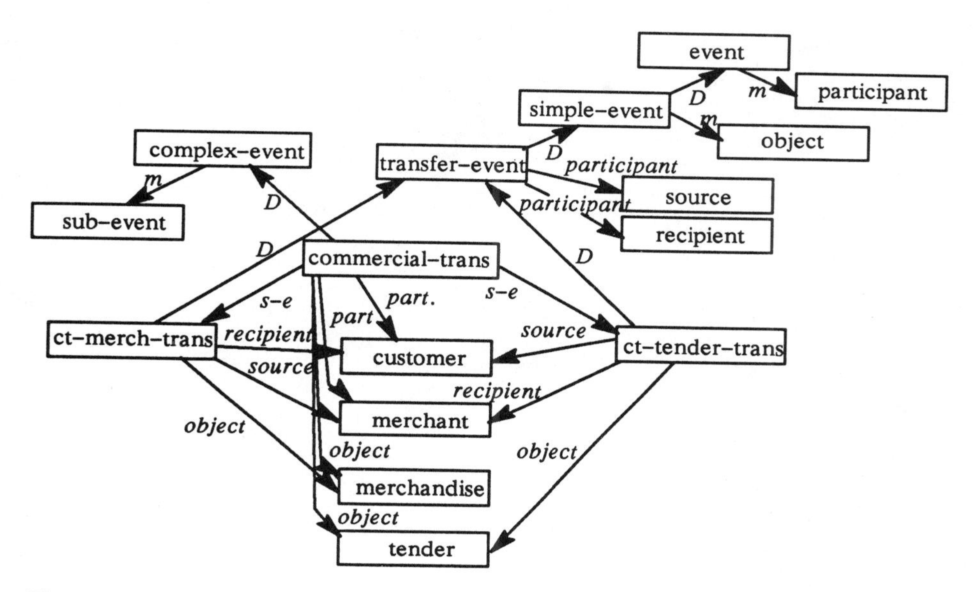

Figure 18.2: The *commercial-transaction* concept

Figure 18.2 illustrates the ACE representation of the *commercial-transaction* concept. [Jacobs, 1987b] more fully covers the details of this diagram. The reason for its complexity is that verbs like "buy," "sell," "charge," and "pay" can all describe the same event, while the roles associated with the verbs vary. The labeled diagonal links in the diagram associate roles of various ways of expressing the *commercial-transaction* with the underlying event. For example, the diagonal link between *ct-merch-trans* and *merchandise* indicates that the direct object of "buy" or "sell" will express the *merchandise* of the transaction, while the link between *ct-tender-trans* and *tender* shows that the object of "pay" or "charge" will express the *tender* (or amount paid).

In Figure 18.2, two subevents (labeled s-e) make up the generic *commercial-transaction*—the transfer of merchandise *ct-merch-trans*, and the transfer of money *ct-tender-trans*. Each of these subevents is a subcategory of the *transfer-event* concept (indicated by the "D" links), and thus has *recipient*, *source*, and *object* roles. The arrows labeled with the names of these roles point directly to the roles of the *commercial-transaction* event because the fillers of these corresponding roles must be identical. This representation captures the gist of the *commercial-transaction* event: *The merchant gives the customer the merchandise*, and the customer gives the merchant the payment. This representation also sets up most of the default roles

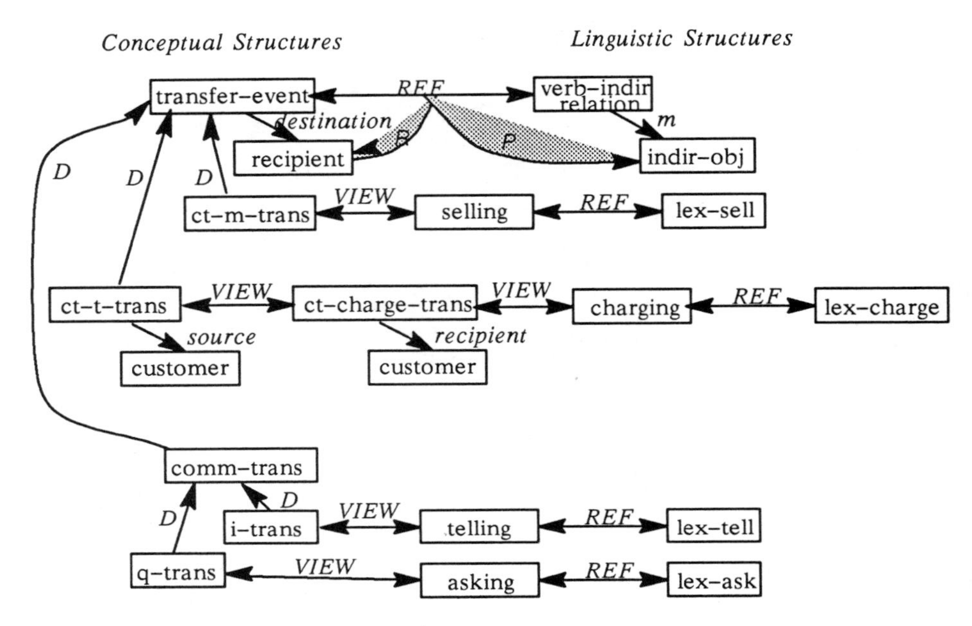

Figure 18.3: VIEWs of events as actions

for verbs that describe the event, while creating underlying roles such as *merchant* and *customer* to help express the common meaning of (6a) and (7a) as well as allow for default inferences (such as who gets paid).

This accounts for some of the different ways of expressing the event but still does not distinguish the verbs "buy" and "sell" or explain why the indirect object of "charge" *doesn't* get the money. These details require another knowledge structure, called VIEW, which relates concepts like *buying* and *selling* to the "deeper" events they express.

VIEW is like REF except that it associates concepts to concepts instead of concepts to linguistic structures. VIEWs help to define core word senses as well as relating core senses to their "extended" or related senses. The verbs "buy" and "sell," for example, express two different VIEWs of the *ct-merch-transfer* event—the two VIEWs share a common meaning except for the agent or *actor* role of the event. The verbs "give" and "take," similarly, are VIEWs of a generalized transfer event.

Figure 18.3 shows how VIEWs fit with some of the concepts shown earlier, such as the concepts expressed by "sell," "charge," "tell," and "ask." The distinction between the *selling* action and *ct-merch-transfer* (abbreviated *ct-m-trans* in Figure 18.3) is that *selling* VIEWs the merchant as an *actor*. The *buying* VIEW (not shown) is the same except that the *customer* is the actor. Except for "charge," the VIEWs preserve the *source*, *recipient* and *object* roles of the underlying transfer. In the case of "charge," the VIEW reverses the *source* and *recipient* roles. While the verb "charge" can indirectly express the same event as "pay," for example, *charging* expresses it as a transfer from the *merchant* to the *customer*, while *paying* expresses it as a transfer from the *customer* to the *merchant*.

The lower part of Figure 18.3 shows the communication transfer event *comm-trans* and two more specific events, *q-trans* (for question transfer) and *i-trans* (for information transfer) The extra level of concepts, including *telling* and asking, allows for the expression of a particular event using a variety of verbs and case structures. While *q-trans* (for question transfer) may not seem like much of a transfer event, it is often expressed as such, as in "I'll take questions from the audience."

The complexity of the representations in Figure 18.2 and Figure 18.3 might lead one to think, incorrectly, that the REFs and VIEWs of ACE are no more efficient than the specific mapping rules they avoid. This is not so, because the diagrams mainly illustrate abstract relationships that apply across broad classes of verbs. Adding a new word to the lexicon usually means linking the lexical entry to a concept appropriately placed in this hierarchy of abstract relationships, following the model of the concepts that are already in the hierarchy. The role relationships, which otherwise could make up most of the lexicon, usually come along for free. Section 18.5 will discuss some of the practical results of applying this model.

Relating the meanings of words such as "buy" and "sell" or "tell" and "ask," along with associated roles, is only a part of the representation problem. Examples such as these are "core" senses of words, but many words have multiple senses. An *extended* word sense is one that derives some part of its meaning from a core sense. For example the core sense of "give" is a transfer of possession, while most of the communication senses of give (as in "give an argument") are extended senses. In practice, extended senses are just as common as core senses, especially for some of the most frequent verbs, as illustrated in the following pair of examples:

- (8a) Mary gave John a hug.
- (8b) Mary gave John a headache.

Clearly (8a) and (8b) are common uses of the word "give." One could treat them as special cases, distinct from the core "transfer" sense, but this would fail to address examples like "John got a hug from Mary" and "John has a headache," which seem consistent with the expression of an action or state change using a transfer verb. To treat "give a hug" and "get a hug" as independent seems to miss an important generalization, since so many expressions are similar. At least, we want to know that, in general, if X *gives* Z to Y, then Y *gets* Z from X, even if the senses of "give" and "get" are extended.

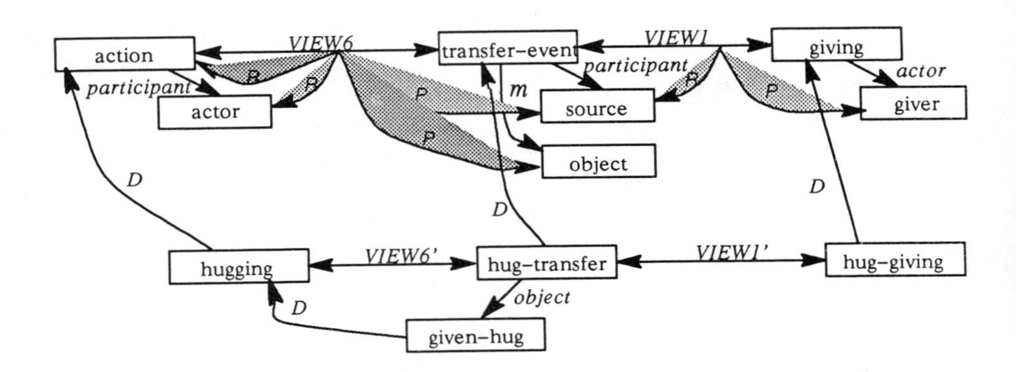

Figure 18.4: The "giving a hug" VIEW

The ACE VIEW accounts for the expression of an action as a transfer in (8a), but not the relationship between transfer metaphors and the underlying possession metaphor in (8b). Martin's computational model [1988] has recently provided a more complete explanation of these examples.

Figure 18.4 illustrates the representation of the "hug giving" metaphor. This structure of this sense of "give" derives from the composition of the *action as transfer-event* VIEW (VIEW6) with the *transfer-event as giving* VIEW (VIEW1).

VIEW6, the most important relation in Figure 18.4, relates actions to transfers, indicating that when transfer verbs such as "give" and "take" express actions, the default roles will express the underlying *actor* as the *source* and the action itself as the *object*. Any sense of "give," "take," "get," or "receive" that expresses an action will inherit these role relationships.

Generalized VIEWs, such as VIEW6 and VIEW1, accomplish two objectives: (1) they account for the range of lexical items (word roots or phrases) that can be used to express a particular concept, even where that concept is not a subcategory of the core sense of the lexical item, and (2) they represent relationships among conceptual roles that form the basis for broad classes of linguistic expressions, so a program need not apply overly specific knowledge in mapping surface roles onto concepts roles, even in extended senses.

The obvious problem with these generalized VIEWs is that they seem to underspecify or underconstrain the language; for example, "Mary gave the button a push" is fine, but "Mary gave the button a press" is not. Especially for generation, this will not do, because the program will not have enough information to choose preferable expressions. A similar problem applies to the REF examples in the previous section. In both cases, the knowledge structures provide the basis for relating certain classes of linguistic expressions to certain classes of concepts, but the appropriate use of the general relationships in either analysis or generation demands some more specific information in the lexicon. This specific knowledge, which combines linguistic and conceptual structures, is the next topic.

18.4 COMBINING LEXICAL AND CONCEPTUAL STRUCTURES

Structured associations such as REF and VIEW may represent the lion's share of relationships between language and meaning by extending word senses and linking conceptual roles to surface forms. But language is idiosyncratic; using these general relationships wherever they seem to fit will result in uncontrolled ambiguity in analysis and near gibberish in generation. The structured associations must be building blocks whose correct assembly depends on a linguistic trigger for analysis and a specific realization for generation. This more specific information comprises a hierarchical phrasal lexicon [Besemer and Jacobs, 1987].

Lexical representation benefits from the uniformity of ACE. Where constructs seem to defy either a strict syntactic or strict conceptual generalization, the combined hierarchy makes it easier to apply linguistic and conceptual constraints simultaneously, without losing the distinction between linguistic and conceptual entities. For example, the "give a hug" construct in (8a) is difficult to constrain using strictly syntactic structures, because it can appear in a range of surface forms, including passives. On the other hand, the construct is clearly lexical as much as it is conceptual, because "give a smooch" doesn't work well.

Figure 18.5 shows the relationship between the lexical hierarchy and the *hug-giving* expression. The relation *lc-give-hug* falls in the class of linguistic-conceptual relations, which are linguistic structures constrained in part by the concepts that they describe. The use of the noun "hug" as the object of a "giving" concept characterizes the *lc-give-hug* relation. A REF link associates this lexical relation to the concept of *hug-giving*, and thus indirectly to *hug-giving*.

The "give a hug" expression is a simple example of where linguistic and conceptual knowledge come together, with the conceptual structure of the extended sense explaining much of its linguistic structure. While it would be relatively easy to use a set of purely linguistic triggers in place of the linguistic-conceptual relation in Figure 18.5, the ability to combine linguistic and conceptual constraints helps to express different lexical forms using a common trigger. It may seem that passive constructions and variations on common expressions are rare, but such constructs actually appear quite frequently in text. For example, in news stories, the passive voice of "give" is about as common as the active voice, and almost all uses represent extended senses.

We are extending the hierarchical lexicon to cover a broad range of expressions and a rich set of senses for 10,000 common roots. In many cases, even specific phrases share common conceptual foundations (e.g., "the head of the stairs," "the foot of the stairs"). The knowledge representation problem is to encode

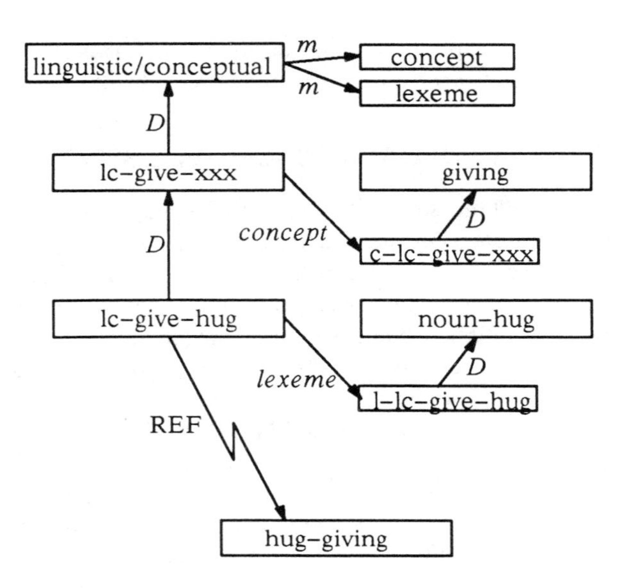

Figure 18.5: The linguistic-conceptual relation *lc-give-hug*

these foundations in a general way while providing adequate constraints for both analysis and generation. While this knowledge representation effort continues, a number of large-scale systems use the foundations described here. The next section will briefly summarize these applications.

18.5 CURRENT APPLICATIONS

A number of different natural language projects within the General Electric Company currently use a common core ACE knowledge base, including several hundred linguistic entries with about a thousand core concepts, in addition to about 15,000 core word senses. Most applications augment this knowledge base with a few dozen domain-specific lexical entries and some hundreds of concepts. The TRUMP analyzer, KING generator, and several other software tools access the knowledge base. The largest projects using ACE are several text processing applications, ranging from diagnostic reports to financial news. A typical application requires several weeks of knowledge base customization and extracts key conceptual features from texts with about 80–90% accuracy at a rate of a few hundred paragraphs per hour [Jacobs and Rau, 1990]. Direct funding from GE businesses has been the principal source of support for the project.

It is difficult to measure the performance of natural language systems and even more difficult to attribute their performance to fundamental technologies. However, we believe that the knowledge representation principles described in this chapter have been the key to scaling up our systems and extending them to real natural language tasks.

18.6 SUMMARY AND CONCLUSION

Encoding linguistic knowledge is a knowledge representation problem and benefits from the framework of structured inheritance networks. Some simple extensions to these networks, including relating linguistic and conceptual structures and representing associations among concepts that indirectly express other concepts, provide a basis for linguistic knowledge representation that encompasses the information necessary for both analysis and generation. These structured associations help to represent word senses in a hierarchy and to link conceptual roles to linguistic expressions.

References

Allen, J. 1987. *Natural Language Understanding*. Benjamin/Cummings, Redwood City, CA.

Besemer, D. and Jacobs, P.S. 1097. FLUSH: A flexible lexicon design. In *Proceedings of the 25th Meeting of the Association for Computational Linguistics*, Palo Alto, CA.

Bobrow, R. and Webber, B. 1980. Knowledge representation for syntactic/semantic processing. In *Proceedings of the National Conference on Artificial Intelligence*. AAAI, Menlo Park, CA.

Brachman, R. and Schmolze, J. 1985. An overview of the KL-ONE knowledge representation system. *Cognitive Science*, 9(2):171–216.

Hirst, G. 1987. *Semantic Interpretation and the Resolution of Ambiguity*. Cambridge University Press, Cambridge, U.K..

Jacobs, P.S. 1987. A knowledge framework for natural language analysis. In *Proceedings of the Tenth International Joint Conference on Artificial Intelligence*. IJCAI proceedings are available from Morgan Kaufmann Publishers, San Mateo, CA.

———. 1987. Knowledge-intensive natural language generation. *Artificial Intelligence*, 33(3):325–378.

Jacobs, P.S. and Rau, L.F. 1985. ACE: Associating language with meaning. In *Advances in Artificial Intelligence*, O'Shea, T. (ed.), pp. 295–304. North Holland, Amsterdam.

———. 1990. SCISOR: Extracting information from on-line news. *Communications of the ACM*, 33(11):88–97.

Martin, J. 1988. *A Computational Theory of Metaphor*. Ph.D. thesis, University of California, Berkeley.

Neal, J.G. and Shapiro, S.C. 1987. Knowledge-based parsing. In Natural Language Parsing Systems, Bolc, L. (ed). Springer-Verlag, NY.

Sondheimer, N., Weischedel, R., and Bobrow, R. 1984. Semantic interpretation using KL-ONE. In *Proceedings of the Tenth International Conference on Computational Linguistics*, Palo Alto, CA.

Wilensky, R. 1986. Knowledge representation—a critique and a proposal. In *Experience, Memory, and Reasoning*, Kolodner, J. and Riesbeck, C. (ed.s), pp. 15–28. Lawrence Erlbaum Associates, Hillsdale, NJ.

19

A FRAME-LIKE KNOWLEDGE REPRESENTATION INTEGRATING ABSTRACT DATA TYPES AND LOGIC

Douglas Skuce
(University of Ottawa, Canada)

Abstract

This paper describes a very general, formal knowledge representation based on algebraic ideas from abstract data types, i.e., on ideas originating outside the AI literature in research on foundations for programming and specification languages. Nevertheless, the representation incorporates practically necessary features found in inheritance systems such as AI frame systems used for natural language understanding, while offering a precise algebraic semantics. We term the approach *conceptually oriented description.*

The contribution of this chapter is (1) to reformulate and simplify these ideas for AI applications, incorporating the useful features found in many practical AI inheritance systems, while retaining the theoretical foundation, and (2) to show how the approach is valuable in natural language semantics applications. This chapter will use some difficult examples motivated by natural language applications, but the formalism is very general and could be used for other applications, such as software requirements specification.

The approach is based mainly on ideas from the language LOTOS, intended for the formal specification of concurrent systems, and also on similar work by Goguen and Meseguer [1987] on algebraically based functional specification. LOTOS adds to basic ADT concepts additional concepts for defining the notions like state, event, and temporal relationships including *causality* and *synchronization.*

The main components of a software system for creating and debugging conceptual definitions using the formalism have been implemented and are briefly mentioned.

19.1 INTRODUCTION

There is currently a rapid growth of interest in inheritance-based systems such as "frame," object-oriented programming (OOP) and other related systems, both in and outside of artificial intelligence. Yet much remains to be done to clarify the semantics of such systems and to integrate features and constraints from various sources while still retaining practical usefulness. Attempts to formalize inheritance and related semantic network systems fall into several categories, primarily:

- Inheritance-based semantic nets (e.g., [Brachman et al., 1985; Touretzky, 1986; Touretzky et al., 1987])
- General semantic nets with an associated logic (e.g., [Sowa, 1984; Shapiro, 1979])
- Nonmonotonic and other nonstandard logics (e.g., [Reiter, 1988])

Most of these approaches use some form of logic as their bases but add no additional mathematical machinery. However the point of this paper is that ideas derived from research on formal computer languages, which adds additional machinery, can serve a valuable purpose in trying to unify such diverse ideas as frames, objects (in the OOP sense), functions, logical constraints, and temporal phenomena.

The literature on theoretical foundations for programming languages and semantics uses additional mathematical ideas for formal semantics, usually termed *algebraic*, *functional*, or *denotational*. This literature includes integrations of more mathematical notions like functions, including varieties of lambda calculus, rewrite systems, type theories, partial orders, even categories. Some of these, abstract data types (ADTs), are being augmented with class- and inheritance-related notions (e.g., [Goguen and Meseguer, 1987]), indicating a cross-fertilization in the inverse direction to that we propose here. However, many of these mathematical approaches are too limited in scope, do not address important practical AI issues, or require excessive mathematical knowledge (of humans) or deduction power (by machines) to be usable in typical AI knowledge representation situations. Yet we believe that these approaches are very promising in terms of becoming both practically usable yet theoretically well founded, and therefore warrant further study to adapt them for AI needs. After considerable searching of this literature to find approaches that would seem amenable to integration with more conventional and practical inheritance-based ideas and requirements, both from the AI and the OOP perspective, we have selected those based on algebraic techniques, particularly those found in LOTOS [LOTOS, 1987] and in the work of Goguen and Meseguer [1987].

In this chapter we shall demonstrate the potential of these algebraic approaches for AI purposes. The research referred to above is recast, simplified, and given a syntax and additional features more in line with practical AI knowledge representation requirements, oriented toward natural language semantics. Unfortunately, space limitations prevent reviewing this work first. The AI reader should at least be familiar with some of the technical ideas from functional, relational, and object-oriented programming in general (e.g., [DeGroot and Lindstrom, 1986]), and the notion of an ADT.

The knowledge structure that we propose is termed a *conceptual descriptor* (cd). A cd is a frame-and-object-like syntactic framework for describing a concept, with a precise semantics given by a mapping into abstract data types (ADTs). Thus the foundations of the representation are essentially algebraic, i.e., based on functions. Logic serves as the language to define constraints on cds. Thus cds can be thought of as syntactic sugar for ADT notations such as LOTOS and GM's. They are given their semantics by specifying a mapping into these other forms of ADTs, whose semantics are known. Thus cds are an "AI version" of ADTs. The latter are derived from functional programming concepts and hence are not well suited as an AI knowledge representation language, nor are they accessible to many AI workers.

In our approach, we use a combination of features from both LOTOS and GM's FOOPS language. The former is the richer language, having most of the features of FOOPS, plus many primitives intended for the specification of *processes* in the sense of concurrent systems. Both have an associated logical language, which we also use: L1 is Horn clauses with equality, used for specifying functional *behavior* in those systems as well as ours. We have added a second logical language: L2, full first-order logic with equality, which we use for specifying constraints, while GM uses L1 for this as well. LOTOS does not have an explicit constraint language, but it does allow certain kinds of constraints like types and inequalities. The cd approach is nevertheless generic, in that other logical languages could be substituted should they turn out to have better properties than this choice.

This chapter is organized as follows: Section 19.2 describes the ADT approach briefly, and relates ours to it. Section 19.3 introduces the basic notions, particularly that of a "property," in terms of which one may develop descriptions of 'class' and 'instance' concepts and construct inheritance taxonomies using cds. Section 19.4 presents several natural language examples, and in particular shows how state and event notions may be described. Section 19.5 briefly mentions a knowledge acquisition system we are implementing which is intended to behave according to the principles we describe. Several similar systems are noted. Section 19.6 concludes with some suggestions for further research.

We have attempted to make the chapter self-contained. It is based primarily on examples, without allowing space for details of syntax or semantics. We use a very simple syntax for cds; their screen views are much more complex. Keywords are in bold or suffixed with ":." Comments follow semicolons.

19.2 ABSTRACT DATA TYPES AND CONCEPTUAL DESCRIPTORS

An ADT is a small, "frame-like" package of knowledge, based on algebraic ideas, which specifies precisely the behavior (in terms of how certain functions interact) of a "data type," i.e. a computer data structure such as a list or stack. Recently, some ADTs have become more sophisticated, taking on inheritance structure that bears a considerable resemblance to (OOP) *objects*, which in turn are very similar to the AI notion of *frame*. GM have very elegantly amalgamated the essential ideas of functional, relational (logic) and object-oriented programming in the language FOOPS. LOTOS (the work of an ISO committee) is quite similar in this respect.[1] We use the term *object* in the OOP sense, as a generic module of encapsulation, integrating memory, constraints, and function. Both FOOPS and LOTOS permit one to make definitions based on the notion of an *algebra*, which relates *sorts* (abstract collections of data values) and associated *operations*. The notion of *state*, i.e., local memory, captures the persistent properties of objects and provides the basis for defining *processes*, *events*, and hence all temporal relationships. The state of an object is defined by how it responds to certain events, and only some events can change its state. *Definitions* or *specifications* impose structure on sorts by adding functions, predicates, attributes, and associated processes and events, often including some logical assertions. However the machinery and notation used by ADT systems are not intended for AI purposes, hence our desire to adapt them for practical AI purposes.

19.3 BASIC PRINCIPLES OF CONCEPTALLY ORIENTED DESCRIPTION (COD)

19.3.1 Conceptual Descriptions

A *concept descriptor* (cd) is a notation for defining some concept at the class or instance level by specifying a number of properties that describe it either totally or partially. Properties are of various property types, most typically *attributes* (atomic values or pointers to other cds), which store the state of a conceptual

---

[1] The main differences: FOOPS is more "object oriented," whereas LOTOS has primitives for concurrency, as we noted. FOOPS directly incorporates memory for *state*, but LOTOS achieves this effect by infinite processes.

object; *functional*, which defines functions; *behavioral* (process knowledge), which defines events; and *logical*, which imposes constraints on values.

The most general *sort* and hence cd (a textual unit or module of defining information) is termed *T*. "Class" concepts (subsorts of *T*) normally have *instances*, also defined by cds. Concepts are defined (or *described*, if defined is too strong a term) by their *properties*, by which we describe their internal structure and their relations to other concepts, using a cd as the syntactic device. Typically, a subconcept or instance of a concept *inherits* suitable properties (those that are inheritable and not contradictory) from that concept. Thus every cd (except *T*) has one or more other cds of which it is a subconcept or instance and from which it normally inherits properties. Clarifying what a concept *is* means clarifying what properties it and its instances have, how it got them, and what instances it has or can have (if any); this is the *raison d'etre* of cds. To clarify the notion of a concept and a cd (which describes a concept), we must clarify exactly what the notion of property means. Cds provide a framework in which to do this with some precision.

The cd for *T* is:

(T)

The meaning of this (or any) cd is defined by mapping it to an ADT such as the GM module:[2]

```
module: T
        sorts: T
endmod: T
```

We use the same symbol for the sort and the ADT *module* (GM's term), assuming that *T* is a primitive "universal" sort: everything is a *T*. We make the assumption that each module has one *principle* sort of the same name associated with it, and *vice versa*. The meaning of this module *T*—which says very little—is, intuitively, that there exists a collection of "concepts of interest" denoted by *T*.

As a slightly larger initial example, the following is a cd for the concept 'person' (details explained below).

```
(person
 specOf:       T
 comment       the concept 'person'
 hasa          ;attributes of person
 age:          an integer
 constraints
  1:           age > 0
  2:           age < 115)
```

---

[2]Space does not permit showing mappings of all our cds to ADTs.

The mapping to a GM module would be:

```
module:        person
sorts:         person
attrs:        age: person -> integer
vars:          P: person
constraints:
               age(P) > 0
               age(P) < 115
endmod:        person
```

The name of this cd is 'person'. The variable *P*, termed the "self" variable, denotes "a person" in the cd. The user-supplied *attribute* 'age' that persons have is denoted functionally in both notations. Such attributes are the sole basis for defining the notion of *state*, and correspond to ordinary "value" slots in a frame, or instance variables in an OOP object. Finally, the *logical* or *constraint* properties tell us that the age of persons must be between 0 and 115. ADTs do not permit referring to (naming) logical properties (reflecting a lack of influence from object-oriented thinking), but we find this very useful for inheriting logical properties "in pieces," i.e., subconcepts often specialize some of the logical pieces (properties) of their ancestors, but usually not all. The constraints guarantee that certain conditions always are true of the values. Constraints are written in L2 (full first-order logic with equality).

A subconcept of person, 'employed adults', would be defined by:

```
(employed adult: P
      specOf:          person
      comment          the concept 'employed adult'
      hasa
      age:             an integer
      jobStatus:       'employed'
      constraints
       1:              age > 17
       2:              age < 115)
```

The basic inheritance operation can be described loosely thus: Properties of an ancestor (in the inheritance hierarchy) are present in a cd, provided that each implies the corresponding ancestor property, as is the case for age and constraints 1 and 2 above (see Section 19.3.4 below). The new property 'jobStatus', and the change to constraint 1, have been introduced by a knowledgable source, presumably a human.

An instance of this concept, Bill, age 23, can be described by the cd:

```
(employed adult: Bill
 instanceOf      employed adult
 comment:        the concept of "Bill"
```

```
hasa
 age:              23
 jobStatus:        'employed'
constraints
 1:                age > 17         ; "Bill's age > 17"
 2:                age < 115)
```

19.3.2 Properties

A cd relies mainly on the notion of a property to clarify what it means both intuitively and formally. A *property* is basically a pair consisting of a *property name*, which is an index or symbol used to refer to the property and a name for a function in the case of attributes, and a *property body*. There are four main kinds of *property body*:

```
propertyBody=        functionalProperty
                     | logicalProperty
                     | attrProperty
                     | specialProperty
```

1. a *functional* property (body) is a partial or complete *specification* of a function,[3] following the keyword **functions (funs)**. The functional specification takes two parts: the *signature*, stating the types of the arguments and the result; and a set of assertions in L1, which defines the functional result.

   Example:
   ```
   head: list -> element     ; the signature for the head of a list
   head(cons(X,Y)) = X       ; an equation for head:
   ```

2. a *logical* (or *constraint*) property (body) is a wff in L2:

   Examples:
   ```
   integer(X) & X < 100
   man(X) iff adult(X) & sex(X) = male
   setOf(X) intersectWith setOf(Y) = empty if X ≠ Y.
   ```

   Logical properties have the keyword **constraints**. They require a *signature* for the predicates, indicated by the keyword **preds**. We often leave these out where they can be inferred. A logical property can be any wff relevant to relating any attributes in a cd to the *self* concept, which can be denoted by the symbol #, or to each other. Variables are local to the constraint unless declared by 'vars'.

[3] We do not emphasize functional definitions here, since (a) many concepts of interest in AI do not have many functions, and (b) this aspect is the most well developed in the functional programming and ADT literature, as in GM's work.

3. an *attribute* property represents a function of one argument (the concept having the property), defined by storing the function value explicitly, i.e., a finite map. The keyword is **attributes** or **hasa**. The value is usually (but not necessarily) intended to be updated. For example, a person has an age, i.e., 'age' is a function on persons, which is unfortunately updated every year. Updating rules can be specified as functional properties in L1, with constraints in L2. To specify an attribute, an expression of 1 to 3 components is given (we assume no syntactic ambiguity arises) as follows:

   ```
   value |
   (value sort |= initialValue)
   ```

   Examples:

   ```
   5                  ; a value of 5
   (integer |= 4)     ; number of legs on a pet, default 4
   ```

   These expressions translate easily into ADTs.

4. *Special Properties* There is a small number of special, primitive properties that have unusual uses. Many of these have no correspondence in modules. The following properties concern inheritance, described further below:

instances	a list of cds that are instances of the cd.
specializationOf	Super concepts (also written **super** or **specOf**).
correspondsTo	indicating mappings between components of different cds (See Section 19.3.4).
events	described in Section 19.4.2

   Several other minor special properties are used later without explanation.

19.3.2.1 User Properties; Property Groups

User properties are definable at two levels by the user. First, he may create a new *category* of properties, normally a subclass of one of the categories above. Given any such user property category (upc), he may create *instances* of it, by giving actual properties to some cd. All property instances in a cd from the same category are called a *property group*. Hence we need to ask: "What is the structure of user properties in general, and particularly, of the large, generic categories identified above?"

We believe that any upc will require (most of) the following:

a *name* a symbol, number, or string that distinguishes it from any other property within the cd

a set of *flags*, possibly empty (see Section 19.3.2.2 for a description of flags)

a *body* the main semantic content of the property, which is represented at the surface level as a character string. The semantics of the body are dependent on the system which is available to analyse (check or compile) it. For example, logical properties are checked by our L2 engine, while functional properties can be checked by a L1 engine.

a *source* most properties in a cd will have been inherited from some more general cd, termed the *source*. If the property originates in (is first introduced in) the cd that has it, then this cd is the source.

a *comment* for human use only

Example 1: ; in any subconcept of 'entity'
attributes ; the group "header", i.e. attributes follow
age(in): an integer <entity> ; the age attribute inherited from entity

here:

age	is the name
i	is a flag (see below) indicating an instance property
n	is a flag meaning that this property is necessary (any entity must have an age)
an integer	is the body, here meaning that this is an attribute having an integer as value
<entity>	is the source, i.e all entities have an age

Example 2: Formal specification languages like LOTOS require signatures to be given for every function and predicate that is introduced. So they would need a property group as follows:

```
signatures      ; header
1:  X cons list -> list          ; a signature in an ADT specification
```

here:

1	is used as the name. There are no explicit flags.
X cons list -> list	is the body, meaning that something X consed with a list yields a list

19.3.2.2 Property Flags

Properties may be flagged with certain property *flag* keywords, placed in parentheses after the index. We have used the term "flag" for want of a better one; terms like "facet" or "subproperty" are sometimes used. The idea is that properties can have a number of modifying codes, attributes, or flags attached to them to indicate certain uses for the property, each highly dependent on the type of property. For example, 'n' above meant that the property is logically necessary. A number of widely applicable flags are:

instance 'i'	the property belongs to instances of the concept
class 'c'	the property does not belong to instances, but only to classes.
necessary n	logically necessary
sufficient s	logically sufficient
optional o	subclasses and/or instances do not have to have this property
typical t	subclasses and/or instances usually have this property
mutable m	can be changed in any way after inheritance
refinable r	can be *refined* after inheritance, i.e., the inherited property can be updated but only such that it implies the parent's restrictions on it, e.g., if the parent says "type is integer" then the child may have 'positive integer' or '5'.
has h	the property will be copied by inheritance, but with a nil body, i.e., a new body must be supplied. Thus subconcepts or instances "have" such a property, but determine its body themselves.
fixed f	the property cannot be changed after inheritance
private p	the property does not inherit at all, and the subconcepts and instances have no property of this name

A number of defaults are useful. For example, attributes are normally necessary and refinable.

19.3.4 Property Inheritance

The formal basis for defining inheritance is the purely syntactic process of copying properties, with suitable changes of names from one cd to another to avoid clashes, followed by a logical verification that no contradiction has occurred. In practice, logical conflicts between properties must be detected; our system has considerable machinery for doing this.[4] Each cd (except T) has one or more cds from which it may inherit properties, termed its *parents*. Most properties have some inheritance behavior; exceptions include 'private' properties, and most special properties.

Three kinds of inheritance *links* between cds are available, each in *full* and *partial* versions:

subconcept (s)	all inheritable properties inherit; normally new properties are added in the subconcept by a knowledge source such as a person

---

[4] Our current system uses an interpreter for full first-order logic written in PROLOG for detecting contradictions and logical dependencies between properties.

correspondence (c)	like s, only one or more symbols are replaced, throughout the cd, by other symbols in the subconcept, but nothing is added
instance (i)	only inheritable instance properties inherit.

Thus we say a cd is either a subconcept, a correspondent, or an instance of one of its parents. It may have all three kinds of parents.

In *full* inheritance, all inheritable properties follow the above rules. In a *partial* inheritance link, some of these properties, associated with this link, may be singled out as not inheriting (blocked). Thus a cd is only "partially" the child of such a parent and should not be considered a subset but an exception. A cd could thus have many inheritance links, of all six varieties. In practice, most cds have two or three links.

In correspondence inheritance, a subconcept cd inherits all inheritable properties of its super concept, except that some symbols have been renamed. These may be *formal* parameters, indicated by symbols prefixed with "$," which have been replaced by actual symbols. This mechanism is typically used with type names, corresponding to the notion of a parameterized type definition in ADTs. (This is illustrated in the cd for "collection.")

The question of how to deal with conflicting properties is application-dependent. A simple case is when two parent cds are offering a different property with the same name; a difficult case is resolving outright logical contradictions. We have made no commitment in our system as to how to deal automatically with such conflicts (except to report them); this has been extensively discussed in the literature on inheritance and nonmonotonic logic. Our representation can be provided with whatever additional inheritance behavior is appropriate to the application.

19.4 EXAMPLES

In this section, we will illustrate the utility and flexibility of the cd notation for defining some problematic concepts that many natural language systems often need to represent. The cd notation facilitates specifying or learning what the semantics of these concepts are.

19.4.1 Count Nouns, Plurals, and Sets

Our first example is a representation that shows how one might specify the essential semantic properties for any concept referred to by a count noun, and some special cases of this. The reader should not confuse the message with the medium: Our opinions about what is linguistically correct and relevant are not the issue here, only the expressive convenience of the cd formalism for communicating them is.

Hence we are making no claims about the linguistic correctness and generality of these definitions, only about the utility of the cd formalism for *stating* such claims.

First, we propose a semantic category *countConcept* corresponding to the syntactic category *count noun*, i.e., concepts for which one may speak of individual instances and use the plural to refer to collections.

```
(countConcept
        specOf              T
        hasa
        roughSize(o):       oneOf no, one, some, few, many, most, all
                            ; oneOf is a syntactic sugar for a list of
                            constants
        countSize(o):       integer

         constraints
        c1:                 countSize >= 0
        c2:                 countSize = 0 iff roughSize = no
        c3:                 countSize > 0 if roughSize \= no
        c4:                 countSize = 1 if roughSize = one ; etc)
```

Thus we can easily see some of the assumptions about this concept.[5] Here, we specify that we usually expect (but don't insist on) a count concept to have a "rough size" and/or "count size" attribute. If an instance is being described, the countSize = 1 and the roughSize = one. (A full characterization of the interaction of these two attributes might take tens of equations.)

An interesting exercise is to write the equivalent cd for a *massConcept*. Clearly, it should not have the countSize attribute, but probably has many of the same values for the roughSize. Indeed, if we wrote:

```
(massConcept
        specOf              T
        hasa
        roughSize(o):       oneOf no, some, most, all)
```

we might be tempted to make 'countConcept' a subconcept of 'massConcept', since it seems to have all its properties. (Would this make linguistic sense?)

Next, we specialize 'countConcept' to any *plural* count concept (inherited properties are shown):

[5] It is a telling exercise to attempt to discover such assumptions in most typical linguistics texts, articles, or AI systems.

```
(collection of $T   ; $T is a sort (or type) parameter.
                    ; It determines what this collection is "made up of"

    specOf          countConcept

    hasa
    type:           $T
    roughSize(o):   oneOf no, some, few, many, most, all
    countSize(o):   an integer

    preds
                    _:$T isOneOf #     ; _:$T is an instance of sort $T
                    _:# areSomeOf _:# ; # means "this concept", i.e.,
                    collections partake in the 'areSomeOf' relation

    constraints      (Y,Z:#) ;Y and Z are of type 'collection of'
                            ; inherited constraints c1 to c4 not shown

                     c5:   Y isOneOf # if Y isOneOf Z & Z areSomeOf #
                              ; a "set" property)
```

This cd is intended to capture some minimum requirements for any plural reference, e.g., there are predicates which say "something or things belong to this collection." (This type of property corresponds closely to the collocational properties that are found in some more modern dictionaries, e.g., the ECD of Mel'cuk and his associates [Mel'cuk, 1984].) Clearly more properties should be added. The parameter T, permits a sort to be specified, which in this case determines the "type" of the collection, such as a collection of persons if T = person. The phrase "collection of persons" could be represented as the following correspondent of this cd using T=person:

```
(collection of person                ; the type is specified here to
                              ; create a unique name
        type:   person)       ; other properties omitted
```

Note that this cd does not have any properties from 'person', yet surely it should have some relation to the 'person' cd, which represents the class of persons. But instances of the former are individual collections of persons (e.g., "the persons in this room") while instances of the latter are individual persons (e.g., "Bill"). Clearly, Bill does not have any properties collections in general, but are there properties of 'persons' that 'collections of persons' should have? We would say "yes": e.g., collections of persons can have a sex property, if they are all the same sex, and an 'average weight' property, if persons have 'weight'. However capturing such relations between properties can be done automatically for only a few very generic properties, we suspect, such as:

X: $T if X isOneOf #

Here, X:T is a primitive predicate meaning "*X* is an instance of cd *T*" (*X* is of type *T*, or X:T). In the context of the above cd, it reads: "*X* is an instance of a person if *X* isOneOf a collection of persons." Other relations can be specified specially for certain properties by suitable logical assertions, such as (for 'collections of persons'):

sex(#) = S if (forAll(P) sex(P) = S if P isOneOf #)

meaning "a collection of persons, having the property 'sex', will have the value *S* for this property if all persons *P* who are in this collection (a generalization of set membership), have *S* as their sex."

19.4.2 Events

The notions of *state* and *event* are very problematic in both the theoretical linguistic literature and in practical nl understanding systems. Usually in the latter, the state of an object or an event is represented informally by some frame (e.g., a LISP structure) or set of logical expressions, like other concepts, without adequate clarification of its formal properties or relations to other similar ideas. Hence any formal analysis of states and events is usually difficult or impossible, and the system may therefore have undiscovered bugs. Even logical systems that can reason about, for example, unfortunate events like in the Yale Shooting Scenario often represent events formally just as predicates in a "logical" language (one whose constructs derive solely from research in logic). Such languages have limitations on the kinds of relations between events they can conveniently express, and, worse, usually do not have any implemented inference engine that can process them.

We believe that cd concepts and notation derived from a language like LOTOS may provide better facilities for specifying the meaning of events, and debugging these expressions practically. In a sense, LOTOS can be viewed as a logical language at least syntactically, since it has a large number of syntactic "inference rules," which are executed by the LOTOS interpreter (see Section 19.5 below). Thus LOTOS proofs are sequences of possible actions, and are a kind of "forward deduction," in that the interpreter gives all possible results of some initial situation. The branching comes from any nondeterminism in the specification. However LOTOS' semantics, at least so far, are given operationally by describing the behavior of the constructs in terms of an abstract machine.

We first require a definition of state. Only cds with attributes have a state, which is defined by their attribute values alone. We will term such cds *objects*, after OOP parlance, as GM do. An object is modeled by a *persistent process* in LOTOS, exactly analogous to the notion of *actor* developed by Hewitt and his associates [Agha, 1987], or as in concurrent PROLOG [Takeuchi and Furakawa, 1986]. (In fact, one might say that LOTOS is "actors with real semantics.") The values can only be changed by certain events, and have initial values whenever an object is created. The term *event* then means a change of state, i.e., a message (to use OOP parlance again) sent to an object that modifies its attributes. The only updates that are allowed on an object are those performed by the allowed events associated with the object, which in turn must respect the logical constraints of the object. Any complex event must ultimately be defined in terms of the atomic events of attribute updates in the participating objects. Objects can also accept *queries*, pure functions which return values without having any side effect. Thus there are two classes of messages: events and queries.

Take for example the event *pushing something toward something*. To guide us in defining a general *push* event, we first consider a standard example from the computer world: *pushing something on a stack*. This example is interesting because there is wide agreement on how to deal with this by using an abstract data type (ADT) description such as one sees in any good undergraduate text on computer languages. However AI knowledge representation researchers have widely varying ideas on how to represent this. Our approach advocates a semantic basis derived from the ADT tradition. But classic ADTs do not usually represent state information *explicitly*; i.e., state is only implicit in the behavioral equations that say, e.g., that a *push* followed by a *pop* will yield the thing pushed. They don't say "where the thing is stored," because the "pure" or classical idea of an ADT is to leave the idea of "state" undefined, with no commitment to any representation, specifying only the external behavior. However modern versions of ADTs such as in LOTOS do have some commitment to representing state in terms of simple primitives like arithmetic and list operations, while retaining the requirement that the set of message interactions be well defined by equations and wffs. The basic ADT requirement is that all message interactions must be well defined, else some sequence of messages will have an undetermined effect. This is precisely what we seek to avoid.

We will generalize the ADT approach to representing concepts to the level of typical AI needs, and will "show where the state is" by explicitly connecting the external state-changing events to the attributes. (GM do the same in the example, a bank account, as do all large AI systems.) However lacking any concurrent constructs, GM employ functions to represent events: the functions they define, "bank account events," are defined in terms of known functions (arithmetic) that explicitly update the attributes. So this is our point of departure from GM's approach: We prefer the mechanisms of LOTOS for this purpose, because a LOTOS event is a *rendezvous*; the sender and the receiver "meet," at a place (called a *gate*) and at a time acceptable to both, and the participating objects are entirely independent otherwise. At rendezvous time, they may exchange values of attributes, in either direction, almost a *mating*. Thus LOTOS wraps concurrency notions around traditional functional ones. A typical LOTOS rendezvous situation looks like:

g1 !3 ; **stop**

|| g1 ?x ; **stop**

This says that there are two processes in parallel, sharing gate g1. At this gate, the first object (process) meets the second and the second gets its 'x' attribute (called a *variable* in LOTOS) set to the value '3'. The variables are true "logical" variables in that they cannot be reassigned (similar to PROLOG). Both of these objects "die" afterward, a short-lived affair ("we can't go on meeting like this"), due to the 'stop' event.

Thus we model an event verb in natural language by a LOTOS event, analogous to *push* for a stack. The effect of a push, in this case on a stack, is defined by the effect on the stack's attributes in terms of known functions. Hence for a stack, we will assume there is an attribute called its *contents*, modeled by a simple primitive data structure, a *list*. Thus we assume that it is desirable to assume the existence of a small set of primitive data structures and operations upon them. Of course, this is what any theory or implementation usually does, only it is often either left unclear, or it is something extremely complex and hard to process formally, e.g., "all of LISP." Hence we would permit formal lists, defined as an ADT in LOTOS, to be used as a state-holding device.

First, a (simple) stack process in LOTOS looks (almost) like:

```
process stack [push, pop] (contents:list): noexit :=

(             push ?x:Type; stack [push, pop] (cons x contents)
[]
              [contents =\= nil] ->
             pop !(car contents); stack [push pop] (cdr contents)
)
endproc
```

This definition says that a stack can respond to either a push or a pop event, but an empty stack will not respond to pop. The symbol 'Type' is a formal parameter to be replaced by an actual type of the thing to be pushed, typical of parameterized ADTs. A push conses the argument of the push onto the contents list, its sole attribute, in a recursive reincarnation of a new stack. This new stack is like an actor: Its parent no longer exists, since it (the parent) had nothing left to do but reincarnate itself. A pop communicates *back* (indicated by "!") the contents as a value, and again begets a new stack. (We prefer think of the "new" stack as being "the old stack reincarnated with a change.") Thus a stack is a concurrent object that can communicate with other such objects. We believe that it (and similar objects) offers a good formal model for the objects needed for typical AI purposes, with considerable precision. Indeed, one could write a very precise "restaurant script" in LOTOS, with 'restaurant', 'customer', and 'server' objects and their associated events. The semantics would be absolutely clear, and formally analyzable. (We abhor faulty restaurant scripts, in which one could wait forever for service.)

But however elegant and acceptable the LOTOS notation may be for specifying communication protocols (its original purpose), it needs considerable repackaging for AI purposes, which is what we are about. Consider:

```
(stack
        attributes
        contents: a list |= nil     ; '|=' means "initially"

        events
       push:        (push X on #)
                    contents <- (cons X contents)

       pop:         (pop !X from #) ; '!' means "returns"
                     if   contents =\= nil
                     then X = contents
                          contents <- (cdr contents))
```

This cd says the same thing as before, only more readably. A stack has one attribute, its contents, which is a list that is initially nil. It responds to two events; the syntax '(push X on #)' means that the verb "push" expects two arguments, 'on' being a convenient constant to distinguish this meaning of push from another. Attribute updates are indicated by an "assignment" arrow, but this is not ordinary assignment, it is "single assignment," prior to tail recursion. This cd can be compiled into the LOTOS shown above.

Now we would like to be able to define a cd for the events themselves, in a manner consistent with the usage we have permitted them with stacks. For example:

```
(push X on Y
        super:       event

        actants
        agent: a stack user
        pushee: a $Type X            ; sugar for X:$Type
        target: a stack Y
        mechanism: a cons

        behavior
                     contents(Y) <- (cons X contents(Y)))
```

The actants correspond to normal case roles for a verb; the agent is the object(s) (read: LOTOS process) that is allowed to have a push event communicating with a stack. The equations so far are particular to stacks, since this event is only for stacks.

Now we should generalize it:

```
(push X on Y
        super:              event

        actants
        agent:              an entity ; entity is a very general type
        pushee:              a $Type X
        target:              an entity Y
        targetAttribute:    an attribute A of Y
        mechanism:          a function F

        behavior
            A(Y) <- (F(X, A(Y))))
```

Now we have a very general 'push' event that pushes anything onto anything in any manner specifiable by a function of the pushee and some attribute of the target. In English:

> "pushing something *X* on something *Y* somehow causes some attribute *F* of *Y* to change depending on *X*"

If the reader finds this definition either too formal, too simple, or too removed from real language requirements and dictionary entries, we recommend that he compare it with the *Explanatory Combinatorial Dictionary* (ECD) developed by Mel'cuk and his associates [Mel'cuk, 1984]. This new and very formalized type of dictionary is nevertheless intended to be used by humans without any formal training, but it exhibits many of the features of our definitions. It also could form the basis for a machine-usable dictionary, but we believe cds are a considerable improvement.

19.5 IMPLEMENTATION AND USE; RELATED SYSTEMS

Many of the main concepts discussed in this chapter have been implemented on a SUN/3 in a prototype system. The user can quickly create windows that display cds in a format like that used in this chapter, using a highly graphical user interface, written in Smalltalk. Certain expressions can be selected and sent to two subsystems for various types of evaluation. One of these systems is a kind of theorem prover for L2, written in PROLOG. We say "kind of," since it is designed to be used interactively to debug sets of assertions in L2. It does all deduction automatically, however, with the user making decisions about how to modify the rule set when problems such as contradictions are encountered. The other is the LOTOS system, also written in PROLOG, intended for debugging specifications of concurrent systems [Guillemot et al., 1988]. It too is fully usable.

The system is intended to permit rapid conceptual knowledge acquisition by a skilled knowledge engineer and/or domain expert, including experimentation with major ontological choices. It can be compared with the following systems: ONTOS [Nirenburg et al., 1988], CYC [Lenat et al., 1990], KREME [Abrett and Burstein, 1987], and KEATS [Lenat et al., 1990]. The features of the implementation have not been explained in this chapter, which is intended only to give an overview of the conceptual basis; they are discussed at length in [Skuce and Wang, 1989].

Several hundred cds, in subjects as diverse as the UNIX operating system, a commercial concurrent OOP design environment, a database design problem involving registering automobiles, and family relationships, have been written. In fact, the current version of the system is being used to help design the next version. Over one hundred cds have been entered into the system and partially debugged.

19.6 CONCLUDING REMARKS

We have advocated a formal approach to knowledge representation that builds on ideas originating outside the AI literature in research on foundations for programming languages. The ideas can be seen as coming from three somewhat distant sources: AI frame systems for natural language, algebras for concurrent systems, and Mel'cuk's ECD. We have argued that, with suitable repackaging, these ideas can serve as very useful basis for practical AI purposes.

The approach described can be developed in several directions.

- It could form the basis for an interactive, general-purpose knowledge acquisition system, which is the main intent of the system we are implementing. Since our approach is more formal than most existing systems, this might be seen as a disadvantage, i.e., that in practical applications, particularly for natural language, one simply does not need this much formality. But the user need not use any more formality than desired; one can create cds with no constraints or functional equations if one wishes, whose properties are just English sentences, for later translation by a knowledge engineer or programmer. Or the formality could be hidden from unsophisticated users, while still retaining the format, which then would look more or less like many other frame-like representations, except that a formal basis would exist for defining what is a correct input.
- It could be used as a knowledge representation underlying some other type of AI knowledge system, such as a natural language understanding system, or an expert system. For the immediate future however, due to the slowness of formal logical processing, this application may not be practical when fast response times are necessary.

- It could be used as a basis for formally specifying and documenting the ontological structure of other knowledge representation systems, i.e., that are built on different principles but which could benefit from a formal description technique. It could hence be used for verifying the correctness of definitions in the system. Thus one could first specify and acquire knowledge using a cd system, and then transfer at least some of it, largely automatically, in a "compilation" process into another less formal representation that would probably be more efficient. The cd version would serve as a formal source knowledge document that had been machine analyzed for semantic errors. (This point is essentially the AI version of the following one.)
- The system could be used for software engineering purposes. There is an increasing awareness of the potential for applying "AI" techniques to software engineering problems, most typically for specification and design. Specifically, there is a need for more formal and unified specification languages (i.e., that integrate the various "paradigms") which can be checked for semantic errors. Some of the research in this area overlaps ideas in this chapter (e.g., [Markosian, 19??] (sic)).
- The system could be specialized for various other purposes, such as constructing dictionaries, documentation, institutional regulations, or for teaching purposes, i.e., to convey knowledge using cds as a knowledge explication tool. The current version of the system is intended to be easily specialized in this manner.

References

Abrett, G. and Burstein, M. 1987. The KREME knowledge editing environment. *International Journal of Man–Machine Studies* 27:103–126.

Agha, G. 1987. *ACTORS: A Model of Concurrent Computation In Distributed Systems*. MIT Press, Cambridge, MA.

Bolognesi, T., and Brinksma, E. 1987. Introduction to the ISO Specification Language LOTOS. *Computer Networks and ISDN Systems* 14:25–59.

Brachman, R., Gilbert, V., and Levesque, H. 1985. An essential hybrid reasoning system: knowledge and symbol level accounts of krypton. In *IJCAI 85*, pp. 532–539. IJCAI proceedings are available from Morgan Kaufmann Publishers, San Mateo, CA.

Computational Intelligence. 1987. (Special Issue on Nonmonotonic Reasoning), 3(3).

DeGroot, D. and Lindstrom. 1986. *Logic Programming: Functions, Relations and Equations*. Prentice Hall, Englewood Cliffs, NJ.

Goguen, J. and Meseguer, J. 1987. *Unifying Functional, Object-oriented, and Relational Programming with Logical Semantics.* Technical Report CSLI-87–93, Center for the Study of Language and Information, Stanford, CA.

Guillemot, R., Haj-Hussein, M., and Logrippo, L. 1988. Executing Large LOTOS Specifications. In *Protocol Specification, Testing, and Verification*, VIII, Aggorwal, S. and Sabnami, K. (ed.s). North Holland.

Lenat, D., and Guha, R. 1990. *Building Large Knowledge-based Systems.* Addison-Wesley, Reading, MA.

LOTOS—A Formal Description Technique Based on the Temporal Ordering of Observational Behaviour. ISO document DIS 8,807, 1987.

Markosian, L., and Abraido-Fandino, L. 19?? (sic). Knowledge-Based Software Engineering Using REFINE. Reasoning Systems Inc., Palo Alto.

Mel'cuk, I. 1984. *Dictionnaire Explicatif et Combinatoire du français contemporain.* Les Presses de l'Universite de Montreal, Montreal, 1984.

Nirenburg, S., Monarch, I., Kaufmann, T., Nirenburg, I. and Carbonell, J. 1988. *Acquisition of Very Large Knowledge Bases: Methodology, Tools and Applications.* Technical Report CMU- CMT-88–108, Carnegie Mellon University.

Reiter, R. 1988. Nonmonotonic Reasoning. In *Exploring Artificial Intelligence*, Shrobe, H. and AAAI (ed.s). Morgan Kaufmann Publishers, San Mateo, CA.

Shapiro, S. 1979. The SNePs Semantic Network Processing System. In *Associative Networks: Representation and Use of Knowledge*, Findler, N. (ed). Academic Press, New York.

Skuce, D. 1991. *A Knowledge Acquisition and Verification Environment Integrating Objects, Logic, and Natural Language.* In preparation.

Skuce, D. Forthcoming. A synthesis of objects, logic, and natural language for software production. Submitted to *IEEE Software.*

Sowa, J. 1984. *Conceptual Structures: Information Processing in Mind and Machine.* Addison-Wesley, Reading, MA.

Takeuchi, A., and Furakawa, K. 1986. Parallel logic programming languages. *Proceedings of the Third International Conference on Logic Programming*, London.

Touretzky, D. 1986. The Mathematics of Inheritance Systems. Morgan Kaufmann Publishers, San Mateo, CA, copublished with Pitman, London.

Touretzky, D., Horty, J. and Thomason, R. 1987. A clash of intuitions: The current state of nonmonotonic multiple inheritance systems. In *IJCAI 87*, pp. 476–482. IJCAI proceedings are available from Morgan Kaufmann Publishers, San Mateo, CA.

INDEX